Professional Development
and Supervision
of School
Psychologists

SECOND EDITION

We would like to dedicate this book to our families—particularly Tim Dawson, Richard Struzziero, Karen Harvey, Jenny Dawson, Rick Struzziero, and Alex and Alison Todd—without whose love, support, patience, and encouragement our professional lives, and this book, would not have been possible.

Professional Development and Supervision of School Psychologists

From **INTERN** to **EXPERT**

SECOND EDITION

VIRGINIA SMITH HARVEY

JOAN A. STRUZZIERO

Foreword by Kenneth W. Merrell

A JOINT PUBLICATION

NASP

NATIONAL
ASSOCIATION OF
SCHOOL
PSYCHOLOGISTS

CORWIN PRESS
A SAGE Company
Thousand Oaks, CA 91320

For information:

 Corwin Press
A SAGE Company
2455 Teller Road
Thousand Oaks, California 91320
www.corwinpress.com

SAGE Ltd.
1 Oliver's Yard
55 City Road
London EC1Y 1SP
United Kingdom

SAGE India Pvt. Ltd.
B 1/I 1 Mohan Cooperative Industrial Area
Mathura Road, New Delhi
India 110 044

SAGE Asia-Pacific Pte. Ltd.
33 Pekin Street #02-01
Far East Square
Singapore 048763

Printed in the United States of America

Library of Congress Cataloging-in-Publication Data

Harvey, Virginia Smith.
Professional development and supervision of school psychologists: From intern to expert/Virginia Smith Harvey, Joan A. Struzziero.—2nd ed.
    p. cm.
Rev. ed. of: Effective supervision in school psychology. 2000.
"A joint publication with the National Association of School Psychologists."
Includes bibliographical references and index.
ISBN 978-1-4129-5326-9 (cloth)
ISBN 978-1-4129-5327-6 (pbk.)

   1. School psychologists—In-service training—United States. 2. School psychologists—Supervision of—United States. I. Struzziero, Joan A. II. Harvey, Virginia Smith. Effective supervision in school psychology. III. Title.

LB3013.6.H37 2008
371.7'130683—dc22   2007052910

This book is printed on acid-free paper.

08 09 10 11 12   10 9 8 7 6 5 4 3 2 1

Acquisitions Editor:	Jessica Allan
Editorial Assistant:	Joanna Coelho
Production Editor:	Libby Larson
Copy Editor:	Rachel Keith
Typesetter:	C&M Digitals (P) Ltd.
Proofreader:	Victoria Reed-Castro
Indexer:	Jeanne R. Busemeyer
Cover Designer:	Michael Dubowe
Graphic Designer:	Lisa Riley

Contents

Foreword

*Moving Supervision and
Development of School Psychologists
From the Sidelines to Center Stage*

Kenneth W. Merrell

University of Oregon

Supervision of school psychological services, and of the professionals who deliver these services, is a critically important endeavor in our field. From the time that beginning graduate students enroll in their first assessment course or enter their first practicum experience until the time that they retire or leave the profession, they will have supervisors assigned. Every person in this profession—regardless of his or her point in the professional development continuum—has experienced supervision, either as a recipient of supervision or as one assigned to supervise, or both.

Those of us who have been in the field for a decade or more have probably experienced our participation as a supervisee in this process in a variety of ways, ranging from active and intense involvement by our supervisors to a laissez-faire approach where our supervisor occasionally checks in with us but seldom takes an active role in the process. In some cases our supervision experiences have been constructive, insightful, and thoughtful and have helped us to reevaluate how we are going about our work and to consider better ways to do what we do. In other cases our supervision experiences may have been negative and stressful, causing us to reevaluate our professional efforts in ways that have not been particularly helpful.

If you have been the supervisor in these exchanges, you have likewise probably had a mix of supervision experiences. Personally, I have had supervisees who were eager to hang on to every observation or word I provided them in my supervisory role, in a sincere effort to improve their results as a professional and perhaps even their attributes as a person. I have also had supervisees who were resistant to my efforts to work with them, or worse yet, were defensive and even hostile recipients of my efforts and my general involvement as their supervisor. And in this vein I will admit that my efforts as a supervisor have been mixed. There have been times where I have been engaged in the supervision process with energy, prior preparation, and careful planning to make the supervision experience as constructive and useful as possible. And there have been other times where my lack of prior preparation, personal investment, or insight resulted in something more like the laissez-faire approach

I mentioned previously and did not make much of an impact on the professional development of the person I was charged to supervise. Let's face it: Supervision can be difficult and complicated, regardless of what our particular role is in the process.

There is no question that the organizations, accrediting bodies, and professional culture within the field of school psychology value the supervision process and strive for its effective perpetuation. The National Association of School Psychologists and the American Psychological Association both have explicit expectations and requirements about supervision within their training standards as well as their codes of ethical and professional conduct. At the doctoral level of training, programs are required by both of these professional organizations to include education in supervision as part of their core curriculum, with the assumption that program graduates will have developed basic knowledge and skill competencies in the supervision process. And although I have seen a variety of presentations on the topic of supervision on the slate at professional conventions, I have never seen one of these presentations aiming to devalue or question the value of supervision. In fact, I can't recall ever hearing a serious professional conversation in which the importance of supervision was questioned.

Given the importance of the topic of supervision, the esteem with which it is held in our profession, and the many challenges that seem to inherently be part of the process, one would think that the area of supervision of school psychologists and the services they provide would be on some sort of pantheon within our field, or at the very least, occupy a place of extensive attention and productivity. Unfortunately, I am not so sure that this prized view of supervision is actually the case in our field. Rather, I tend to see the coverage of professional development and supervision of school psychologists afforded a place of secondary importance, with most of our efforts focused on the types of services we provide rather than our skill and competence in how we are going about providing or evaluating them. My estimation is that although training programs tend to place high importance on clinical supervision of students, relatively little effort is expended on how to train students to be effective supervisees or supervisors. At the doctoral level of training, where coverage of supervision is required, many of the curriculum offerings in these areas appear to be added on to the list of requirements as a concession to the standards of the accreditation bodies rather than strategically placed in the curriculum as a core part of the program.

Increasingly, it seems that the relative lack of attention to supervision within our training programs and profession in general is a problem. It is well known from various surveys regarding job role satisfaction of school psychologists over the past three decades that the quality of supervision they receive in their professional lives is one of the important factors associated with their satisfaction or dissatisfaction. And perhaps even more striking is the fact that most school psychology interns and many school psychologists are supervised by school psychologists who have not received any formal training in supervision. The flip side of this fact is that many school psychologists who have not received any formal training in the supervision and development process are being asked to take on supervisory roles. Of course, some and perhaps most professionals in this situation do just fine, and I would be hard pressed to identify a scientific study showing that taking a class or seminar in supervision led to significantly better outcomes in supervision. That said, it's unfortunate that so little attention is being paid to an activity that is part of our collective professional experience in school psychology and that may play a large role in our job satisfaction and professional development.

Perhaps part of the challenge regarding the placement of a systematic training focus on the process of supervision within our field is that most of the work in this area has evolved outside the field of school psychology. There have been relatively few books written on supervision of school psychology services, and this area scarcely appears as the topic of research reports in our field's professional and scientific journals. Much of the basic theoretical, scientific, and applied work on supervision processes and training has come from our sister fields of clinical psychology and especially counseling psychology, where the topic has been one of serious focus and attention in the literature. Perhaps we want and need our *own voice* in addressing this area of need, perceiving that the situations that are so unique to our field define us, and require a specific approach from within.

Virginia Smith Harvey and Joan Struzziero's *Professional Development and Supervision of School Psychologists: From Intern to Expert* is in my estimation a landmark work that has the potential to move professional development and supervision of school psychologists to center stage in our field. Here, we have our own voice, our own examples, situations to which we can easily resonate and relate. Written in an engaging manner that often approximates a conversation with the reader, this work provides the most comprehensive guide to supervision and development of school psychologists that I have ever seen. It is much more than a revision of the previous volume from which it sprang. Rather, this book offers a bold new vision of training in the process of supervision that is simultaneously personal and universal, specific and general, practical and theoretical, accessible and challenging. Covering a diverse array of topics within the general areas of foundations of supervision, clinical supervision, and administrative supervision, the authors have created a volume that should receive serious consideration for adoption in courses that introduce the profession in our training programs, for use in supervisory training, and to hold a place on the bookshelves of any one of us who is expected to provide supervision. Stated simply, this book is a superb resource and holds the promise of serving as a catalyst for moving our professional discourse and practice forward in the area of supervision.

Every book or chapter on supervision that I have seen includes coverage of various models of supervision as well as a fairly heavy emphasis on methods of clinical supervision. *Professional Development and Supervision of School Psychologists* includes detailed coverage of these two areas and much more. Some of the innovative topics covered in this volume include an emphasis on systems that is woven throughout the book, an expansive view of multicultural competency issues in supervision that goes well beyond race and ethnicity, the use of technology in supervision, methods and models for conducting performance evaluations, issues in leadership, and successful approaches to recruitment of school psychologists. Some of the engaging tools in the book include the systematic use of vignettes, reflective questions for readers, suggested activities for further development of knowledge and skills, and an illustration of numerous "supervisory dilemmas" that are realistic and compelling. In short, this book covers all of the important areas in supervision and development of school psychologists and moves our professional vision to a new level.

The need for increasing attention to be placed on our practices and processes in supervision and development of school psychologists can be addressed in many ways. Perhaps this area will receive more emphasis in the future within our professional training standards, but I'm not suggesting that this course of action is necessarily the best or only solution, or that we should wait until it happens before we begin to be more systematic in our efforts for improvement. Rather, a proactive and grassroots renewed emphasis on supervision and development in our field has the potential to result in dramatic improvements in this area. This book is one tool that can help make this vision a reality, and I commend the authors for their extraordinary vision and effort that is so evident from cover to cover of *Professional Development and Supervision of School Psychologists*.

Preface

*P*rofessional Development and Supervision of School Psychologists is a practical guide to foster the professional growth of school psychologists, whether they are beginners, interns, experts, or supervisors. It comprehensively addresses the necessary administrative supervision, clinical supervision, and systemic leadership required for school psychologists to provide effective services across the domains of practice.

Professional Development and Supervision of School Psychologists succeeds our previous book, *Effective Supervision in School Psychology* (Harvey & Struzziero, 2000). Both books were written with the assumptions that practicing as a psychologist in schools is complex, changes constantly, requires lifelong professional development, and is greatly facilitated by effective supervision that employs unique, identifiable, and learnable skills.

However, this book has such substantial differences from our previous work that it merits a different title. It has a much greater emphasis on the support needed by school psychologists and their supervisors as they undertake the paradigm shift to provide evidence-based practice, prevention services, and demonstrable outcomes. This paradigm shift is required by ethical standards, recommended by research evidence, and supported by general and special education laws mandating accountability within the educational system. This book also has an increased focus on systems-based delivery, multicultural issues, clinical supervision, and systemic leadership.

The wide variety of skills needed by psychologists working in schools are related yet independently developed and cannot be fully mature by the end of graduate training. Both novice and veteran psychologists are likely to be "beginners" in some skills, such as crisis intervention counseling, and simultaneously "proficient" in other areas, such as assessment and Curriculum-Based Measurement. Professional development and effective supervision can help psychologists develop in all areas of practice and ensure that they keep abreast of constantly emerging knowledge, research, and skills. Throughout their careers, effective school psychologists continuously expand their expertise across broad ranges of knowledge and skills by maintaining an active approach to their own professional development. Their professional lives are characterized by ongoing learning, integrated case conceptualization, clearly defined professional boundaries, and the ability to see complex situations clearly. Effective supervisors display these attitudes and approaches and encourage their supervisees to do the same.

Similarly, supervisors benefit from ongoing professional development in supervisory skills. Just as effective coaching requires a different skill set than being an expert athlete, effective supervision requires a different skill set than expert practice. Furthermore, these skills can be learned. This book is intended to provide guidance in the acquisition of supervisory values, attitudes, and skills necessary for effective supervision of psychologists working in schools.

Professional Development and Supervision of School Psychologists will be useful for individuals who provide professional development for and supervision of psychologists working in schools and educational settings in a wide variety of roles. It is appropriate for supervisors in any of the following situations:

- Field and university supervisors of school psychology interns and practicum students
- Coordinating psychologists who provide clinical supervision for school psychologists
- Supervising psychologists who provide both administrative and clinical supervision for individuals providing psychological services in schools
- Principals, special education directors, and other school administrators who provide administrative supervision for those providing psychological services in schools
- School psychologists who participate in peer supervision and collaboration
- Students enrolled in a school psychology supervision course
- School psychologists engaged in self-supervision via self-study and professional development activities
- Practitioners seeking helpful forms, details, and ideas to enhance their day-to-day practice

There is considerable overlap in the foundational knowledge required across the above roles. All supervisors need proficiency in interpersonal skills, multicultural competencies, data-based decision making, and application of ethical standards and laws. They also need to use systemic leadership to address the challenges particular to the supervision of psychological services in schools. These foundational topics are covered in Chapters 1 through 6. Chapters 7 through 12 focus on clinical supervision and are designed for those who closely supervise the provision of prevention services, consultation, assessment, intervention design, and student progress monitoring. Chapters 13 through 15 are designed for administrative supervisors—intern supervisors as well as administrators—who hire and evaluate school psychologists.

Throughout the book the reader is provided information on several levels. We provide relevant theories, research, and policies drawn from the fields of school psychology, educational psychology, counseling psychology, industrial and organizational psychology, and education. Every chapter has multiple vignettes (using pseudonyms and disguised information) illustrating the principles discussed. We then provide suggestions for supervision and tools to use in appraising supervisor effectiveness and close each chapter with supervisory dilemmas to facilitate lively discussions.

Acknowledgments

We have many individuals to acknowledge and thank for direct and indirect contributions to this book. These include our supervisors and mentors, past and present. These also include individuals who read and commented on our previous book, *Effective Supervision in School Psychology* (Harvey & Struzziero, 2000); those who have attended our supervision workshops and classes during the past 10 years; those who participated in interviews regarding the challenges of supervising school psychological services; and those who participated in the NASP Supervision Interest Group (a special thanks to Barbara Fischetti for her dedicated leadership of this group). The rich discussions that ensued in all of these settings were illuminating and thought provoking and have had a substantial impact on our thinking and writing.

We would like to extend particular thanks to Cynthia Adamchek and Sarah Raley, who were our graduate assistants as we prepared this manuscript. We would also like to thank individuals who reviewed and provided suggestions for early versions of this manuscript, including MaryAnn Byrnes, Bob Lichtenstein, Gayle Macklem, Mark Swerdlik, and Susanne Toomajian. Finally, we would like to thank our students and colleagues at our respective universities and school districts, all of whom have contributed to our professional growth.

Corwin Press wishes to gratefully acknowledge the following peer reviewers for their editorial insight and guidance:

MaryAnn Baldwin, PhD
Counselor and AP Coordinator
Chamberlain High School
Tampa, Florida

Sharon Gorenstein, PhD, NCSP
Psychologist
Baltimore City Public School System
Baltimore, Maryland

Katy Olweiler, MA, MPA, NCSC, NCC
Counselor
Lakeside School
Seattle, Washington

Charles J. Russo, JD, EdD
Panzer Chair in Education
University of Dayton
Department of Educational Leadership
Dayton, Ohio

Diane P. Smith
Counselor
Smethport Area School District
Smethport, Pennsylvania

About the Authors

 **Virginia Smith Harvey, PhD**, is professor and director of the School Psychology program at the University of Massachusetts, Boston. Before becoming a university professor, she was a practicing school psychologist for 18 years and supervised school psychologists and interns throughout those years. During her 15 years as a professor she has supervised practicum, intern, and postgraduate students. She has written numerous articles and book chapters, and she is coauthor of *Effective Supervision in School Psychology* (2000, with J. A. Struzziero) and *Fostering Independent Learning: Practical Strategies to Promote Student Success* (2007, with L. A. Chickie-Wolfe). Dr. Harvey is currently chair of the ethics committee of the New Hampshire Association of School Psychologists and serves on the Standards Revision Writing Group of the National Association of School Psychologists.

 **Joan A. Struzziero, PhD**, is an adjunct professor at Northeastern University and a school psychologist in the Scituate Public Schools in Massachusetts. She has worked as a school psychologist for 18 years and as a field and university supervisor of interns for 15 years. She has also been a supervisor for the Global School Psychology Network and has researched the use of the Internet in supervision. Dr. Struzziero is coauthor of *Effective Supervision in School Psychology* (2000, with V. S. Harvey), cochair of the ethics committee of the Massachusetts Association of School Psychologists, and the Northeastern representative of the ethics committee of the National Association of School Psychologists.

PART I

Foundations of Supervision

1

Overview

Vignette 1.1

Anne, a fourth-year school psychologist in the Smithville Public Schools, has been asked by the district's lead psychologist to supervise a school psychology intern, **Zoe**. She is excited yet daunted by the prospect. Anne's principal, **Bob**, appreciates the Second Step prevention and evidence-based response to intervention (RTI) programs Anne coordinates. He is apprehensive about her being responsible for an intern in addition to these other responsibilities.

Catherine, the district's lead psychologist, coordinates psychological services, but since she is in the same union bargaining unit as the other school psychologists, she is not the line supervisor who hires and evaluates them. **Dottie** is the district's special services director and hires and evaluates 53 individuals (special education teachers, reading teachers, school psychologists, counselors, social workers, speech pathologists, and nurses). Although trained as a school psychologist, Dottie has little time to provide direct supervision.

The district superintendent, **Paul**, values psychologists' reports that appease angry parents. When drawing up the district budget, he mentions the number of psychoeducational reports generated, and he believes that Catherine should assign school psychologists' time according to the number of reports they generate. He is unaware of the prevention and intervention programs that Anne coordinates.

Are psychological services in Smithville District well supervised? What is working? What isn't? How can the individuals who supervise psychological services in this district—Anne, Bob, Catherine, Dottie, and Paul—better coordinate their efforts? How can they maximize the effectiveness of school psychologists' work with children, adolescents, parents, and educators?

This book addresses these questions in considerable detail. This introductory chapter provides an overview of effective supervision of psychological services in schools and its accompanying challenges.

BASIC CONSIDERATIONS

Schools tend to be hierarchically arranged with clearly designated administrative assignments wherein every employee has a supervisor responsible for completing periodic evaluations. Often these evaluations are defined by district and union policies. In many administrative units, formal observations and evaluations are mandated several times during the first years of employment and less frequently in subsequent years. Despite these extant structures, there have been repeated calls for increased supervision of psychological services in schools (Fischetti & Crespi, 1999; Knoff, 1986; Murphy, 1981; National Association of School Psychologists [NASP], 2004). Several surveys have revealed that school psychologists receive insufficient supervision relative to both personal needs and professional standards (Chafouleas, Clonan, & Vanauken, 2002).

To understand these calls for increased supervision, it is necessary to first consider definitions and rationales for supervision of psychological services in schools, characteristics of effective supervision, and challenges in providing supervision. To implement appropriate supervision, such challenges must be addressed, needs assessed, and appropriate supports provided.

DEFINITIONS OF SUPERVISION OF PSYCHOLOGICAL SERVICES

Supervision of psychological services has been defined as

> an intervention provided by a more senior member of a profession to a more junior member or members of the same profession. This relationship is evaluative, extends over time, and has the simultaneous purposes of enhancing the professional functioning of the more junior person(s), monitoring the quality of professional services offered to [clients], and serving as a gatekeeper of those who are to enter the particular profession. (J. M. Bernard & Goodyear, 2004, p. 8)

Supervision of psychological services in schools has been defined as

> an interpersonal interaction between two or more individuals for the purpose of sharing knowledge, assessing professional competencies, and providing objective feedback with the terminal goals of developing new competencies, facilitating effective delivery of psychological services, and maintaining professional competencies. (D. E. McIntosh & Phelps, 2000, pp. 33–34)

The National Association of School Psychologists adds to this definition the ultimate goal of improving the "performance of all concerned—school psychologist, supervisor, students, and the entire school community" (NASP, 2004, p. 1).

Supervision is both similar to and different from teaching, consulting, and providing therapy (J. M. Bernard & Goodyear, 2004; Evangelista, 2006). Supervision is similar to teaching in that it enhances learners' knowledge and skills and evaluates the same. It differs in that teaching usually is directed toward a group and follows a set curriculum, while supervision is usually individualized and open ended. Supervision is similar to consultation in that it helps supervisees explore new ways to think about issues, identifies resources that enable supervisees to problem solve, and examines skills and needs.

It differs from consultation in that supervision partners are not equal and in that supervision can be imposed rather than requested. Finally, supervision is similar to therapy in that it encourages the individual to see patterns of behavior, set targets for change, and use interventions to bring about that change. It differs from therapy in that it is evaluative and addresses professional rather than personal issues.

To reconcile these different perspectives regarding supervision, it is necessary to discuss the primary roles of supervisors. Much of the counseling psychology literature differentiates these primary roles into *administrative supervision* and *clinical supervision*. There is evidence that an effective supervisor of school psychologists adopts the additional role of *systemic change leader* because of school psychology's highly contextual nature (Harvey, 2008). Thus we will describe a *clinical-administrative-systemic model* of supervision.

All effective supervisors give supervisees helpful comments and provide supervision in a manner that is responsive to the supervisee's developmental level. They help supervisees problem solve, reflect on practice, engage in continuous learning, maintain professional and ethical standards, uphold appropriate laws and statutes, and manage difficult situations such as due process hearings. They also promote school psychological services by, for example, preparing documents regarding the provision of services for school administrators or state and federal departments of education.

Clinical (professional) supervision involves the oversight of professional practice and requires discipline-specific training and knowledge. Clinical supervisors demonstrate and teach techniques and skills, examine student work with supervisees, help supervisees conceptualize cases, assist supervisees as they disaggregate and interpret data, ensure that supervisees practice only within areas of professional competence, assist supervisees as they design intervention strategies, help supervisees learn how to work with different types of clients and colleagues, debrief supervisees after difficult or crisis situations, provide second opinions, help supervisees address their blind spots resulting from personal experiences, and supervise the provision of a broad range of clinical services. Furthermore, clinical supervisors provide formative evaluations of supervisees, provide training and professional development opportunities, reduce feelings of professional isolation during supervision itself by supporting peer collaboration, and encourage induction into the profession via membership in professional organizations. They help supervisees become more aware of what they are doing well and what they need to change and to avoid becoming professionally stagnant. In sum, good clinical supervision plays a pivotal role in fostering professional growth, reducing stress and burnout, and strengthening practice (McMahon & Patton, 2000). Although clinical supervisors do not have a primarily evaluative role, they do evaluate whenever they indicate that supervisees are fit to be licensed or certified or to continue practicing. In contrast to administrative supervision, professional (clinical) supervision must be provided by a credentialed school psychologist or the equivalent (NASP, 2004). In the opening vignette, Anne and Catherine provide clinical supervision. As a trained psychologist, Dottie could provide clinical supervision but cannot do so due to time constraints.

Administrative supervisors provide leadership, recruit and hire, delegate assignments, conduct formal personnel evaluations, design corrective actions, and take ultimate responsibility for services provided by supervisees. They focus

> on the functioning of the service unit, including personnel issues, logistics of service delivery, and legal, contractual and organizational practices. Administrative supervision addresses the performance of job duties in accordance with conditions of employment and assigned responsibilities, and is primarily concerned with outcomes and consumer satisfaction rather than discipline-specific professional skills. (NASP, 2004, ¶ 5)

In that administrative supervision is not discipline specific, it may be provided by individuals who are not trained in school psychology. In fact, most administrative supervision of school psychologists is not provided by school psychologists. More than 75% of school psychologists are evaluated by administrators (district level administrators evaluate 59% and principals evaluate 18%) in contrast to the 18% evaluated by supervising school psychologists (Hunley et al., 2000). In the opening vignette, Bob, Dottie, and Paul provide administrative supervision.

Finally, when serving in the role of systemic change leaders, supervisors act as change agents within the district. They respond to a comprehensive view of school procedures, cultural issues, and school system concerns. In this role, supervisors promote the effective practice of their supervisees by promoting effective educational practices at the district or state level. They conduct program evaluations, not only of school psychological services but also of district-based educational programs and practices.

Within the psychology supervision literature, there is no consensus regarding whether the same individual can fulfill all of these major roles. To provide both administrative and clinical supervision, one must "walk the fine line between the demands for monitoring and the need for support" (Chan, 2004, p. 66). Supervisees might be reluctant to reveal shortcomings to their evaluators (J. M. Bernard & Goodyear, 2004), or supervisors might experience conflicts between professional standards and administrative responsibilities (Le Maistre, Boudreau, & Paré, 2007; Pennington, 1989). On the other hand, combining roles can be beneficial. In a study conducted by Tromski-Klingshirn and Davis (2007), counselors whose supervisors took both administrative and clinical responsibilities reported no difference in satisfaction compared with those who received only clinical supervision. Further, 82% of the supervisees receiving clinical and administrative supervision from the same person did not view this dual role as problematic, and 72.5% perceived it as beneficial.

Considering the supervision activities of clinical supervisors, administrative supervisors, and systemic change leaders helps explain the calls for increased supervision. Only 10% of school psychologists receive formal clinical supervision by a trained school psychologist who is able to provide adequate clinical supervision, yet 70% indicate a perceived need for clinical supervision (Chafouleas et al., 2002; Fischetti & Crespi, 1999).

Therefore, all too often school psychologists do not have sufficient clinical supervision to meet their needs for professional growth. Furthermore, school psychologists' work is frequently compromised when they do not have the support of a systemic change leader to facilitate appropriate district policies.

RATIONALES FOR SUPERVISION

Research Supporting Supervision

A growing body of research in psychology and education provides empirical support for effective supervision. Demonstrated outcomes have included skill maintenance, skill improvement and expansion, professional development, reduced stress, and enhanced accountability.

Skill Maintenance

"Experience without feedback on how to improve is unlikely to lead to high levels of functioning" (Palmer, Stough, Burdenski, & Gonzales, 2005). Expert musicians, athletes, and scientists inevitably seek, obtain, and incorporate corrective feedback regarding their performance. For example, it is difficult to imagine a world class orchestra without a conductor, or a professional athlete without a coach and personal trainer. In fact, research has repeatedly demonstrated that many hours of practice *accompanied by corrective feedback* is more closely correlated with the development of expertise than is "talent" (Ericsson & Charness, 1994; Ericsson, Krampe, & Tesch-Romer, 1993).

One of the reasons that supervision is needed is because beginners and experts see problems differently. Novices tend to have difficulty identifying important problem components and often respond to surface features rather than underlying concepts and principles. Expert practitioners think so differently from novice professionals that it sometimes interferes with their ability to mentor. Because proficient practitioners and experts no longer think in terms of simple solutions and rules, they can have difficulty providing "rules" and breaking down the big picture into the components novices need (Benner, 1984). Thus supervisors need to take care when they communicate their thought processes to supervisees.

Vignette 1.2

After 25 years as a practicing school psychologist, **Velda** accepted a part-time teaching position at the local university. As practicum students and interns brought in cases to discuss, she found herself making suggestions regarding possible problem areas on the basis of very little information. The students were amazed when her hunches proved correct. Velda realized that, as a highly experienced practitioner, she recognized patterns much more quickly than her students did. To avoid mystifying (and overimpressing) them, she forced herself to break down thought processes into manageable steps that the interns could follow.

Novices require frequent and direct supervision (Stoltenberg, McNeill, & Delworth, 1998). Furthermore, individuals regress to novice status whenever they are learning a new skill, and remain novices for some time. Expert performance takes about 10 years of corrected practice to develop (Ericsson & Charness, 1994).

A meta-analysis of 200 studies analyzing skill acquisition in teachers found that effect sizes averaged zero unless the teachers received ongoing supervision and coaching (Joyce & Showers, 1995). Similarly, although school counseling graduate students demonstrated skill acquisition during training, without ongoing support the skills had little transfer and were maintained for less than a year (Baker, Daniels, & Greely, 1990; Spooner & Stone, 1977). Supervision that includes direct instruction, corrective feedback, and appropriate rewards can prevent skill deterioration (Beck, 1986; Dodenhoff, 1981; Kavanagh et al., 2003). It is unreasonable to expect skills developed during graduate school training to be maintained without additional support.

Increasing recognition of this phenomenon has led to the recommendation to designate and train mentors for beginning teachers (Sprinthall, Reiman, & Thies-Sprinthall, 1993, 1996) and school counselors (Agnew, Vaught, Getz, & Fortune, 2000; Benshoff & Paisley, 1996; Borders, 1991; Crutchfield & Borders, 1997; Herlihy, Gray, & McCollum, 2002; Peace & Sprinthall, 1998). It has also led to multi-level licensure and certification by state departments of education, wherein "professional" credentials are awarded only after several years of practice. Clinical supervision has been identified as necessary for professional growth to occur (Wiley & Ray, 1986) and to prevent the deterioration of performance through lack of practice, carelessness, or inaccurate practice without correction (Franklin, Stillman, Burpeau, & Sabers, 1982).

The same issues are relevant to school psychology. The more school psychologists in training receive supervision using a specific technique, the more likely they are to use that technique effectively in professional practice (E. S. Shapiro & Lentz, 1985). "Simply reading or hearing about empirically supported treatments will not be sufficient to get psychologists to use them; rather, skill development strategies that reflect good models of professional development are also required" (Rosenfield, 2000).

Skill Improvement and Expansion

Graduate training cannot provide all of the attitudes, knowledge, and skills necessary for optimal functioning as a school psychologist. As articulated in *School Psychology: A Blueprint for Training and Practice III* (Ysseldyke et al., 2006), competence emerges over time. School psychologists are likely to demonstrate a novice level of competence at the end of coursework and competence in some areas after completing their internships. Only after 5 to 10 years of practice are school psychologists likely to demonstrate expertise across broad domains of practice in multiple delivery systems as prescribed by best practice, as illustrated in Figure 1.1.

Figure 1.1. Training and practice in school psychology.

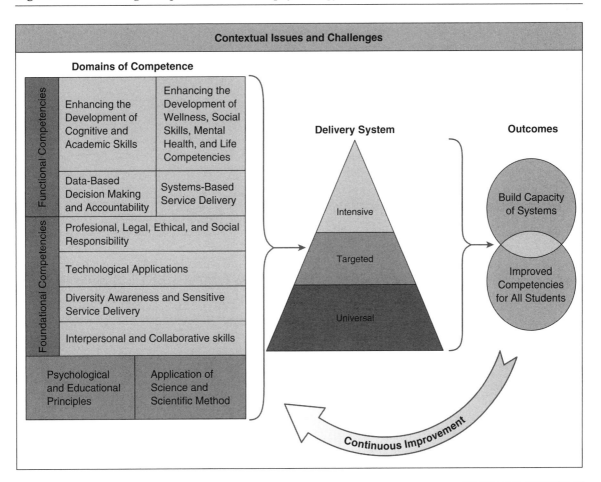

From Ysseldyke, J. E., Burns, M., Dawson, P., Kelley, B., Morrison, D., Ortiz, S., et al. (2006). *School psychology: A blueprint for training and practice III.* Bethesda, MD: National Association of School Psychologists. Copyright © 2006 by the National Association of School Psychologists, Bethesda, MD. Use of this material is by permission of the publisher, www.nasponline.org.

Furthermore, to be effective practitioners, school psychologists must constantly keep abreast of new knowledge, research, and skills that emerge throughout their professional careers. Clinical supervision is essential for skill development and expansion throughout an individual's career, and school psychologists need an organizational framework for life-long professional development (Rosenfield, 1985). Typically, professional development opportunities are fragmented, discontinuous, haphazard, and not integrated into practice. Attending professional development workshops is not sufficient, for after hearing about new knowledge and skills in professional development workshops, few participants apply the information to their practice unless they receive feedback and supervision in their application. For example, both doctoral and specialist level school psychologists in more than 60 schools required extensive support to develop and sustain effective instructional consultation teams, even though they were well trained and knew that the method improved student functioning (Rosenfield, 2000; Rosenfield & Gravois, 1996).

Furthermore, regardless of years of experience, practitioners require supervision whenever they enter situations in which they have no previous experience. As indicated by J. M. Bernard and Goodyear (2004), often the most troublesome employees are those with extensive, unsupervised experience. School psychologists can experience significant stress as they learn and implement new approaches. Without considerable support, they can be tempted to continue ineffective or outdated practice because it is familiar and feels safe (Harvey, 2008). School psychologists need ongoing support to sustain best practices.

Vignette 1.3

Prudence, a veteran school psychologist, inappropriately administers the exact same tests to every child regardless of the referring problem—the WISC, WRAT, Bender Gestalt, and House-Tree-Person that she learned in graduate school some years ago. She feels comfortable with these tools and thoroughly enjoys being the "expert" during team meetings. Her district is now mandating that school teams adopt the response to intervention model for diagnosing learning disabilities. Prudence is panicking at the thought of this change and is counting the days until she can retire. Unfortunately, her retirement is 12 years in the future!

It is imperative to provide every staff person support sufficient for practice improvement. Such support requires an appraisal of supervisees' knowledge, skills, confidence, objectivity, and interpersonal interactions and then systematic facilitation of professional development in each area.

Stress Reduction

School psychologists work in complex and emotionally challenging situations that can result in "performance fatigue." They can develop blind spots in their work or be unable to independently address difficult situations, and even expert practitioners need supervision to maintain objectivity. Good supervision promotes job satisfaction and reduces stress for individuals who provide psychological services in highly stressful settings (Hyrkäs, 2005). The research in school counseling supervision over the past 30 years has consistently revealed that school counselors perceive that clinical supervision provides support, ongoing learning, and professional development and therefore reduces professional isolation and burnout. High-quality supervision provides the opportunity to obtain praise and empathy for successfully resolving challenging problems as well as to obtain support and ideas for problem resolution itself (Kavanagh et al., 2003).

As McMahon and Patton (2000) indicated, the ability to positively adapt to changing situations, or to be resilient, is enhanced through participation in supervision. Individuals working in isolation are less adaptable and more likely to experience stress and burnout. Without supervision, it is difficult to "be resilient enough to endure the challenges of work in the 21st century" (p. 349).

Increased Self-Reflection

Effective school psychologists employ executive functions such as planning and appraisal to reflect on their practice and modify future practice according to their findings. It is very difficult to sustain reflective practice alone, particularly in the face of the time pressures experienced in schools (Sergiovanni & Starratt, 2007). School psychologists are almost always the only psychologist in their assigned building and thus suffer from extreme professional isolation. This isolation, combined with little time for reflection and self-appraisal, means that school psychologists often do not determine which of their practices actually result in improved student functioning. As Carrington (2004) indicated, supervision can ameliorate professional isolation and provide the support necessary to foster self-reflection, an activity that is often neglected, and thereby improve practice.

Particularly when learning new skills, reflective school psychologists monitor their progress by self-applying supervisory techniques normally used with novice supervisees. These include taping and analyzing counseling, consultation, and assessment sessions; obtaining evaluative information from students, teachers, and administrators; and evaluating the effectiveness of services. Reflective school psychologists thereby compare their functioning with best practices described in current publications such as *School Psychology: A Blueprint for Training and Practice III* (Ysseldyke et al., 2006), *Best Practices in School Psychology V* (A. Thomas & Grimes, 2008), the *Professional Conduct Manual* of the National Association of School Psychologists (2000a), and the Guilford School Practitioner Series, as well as professional Listservs and Web sites. In addition to consulting these and other professional resources, self-supervising school psychologists foster a network of experienced psychologists, counselors, teachers, and others with whom they can consult regarding new skills and difficult cases.

Increased Accountability

Through the implementation of the above practices, supervision fosters appraisal of the effectiveness of services. As service effectiveness is established, these results can be made public and used to support the funding of both psychological services and their supervision.

Professional Standards Supporting Supervision

The importance of supervision of psychological services has been supported by professional practice standards and ethical guidelines as defined by both the National Association of School Psychologists (NASP) and the American Psychological Association (APA).

NASP Position Paper

In 2004, the Delegate Assembly of the National Association of School Psychologists passed a formal position statement entitled "NASP Position Statement on Supervision in

School Psychology" (NASP, 2004). This statement defined professional (clinical) supervision as essential to school improvement and student success in that supervisors observe, monitor, and evaluate the practice of school psychologists to ensure that they provide appropriate services. As such, NASP recommends that school psychologists obtain supervision from trained school psychologists, because it is believed that supervisors who are knowledgeable about and experienced in the delivery of school psychological services will promote adherence to high standards, ensure the provision of appropriate and high-quality services to children and adolescents, provide appropriate evaluations, promote ongoing professional development, and adapt roles to meet changing needs of the school community.

NASP Professional Standards

Guidelines regarding supervision are described in professional practice standards (NASP, 2000b). These standards indicate that interns and first-year school psychologists, as well as others in need of such supervision, must receive at least 2 hours of supervision per week. After the first year of employment, NASP standards indicate, professional supervision and/or peer review *should be available* to ensure ongoing professional development, regardless of level of experience. This is necessary because individuals may not be proficient in skills across the domains of practice. NASP recommends that psychologists' professional functions be supervised by a qualified psychologist who holds an appropriate credential; has at least 3 years of successful, supervised experience as a school psychologist; and is designated by the school district as the supervisor responsible for school psychological services.

APA Standards and Policies

APA standards indicate that nondoctoral school psychologists should receive face-to-face supervision throughout their careers. More than 20 years ago, the "Specialty Guidelines for the Delivery of Services by School Psychologists" (APA, 1981) expressed concern regarding the supervision of school psychologists by nonpsychologists because such supervisors are unfamiliar with relevant ethical responsibilities and professional standards, which is thought to result in conflicts between professional and administrative expectations. APA (2007) also specified that internships should be fully integrated into the organization and governed by written policies. Training should be experiential, sequential, cumulative, graded, respectful of diversity, and consistent with the training program's philosophy, and it should enable interns to integrate science with practice. During the internship, APA mandates at least 4 hours of supervision per week, 2 hours of which must be face to face and individual. Each intern should have at least two supervisors who are appropriately skilled, hold doctoral degrees, are integral members of the organization, and participate actively in the development and evaluation of the internship.

Ethical Standards

Supervision of school psychological services promotes adherence to professional ethical mandates by providing protection for the children and adolescents with whom supervisees work. As supervisors review cases, they help their supervisees sustain interpersonal skills and maintain objectivity in the face of potential bias and covert pressures. To adequately protect clients, supervisors master and apply a complex array of legal and ethical principles. Supervisors are legally responsible for monitoring the welfare of the supervisee's clients, particularly when the supervisee is not licensed or certified to practice independently (J. M. Bernard & Goodyear, 2004).

EFFECTIVE SUPERVISORY STRUCTURES

School psychology and the supervision of psychological services are dynamic, as are all systems and systemic relationships. Effective supervisors consider internal and external strengths and weaknesses and then alter the structure of supervision, professional development, and service delivery. The altered structure, in turn, modifies strengths and weaknesses and consequently changes the strategies of choice. This again affects structure. Thus effective supervisors consider the context in which supervision occurs and plan accordingly, change that context by providing supervision, and then revise supervision within the changed context. Each component feeds into and affects the next, as shown in Figure 1.2.

Successful supervision of psychologists in schools requires contextually responsive supervision. This contextual aspect is unique to schools, going beyond the clinical and

Figure 1.2.   Systemic supervision cycle.

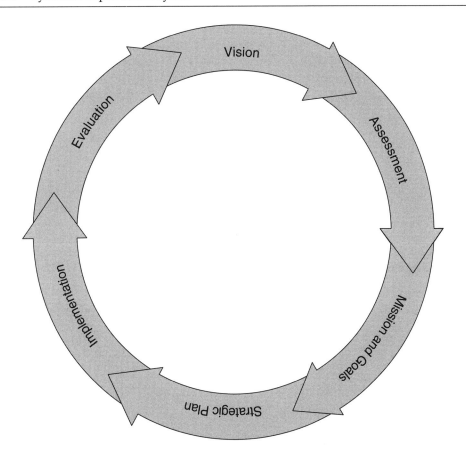

administrative supervision appropriate in clinical settings. Because of the highly contextual nature of school psychology, supervisors are challenged by the necessity to assess the needs of each school and school district, determine the needs that could and should be met by school psychologists, take into consideration the professional development of each psychologist as well as the broader context, and then ensure that the school psychologist has sufficient expertise to meet school and school district needs.

Appropriate supervision structures are characterized by several components. As described by Fischetti and Lines (2003) and Harvey (2008), these components include:

- A primary focus on meeting the needs of students
- Coordinated psychological services that respond to the needs of district students, teachers, parents, and administrators in terms of the practice of school psychology and the development of school district policies
- Psychological services permeated by a commitment to ethically responsive educational and school psychological practices that translate theory and research into practice
- Practices that help supervisees cope with rapidly changing knowledge, increasing diversity, and ever-expanding technologies by providing continuing education, facilitating information dissemination, encouraging affiliation with professional organizations, and promoting staff development
- Clearly articulated supervision employing evaluation methods that reflect best practices in school psychology
- Supervisory policies and practice that respect and maximize the unique skills and strengths of each contributing professional and foster self-appraisal, goal setting, and progress monitoring
- Cross-collaboration among staff within small "communities of learning" that network, consult, and team with others
- School psychological services oriented to meeting the needs of all school administrators, general education teachers, special education teachers, parents, and other constituents rather than limited to special education placement
- School psychology staff who regularly meet to discuss difficult cases and to develop position statements on controversial issues such as identification of learning disabilities; these position statements are later used to guide practice, as in-service tools, and to facilitate intra-unit communication (Murphy, 1981)
- Supervising and lead school psychologists who regularly collaborate at the district level to help set policies regarding controversial issues such as curriculum adoption, English language learners, and retention
- An ongoing mentoring program that provides planned intern supervision, mentoring for novice school psychologists, and skill development for supervisors and mentors
- Collaboration with state departments of education and, when possible, university training programs

It is very helpful when a clinical supervisor is an employee of the same school district as a supervisee, because that increases knowledge regarding district issues and personalities as well as affords greater opportunities for systemic leadership. However, where that is not possible, alternative models such as part-time supervisors, the sharing of supervisors among school districts or between districts and community agencies, or online supervision can be used appropriately (NASP, 2004).

CHALLENGES IN SUPERVISING SCHOOL PSYCHOLOGICAL SERVICES

The NASP logo, designed by former president Fred Dornbeck, depicts two interlocking circles: one containing the Greek letter psi (for psychology) and the other containing the lamp of learning (for education). Not surprisingly, the supervision of psychological services in schools is complicated by factors stemming from both the educational context and the field of psychology.

Educational Context

School psychology takes place in schools and concerns the interaction between students and their learning and learning environments. This highly contextualized nature renders the practice of school psychology and its supervision extremely complex.

Funding

Funding affects the supervision of school psychological services in at least two ways: the expense of supervision, and the funds used to underwrite psychological services in general. "Good" clinical supervision requires considerable contact between the supervisor and supervisee, and this time requirement is difficult to reconcile with the high needs of schools. While NASP mandates only 2 hours of face-to-face supervision per week for interns and beginning school psychologists, most skilled supervisors provide much more, particularly at the beginning of the year. In fact, supervisee perception of supervision quality has been found to be tied to frequent supervisee-supervisor contacts (Allen, Szollos, & Williams, 1986). On the other hand, both school psychologists and their supervisors are often severely taxed for time, and geographic separation across the school district exacerbates this difficulty. For school districts to justify this expenditure, supervisors of school psychologists must believe and convince administrators that supervised school psychological services are more cost effective than unsupervised services. Some consider it ethically imperative to experience weekly clinical supervision by a person who "not only knows how to manage others to do a good job but also is . . . able to demonstrate how it can be done" (Chan, 2004, pp. 63–64). Others consider such supervision less valuable than direct service, perceive it as a luxury rather than a necessity, and are unwilling to allocate necessary resources. There is no question that clinical supervision is expensive, because it takes significant time on the part of both supervisors and supervisees. On the other hand, research and professional standards support this expenditure.

In addition, school psychologists are often funded through special education departments. This funding structure has led some to mistakenly believe that school psychologists should work with students only as they are deemed eligible for, or as they receive, special education services (Sheridan & Gutkin, 2000). This practice inappropriately ignores the needs of students in the general population for psychological services such as mental health promotion and crisis prevention and intervention. In their role as systemic change leaders, supervisors who find that their school psychologists are so constrained can work with district administrators to broaden school psychologists' connection to general education programs and students. For example, the job descriptions of school psychologists can be revised to include regular participation in general education child study and student support teams.

Educational Mandates and Legislation

Legislative and educational mandates institute multiple changes in educational practices. For example, the Individuals With Disabilities Education Improvement Act of 2004 (IDEA 2004) and the No Child Left Behind Act of 2001 (NCLB) emphasize accountability for teachers and administrators by requiring universal student outcomes; mandate the use of evidence-based educational practices such as scientifically established reading programs; require students—including those identified as eligible for special education services—to achieve certain levels of performance on achievement tests; and demand increased integration between general and special education (for instance, requiring that special education individualized education plans reflect general education curriculum benchmarks). These changes have a profound impact on the work of many school psychologists and on their professional development and supervision needs (Ysseldyke et al., 2006).

General Education Curriculum

The universal adoption of specified general education curricula across schools, districts, and states can have many unintended side effects. For example, many students who were exposed to but unresponsive to whole language reading instruction never developed strong reading skills. Students taught math using strategies completely unfamiliar to their parents are not able to obtain homework help from their parents. These variables affect the practice of school psychologists because they result in "curriculum casualties" and subsequent referrals for special assistance. In their role as systemic change leaders, supervisors can employ a number of strategies to address this challenge. For example, they can serve on curriculum adoption committees to advocate evidence-based curricula, provide professional development programs regarding evidence-based practices for teachers, and help administrators to develop prevention and targeted intervention programs and to evaluate program outcomes.

Increased Demands in Promoting Students' Mental Health

Increased focus on the necessity for schools to address the mental health needs of all students, particularly in the wake of tragic school violence and high rates of suicide, school dropout, and other mental health situations (Sheridan & Gutkin, 2000), has resulted in the need for school psychologists to increase the time they devote to these issues. However, schools do not have a tradition of providing clinical supervision necessary for adequate mental health services and actually have been found to sustain a pervasive anticlinical bias from higher level administrators (Breiman, 2001). The importance of incorporating systemic change leadership into the supervisory role when supervising in a school setting is well illustrated by these considerations.

Evaluation Procedures

Because school psychologists are often evaluated by educational administrators using instruments designed for the evaluation of teachers, they are not evaluated using criteria specific to their role (Chafouleas et al., 2002). To change this, more appropriate evaluation methods that specifically address school psychologists' "standards of performance" must be developed through participation in the collective bargaining process (Clarke, 2006). Successful supervisors address the evaluation system used with school psychologists and ensure that they address the skills needed for effective practice.

Supervisory Structures

Typical school administrative structures complicate adequate supervision of school psychological services considerably. As mentioned previously, most often school psychologists have administrative supervisors who are not psychologists and who are unable to address professional components unique to the provision of school psychological services. This results in school psychologists' receiving very little supervision regarding the activities at which they spend the majority of their time.

Since school psychologists are almost always the only school psychologist in a building, they often do not have opportunities for professional collaboration or peer supervision. Therefore, they are often not members of a "community of learners," essential to professional growth (Sergiovanni & Starratt, 2007).

As is common for middle managers, supervisors of school psychological services must balance the expectations of upper administration and the needs of the school psychologists whom they supervise. They must resolve conflicting components of professional identity, ethical guidelines, policies of the school district, and expectations and desires of teachers, parents, students, and principals.

Further, the "unity of command" principle indicates that each supervisee should have only one immediate supervisor (Rue & Byars, 1997). Yet in the practice of school psychology there is often more than one administrator (e.g., multiple principals, directors of special education, and superintendents) involved in prioritizing the time and activities of school psychologists.

Finally, schools sustain an extremely high supervisor-supervisee ratio in general. The "span of management" referred to in business literature addresses the number of supervisees a manager can effectively supervise. Urwick (1938) originally indicated that no one should attempt to supervise more than six individuals at a time. This number is not absolute, for it is reduced by the complexity and variety of jobs held by the supervisees and increased by physical proximity and high personnel quality (Rue & Byars, 1997). Nonetheless, this figure is much lower than the number of supervisees typically supervised by a single individual in school settings. For example, in a school of 500 children one principal probably attempts to supervise more than 30 individuals (20 teachers, a half dozen special service and support personnel, and several secretaries and custodians). In a classroom a teacher is expected to supervise the learning of about 25 children at a time, and in the vignette that opened this chapter, Dottie is expected to supervise 53 individuals. The level of supervision possible with such ratios is reminiscent of industrial factories and is far below the level of supervision appropriate for complex settings and professions. In schools, supervision is seen as a low priority and is not well funded, whether the supervisee is a teacher, counselor, or school psychologist.

Confusion Regarding the Appropriate Roles of School Psychologists

Gilman and Gabriel (2004) discerned fundamental differences among teachers', administrators', and school psychologists' perceptions of what school psychology is and what school psychologists should do. School administrators were frequently satisfied with the traditional services provided by school psychologists. Despite this satisfaction, and without regard for time constraints, administrators also endorsed school psychologists' devoting additional time to parent workshops, in-service training, and teacher consultation. On the other hand, teachers believed that school psychologists should increase the time they devoted to individual counseling, group counseling, crisis intervention, work with general education students, teacher consultation, parent consultation, and parent workshops, while administrators expressed less interest in school psychologists devoting additional time to counseling, crisis intervention, working with general education students, and curriculum development. Despite these additional expectations, on average both teachers and administrators indicated that the amount of time school psychologists spend in special education assessment should remain the same, and at least one third preferred that school psychologists participate in more assessment activities!

On their part, school psychologists tend to endorse spending less time on special education assessment and more time on individual counseling, group counseling, working with general education, and curriculum development (Gilman & Gabriel, 2004). These endorsements are substantiated in professional practice guidelines (Ysseldyke et al., 2006) and professional literature (Sheridan & Gutkin, 2000), which indicate that relying on special education assessment, written reports, and very brief team meetings to communicate complex intervention information results in intervention failure. This finding is particularly troubling given the lack of evidence regarding benefits of full-time special education and the considerable research evidence supporting increased involvement in evidence-based preventative measures, intervention development and monitoring, and policy development.

Therefore, conflicts exist between the expectation of administrators and the desires of teachers, the interests of psychologists, and best practices as defined by research literature. Even though school administrators would like increased teacher consultation, parent workshops, and in-service training, they expect and favorably view the current functions of school psychologists. Time constraints profoundly impact school psychologists' ability to expand their role while simultaneously completing already required paperwork. Since administrators are the individuals who complete the school psychologists' evaluations, their viewpoints are pivotal and must be addressed.

Vignette 1.4

As a clinical supervisor, **Carrie** co-supervises six school psychologists with their administrative supervisors, the district principals. One principal perceives that the school psychologists' primary role is to identify troublesome students as eligible for special education—then recommend placement in self-contained classes located in another school. In contrast, Carrie perceives that their primary role is to develop and monitor interventions enabling those same students to successfully stay in their home school. Clearly, until the clinical supervisor and the administrative supervisor reconcile these fundamental differences, their conflicting viewpoints put one school psychologist in a very difficult position!

Variability in Available School Personnel

Supervision of psychological services in schools is additionally complicated by a high degree of variability in personnel available to provide prevention and intervention programs. In some elementary schools, school psychologists are the only mental health professionals, and they provide preventative and classroom-based services as well as targeted small group mental health interventions. In other schools, these services are provided by school counselors. In some secondary schools, counselors provide guidance relative to course selection and college admissions while school psychologists provide individual counseling, group counseling, and crisis intervention for students with acute mental health issues. In yet other schools, social workers are employed to interface with families and community agencies, but in some settings this responsibility falls to school psychologists. In some schools reading teachers measure the reading skills of the general student population using Curriculum-Based Measurement tools and then monitor the progress of students enrolled in small group interventions, while other schools do not have reading specialists and this responsibility is assumed by school psychologists. In some schools teachers of students with learning disabilities play a major role in the assessment of academic and cognitive strengths and weaknesses, while in other schools that role is the province of school psychologists. In many districts school psychologists design and monitor behavior intervention plans, while other districts employ behavioral specialists to do the same; similarly, in some settings school psychologists oversee programs for students with emotional handicaps, while in other settings a special education teacher is assigned that responsibility. This variability clearly affects and creates extraordinary disparities in the practice and supervision of school psychology.

Variability in Community Resources

Variability in community resources also affects the practice and supervision of school psychology. Extreme diversity exists in terms of student needs, socioeconomic status, and community supports. For example, a school psychologist working in a small city with supports for students and their families (e.g., an active and involved counseling center that has a sliding scale and appeals to adolescents and low-income families, and a Boys & Girls Club that provides homework support, after-school care, dinner for students, and social work services for families) has resources unavailable to a school psychologist working in an isolated suburb or rural area. In the latter setting, school psychologists may well be called upon to coordinate or even provide such services.

Multiculturalism

Increased multiculturalism in schools and communities has resulted in multiple challenges. First, multiculturalism impacts the practice of school psychology, and supervisors are responsible for helping their supervisees respond appropriately to multicultural issues in counseling and assessment as well as large system issues (e.g., large numbers of English language learners failing high-stakes testing, being refused high school graduation, and dropping out of school). Furthermore, as the field of school psychology becomes increasingly diverse, supervisors of school psychologists face the challenge of supervising individuals from cultures quite unlike their own. Because of the power differential inherent in the supervisory relationship, supervisors must directly bring up and facilitate discussions regarding multicultural issues in supervision, such as cultural sensitivity, respect, and cross-cultural mistrust (Nilsson & Anderson, 2004).

Novice Psychologists' Difficulty Dealing With Complexity

Novices have difficulty dealing with complexity in general. Consequently, one of a supervisor's tasks is to help clarify complex cases for novice psychologists (Stoltenberg et al., 1998). Supervisors of school psychological services must address this challenge on the systems level as well as the individual case level, since the complexity of schools is multifaceted. If supervisors address this issue only at the case level, they will not enable their supervisees to master the complexity of working in schools sufficiently to be able to provide the full range of services.

Concomitant Changes in Psychology

Leaders in the field of school psychology are advocating a paradigm shift in the provision of school psychological services away from assessment-focused practice and toward the provision of empirically supported, outcomes-focused interventions (Sheridan & Gutkin, 2000). This position stems from the belief that, to have meaningful impact on students' lives, school psychologists

> must move away from service delivery systems based on medical models and commit to models that emphasize (a) the development of healthy systems and environments where children spend most of their time (e.g., families, schools, communities); and (b) individual, group, and system-level services that are based in problem-solving methodologies. (Curtis, Grier, & Hunley, 2004, p. 63)

At the 2002 Conference on the Future of School Psychology, critical outcomes on which to focus the practice of school psychology were identified as:

- Improved academic competence and school success for all children
- Improved social-emotional functioning for all children
- Enhanced family-school partnerships and parental involvement in schools
- More effective education and instruction for all learners
- School-based child and family services integrated with community services that promote health and mental health (Cummings et al., 2004)

This shift clearly supports the outcomes-based mandates inherent in legislation such as NCLB and IDEA 2004. However, this shift also creates major challenges for supervisors of school psychological services.

Experience and Comfort Levels

Many school psychologists were trained and have years of experience in a medical model in which they are expected to be assessment experts, particularly in the diagnosis of special education eligibility. Further, many school psychologists are not skilled in understanding systems, effecting systems change, or conceptualizing and delivering prevention programs. Supervisors can deliberately foster supervisees' professional development in these areas through systematic, districtwide support systems that augment traditional workshops.

In supporting a role change, supervisors are challenged by the comfort of the status quo. Many school psychologists are comfortable in the role of special education evaluator, and it is very difficult for individuals who have been experts for some time in one role to accept the considerable discomfort inevitably resulting from assuming new roles and once again performing at the novice level. Supervisors can openly discuss these issues with supervisees and overtly address critical variables such as expectations, time allocation, and criteria for success.

Limited Availability of Appropriate Field Placements

In some settings (e.g., Illinois, Iowa, Wisconsin, and Florida) school psychologists have readily stepped into roles reflective of this paradigm shift. They routinely serve on non–special education problem solving teams, coordinate curriculum-based assessments, monitor intervention results, provide preventative mental health services, and provide intensive evidence-based mental health services. In other settings, these roles are not yet recognized or valued by the school district or state. This variability makes it quite difficult for training programs to have a universal outcome. Training programs can easily provide didactic coursework and even practica in the expanded role, but without internship settings providing sufficient practice to attain some degree of proficiency, the skills will not be sustained. Furthermore, when the school psychologist is employed, particularly in isolated settings, it is very difficult to sustain the expanded role without supervisory or contextual support.

Internship Experiences

Despite many years' emphasis on expanded roles during school psychology training, typical internships still emphasize assessment. This results in interns' and practitioners' experiencing low self-efficacy and low self-esteem regarding other roles such as counseling and consultation (Trant, 2001). Clearly, internships must be carefully structured, organized, and supervised such that sufficient training and supervision in the full spectrum of services occurs and graduates feel effective across all domains.

Shortage of School Psychologists

A shortage of school psychologists has existed for some time and is likely to be exacerbated by a large number of retirements in the near future (Curtis et al., 2004). This shortage adds yet another dimension to the complexity of supervising psychological services. Many positions go unfilled, resulting in unacceptably high student–school psychologist ratios. It can be overwhelming for already overtaxed school psychologists to devote time to acquiring new skills or initiating new programs, even if they save time in the long run. This is particularly problematic when "old" procedures are maintained in the meantime.

Vignette 1.5

Anne, whom we met at the beginning of the chapter, knows that the number of students eligible for special education services will decrease as academic difficulties are identified and addressed in the primary grades. In the meantime, however, she struggles to respond to referrals and reevaluations in the intermediate grades, required for those students who did not benefit from the early intervening program.

Supervision Complexity

Because supervision occurs at multiple levels, a supervisor's skill development must also develop at multiple levels. Supervision training at the graduate level will be almost unavoidably limited to the development of microskills, such as discrete consultation, assessment, and counseling skills, because graduate students have not developed sufficient experience as school psychologists to be able to provide adequate clinical supervision regarding complex services such as systems change. This can usually occur only after additional years of successful experience have afforded sufficient knowledge regarding schools and education as well as sufficient credibility in the eyes of teachers and administrators. At that point, school psychologists are in a position to provide systemic leadership that can inspire effective school psychology programs and serve as an impetus for appropriate systems level change (Harvey, 2008).

Lack of Supervision Training

According to a demographic survey by Hunley et al. (2000), 90% of supervising school psychologists had not completed coursework in supervision and 83% had not taken part in substantial additional training in supervision. Doctoral level programs supply coursework in supervision and some state associations provide ongoing professional development in supervision (M. E. Swerdlik, personal communication, April 9, 2007). However, most interns are supervised by specialist level school psychologists who are not obligated to complete supervision training. Furthermore, because no supervision credential is required for either clinical or administrative supervision in school psychology, there is little incentive to complete coursework in clinical supervision after a few years of practice. There may be little incentive to complete coursework in administrative supervision unless such coursework is provided or required by the school district or state.

Ambiguous Prioritization of Supervision by Professional Organizations

Supervision has been identified as a central domain of training in psychology (APA, 2007), proposed as a core competency in clinical psychology (Falender et al., 2004), and adopted as a core competency for mental health counselors (Dye & Borders, 1990). Clinical supervision of master's level mental health professionals who work in private practice or clinical settings (Herlihy et al., 2002), and of APA-licensed doctoral level psychologists, is mandated through initial years of work in the field. These standards reflect the pivotal role that supervision plays in the training and credentialing of many psychologists and counselors (Falender et al., 2004).

In contrast, credentialing and training regarding supervision has not been universally supported in the field of school psychology. While NASP adopted a position paper in support of supervision, a supervisory credential has not been established and supervision has not been identified as a core competency. This may stem from a desire of school psychologists to be autonomous and avoid the inherently hierarchical nature of supervision (D. E. McIntosh & Phelps, 2000). Or it may stem from a desire to avoid the discomfort of having one's work scrutinized (Herlihy et al., 2002).

Because of the lack of identification of supervision as a core competency and because of the lack of a supervisory credential, few training programs provide comprehensive training in supervision, and consequently few school psychologists are adequately prepared for this role. R. P. Ross and Goh (1993) found that although most school psychologists supervise other school psychologists or interns at some point, only 25% of supervising school psychologists received graduate training in supervision and only 11% received this training within their school psychology programs. Hunley et al. (2000) found that only 10% of school psychologists identifying themselves as supervisors had received training in supervision prior to becoming a supervisor. Furthermore, since clinical supervision is so rarely provided, few school psychologists have received clinical supervision beyond their internship. Even in situations where supervision does occur, many supervisors have received neither supervision training nor supervision-of-supervision (Illback & Morrissey, 1985).

The lack of training in supervision typical for school psychologists is in direct contrast to the fields of family therapy, counseling psychology, clinical psychology, and school administration, all of which provide training in and have developed a body of literature about supervision. Furthermore, the lack of training in supervision directly contradicts the dictates of professional organizations. Both NASP and APA professional standards indicate that psychologists should not provide services for which they have not had adequate training. Knowledge and skills in supervision have been identified as distinct competencies that must be developed through systematic education and training (Falender et al., 2004), yet as a whole the field of school psychology lacks such training.

SUPERVISOR QUALIFICATIONS, VALUES, KNOWLEDGE, SKILLS, AND TRAINING

As previously indicated, while administrative supervisors do not need training as school psychologists, it is important that clinical supervisors have training, credentials, and at least 3 years of successful experience as a school psychologist (NASP, 2000b). APA standards indicate that supervision should be provided by doctoral level psychologists, and school psychologists who identify themselves as supervisors indeed hold doctoral degrees more often than school psychologists in general (45% vs. 21%; Hunley et al., 2000). NASP (2004) does not mandate the doctoral degree. Nonetheless, professional standards clearly indicate that training in the supervision of school personnel is desirable. This need is reinforced by school psychologists who identify themselves as supervisors and state that they would like to receive additional support, such as training in supervision, meetings with other supervisors, participation in mentoring programs, and membership in Listservs (Hunley et al., 2000).

Regardless of the educational background of the supervisor, supervision is unfortunately not always effective. As Sergiovanni and Starratt (2007) stated, for many,

> experiences of supervision are anything but uplifting. Again and again, [educators] tell of being placed in a win-lose situation and of experiencing powerlessness, manipulation, sexual harassment, and racial and ethnic stereotyping. At best, their encounters with supervisors lead directly to evaluative judgments based on the skimpiest of evidence. At worst, these encounters can destroy autonomy, self-confidence, and personal integrity. Unfortunately, supervision as practiced by some supervisors is not only nonprofessional, it is dehumanizing and unethical. (pp. 66–67)

School psychologists report similarly negative supervisory experiences resulting from defensive, domineering, incompetent, or uninvolved supervisors. They might be required to "figure out things for themselves," subjected to overly critical feedback and insensitive supervision, or receive supervision characterized by a lack of awareness of critical issues such as multicultural concerns (Hunley et al., 2000).

Negative supervision experiences result from "supervision mismatches" (S. M. Gross, 2005). Mismatches can occur because the provided supervision does not match the developmental level of the supervisee; because the supervisee and supervisor differ in terms of desired supervision structure, time allocation, privacy of supervisory communications, theoretical orientations, or reliance on empirically based decisions; because the supervisee has multiple supervisors with conflicting expectations; or because supervisees are unhappy with workloads (perhaps because they feel exploited relative to other practitioners or because they feel they are given the least desirable assignments, or because they feel underutilized). To avoid such mismatches, it is essential to foster the values, knowledge, and skills necessary for effective supervision.

Critical Supervision Values

Effective supervisors maintain and uphold the ethical principals mandated by their profession. They assume responsibility for the welfare of the student and for the practice of the supervisee. They are respectful, sensitive, and responsive to supervisee development. They balance challenges and supports and are committed to respecting diversity. They are committed to lifelong learning and professional growth for their supervisees and for themselves, both in terms of clinical skills and supervision. They also are committed to translating research into practice and advocating service delivery that maximizes student development.

Effective supervisors demonstrate a thorough knowledge and commitment to ethical practice by applying ethical principles in complex situations, fostering the ethical development of supervisees, and ensuring that nonexploitative relationships are maintained between themselves and supervisees as well as between supervisees and clients. They are skillful in conflict management by listening, avoiding blame, suppressing personal needs, and achieving conflict resolution.

Critical Supervisor Knowledge

Professional Knowledge

Effective supervisors maintain current knowledge regarding professional areas, including school psychology, counseling and clinical psychology, educational psychology, neuropsychology, developmental psychology, and general and special education. They regularly read *School Psychology Review*, the *Communiqué*, and other journals such as *American Psychologist, Exceptional Children, Educational Leadership, Educational Psychology, Learning Disabilities: Research & Practice, Behavioral Disorders*, and *Psychology in the Schools*. They are quickly able to find information and research articles through online or library literature searches.

Systems Knowledge

Effective supervisors have considerable knowledge regarding the schools, district, community, and sociopolitical contexts in which their supervisees practice. They have thorough knowledge of educational organizational structures and policies and the delegation of duties and responsibilities in their employing school systems (Curtis & Yager, 1981, 1987).

Supervision Knowledge

Effective supervisors are additionally knowledgeable regarding models, theories, modalities, and research on supervision. They are skilled in supervision techniques and knowledgeable regarding supervisee development, ethics, legal issues, evaluation, and diversity.

Critical Supervisor Skills

Interpersonal and Communicative Skills

Effective supervisors demonstrate complex interpersonal and communicative skills. They are skilled in working with diverse individuals, conflict resolution, providing individual and group supervision, and advocating for the profession with administrators. Effective supervisors also demonstrate multicultural competencies in working with students, parents, teachers, and supervisees. They have skills relevant to consultation, group dynamics, and decision making, including excellent listening skills and the ability to perceive underlying issues at a deep as well as surface level. They are able to develop strong supervisory alliances by engendering trust and honesty, conveying warmth and acceptance, and eliciting feelings of safety such that supervisees honestly disclose difficulties and subsequently make professional growth and gain confidence (Worthen & McNeill, 1996).

Effective supervisors attend to the developmental level of supervisees by providing beginner supervisees with attention to discrete skill development while simultaneously refining their ability to conceptualize cases. They provide intermediate supervisees with assistance with conceptualization skills, personal development, and theory development, and they provide advanced supervisees with assistance in dealing with complex cases (Stoltenberg et al., 1998; Worthen & McNeill, 1996). They help supervisees perceive the complexity of clients' issues, yet simultaneously render complex and confusing situations more coherent. Good supervisors delegate effectively and motivate their supervisees to high levels of performance. They help supervisees develop a game plan to address challenging situations. They also provide supervisees with the impetus to develop a positive professional identity.

Professional Skills

Clinical supervisors should provide supervision only in those areas in which they are proficient. They therefore should assess their own skill proficiency, find ways to increase their proficiency in less developed areas, and seek support from more proficient professionals when appropriate.

Skills in Systemic Leadership

Effective supervisors are also skilled in providing systemic leadership. They develop and implement programs, serve as change agents at multiple levels to implement scientific problem solving, and translate current research results into educational and psychological practice (Harvey, 2008). While so doing, they consider the impact of local variables such as personnel, budgets, curricula, organizational structure, and changing contexts (Rosenfield, 2000).

Supervisory Skills

Effective supervisors are skillful teachers in that they identify learning needs, write learning goals, devise instructional strategies, present material didactically and/or experientially, evaluate learning, take an authoritative role, and give constructive comments. They skillfully implement supervision methods and techniques, provide effective formative and summative evaluations, and promote professional growth and self-assessment.

They accurately assess their own skills, solicit and respond to supervisee feedback, and seek consultation when they encounter issues beyond their competence. They also balance multiple roles and set appropriate boundaries.

Training Supervisors

To attain the values, attitudes, knowledge, and skills described above, it is highly likely that supervision training is necessary. While many doctoral level programs now include courses in supervision, relatively few specialist level programs do, even though graduates are likely to become intern supervisors within a few years of graduation. The widespread lack of training and supervised practice in the supervision of school psychology is extremely unfortunate and verges on unethical practice, since practicing as a supervisor without adequate training can be construed as practicing outside the area of expertise.

The concept of training and supervising supervisors is not new in counseling psychology (J. M. Bernard & Goodyear, 2004; Mead, 1990; Storm, 1997; Storm, Todd, McDowell, & Sutherland, 1997). The Approved Clinical Supervisor credential put forth by the Center for Credentialing and Education (2001) recommends training processes and content for mental health supervisors. Further, the clinical psychology literature indicates that supervisors should be able to provide verification that they have received training and supervision-of-supervision, as well as documents that reflect feedback regarding their supervisory skills and readiness to supervise independently (Falender et al., 2004). Gizara and Forrest (2004) recommended that supervisor training include the following:

1. Mandated supervision courses and practica that focus on evaluative processes

2. Close examination of and adherence to standards of practice

3. Development of the supervisor's ability to recognize and address ethical issues

4. Development of a professional norm to confront inadequate practice

5. Maintenance of a collegial supervision group characterized by trust and respect, sustained dialogue, and regularly scheduled meetings with other supervisors during the workweek, particularly for novice supervisors

Vignette 1.6

Barbara has been working as a school psychologist for 10 years and feels reasonably capable and competent in the position. This year one of her schools is entering into an agreement with a nearby university to become a Professional Development School, which means that she is now expected to supervise interns. She feels that the supervision she received as an intern was excellent, but that was a long time ago. She is not sure her skills are completely up to date, she no longer has a supervisor, and she has neither had a course in supervision nor ever worked in a setting in which she received supervision other than her internship. She feels that having interns would be exciting and enriching but is concerned that she is being asked to practice in an area beyond her expertise.

Supervising the novice practitioner offers a challenging responsibility. Effective supervision of interns requires proficient teaching abilities, expert clinical knowledge, and strong technical expertise. Perhaps no other component of professional training has a greater impact on a student's skills and potential. During this structured learning experience, a foundation for future ethical practice and professional knowledge development is established. Just as student teachers tend to teach in a manner similar to that of their supervising practitioners (Henry & Beasley, 1982), the model of practice demonstrated by the supervising school psychologist often becomes the model followed by the intern. Thus internship supervision has perpetuity, because professionals tend to supervise others in the manner in which they were supervised.

Regrettably, despite the intensely demanding nature of this supervisory role, most internship supervisors have received little or no formal academic training in supervision and do not receive supervision of their supervision (Knoff, 1986; Ward, 1999; Zins, Murphy, & Wess, 1989). This important role is customarily undertaken with little knowledge and insufficient ongoing support. In response to this quandary, novice supervisors can obtain training in a number of ways. They can participate in professional workshops followed by informal self-study and peer supervision networks, attend university-run training for field supervisors, enroll in professional workshops, or complete formal coursework.

Workshops, Informal Self-Study, and Peer Supervision Networks

Attending supervision workshops at professional meetings is a good introduction to critical issues but must be supplemented by deliberate self-study and participation in a peer supervision network. All supervisors should seek consultation and collegial supervision from other supervisors or expert psychologists, particularly when supervising in relatively unfamiliar areas. When they self-supervise, supervisors protect the welfare of both clients and supervisees by monitoring and improving their own performance so that it resembles the practice of experienced supervisors (Knoff, 1986; Mead, 1990; Todd, 1997b).

University-Run Training for Field Supervisors

As indicated by Abramson and Fortune (1990), to provide an effective learning environment field, supervisors and university trainers should share common knowledge bases, teaching strategies, and evaluation processes. University-sponsored training sessions for field supervisors can help foster these commonalities. McMahon and Simons (2004) utilized a 4-day, 6-hour-per-day training program that included personal reflection, small group discussions, case discussions, role plays, practice supervision sessions, lectures, readings, and tapes of supervision sessions. Relative to a control group, participants significantly increased their levels of confidence, self-awareness, skills, techniques, and knowledge.

Gourdine and Baffour (2004) described a variety of studies that demonstrate effective university-run training sessions for developing field supervisors' critical thinking skills, ability to conduct process monitoring of discrete clinical skills, knowledge of single-system research design, goal-directed supervision ability, and multicultural skills. Participation in even one training session increased supervisors' perception of their ability to supervise, integrate theory and research into fieldwork, and promote professional socialization. They recommend that competency-based sessions for field supervisors focus on increasing their understanding of professional codes of ethics, core competencies, and basic supervisory skills. Essential competencies for field supervisors, adapted from Gourdine and Baffour, are included in Handout 1.1.

Handout 1.1

FIELD SUPERVISOR COMPETENCIES

(Adapted from Gourdine & Baffour, 2004)[1]

1. Understand internship requirements and evaluation criteria by studying university fieldwork handbooks

2. Review university course syllabi and master training program content to help supervisees integrate theory and current research into practice

3. Review and monitor interns' work both directly (e.g., observe, listen to tapes, and read reports) and indirectly (e.g., read case process notes)

4. Deliver structured learning activities during which district policies are explained and professional tasks are modeled

5. Develop personal problem solving skills and foster them in supervisees through modeling and structured learning activities

6. Improve one's own and supervisees' multicultural skills

7. Promote supervisees' professional identity through mentoring, providing opportunities for interactions with other professionals, modeling professional and respectful behavior, and discussing appropriate professional behavior

8. Structure appropriate internship experiences by specifying tasks, roles, responsibilities, and case presentations

9. Provide interns with opportunities to demonstrate knowledge of district policies, practices, and procedures

10. Assess relevant community and district services, model consultation for interns, and foster their understanding of consultation processes

11. Provide well-structured supervision sessions that facilitate interns' ability to evaluate their own learning

12. Foster interns' understanding of ethical practice by discussing ethical dilemmas and relating them to professional codes

13. Help interns successfully transition from student to practitioner by managing personal and professional stresses

14. Remain aware of the levels of stress that interns may be experiencing and arrange for additional support when appropriate; maintain the roles of mentor and teacher without taking on the role of therapist

---

[1]Gourdine, R., & Baffour, T. (2004). Maximizing learning: Evaluating competency-based training program for field instructors. *Clinical Supervisor, 23*, 33–53.

Formal Coursework in Supervision or Administration

Formal training in supervision that includes didactic coursework and in supervision-of-supervision that incorporates observations (direct or via taping) followed by critical feedback has repeatedly been recommended (Falender et al., 2004). Such training addresses knowledge of supervision research and theoretical literature, peer group supervision, training in individual and group supervision, observations of skilled supervisors providing supervision, monitoring and feedback of supervision sessions, consideration of the developmental level of supervisees, multicultural skills of supervisors and supervisees, accountability of supervision, and assessment of supervision skills by supervisees.

Peace and Sprinthall (1998) described a two-semester course in supervision. During the first semester, supervision skills are taught by providing a rationale, modeling the skill, giving opportunities to practice with peers, and generalizing the skill. Topics include:

1. Needs of novice practitioners

2. Techniques for building positive supervisory relationships

3. Models of adult and professional development

4. Differentiating supervision according to supervisee development

5. Updating clinical skills of supervisors

6. Observing, collecting data, and conferencing about clinical skills

7. Analyzing interactions between supervisee and supervisors

During the second semester, supervision students apply the above skills to supervision itself. They keep supervision journals, tape supervision sessions, and review journals and tapes in supervision-of-supervision sessions to obtain corrective feedback. Some supervisors, at a higher developmental level, were easily able to apply skills and analyze them at a complex level, while others required more structured instruction to foster growth (Peace & Sprinthall, 1998).

A NOTE TO THE READER

As evidenced in this chapter's discussion of supervision challenges, enhancing school psychologists' professional development and providing appropriate supervision can be quite challenging. As supervisors adopt the new strategies described in this book, they will need to obtain support in order to tolerate the anxiety and incremental progress that inevitably accompany learning. Furthermore, given the complexity of providing adequate supervision, novice supervisors should either obtain supervision-of-supervision or collaborate with one another to provide mutual support. As they learn, to avoid feeling overwhelmed, supervisors will need to themselves employ executive functions in planning, selecting, implementing, appraising, and modifying their supervision.

While providing supervision is a daunting task that requires both technical expertise and interpersonal skills, it also represents an extraordinary opportunity to truly make a difference. Continuously developing and honing one's own skills while fostering an optimal learning environment for supervisees is a tremendously satisfying way to bequeath one's professional legacy and ultimately benefit the children and adolescents we serve.

SUMMARY

Supervision includes evaluation, skill enhancement, feedback, maintenance of professional competencies, and development of new competencies. The goal of supervision is to improve not only the performance of school psychologists but also the performance of supervisors, students, and the school community as a whole. Supervision has some similarities to teaching, consulting, and providing therapy but is also very different.

Effective supervision assists supervisees with problem solving, reflecting on practice, continuous learning, maintaining professional and ethical standards, upholding laws and statutes, and managing difficult situations. It also provides feedback and training in a manner that is responsive to the supervisee's developmental level. Clinical supervisors are responsible for the oversight of professional practice and the provision of discipline-specific training and knowledge. Administrative supervisors provide leadership, recruit and hire, delegate assignments, conduct formal personnel evaluations, design corrective actions, and take ultimate responsibility for services provided by supervisees.

The importance of supervision is reflected in the professional practice standards and ethical guidelines of both the National Association of School Psychologists (NASP) and the American Psychological Association (APA), but school psychologists often do not receive adequate supervision. Clinical supervision is often absent or given by supervisors who have no training in school psychology and therefore lack the necessary clinical skills. Furthermore, multiple challenges confront those providing administrative supervision and systemic leadership. Nonetheless, it is critical that effective supervision be established and maintained for school psychologists. Furthermore, it is important that psychologists receive training in the provision of supervision.

REFLECTIVE QUESTIONS

Q1.1. In what ways is supervision both similar to and different from teaching, consulting, and providing therapy?

Q1.2. What are the similarities and differences between administrative and clinical supervision? Which responsibilities fall under each?

Q1.3. Why is clinical supervision neglected? Why is it critically important?

Q1.4. Discuss how professional standards and ethical guidelines support the need for administrative and clinical supervision. What are the specific recommendations of NASP and APA?

Q1.5. What are the features of an effective supervisory structure?

Q1.6. What factors complicate and challenge the supervision of school psychologists?

Q1.7. Why does the supervision of school psychologists require systemic leadership in addition to administrative and clinical supervision?

Q1.8. Discuss the critical needs, skills, and training of supervisors and why these present their own challenges.

Q1.9. Design a supervision training program.

2

Interpersonal Relationships

A positive supervisory relationship is critical to effective supervision.

Vignette 2.1

After 3 years, **Timothy** was so happy with his position as a school psychologist in Turner City that he expected he would work there until retirement. His supervisor, **Rowena**, was very supportive whenever he suggested new ideas, and Timothy was thrilled that he had already developed two innovative and successful programs—an after-school care program at the elementary school that resulted in increased homework completion and improved grades, and a social-academic support program for at-risk high school students that reduced dropout.

Two years later, Timothy abruptly quit his job in Turner City to take a job in a neighboring district. Timothy explains, "Rowena quit last year, and my new supervisor, **Babs**, was awful. She closed the programs I had started, saying I had to devote all of my time to special education students. She was impossible to communicate with. Whether I wrote a memo, e-mailed, or met her in person, she did not listen or follow through. She infuriates principals and parents—and I caught the flak when they were unhappy. I've had it. Life is too short." On her part, **Babs** has no idea why Timothy left and is angry at being left with an unfilled position.

Unlike Babs, effective supervisors of school psychological services are adept at complex interpersonal relationships. Whether working with an individual supervisee or communicating with school administrators, they have excellent listening skills, are proficient problem solvers, and respond to issues at both deep and surface levels. This chapter addresses these essential interpersonal supervision skills. The subset of these skills relevant to multicultural competencies is addressed in Chapter 3.

BASIC CONSIDERATIONS

Just as the ability to develop effective consultative relationships is essential to consultation with teacher and parents and the ability to develop effective therapeutic alliances is essential in counseling, the ability to develop effective working alliances with supervisees, teachers, parents, and school administrators is integral to effective administrative supervision (Sergiovanni & Starratt, 2007), clinical supervision (Frawley-O'Dea & Sarnat, 2001; Gill, 2001; Kaiser, 1997), and internship supervision (Perrotto, 2006). A positive supervisor-supervisee working alliance is reflected in increased supervisee adherence to supervisory recommendations, improved alliances between the supervisee and students, and subsequent student progress (M. J. Patton & Kivlighan, 1997).

Interpersonal difficulties with supervisors are among the most frequently mentioned factors contributing to supervisees' stress. Counseling supervisees describe helpful supervisors as supportive, collegial, respectful, nonjudgmental, and anxiety reducing, while negative supervisors are described as rigid, critical, inattentive, and demeaning (L. A. Gray, Ladany, Walker, & Ancis, 2001). Ramos-Sanchez et al. (2002) described poor supervisee-supervisor working alliances as manifested in personality conflicts; overly critical, judgmental, and unsupportive supervisors; conflicts regarding supervision activities, goals, and content of supervision sessions; insufficient supervision; and inadequate supervisor knowledge and skills. Conflicted supervisory relationships can also be characterized by disengaged or irresponsible supervisors, role confusion, power struggles, excessive supervisee workloads, sexual harassment, misunderstandings, and even supervisor expectations that supervisees will provide *them* personal support. School psychologists describe additional sources of interpersonal difficulties: supervisors who devalue best practices, conflicting expectations from multiple supervisors, ethical conflicts, too little delegation, too much delegation, and supervisors who have excessive need for power (Harvey, 2005b).

Poor interpersonal skills on the part of supervisors can actually harm individual supervisees, service delivery by the entire department, program delivery, and student progress. Unfortunately, supervisors can respond to such conflicts with anger or acts of revenge, such as negative or withheld evaluations (Nelson & Friedlander, 2001). A poor supervisory relationship can increase shame and exacerbate supervisees' tendency to conceal essential information from supervisors (Yourman, 2003). Supervisees can respond to conflict by withdrawing, losing trust, developing health problems, demonstrating diminished self-efficacy, engaging in increased self-reflection, and experiencing feelings of fear, powerlessness, and anxiety (Nelson & Friedlander, 2001). With or without intent, supervisors can neglect, harass, and provide demeaning or destructive supervision, which in turn undermines supervisees' work. Supervisors of school psychological services with poor working relationships can undermine efforts of the district school psychologists, as illustrated in the vignette that opened this chapter.

It is critical that all supervisors of school psychological services develop interpersonal skills that foster positive working alliances across the school district. Such alliances are affected by characteristics of the context in which supervision takes place, supervisor characteristics, supervisee characteristics, and dynamics of the supervisee-supervisor relationship.

CHARACTERISTICS OF THE SUPERVISORY CONTEXT

The context in which supervision occurs affects the supervisory relationship (Holloway, 1995). Any mentoring relationship is affected by the organization and culture in which it occurs (Ralph, 2002). This is particularly the case in settings where the organization has power over the professional careers of both supervisors and supervisees (Gediman, 2003), which of course is the case in school districts. Many of the contextual variables that affect the supervision of school psychological services were discussed in Chapter 1. These include the pervasive lack of time; the educational context, including funding of supervision (or lack thereof), funding of psychological services, educational mandates and legislation, competing educational priorities such as high-stakes testing, the general education curriculum, increased dependence on schools to address students' mental health needs, evaluation procedures used for school personnel, typical school administrative structures, confusion regarding the appropriate roles of school psychologists, variability in school personnel available to provide prevention and intervention programs, variability in community resources, and increased multiculturalism in schools; the shortage of school psychologists; and the marginalization of school psychological services.

When severe, contextual variables can cause supervisors themselves to experience marginalization and procedural injustices, such as the inability to influence decisions, disrespectful treatment, and unjust resource allocation. These result in supervisors' experiencing depression, apathy, and feelings of powerlessness and can even result in their becoming verbally hostile and abusive toward supervisees (Tepper, Duffy, Henle, & Lambert, 2006). Such a situation is clearly unacceptable and is one reason that all supervisory agreements should include recourses for supervisees to turn to in such an eventuality.

SUPERVISOR CHARACTERISTICS

Personal Characteristics

The personal characteristics of supervisors obviously affect the quality of supervision. Strong supervisors have *integrity.* They are truthful, honest, and in touch with reality; focus on quality work; are strong problem solvers; and consistently strive for improvement (Cloud, 2006). Supervisors who are able to forge positive affiliative attachments with others and have *secure attachment styles* (Bowlby, 1982) develop stronger working alliances than those with insecure attachment styles (Riggs & Bretz, 2006; White & Queener, 2003). Strong supervisors also have sufficient *cognitive development* to deal with complexity and conceptualize at a high level (J. M. Bernard & Goodyear, 2004) and are therefore able to deal with complex problems endemic to school psychology and empathize with supervisees, school administrators, teachers, and parents with whom they work. Strong supervisors are *mentally healthy* and do not suffer from disabling psychiatric disorders, such as severe personality disorders or substance dependency, that render professional functioning impossible. Furthermore, they are sensitive and responsive to *multicultural issues* (both their own and those experienced by others) such as age, socioeconomic class, ethnicity, race, gender, sexual identity, and religion.

Steps can be taken to foster personal traits relevant to supervisors' interpersonal skills. To foster the development of supervisors' integrity and ethical problem solving skills, it is useful to discuss and address ethical dilemmas. Since practitioners' ability to work at a higher cognitive level is fostered by supervision, it follows that supervisors' ability to work at higher cognitive levels would similarly be fostered by supervision-of-supervision and the development of metacognitive skills involved in supervision (J. M. Bernard & Goodyear, 2004). Finally, while it is hoped that individuals who suffer from disabling psychiatric disorders such as severe personality disorders or disabling substance dependence disorders are not promoted to become supervisors of school psychological services, in such an event the same procedures that are used to deal with any impaired employee should be used.

Supervisory Experience

Supervision experience and development also affects the supervision process. A number of models describe stages through which individuals progress as they advance from novice to expert in complex skills or professional development (Benner, 1984; Dreyfus & Dreyfus, 1991; Rønnestad & Skovholt, 2003; Stoltenberg, 2005; Stoltenberg, McNeill, & Delworth, 1998). Novice characteristics are addressed more fully later in this chapter, since they are critical supervisee characteristics, but they are mentioned as supervisor characteristics because all supervisors are novices when they begin to act as a supervisor.

Motivation

Motivation for assuming the responsibility of supervising others is another supervisor characteristic of interest, given the increased liability and workload associated with the position. Individuals might be motivated to become supervisors by an interest in mentoring and altruistically helping others. Supervisors may also have a desire for personal growth through positive relationships with others, as suggested by relational theory (C. Rogers, 1951). They might be motivated by the anticipation of increased pay or status, as suggested by behaviorists (Bandura, 1986; Skinner, 1953). Supervisors might be motivated by the drive for self-actualization (Maslow, 1954, 1970) or increasing self-efficacy (Bandura, 1997; Wolters, 2004), since supervising others often leads to opportunities to learn from supervisees or university connections. Thus supervisors might be extrinsically motivated to achieve an end result, intrinsically motivated to participate in the activity for its own sake, or both extrinsically and intrinsically motivated. As is true in other settings, supervisors can demonstrate mastery goal orientations, approach or avoidance performance goal orientations, or work avoidance goal orientations. Individuals with mastery goal orientations are intrinsically oriented, focus on improving their knowledge and skills, use effective strategies, prefer challenging tasks, and display greater persistence. Those with approach orientations strive to please and impress others or obtain rewards. Individuals with avoidance orientations focus on "not looking bad," and those with work avoidance goal orientations minimize the amount of time and effort they expend. The last two orientations have the poorest achievement level (Pintrich & Schunk, 2002). Logically, supervisors with mastery goal and approach orientations would be most effective in their roles, while those focusing on not looking bad would have the least positive outcomes.

Since altruistic, mastery goal, and positive approach orientations are associated with the best outcomes, as much as possible supervisors should be encouraged to be altruistically and intrinsically motivated, to focus on improving knowledge and skills, and to monitor the effectiveness of their strategies in order to foster continual improvement. They should be encouraged to focus on helping their supervisees and the entire department, and to "look good" as opposed to "not looking bad." This involves taking an active and positive leadership role, initiating new structures and procedures to accomplish goals, enlisting the enthusiastic participation of others in meeting these goals, and delegating by assigning work, responsibility, power, and sufficient authority—along with support—so that supervisees can satisfactorily complete delegated tasks (Rue & Byars, 1997).

Leadership Skills

A supervisor's systemic leadership skills are relevant, since they affect success within the school district (Harvey, 2008). Effective leaders initiate new structures and procedures to accomplish goals and are able to enlist the enthusiastic participation of others in meeting these goals. They help others perceive the complexity of situations yet simultaneously render the same situations more coherent. They have a firm grasp of decision making and conflict resolution. They are skillful advocates for those whom they lead, yet also delegate and effectively motivate supervisees. Effective leaders collaboratively set high and appropriate goals, manage organizational elements to free supervisees to work up to their potential, foster a democratic atmosphere that encourages individual participation, and work continually to expand supervisees' self-direction. They provide opportunities for supervisees' personal growth, and they help individuals move from a dependent role with a limited repertoire and a short-term perspective to a more mature, autonomous role with a varied repertoire and a long-term perspective. They provide staff with appropriate reinforcement, clear direction, and psychological support. Effective educational leaders treat staff as independent, mature, responsible professionals who have worked hard to attain their positions and are interested in performing well not only for themselves but in the service of students (Sergiovanni & Starratt, 2007).

Delegation Skills

Effective supervisors assign work, responsibility, power, and sufficient authority such that supervisees can satisfactorily complete delegated tasks (Rue & Byars, 1997). On the other hand, they also provide enough direction and support that supervisees can succeed with new challenges. In delegating, supervisors analyze how they spend their time, decide which tasks can be delegated, determine which supervisees can handle the tasks, assign authority, create a sense of responsibility for the task, provide ongoing support as necessary, and control and monitor the delegation. When determining whether to delegate a task, effective supervisors consider the supervisee's training or ability to do the job, the adequacy of time and resources, and the reality of an open communication system. Most individuals are capable of and interested in carrying considerable responsibility, but it is important that assignments encourage the personal growth of the school psychologist.

Supervisors sometimes are reluctant to delegate tasks because they fear supervisees will not be successful, because they believe it is easier or more comfortable to do tasks themselves, or because they are unwilling to relinquish power or recognition. However, by delegating, supervisors free themselves from routine tasks and have time and energy to spend on exceptional situations. Even more important, when supervisors delegate to supervisees' maximum ability, supervisees are more committed and are better positioned to grow professionally.

Vignette 2.2

Emily, a veteran school psychologist who provides clinical supervision for six school psychologists, has been finding herself "taking over" cases from her supervisees that have become "difficult." After reading an article on supervision, Emily realizes that her practice of taking over undermines her supervisees, prevents their professional growth, lowers their self-worth, and needlessly assigns her to cases all over the district. She decides to employ extensive coaching strategies to help her supervisees work through difficult cases, and on occasion she sits in on team meetings to provide support, but she no longer assumes responsibility for the cases or works directly with the administrators, parents, teachers, or students.

A primary delegation responsibility for supervisors of school psychological services is assigning individual school psychologists to particular schools and programs within the district. In making assignments, the strengths of the individual school psychologist and the needs of each school or program should be matched as closely as possible. In addition, it is important that the assignments are equitable, but equitable does not mean identical.

Activity 2.1

Delegating

With your supervisees, review specific situations in which you delegated responsibility. Identify situations in which they felt that:

- Tasks were delegated to them prematurely
- They were not given adequate responsibility
- They needed more detailed or frequent guidance
- They were managed too closely

SUPERVISEE CHARACTERISTICS

Personal Characteristics

As is true for supervisors, personal characteristics of supervisees have a considerable impact on the supervisory relationship. *Integrity* is essential for supervisees in that their openness, honesty, and professional competence makes it possible for supervisors to trust them, depend on their skilled professional practice, and minimally fear vicarious liability (J. M. Bernard & Goodyear, 2004). *Disabling psychiatric disorders* such as a supervisee's personality disorder or substance dependency can have a negative impact on the supervisory relationships. For example, supervisees prone to perfectionism can be so anxious that they become overwhelmingly self-critical, making it difficult for the supervisor to provide constructive support (Arkowitz, 2001). Supervisees' *cognitive development* affects the supervision processes, because practitioners who are able to conceptualize at a high level and deal with cognitive complexity are better able to empathize and conceptualize cases (J. M. Bernard & Goodyear, 2004). Furthermore, *multicultural issues* (both the supervisee's own and those experienced by others) such as age, socioeconomic class, ethnicity, race, gender, sexual identity, and religion can affect a supervisee's responses to supervision.

Experience

The personal experiences of school psychologists vary widely and consequently affect the supervision needed. For example, a first-year school psychologist who has worked for multiple years as a therapist in a mental health center will need considerably less supervision regarding mental health services and crisis intervention than a first-year school psychologist without those years of experience. Similarly, a school psychologist with prior experience working as a teacher will have a much deeper understanding of curricula and will be more readily able to relate to teachers than a psychologist without that experience.

Vignette 2.3

Albert, an administrator who supervises school psychologists and counselors, firmly believes that his supervisees must "join" with the teachers to gain their respect and cooperation. He finds that otherwise the teachers view them as "self-styled experts in an ivory tower." He therefore requires that supervisees observe in multiple schools and classrooms, attend faculty meetings, and be very familiar with the curricula. He encourages all school psychologists and counselors to "partner" with specific teachers and spend a great deal of time in their classrooms. He even encourages those without personal teaching experience to serve as substitute teachers!

Development

There are several models of professional development that differ in the number of stages or phases described yet contain substantial similarities. We will discuss two models. The Supervisee Experience and Development Model put forth by Rønnestad and Skovholt (2003) focuses on the psychosocial development of supervisees. As in Erik Erikson's (1950) model of psychosocial development, the individual is described as positively or negatively resolving predictable conflicts at each stage of development. The Integrated Developmental Model put forth by Stoltenberg and Delworth (1987) focuses on cognitive and affective development evident with skill acquisition. As in Piaget's model (Piaget & Inhelder, 1969) of cognitive development, qualitatively different thought processes are thought to exist at different stages. Individuals do not automatically attain the highest level of cognitive development; doing so depends upon environmental and personal variables.

Supervisee Experience and Development Model

Rønnestad and Skovholt (2003) developed the Supervisee Experience and Development Model after conducting a longitudinal study across the entire professional life. Their study, as well as studies suggesting that expertise requires at least 5 to 7 years of corrected experience (Ericsson & Charness, 1994), suggests that a model incorporating multiple years of professional practice is warranted. Rønnestad and Skovholt found that professional development was lifelong, slow, continuous, and erratic. Positive professional growth was propelled by an intense commitment to learn, continuous reflection, and moving between internal and external foci. Personal life influenced professional functioning. Interpersonal relationships, including those with students, influenced development more than "impersonal" sources such as workshops.

Six stages of professional growth were identified. Before most psychologists begin their professional training, they act as *lay helpers* who attempt to help parents, friends, children, and colleagues make decisions and improve personal relationships. Typically, lay helpers quickly identify the problem, offer emotional support, and provide advice based on personal experience. Lay helpers help in a way that feels natural to them and are guided by common sense. Often the lay helper strongly identifies with the person he or she is helping, does not take time to reflect, and is sympathetic rather than empathic (understands the experience of the other person, but loses the ability to regulate his or her own personal emotional involvement). This results in strong, specific, and often inappropriate advice (Rønnestad & Skovholt, 2003, pp. 10–11).

Beginning students, starting their professional training, find the combination of theories, research, students, professors, mentors, personal life, peers, and the social environment to be both exciting and overwhelming. They are challenged as they begin practicum work and move from the familiar role of "lay helper" to the unknown role of "professional." They tend to doubt their ability to pull it all together and therefore rely heavily on mentors and supervisors. They can have significant anxiety, sometimes to the point that they have difficulty concentrating and simultaneously remembering details about a case. Their anxiety tends to be mitigated by positive feedback from supervisors, teachers, administrators, parents, and students. Similarly, their anxiety can be significantly exacerbated by any criticism or negative feedback from any of those sources. Typically students in this phase are anxious both in their professional work and during supervision. They are appropriately unsure how to approach tasks and do not have confidence that they are effective. Consequently, they can feel distressed, troubled, irritated, or guilty. They are likely to closely imitate those they feel are experts. They also do best when assigned easily mastered and straightforward methods, models, systems, approaches, and frameworks that can be applied universally. While this tendency to prefer simplification is normal and characteristic, those who later grow professionally maintain an "active, searching, trying-out" approach. In contrast, those who later stagnate are less concerned with long-term development and are primarily concerned with reducing anxiety, limiting experience, and saving face (Rønnestad & Skovholt, 2003, pp. 10–11).

Advanced students, or interns, are expected to function at a basic professional level. Many aspire to function higher than this basic level and to excel by avoiding any mistakes. This can result in their acting cautiously, conservatively, and with excessive thoroughness. They tend to feel excessively responsible. Typically, advanced students realize that they still have a great deal to learn. They often feel vulnerable and insecure and seek approval from peers and supervisors, so negative supervisory experiences can be quite detrimental. Conflicts in supervision are frequent, because advanced students are simultaneously trying to meet expectations of the training program and trying to be autonomous (somewhat like an adolescent striving to be both autonomous from and dependent on parents and peers!). They continue to learn from observing and imitating supervisors and senior practitioners and can be frustrated if they do not have sufficient opportunities to observe experts demonstrating their work. Moving away from reliance on easily learned models and methods, advanced students start to evaluate models of practice and to differentially accept or reject components. While they still have external foci, advanced students focus internally as well and begin to analyze how their personality and background affect their work (Rønnestad & Skovholt, 2003).

Novice professionals typically are intensely engaged in their professional practice. After initially enjoying the freedom of being on their own and confirming the validity of their training, they often become disillusioned when they realize that they are facing challenges for which their training did not prepare them. This disillusionment can be surprising, scary, and disappointing. After this disillusionment, novice professionals who adapt well intensely explore their profession to acquire additional models, methods, and techniques needed to work effectively. Those who do not adapt well become overwhelmed by the complex contexts of schools, districts, communities, and families and consequently feel inadequate. Successful novice professionals begin to integrate their personal and professional selves and may respond to identifying a personal deficiency that is affecting their professional work by entering therapy. Novice professionals are often increasingly aware of relationship issues in their work and struggle to defend appropriate boundaries (Rønnestad & Skovholt, 2003, pp. 17–20).

Experienced professionals have practiced for a number of years and have worked with a wide variety of populations and problems. Their work has become more coherent and cohesive. They tend to integrate and consolidate their case conceptualization, "throwing out the clutter," and to have an even better understanding of the importance of their role in their work. Techniques and methods are no longer applied rigidly and rules are abandoned for increased flexibility. Experienced professionals typically trust their professional judgment, feel competent in their work, feel comfortable challenging others, and have clearly defined professional boundaries. If they can accept that there are no clear answers for the complex problems that face children and adolescents, they can avoid becoming burnt out. Successful experienced professionals tend to separate their personal from their professional lives, yet also integrate their professional expertise with their values, interests, and attitudes. They may become less tolerant of working in an environment that "doesn't fit." Experienced professionals report learning from their students, from their personal lives, from mentors and supervisors, and from mentees and supervisees; they also report learning about human behavior from sources such as movies, theater, and novels. Unfortunately, they can be more likely to rely on their past experiences with similar students than to turn to current research literature for information. Experienced professionals may have the impression that "there is not much new in the field" and consequently have little interest in attending workshops, feeling that they are targeted toward beginners (Rønnestad & Skovholt, 2003, pp. 20–25).

Vignette 2.4

Elizabeth, a supervisor of a small school psychology unit, considers herself an experienced professional; she feels competent and accepts that there are no simple answers for complex problems. Unfortunately, one of her supervisees, **Molly**, has not herself successfully navigated the challenges of professional development. She is obviously burnt out and disengaged. Molly "acts out" in group supervision meetings by contributing only negative comments. When she sets her wristwatch alarm to sound the moment a group supervision meeting is scheduled to end, thereby interrupting an important supervisory moment, Elizabeth knows that she has to take action. She asks Molly in for an individual meeting and clarifies her expectations regarding Molly's supporting others' professional growth. Elizabeth then seeks ways to help Molly feel more positive, initially by helping her remember positive reasons why she initially entered the field and aspects of the position that she most enjoys, and then by finding strategies to help her focus on increasing positive experiences.

Senior professionals typically have practiced 20 years or more. Some senior professionals enjoy mentoring the next generation, while others find it difficult. Professionals in this phase often continue to struggle with the same issues addressed by experienced professionals. Additionally, many of them experience grief at the deaths of mentors and family members. Even retirements of cohort members can create a sense of loss and stress for senior practitioners.

Many senior professionals lose idealism and develop an "increased sense of reality in terms of what can be accomplished professionally. Also, there is a sense that there is and will not be any significant new knowledge in the field" (Rønnestad & Skovholt, 2003, p. 27). Observing "wheels being reinvented" and the introduction of "new" ideas that the senior professional has known about for years can result in frustration, cynicism, apathy, boredom, and disengagement. On the other hand, many senior professionals continue to grow professionally, to be highly productive, and to become increasingly creative. These individuals feel and demonstrate self-acceptance, decreased anxiety, competency, and modesty (pp. 25–27).

Vignette 2.5

Sally first encountered a totally disengaged senior school psychologist as an intern. During a peer supervision meeting, a school psychologist with 22 years' experience confessed that he had become so bored administering the WISC-IV that he found himself giving it "automatically," reaching the end of the test without remembering either administering the test or recording the results, similar to driving automatically along a familiar route. Even worse, he admitted that he often nodded off while administering the battery just after lunch. Sally was appalled and immediately decided that she would never find herself in a situation where she was that bored—nor where she would treat students so disrespectfully. She thereafter engineered her career so that she was stimulated and challenged and kept the needs of students paramount.

Developmental Stages Model

The Integrated Developmental Model (Stoltenberg & Delworth, 1987; Stoltenberg et al., 1998) assumes that supervisees progress through stages of cognitive development as they acquire skills, much like moving from concrete operations to formal operations thinking (Piaget & Inhelder, 1969). Another developmental model, proposed by Benner (1984), indicates that as individuals pass through the novice, advanced beginner, competent, proficient, and expert levels, they shift from rule-based to intuitive behavior, from an analytical to a holistic perspective, and from a "skill-performing" to an "involved" self-image. This shift does not result simply from an accumulation of skills or a passage of time; practice is transformed by skill integration, affect and intellect integration, and qualitative changes in thinking. The stages described in the following pages integrate the work of Benner and Stoltenberg.

Vignette 2.6

Mike, a driver education teacher, notices that as novices, students in driver education classes are so rule oriented that they get lost in the details. For example, they might ask, "How many feet before you want the car to turn do you start to turn the steering wheel?" After many years of practice, experienced drivers are not even aware of such details. Without thinking about it, they adjust the point at which they turn the steering wheel to the road conditions, speed of the car, size of the car, other cars and objects in the vicinity, and many other factors. They integrate their own skills, variables to do with the car, and environmental variables in a transformative manner.

Novices (Stoltenberg, 2005, Level 1) have no previous experience in the field in which they are training. They rely on abstract principals, objective attributes, and "rules" to govern behavior. Novices see situations as compilations of bits of information, tend to act as detached observers, and "know about" rather than "know how to" (Benner, 1984). Novices focus on skill acquisition. Their rule-governed behavior tends to be inflexible, which hinders actual performance because it interferes with the ability to look ahead and to respond to the entire context. They integrate schemata inaccurately or slowly and have a simplistic understanding of complex constructs. While highly motivated, novices may experience so much anxiety that they have difficulty empathizing. They tend to experience diminished self-confidence and self-efficacy, which in turn has a negative impact on performance (M. L. Friedlander, Keller, Peca-Baker, & Olk, 1986). If they have had experience in a related field, they may inappropriately reconceptualize current situations to fit their prior experiences. Novices tend to have limited self-awareness and are inaccurately aware of their strengths and weaknesses. They depend on supervisors for direction in determining most important or relevant tasks to perform and may uncritically accept supervisory suggestions without understanding. This can result in dependency, inappropriate generalization, and inadequate learning.

Advanced beginners (Stoltenberg, 2005, Level 2) demonstrate marginally acceptable performance and begin to take into account contextual aspects as well as objective attributes (Benner, 1984). Advanced beginners continue to have difficulty distinguishing the relative importance of student and contextual attributes. They need ongoing support and close supervision in prioritizing. They continue to be concerned with learning and mastering technical aspects, which results in emotional disconnection. At the same time, they are improving in their ability to empathize, which sometimes results in difficulty balancing their level of involvement. They begin to perceive recurring situations and to take context into account but still have difficulty taking in an entire situation and distinguishing the relative importance of various attributes. Their anxiety level decreases and confidence increases, but their understanding is limited in complexity. This can result in confusion and discouragement. Advanced beginners start to function more independently and demonstrate marginally acceptable performance, but they often hesitate to take responsibility and continue to rely on supervisors to help make decisions, particularly in terms of prioritizing. In supervision, they can be assertive with their own agenda, desire more autonomy than warranted, or have a dependency-autonomy conflict. Generally, school psychologists are in this stage during internships and the first few years of employment.

Competence (Stoltenberg, 2005, Level 3) is achieved after 2 or 3 years of professional practice. At this point, school psychologists are better able to see relationships between situational components. They shift from preoccupation with their own performance to greater student awareness; they can be simultaneously oriented to their own skills, engaging others, and encouraging improved functioning. Competent practitioners desire to limit the unexpected and therefore engage in planning and goal setting. They feel a sense of mastery, are efficient and organized, and possess sufficient skill to perform automatically. They are able to perceive patterns and makes insights that appear to be intuitive to novices. They quickly make decisions about avenues to explore, develop schemata, and make links to related concepts. Often they have stable motivation, doubts that are not disabling, and firm professional identity. They accept their own strengths and weaknesses, have a firm belief in their own autonomy, retain responsibility for outcomes, yet know when to seek consultation. Many individuals remain at the competent level throughout their careers (Benner, 1984).

Proficiency can be reached after 3 to 5 years of practice but does not come from practice alone (Benner, 1984). Psychologists progressing to this stage move from focusing on analytical processes and technical issues to focusing on systemic issues. Proficiency requires reflective and integrative practice. Such reflection and integration usually requires ongoing supervision and participation in communities of learning (Sergiovanni & Starratt, 2007). Unfortunately, school personnel "in most schools are not supported in ways to improve their thinking. The only alternative for [an educator] in a complex environment who cannot adjust to multiple demands and is not being helped to acquire the ability to think abstractly and autonomously is to simplify and deaden" the work environment by establishing and maintaining routines and ignoring situational and individual differences (Glickman, Gordon, & Ross-Gordon, 2006, p. 52). In some school districts, innovation and change are openly discouraged. The individual school psychologist needs personal strength and conviction to stand up to this type of challenge, and effective supervision can significantly bolster a supervisee's resilience in this regard.

In contrast, individuals who move to the proficient level recognize patterns, see what is of primary importance, and perceive whole situations rather than component parts. They are guided by nuances, perceive the meaning of situations in terms of long-term implications, know typical events to expect in given scenarios, recognize when something doesn't "fit," and make decisions with less labor. They hone in accurately on problem areas and consider few options. As Holloway (1995) indicated, their work is very contextual and they are frustrated when information is presented without a context. In supervision, proficient practitioners might resist analyzing decisions because they see it as unnecessary. They tend to be accurate in self-assessment but still need support.

Experts see situations as a whole and act as involved performers (Benner, 1984). They have transformed their thinking so that they grasp entire situations, attend to context and environment, and base decisions on qualitative distinctions rather than on rules or multiple facts. The expert is at home in complex and rapidly changing situations and no longer relies on analytical principles or rules, guidelines, or maxims. Experts intuitively grasp situations without wasteful consideration of a large range of alternatives. Their skills are transformed to become an extension of the self; they are involved performers rather than observers. Experts efficiently assess factors that initially seem unrelated, moving quickly through assessment to treatment. They understand multiple domains of practice and can bring in information from other fields and experiences. Experts often perceive the need to become change agents and therefore become involved in public policy issues related to professional practice. Experts tend to be accurate in self-assessment but still need support. Without any diminution of their self-esteem and with eagerness for collaboration and teamwork, they often benefit from and actively seek peer supervision.

Activity 2.2

Assessing Personal Professional Development Levels

Consider each of the skills delineated in the NASP domains of practice, as in Handout 15.8, School Psychologist Evaluation Form (pp. 451–458). Then develop a time line of your own professional history with several different strands. At what point were you a novice, competent, and expert in each of the skills and domains contained in the *Blueprint?* How did your graduate school training, professional development workshops you have attended, and/or supervision you have received (or the lack thereof) affect your acquisition of skills and integration of each domain into professional practice?

Developmental Supervision

According to developmental models, each developmental stage requires a unique supervisory approach (Cagnon & Russell, 1995; Dreyfus & Dreyfus, 1991; Stoltenberg & Delworth, 1987). However, it is important to keep in mind that a practitioner's developmental stage is task specific. *All school psychologists are beginners when they enter situations in which they have no previous experience, either in terms of the population with which they are working or with regard to the procedures and/or tools used.* For example, the same school psychologist may be an experienced diagnostician yet a beginner in monitoring intervention effectiveness. Therefore, in the same session with the same supervisee, a supervisor may need to call upon the supervisory methods appropriate for work with beginners *and* those appropriate for work with experienced professionals.

Novice supervisees are thought to need very close supervision, structure, positive feedback, and students with mild problems. However, despite their need for close supervision, they tend to have a weaker working alliance with their supervisors than supervisees at higher levels of development, which suggests that supervisors must take particular care to foster a positive working relationship at this level (Ramos-Sanchez et al., 2002). The best supervisory interventions at this level are facilitative (encouraging), prescriptive (suggesting approaches), or conceptual (tying theory to diagnosis and intervention).

Self-reports of novices are notoriously inaccurate, because novices have difficulty determining what should be reported, unconsciously leave out important material, and sometimes deliberately omit significant material to "look good." Therefore, supervisors should use supervisory techniques that result in raw data, such as videotapes, audiotapes, live observation, role playing, interpretation of dynamics, readings, and group supervision. Providing opportunities for supervisees to shadow supervisors or collaborate in providing services (i.e., coleading groups, cooperatively assessing students, and collaborating on consultation cases) is very effective. To alleviate excessive anxiety when providing feedback, supervisors should acknowledge supervisee strengths before areas of weaknesses. Supervisors should closely monitor student functioning to ensure adequate care.

Advanced beginner supervisees need less structure and more autonomy than novices. Supervisors should provide guidelines for recognizing patterns and help supervisees formulate guidelines that dictate actions. Advanced beginners should be assigned students with more severe problems, such as personality disorders, and start to address more complex (e.g., multicultural) issues. Supervisors should continue to monitor student functioning to ensure that their needs are met. Supervisors should rarely use prescriptive interventions—they should primarily use facilitative supervisory interventions. Confrontational, conceptual (introducing alternative views), and catalytic (providing comments regarding processes) supervision can also be helpful. Appropriate supervision techniques include tapes, live observation, role playing, interpretation of dynamics and parallel process, and group supervision.

Competent supervisees should be encouraged to structure supervision sessions themselves. At this level, supervision focuses on the discussion of cases that the supervisee finds particularly challenging, the development of specialized knowledge, and integration of the supervisee within the context of a complex organization. Supervision can be provided by a peer (another staff school psychologist who has sufficient expertise to provide supervision), an administratively appointed supervisor (whose job includes the supervision of school psychological services and staff implementing such services), or an external supervisor (who has appropriate background but is based in the community rather than the school system; Knoff, 1986). Supervisors should employ facilitative, confrontational, conceptual, and catalytic supervisory interventions and should continue to use direct observation (observation, videotapes, and audiotapes). It is also helpful to work with administration to ensure that effective supervision is supported in the budget.

Proficient and expert supervisees continue to benefit from supervision to help maintain subjectivity, deal with resistance, choose appropriate methods of advocacy, and continually upgrade skills. At this level, school psychologists benefit from inductive instruction using complex case studies at a higher level of conceptualization than those dealt with at the earlier levels. It is helpful for supervisors and supervisees to collaboratively analyze case studies—both those with whom supervisees felt success and those with whom they were frustrated. Furthermore, at these levels, the school psychologist is in a position to supervise school psychologists at levels of lesser expertise. Supervision of supervisors focuses on "metasupervision" and increasing the supervisor's conceptual, interpersonal, and technical skills (Knoff, 1986).

Motivation

Motivation is best understood as a three-step process: a need experienced by an individual, an action taken by that individual, and the resolution of that need. Both needs and motivators are highly individualized. Fundamental aspects of motivating others include providing a sense of empowerment, expecting quality performance, giving meaningful recognition, training and encouraging self-development, asking individuals about job expectations, and helping individuals to meet their own needs. To foster supervisees' motivation, it is essential that supervisors attend to supervisees' needs and refrain from assuming that those needs are largely similar to their own. Beginning practitioners are often motivated to acquire and demonstrate expertise. Supervisors can tap into beginning practitioners' motivation to acquire and demonstrate expertise by implementing supervision strategies that foster clinical skills.

Experienced school psychologists may feel they have sufficient expertise, but they may become bored and need to find ways to make their work less routine. Furthermore, a given individual will have different levels of motivation for different aspects of the job; some school psychologists, for example, have difficulty mustering the motivation to write required reports but have no difficulty motivating themselves to meet with students. The ability to self-motivate is essential in the practice of school psychology, because school psychologists work independently much of the time. To self-regulate motivation, successful individuals use a variety of cognitive, social, volitional, and extrinsic and intrinsic strategies and vary them according to need and context (Wolters, 1998). Maslow's (1954) theory of motivation can be a useful framework to consider when working with supervisees.

Supervisees' basic physiological and safety needs are generally met by steady employment. However, in school districts where job security is threatened, the unmet safety need can result in dissatisfaction, expenditure of energy in job seeking, or a search for job security through union involvement. The next level of needs, social needs, can be thwarted when school psychologists feel isolated and can result in resistance, antagonism, and lack of cooperation.

More advanced needs include self-esteem (self-confidence, independence, achievement, competence, and knowledge), regard (status, recognition, appreciation, and respect), and self-fulfillment (realizing one's potential, continued self-development, and creativity). Whether school psychologists have the resources to meet higher-order needs through their professional lives is largely dependent on the characteristics of the school psychology department, school district, and state. Union contracts tend to target extrinsic rewards, such as fringe benefits. However, industrial research (Halloran, 1981) indicates that the most important motivators are interesting work, sufficient help and equipment, sufficient information, enough authority, adequate pay, appreciation, advancement opportunities, and opportunities for successful achievement. Motivation decreases when supervisees feel they have insufficient skills, are overburdened, lack resources or information required to do well, anticipate criticism, have insufficient self-confidence, receive insufficient incentives, or do not want responsibility for outcomes. It is important for supervisors, as systemic leaders, to address such issues because quality services for children depend on highly motivated staff who respond to new situations and want to continually update skills (Sergiovanni & Starratt, 2007).

Assessing Goals

Since both motivation and achievement are higher when individuals develop their own goals rather than strive to meet others' expectations (Mithaug & Mithaug, 2003), it is important to help supervisees develop appropriate goals. This can be accomplished using a variety of tools. *Core goal determination* is accomplished by listing up to 25 satisfying activities and experiences, examining 15 of those experiences and activities according to their associated feelings, and grouping these according to feelings. These groupings identify the individual's core goals and encourage the consideration of positive and negative aspects of each core goal (Nichols, 1991).

In completing a *visualization exercise*, the supervisee visualizes "the very best school psychologist in the world," delineates what that school psychologist does, compares that image to her or his own practice, and determines which of the "best school psychologist's" positive habits and behaviors could be adopted (adapted from Harvey & Chickie-Wolfe, 2007).

Goal setting is begun with a relaxed brainstorming session during which supervisees discuss desired accomplishments but refrain from making any value judgments until the end of the session. Activity 2.3 can facilitate this process.

Activity 2.3

Goal Setting

1. Quickly write down long-term (5- or 10-year) career and personal goals, then star the most important goals.

2. Quickly write down short-term (6 months to a year) career and personal goals, add additional short-term goals necessary to begin to meet important long-term goals, and star the most important short-term goals.

3. List activities that hinder achievement of important goals and brainstorm methods to reduce time spent on these barriers.

4. List activities and people that help achieve important goals, and brainstorm methods to increase time spent on these aids and with people who facilitate meeting the goals.

To help supervisees meet basic, social, self-esteem, regard, and self-fulfillment needs, supervisors can tap suggestions included in Handout 2.1.

Handout 2.1

SUPERVISORY STRATEGIES TO MEET SUPERVISEES' PSYCHOLOGICAL NEEDS

To help their supervisees meet *basic needs*, supervisors can:

- Work to minimize insecurity engendered by threats to job security (e.g., provide accurate information regarding potential layoffs during budget cuts)
- Work openly and assertively toward just compensation for supervisees

To help their supervisees meet *social needs*, supervisors can:

- Take steps to reduce professional isolation by fostering group cohesion among school psychologists and encouraging contact with other school psychologists
- Support participation in local and state professional organizations
- Encourage supervisees to build strong relationships with building personnel, including general education teachers, speech pathologists, department heads, lead teachers, occupational therapists, assistant principals, and principals
- Encourage interdisciplinary professional relationships with district school personnel other than school psychologists

To help their supervisees meet their *need for self-esteem* (self-confidence, independence, achievement, competence, and knowledge), supervisors can:

- Respect individuals' needs and unique talents
- Provide sufficient help and equipment
- Work to minimize frustrating job components that are time consuming yet do not help students directly (e.g., excessive clerical work might be minimized by tracking hours spent filing, copying, and preparing mailings and then completing a cost analysis to present to administrators in support of hiring clerical staff)
- Clearly delegate tasks along with sufficient authority and supports necessary for successful completion
- Communicate well by providing supervisees with information regarding events and district policies, by providing administrators with supervisee input, and by involving supervisees in decisions
- Encourage supervisees to use effective time management and organizational strategies, seek help when needed, and regulate their work environment (e.g., by choosing a time and place in which to write reports where there will be no interruptions)
- Encourage supervisees to develop self-reward systems, such as allowing oneself a pleasant break after completing unpleasant work
- Encourage supervisees to spend energy on tasks and strategies that result directly in improved student success

- Assign challenging yet manageable tasks
- Structure, restructure, and rotate assignments to provide variety and interest
- Give supervisees some control over assignments

To help their supervisees meet their *need for regard* (status, recognition, appreciation, and respect), supervisors can:

- Work toward policies that permit flexible work hours to compensate providers for evening work with parents
- Seek out and support advancement opportunities for supervisees
- Encourage experienced professionals to accept the challenge of mentoring or supervising beginning practitioners
- Make expectations and standards clear
- Give frequent feedback that stresses positive support
- Encourage supervisees to spend time in activities that increase their visibility and status, such as writing articles for school newsletters, writing articles for local newspapers, presenting at parent-teacher meetings, writing for the school Web site, and participating in school events and student clubs
- Encourage supervisees to become standing members of the school teams that have decision making power, including crisis teams, child study teams, student support teams, and teacher assistance teams
- Ensure that supervisees are given reinforcement when they expend effort and produce accurate work
- Evaluate using competency-based rather than criterion-referenced measures

To help their supervisees meet their *need for self-fulfillment* (realizing one's potential, continued self-development, and creativity), supervisors can:

- Help develop and prioritize short- and long-term goals for each individual and the department
- Foster optimism, constructive attributions, internal loci of control, and positive belief systems regarding the potential of each supervisee and of the entire department
- Foster having fun and find ways to make tasks more enjoyable, interesting, and easier
- Encourage supervisees to volunteer for work groups that interest them (e.g., join a playground committee, plan summer reading activities, or design new programs)
- Encourage supervisees to participate in research and program evaluations
- Increase task value by focusing on relevance and utility to self and others

Addressing Anxiety

Anxiety is a common supervisory issue because novices are inevitably (and appropriately) anxious and even advanced practitioners become anxious, particularly during evaluative processes. As in all learning, moderate anxiety is helpful in that it raises motivation, accentuates attentiveness, and enables the individual to identify areas in need of attention. On the other hand, excessive anxiety diminishes the ability to learn, has a detrimental effect on performance (especially when a skill is newly being learned), and can have a deleterious effect on the supervisor-supervisee relationship in that it can cause supervisees to hide areas of weakness, thus reducing learning opportunities. Supervisors who have a supportive style that reduces anxiety are perceived as better teachers (Cresci, 2001). A number of authors have suggested methods that might help supervisees maintain anxiety at the level that is optimal for learning (Arkowitz, 2001; Costa, 1994; G. Macklem, personal communication, April 2007; Pearson, 2000). A compilation of these suggestions can be found in Handout 2.2.

Addressing Personal Problems

Some supervisees suffer from such excessive anxiety that the above suggestions do not suffice. Although it is extremely important for a supervisor to avoid taking the role of therapist with supervisees, supervisors almost inevitably find themselves providing some personal advising for supervisees. It is important that this be provided in response to early warning signals rather than only in crisis situations. As in any counseling or consultation situation, basic steps include active and responsive listening followed by an exploration of alternatives and solutions.

At some point in life, almost everyone has a personal problem so great that it seriously impacts his or her ability to work. School psychologists are no different. When individuals experience severe personal problems, they generally display signs of emotional distress such as exaggerated behavior, overly controlled behavior, irrational behavior, an inability to concentrate, agitation, lack of sleep, loss of weight, irritability, or crying. Frequently a school psychologist with a personal problem will share this problem with his or her supervisor. The appropriate role of the supervisor is to listen carefully, provide support, and refer the supervisee for additional counseling as appropriate. The amount and duration of support necessary is highly individualized and not easily quantifiable. For example, it is a mistake to assume that a bereaved person should be "back to normal" in a specific amount of time, since a person's reaction to a loss depends on many variables.

On the other hand, individuals who experience long-term personal problems that are considered shameful often avoid talking about them with supervisors. For example, alcoholism, drug abuse, and mental illness are stigmatizing and frequently not disclosed. Unfortunately, these disorders are common, occurring in more than 10% of the general population. From the perspective of employers, an alcoholic or substance abuser is a person whose repeated overindulgence in alcoholic beverages seriously reduces effectiveness and dependability in completing work assignments. Although supervisors tend to view alcoholics as having severe personal problems, they are highly ambivalent about dealing with the problem directly.

Another example is supervisees with undisclosed (or undiagnosed) learning disabilities that affect their work as school psychologists. For example, supervisees with verbal learning disabilities may have intense difficulty writing, causing them considerable stress and anxiety as they write reports.

Handout 2.2

STRATEGIES TO REDUCE SUPERVISEE ANXIETY

- Openly express that anxiety is normal for beginners and novices

- Balance support and giving challenging (yet manageable) assignments

- Provide greater structure and guidance in areas in which the supervisee is inexperienced or less confident

- Provide greater structure and guidance in areas that are particularly challenging, such as crisis response

- Clarify expectations through modeling and providing work samples

- Share ongoing cases with supervisees and share imperfect case conceptualizations, diagnoses, treatment, and intervention implementation

- Increase positive feedback

- Change supervision techniques

- Modify evaluation tools

- Discuss the challenges and dangers of perfectionism with the supervisee

- Challenge the supervisee's irrational cognitions regarding the need for perfection or unconditional approval and help the supervisee replace them with more rational thoughts

Maintaining logs regarding performance adequacy, providing frequent feedback to the supervisee regarding performance, and referral to a treatment program are all highly appropriate. If the supervisee is not sufficiently rehabilitated and job performance remains unsatisfactory, the supervisor must take the steps that would be appropriate for dismissal for unsatisfactory job performance for any reason (Noe, Hollenbeck, Gerhart, & Wright, 1996). Taking these steps can be particularly difficult for the supervisor of school psychologists because of a general orientation toward positive support. Nonetheless, if performance does not improve after corrective interviews, the supervisor must continue through additional steps as delineated in school district policy, because the welfare of the children served must be paramount. This topic is addressed more fully in the section of Chapter 15 that addresses supervisee impairment.

SUPERVISOR-SUPERVISEE RELATIONSHIP

The supervisor-supervisee relationship can be conceptualized as having three phases (Holloway, 1995). During the *early* phase the working alliance is established and maintained, the nature of the supervisory relationship is clarified, strategies for collaborative work are devised, a supervision contract is developed, supervision techniques are selected, and clinical competencies are assessed and developed. During the *mature* phase, the relationship is individualized, social bonding is emphasized, supervisees advance in their case conceptualization, ruptures to the working alliance are repaired as necessary, and the supervisee's personal experiences, insofar as they relate to professional practice, are explored. The supervisor and supervisee become more collaborative as the supervisee learns to link theory and practice. During *termination*, supervisors and supervisees discuss termination, associated thoughts and feelings, and future professional goals.

Building Working Alliances

Strong supervisee-supervisor working alliances result in positive outcomes for supervision, services provided, and student functioning (L. A. Gray et al., 2001). A working alliance that leads to disclosure by the supervisee is essential for a number of reasons. Without it, supervisors cannot provide support that enables supervisees to make professional growth because they are not aware of areas of difficulty. Positive working alliances also increase the likelihood that supervisees will adhere to appropriate recommendations made by the supervisor (J. M. Bernard & Goodyear, 2004; Yourman, 2003). As defined by Bordin (1983), three essential components of forming strong working alliances are (a) developing mutually agreed-upon goals, (b) agreeing upon methods to meet goals, and (c) fostering caring, liking, and trusting through shared experiences.

To build effective working alliances, supervisors should employ the same basic communication strategies (attending, reflecting, responding, and following up) used when effectively consulting with teachers, parents, and administrators. Supervisors should prevent interruptions, avoid attempts to communicate during times of high emotion, listen effectively by focusing attention, and reinforce oral communications with written notes.

Attending to the supervisee's words and nonverbal cues, including omitted material, requires focusing attention. Attending includes evaluating and responding to the supervisee's need for partnership, empathy, apology, respect, legitimization, or support (PEARLS; Milan, Parish, & Reichgott, 2006). It should be minimally necessary to ask for repetition and the supervisor should take care to listen to the entire message before formulating a response. Many supervisors find it helpful to take notes to remind them of future questions or comments so that it is not necessary to keep them in working memory. *It is not possible to listen and simultaneously answer telephone calls, respond to e-mails, or read files.* In busy school environments, it is challenging but essential to remove such distractions.

Reflecting, pausing to process both the content of the communication and the affect of the supervisee, enables supervisors to convey respect, clarify their thinking, and take time to formulate appropriate responses. Appropriate *responding* begins when the supervisor restates the communication, invites elaboration, obtains feedback regarding perception accuracy, and conveys thoughts and feelings about what was heard. *Following up* consists of respectfully and nonjudgmentally asking for additional information; exploring supervisee assumptions, beliefs, and feelings; and investigating the supervisee's thoughts regarding possible future actions. Probes for additional information are most effective when they assume that the supervisee has already considered the information. In contrast, probes for possible future actions are most effective when they emphasize the deepening and integration of knowledge rather than provide explicit direction, although the degree of direction needed depends on the developmental level of the supervisee regarding the given task.

Useful feedback involves written as well as oral comments, since research indicates that 48 hours after a 10-minute oral presentation, only 25% of the information is retained, and less than 10% is retained after a week (Ailes, 1988). To minimize common communication failings, supervisors should seek verbal and nonverbal feedback from supervisees regarding whether clarity has been achieved. After a supervision session regarding a given topic, the supervisor should periodically check progress and eventually evaluate both the process and the resultant product (Loen, 1994). Some supervisors find it helpful to schedule these follow-up conversations in their own appointment books.

Activity 2.4

Taping Supervision Sessions

With your supervisee's permission, tape record supervisory sessions. Then transcribe the tape and analyze the tape and transcripts for process and content as you were taught in introductory counseling courses. What can you discern about your supervisory communication skills? Identify at what points you:

- Obtain feedback regarding the accuracy of perceptions
- Listen without evaluating
- Restate
- Actively listen
- Review

A supervisee's *positive affect* is supported by ethical and appropriate behaviors of the supervisor (e.g., respect toward the supervisee, maintaining confidentiality; Ladany, Lehrman-Waterman, Molinaro, & Wolgast, 1999); emphasizing the consultative aspect of supervision to a greater extent than the teaching and counseling aspects (Ladany, Walker, & Malincoff, 2001); a moderate degree of self-disclosure by the supervisor regarding personal issues and professional struggles (Ladany & Lehrman-Waterman, 1999); an emphasis on the use of expert and referent power rather than reward, coercive, or legitimate power (Schultz, Ososkie, Fried, Nelson, & Bardos, 2002); supervisor-initiated, open discussions of supervisor-supervisee ethnic differences (Gatmon et al., 2001); and refraining from exploiting the supervisee to meet the supervisor's own needs (J. M. Bernard & Goodyear, 2004). When supervisors are skillful at developing working alliances, they engender trust and honesty, convey warmth and acceptance, and elicit sufficient feelings of safety such that supervisees honestly disclose difficulties (Ladany, Hill, Corbett, & Nutt, 1996).

Contracts

Communication within the supervisory process can be greatly facilitated by developing a formal supervisory agreement prior to the onset of supervision in the form of a written and signed supervisory contract. Contracts clarify expectations, outline the responsibilities of each person, promote shared responsibility, provide direction when difficulties arise, maximize the fit between supervisee and supervisor, and provide a concrete method to measure the performance of both supervisees and supervisors. Contracts are useful for both administrative and clinical supervisors. Well-written contracts include:

1. Credentialing, licensing, or professional organization requirements to be met by the supervision

2. The logistics of supervision, including the frequency, time, place, length, and schedule of meetings; the legal responsibilities of supervisors; separation of responsibilities when more than one supervisor is involved; methods of dealing with canceled supervision sessions; methods of notifying students and parents that the individual providing services is being supervised; and the supervisor's name and credentials

3. Clarification of the supervisory process, including theories and models espoused by the supervisor; the supervisor's willingness to explore additional ideas, methods, or styles; relationship power differentials; and conflict resolution methods

4. Supervision goals

5. Anticipated methods of supervision, such as audiotapes or videotapes, collaborative work on cases, case presentations, and observations

6. Legal and liability information, including what responsibility the supervisor has for the supervisee's work, what procedures are appropriate to follow when students are a danger to themselves or others, what information the supervisor will need to intelligently consult about a case, and what method the supervisor will use to review the supervisee's cases

7. Methods of individual performance evaluation, performance evaluation distribution procedures, the involvement of the supervisee in the evaluation process, and the method to be used to evaluate supervision itself

Handbooks

Communication can be greatly enhanced by developing a handbook to ensure that important information is readily and repeatedly accessible. They are most effective when kept in a loose-leaf binder so that individual pages are easily updated. Appropriate contents vary according to the orientation of the department, the job descriptions of district personnel, available resources, and environmental factors but often include:

1. District information (calendar, school phone numbers and Web sites, map, organization chart, job descriptions)

2. District services (child study team procedures; English language learner [ELL] services; alternative and vocational programs; remedial, Section 504 [Rehabilitation Act of 1973], and special education services; itinerant specialist schedules)

3. School psychology services (goals; brochure; procedures regarding providing prevention, consultation, assessment, and intervention services; blank and sample forms; assessment of ELL, Section 504 [Rehabilitation Act of 1973], and special education students; National Association of School Psychologists [2000a] *Professional Conduct Manual*)

4. Additional resources (community services contacts, support groups, crisis intervention strategies and resources)

5. State information (licensure/certification information, state curriculum frameworks, standards for special education)

Activity 2.5

Developing a Handbook

Develop a list of materials to include in a handbook that you believe matches the needs of your setting, compile the handbook, obtain feedback from your supervisees and your own supervisors regarding its content, and revise accordingly.

Developing Mutually Agreed-Upon Supervision Goals

Supervisory alliances are supported by developing clinical skill and supervision goals that are aligned with supervisees' developmental level (Stoltenberg, 2005); clear and fair evaluative processes (Lehrman-Waterman & Ladany, 2001); clearly written supervision contracts at the onset of supervision (Mead, 1990); and open discussions regarding the purpose of supervision, the role of psychological services, and the outcomes desired as a result of these services.

Methods to align supervision goals include seeking supervisee input regarding what could be done during supervision sessions to reduce any shame they feel during supervision sessions (Yourman, 2003); aligning supervision goals through a supervision contract; assessing the supervisee's expectation for supervision; and teaching the supervisee appropriate supervision behaviors by sharing tapes of successful supervision sessions (J. M. Bernard & Goodyear, 2004). Furthermore, supervisors can explicitly state that supervisees can and should see things differently from the supervisor and that supervision is improved by discussing these differences (Yourman, 2003).

To ensure supervision goal alignment, Briggs and Miller (2005, p. 203) suggested that at the beginning of each supervision session the supervisor determine the supervisee's immediate goals by asking what her or his goals and hopes for the session are. During the supervision session, it is helpful to employ "problem solving supervision" that focuses on supervisee strengths to foster self-efficacy. Briggs and Miller indicated that this is a more effective use of supervision time than focusing on student issues, since effort devoted to student issues is not likely to be generalized from one student to another. This focus is not automatic, in that supervisees tend to bring problems rather than successes to supervision sessions. Briggs and Miller also suggested pointing out what the supervisee does well as tapes of sessions are reviewed and encouraging the supervisees to do the same by comments such as "That was really good! How did you do that?"

Briggs and Miller (2005) acknowledged problems identified by supervisees but reframed them as solvable setbacks, conveying confidence that the supervisee will be able to cope successfully. When supervisors recognize a problem that needs addressing, they help the supervisee identify the problem, her or his intent, and alternative actions. Supervisees' responses to designated questions provide material to use in forging positive comments and affirmations. After identifying a problem, it is important to conclude with compliments regarding problem recognition and solution. Briggs and Miller further recommended that supervisors take a break during each supervision session to construct, and then give feedback to the supervisee that includes compliments, bridging statements, and tasks. They recommend that supervisors ask the supervisee to evaluate the success of the supervision session. Questions contained in Handout 2.3 can be asked of supervisees to direct supervision sessions in a positive, problem solving way.

Agreeing upon methods to meet supervision goals occurs by aligning supervision techniques with supervisees' developmental levels; clearly writing supervision contracts; frequently communicating regarding the effectiveness of supervision sessions; openly discussing supervision techniques; and openly discussing approaches to clinical practice.

Activity 2.6

Giving Instructions

Review two situations in which you gave instructions a month ago, once in a written format (perhaps a memo) and once orally (perhaps in a supervisory session, from supervisory session notes). Analyze them for how well you timed the request, communicated the rationale, delineated responsibilities, described the results expected and the method for reporting them, set deadlines, checked to make sure that the task was progressing, and evaluated the result. Identify the communication method that is clearest and most effective.

Maintaining Appropriate Use of Power

Effective supervisors attend to complications in supervision that naturally arise from the intersection of axes of power related both to the supervisory relationship and to issues of class, gender, race, religion, and sexual identity (Turner & Fine, 1997). Expert and referent power are most closely associated with high supervisee performance and satisfaction, whereas the use of coercive, legitimate, and reward power tends to be viewed quite negatively by supervisees and results in decreased performance and satisfaction (Sergiovanni & Starratt, 2007). Clinical supervisors are encouraged to foster expert and referent power by ensuring that they have the proper technical, conceptual, and interpersonal skills.

Handout 2.3

PROBLEM SOLVING SUPERVISION
(Adapted from Briggs & Miller, 2005)[1]

Before beginning the supervision session, ask:

- What is your goal in coming to supervision today?
- What would you like to accomplish in supervision today?
- What should happen in the next hour so that you don't feel this supervision session was a waste of time?
- What are your best hopes for today's meeting?

Before reviewing tapes and other work, ask:

- What are strengths you showed in the work we are about to discuss?
- It is useful to hear your description of times when your work isn't going as well as you would like. Could you also tell me about times when you do not experience these difficulties?
- What is different about this situation compared to times when you have success with this or similar students/parents/teachers?

When reviewing a "problem," ask:

- What do you think you did?
- What were you trying to accomplish? How would that be helpful?
- What would you like to have done differently?

At the end of the session, ask:

- On a scale of 1 to 10, where 10 is the best supervision session you could possibly have, where would you rate this session?
- What would be different if the session were a point or two higher?
- How will you change future sessions?

---

[1]Briggs, J., & Miller, G. (2005). Success enhancing supervision. *Journal of Family Psychotherapy, 16,* 199–222.

Because of the substantial power differential inherent in the supervisory relationship, a supervisee can easily perceive supervisors as bullies if they are not careful to be sensitive to the supervisee (Peyton, 2004). Coercive (punitive) power should be used only in extreme situations.

However, supervisors can effectively use reward power. School psychology supervisors generally have limited ability to affect the pay of their supervisees, but they do have other rewards at their disposal. For example, they can write letters of recognition and commendation, nominate individuals for local and state awards, obtain improved equipment, and assign work and schedules that meet the personal needs and professional strengths of individuals.

Because of the innate power differential in the supervisory relationship, supervisees are unlikely to feel that they have the power to initiate difficult conversations, so it is incumbent upon the supervisor to raise issues of power differences (Turner & Fine, 1997). For the same reason, supervisors should initiate conversations regarding race, class, gender, social status, disabilities, sexual orientation, theoretical orientation, and religion with their supervisees (J. M. Bernard & Goodyear, 2004; Lappin & Hardy, 1997).

Improving Supervisory Relationships

Ameliorating interpersonal conflicts, miscommunication, ruptures in working alliances, and other interpersonal supervisory problems are important aspects of a supervisor's interpersonal and communication skills. Supervisory relationships are challenged when supervisees perceive that supervisors dismiss their thoughts and feelings (L. A. Gray et al., 2001). Communication failures can result from inattentive listening, attempting to communicate during periods of high emotion, erroneous perception of nonverbal cues, different understandings of word meanings, insufficient feedback, and inaccurate assumptions (Rue & Byars, 1997). Some supervisees perceive their supervisors as disrespectful, verbally abusive bullies (Peyton, 2004).

As previously mentioned, many novices are so highly anxious that they do not sufficiently disclose to their supervisors, which threatens the working relationship and supervision effectiveness. The evaluation process particularly challenges supervisor-supervisee relationships as it increases both supervisee and supervisor anxiety. Supervisors and supervisees sometimes attempt to deny the reality of the evaluative component in supervision (J. M. Bernard & Goodyear, 2004), which results in supervisors' making superlative comments and conducting overly positive, meaningless evaluations (e.g., all 5s on a 5-point scale). Such evaluations are dishonest and do not provide supervisees with enough feedback to improve. This can be a problem with both novice and veteran practitioners (Burke, Goodyear, & Guzzard, 1998) when supervisees and supervisors collude to ignore problems such as professional performance and inadequate supervision preparation in order to avoid conflict (Todd, 1997a).

Vicarious liability held by supervisors for their supervisees' work further threatens the working relationship because it raises supervisor anxiety and makes it difficult for supervisors to trust supervisees. Supervisors are held accountable, yet they have few ways to know that their supervisees have behaved appropriately. They must walk a careful line between keeping appropriately informed and inappropriately "policing" (Pearson, 2000).

Conflict Resolution

According to Moskowitz and Rupert (1983), almost half of supervisees experience significant conflicts with supervisors. Conflicts can be goal, method, or relationship conflicts.

Goal conflicts occur in supervision in a number of ways. Supervisors and supervisees may disagree on goals relating to practice; for example, a supervisee may have a goal of increasing prereferral intervention activities, but his or her supervisor may not respect that process. Or supervisors and supervisees may disagree on goals related to supervision. A supervisee may consider supervision to be an opportunity to obtain support, while a supervisor may consider it an opportunity to provide correction. These differences can be highlighted when supervisors take the evaluative role (J. M. Bernard & Goodyear, 2004).

Supervisors may also experience goal conflicts stemming from the context. For example, administrator expectations may conflict with professional standards, or administrator expectations may conflict with university training requirements. Supervisors may be challenged to help supervisees resolve conflicts with other school personnel, such as administrators who attempt to dictate inappropriate tests. Supervisors may also experience conflicts when they hold dual roles in the school district, such as both school psychologist and special education team leader.

Method conflicts occur when supervisors disagree with supervisees regarding appropriate supervision methods. For example, a supervisor may feel that access to raw data such as audiotapes of counseling sessions is essential for adequate supervision, while the supervisee may see such activities as too intrusive. Method conflicts also occur when supervisees withdraw or are confrontational when given direction, particularly in response to controlling supervisors (Safran & Muran, 2000). Additionally, method conflicts occur when supervisees are reluctant to give negative feedback to supervisors for fear of repercussions (L. A. Gray et al., 2001). With novice supervisees, ruptures of the supervisory alliance often occur around their lack of skill, while with more advanced supervisors, ruptures tend to occur due to differences in theoretical orientation, personal style (e.g., verbosity, tardiness, pace), and opinions regarding appropriate interventions (Burke et al., 1998).

Union conflicts can occur in settings where school psychologists are unionized. The school psychologist may take an unresolved complaint to the union and file a grievance, which can progress up through the administration. To handle complaints and grievances well, it is important that supervisors treat grieving supervisees respectfully by listening carefully, uncovering the true concern, remaining calm, getting all of the facts, asking for suggested solutions, explaining reasons for decisions, explaining how to appeal, and following up after the resolution. To avoid grievances, Halloran (1981) suggested that supervisors communicate clear expectations, conduct frequent evaluations, give credit for good performance, give clear direction for areas in need of improvement, make use of each school psychologist's strengths, encourage professional growth and responsibility, solicit problem solving from supervisees, suggest policy changes to administrators, and enlist supervisee participation in policy changes.

Conflict resolution takes place in three stages: exploration, discussion/communication, and resolution. During exploration, the objective is to identify the disputants and specify the areas of conflict (Maher, 1984). During discussion/communication, the disputants brainstorm a generous number of possible solutions without commentary. The benefits and associated costs are then discussed and one or more solutions selected. During the resolution stage, responsibilities and time frames are designated and the plan is formalized, implemented, and evaluated (Fleming, Fleming, Roach, & Oksman, 1985). After the conflict is resolved, it is important to evaluate the outcome through data collection and incorporate the results into future practice. To make such an assessment and address further conflicts, McInerney (1985) recommended that supervisors:

1. Consciously observe those involved and ask them to provide information about their thoughts and feelings, looking for anger, persistent job dissatisfaction, limited future expectations, depression, and self-defeating actions, feelings, or thoughts.

2. Assess whether overwork or underwork is contributing, since either can lead to depression and job burnout.

3. Observe their own behavior as they exercise authority, looking for evidence that they avoid exercising authority; that they are authoritarian, sarcastic, or hostile; that they are inconsistent; or that they do not follow up on requests. If these traits are apparent, they may need to investigate their own feelings about the individuals involved as well as about exercising authority in general.

4. Brainstorm a number of potential solutions and designate them as minor challenges (able to be accomplished in less than a month with available resources), moderate challenges (under the control of the group, possible with available resources, and able to be accomplished within 6 months), or major challenges (involving individuals not in the group, requiring additional resources, and/or taking more than a year).

5. Target one moderate goal per quarter, obtain help with major goals, and determine appropriate minor goals.

6. Plan and implement action plans with staff.

7. Evaluate the results.

8. Repeat the process on an ongoing basis.

Effectively resolving interpersonal conflict and communication barriers in the supervisory setting involves seeing differences as natural and appropriate, honest confrontation, objective problem solving, and striving to integrate both views into a common good (Sergiovanni & Starratt, 2007). This sometimes requires "stepping back" progressively until common goals are evident. Optimism is critical to success and can be fostered by focusing on one step at a time and perceiving "failures" as temporary setbacks.

Vignette 2.7

Rose works in a highly contentious school district in which teachers, administrators, and parents are frequently at odds. To help herself stay child focused and keep student needs paramount, she has a poster on her office wall that asks: "What is best for the kids?"

Parallel Processes, Transference, and Countertransference

Parallel processes, transference, and *countertransference* are terms that describe the tendency to respond to an individual in one setting as though one were relating to a different individual in a different setting. These may refer to responses within the settings of either professional practice or supervision. While these terms are commonly used in psychotherapeutic literature, they also describe events that occur in the practice and supervision of school psychology.

Parallel processes occur when events within supervision reflect events occurring in the relationship between the supervisee and the student. For example, supervisees who are dealing with teachers who are particularly oppositional and respond with "Yes, but . . ." to every suggested intervention may be similarly oppositional toward suggestions made by their supervisors. Parallel processes are often triggered by countertransference experiences on the part of the supervisee or supervisor (Falender & Shafranske, 2004).

Transference and *countertransference* refer to the tendency to transfer feelings and responses from the past into the present, usually manifested in distorted, exaggerated, irrational, or unrealistic reactions. For example, a student might transfer feelings regarding a parent onto a school psychologist. In turn, a school psychologist might countertransfer strong negative feelings regarding an ex-spouse onto an administrator who reminds her or him of that spouse. Similarly, in supervision, countertransference might occur when supervisors relate to supervisees as though they were their children, while transference might occur when supervisees respond to supervisors as though they were their parents.

Transference and countertransference affect every interpersonal relationship to some degree, because every relationship is influenced by personal meaning and culture (Falender & Shafranske, 2004). When they occur to an excessive degree, they are usually triggered by both characteristics of the targeted person (defensiveness, a "fighter mentality," passivity/vulnerability, or engaging manner/attractiveness) and unresolved personal issues on the part of the person experiencing the transference or countertransference (either previous relationship patterns or the tendency to maintain either a highly critical or a "peacemaker" style; Ladany, Constantine, Miller, Erickson, & Muse-Burke, 2000, p. 106). They can be exacerbated by concerns regarding competency, overly high self-expectations, an excessive desire for approval, or past professional experiences (J. M. Bernard & Goodyear, 2004).

Vignette 2.8

Everything about **Carla** bothered her internship supervisor, **Matt**. He saw her as a perfectionistic, whining, self-absorbed, materialistic "Valley girl." The more she tried to please, the angrier he became. He found himself avoiding answering her phone calls and e-mails, being very curt, and arriving late to or even missing supervision sessions. He was somewhat bewildered by his atypical behavior until one day he almost called her by his ex-wife's name. "Ah," he thought. "I need to work on this!"

Transference and countertransference are manifested by affective, cognitive, and behavioral components (Ladany et al., 2000). Affective components are most often made evident by the experience of very strong feelings and reactions to the student, parent, teacher, administrator, supervisee, or supervisor in question ("She pushes my buttons"). These might be distress, frustration, anger, irritation, anxiety, negative feelings about oneself, confusion, or surprise. Cognitive components might include thinking excessively about the person, questioning one's abilities, being concerned about understanding the person, feeling a need to proceed with caution, or perceiving a need to protect the person. Behavioral components might include disengaging, repeatedly discussing the situation with others, changing the environment (Ladany et al., 2000), having a physical reaction (jaw clenching), dressing more attractively when meeting with the individual, treating the individual atypically, or recognizing that this individual behaves differently toward you than he or she does toward others in the same role (Pearson, 2000). Countertransference in supervision can be manifested by favoritism, encouraging a supervisee to act out, competing for a supervisee's attention, or holding exaggerated expectations for the supervisee. These cognitions, affect, and behaviors most commonly manifest themselves within a month into supervision, although it may take the supervisor longer to recognize them. While they initially weaken the supervisory working alliance, they eventually can strengthen it (Ladany et al., 2000). However, because they can render supervision ineffective, it is important to be sensitive to and address parallel processes, transference, and countertransference.

Vignette 2.9

Marjean provides clinical supervision for a department of 12 school psychologists. Last year one of her veteran psychologists, **Linda**, tearfully confided that her husband had abruptly left her after 25 years of marriage, telling her that he hadn't loved her for the past 10 years. Marjean fully sympathized and tried to give Linda considerable support. When the principals at Linda's schools complained that she was frequently late and unprepared for meetings, Marjean indicated that Linda was going through some rough patches and that she was sure things would work out. She did not convey the concerns to Linda. When the principals marked Linda lower than she had ever scored on their administrative evaluations, Linda was distraught. She was even more upset when she found out that Marjean had known about the principals' concerns but had not told her about them because she wanted to avoid causing her further distress. In hindsight, Marjean realizes that she should have been more open with Linda.

Rather than thinking of parallel processes, transference, and countertransference as problematic, supervisors and supervisees should think of them as helpful tools that indicate areas in need of work. Sometimes transference and countertransference indicate deficient clinical skills. Other times, they indicate areas the individual should address in personal counseling. When supervisors notice their supervisees experiencing countertransference toward students, they can work with them to understand the feelings and their significance in their work, simultaneously being careful to respect the supervisees' personal boundaries (Epstein, 2001; Hunt, 2001).

Self-disclosure by supervisors may facilitate effective practice (Ladany & Walker, 2003). On the other hand, quality supervision depends on safe boundaries between supervisors and supervisors. Supervisees can be made uncomfortable by "too much" self-disclosure on the part of supervisors, such as discussion of the supervisor's own job struggles, alcohol dependency, personal therapy, or sexuality (Heru, Strong, Price, & Recupero, 2004). Supervisors' self-disclosure should be limited to information that is appropriate to the topic at hand and is constructive for the supervisee (Haynes, Corey, & Moulton, 2003).

Noncompliance and Resistance

Noncompliance or *resistance* occurs when an individual rejects sound advice and therefore acts in a manner that is not in her or his best interest. It is common in both counseling and consultation, and unfortunately it is also common in supervision. It can be a source of considerable frustration (J. M. Bernard & Goodyear, 2004; McColley & Baker, 1982). Noncompliance or resistance can be manifested by excessive supervisee self-criticism that deflects supervisor feedback; focusing on technical issues to the detriment of resolution of process issues; missing all or part of supervision sessions; "forgetting" or neglecting to complete supervision tasks, especially those that are particularly anxiety provoking (e.g., not taping sessions and using school-based excuses); not disclosing important information; deflecting discussions away from certain topics; engaging in power struggles; or neglecting to implement mutually agreed-upon interventions (J. M. Bernard & Goodyear, 2004; Pearson, 2000).

Rather than thinking of supervisees as "noncompliant" or "resistant," however, it is most useful to consider in what ways such refusals to follow a supervisor's advice, whether through passive neglect or overt refusal, serves a positive function for the supervisee. Noncompliance or resistance might be a reaction to an overly directive supervisor who gives insufficient freedom of choice, a method to individuate or separate from the supervisor when the supervisee is personally or developmentally in need of greater autonomy, or an indication that the goals of the supervisee and supervisor are not aligned (J. M. Bernard & Goodyear, 2004). Noncompliance or resistance might serve as a method of self-protection in response to a perceived threat, particularly when the supervisee has insufficient trust in the supervisor, when the supervisees feels guilt for not completing a task, or when the supervisee feels ashamed of personal inadequacy that is exposed during the supervision sessions—especially because supervisees are "expert" in one setting (professional practice) and "learners" in another (supervision; Gill, 2001).

Some supervisees are particularly sensitive to a perceived lack of approval by a supervisor. For example, while some supervisees might perceive the question "Why did you do that?" as an interesting invitation for self-reflection, others might perceive it as shaming. Those who perceive it as shaming will be less forthcoming in future supervision sessions, which can have a seriously detrimental effect on both supervision and professional practice (Yourman, 2003).

Noncompliance and resistance can be countered by fostering a supervision atmosphere characterized by trust, respect, and acceptance; providing consistent feedback and support; acknowledging and normalizing feelings of inadequacy, including those of the supervisor; and focusing on the student, teacher, or parent with whom the supervisee is working rather than on the supervisee (Alonso & Rutan, 1988; J. M. Bernard & Goodyear, 2004; Bridges, 1999). If noncompliance is a reaction to a supervisee who perceives a supervisor as overly directive, or who feels a need for greater autonomy, it can be countered by being less directive and emphasizing the consultation role in the supervisory process (J. M. Bernard & Goodyear, 2004).

Terminating Supervisory Relationships

Supervisory relationships inevitably terminate. Intern supervision naturally terminates at the end of the internship year. Other supervisory relationships terminate when either the supervisee or supervisor moves, retires, or changes position. In these naturally occurring terminations, the same processes that are used to terminate counseling relationships should be used. It is important to discuss the upcoming termination, address the feelings involved, take into consideration the shifting of tasks and responsibilities, and reach a sense of closure. Supervisors should summarize the progress made by the supervisee, discuss the supervisee's need for additional supervision and training, draw generalizations from the supervision, resolve interpersonal issues, review the written evaluation with the supervisee in a personal interview, and bring supervision to a closure (Mead, 1990; Todd, 1997a). These activities are generally completed in conferences between supervisors and supervisees, but others are involved as appropriate. For example, it is likely that university supervisors will be involved with interns, and that future supervisors will be involved in problematic situations.

On rare occasions, the supervisory relationship ends on a negative note. Supervisors may recommend that an intern not receive credit for an internship, or that a supervisee leave the profession of school psychology altogether due to clinical incompetence, academic status, ethical violations, or legal grounds. Clearly defined standards, evaluation methods, and procedures for dismissal should be made available to supervisees at the beginning of a placement or job to adhere to ethical principles and to minimize objections and legal challenges to such unpleasant but necessary steps (Todd, 1997a).

APPRAISING COMMUNICATION AND INTERPERSONAL SKILLS

Supervisors should assess their own communication and interpersonal skills, develop a plan to address them, implement that plan, and appraise the resulting change in order to determine the need for future change. Even veteran supervisors should appraise their communication and interpersonal skills on an ongoing basis. Inevitably, changes in circumstances, such as new administrators or supervisees, will necessitate adjustments by the supervisor in these variables. Therefore, supervisors would appropriately include at least one communication and interpersonal skill goal in their annual goals to ensure continual attention to these critical variables.

Supervisors' interpersonal skills can be improved through systematic assessment, development of targeted interventions to improve specific skills, and appraisal of the success of these interventions. One method of assessment is to observe the supervisor interact with supervisees and others, either directly or through taped sessions. In addition, a number of instruments can be employed. These include the Supervisory Working Alliance Inventory (Efstation, Patton, & Kardash, 1990), which has one scale for the supervisee and one for the supervisor. It measures working alliance in terms of rapport and perceptions of the supervisee's work with students. The scale is reported to have reliability coefficients ranging from .71 to .90. The Working Alliance Inventory—Modified (WAI-M; Burke et al., 1998) is a modification of Horvath and Greenberg's (1989) Working Alliance Inventory. Supervisors and supervisees report impressions of the strength of the working alliance in terms of goals, tasks, and bonds. The scale has been found to have coefficient alphas between .78 and .86. The Supervisory Styles Inventory (SSI; M. L. Friedlander & Ward, 1984) has supervisees evaluate their supervisors on Likert-type items that fall in three scales: attraction, interpersonal sensitivity, and task orientation. Reliability has been found to range from .76 to .93, and the inventory has been found to predict supervisees' perception of supervision's effect on their professional development. Additional instruments include the Role Conflict and Role Ambiguity Inventory (RCRAI; Olk & Friedlander, 1992), a 29-item questionnaire that measures supervisees' perceptions of clarity regarding supervisor expectations and evaluation criteria. The supervisee's developmental level can be assessed using the

Supervisee Levels Questionnaire—Revised (SLQ-R; McNeill, Stoltenberg, & Romans, 1992). Reliability has been found to range from .64 to .83 on the scales of Self and Other Awareness, Dependency-Autonomy, Motivation, and Total. The Supervision Attitude Scale (Kavanagh et al., 2003) was developed to assess supervisee-supervisor relationships. It has been found to have internal consistency of .90 and .94. It asks supervisees and supervisors to rate each other, using a 4-point scale, on positive items such as "They are easy to get along with," "They listen to me," and "They appreciate what I do for them," as well as on negative items such as "They make me feel drained," "They are becoming harder to work with," and "They deliberately cause me problems."

The Session Evaluation Questionnaire (SEQ; Stiles, 2006) measures post-session thoughts and affect. It can be used to assess sessions with supervisors, supervisees, or students on four factors: depth, smoothness, positivity, and arousal. It has been found to have internal consistency above .90, has been used in a number of research studies (Burke et al., 1998), and is available at www.users.muohio.edu/stileswb (scroll down and click on "Session Evaluation Questionnaire") in English, German, French, Dutch, Greek, Chinese, Thai, and Bahasa Malaysia.

SUMMARY

Effective supervisors understand the importance of building strong working alliances and are adept at interpersonal relationships. Interpersonal difficulties with supervisors are among the most stressful situations for supervisees. In addition to harming supervisees, a supervisor's poor interpersonal skills can negatively affect service delivery, program delivery, and student progress. A poor supervisory relationship can increase shame and exacerbate supervisees' tendency to conceal essential information regarding professional practice from supervisors. Supervisee responses can include withdrawal, loss of trust, development of health problems, diminished self-efficacy, increased self-reflection, and feelings of fear, powerlessness, and anxiety. Even if not intentionally, supervisors can neglect, harass, and provide demeaning or destructive supervision that in turn undermines supervisees' work.

The ability to provide good supervision is affected by personal characteristics and supervision experience and motivation as well as skills in leadership and delegating. Supervisors and school psychologists typically pass through developmental phases of professional development during which they increase and refine their skills and abilities. This professional development is a lifelong process. In fact, regardless of developmental stage, all school psychologists are beginners when they enter situations in which they have no previous experience. It is clear that strong supervisee-supervisor working alliances result in positive outcomes for supervision. There are many challenges to positive interpersonal relationships between supervisors and supervisees, including goal conflicts; method conflicts; negative affect; occurrences of parallel processes, transference, and countertransference; and noncompliance and resistance.

Supervisors' interpersonal skills can be improved through systematic assessment, the development of targeted interventions to improve specific skills, and the monitoring of whether these interventions are successful. In addition to direct observation of a supervisor's interpersonal skills, a number of instruments exist that can measure such skills as well as the degree of working alliance between supervisor and supervisee. Interventions may focus on multiple areas, including improving the supervisory context, improving communication skills, addressing motivation, responding to supervisee developmental levels, developing supervision session goals, fostering effective problem solving, addressing countertransference, addressing noncompliance or resistance, addressing supervisee anxiety and personal problems, maintaining appropriate supervisory boundaries, using power appropriately, and terminating supervisory relationships.

REFLECTIVE QUESTIONS

Q2.1. What are the characteristics of conflicted supervisory relationships?

Q2.2. Describe the personal characteristics and skill set of a good supervisor.

Q2.3. Describe the phases of professional development outlined by Rønnestad and Skovholt (2003). Describe the stages of professional development indicated by the Integrated Development Model. What themes are present throughout a professional's development?

Q2.4. How can Maslow's (1954) theory of motivation be a useful framework to consider when working with supervisees?

Q2.5. What are the three phases of the supervisor-supervisee relationship (Holloway, 1995)? What should occur during these phases?

Q2.6. How does context affect the supervisory relationship?

Q2.7. Why do challenges to positive interpersonal relationships between supervisors and supervisees occur, and how do they manifest themselves?

Q2.8. Describe a systematic approach for supervisors to improve their interpersonal skills.

SUPERVISORY DILEMMAS

SD 2.1

In your district, school psychologists are not part of the teachers' bargaining unit. The teachers' union has voted to "work to rule," which means that they strictly adhere to contractual language that states that they must arrive 15 minutes before the start of school and may leave 15 minutes after the students are dismissed. In an attempt to support the teachers, school psychologists are also working to rule. Many team meetings, previously held after school hours to accommodate parents' work schedules, have had to be canceled. The director of special education is pressuring the school psychologists to disregard the current situation and work after school. *What are the supervisory considerations? What should be done?*

Authors' thoughts: Inarguably, the underlying obligation of all school psychologists is to safeguard students' welfare. Hence, any and all work actions must be mediated by this primary professional responsibility. To perform optimally, it is imperative that school psychologists maintain good relationships with teachers. A prudent course of action would be to consider which services are so essential that they should be delivered outside contractual hours in light of the present situation. For example, most team meetings could probably be scheduled to occur during school hours. On the other hand, if a student presented with suicidal ideation at the close of the school day, there would be no doubt that the priority of the school psychologist would be to work with the student. The supervising school psychologist might briefly explain the situation to both the special education director and the teachers' union representative in order to preserve sound working relationships. Simply stated, the collective response of the school psychologists will be influenced by the demands of the situation. While it is important to support the teachers, student welfare will always be the priority.

SD 2.2

Two of your supervisees disagree about the appropriateness of social contacts with school personnel and turn to you for advice. One school psychologist believes that participating in social events outside of school hours is helpful and appropriate in that it enables her to build friendships with colleagues that facilitate her work in the school as a consultant. Therefore, she accepts invitations to dinners, parties, and after-hours socializing in bars. The other believes that participating in social events is an ethical violation that leads to dual relationships. *What are the supervisory considerations? What should be done?*

Authors' thoughts: While dual relationships do form and can indeed pose problems, it does seem to be human nature to form personal relationships at work. Social interaction is, in fact, a workplace benefit. Hence, rather than avoiding all contact, keeping ethical demands at the forefront should be an effective response. (We might suggest real restraint in the bars, however!) Vigilance in guarding confidentiality may present the major challenge!

SD 2.3

You have been supervising a female school psychologist on a weekly basis for 3 years and have noticed a pattern where she almost invariably interprets the behavior of males—principals, teachers, other school psychologists, and parents—as sexually motivated. You suspect that these interpretations may not be accurate and that they are interfering with her ability to generate alternative hypotheses. *What are the supervisory considerations? What should be done?*

Authors' thoughts: Because the apparent misperceptions are adversely affecting the work of the school psychologist, the supervisor has no choice but to directly and immediately confront the issue. This appears to be a case of countertransference, but supervision should never traverse into therapy. Hence, a referral for counseling would be appropriate. Minimally, in the short term, close supervision and careful selection of cases is warranted.

SD 2.4

An intern who is quite enthusiastic and eager—and who looks very young—is under your supervision. The majority of teachers in your school are mature and close to retirement. They have seen many educational fads come and go and have little patience with young enthusiasm. After 6 months, you perceive that the teachers in the school consistently turn to you even regarding those cases handled entirely by the intern. *What are the supervisory considerations? What should be done?*

Authors' thoughts: It takes both time and effort to establish a "power base" in a new setting. In this case, it appears that a more proactive approach may be warranted. As a supervisor, it would be ideal to support the new practitioner in an undertaking that might help to better establish her credibility and demonstrate expertise. In the meantime, it may be helpful to "double-team" in order to address teachers' concerns and then gradually withdraw supervisory participation. Brainstorming with the new school psychologist about ways to handle the situation will be of inestimable importance. It is likely that she is aware that she is being bypassed. Finally, it will be important to determine if the veteran teachers have found her performance to be ineffective or if they just haven't sought out her services.

3

Multicultural Competencies

Both supervisors and supervisees should recognize that they may hold attitudes and beliefs that can detrimentally influence their perceptions of, and interactions with, individuals who are different from themselves.

Vignette 3.1

Jen, a school psychologist working in a city, noticed that a substantial number of parents did not return for second prereferral team meetings to discuss their children. She also noticed that their children were frequently accused of "starting fights for no reason" on the playground. In a supervision session, Jen remarked that the families had migrated from impoverished rural areas, leading her supervisor to suggest that cultural issues might be relevant. She recommended that Jen learn more about the culture of the families. To do so, Jen interviewed students, parents, and teachers originally from the country and also read relevant autobiographies and history books. From this exploratory work, she and her supervisor developed several hypotheses that Jen subsequently checked with the aforementioned interviewees. Jen concluded that several factors should be addressed and made the following recommendations: (a) To help make the parents more comfortable in meetings with school personnel and to respect their cultural standards for good manners, Jen recommended that the team schedule at least 15 minutes' extra meeting time to permit polite socialization before beginning the business part of the meeting. (b) To reduce shame and feelings of being "beholden," Jen recommended that the school social worker charge a very nominal amount for clothing and other items rather than giving them away without charge. (c) To reduce playground fights provoked by name-calling, Jen recommended that the principal include "hillbilly" on the unacceptable list of the schoolwide policy against name-calling. (d) To reduce "unprovoked" playground fights (which typically included an older sibling "standing up for" a younger sibling by attacking the older sibling of the younger sibling's adversary), Jen recommended that school personnel demonstrate respect for family solidarity by regularly involving siblings whenever a student participated in mediation.

Multicultural competencies are a subset of the interpersonal and communication skills addressed in the previous chapter, but because of their significance and complexity they are addressed in this separate chapter. This chapter addresses *general* multicultural competencies that supervisors of school psychological services should foster both in themselves and in their supervisees. More specific multicultural competencies, such as those relevant to assessment and intervention, are addressed in subsequent chapters.

BASIC CONSIDERATIONS

Supervisors are responsible for developing their own and their supervisees' multicultural awareness, sensitivity, and responsivity. Both supervisors and supervisees must be skilled in working with students, parents, and educators of diverse races, ethnicities, and cultures for several reasons.

First, ethical principles and professional standards mandate these skills (American Psychological Association [APA], 2002; National Association of School Psychologists [NASP], 2000a). Concern for the welfare of students supersedes all other concerns, and practitioners who do not possess multicultural competencies will inevitably, although unintentionally, violate this standard.

Societies categorize people according to visible and invisible traits, use such categorizations to deduce behavioral and mental traits, and apply policies and practices that jeopardize some while benefiting others. As a result, gross exaggerations and stereotypes often result. Both positive and negative stereotypes limit our perspective on an entire group of people and result in unjust resource allocation. Power and prestige are differentially applied by category, and racism and discrimination are systemic manifestations of these economic, political, and social power differentials. Since supervisors are ethically mandated to provide supervision only in areas in which they have expertise, it is obviously ethically imperative that they address their own multicultural competencies as well as those of their supervisees.

Second, at this time, most school psychologists are middle class and nondisabled, and in the United States they are predominantly white and monolingually English speaking (Curtis, Grier, & Hunley, 2004). This is in marked contrast to the populations with whom school psychologists work; significantly higher percentages of the general population are ethnic minorities, and a high percentage of culturally diverse children are identified as disabled. Thus, it can be surmised that middle class white school psychologists serve the vast majority of ethnic minority and underprivileged students and that it is critical that school psychologists have the multicultural competencies needed to work effectively with those unlike themselves. Supervisees tend to overestimate their multicultural competencies. However, this can be ameliorated, regardless of race, when supervisors instruct supervisees to address racial and multicultural issues in their work (Ladany, Inman, Constantine, & Hofheinz, 1997). Consequently, supervisors themselves must solidly understand appropriate methods to address multicultural issues.

Third, psychologists are more likely to acquire multicultural competencies in response to personal and professional experience than in response to ethical codes or professional guidelines (Hansen et al., 2006). Therefore, supervised practice is one of the primary modalities through which practitioners acquire multicultural competencies (Ladany et al., 1997). To foster the development of multicultural expertise, supervisors need to explicitly engineer the supervisees' experiences to include *successful* multicultural experiences.

Finally, in response to the increasingly diverse student populations, school psychology graduate programs are deliberately and systematically increasing the number of diverse applicants accepted into school psychology programs (Curtis et al., 2004). Having bilingual and bicultural school psychologists among members of school psychology departments certainly has advantages for ethnic minority children and parents and for the department as a whole. When well-supervised, departments containing individuals of different cultures can develop positive interdependence among members, a group identity based on a common set of values, personal relationships that encourage open discussions, and open clarification of common misunderstandings (Johnson & Johnson, 1994). To facilitate supervisee success as districts build school psychology departments containing psychologists from diverse backgrounds, supervisors will need skills in *multicultural supervision*, or supervision by an individual from a culture other than one's own. Duan and Roehlke (2001) found that 93% of supervisors had no experience with supervisees who were racially or culturally different from themselves. This poses challenges in that multicultural supervision is vulnerable to "cultural variances in communication and behaviors, expectations, values and beliefs, preferences, perceptions, and culturally based assumptions [that] sometimes result in miscommunication, misinformation, and misunderstanding. This can lead to supervisee anger and resistance, supervisor defensiveness, supervisor overidentification, supervisee resistance, supervisor countertransference, or supervisor patronization" and can culminate in a destructive communication breakdown (Garrett et al., 2001, p. 150). On the other hand, supervisors with multicultural competencies have stronger supervisory alliances, are better able to foster supervisees' multicultural competencies, and have supervisees who are more satisfied with supervision (Inman, 2006).

MULTICULTURAL COMPETENCIES

In 2003, the American Psychological Association (APA) published "Guidelines on Multicultural Education, Training, Research, Practice, and Organizational Change for Psychologists." These guidelines explicitly encourage psychologists to develop multicultural awareness, sensitivity, and responsiveness. They explicitly discourage a "colorblind" approach whereby cultural differences are ignored.

When school personnel, including school psychologists, are "color blind," they are, in fact, refusing to accept differences. This truth is demonstrated by imagining school personnel being "disability blind," and refusing to accept differences resulting from disabilities. In reality, accepting differences means making provisions for them. For example, the *Lau v. Nichols* (1974) Supreme Court case decision concluded that instruction of Chinese students in English was not providing an equal educational opportunity because students could not benefit from the instruction. As Miville, Rosa, and Constantine (2005) suggested, the following subset of the APA guidelines are of particular relevance:

1. Psychologists are encouraged to recognize that, as cultural beings, they may hold attitudes and beliefs that can detrimentally influence their perceptions of and interactions with individuals who are ethnically and racially different from themselves. (APA, 2003, p. 382)

2. Psychologists are encouraged to recognize the importance of multicultural sensitivity/responsiveness to, knowledge of, and understanding about ethnically and racially different individuals. (APA, 2003, p. 385)

5. Psychologists are encouraged to apply culturally appropriate skills in clinical and other applied psychological practices. (APA, 2003, p. 390)

6. Psychologists are encouraged to use organizational change processes to support culturally informed organizational (policy) development and practices. (APA, 2003, p. 392)

According to Hansen et al. (2006), important manifestations of multiculturally competent practice include personal and professional development, establishment of rapport, case conceptualization, treatment accommodation, and systems change.

Personal and Professional Development

Psychologists and supervisors are multiculturally competent when they take responsibility for transcending their own cultural conditioning, both positive and negative; determine when assumptions, values, and biases impact practice; assess personal multicultural competence and determine areas of weakness; and implement a professional development plan to improve these skills.

Establishing Rapport

Psychologists and supervisors are multiculturally competent when they respect others' worldviews; avoid idealizing any group; establish rapport in racially/ethnically/multiculturally sensitive ways; initiate and explore issues of cultural differences among students, teachers, parents, and others; and respect individual differences within cultural groups.

Case Conceptualization

Multicultural case conceptualization is the ability to identify and integrate cultural factors into problem analysis, assessment strategies, and intervention plans. Psychologists and supervisors are multiculturally competent when they consider the impact of race, ethnicity, sociopolitical factors, and other multicultural issues on cognitive development, personality development, gender roles, and psychological disorders; routinely evaluate language proficiency; develop culturally relevant case conceptualizations; employ culturally sensitive data gathering techniques; consider cultural issues during diagnosis; and use literature, translators, indigenous resources, community resources, and other multicultural resources to augment practice.

Treatment Accommodations

Psychologists and supervisors are multiculturally competent when they negotiate psychologist-client language differences; refer clients to culturally more qualified providers when appropriate; seek culture-specific consultation and feedback; use translators when linguistically appropriate; modify interventions to take into account the client's help-seeking style, beliefs about illness, and psychological effects of oppression/discrimination; help students and parents develop skills to interface with other cultures and with institutional barriers; and assess and address students' and parents' level of acculturative stress.

Systems Change

Psychologists and supervisors are multiculturally competent when they recognize and address school, district, and societal stereotyping, prejudice, and discrimination.

CHALLENGES TO DEVELOPING SUPERVISEES' MULTICULTURAL COMPETENCIES

There are several variables that challenge supervisors of school psychological services as they strive to develop supervisees' multicultural competencies. These include discomfort regarding discussion of multicultural issues, the challenge of acquiring knowledge regarding peoples of other cultures without overgeneralizing such knowledge to the point that it becomes bias or stereotyping, bias in the field of psychology, deficient graduate training, deficient professional development programs, biased laws, bias in K–12 education, and insufficient knowledge regarding the complexity and components of culture.

Overcoming Discomfort

First and foremost, open discussions regarding cultural differences, particularly those relating to oppressed groups, are avoided by many individuals because they are uncomfortable or even perceive these topics as taboo, even within a supervisory relationship (Utsey, Gernat, & Hammar, 2005). Individuals from majority groups tend to be unaware of the privilege afforded on the basis of their group memberships, or to be afraid of offending or angering members of minority groups by broaching the subject. Individuals from oppressed groups are likely to be wary of being perceived as using their group status as a defense or excuse for poor performance.

Unfortunately, supervisors tend to believe that they conduct discussions regarding cultural issues more frequently than their supervisees perceive that they do (Duan & Roehlke, 2001), and cultural issues regarding multicultural supervisory relationships are addressed less than half the time by supervisors (Burkard et al., 2006). Supervisors tend to be relatively unaware of negative events in multicultural supervision, such as cultural insensitivity, questioning of supervisees' clinical abilities, challenging of the use of interventions with culturally diverse clients, negative communication, and lack of intervention by the supervisor. In one study, only 7% of supervisors reported such negative events, compared with 16% of supervisees (Burkard et al., 2006).

Balancing Multicultural Knowledge and Stereotyping

Knowledge of general cultural differences is an important initial step in multicultural understanding. On the other hand, assuming that "known" cultural differences are invariant is stereotyping. Therefore, supervisors and supervisees are challenged to increase knowledge regarding cultural groups other than their own while simultaneously refraining from making the assumption that all group members are identical. If mishandled and focused on *multiculturalism* rather than multicultural skills, attempting to develop multicultural sensitivity can actually be detrimental. This can occur when individuals devote effort to understanding and appreciating cultural differences without also addressing skills needed to relate and communicate. It also can occur when the "diversity paradox" (attending to group differences while simultaneously respecting individual differences) is ignored (Frisby, 2005).

The Field of Psychology

The field of psychology has a pervasively white, Eurocentric basis, as evidenced by Guthrie's 1998 book *Even the Rat Was White: A Historical View of Psychology* (Falender & Shafranske, 2004). Therefore, psychologists and supervisors must transcend the very academic, research, and therapeutic foundations of their field, as well as the pervasive culture, to develop and realize multicultural competencies.

Graduate Training

Many graduate programs are deficient in multicultural courses, faculty conducting multiculturally oriented research, and field placements serving multicultural clients. They are particularly likely to neglect differences in religion, gender, and sexual identity (Falender & Shafranske, 2004). Supervisors are likely to be even less prepared to deal with multicultural situations than their supervisees because they attended graduate school prior to the infusion of multicultural issues into the curricula and/or completed their training and internship in homogeneous settings. Constantine (1997) found that only 30% of supervising psychologists had completed multicultural coursework during their graduate programs, in comparison to 70% of their interns. Thus supervisors of psychological services in schools are very likely to need to address the development of their own multicultural competencies as well as that of their supervisees. Supervisors undergo several stages in the development of their ability to provide effective multicultural supervision (T. L. Brown, Acevedo-Polakovich, & Smith, 2006; Helms & Cook, 1999; Porter, 1994). Although there are variations among models, several broad stages have been identified:

- Stage 1: Supervisors ignore race and culture and assume that their worldview does not affect their supervision. They focus only on "common humanity" and may claim "scientific objectivity."
- Stage 2: Supervisors recognize that their views and practice have been influenced by their culture of origin and that individuals from other cultures have valid, although different, worldviews. They have difficulty incorporating differences into practice.
- Stage 3: Supervisors perceive client culture as a valid characteristic and "explore how discrimination, oppression, power and other socioeconomic forces affect the mental health of minorities. Supervisors understand that some behaviors that appear pathological may be culturally embedded or may even be adaptive ways of coping with real sociocultural problems" (T. L. Brown et al., 2006, p. 76). At this stage, supervisors explore their own biases through honest self-reflection in response to cross-cultural challenges and come to respectfully acknowledge the culture of clients, supervisees, and themselves. They are aware of cultural assumptions and attitudes, incorporate sociopolitical implications of culture in practice, acknowledge racial and cultural differences, integrate their personal cultural values as well as those of supervisees and clients, and effectively address cultural differences in supervision.
- Stage 4: Finally, supervisors advocate for oppressed groups in larger contexts by addressing school and districtwide policies; they move beyond the individual to the systems level (J. M. Bernard & Goodyear, 2004; T. L. Brown et al., 2006).

Professional Development Programs

Just as university programs have historically neglected to adequately address multicultural issues, professional development programs in school psychology are similarly deficient

(Falender & Shafranske, 2004). In this field, unlike domains of practice in which veteran psychologists within the department have high levels of expertise they model for novice psychologists, veteran psychologists often do not feel multiculturally competent (K. W. Allison, Echemendia, Crawford, & Robinson, 1996) and do not perform behaviors that demonstrate multicultural awareness, sensitivity, and responsivity (Hansen et al., 2006). Consequently, supervisors must address insufficient multicultural competencies in veteran practitioners across the department in addition to fostering skills in novice school psychologists.

Challenges That Minority School Psychologists and Supervisors Encounter

Even in schools with a plurality of minority students, a minority school psychologist may work almost entirely with majority culture teachers and administrators. This may affect her or his feelings of empowerment and efficacy when practicing consultation, and supervisors can be challenged to provide sufficient support to such supervisees. Supervisors who are themselves members of racial or ethnic minority groups have additional issues to address. Dickens and Dickens (1991) indicated that minority supervisors progress through four stages as they adjust to the supervisory role. A false sense of security, relief at the appointment, and a lack of personal goals characterize the *entry* phase. The second phase, *adjusting*, is characterized by dissatisfaction, frustration, testing of the organization, and anger. During the third phase, *planned growth*, the supervisor develops a concentrated and strategic effort to succeed. The fourth phase, *success*, is characterized by achieving confidence, reaching goals, and setting new goals for the future.

Laws

While well intended in terms of improving schools and raising educational standards, laws such as No Child Left Behind are biased against English language learners (ELLs) because they require that students be administered high-stakes achievement tests in English after a minimum number of years of schooling in English. After this level of exposure to English, students are likely to have acquired Basic Interpersonal Communication Skills (BICS), or the ability to communicate basic wants and needs and carry on conversations. They are unlikely to have acquired Cognitive Academic Language Proficiency (CALP), or the degree of language proficiency necessary for academic success, because that takes approximately 6 years to develop (Krashen, 1982). Particularly with minority and ELL students, requiring passage of high-stakes exams in order to graduate from high school appears to increase the number of students who drop out of high school (Amrein & Berliner, 2003; Haney, 2000; B. A. Jacob, 2001). Supervisors must help their supervisees cope with this bias as they are asked to provide services for the increasingly high percentage of students who arrive at school as nonnative English speakers and the shamefully high proportion of nonnative English speakers who drop out of high school.

K–12 Education

As Nieto (2004) indicated, multiple structural factors in schools in the United States combine to render schools hostile environments for students who are not middle or upper class English-speaking Euro-Americans. These factors include tracking that discriminates on the basis of social class, testing that favors individuals from cultures favoring autonomy, curriculum content that ignores pluralism and favors Euro-American history and literature, teaching methods that do not favor multiple learning styles, disciplinary policies that ignore cultural imperatives, negative attitudes toward students who speak languages other than English (unless they are native English speakers studying a second language in school), and the limited role of students, teachers, parents, and community members in developing school policies. Nieto pointed out that while the education system was designed to tear down barriers of class and caste and provide all with equal education, the schools are unsuccessful with many students, particularly those from cultural minority, linguistically diverse, and poor families. Sometimes what is valued by a culture is devalued in schools, forcing a child to choose alienation from either school or family. For example, if a culture values cooperation but children attend a school that values competition, they may be forced to abandon cultural values to be successful in that competitive school. Therefore, one of the prices of successful assimilation into the educational system can be abandonment of culture of origin.

Another example of conflict between cultural values and schools is found in migrant families. The value placed on financially supporting the family, starting at ages 10 to 12, is so strong in migrant families that it interferes with school attendance, school completion, and community attachment. Additional challenges faced by migrant children include minimal health care despite considerable health risks, minimal income, multiple languages, and an extremely high rate of school transfers (Henning-Stout, 1996).

Harry, Allen, and McLaughlin (1996) described another example of a cultural conflict with education. They found that parents of African American preschool children saw school as the root of success and perceived schools as "doing their job" when the children learned basic reading, writing, and arithmetic through explicit instruction, repeated drill, and practice. The parents had faith in phonics and perceived sight-reading as illogical. Parents also expected their children to receive explicit instruction in the dominant English dialect. They defined the purposes of school as teaching reading, writing, and math; teaching the child social and personal behaviors needed for success in school and life (share, sit down, pay attention); and providing a safe haven. They were not concerned that the schools teach problem solving and practical skills, since those were thought to be more appropriately learned at home or in the community. A "good teacher" was described as having a sincere interest in the children, implementing firm classroom and behavior management, using structured teaching methods, facilitating the acquisition of basic skills, and assigning and promptly grading regular homework. "Pushing" by a teacher was seen as evidence of "caring." A "good school" was defined as orderly and traditional, with firm discipline, a principal who wasn't afraid of the kids, and a focus on explicitly teaching children the behaviors that would make them more acceptable (and therefore safer) in mainstream society. Schools and teachers that do not match parental definitions of "good" are likely to suffer from insufficient parental and community support.

Insufficient Understanding of the Complexities of Culture

Many individuals misunderstand the number of variables that contribute to an individual's culture, and supervisors are challenged to help supervisees understand the complexity of this concept. Misconceptions regarding culture can range from "whites don't have a culture" to believing that individuals from a given demographic group all have the same culture. There are vast differences among the subcultures of any demographic group. Furthermore, even more variance is found at the individual level. A person's culture arises from a broad spectrum of characteristics, including age, ethnicity, race, socioeconomic status, gender, sexual identity, religion, and acculturation.

COMPONENTS OF CULTURE

Culture is defined as patterns of attitudes, living, norms, traditions, and values developed and influenced by parents and community (Mosley-Howard, 1995). Culture involves the ever-changing values, traditions, social relationships, politics, and worldwide views created and shared by a group of people bound together by factors such as common history, geographic location, language, social class, and religion. It is expressed tangibly in foods, holidays, dress, and artistic expression and less tangibly in communication style, nonverbal behavior, attitudes, values, family relationships, and gender role expectations. Hofstede (1993) identified several dimensions on which cultures typically differ:

1. *Individualism versus collectivism* indicates the degree to which individuals act in their own interest as opposed to the interest of the group.

2. *Power distance* describes the degree to which a culture attempts to reduce inequalities in power and wealth.

3. *Uncertainty avoidance* describes the degree to which cultures deal with the unpredictability of the future by turning to technology, law, and/or religion.

4. *Masculinity-femininity* describes the extent to which traditionally male traits (assertiveness, competitiveness, performance, and success) and female traits (care, service, and solidarity) are valued.

5. *Long-term/short-term orientation* describes the degree to which the culture focuses on and plans for the future over short-term gains.

It should be emphasized that all individuals in the same culture are not identical. While identification with a particular race or ethnic group is often reflected in culture, there are multiple cultures in any race or ethnic group. For example, there are multiple cultures among the individuals who identify themselves as Latino or Latina that reflect variables such as country of origin, class, urban versus rural living, acculturation, and geographic location. Furthermore, culture is integral to the individual but affects every individual differently. Thus, generalizing from group membership to the individual can be misleading and damaging.

Vignette 3.2

Linda supervised two Latinas, one a third-generation Cuban expatriate from Miami and the other a child of a first-generation Mexican immigrant migrant worker. Aside from their language, Linda found that these two supervisees had culturally little in common. They had completely different socioeconomic backgrounds and degrees of acculturation. Even their traditional foods differed markedly.

Age

School psychologists are unlikely to encounter diversity issues relative to age among K–12 students. On the other hand, both school psychologists and supervisors encounter diversity issues relative to age as they consult with parents, teachers, administrators, and each other. Younger adults frequently have stereotypes regarding older adults and vice versa. Furthermore, because of the cohort effect, an ethnically identical supervisor who is close to retirement is likely to be from a different culture than a supervisee 40 years younger; individuals who came of age during the Vietnam War era had a considerably different life experience than individuals who came of age during the early 21st century. In this situation, and in other relationships (e.g., school psychologist–consultee teacher) with considerable age differences, individuals will need to foster the same empathy and understanding that they employ in other multicultural settings in order to effectively communicate.

Furthermore, developmental psychology courses in school psychology programs may focus primarily on child and adolescent development and exclude information that school psychologists need to effectively work with parents, teachers, and administrators who are themselves experiencing adult developmental issues. It is important that supervisors ensure that they and their supervisees are well versed in psychological development across the life span.

Socioeconomic Status and Class

Socioeconomic class affects identity, feelings of loyalty, and expectations about education, lifestyle, and many other variables. Classism is exacerbated by the American attribution of individual responsibility for class membership ("Anyone can make it if they try."). Classism can have a profound impact on the practice of school psychology, because inattention to class can result in "blaming the victim" (Lappin & Hardy, 1997). Class differences and classism may arise because of different backgrounds between the supervisor and supervisee, and they almost inevitably will arise because of differences between supervisees and their clients. Furthermore, even when school personnel themselves are not originally from middle class families, they may adopt the middle class values and stereotypes endemic in schools and become intolerant or disparaging of the values of other classes.

Disabilities

As does society at large, schools can maintain prejudices toward and a devaluation of individuals with disabilities, or "ableism" (Hehir, 2002, 2007). This devaluation contributes to low levels of academic achievement. It becomes particularly problematic when educational programs for students with disabilities focus exclusively on overcoming their disability rather than on providing them with learning opportunities that foster the broad spectrum of educational opportunities and thereby *enable* them to eventually fully participate in society.

Although identifying and working with students with disabilities is a major responsibility of school psychologists, they can nonetheless harbor considerable prejudices and preconceptions regarding handicapping conditions. We have observed school psychologists demonstrate such biases by assuming that all children with IQ scores below 85 "will find it difficult if not impossible to achieve in general education classes" regardless of motivation or other personal variables; disregarding ophthalmologists' evaluations of students identified as blind with the mistaken assumption that any child so identified is totally without vision; assuming that all children who have difficulty focusing attention have neurologically based attention deficit disorder and are in need of stimulant medication, rather than investigating other possible causes of attention deficits, such as anxiety, posttraumatic stress disorder, and distracting environments; assuming that children diagnosed with Down syndrome are inevitably mentally retarded or handicapped; and assuming that any learning difficulty experienced by an English language learner is a result of language differences.

Ethnicity and Race

Although a pivotal source of identity, issues of ethnicity and race are often marginalized, denied, ignored, and inappropriately left unspoken, particularly by members of the majority culture (Lappin & Hardy, 1997). Consequently, both supervisees and supervisors tend to be disinclined to raise the issue, particularly if they are white. When discussing racism, whites often react with anger, apathy, or intellectual detachment (D'Andrea & Daniels, 2001). This is problematic in that initiating open and supportive discussions regarding race facilitates both supervisory and therapeutic alliances. Such discussions can be critical in creating a trusting relationship and providing both effective interventions and supervision (Cardemil & Battle, 2003; Helms & Cook, 1999). Race can be an extraordinarily difficult topic for many individuals to address. This is in part because the topic of race raises considerable negative emotions, including shame on the part of individuals who belong to the group whose ancestors were racist and anger on the part of individuals whose ancestors were enslaved, oppressed, or murdered. Furthermore, many individuals are so afraid of being perceived as racist that they pretend not to notice race to an absurd degree.

Vignette 3.3

Emily, a school psychologist working in a suburban town, met regularly with the student support team. During one meeting the team discussed **Robert**, a student new to the school who was reportedly having considerable difficulties adjusting and had not made any friends. When Emily entered the classroom to make her observation, she was surprised to find that he was the only African American student in the entire school. Emily was struck by the fact that, in attempting to be "color blind," the team appeared oblivious to the challenges Robert faced as an "only" in the school.

As P. McIntosh (1989) indicated, destructive racism consists not only of individual acts or statements of racism, but also of taking advantage of "white privilege" afforded on a daily basis. Such advantages may include freedom of choice in public accommodations, travel, residence, schooling, and employment—privileges that many individuals take for granted.

Supervisors have a mandate to address racism on multiple levels. First, to minimize the ill effects of racism, supervisors must develop their own awareness of these factors and encourage a similar awareness in supervisees. Second, as systemic leaders, supervisors of school psychologists are in a position to positively influence school policies that affect children from minority groups.

Gender

Gender stereotypes are so culturally pervasive that they inevitably affect supervision and supervisory relationships. For both supervisors and supervisees, patriarchy can result in men's contributions being heeded more respectfully and women's contributions being devalued (J. M. Bernard & Goodyear, 2004; Turner & Fine, 1997). This devaluing can occur in interactions with administrators, teachers, and parents as well as in supervisor-supervisee relationships. As J. M. Bernard and Goodyear indicated, gender issues in supervision can be manifested when:

- A supervisor assumes only the female, supportive "voice of care" or only the male, challenging "voice of justice" (Gilligan, 1982), since effective supervision requires both voices (Ellis & Robins, 1993)
- Male supervisors violate cultural norms that promote competition, autonomy, and emotional constriction and therefore experience gender role conflict (Wester & Vogel, 2002; Wester, Vogel, & Archer, 2004)
- Miscommunication occurs due to typical gender differences in conversational rhythms, tendencies to interrupt, and listening patterns

Sexual Orientation

Sexual orientation is relevant to the supervision of school psychological services for several reasons. Supervisors need to help supervisees understand how to create a safe environment for self-disclosure and support for students, since they are very likely to encounter students of diverse sexual orientations (Long, 1997). Additionally, supervisees may be of a different sexual orientation than their supervisors, and it is important that supervisors create a safe environment for self-disclosure within the supervisory relationship. Finally, it is important for supervisors to help supervisees with minority sexual orientations understand the implications and repercussions, if any, of self-disclosure to administrators and to others within the school district.

According to the "Guidelines for Psychotherapy With Lesbian, Gay, and Bisexuals Clients" (APA, Committee on Lesbian, Gay, and Bisexual Concerns, 2000), relevant skills include an understanding of:

- Normal developmental stages in sexual identity, including the development of normal lesbian/gay/bisexual (LGB) identity
- How assessment and interventions may be varied when working with LGB clients and how prejudice, discrimination, and threats of violence affect their mental health and presentation to psychologists
- The unique challenges experienced by parents of LGB individuals and the impact that LGB identity has on a person's family of origin
- The similarities and differences between LGB relationships and those of heterosexuals, including same-sex friendships, intimate relationships, familial relationships, and the reliance of LGB individuals on "family" members who are not legally or biologically related
- Unique challenges experienced by LGB youth, adults, and elderly
- Unique challenges experienced by LGB disabled
- Unique challenges experienced by bisexual individuals
- Community resources available to LGB individuals
- When to seek consultation, referrals, professional development, and additional training

Religion

Given the long history of wars and atrocities stemming from intra- and interreligious differences, these differences obviously play a major role in multicultural misunderstandings and abuses. However, psychologists and psychology training programs have typically neglected religious issues as well as religious diversity. Supervisors, particularly in diverse settings, are likely to find that their supervisees have extremely limited knowledge regarding the religious lives of students and families with whom they work. In the United States, addressing religion within psychological services in schools is made even more complicated by the interpretation of laws disallowing government-supported religion, which has been extended to include the banning of discussions regarding religion in public schools.

However, to ignore this topic is to ignore a significant contributor to student, family, and community life. Surveys have repeatedly indicated that the majority of the population believe in God, define religion and spirituality as important factors in their culture and identity, and would appreciate a psychologist who integrated religious matters into therapy (Hage, 2006). Furthermore, healthy spirituality and religious practices are associated with positive mental heath, well-being, and life satisfaction (Plante & Sharma, 2001), while religious practice that is less positive (e.g., that focused on negative aspects of other religions or on negative human attributes) has been associated with depression, stress, and other negative outcomes (Pargament, 1997).

Acculturation

Acculturation is the degree to which a person who is living among peoples of another culture (a) retains the values, beliefs, behaviors, and other aspects of his or her culture of origin and (b) pursues relationships with members of the new culture. It is possible to become "culturally integrated" by retaining aspects of the culture of origin while developing relationships with members of the new culture. It is also possible to be "culturally assimilated" by giving up the culture of origin. Not every member of a family is acculturated to the same degree as other members. Furthermore, a given individual is likely to be more and less acculturated in different settings (Falender & Shafranske, 2004).

Vignette 3.4

When investigating high school senior **Igor**'s degree of acculturation, **Jane** discovered that he was much more acculturated at school than he was at home. In school he spoke English fluently and appeared to be socially integrated into the student population. At home, Igor spent all of his time with other Russians, spoke only Russian, and felt very inhibited about leaving his close-knit neighborhood. This resulted in severely restricted job and postsecondary learning opportunities.

Some successful minority students interviewed by Nieto (2004) said they felt unable to identify both as American and as part of their own cultural group. These feelings sometimes resulted in students "creating new cultures," or selecting from an array of values and behaviors. Most students are proud of their own culture and resist complete assimilation, but they are also aware that their culture may be devalued in school. For some students, the more they resisted assimilation while maintaining their culture and language, the more successful they were in school.

APPLICATIONS TO SUPERVISION

As can be surmised by the above discussion, to optimize success, supervisors of school psychological services must address multicultural competencies at multiple levels and from various perspectives. Supervisors must assess and address their own multicultural competencies, those of their supervisees, and those of their department. Furthermore, as systemic leaders, supervisors of psychological services must assess and address the multicultural climate of the school, district, and community.

Assessing Individual Skills

Questions regarding multicultural competencies are often appropriately included in evaluation forms developed to appraise both supervisors and supervisees. In addition, some self-report instruments have been developed that may be useful in helping supervisees and supervisors appraise their multicultural competencies, with the understanding that they will be subject to the biases inherent in any self-report instrument. These are typically available through research literature rather than test publishers and have not been reviewed in the *Mental Measurement Yearbook*s as of 2007. These include the Multicultural Supervision Inventory—Supervisor Version (Pope-Davis, Toporek, & Ortega, 1999; Pope-Davis, Toporek, & Ortega-Villalobos, 2003), developed to help supervisors assess their own multicultural competencies; the Multicultural Counseling Knowledge and Awareness Scale (Ponterotto, Gretchen, Utsey, Rieger, & Austin, 2002), which assesses supervisors' awareness of their own cultural socialization as well as their knowledge of cross-cultural counseling issues and information; the International Student Supervision Scale (ISSS; Nilsson & Dodds, 2006), a pilot instrument designed to measure cultural issues and relationship dynamics in supervisory relationships with international students; the Bem Sex-Role Inventory (BSRI; Bem, 1974), which assesses the degree to which individuals describe themselves as having a global "instrumental," "dominant," or "assertive" (male) disposition versus "expressive" or "nurturant" (female) tendencies and can be used to uncover and address male supervisors or supervisees who are experiencing gender role conflict; the American-International Relations Scale (AIRS; Sodowsky & Plake, 1991), which measures acculturation of international students into U.S. culture as well as perceptions of prejudice and language use; the Cross-Cultural Counseling Inventory—Revised (CCCI-R; LaFromboise, Coleman, & Hernandez, 1991), which assesses supervisees' cross-cultural competencies; the Multicultural Awareness, Knowledge, and Skills Survey (D'Andrea, Daniels, & Heck, 1991); the Multicultural Counseling Inventory (Sodowsky, Taffe, Gutkin, & Wise, 1994); and the Self-Assessment Checklist for Personnel Providing Services and Supports to Children and Their Families (Goode, 2002). The last is available at www.nasponline.org and is reproduced in Handout 3.2 at the end of this chapter.

Assessing Departmental Variables

In addition to assessing their own multicultural skills and those of their supervisees, supervisors of school psychological services should assess broad departmental variables as compared to the needs of the district. A department's capacity to address multicultural variables is affected by the following:

- Cultural proficiency of psychologists, social workers, counselors, and behavior therapists relative to student cultures
- Linguistic proficiency of psychologists, social workers, counselors, and behavior therapists relative to the students' native languages
- Adequacy of district-owned assessment tools in terms of both translated and nonverbal instruments

Assessing School, District, and Community Variables

Supervisors of school psychological services should assess multicultural issues relevant to school, district, and community variables, because schools and districts that do not promote and value cultural diversity are likely to undermine supervision and development of multicultural skills (T. L. Brown et al., 2006). To determine appropriate areas in which they might advocate more appropriate policies and procedures, supervisors can consider:

- What are school and district failure rates of English language learners on high-stakes tests relative to native English speakers? What supports are in place for ELL students?
- How well do school policies, curriculum, and evaluation procedures match parental definitions of "good teachers" and "good schools"?
- What are the district's needs relative to its students, teachers, paraprofessionals, cafeteria workers, bus drivers, and administrators in terms of multicultural knowledge, sensitivity, and communication strategies? Have changes in community demographics (e.g., a recent influx of immigrants) or world events (e.g., a war) led to a need to better understand a particular group? How can providers of school psychological services help meet these needs through general education programs and professional development programs?
- What community supports are there for cultural groups represented in the district? To what resources and individuals can providers of school psychological services turn for translating and other multicultural support?

DEVELOPING MULTICULTURAL COMPETENCIES

Whether cultural diversity is a result of race, ethnicity, class, religion, gender, or sexual orientation, supervisors can facilitate respect for diversity in themselves and their supervisees. Majority educators who are successful in working with minority children employ a number of distinctive strategies. They refuse to buy into myths such as meritocracy and cultural superiority, they emphasize the positive aspects of minority cultures and the negative aspects of the majority culture, and they openly discuss cultural and language differences and politics (Bartholeme, 1998). Supervisors can foster these approaches by creating a safe supervisory environment, raising their own and their supervisees' personal consciousness, ensuring the success of minority supervisees, increasing their own and their supervisees' knowledge regarding many aspects of culture, fostering appropriate case conceptualization, and nurturing multicultural contacts. To ensure that their supervisees meet the standards suggested by APA (2003), supervisors and supervisees can use Handout 3.1 as a checklist.

Creating a Safe Supervisory Environment

As Miville et al. (2005) indicated, a critical task of clinical "supervisors is to create an environment in which supervisees feel safe to describe the details of their experiences, including biases, stereotypes, fears, and transference and countertransference. This environment should involve the expression of feelings around racial and cultural issues" (p. 194). Supervisors can raise their own and their supervisees' personal consciousness of issues through ongoing reflections on expectations as well as on the complex power dynamics related to class, gender, race, religion, and sexual identity during supervision and during work with students, teachers, parents, and others (Turner & Fine, 1997).

Handout 3.1

MULTICULTURAL PRACTICE CHECKLIST

- Provide services and materials in a language that is understandable to students and parents, refer to mental health workers fluent in each client's language as appropriate, and, when this is not possible, use a translator who has appropriate training

- Keep abreast of current research and recommended practice regarding various ethnic and racial groups

- Seek out educational and training experiences to enhance knowledge of cultural, social, psychological, economic, and historic experiences and enhance ability to understand and address various populations' needs

- Recognize personal limits in competency and expertise and respond to such limits by consulting with more knowledgeable colleagues or referring the student or parent to appropriate persons

- Consider the validity of assessment instruments given the cultural and linguistic characteristics of the assessed student and keep abreast of current best practices regarding the assessment of English language learners

- Foster awareness of your own background and an understanding of how this background affects your experiences, attitudes, values, and biases

- Make efforts to correct prejudices and biases

- Incorporate understanding of ethnic and cultural background into practice

- Help students increase awareness of their own background; understand how this background affects their experiences, attitudes, values, and biases; and foster the ability to apply this knowledge to their lives and to society

- Help students avoid inappropriately personalizing racism or bias in others

- Consider cultural beliefs and values in diagnosing and addressing problems

- Respect the roles of family members, community structures, values, beliefs, and hierarchies in students' cultures

- Become familiar with and respect students' religious beliefs as they affect their values, attributions, psychosocial functioning, and taboos, including consultation with or inclusion of relevant religious leaders and practitioners

- Match interventions to students' level of need according to Maslow's (1954) hierarchy and consider adverse social, environmental, and political factors during both the assessment of problems and the development of interventions

- Work within the cultural setting to improve the welfare of all

- Attend to and work to eliminate biases, prejudices, and discriminatory practice

- Document cultural factors in student records, including the number of generations the student's family has lived in the country of residence, the number of years the student has been in the country of residence, fluency in English, the extent of family support, relevant community resources, level of education, change in social status due to immigration, relationships with individuals from other cultures, and stress associated with acculturation

Culturally responsive supervision, during which supervisees feel support for exploring cultural issues, results in improved supervision and client outcomes (Burkard et al., 2006). Culturally unresponsive supervision, in which cultural issues are ignored, discounted, or dismissed, has a negative impact on the supervisee, the supervision, and client outcomes. Culturally responsive supervision is most likely to occur when the supervisor has a more advanced (progressive) racial identity, regardless of her or his own race (Constantine, Warren, & Miville, 2005). In general, because of the power differential, it is the supervisor's responsibility to raise cross-cultural issues. This discussion can be opened by initiating a conversation regarding differences and similarities among the cultures of the supervisor and the supervisees (T. L. Brown et al., 2006).

To develop a safe supervisory environment, it is also important for supervisors to adapt their communication style to the supervisees' needs. Many cultural variables (e.g., age, ethnicity, race) result in differences in communication style that can in turn result in misunderstanding and miscommunication. Differences can include body language, rate of speech, volume of speech, tone of voice, hand gestures, reliance on context, and the use of subtle and indirect communication versus the expectation of direct communication. Supervisors need to be alert to these differences as they provide supervision (T. L. Brown et al., 2006).

Ensuring the Success of Minority Supervisees

When supervisors provide supervision for diverse supervisees, it is important that they pay particular attention to developing a strong supervisory alliance while being culturally sensitive and respectful of possible mistrust. Supervisors can facilitate conversations regarding similarities and differences between their supervisee's culture and the dominant culture in terms of educational expectations, the meaning of mental health and mental illness, and the role of schools and education. As mentioned earlier, it is important for supervisors to initiate conversations regarding multicultural issues because the power differential inherent in a supervisory relationship makes it very difficult for supervisees to initiate such conversations (Nilsson & Anderson, 2004).

Matching supervisors and supervisees by culture and ethnicity does not seem to be correlated with increased satisfaction. Instead, culturally sensitive supervision appears to be paramount regardless of the identity of the supervisor and supervisee. Supervisees of color report experiencing culturally unresponsive supervision more frequently than white supervisees, and its impact was more adverse. On the other hand, culturally responsive supervision has positive effects, such as improved ability to include cultural issues in case conceptualization and increased awareness of cultural issues (Burkard et al., 2006).

When working with supervisees from minority cultures, supervisors should assess the supervisees' level of acculturation. When appropriate, supervisors should foster supervisees' understanding of and ability to manage the differences between their culture and the dominant culture, particularly insofar as it is manifested in schools. They also should help their supervisees identify and manage language barriers and should routinely check at the end of every supervisory session to make sure that the supervisee clearly understands the supervisor's expectations, make sure that there is agreement regarding what has been discussed, and address any remaining questions (Nilsson & Anderson, 2004).

Furthermore, supervisors can help their supervisees cope with being members of a minority within the professional community. As Dickens and Dickens (1991) indicated, minority supervisees can cope with being in a majority culture environment by:

- Obtaining a solid knowledge base
- Clarifying others' expectations regarding their performance

- Finding areas of mutual interest
- Increasing their own comfort by focusing on being an integral part of meetings
- Focusing on responsibilities and results
- Cultivating two support networks, one with majority culture colleagues and the other (off-site if necessary) with members of their own minority group

---

Vignette 3.5

Dawn, a special education director in a small city, was thrilled when she was able to hire a male school psychologist bilingual in English and a language native to many of the students in the district. She was equally dismayed when she began to get vociferous complaints regarding this school psychologist—teachers complained when he took twice as much as the allotted time during a classroom lesson on violence prevention, and team leaders complained that he was late to meetings with parents. Dawn recognized that the school psychologist's culture placed much less importance on time than did the school, where a disregard for punctuality was considered extremely disrespectful (and punished, in students, by demerits and suspensions). Dawn addressed this as a cultural difference with her supervisee, explaining that for professional success in this school he needed to foster biculturalism, including punctuality.

Raising Personal Consciousness

A critical first step in acquiring multicultural competence both for supervisors and supervisees is increasing self-awareness regarding cultural issues. This can be accomplished by answering the questions in Activity 3.1.

Activity 3.1

Raising My Personal Consciousness

Reflect on the following questions:

1. What demographic variables (e.g., age, class and socioeconomic status, disabilities, ethnicity/race, gender, sexual orientation, religion, country of origin, other physical characteristics) influence my cultural identity? What worldviews (assumptions, biases, values) do I bring to my professional work based on these cultural identities? What knowledge do I possess about the worldviews of those whose cultural identities differ from mine? What skills do I possess for working with them? What challenges do I face? How do I resolve these challenges? How would I like to improve my abilities in working with culturally diverse individuals? (Adapted from Miville et al., 2005)

2. What prejudices was I taught in childhood regarding age, race, ethnicity, disabilities, gender, sexual orientation, and religion? How and when did I first discover that classism, racism, sexism, religious prejudice, prejudice against LGB individuals, prejudice against individuals with disabilities, and other prejudices existed? How have I accepted or rejected the prejudices I was taught?

3. What are the characteristics of the cultures with which my parents, grandparents, and great-grandparents identified? In which of these cultures was I predominately raised? What do I know of how my family resolved cultural differences? What do I know of how my family assimilated or acculturated to the dominant culture?

Helping Supervisees Acquire Knowledge

Supervisors should ensure that they themselves and their supervisees are familiar with the cultures of the students, parents, teachers, and administrators with whom they work. Supervisees and supervisors can both become better informed about cultural similarities and differences and increase their understanding of the complexity of cultural questions by attending professional workshops and reading professional books. A number of recently published books are excellent resources. These include the *Handbook of Multicultural School Psychology: An Interdisciplinary Perspective* (Esquivel, Lopez, & Nahari, 2007); *Strategies for Building Multicultural Competencies in Mental Health and Educational Settings* (Constantine & Sue, 2005); and the *Comprehensive Handbook of Multicultural School Psychology* (Frisby & Reynolds, 2005). Additional helpful books include *Assessing Culturally and Linguistically Diverse Students: A Practical Guide* (Rhodes, Ochoa, & Ortiz, 2005); *Developing Cross-Cultural Competence: A Guide to Working With Children and Their Families* (Lynch & Hanson, 1998); *Intentional Interviewing and Counseling: Facilitating Client Development in a Multicultural Society* (Ivey & Ivey, 2006); and *Confronting Prejudice and Racism During Multicultural Training* (Kiselica, 1998).

Counseling literature is replete with information regarding the implications of multicultural counseling, and entire journals are devoted to such concerns (e.g., *Journal of Multicultural Counseling and Development, Journal of Non-white Concerns*). Books to consider are *Addressing Cultural Complexities in Practice: A Framework for Clinicians and Counselors* (Hays, 2001); *Promoting Cultural Competence in Children's Mental Health Services* (Hernandez & Issacs, 1998); the *Handbook of Multicultural Counseling* (Ponterotto, Casa, Suzuki, & Alexander, 2001); the *Handbook of Multicultural Competencies in Counseling and Psychology* (Pope-Davis, Coleman, Liu, & Toporek, 2003); *Counseling the Culturally Different: Theory and Practice* (Sue & Sue, 1999); *Counseling American Minorities* (Atkinson, 2004); *Culture in Psychology* (Squire, 2000); *Psychotherapy Relationships That Work: Therapist Contributions and Responsiveness to Patients* (Norcross, 2002); *A Guide to Treatments That Work* (Nathan & Gorman, 2002); *Re-visioning Family Therapy: Race, Culture and Gender in Clinical Practice* (McGoldrick, 1998); and *What Works for Whom? A Critical Review of Treatments for Children and Adolescents* (Fontagy, Target, Cottrell, Phillips, & Kurtz, 2002). To increase knowledge regarding specific cultural variables, it is also helpful to read targeted literature, conduct interviews, and broaden experiences in a number of ways. Each variable will be addressed separately below.

Age

When supervisees are insufficiently knowledgeable regarding life span development, supervisors can encourage them to obtain and review a copy of a comprehensive book such as *Life-Span Human Development* (Sigelman & Rider, 2006). Supervisors can also remind supervisees to consider age variables as they discuss consultation with teachers, parents, and administrators in group and individual supervision.

Socioeconomic Status and Class

Because class is an important aspect of self-image and permeates interpersonal interactions, it is important for both supervisors and supervisees to be aware of their attitudes toward class. Supervisors can encourage their supervisees to read books such as *Children at Risk: Poverty, Minority Status, and Other Issues in Educational Equity* (Barona & Garcia, 1990); *The Shame of a Nation: The Restoration of Apartheid Schooling in America* (Kozol, 2005); *A Framework for Understanding Poverty* (Payne, 2001), and *Savage Inequalities: Children in*

America's schools (Kozol, 1991). Using ethical problem solving strategies (S. Jacob & Hartshorne, 2007), supervisors and supervisees can consider class-related supervisory dilemmas, such as those contained at the end of the chapter. Another approach is to investigate one's own concept of class. Both supervisors and supervisees may benefit from completing Activity 3.2.

Activity 3.2

Uncovering Attitudes Regarding Class

(Adapted from Lappin & Hardy, 1997; J. Ross, 1995)

Answer the following questions:

1. With what class did you identify as a child?

2. What were your experiences with persons from a class other than your own?

3. At what age did your class of origin expect you to: Finish with education? Be financially independent? Get married? Have children?

4. With what class do you identify as an adult?

5. In what class are you raising your children?

6. What does "your" class say about other classes?

7. What do you think "other" classes say about yours?

8. How do you determine the class of another person? (Occupation? Level of education? Size or location of home? Clothing? Taste in music?)

9. Would you say your class expects individuals to: Act in their own interest? Share with less fortunate persons? Rely on the structures of technology, law, or religion? Value traditionally male traits of assertiveness, competition, performance, and success? Value traditionally female traits of care, service, and solidarity? Focus on and plan for the future over short-term gains?

10. If you are currently in a socioeconomic class different from that in which you were raised, how does this affect your personal and professional life? What do you believe happens when individuals from two different classes marry? Not infrequently after divorce, one parent changes class—what do you think is the experience of children living simultaneously in two different classes? What do you think happens in a family that is not college educated when one member receives a college scholarship? How would it change your family relationships if you suddenly had to immigrate to another country and live in a lower class?

Disabilities

To help supervisees become more familiar with the experiences of individuals with disabilities, supervisors can encourage them to read first-person accounts written by individuals with disabilities. Many such books exist; a few examples are *Learning Outside the Lines* (learning disabilities; Mooney & Cole, 2000); *The Unquiet Mind* (bipolar disorder; Jamison, 1995); and *Thinking in Pictures* (autism; Grandin, 2006). Although not a first-person account, *Surviving Schizophrenia: A Manual for Families, Parents, and Providers* (Torrey, 2006) powerfully conveys the experiences of schizophrenics and psychosis.

Activity 3.3

Uncovering Perspectives on Disability

Interview adults and older adolescents with a wide range of disabilities and ask: Which educational experiences did you find helpful? Which educational experiences were detrimental? How do you accommodate yourself to your disability now? How does it affect your current functioning? How could school psychologists have better met your needs while you were in school?

Ethnicity and Race

To help supervisees become more familiar with the experiences of individuals from ethnic and racial groups different from their own, supervisors can encourage them to read first-person accounts such as *YELL-oh Girls! Emerging Voices Explore Culture, Identity, and Growing Up Asian American* (Nam, 2001); *Black Baby White Hands: A View From the Crib* (John, 2002); *Living in Spanglish: The Search for Latino Identity in America* (Morales, 2003); and *Americanos: Latino Life in the United States* (Fuentes, Olmos, & Ybarra, 1999). In addition, it can be very helpful to read professional books such as *Affirming Diversity: The Sociopolitical Context of Multicultural Education* (Nieto, 2004); *Understanding Diversity* (Okun, Fried, & Okun, 1999); *Working With Culture: Psychotherapeutic Interventions With Ethnic Minority Children and Adolescents* (Vargas & Koss-Chioino, 1992); *Overcoming Our Racism: The Journey to Liberation* (Sue, 2003); and *Why Are All the Black Kids Sitting Together in the Cafeteria?* (B. D. Tatum, 1997).

Additional information can be obtained from professional Web sites designed to promote cultural competence, such as:

- www.aapaonline.org (Asian American Psychological Association)
- www.abpsi.org (Association of Black Psychologists)
- www.nasponline.org (National Association of School Psychologists)
- www.nlpa.ws (National Latina/o Psychological Association)
- www.nmtp.org (Network of Multicultural Training Professionals)
- www.apa.org/divisions/div45 (Society for the Psychological Study of Ethnic Minority Issues)

In addition, the activities contained in Activity 3.4 are illuminating.

Activity 3.4

Uncovering Perspectives on Ethnicity and Race

1. Interview adults from different ethnic and racial groups. Ask: Which educational experiences did you find helpful? Which educational experiences were detrimental? How could school psychologists have better met your needs while you were in school?

2. Interview a biracial individual regarding his or her experiences growing up.

3. Conduct focus groups with parents from diverse ethnic and racial groups and determine their definitions of a "good teacher," "good teaching," and a "good school." Then work to match the school's instructional and disciplinary practices with parental values.

Language

Supervisors can help supervisees become more familiar with the experiences of individuals as they struggle to learn the dominant language. Since children whose native language is not the dominant language must be explicitly taught written, spoken, and nonverbal language for effective participation in the mainstream culture, supervisees can consider methods schools can develop and implement that encourage rather than discourage bilingualism and biculturalism in students, faculty, and parents. The intent is not to eliminate students' home language but rather to add other voices to their repertoire (Delpit, 1995). Activity 3.5 may also be helpful.

Activity 3.5

Considering Language Acquisition

Consider a foreign language you studied in high school or college. How many years of study did it take before you felt comfortable attending a lecture or taking a course given in that language about a topic with which you were very familiar (e.g., psychology)? In a topic with which you were unfamiliar (e.g., chemistry)?

Gender

Supervisors can help supervisees of both sexes increase their knowledge regarding women and power equity issues. They can also ensure that male supervisors treat women supervisees appropriately, that women supervisors are accorded respect by male supervisees (Turner & Fine, 1997), that miscommunication is minimized, and that the effects of gender role confusion are minimized.

Sexual Orientation

Supervisors can help supervisees increase their knowledge regarding gender identity in several ways. They can increase supervisees' understanding of the heterosexual bias in psychology theories and research as well as the inappropriateness of application of heterosexuality as a source of normative standards. Professional books such as the *Handbook of Counseling and Psychotherapy With Lesbian, Gay, and Bisexual Clients* (Perez, DeBord, & Bieschke, 2000) can be helpful. Supervisors can also assist supervisees in acquiring a greater understanding of the great psychological energy needed to maintain invisible relationships, of the "coming out" process in both the personal and professional spheres, of the gay rights movement and current social battles, and of the effects of homophobia, including the threat of physical harm or death. First-person accounts, such as *The Velvet Rage: Overcoming the Pain of Growing Up Gay in a Straight Man's World* (Downs, 2005), can be particularly illuminating.

During individual and group supervision sessions, supervisors can help supervisees relinquish stereotypes through knowledge of pertinent research findings. As reported by Long (1997), research has demonstrated that approximately 63% of lesbians and 50% of homosexuals are in steady relationships (Peplau & Cochran, 1990); that many gays and lesbians establish lifelong partnerships (Blumstein & Schwartz, 1983; Bryant &

Demian, 1994; McWhirter & Mattison, 1984); that relationship satisfaction of homosexual couples is comparable to satisfaction of heterosexual couples (Duffy & Rusbult, 1986; Kurdek & Schmitt, 1987; Peplau & Cochran, 1990); that no differences have been found between homosexuals and heterosexuals in effective parenting practices (Flaks, Ficher, Masterpasqua, & Joseph, 1995; Harris & Turner, 1985–1986; Kirkpatrick, Smith, & Roy, 1981); that children of homosexuals do not experience sexual identity confusion and are appropriately popular, socially adjusted, and socially competent (Golumbok, Spencer, & Rutter, 1983; R. Green, 1982; Kirkpatrick et al., 1981; C. J. Patterson, 1994); and that children exposed to persons with minority sexual orientations are not more likely to be molested (Finkelhor, 1986; Riveria, 1987). Throughout individual and group supervision, supervisors should ensure that supervisees refrain from trying to "convert" homosexuals to heterosexuality and refer them to other psychologists when the supervisee has insufficient knowledge or a conflict in values.

Religion

Supervisors can help supervisees increase their knowledge of religion by encouraging them to read accurate information regarding the world's religions. Supervisees can improve their understanding of professional issues relative to religion by reading professional books such as the *Handbook of Psychotherapy and Religious Diversity* (P. S. Richards & Abergin, 2000); *The Spirit Catches You and You Fall Down* (Fadiman, 1997); and *Encountering the Sacred in Psychotherapy: How to Talk With People About Their Spiritual Lives* (J. L. Griffith & Griffith, 2002). Activity 3.6 will also be helpful.

Activity 3.6

Learning About Religion

Visit a place of worship attended by children in the community and take part in a tour given by a clergyperson. With permission, attend services, being careful to be respectful of the religion's values by participating or refraining from participating as appropriate.

Interview an individual whose religion is unfamiliar, focusing on how religious orientation informs the individual's overall understanding, including her or his values, beliefs, and worldview. Interview a psychologist or social worker who works with individuals who identify with the religious group being studied. Ask about the religious group's experiences with discrimination, bias, and oppression and request recommendations for psychologists.

Design a workshop to help other school personnel understand the religion and how knowledge of the individuals in the context of their religious beliefs may inform education and psychological treatment (V. Konstam, private communication, June 2006).

Acculturation

School psychologists can also consider the role of extracurricular activities in a student's acculturation. Success in high school is frequently associated with activities beyond academics, such as hobbies, religious group membership, and sports. These activities serve to focus the student, develop critical thinking and leadership skills, and provide a feeling of belonging. Supervisors should encourage school psychologists to consider these issues as they develop prevention and intervention plans for students. Many successful bicultural and multicultural students speak of having teachers who showed they cared by preparing for classes, making classes interesting, being patient, and providing curriculum that affirmed their language, culture, and concerns (Nieto, 2004).

Fostering Appropriate Case Conceptualization

Supervisors should regularly and consciously include multicultural case studies and readings in supervisory sessions. Also, supervisees should be asked to review role-plays and audiotapes for lack of sensitivity and language biases. Supervisors can support multicultural assessment methods by ensuring that the district has and uses assessment tools that address multiple facets of ability and that respect cultural and linguistic diversity (e.g., qualitative and authentic assessment tools). Supervisors can develop focus groups composed of families and community support systems to discuss and help develop appropriate interventions. Questions contained in Activity 3.7 may be helpful.

Activity 3.7

Determining Whether Clients From Minority Populations Feel Respected

(Adapted from Rambo & Shilts, 1997)

Have your clients answer the following questions:

1. Does your psychologist understand your situation?

2. Is your psychologist missing anything?

3. What has been happening differently for you since you started seeing the psychologist?

4. What would you like to see different?

5. Do you have any ideas on how to make that happen?

6. Do you have any suggestions for the psychologist?

7. Do you or your child feel your psychologist is sensitive to your loss of time, money, and privacy?

Developing Multicultural Consultation Contacts

T. Thomas (1992) added that school psychologists can help immigrant children in the United States by familiarizing themselves with the cultural practices and history of the children they serve, identifying ways schools can develop programs for helping students gain functional understanding of American educational and cultural practices, acting as liaisons with public programs outside of schools, conducting careful interviews with parents and observations of children in familiar settings, and actively educating school staff in both the educationally relevant issues faced by immigrants and the richness immigrant families bring to classrooms. When a school psychologist develops multicultural consultation contacts, these activities are greatly facilitated.

ASSESSING THE IMPACT OF MULTICULTURAL SKILLS DEVELOPMENT

Supervisors can assess the impact of multicultural skill development on their supervision by reviewing tapes of supervisory sessions and reviewing those tapes for evidence of multicultural awareness, sensitivity, and responsivity. It can be particularly helpful to ask a colleague or supervisor from a different culture (e.g., age, class, ethnicity, race, gender, sexual orientation, religion) for feedback regarding the taped sessions (Borders & Brown, 2005). After a supervisor has assessed his or her multicultural skills, developed a plan to address them, and implemented that plan, the resulting change must be appraised to determine the need for future change. The same instruments used in the initial assessment can be used for such an appraisal, as can global assessments of supervisor skills.

Furthermore, even veteran supervisors should appraise their multicultural skills on an ongoing basis. Inevitably, changes in circumstances, such as changing school system demographics or the hiring of a supervisee with a unique background, will require supervisors to make adjustments in their multicultural skills. Therefore, it is appropriate for supervisors to include improvement of multicultural skills in their annual goals.

SUMMARY

To work effectively with students, parents, and other educators of diverse races, ethnicities, and cultures, school psychologists must be aware of, sensitive to, and responsive to multicultural issues. Supervisors must develop their own skills in this area and also ensure the same for their supervisees. This is important for several reasons: First, multicultural skills are mandated by the ethical principles and professional standards of both NASP and APA. Additionally, most school psychologists are middle class, white, monolingually English speaking, and nondisabled, which is markedly different from the populations with which school psychologists work. Third, since experience is one of the primary ways in which school psychologists acquire multicultural competencies, supervisors need to provide experiences that increase successful multicultural experiences.

Multicultural competency includes personal and professional development in multiculturalism; establishing rapport with members of diverse groups; incorporating multicultural issues into problem analysis, assessment strategies, and intervention plans; and making treatment and system changes as appropriate. Challenges exist in the development of multicultural competencies in supervisees. These include discomfort; overgeneralization; deficient graduate training and professional programs; bias in law, education, and psychology; and lack of knowledge and understanding of the complexity of culture.

Various cultures differ from one other in a number of areas, yet individuals within any culture are not identical, and one must therefore be wary of generalizing among members of the same culture. Areas of diversity that school psychologists work with include age (parents, teachers, and other school personnel), socioeconomic status and class, disabilities, ethnicity and race, gender, sexual orientation, and religion. Supervisors should assess and address multicultural competencies at multiple levels, including themselves, their supervisees, their department, and the school, district, and community in which they practice. It is important that supervisors create a safe supervisory environment in which supervisees can discuss their own experiences, including their biases, stereotypes, fears, and transference and countertransference. Cultural sensitivity, the addressing of possible mistrust, and the development of a strong supervisory alliance are particularly important when supervisors provide supervision for supervisees from diverse cultures. To encourage the development of multicultural competencies, supervisors should help supervisees acquire knowledge of specific cultural variables while increasing self-awareness of diversity issues. Outside the supervisory session, supervisors can encourage the development of multicultural competencies by utilizing culturally relevant assessment tools, forming focus groups, and developing multicultural consultation contacts.

REFLECTIVE QUESTIONS

Q3.1. Discuss what you have learned from this chapter that is most surprising. What is most relevant to your practice of supervision? What can you change? How do you plan to do it?

Q3.2. How can supervisors meet the challenge of being sensitive to culture while requiring minority supervisees to meet universal performance standards as they work in majority culture school settings?

Q3.3. Why is multicultural competence included in principles of ethical and professional practice?

Q3.4. Describe the challenges to developing supervisees' multicultural competencies. How can supervisors deal with these challenges?

Q3.5. What are the dimensions on which cultures typically differ?

Q3.6. What are the areas of diversity with which school psychologists work? How can supervisors ensure that both they and their supervisees understand these issues and their implications?

Q3.7. How do school psychologists assess multicultural competencies in themselves and their supervisees? What tools are available? How can multicultural competencies be assessed in school psychology departments as well as in schools, districts, and communities?

Q3.8. What are the means by which multicultural competencies can be developed?

Q3.9. What is a safe supervisory environment, and why is it important to the development of multicultural competencies? How can supervisors facilitate such an environment?

Q3.10. What issues may exist when supervisors provide supervision for supervisees of diverse cultures? How can supervisors address these issues?

Q3.11. How can individuals acquire knowledge of specific cultural variables?

SUPERVISORY DILEMMAS

SD 3.1

For several years, your supervisee has been working in a school composed of two distinct classes: students from wealthy families and students from impoverished families. He has noticed that one particular teacher invariably refers every boy from the impoverished families for psychological testing and is quite contemptuous toward these boys and their families. *What are the supervisory considerations? What should be done?*

Authors' thoughts: Discriminatory, harmful behavior is emanating from prejudice. It will be critical to determine whether or not the teacher has an awareness of her referral patterns and prejudicial attitude. If she is unaware of her behavior, perhaps some consciousness raising will be fruitful. The intern might offer to supply information on the effects of poverty as well as the potentially negative effect of referral to special education. Examining the "hit rates" (i.e., the percentage of referrals made by the teacher that resulted in eligibility for special education services) might be a fruitful exercise. Ultimately, the intern and supervisor have an obligation to the students to assure that this pattern of referrals ends. More important, any prejudicial or contemptuous behavior must immediately end. Administrative support will be essential.

SD 3.2

You are a supervisor of school psychology working in a small city whose population has changed dramatically in the past 10 years. The population, formerly primarily American-born blue collar workers, has become 80% immigrant, primarily from the Caribbean and Southeast Asia. One of the school psychologists you supervise is only a few years from retirement. Although she is generally capable, she not only has neglected to become knowledgeable about the new populations but also frequently makes ethnic and racial slurs about the changing populations. She has not been responsive to your attempts at sensitization and education. *What are the supervisory considerations? What should be done?*

Authors' thoughts: While it is impossible to legislate understanding and respect for racial, ethnic, and cultural diversity, it *is* possible to demand an immediate cessation of disparaging remarks. Racial and ethnic slurs are intolerable and without doubt harmful to staff and students alike. Clearly, a mandate to stop such behavior is warranted. If an appropriate response is not forthcoming, a discussion of early retirement or dismissal might occur. At this point, documentation that complies with local and state law and policy should be initiated. Another concern emerges in regard to the ethical obligation of school psychologists to seek training or education to effectively meet the needs of a changing population. In this scenario, it is evident that this has not occurred. Students cannot be effectively served without consideration of myriad ecological factors that impact learning and behavior. Finally, the question of whether your supervisee's attitude or remarks have resulted in actual harm to students must be considered. Serious impediments to effective practice are embedded in this scenario. Given the failed past attempts at remediation, it is highly likely that the situation will not respond to intervention. You may want to show her the door and cross your fingers!

SD 3.3

You, a supervising school psychologist, realize that the goals of the school system are contradictory. That is, the first stated goal of the school system is to improve the group test scores of the students in the district, while the second goal is to reduce dropout rates. The district is largely composed of students from diverse racial, linguistic, and cultural backgrounds. In fact, a significant number of students are recent immigrants and English is not their primary language. Many of these students struggle with receiving academic instruction in English and their grades are low. You realize that, logically, as more low-achieving students stay in school and take standardized tests, scores will be likely to decrease. *What are the supervisory considerations? What should be done?*

Authors' thoughts: This situation is fraught with inherent difficulties. The school psychologist is in a unique position to educate administrators about the negative impact of testing for many students. Gathering data regarding these results, culling research studies on the same topic, and consulting with other educators and school psychologists facing the same issue would all be fruitful endeavors. It is likely that school psychologists will need to become active at the policymaking level to redress this wrong.

Handout 3.2

SELF-ASSESSMENT CULTURAL SENSITIVITY CHECKLIST

This checklist is intended to heighten the awareness and sensitivity of personnel regarding the importance of cultural diversity and cultural competence in human service settings. It provides concrete examples of the kinds of values and practices that foster such an environment.

Directions: Select A, B, or C for each numbered item listed.

A = Things I do frequently

B = Things I do occasionally

C = Things I do rarely or never

Physical Environment, Materials, and Resources

_____ 1. I display pictures, posters, and other materials that reflect the cultures and ethnic backgrounds of the students and families served by my school.

_____ 2. I ensure that magazines, brochures, and other printed materials in reception areas are of interest to and reflect the different cultures of students and families served by my school.

_____ 3. When using videos, films, or other media resources for health education, treatment, or other interventions, I ensure that they reflect the cultures of students and families served by my school.

_____ 4. I ensure that meals provided include foods that are unique to the cultural and ethnic backgrounds of students and families served by my school.

_____ 5. I ensure that toys and other play accessories in reception areas and those used during assessment are representative of the various cultural and ethnic groups within the local community and the society in general.

Communication Styles

_____ 6. For students who speak languages or dialects other than English, I attempt to learn and use key words in their language so that I am better able to communicate with them during assessment, treatment, and other interventions.

(Continued)

(Continued)

_____ 7. I attempt to determine any colloquialisms used by students and families that may impact assessment, treatment, and other interventions.

_____ 8. I use visual aids, gestures, and physical prompts in my interactions with students who have limited English proficiency.

_____ 9. I use bilingual staff or trained and certified interpreters for assessment, treatment, and other interventions with students who have limited English proficiency.

_____ 10. I use bilingual staff or trained and certified interpreters during assessments, treatment sessions, meetings, and other events for families who require this level of assistance.

_____ 11. When interacting with parents who have limited English proficiency, I always keep in mind that:

_____ Limitations in English proficiency do not reflect intellectual functioning.

_____ Limited ability to speak the language of the dominant culture has no bearing on ability to communicate effectively in the language of origin.

_____ A person may or may not be literate in her or his language of origin and also may or may not be literate in English (i.e., the presence or absence of literacy in one language is not an indicator of the presence or absence of literacy in another).

_____ 12. When possible, I ensure that all notices and communiqués to parents are written in their language of origin.

_____ 13. I understand that it may be necessary to use alternatives to written communications for some families, as word of mouth may be a preferred method of receiving information.

Values and Attitudes

_____ 14. I avoid imposing values that may conflict or be inconsistent with those of cultures or ethnic groups other than my own.

_____ 15. I discourage students from using racial and ethnic slurs by helping them understand that certain words can hurt others.

_____ 16. I screen books, movies, and other media resources for negative cultural, ethnic, and racial stereotypes before sharing them with students and their parents.

_____ 17. I intervene in an appropriate manner when I observe other staff or parents within my school engaging in behaviors that show cultural insensitivity, bias, or prejudice.

_____ 18. I understand and accept that "family" is defined differently by different cultures (e.g., extended family members, kin, godparents).

_____ 19. I recognize and accept that individuals from culturally diverse backgrounds may desire varying degrees of acculturation into the dominant culture.

_____ 20. I accept and respect that male-female roles in families may vary significantly among different cultures (e.g., who makes major decisions for the family, what kinds of play and social interactions are expected of male and female students).

_____ 21. I understand that age and life cycle factors (e.g., high value placed on the decisions of elders or the role of the eldest male in the family) must be considered in interactions with individuals and families.

_____ 22. Even though my professional and moral viewpoints may differ, I accept the family/parents as the ultimate decision makers regarding services and supports for their students.

_____ 23. I recognize that the meaning and value of medical treatment and health education may vary greatly among cultures.

_____ 24. I recognize and understand that beliefs and concepts of emotional well-being vary significantly from culture to culture.

_____ 25. I understand that beliefs about mental illness and emotional disability are culturally based. I accept that responses to these conditions and related treatment and interventions are heavily influenced by culture.

_____ 26. I accept that religion and other beliefs may influence how families respond to illness, disease, disability, and death.

(Continued)

(Continued)

_____ 27. I recognize and accept that folk and religious beliefs may influence a family's reaction and approach to a student born with a disability or later diagnosed with a physical or emotional disability or special health care needs.

_____ 28. I understand that traditional approaches to disciplining students are influenced by culture.

_____ 29. I understand that families from different cultures will have different expectations of their students for acquiring toileting, dressing, feeding, and other self-help skills.

_____ 30. I accept and respect that customs and beliefs about the value, preparation, and use of food are different from culture to culture.

_____ 31. Before visiting or providing services in the home setting, I seek information on acceptable behaviors, courtesies, customs, and expectations unique to families of specific cultures and ethnic groups served by my school.

_____ 32. I seek information from family members and other key community informants that will assist in service adaptation to respond to the needs and preferences of culturally and ethnically diverse students and families served by my school.

_____ 33. I advocate review of school and district mission statements, goals, policies, and procedures to ensure that they incorporate principles and practices that promote cultural diversity and cultural competence.

There is no answer key with correct responses. However, if you frequently responded "C," you may not necessarily demonstrate values and engage in practices that promote a culturally diverse and culturally competent service delivery system for students with disabilities or special health care needs and their families.

Adapted from Tawara D. Goode, *Promoting Cultural Competence and Cultural Diversity in Early Intervention and Early Childhood Settings*—June 1989. Revised 1993, 1996, 1999, 2000, and 2002. Copyright © 2000 by the National Association of School Psychologists, Bethesda, MD. Use of this material is by permission of the publisher, www.nasponline.org.

4

Data-Based
Decision Making
and Accountability

We have an ethical and moral responsibility to ensure that psychological services actually benefit students.

Vignette 4.1

Anne, the supervisor we met in Chapter 1, was surprised to learn that her intern, **Zoe**, was required to complete six case studies using a research design, adhering to treatment integrity, and demonstrating positive student outcomes. Just a few years before, Anne's own internship had required that she demonstrate proficiency in consultation, counseling, assessment, and providing in-service programs—but not that she show that her recommendations actually improved student functioning. The current requirements shifted the emphasis away from Zoe's skills to the academic skills and behavior of the students with whom she worked.

Evidenced-based education programs are mandated by laws such as the Individuals With Disabilities Education Improvement Act of 2004 (IDEA 2004) and the No Child Left Behind Act of 2001 (NCLB). Research-based practices, rather than those dictated by popularity, are promoted by Web sites maintained by professional organizations, including the Institute for the Development of Educational Achievement (n.d.); the National Association of School Psychologists (2005); the National Council of Teachers of

Mathematics (n.d.); the National Reading Panel (2001); the Institute of Education Sciences (Institute of Education Sciences, What Works Clearinghouse, n.d.); the National Institute of Mental Health (Riley et al., 2007); and the Substance Abuse and Mental Health Services Administration (n.d.). Additionally, evidence-based psychological practice is mandated by the National Association of School Psychologists (NASP; 2000b) and the American Psychological Association (APA; 2007) as described by the APA Presidential Task Force on Evidence-Based Practice (2006).

Ysseldyke et al. (2006) indicated that effective school psychologists are "good problem-solvers who collect information that is relevant for understanding problems, make decisions about appropriate interventions, assess educational outcomes, and help others become accountable for the decisions they make" (p. 17). They proceeded to suggest that school psychologists should (a) be leaders in identifying environments and factors that promote student success, (b) assess the environment to identify factors that affect student learning and behavior, (c) use information to promote student competence and prevent difficulties and disabilities, (d) serve as school-based leaders in data collection and interpretation, and (e) help design appropriate assessment practices for school accountability.

School psychologists receive training in research methods, statistics, and program evaluation to enable them to perform these activities and thus are among the best-trained educators to help students, parents, teachers, schools, and districts evaluate outcomes and make data-based decisions. However, graduate programs can provide limited opportunities for the application of these skills. Considerable guided practice and supervision must occur during the internship and initial years of practice for school psychologists to attain expertise in this area. Furthermore, as suggested by the vignette that opened this chapter, supervisors themselves may have underdeveloped skills in evidence-based practice, particularly if their work has focused on special education gatekeeping and minimally addressed progress monitoring. Therefore, this is an area of critical need.

BASIC CONSIDERATIONS

As Kratochwill and Stoiber (2002) indicated, the research-to-practice gap, or the disinclination of practitioners to employ empirically based practices, stems from various sources. First, practitioners employ clinical judgment rather than research regarding treatment efficacy when designing and evaluating interventions. Second, many practitioners believe that interventions are equally effective and that doing "something" is better than doing nothing. Therefore, they do not analyze intervention plans, decisions, or outcomes. Further, because of the intense demands on practitioners, inserting "an empirical basis into practice does not match the day-to-day demands of practitioners' lives" (p. 368). To overcome these barriers, practitioners must experience evidence-based practice as both more *efficient* and more *effective* than practice that is not evidence based.

Data-based evaluations can serve various purposes (Royse, Thyer, Padgett, & Logan, 2006):

- *Needs assessments* establish the need for a program and suggest the form a new intervention or program might take.
- *Formative evaluations* determine whether the processes being used in program or intervention implementation are appropriate and which modifications are warranted.
- *Summative evaluations* ascertain whether goals have been achieved and whether the program is cost effective and accountable.

Whether working at the individual, group, or systemic level, the same procedures are followed. During the preparation phase, the problem is defined, needs and assets are explored, and current functioning is determined. During the implementation phase, the conclusions reached during the preparation phase are used to select and implement data-based interventions with integrity. During the appraisal phase, outcomes are evaluated and processes appraised, and then those results are used to inform future actions.

ENSURING ADEQUATE KNOWLEDGE, SUPPORT, AND PRACTICE

Although many individuals are apprehensive about adopting the evidence-based practice model, in truth it calls on the very skills in which school psychologists already excel: gathering data, analyzing data, and comparing data against criteria. The difference is that the type of data, the type of analysis, and the criteria are somewhat different. To feel comfortable with this approach, supervisors might need to (a) increase their knowledge and skills, (b) ensure that they have access to sufficient support, and (c) obtain sufficient practice.

Increasing Knowledge and Skills

A large number of resources are available to help supervisors augment their knowledge in this area. These include those that identify evidence-based interventions, those that help determine whether an applied intervention has been successful, and those that facilitate "number crunching." They are reviewed throughout this chapter.

Increasing Support

As supervisees and supervisors move into single-case designs and other forms of evidence-based practice, they need support for two reasons: First, as in implementing any new process or procedure, support is needed during the learning period. Second, there may initially be resistance from other school personnel or parents when school psychologists implement interventions prior to administering norm-referenced assessment tools. However, such resistance erodes when psychologists present data that demonstrates student improvement after successful interventions (Reschly, 2006).

SINGLE-CASE DESIGNS

Whether or not an intervention is successful can be determined using a *single-case design* (also called *time series analysis*). This method can be used with an individual or a group of students; the term "single case" refers to the lack of a control group. Instead, baseline data are gathered, an intervention is introduced, and often a reversal phase is included wherein the intervention is removed and reintroduced. Throughout all of these phases, data are gathered and compared to confirm the efficacy of the intervention.

Case study design, as described by Brown-Chidsey, Steege, and Mace (2008), is a type of single-case design that often does not include a reversal phase. Further, case studies often address multiple hypotheses with targeted interventions rather than implementing just one intervention. They have limitations, the most notable being that they do not determine whether a particular intervention caused a change (or lack thereof). Confounding variables such as multiple simultaneous interventions, maturity, testing effects, and co-occurring events can result in observed changes. Nonetheless, case studies provide valuable information and are more easily applied in schools than more rigorous designs. Furthermore, they are appropriate in situations where regression is unlikely when an intervention is removed (e.g., students do not typically "unlearn" math facts during a reversal phase). Finally, they are a decided improvement over the more traditional approaches that ignore outcomes altogether.

To illustrate the case study steps, listed in Handout 4.1, this chapter includes an example case study regarding Minnie M., a seventh-grade student suffering from separation anxiety. This case is based on a case study completed by Kristen Orlandella, a novice school psychologist. Details have been changed and the case study has been adapted and used with Ms. Orlandella's permission.

Problem Identification

To clearly define a problem, it is helpful to begin by asking all stakeholders, including students, the questions contained in Handout 4.2. The answers lead directly to a defined problem, an understanding of expectations and goals, and appropriate data measures.

Academic and behavioral problems are defined in operational terms and compared with relevant expectations. To do this, school psychologists observe, interview, employ standardized norm-referenced tests, conduct functional behavioral assessments, use Curriculum-Based Measurement tools, assess ecological and environmental variables, and monitor student progress.

At least three points of data are gathered during the baseline period prior to any intervention. Data are collected using sensitive and reliable methods daily or weekly. Often data are collected using a direct observation system, such as event recording, that indicates whether a behavior did or did not occur during a specified period and contrasts the targeted student's behavior with that of comparison students. At least three data points are graphed to provide visual manifestations of paths, trends, and stability. Data that are stable and flat predict that the behavior will remain at that level without an intervention, while data showing a stable trend of increasing or decreasing predict a continuous trend in the same direction in the absence of intervention (Alberto & Troutman, 2006; Tawney & Gast, 1984). Possible outcome measures include, but are not limited to:

- Achievement test scores
- Attendance or days tardy
- Curriculum-Based Measurement (weekly, monthly, quarterly) in reading, spelling, writing, math
- Discipline reports and suspensions
- Emotional status (subjective self-reports, parent and teacher feedback)
- Grades on weekly quizzes, unit tests, progress reports, report cards
- Hours per week assigned to services
- On-task behaviors
- Positive social interactions
- Positive behavior tallies

Handout 4.1

CASE STUDY CHECKLIST

1. Problem Identification

___ The student's behavior is operationally defined in the context of appropriate grade and/or peer expectations, for example, local norms. A clearly defined problem with testable questions is stated.

___ The problem is collaboratively defined; parents/guardians and teachers are involved in the problem identification process.

___ The behavior is operationally defined or quantified in terms of both current and desired levels of performance, and the difference is explained.

___ Baseline includes the student behavior, peer/grade norms and expectations, and computed trend lines. At least three time points are included.

___ The student behavior is identified as a skill and/or performance deficit.

___ Appropriate parent and student informed consent is obtained for programs.

2. Problem Analysis

___ One or more hypotheses are generated through collaboration with teacher and/or parent.

___ There are multiple sources of data (record review, interview, observation, testing, and self-report) that converge on each proposed hypothesis.

___ Hypotheses reflect an awareness of issues of diversity (e.g., physical, social, linguistic, cultural).

3. Intervention

___ Intervention is linked to observable, measurable goal statement(s).

___ Intervention selection is based on data from problem analysis and hypothesis testing.

___ Intervention is evidence based (e.g., research literature, functional analysis, single-case design analysis).

___ Intervention is developed collaboratively.

___ Intervention reflects sensitivity to individual differences, resources, classroom practices, and other system issues. Acceptability of intervention is verified.

___ Logistics of setting, time, resources, and personnel are included in the intervention plan.

___ Intervention selection considers unintended outcomes or limitations.

___ Intervention is monitored and data are provided to ensure that it is implemented with integrity.

___ Intervention is monitored and intensity is varied appropriately.

4. Evaluation

___ Data are used to inform further problem solving and decision making (i.e., continuation of intervention, modification of intervention, maintenance of intervention).

___ Progress monitoring data are demonstrated on a chart that includes student performance trend lines and/or goal lines.

___ Progress monitoring data are demonstrated to be effective when compared to baseline data generated from multiple sources/settings.

___ Responses to intervention data are used to inform problem solving and decision making. Single-case design was specified (e.g., changing criterion, parametric, component analysis, multiple baseline, alternating treatment).

___ Strategies for transfer/generalizing outcomes to other settings are addressed and documented as effective.

___ Modifications for future interventions are considered based on collaborative examination of effectiveness data.

___ Effectiveness of intervention is shared through collaboration with parents, teachers, and other personnel.

___ Strategies for follow-up (e.g., continued progress monitoring, transition planning) are developed and implemented.

Handout 4.2

PROBLEM IDENTIFICATION QUESTIONS

1. What isn't going well?

2. How do you know this is a problem?

3. What would you like to be different?

4. How can we measure this difference?

5. What is contributing to this problem?

6. What is going well?

7. How can we make it go better?

Example Case Study: Problem Identification

Minnie M. was referred to the school's student support team prior to the beginning of her seventh-grade year by her mother, who reported that Minnie had a history of poor school attendance due to excessive anxiety. In the past, Minnie's academic achievement had suffered because of her anxiety, and her sixth-grade teachers reported that Minnie was not able to grasp concepts because she was not present. Her mother, who also suffered from anxiety, was concerned that the move to junior high would escalate Minnie's anxiety even further. Minnie had been referred to the student support team at her elementary school and was found to have grade level academic skills.

The school psychologist selected academic achievement and attendance as baseline data. Minnie's previous year's attendance and days tardy were compared to those typical of her classmates, as were her previous year's grades. Minnie had attained "needs improvement" in effort, academic grades in the C range, and 54 absences over the year. Other students in her sixth-grade class averaged academic grades of B, work and effort grades in the satisfactory range, and 12 absences per year. Baseline data were as follows:

Class	Term 1	Term 2	Term 3	Term 4	Mean	Peers Mean
English/Language Arts	C+	B−	B+	B	B−	B
Mathematics	C	C	C+	B−	C+	B
History	C+	C+	B	C+	C+	B
Science	C+	C+	B	C	C+	B
Overall Effort	4	4	4	3	3.75	2.8
Completes Work	4	4	4	4	4	2.5
Completes Homework	4	4	4	4	4	2
Days in Attendance	30	31	33	32	32	42
Days Absent	15	14	12	13	13.5	3
Days Tardy	3	5	4	4	4	1

Overall Effort, Completes Work, and Completes Homework scales:
1 = Excellent, 2 = Good, 3 = Satisfactory, 4 = Unacceptable

Problem Analysis

After the problem has been defined, one or more reasons for the problem are hypothesized. Using multiple sources of data, each hypothesis is either ruled out or considered an area to address.

> **Example Case Study: Problem Analysis**
>
> Assessment methods included informal observations of Minnie, an interview with Minnie's mother, a record review, and an interview with Minnie. During the interview, Minnie was asked to rate her anxiety in various situations on a scale of 1 to 10 (1 being not anxious at all and 10 being the most anxious possible). Minnie rated the following items as 10s on her anxiety rating scale: not knowing where a class is located, getting lost in school, having a teacher not allow her to leave class, and not being able to contact her mother. She did not rate attending school, completing schoolwork, completing homework, or any specific subject area higher than 4. She also did not indicate any anxiety regarding relationships with peers, and her mother similarly reported that Minnie had two close friends with whom she spent much time. The results suggested several hypotheses regarding Minnie's anxiety:
>
> 1. It is provoked by starting middle school (ruled out because anxiety was present in her old school).
> 2. It enables her to avoid tasks she doesn't like (ruled out because Minnie indicated she enjoyed schoolwork and would like to be able to attend class).
> 3. It is due to schoolwork being too difficult (ruled out because previous evaluations had determined that she was able to complete curriculum materials and her performance on tests was commensurate with grade expectations).
> 4. It is social anxiety (probably ruled out because both Minnie and her mother reported positive friendships and her friends were scheduled to start junior high as well; however, she might have social anxiety regarding other students).
> 5. It is a symptom of attention seeking (possible—could be addressed by using positive attention as a reinforcement for appropriate behavior).
> 6. It is in response to unsupportive staff in her previous school (possible—could be addressed by fostering positive relationships with staff).
> 7. It is exacerbated by classroom pressures (possible—could be addressed by a formal procedure whereby she could leave the classroom for short periods).
> 8. It is separation anxiety in response to leaving her mother (possible—could be addressed by allowing her to have limited telephone contact with her mother during the day but not allowing her to return home).

Intervention Selection and Implementation

After the appropriate preparation for data-based decision making has been completed, the next step is to select and implement a data-based intervention. Kendall and Beidas (2007) differentiated among the strengths of scientific foundations for interventions. *Evidence-based practices* synthesize scientific findings with clinical judgment; they have some scientific foundation but are not rigorously proven. *Empirically based treatments* utilize scientifically determined findings to inform treatment. The most rigorous, *empirically supported treatments,* are detailed procedures that have been evaluated using scientific methodology—randomized trials with real clients yielding consistent results across studies in more than one setting. These treatments are referenced in the *Procedural and Coding*

Manual for Review of Evidence-Based Interventions (Task Force on Evidence-Based Interventions in School Psychology, 2003).

Examples of empirically based treatments include helping depressed, aggressive, and anxious students change their cognitions; testing depressed students' accuracy of self-deprecating beliefs; challenging aggressive students' negative attributions of others' intentions through perspective taking; and helping anxious students strengthen their abilities to accurately ascertain threats, self-regulate emotions, and resist avoidance of anxiety-provoking situations. Implementing empirically supported treatments often requires close adherence to treatment protocols using manuals or detailed formats. Instituting empirically supported treatments requires supervision until the psychologist can provide the treatment with fidelity (Kendall & Beidas, 2007).

While empirically supported procedures are preferable, educators and school psychologists can use weaker evidence-based practices when no empirically supported practices have been established, when empirically supported programs do not fit the situation, when empirically supported procedures are too complex to be implemented in the school setting, or when their cost is prohibitive. Regardless, *in all cases school psychologists should gather and monitor data from the particular case(s) at hand to determine whether the intervention is indeed effective with the student or students involved.* This requires ongoing monitoring throughout and beyond intervention implementation.

Ongoing data collection throughout intervention implementation permits replication under a variety of conditions to ensure that the desired change is not a result of confounding variables. Replication of the effectiveness of a given intervention is best established through rigorous designs such as reversal, changing criterion, multiple baselines across participants, and alternating treatment (Bailey & Burch, 2002; Cooper, Heron, & Heward, 1987; Tawney & Gast, 1984). Care is taken to ensure that the intervention is applied using the appropriate level of intensity and with integrity.

Example Case Study: Intervention Selection and Implementation

The school psychologist working with Minnie conducted a literature review, which revealed that evidence-based treatments for separation anxiety include reinforced practice, relaxation training, in vivo exposure, modeling, cognitive behavior therapy, and family anxiety management. The school psychologist, counselor, Mrs. M., and Minnie collaboratively decided to use relaxation training, in vivo exposure, reinforced practice, and family anxiety management. The combination of relaxation training and in vivo exposure, also known as systematic desensitization, allows the person to experience typically anxiety-producing events, situations, or locations while remaining safe and anxiety free. The procedure has the person experience the same situation over and over while using strategies to reduce stress and anxiety. Over time, the person usually is able to report a decrease in anxiety and eventually become desensitized to the once anxiety-producing event.

It was determined that the focus of the intervention would be to improve Minnie's attendance, increase her time in class, reduce her anxiety, and raise her academic achievement. Attendance records and grades would serve as quantifiable data. Short-term progressive goals for Minnie consisted of entering school, coming into the counseling suite, going to her locker, going to class, remaining in class, completing her work, and learning to seek appropriate resources when in need of help. An additional goal consisted of learning to cope with anxiety through the use of progressive

(Continued)

(Continued)

relaxation exercises. Much of this work would be accomplished jointly with the school counselor and school psychologist in order to avoid Minnie's becoming entirely dependent on one person. The intervention plan included intense intervention at the beginning of the school year with gradual fading as time progressed. Thus a schedule was developed whereby the counselor and school psychologist met with Minnie multiple times per day initially, then daily, every other day, and finally weekly.

To decrease anxiety associated with school, Minnie toured the school before the start of the year to become familiar with the physical setting and establish rapport with staff. Once school began, systematic desensitization was used with the progressive goals listed above. Additionally, during the fall Minnie worked toward identifying her anxiety and using relaxation strategies to handle her anxiety when it escalated. Each small success was rewarded, using time and attention from the counselor and school psychologist as reinforcers. She was also encouraged to come to the counseling suite to build relationships with both the school psychologist and the counselor. In the suite, she was able to call her mother. These phone calls helped Mrs. M. cope with her own anxiety regarding her daughter's status during the day, as did frequent contact with the staff. To the same end, the school psychologist and counselor met frequently with Minnie's mother to alleviate her concerns. This open and ongoing home-school collaboration informed school personnel about when to push Minnie and when to allow her space. The school psychologist also worked closely with Minnie's teachers so that they understood her situation, were supportive of her progress, and set appropriate limitations.

Because *treatment integrity* (also known as treatment fidelity) is critically important to intervention success, we will address it in some depth. Treatment integrity refers to the extent to which an agreed-upon course of action is implemented as intended (Gresham, 1989). Gresham, MacMillan, Beebe-Frankenberger, and Bocian (2000) stated that "treatment integrity is concerned with the *accuracy* and *consistency* with which independent variables constituting the treatment (as opposed to subject characteristics) are implemented" (p. 198). Treatment integrity determines the effectiveness of an intervention at the individual level and also helps determine feasibility and effectiveness for future use. Treatment integrity is affected by (a) the complexity of any given treatment, (b) the time necessary to implement chosen interventions, (c) accessibility of necessary resources and materials, and (d) perceptions of probable effectiveness (Gresham et al., 2000). Without consideration of the degree of intervention implementation (*what* is done, *where* it is done, *when* it is done, by *whom* it is done, etc.), there can be no internal validity and it is impossible to accurately determine intervention effectiveness. Inadequate consideration of treatment fidelity prevents both generalization of interventions and the development of evidence-based interventions.

There is substantial evidence to suggest that treatment integrity is often disregarded, despite the assumption that it directly impacts treatment outcome (Noell, Duhon, Gatti, & Connnell, 2002, Power et al., 2005). Dufresne, Noell, Gilbertson, and Duhon (2005) found that implementation of interventions tends to vary across teachers regardless of training, available materials, and remuneration. Notably, Wickstrom, Jones, LaFleur, and Witt (1998) determined that teachers collected only half of the progress monitoring data and that implementation of the intervention occurred only 4% of the time!

Vignette 4.2

Mrs. Robb, a teacher, agreed to work with **Elise**, a school psychology practicum student, to complete an academic consultation project. **Johnny**, a feisty third-grader, was the targeted student. During reading he acted out and refused to complete any work, and he was falling farther and farther behind his peers. Elise collected preintervention data and a behavior management plan was designed and agreed upon. Two weeks later Elise stopped by to pick up the data, but the teacher said she had been too busy to initiate the interventions. Elise realized that she should have stopped by the classroom every day until the program was implemented. Valuable time had been lost!

Merrell, Ervin, and Gimpel (2006) suggested that enhancing treatment integrity requires mutual understanding among all participants regarding "the intervention steps, roles, and responsibilities, as well as monitoring and evaluation techniques" (p. 154). For supervisors of school psychologists, maintaining and assessing treatment integrity is an effortful but necessary support task. Supervisors of school psychologists should anticipate—and account for—the inevitable deviations that will occur. In addition to vigilance and patience, this requires sound consultation skills and technical expertise. To that end, it is recommended that an "integrity check" of interventions be conducted. Relevant questions are included in Handout 4.3.

Example Case Study: Treatment Integrity

Because the school psychologist stayed in very close contact with Mrs. M., the teachers, and Minnie, she was able to ensure that the interventions were implemented with integrity. As a result, the school and home environments were consistent in their expectations for attendance and academic success. All of these factors helped Minnie feel confident in her ability to handle her anxiety. It also helped Minnie to generalize her coping strategies to other environments, such as the community.

Evaluation

After an intervention has been implemented, its success should be determined to ascertain whether to keep the intervention in place or change the focus. If the implemented intervention is effective, it is continued and steps are taken to (a) generalize its benefits across settings and (b) involve the student in applying self-regulation strategies to maintain the change.

If an intervention is insufficiently effective and it is decided to change the focus, the same steps described previously are used. A plan of action to remedy areas of weakness is developed and specific and measurable goals are developed and prioritized. Persons responsible for action items, time lines, and methods of goal measurement are designated. This plan of action is presented to all stakeholders, and their feedback is taken into consideration in the development of the final plan.

It is very important for school psychologists to play an active role in data collection and analysis at this stage. Teachers do not have the time, and often do not have the expertise, to conduct an analysis of data sufficient to determine whether an intervention has been successful.

Handout 4.3

INTERVENTION INTEGRITY CHECKLIST

Preparation

___ The individual who designed the intervention is expert in designing this type of intervention.

___ If not, the design was reviewed by an expert before it was implemented.

___ The classroom teacher and/or parent(s) were involved in the design of the intervention and their preferences were included.

___ The individual designated to implement the intervention was consulted during the design period.

___ The individual designated to implement the intervention was given a demonstration and trained until competency was achieved.

___ The individual designated to collect the data was trained in collection methods.

___ The data collection method design is practical.

___ The monitoring method design is practical.

___ The monitoring method design is appropriate for the intervention.

Intervention Implementation

___ The intervention was implemented in the *manner* agreed upon.

___ The intervention was implemented as *often* as agreed upon.

___ The individuals designated to implement the program, monitor progress, and collect data did so.

___ Detailed monitoring of the intervention occurred.

___ Monitoring data were collected on schedule.

___ Selected outcome data were appropriate for the intervention design.

Appraisal

___ Data collection has been complete.

___ Aspects of the intervention that worked well have been determined.

___ Aspects of the intervention that did not work well have been determined.

___ The raw data have been collected and preserved so that they can be reviewed.

___ The evaluation team has determined what should be done to modify the plan so that it can be successfully implemented.

___ Appropriate conclusions have been drawn.

Example Case Study: Evaluation

To continue to monitor Minnie's progress, the school psychologist held a brief meeting with her once every 6 days during the first semester and decreased that to once every 12 days during the second semester. She also obtained reports on Minnie's grades, effort, and work completion during the team meeting time for her teachers once every 6 days during the first semester and once every 12 days during the second semester. Additionally, her mother called or came to the school with any concerns. As time passed, the monitoring became less frequent; however, if the need arose, intervention intensity could be increased. Summative results are indicated in the chart below.

Class	Minnie—Sixth Grade				Minnie—Seventh Grade		
	Term 1	*Term 2*	*Term 3*	*Term 4*	*Term 1*	*Term 2*	*Term 3*
English/Language Arts	C+	B–	B+	B	A–	A	A+
Mathematics	C	C	C+	B–	B–	B	B
History	C+	C+	B	C+	B+	B	B+
Science	C+	C+	B	C	A–	A	A
Overall Effort	4	4	4	3	1.5	1.25	1
Completes Work	4	4	4	4	1.25	1.25	1
Completes Homework	4	4	4	4	1	1	1
Days in Attendance	30	31	33	32	36	40	41
Days Absent	15	14	12	13	9	5	4
Days Tardy	3	5	4	4	2	1	1
Mean Anxiety Self-Rating (by month)	NA	NA	NA	NA	8.5 6.7	4.2 2	2.2 1 2 2 3

Overall Effort, Completes Work, and Completes Homework scales:
1 = Excellent, 2 = Good, 3 = Satisfactory, 4 = Unacceptable

Anxiety rating scale: 0 = No anxiety, 10 = Highest anxiety possible

As is evident in the above chart, outcome data revealed a marked improvement compared to the previous year. Grades in all areas moved to the acceptable range, and the changes in effort, conduct, and homework grades are particularly noteworthy. Attendance improved steadily, and both absences and days tardy similarly decreased. There was no anxiety self-appraisal available prior to the start of the intervention. However, over the course of the intervention Minnie's self-rated anxiety level

(Continued)

(Continued)

> decreased markedly. Staff similarly observed a marked decrease in manifested anxiety. The data, Minnie's input, and Mrs. M.'s reports all suggest that the intervention was successful. At the end of the year, plans were made to promote transfer to the next year. It was anticipated that Minnie would need to check in with the school psychologist on an as-needed basis. The school psychologist also agreed to meet with the eighth-grade teachers to alert them to the program of the previous year and ask them to immediately contact her if they noticed a recurrence of Minnie's anxiety.

Supervision Issues

School psychologists conducting case studies to determine whether a particular intervention is successful will require ongoing supervisory consultation in which the supervisor addresses the points raised in Handout 4.1.

To help school psychologists move toward evidence-based practice, NASP-approved school psychology programs require demonstration of case study application skills. NASP also requires that psychologists seeking the Nationally Certified School Psychologist credential submit case studies in their portfolios. To that end, NASP has developed a Case Study Evaluation Rubric, reproduced as Handout 4.4 at the end of this chapter, to evaluate the quality of case studies.

Activity 4.1

Application of the Case Study Evaluation Rubric

In individual or group supervision sessions, use the Handout 4.4 Case Study Evaluation Rubric to assess supervisees' case studies. Determine which areas are the most problematic, consider sources of those difficulties, and develop a professional development program to ameliorate those areas.

PROGRAM EVALUATIONS

School psychologists can directly impact educational policy as consumers, distributors, or conductors of research (Keith, 2008). Furthermore, research in the form of program evaluations is easily conducted, feasible, and effective and can result in remarkable systemic changes.

Conducting a program evaluation is very similar to conducting a case study with an individual student. The first step is to determine a need for the evaluation. The evaluator discusses the identified problem with staff and supervisors, obtains consensus that a program evaluation is desired, and formulates clearly defined, testable questions. The next step involves recruiting an evaluation team composed of staff, supervisors, and representatives of other constituent groups who are stakeholders in the evaluation outcome. The more groups represented in the evaluation team, the more likely the findings will result in meaningful change. It is particularly helpful to include individuals who "write the checks" (i.e., administrators). Persons invited to be evaluation team members should believe that the evaluation is worthwhile, have an interest in the appropriate use of the results, and have the authority and capability to implement the findings. They are most likely to agree to serve when reassured that the time commitment will be reasonable. The chair of the evaluation team supervises the evaluation process and facilitates meetings.

The evaluation team determines the purposes of the evaluation and chooses one or two questions to be addressed. After testable questions are clearly formulated, the evaluation team chooses the evaluation components. Appropriate data collection methods and procedures are determined after the questions have been planned and the sources of data identified. It is helpful to develop forms and spreadsheets to facilitate data collection and organization. The costs of conducting the evaluation in terms of time, supplies, and data analysis are roughly calculated. Evaluation components can include but are not limited to questionnaires, interviews, file reviews, and outcome data.

While it is possible to conduct an "inside" program evaluation without the sanction of upper level administration, ensuing recommendations are much more likely to be implemented if upper level administration has approved the project. Furthermore, the administration is responsible for acting as the equivalent of a human subjects institutional review board and giving official approval for any study conducted in a district. Therefore, before proceeding with an evaluation, a proposal should be presented to key decision makers in the school district. The proposal need only be a few pages long to address the critical information. Components should include the purpose of the evaluation, questions to be posed, a summary of the model to be employed, a plan for data analysis, discussion of the planned dissemination of results, the estimated cost in terms of time and resources, a description of methods that will be used to obtain informed consent, sample consent forms, sample questionnaires and interview questions, and a request for a letter indicating administrative sanctions and support. After obtaining permission to proceed with the evaluation, the evaluation team designs the procedures more fully, establishes time lines, and designates persons responsible for each step.

Questionnaires

If questionnaires are to be used, the committee may choose to send one set of questions to parents, another to administrators, and yet another to teachers. They may also choose to send the same questions to each group. A cover letter should be included that (a) explains the project well enough so that any consent given is fully informed, (b) suggests the possibility of nonparticipation at any point, (c) indicates upper administration approval, (d) urges completion of the questionnaire in a timely fashion, and (e) provides contact information for the program evaluator and district administrators should questions arise. Requesting that questionnaires be returned anonymously may help to increase the response rate. Easily modified survey forms to generate questionnaires are available from a variety of sources, including Microsoft Office Online (http://office.microsoft.com). Surveys can be efficiently conducted using an electronic system that enables anonymous responses, such as SurveyMonkey.com. When professional staff are asked to complete lengthy paper surveys, response rates can be increased by awarding professional development credit for participation (anonymity can be maintained by having a secretary record the names of respondents).

Interviews

The evaluation team decides who will conduct interviews, what format the interviews will take, and what questions will be asked. It is particularly helpful to field test interview questions on a few persons to ensure that the questions elicit the desired information. After field testing, the questions can be refined and interviewers trained. Helpful information regarding the use of interviews to pursue qualitative data is contained in *Interviewing as Qualitative Research: A Guide for Researchers in Education and the Social Sciences* (Seidman, 2006) and *Program Evaluation: An Introduction* (Royse et al., 2006).

File Reviews

Examination of student files can provide a great deal of pertinent demographic and historical information. For example, evaluating whether a junior high program in study skills is effective may require knowing which elementary schools were attended by participants, since the program may be more effective with students who attended an elementary school with weak study skill curricula.

Outcome Data

Selected student outcome measures should reflect the initially identified problem. Because controlling samples and random treatment assignment is very difficult in schools, outcome data analysis often uses a single-subject (repeated time series) design employing at least three data points prior to and at least three data points following the intervention.

Vignette 4.3

The school psychologists in Small City School System were heavily involved in a systemwide program evaluation of special and general education services. Initially, an evaluation team composed of special and regular educators met to determine the evaluation process. The proposed process was approved by the administration, including the school board, central administration, and principals. Secretarial staff tabulated outcome data (grades, attendance, suspension rate, and dropout rate) for all special education students and a sample of non–special education students at each level.

Questionnaires were distributed to all teachers, administrators, and one third of the parents of special education students. The questionnaires asked respondents to indicate on a Likert-type scale whether positively worded indicators of effective education were adhered to "almost always," "frequently," "sometimes," "seldom," or "never." For example, a positively worded indicator was that "special and general education staff communicate and plan together." A selected sample of parents and staff were also interviewed.

The results of the outcome data, questionnaires, and interviews were tabulated and distributed in paper copy to administrators, school board members, and teachers. The results were also presented orally at administration, faculty, and school board meetings. Subsequently, a team of special education teachers, administrators, parents, and school board members reviewed the data, determined areas of strength and weakness, and developed recommended courses of action in a series of goals and objectives much like a student's individualized education plan. The evaluation results demonstrated that concerns were expressed repeatedly. Consensus on goals and objectives was reached easily, and steps to attain these were subsequently implemented.

Applications of Supervision to Program Evaluations

As in performing all other activities, school psychologists conducting program evaluations progress through developmental stages as they become more skilled. Supervision is again necessary, particularly in the beginning stages. Program evaluations are also ideal opportunities to utilize peer supervision and obtain invaluable feedback from colleagues at each stage of the process.

Courses in program evaluation are readily available at most colleges and universities, although often they are housed in administration programs or other programs emphasizing applied research. Normally, program evaluations do not require sophisticated statistical analysis and basic spreadsheet software (such as Lotus 1-2-3 or Microsoft Excel) is sufficient. For more sophisticated analyses, advanced statistical programs such as SPSS and StatView are available at a reasonable cost.

When school psychologists conduct program evaluations, their supervisors should ensure that this activity is seen as part of their job by both immediate supervisors and the general administration. Integration into the role description is essential because it connotes official approval and permits allocation of appropriate resources including school psychologist, clerical, and teacher time. Official sanction also lends authority to the findings and makes it more likely that recommendations will be implemented.

RESEARCH

As consumers and distributors of research, school psychologists are in a ready position to help school districts make informed decisions based on data rather than political forces or fads. As conductors of research, school psychologists are strategically positioned to gather information about a school's strengths and weaknesses and the effectiveness of individual and group programs. In so doing, school psychologists can make a real difference that positively affects large numbers of students.

Applications of Supervision to Research Consumption

School psychologists should be, at the very least, competent consumers of research (Keith, 2008). The development of skills in research consumption is critical for two reasons: First, if school psychologists are not competent research consumers, their skills quickly become outdated. Second, the popular press and the Internet often report subjective conclusions regarding psychology and education research studies that affect the expectations of teachers and parents. Members of the general public do not have the skill to identify a research study as poorly conducted, and this limitation can lead them to unwarranted conclusions. An ongoing need exists, therefore, for every school psychologist to be aware of popularly disseminated research results.

Activity 4.2

Popular Psychology Book Analysis

Select self-help or popular psychology books from a local bookstore and analyze them for evidence-based recommendations. Compare the content with professional textbooks, at least six current empirically based research articles on the same topic, information on the same topic on the Web, and (if available) research by the popular press book's author. Determine whether the information in the book is evidence based enough that you would recommend it to clients. If not, find a better book on the same topic!

Supervisors of school psychologists must encourage supervisees to become skillful research consumers so that supervisees develop these skills to a more advanced level. Most specialist level programs include a research course in the curriculum, resulting in graduates attaining "advanced beginner" status as research consumers. Ideally, these courses focus on conceptual material (Houser, 1998; Keith, 2008), for in a conceptual course school psychology trainees learn how to evaluate the appropriateness of a research design and the generalizability of the results. However, for practicing school psychologists to develop advanced skills as research consumers, they must continue to practice and hone these critical skills. Supervisors can foster these skills by:

- Encouraging supervisees to schedule time to read, discuss, and critique research
- Providing access to journals and online subscriptions to databases regarding school psychology, general education, special education, educational psychology, child and adolescent development, clinical psychology, neuropsychology, counseling, the sociology of schools, and systems theory
- Encouraging attendance at conferences where sound research is presented, including those conducted by NASP, APA, the Council for Exceptional Children (CEC), and the American Educational Research Association (AERA) and their regional and state affiliates
- Encouraging participation in group supervision or peer supervision groups that maintain a focus on research reviews
- Encouraging the establishment of a peer supervision and/or support network whose members develop specific areas of expertise and share their knowledge with others
- Establishing a departmental custom of sharing articles and journals
- Encouraging supervisees to participate in research studies conducted by school districts, psychologists, and local universities
- Including maintenance of current research knowledge as an item in school psychologists' job descriptions and evaluation forms
- Scheduling time for the above activities when allocating time, resources, and supervisory consultation

Practicing school psychologists face critical obstacles in becoming proficient research consumers, particularly time constraints. Results of an informal canvassing of local school psychologists disclosed a wide variety of methods to cope with this difficulty. Some suggestions are included in Table 4.1.

Resources that address selecting evidence-based interventions include *Interventions for Academic and Behavior Problems II: Preventive and Remedial Approaches* (Shinn, Walker, & Stoner, 2002); "Best Practices in Selecting and Implementing Evidence-Based School Interventions" (Forman & Burke, 2008); "Training Psychologists for Evidence-Based Practice" (Hunsley, 2007); and "Evidence-Based Prevention Practice in Mental Health: What Is It and How Do We Get There?" (Rishel, 2007).

Additionally, a number of Web sites maintain current information regarding evidence-based practices, such as www.interventioncentral.com, http://ies.ed.gov/ncee/wwc (what works), www.nctm.org (math programs), http://reading.uoregon.edu/curricula/index.php (reading programs), www.nationalreadingpanel.org (reading programs), and www.wjh .harvard.edu/%7Enock/Div53/EST/index.htm (mental health).

A few resources addressing the evaluation of implemented interventions to determine their effectiveness include *Response to Intervention: Principles and Strategies for Effective Practice* (Brown-Chidsey & Steege, 2005); *Applied Behavior Analysis for Teachers* (Alberto &

Table 4.1   Methods of Keeping Current

- Subscribe to a few journals, or obtain journals in conjunction with organizational memberships to NASP, CEC, AERA, APA, etc.
- Trade journal articles with colleagues
- Participate in a monthly "professional book club" with teachers, administrators, or other school psychologists
- Read abstracts in journals as soon as they arrive
- Subscribe to journal abstracts
- Read article abstracts online
- Keep a journal or two handy in the car and read articles during odd moments (e.g., while waiting at soccer games and music lessons)
- Keep a journal or two handy at work and read them whenever you have some unexpected free time, such as appointment cancellations
- Set aside 2 hours per week to read
- Choose one or two areas of interest and read about them regularly
- Participate in a professional Listserv on the Internet
- Read publications in a variety of fields, for example, *School Psychology Review, Learning Disabilities, Educational Week, Educational Psychology*
- Persuade the school librarian to purchase at least one research-based professional journal subscription

Troutman, 2006); "Responsiveness-to-Intervention: A Blueprint for Practitioners, Policymakers, and Parents" (D. Fuchs & Fuchs, 2005); "Response to Intervention: Empirically Based Special Service Decisions From Single-Case Designs of Increasing and Decreasing Intensity" (Barnett, Daly, Jones, & Lentz, 2004); "Best Practices in Evaluating the Effectiveness of Interventions Using Case Study Data" (Brown-Chidsey et al., 2008); and "Best Practices in Using and Conducting Research in Applied Settings" (Keith, 2008).

Knowledge regarding data analysis can be augmented using *School Counselor Accountability: A MEASURE of Student Success* (Stone & Dahir, 2007); *The Great Ideas of Clinical Science: 17 Principles That Every Mental Health Professional Should Understand* (Lilienfeld & O'Donohue, 2007); *Reading Statistics and Research* (Huck, 2007); and *Counseling and Educational Research: Evaluation and Application* (Houser, 1998).

In terms of "number crunching," single-subject designs, case studies, and program evaluations do not usually include sophisticated data analyses, since usually only trend lines, means, and standard deviations are needed for meaningful interpretation of results. For data presentation, however, it is helpful to know graphing methods. To generate graphs, Microsoft Excel and ChartDog (www.jimwrightonline.com/php/chartdog_2_0/chartdog.php) can be used.

Applications of Supervision to Research Distribution

As previously mentioned, school psychologists are in an ideal position to distribute research findings to other educators and thereby increase the likelihood that teachers and administrators will make data-based decisions. Steps involved include defining primary and secondary research topics, evaluating the research, integrating the findings, drawing one or two appropriate conclusions, and making recommendations based on these conclusions (Keith, 2008).

Effective supervisors frequently take responsibility for distributing research findings to supervisees and other school personnel. They also provide supervision to other school psychologists as they take the steps necessary for distributing research to teachers, administrators, parents, and other school personnel. Such activities have multiple benefits. They increase the visibility of school psychologists, reduce frustration when inadequate programs are suggested, provide practice in research skills, and enhance professional development. Supervisors can facilitate research distribution skills by:

1. Including this activity in job descriptions and personnel evaluations

2. Encouraging supervisees to explore relevant areas of research interest, particularly areas about which the administration is unsure of an appropriate course of action (e.g., "Should we institute a time-out room at our high school?")

3. Facilitating access to research by increasing the availability of conferences, journals, and databases, such as ERIC and PsychLit through the Internet

4. Helping supervisees clearly formulate central and secondary topics to review

5. Regularly meeting with supervisees to facilitate the progress of research distribution projects, ensure that a thorough review is conducted, accurate conclusions are drawn, and appropriate and feasible recommendations are made

Applications of Supervision to Conducting Research

Taking the time to publish successful practices as a research study can be very worthwhile. Final reports of both individual and group programs can be shared in professional newsletters or journals to improve programs or provide guidance to others attempting to deal with the same problem.

Informed consent is mandated when a student participates in any program outside of the general education program. *Additional* consent must be obtained if the results are to be generalized to a broader audience by being published as a research study. The ethical principles of the APA (2002) regarding research are supported by the ethical principles outlined in NASP's (2000a) *Professional Conduct Manual* and mandate the following:

- Obtaining informed consent
- Communicating potential risks to participants prior to obtaining consent
- Taking extra precautions necessary when conducting research with special populations, including minors and individuals with disabilities
- Providing participants with the opportunity to be informed of the results of the study
- Using deception rarely and only when no other methods are available
- Using minimally invasive methods of data collection
- Taking extra precautions when conducting research on socially sensitive topics, such as the effectiveness of sex education programs in promoting the use of birth control
- Providing participants with nonpunitive avenues for withdrawing from the study

In addition, the United States Department of Health and Human Services (2005) provided ethical guidelines that specifically address research with human subjects. These guidelines require the review of proposed research by a human subjects institutional review board that carefully scrutinizes proposals for evidence of informed consent, assesses the risks and benefits to research participants, and evaluates methods of ensuring confidentiality (Houser,

1998). This scrutiny is mandated for any institution receiving federal monies, which clearly includes schools. In school districts, the upper level administration acts as the review board to ensure that all research adheres to the guidelines. Therefore, permission to conduct a research study, whether with an individual student or a group, must be obtained from the administration prior to conducting the project. Expedited reviews, that commonly do not require individual consent, can be used to disseminate results of educational programs.

EVIDENCE-BASED SUPERVISION

Evidence-based supervision addresses multiple embedded systems (Mead, 1990). The student system or level is encompassed by the supervisee system, and both the student and supervisee systems are encompassed by the supervision system.

At each level, data are collected, goals are set, a plan is developed, observations are made, interventions are applied, and progress is determined. At the student level, students make observations about themselves, establish goals, and evaluate the success of their experience. At the supervisee level, supervisees first make observations about themselves and prepare for practice. They then make observations about the student, establish goals for practice, and evaluate the success of their practice. In turn, supervisors first make observations about their readiness for supervision and assess the supervisee's level of preparation. Supervisors determine supervision goals, develop assessment and observation procedures, develop a supervision plan, observe the supervisee's practice, evaluate the success of treatment, modify the assessment of the supervisee, and finally assess the success of supervision. This is graphically depicted in Figure 4.1.

Given that the fundamental functions of supervision are to protect students, enhance services and improve educational outcomes, and provide leadership in developing and evaluating effective and accountable services, it logically follows that evaluation of supervision addresses the functioning of children and adolescents with whom the supervisee works, the effectiveness of the programs the supervisor oversees, the functioning of the supervisee, and the performance of the supervisor. As Sergiovanni and Starratt (2007) indicated, effective supervision should be judged by the results it secures.

Like evidence-based psychology practice, evidence-based supervision has three recursive phases at each level. In the preparation phase, data are collected, goals are set, and a plan is developed. In the implementation phase, data-based interventions are implemented and modified according to pertinent observations. In the appraisal phase, the progress toward meeting goals is assessed, practice is reflected upon, and future plans are revised accordingly. Again, fundamental questions (previously outlined in Handout 4.2) are:

1. What isn't going well?
2. How do you know this is a problem?
3. What would you like to be different?
4. How can we measure this difference?
5. What is contributing to this problem?
6. What is going well?
7. How can we make it go better?

The phases and venues are illustrated in Table 4.2.

Figure 4.1. Systemic supervision.

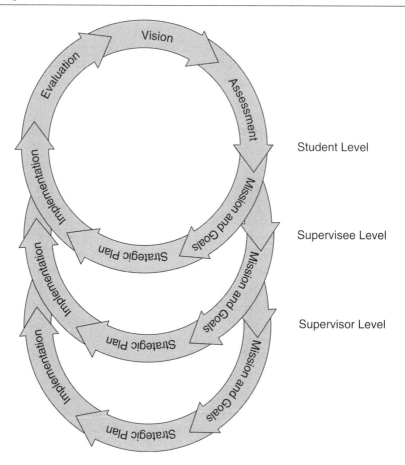

From Harvey, V. S., & Struzziero, J. (2000). *Effective supervision in school psychology.* Bethesda, MD: National Association of School Psychologists. Copyright 2000 by the National Association of School Psychologists, Bethesda, MD. Use of this material is by permission of the publisher, www.nasponline.org

Table 4.2   Outcomes-Based Supervision Matrix

	Student	*Program/School*	*Supervisee*	*Supervisor*
Problem Definition and Analysis	Assess academics and behavior	Assess needs	Assess professional skills and dispositions	Assess professional and supervision skills
	Set goals			
	Develop plan			
Intervention	Implement data-based interventions			
Evaluation	Assess progress			
	Reflect			
	Revise			

SUMMARY

Both NASP and APA mandate evidence-based practice, and many professional organizations maintain Web sites to promote research-based educational practices. As consumers and distributors of research, school psychologists can help school districts make informed decisions based on data rather than political forces or fads. As conductors of research, school psychologists can gather information about a school's strengths and weaknesses, student learning, and the effectiveness of individual and group programs and share this with administrators, encouraging data-based decision making. School psychologists are also among the best-trained school professionals to help others implement and evaluate new types of educational outcomes.

Since graduate programs can provide only limited training in the application of data-based decision making, supervisors must guide school psychologists as they develop expertise in evaluating intervention effectiveness at the individual (single-case) and programmatic levels. Effective evaluations begin with thorough preparation in which the problem is defined, needs and assets are delineated, and current functioning is determined. In the next phase, data-based interventions are implemented. During the appraisal phase, outcomes are evaluated, processes are appraised, and results are used to inform future actions.

Supervisors must help supervisees become competent consumers of research or their skills will quickly become outdated. Supervisors should also distribute research findings to supervisees and other school personnel and encourage supervisees to do the same. When this is done well, the school psychologist may be invited to administrative meetings and asked to consult when important decisions are made in the district.

The effectiveness of supervision can be ascertained by the results achieved. This includes the functioning of students with whom the supervisee works, the effectiveness of the programs the supervisor oversees, the functioning of the supervisee, and the performance of the supervisor. Outcomes-based systemic supervision is recommended as a means of finding answers to such questions as: How do we know what we are doing is working? How can we make it work better?

REFLECTIVE QUESTIONS

Q4.1. Where can one easily find the research-based educational practices promoted by professional organizations?

Q4.2. What are the differences among evidence-based practices, empirically based treatments, and empirically supported treatments?

Q4.3. Describe recommended uses of research in the practice of school psychology.

Q4.4. Describe the three steps of effective data-based decision making as they apply to single-case design and program evaluations.

Q4.5. What are the ethical guidelines in conducting research?

Q4.6. How can supervisors foster the consumption of research by school psychologists?

Q4.7. Describe methods school psychologists might use to find time to keep abreast of current research, select a method, and begin to implement it.

Q4.8. Describe how supervisors can facilitate research distribution skills.

Q4.9. How can supervisors provide consultation for single-case studies and in program evaluations?

SUPERVISORY DILEMMAS

SD 4.1

A school psychologist is evaluating the outcome of a conflict resolution program she has implemented in her high school. An essential question is whether disciplinary actions have been less frequent after the program's implementation. Unfortunately, the school administrators have a practice of deleting all records of disciplinary actions every June, stating that keeping them would violate the students' right to privacy. The school psychologist understands the need for confidentiality but decidedly feels that being denied access to the results of interventions constitutes an ethical violation. *What are the supervisory considerations? What should be done?*

Authors' thoughts: The most salient priority is to determine how to best assess program efficacy. It would appear that discipline referrals of program participants constitute an important outcome measure. With the benefit of hindsight, it is clear that the school psychologist should have discussed the accessibility of these records for the purposes of program evaluation with the administration. One solution would be to collect data prior to record destruction. It may be worthwhile to explore whether it is good practice to routinely destroy these records, since cumulative records may help to determine patterns of behavior on both the individual level and the systems level. To that end, another option is to help the administration understand that deleting records in the service of "a fresh start" may actually be detrimental. Furthermore, consultation with the school attorney regarding the pros and cons of each option may be helpful.

SD 4.2

You and the school principal co-supervise a school psychologist who initiated and continues to direct an after-school program in a community center. The school psychologist has completed a well-designed outcomes-based program evaluation and determined that the program is highly successful. The data are impressive, in fact. Grades of participants have improved, referrals for psychoeducational evaluations have decreased, and neighborhood vandalism has decreased. The school now has a new principal, who believes that the after-school program should be taken over by paraprofessionals and that the school psychologist should not be spending time on this program. *What are the supervisory considerations? What should be done?*

Authors' thoughts: This is a wonderful opportunity to effectively "make a case" for the students we serve! Data gathering, followed by a well-structured presentation of program efficacy, may be the key to success. Asking for support from the exiting principal and other involved parties (police, clergy, parents, etc.) should be explored as well. This scenario also affords an opportunity to discover more about the power and utility of public relations. With a sound presentation of the facts, it is likely that this effective program will obtain support. Moreover, this may be a great time to expand the program to other schools in the district or to look into the possibility of obtaining grant funding. Finally, it will be particularly important to investigate the underlying perceptions of the new principal regarding the roles of school psychologists and paraprofessionals. While utilization of paraprofessionals can certainly be explored, it is doubtful that the same level of success would be achieved without the input of the school psychologist. It may be that the new principal is simply unaware that the talents of school psychologists have greatly expanded beyond the "WISC jockey" role! Clearly, an exemplary program like this is too good to abandon and offers a viable opportunity to illustrate how school psychologists can really make a difference.

SD 4.3

A group of teachers and school psychologists conducts a formative, standards-based program evaluation to determine the effectiveness of in-district programs for students with emotional and behavioral disorders. The evaluation results in several intraprogram recommendations that could easily be implemented by staff. The recommendations requiring schoolwide or districtwide changes are less easily implemented. For example, recommendations include developing standardized referral methods, increasing vocational curricula, institutionalizing planning time, and increasing staff. The administration is resistant to a standardized referral method (preferring the option of "emergency placement"), and, despite acknowledging the need, indicates that it does not have the resources to institutionalize planning time or increase staff. *What are the supervisory considerations? What should be done?*

Authors' thoughts: When concrete recommendations emerge from program evaluation, it is an exciting opportunity to use data to improve services for students. As exemplified in the above scenario, it is typically not possible to do everything immediately. One preliminary step might be for stakeholders to prioritize the recommendations in terms of both their importance and ease of implementation. Simply stated, if an intervention is both feasible *and* important, it could be prioritized for imminent implementation. Astute and pragmatic planning can address the other recommendations. Creating short- and long-term goals allows for efficient allocation of time and resources. In this case, crafting a referral process is seemingly an important but not costly goal. A "planning team" could develop and present a model for referral that avoids a crisis-based approach. Furthermore, the team could collect data to determine if emergency placement actually utilizes more staff time than a more standardized procedure. With an effective presentation of all salient facts, it is probable that effective change could occur. Administrators are often resistant to change because they do not possess adequate information, or because they are so overwhelmed with current crises that they have difficulty seeing the "big picture" and making long-term plans.

SD 4.4

A supervisee is very much abreast of the research literature regarding the importance of early intervention for reading problems. The principal at the elementary school in question is a fan of whole language approaches to reading instruction and forbids his kindergarten through second-grade teachers to teach phonics (some of them hide such materials in closets and bring them out when the principal is supervising the lunchroom). Parents whose students are having reading difficulties are voicing objections to the lack of phonics instruction. Your supervisee has gone to the principal and shared his knowledge of the research literature. He comes to you in extreme frustration because the principal is unwilling to listen and has told him not to divulge the research results to the parents. He wants you, as his supervisor, to battle with the administration on his behalf. *What are the supervisory considerations? What should be done?*

Authors' thoughts: Battles with administration often have few survivors! To reduce "casualties," a far better approach would be to arm oneself with data to support the initiative for change. The critical task is to present information in a way that supports the proposed initiative. Notably, this supervisee is motivated by his responsibility and desire to serve students in a manner that complies with best practices. The question of whether to share research findings with parents is more difficult to answer concretely. Parents' ability to appropriately consume research is most likely quite variable among the population. One recommendation would be to first attempt to procure administrative support for proposed change and determine criteria that would effectively guide placement decisions.

Handout 4.4

CASE STUDY EVALUATION RUBRIC

		Very Effective	*Effective*	*Needs Development*
1. Problem Identification	1.1	The student's behavior is defined in the context of appropriate grade and/or peer expectations, for example, local norms.	The student's behavior is operationally defined.	The student's behavior is identified but not operationally defined.
	1.2		The problem is collaboratively defined.	The problem is not collaboratively defined.
	1.3	The discrepancy between current and desired level of performance is explained.	The behavior is operationally defined or quantified in terms of both current and desired levels of performance.	The behavior is not operationally defined in terms of both current and desired levels of performance.
	1.4	Baseline includes the student behavior and peer/grade norms and expectations with computed trend lines.	A baseline for the student behavior is established using sufficient data.	A baseline for the student behavior is not established or has insufficient data.
	1.5		The student behavior is identified as a skill and/or performance deficit.	The student behavior is not identified as a skill and/or performance deficit.
	1.6		Parents/guardians and teachers are involved in the problem identification process.	Parents/guardians and teachers are not involved in the problem identification process.
2. Problem Analysis	2.1	Hypotheses are generated through collaboration with teachers and/or parents.	One or more hypotheses are developed to identify the functions that the behavior serves and/or the conditions under which the behavior is occurring or has developed in two or more of the following areas: student factors, curriculum, peers, teacher, classroom, home.	Hypotheses are not developed, hypotheses are developed in only one area, and/or hypotheses are not measurable.
	2.2	There are multiple sources of data that converge on each proposed hypothesis.	There is evidence that appropriate data are collected to confirm or reject the proposed hypotheses.	Appropriate data are not collected to confirm or reject the hypotheses.

(Continued)

(Continued)

		Very Effective	*Effective*	*Needs Development*
			Appropriate data include one or more of the following: record review, interview, observation, testing, and self-report.	
	2.3		Hypotheses reflect an awareness of issues of diversity (e.g., physical, social, linguistic, cultural).	Hypotheses do not reflect an awareness of issues related to diversity (e.g., physical, social, linguistic, cultural).
3. Intervention	3.1		Intervention is linked to observable, measurable goal statement(s).	Intervention is not linked to observable, measurable goal statement(s).
	3.2		Intervention selection is based on data from problem analysis and hypothesis testing.	Intervention selection is not based on data from problem analysis and hypothesis testing.
	3.3		Intervention is evidence based (e.g., research literature, functional analysis, single-case design analysis).	Intervention is not evidence based (e.g., research literature, functional analysis, single-case design analysis).
	3.4		Intervention is developed collaboratively.	Intervention is not developed collaboratively.
	3.5		Intervention reflects sensitivity to individual differences, resources, classroom practices, and other system issues. Acceptability of intervention is verified.	Intervention does not reflect sensitivity to individual differences, resources, classroom practices, and other system issues. Acceptability of intervention is not verified.
	3.6		Logistics of setting, time, resources, and personnel are included in the intervention plan.	Logistics of setting, time, resources, and personnel are not included in the intervention plan.
	3.7		Intervention selection considers unintended outcomes or limitations.	Intervention selection does not consider unintended outcomes or limitations.

		Very Effective	*Effective*	*Needs Development*
	3.8		Intervention is monitored and data are provided to ensure that it is implemented as designed.	Treatment integrity is not monitored.
4. Evaluation	4.1	Charting includes student performance trend lines and/or goal lines.	Progress monitoring data are demonstrated on a chart.	Progress monitoring data are not demonstrated on a chart.
	4.2	Progress monitoring data are demonstrated to be effective when compared to data generated from multiple sources/settings.	Progress monitoring data are demonstrated to be effective when compared to baseline data.	Intervention is not demonstrated to be effective through data comparison.
	4.3	Responses to intervention data are used to inform problem solving and decision making. Single-case design was specified (e.g., changing criterion, parametric, component analysis, multiple baseline, alternating treatment).	Data are used to inform further problem solving and decision making (i.e., continuation of intervention, modification of intervention, maintenance of intervention).	Data are not used to inform further problem solving and decision making.
	4.4	Strategies for transfer/generalizing outcomes to other settings are documented as effective.	Strategies for transfer/generalizing outcomes to other settings are addressed.	Strategies for transfer/generalizing outcomes to other settings are not addressed.
	4.5	Modifications for future interventions are considered based upon collaborative examination of effectiveness data.	Effectiveness of intervention is shared through collaboration with parents, teachers, and other personnel.	Effectiveness of intervention is not shared or communicated.
		Strategies for follow-up are developed and implemented.	Suggestions for follow-up are developed (e.g., continued progress monitoring, transition planning).	Suggestions for follow-up are not developed.

Summary of strengths (based on the rubric):
Summary of areas for improvement (based on the rubric):
Comments:

5

Systems-Based Service Delivery

"If you think you're too small to have an impact, try going to bed with a mosquito."

—Anita Roddick, founder of The Body Shop

Vignette 5.1

Crystal, a fourth-grade teacher, is concerned about the mounting behavioral and academic problems she has observed in her classroom. In a conversation with the school psychologist, **MaryAnna**, she expressed extreme frustration. "I have eight students with *awful* behavior during math. The trouble started in January when we began to prepare for the state-mandated testing. I know it's frustrating, but I *have* to give these daily drills. Now that I think about it, I've only had these problems since we started the new math curriculum. I need these kids evaluated *now*." In a subsequent conversation with the principal, MaryAnna finds that *each* of the teachers in the fourth grade has approached the principal with similar concerns and lists of referrals. MaryAnna is faced with the prospect of helping to manage a "quiet crisis"—administrators and teachers are expected to simultaneously deal with an apparently problematic curriculum, manage escalating behavior problems, and meet high-stakes testing requirements. This is an excellent chance for her to provide systems-based services to benefit all students in the school.

Because service-based service delivery provides the opportunity to make a significant difference for large numbers of students, it can be some of the most exciting and rewarding work undertaken by school psychologists. Leaders in the field of school psychology have long advocated a systems, ecological orientation as the most effective and ethical approach to school psychology (Curtis, Castillo, & Cohen, 2008; S. W. Gray, 1963; Knoff, 2000; Plas, 1986; Sheridan & Gutkin, 2000; Woody, LaVoie, & Epps,

126

1992; Ysseldyke et al., 2006). As Curtis et al. (2008) stated, implementing evidence-based practices to improve student functioning almost inevitably requires significant school-wide change involving systems-based services and systems level revisions.

Nonetheless, systems-based service delivery remains elusive for many school psychologists. To work in this area, school psychologists need considerable supervisory support and professional development. Furthermore, as skilled and respected practitioners, supervisors themselves frequently provide systems-based services at the school and district level. Thus supervisors need information in this area both for their own practice and to inform their supervision of others. This chapter addresses the challenges of practicing and supervising in this domain.

BASIC CONSIDERATIONS

In applying the systems approach, psychologists consider multiple factors: biological and neuropsychological elements, individual strengths and needs, family variables, teacher and classroom factors, school climate, neighborhood, community, social issues, and cultural factors. Studying the individual separately can be useful, but only insofar as the psychologist feeds the "part" back into the "whole" before the final analysis. A systems psychologist also looks beyond the comfortable boundaries of psychology. This requires abandoning defensiveness and professional insularity in favor of collaboration and coordinated efforts.

Systems theory originated in scientists' frustration with overspecialization, isolation, and insufficient interdisciplinary communication (Laszlo, 1972). Systems thinkers search for isomorphisms, or common patterns across time or settings, that result from similar causes. They arrange empirical facts hierarchically, starting at the simplest level and extending to the most complex. They also apply a holistic, nonreductionistic, in toto approach to elements, phenomena, and problems (Bertalanffy, 1956; Boulding, 1956). In addition to psychology, the systems approach is applicable to business (Fuqua & Newman, 2002), the physical sciences, the behavioral sciences, education, and the social sciences (Kaufman, 1972; Sarason, 1996; Sutherland, 1973).

A systems-based orientation is necessary in school psychology because students' learning successes and problems belong not only to students, but also to the systems—the schools, families, neighborhoods, and communities—in which they live and learn (Ysseldyke et al., 2006). As Bronfenbrenner (1979) indicated, students' growth and functioning are affected by their microsystems—their classrooms, schools, families, peers, neighborhoods, and communities. Students are further impacted by interactions (the mesosystem) among microsystems—for example, the relationships between their parents and school personnel. Students are even affected by exosystems, or social systems in which they do not directly participate, such as a parent's workplace. Macrosystems—larger cultural systems such as social class, ethnicity, the economy, and war—add yet another layer of influence, as do the chronosystems—unique characteristics of the time period in which the student lives. For example, currently the exploding information revolution is clearly a system with tremendous impact on all students. All of these systems interact reciprocally and influence one another. An adaptation of Bronfenbrenner's model is shown in Figure 5.1.

Yet systems-based practice is challenging for a number of reasons. While most school psychologists freely acknowledge that classrooms, schools, families, peers, neighborhoods, and communities affect students, it can be difficult to maintain a systems perspective. Our training and culture both tend to reinforce first considering the individual rather than the systems as both the cause of difficulties and the platform of change.

Figure 5.1. Students' interactive systems.

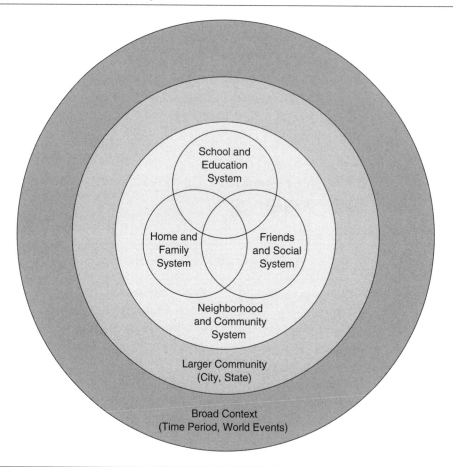

APPLICATIONS TO PRACTICE

School psychologists' work at the systems level can be manifested in many activities. Some examples are designing and implementing problem solving teams, providing programs to train teachers and paraprofessionals, consulting with administrators regarding discipline and grading policies, designing and implementing crisis prevention and intervention programs, designing and implementing programs that help students transition from one aspect of schooling to another, consulting with administrators and teachers to implement programs that promote school safety and positive behavior, designing and implementing programs to improve parenting skills and home-school collaboration, and working with community agencies to systematize wraparound services for students.

As Curtis et al. (2008) indicated, systems-based work requires many skills necessary in consultation: collaboration, effective communication, strategic problem solving (problem identification, analysis, intervention implementation, and evaluation), data gathering and analysis, and appraisal of results. Approaches used by school psychologists must be deliberately tuned. As DeLeon, Ball, Loftis, and Sullivan (2006) pointed out, maintaining a visible presence, being persistent, fostering positive interpersonal relationships, "speaking the language" of those with whom one is working, and maintaining a long-term vision are all required when addressing issues at the school, community, or legislative level.

In order for school psychologists to be able to work effectively at the systems level, supervisors must provide continual support. Supervisors can help their supervisees prioritize improvements, involve other staff in developing new policies, align innovations with school district goals and procedures, institutionalize innovations, and provide staff development in attitudes, knowledge, and skills (Knoff, 2002). They also can serve as systemic change leaders by actively addressing and changing systemic variables at the district level and beyond (Harvey, 2008).

Furthermore, supervisors can help their supervisees acquire the requisite understanding of principles of organizational change. To be effective in this domain, school psychologists must understand how each system works and how they interact with one another, then use this knowledge to facilitate appropriate change in schools, classrooms, families, and communities.

PRINCIPLES OF ORGANIZATIONAL CHANGE

A substantial body of information regarding organizational change exists in business management and educational administration literature. A meta-analysis of organizational development empirical literature by Halfhill, Huff, Johnson, Ballentine, and Beyerlein (2002) revealed that successful organizational change interventions were characterized by several traits. These, along with considerations described by H. Levinson (2002) and Winum, Nielsen, and Bradford (2002), are listed in Table 5.1.

To this list, Curtis et al. (2008) added that systems change in schools, like consultation, is most effective when it focuses on teaching problem solving skills and processes to encourage generalization and transfer after the original problem is resolved.

Regardless of the application level, effective psychologists providing systems-based services establish positive collaborative relationships, assess strengths and weaknesses,

Table 5.1   Characteristics of Effective Organizational Development

1. Needs assessment

2. Goal setting

3. Management by objectives

4. Team building and collaboration

5. Training

6. Work design and redesign

7. A focus on changing the quantity and quality of behaviors

8. A *lack* of focus on changing individual attitudes (e.g., satisfaction)

9. Simultaneous multiple change efforts rather than focusing on one element

10. Outcomes evaluations

11. Feedback in both writing and oral presentations to administrators and stakeholders

reach a consensus regarding needs and goals, select and plan strategies, implement interventions, evaluate progress, and either reach closure or continue to address the same problem by incorporating evaluation results into future work. The list above should be very familiar to the reader in that these are the same steps described as essential to evidence-based practice in Chapter 4. The process is most productively perceived as circular, in which each component feeds into and affects the next.

Systems-based interventions require collaborative problem solving strategies and the enlistment of others (i.e., school administrators and teachers) in actual intervention implementation. The term *consultation* is normally used to describe work with teachers, administrators, and parents regarding individual students or targeted small groups of students. In contrast, systems-based service delivery occurs on a broad and often preventative level. For example, a school psychologist providing a systems-based intervention might work with parents, teachers, and administrators to develop and implement a more effective behavior management system for an entire school rather than for an individual student.

As does evidence-based practice at the individual level, good systems level work is characterized by selecting evidence-based interventions, applying them with integrity, and evaluating the outcomes. Measuring the results of systems-based work should focus both on *effectiveness* (the degree to which goals are accomplished) and *efficiency* (the degree to which goals are met in a cost- and time-effective manner). Carefully selecting appropriate measures is critical. As B. C. Tatum and Nebeker (2002) indicated,

> most organizations collect and process an enormous amount of data every day. Identifying things to measure is usually not the problem. The problem, more typically, is to convert the data into useful information that can be used to make decisions, plan, and act. (p. 698)

B. C. Tatum and Nebeker (2002) recommended that when there is a question regarding "what should be measured," the best strategy is to ask the "customer." However, schools have a wide assortment of "customers," including the state department of education, the local school board, parents, and students themselves. Supervisors are advised to consider the varied interests of all of these constituencies, as well as of the teachers and administrators in the district, as they select (or help supervisees select) data to gather during systems change programs. In addition, effective systems-based practice requires carefully following fundamental principles of planned change. While supervisors and supervisees alike can feel frustrated in taking the time necessary to adequately plan, in the end it is more cost effective than rushing into change without considering all variables, since "faster is slower" (Senge, 2006). During the *planning* stage, according to D. Brown and Trusty (2005), the school psychologist and/or supervisor should:

1. Obtain administrative support

2. Consider contracts, state regulations, and accreditation standards

3. Design a data gathering system to use before, during, and after change implementation

4. Begin using the data gathering system to obtain baseline data at, minimally, three time points to allow a time series analysis

5. Ensure that the proposed change is in accord with current school district goals

6. Ensure that proposed changes cost the same or less than current practice

7. Propose changes that will eventually maintain or diminish current workloads

8. Propose changes that minimally threaten and address issues of status or self-esteem

9. Adopt changes that can be easily explained to others

10. Develop a clear and focused plan of action

11. Explain the proposed changes to school personnel, parents, administrators, and community agencies so that all constituents understand what the changes would be, why they are being considered, what new services would be provided, and what services would no longer be provided

During the *implementation phase* of change, according to R. Allison (2002), the school psychologist and/or supervisor should:

1. Start small and seek ways to find measurable success

2. Encourage individuals to take risks and experiment, reinforcing the attitude that mistakes provide learning opportunities

3. Reward small efforts to move in the desired direction, being careful not to inadvertently punish the same

4. Avoid rewarding undesirable practices

5. Set clear and unambiguous expectations

6. Permit changes in structures (such as schedules) that allow adherence to the new model

7. Anticipate an implementation period of several years

8. Accept that new skills will not be learned in one trial and provide multiple opportunities to learn and obtain feedback

9. Not expect staff to relinquish old practices until they have mastered new skills

10. Encourage input, open communication, and participation in decision making

11. Anticipate and be tolerant of disagreement and discomfort

12. Understand and accept that staff will learn new skills in different ways and implement them at different rates

13. Continuously show staff the intended outcome and provide them with ongoing support until they reach their goals

14. Connect new skills literally and conceptually

15. Provide materials with which to practice new skills rather than expecting supervisees to develop them on their own

16. Provide time for practice and refinement

17. Carefully monitor implementation of innovative practices to ensure implementation integrity

18. Carefully select new staff who can support the innovative practice because of their orientation and skills

19. Take steps to align the innovation with existing concepts and procedures, such as job descriptions, evaluation procedures, accountability paperwork, program evaluations, and rubrics

During the *evaluation phase*, the school psychologist and/or supervisor evaluates the outcomes of the innovation by comparing the postintervention data with the data obtained during the planning phase. This requires program evaluation strategies, described in Chapter 4.

UNDERSTANDING AND WORKING WITH EDUCATIONAL SYSTEMS

To work effectively at the systems level, it is essential to understand the characteristics of the system in question. In truth, understanding schools-as-systems is pivotal in working effectively as a school psychologist. This means that both supervisors and school psychologists must learn about school district, state, and federal educational systems in general as well as of the specific school, district, and state in which they work.

For example, to understand schools-as-organizations, supervisors and supervisees must understand the perpetual clashing views on educational issues. Subscribing to and reading *Educational Week* is an extremely helpful method of better understanding schools, districts, and their interaction with state and federal events. Noll's (2008) anthology *Taking Sides: Clashing Views on Educational Issues* is a helpful overview of diametrically opposed viewpoints that have affected schools over the past 100 years, such as the ongoing debate over whether educational reform should focus on increasing collaboration and teaching for understanding (Darling-Hammond, 2001) or on traditional instruction to meet a prescribed "standard" curriculum (Hirsch, 1999).

It is also beneficial to read professional literature that considers schools-as-systems. Sarason's (1996) classic book *Revisiting "The Culture of School and the Problem of Change"* is an excellent starting point. He described schools from a "Martian's" perspective and in so doing vividly highlighted notable systemic issues. Schlechty's (2005) work, *Creating Great Schools: Six Critical Systems at the Heart of Educational Innovation*, raises awareness of the multiple microsystems that define a school's rules, roles, and relationships and therefore its organizational culture. Analysis of these microsystems can be used to ascertain each school's unique culture as it is defined by the individuals in the schools and by their subsystems, such as recruitment and induction, knowledge transmission, power and authority, evaluation, direction, and boundaries (Schlechty, 2005).

All effective organizations, including effective schools, have certain characteristics. These include smooth functioning, demonstrated by trust and freedom from conflict; stakeholder satisfaction; well-defined and appropriately measured goals; and successful acquisition of resources necessary to meet the goals (Cameron, 1980). A system's ability to interact with internal and external forces is another critical variable.

Systems that are too "closed" and unable to respond to new information can generate substantial tension because they do not adapt to change. Systems that are too "open" cannot screen information and "accept all input and try to response to everything, often with the same level of intensity" (Curtis et al., 2008, p. 890). Working effectively with schools-as-organizations involves considering each of these interacting systems and variables.

Vignette 5.2

The faculty of **Small Town Elementary School**, a relatively "open" system, pride themselves on being cutting edge. Although their students did very well learning writing skills when using writing workshops, they immediately adopted an unproven "new writing method" when it was introduced at a local workshop. In contrast, faculty at **Small Town Junior High School** are very hesitant about trying new methods and procedures. Some of their textbooks are so old that their students find their parents' names inside the front covers!

To determine the areas in which they might provide effective systems-based services, school psychologists must be well informed regarding the schools, districts, and communities in which they work. Some methods school psychologists can use to learn about schools, districts, and state educational systems include:

1. Reading the district curriculum guidelines
2. Reading the state curriculum frameworks
3. Reading the state special education regulations
4. Reviewing information on district and state Web sites regarding the school, district, and neighboring districts
5. Attending local school board meetings
6. Interviewing local school administrators
7. Attending state department of education meetings
8. Attending state legislature sessions at which educational or social issues are discussed
9. Carefully listening to parents, teachers, administrators, and students as they engage in discussions regarding strengths and areas of need
10. Observing in neighboring district schools to garner ideas
11. Observing in all types of schools in the district (preschools, elementary schools, middle schools, junior high schools, high schools, alternative schools, vocational schools, etc.) to become more aware both of challenges faced by students as they transition from one level to another and of available resources

Vignette 5.3

In the last chapter, we introduced the school psychologists in **Small City School System**, who were involved in a systemwide evaluation of special and general education services. As previously mentioned, the results were tabulated and distributed in paper copy and by oral presentation to all stakeholders. Then a collaborative team developed recommended goals, objectives, and action items to address repeatedly described areas of weakness. Because the indicators were worded positively, areas of weakness were positively framed. Using both outcome and process data lent substantial credence to the results. As might be expected, there were instances of distress and anxiety when particular schools were rated less positively than others. However, the positive nature of the questions and the positive focus of the program planning meetings minimized this effect. Since this evaluation focused on program improvement rather than compliance, it eventually resulted in profound, systemic changes in the district's approach to special education and inclusion of students with special education needs in general education classrooms.

CLASSROOMS

Classrooms are microcosms of the education world, and teachers often feel as though they are beleaguered members of these larger systems. Consequently, all of the readings mentioned above aid understanding of individual classrooms. In addition, it is helpful to explore each classroom as a system in itself, composed of additional interacting systems such as informal social groups, reading groups, and dyadic relationships among all members, including the teacher. Doll, Zucker, and Brehm (2004) provided useful strategies for analyzing the culture of an individual classroom and promoting positive social foundations that can foster optimal learning. Similarly, Dawson and Guare (2004) provided tools that encourage the development of teachers' executive functioning, thereby reducing stress in classrooms.

LEVELS OF SYSTEMS-BASED SERVICE DELIVERY: AN ILLUSTRATION

To illustrate the many levels at which systems-based service delivery can address a particular problem, we will consider a multifaceted approach to high-stakes testing. Currently there is considerable public interest in the assessment of all students' academic progress. This approach, mandated by the No Child Left Behind Act of 2001 (NCLB), requires assessments across multiple grade levels and has been made more challenging by students' increased diversity in terms of native language, learning style, emotional needs, disabilities, and socioeconomic background. Multiple intended and unintended outcomes are associated with such testing. At the student level, outcomes include placement decisions, promotion/retention decisions, and graduation opportunities, and disenfranchised groups have clearly been disproportionately affected (Reschly, 2006). At the school level, high-stakes tests affect teachers and administrators when successively more intrusive sanctions are imposed after schools fail to make adequate yearly progress in improving high-stakes test scores (Kruger, Wandle, & Struzziero, 2007). Furthermore, since scores are published in newspapers and on the Web, they impact the entire community at the most fundamental level—home values are affected, and the ensuing publicity fosters competition among grades, schools, and towns.

School psychologists can help educators address these unintended outcomes of high-stakes tests by employing a systems approach at multiple levels (Shriberg, 2007). As Kruger et al. (2007) suggested, a school psychologist might complete the following activities at the state, school, district, community, classroom, and student levels:

1. At the *state level*, school psychologists can work to establish strong and positive leadership to bring together relevant stakeholders, develop a common vision, foster shared language, and bring support services into integral roles (Gysbers, 2006). They can also work to promote an understanding of basic psychometric principles among individuals who design accountability systems.

2. At the *community level*, school psychologists can collaborate and communicate with parents and community members to ascertain dropout rates and other adverse effects of high-stakes testing. They can then systematically help parents and community agencies address the identified issues. For example, community members might be enlisted to provide library-based tutoring to students in need.

3. At the *school and district levels*, school psychologists can engage in systems level consultation with district administrators to identify and target problem areas using a problem solving team. The results of group testing can be used to determine strengths and weaknesses at the classroom, school, and district levels. Those determinations can be used to modify the curriculum and to develop methods to remediate deficits. Consultants can also encourage administrators to eliminate competition and comparisons among teachers by taking care in how scores are reported and fostering collaborative "whole school" goals and strategies, such as school-based positive behavior strategies.

4. At the *classroom level*, school psychologists can help by fostering both preventative strategies and specific test taking measures. Preventative measures include fostering resilient classrooms (Doll et al., 2004), implementing ongoing formative assessments of student achievement (e.g., Curriculum-Based Measurement) and using the results to form groups for targeted interventions, and helping individual teachers cope with the time demands of high-stakes tests (e.g., finding methods to "work smarter," such as using science books for reading instruction to meet demands for test preparation). Classroom-based strategies specific to test taking include helping teachers examine test results so that they can use them as informational tools and providing programs to address symptoms of stress.

5. At the *student level*, school psychologists can help identify and provide additional supports for students who are likely to perform poorly based on past performance and current performance. They can also educate all students regarding the importance of good test taking strategies, such as getting enough pretest sleep and employing techniques to monitor and cope with anxiety (Harvey & Chickie-Wolfe, 2007).

UNDERSTANDING AND WORKING WITH COMMUNITIES AND FAMILIES

Communities

Just as knowledge of the educational system informs effective school psychology services, school psychologists and their supervisors are most effective when they have a comprehensive understanding of the communities in which their students live. Such knowledge enables them to work more effectively with parents, students, and teachers because it fosters understanding. It also greatly facilitates their awareness of resources and in turn their ability to help network and attain services for students and their families.

Vignette 5.4

Every year **Perry**, who works in an impoverished neighborhood, takes his new practicum students and interns on tours of the community and visits local stores, places of worship, and community agencies. He also takes them with him on visits to students' homes. He finds that when his supervisees see how and where the students live, they gain invaluable knowledge. For many practicum students and interns, the experience is a real eye opener.

To obtain critical information about the local community, school psychologists and their supervisors should:

1. Maintain an active curiosity about the world in which the students live

2. Faithfully read local newspapers, visit the public library, scan the telephone book, review the community Web site, and contact information brokers such as information hotlines to better understand the community and ascertain local resources

3. Visit and interview community service providers commonly used by students and their families, such as the Boys & Girls Club, soup kitchens, and shelters

4. Interview local providers of medical and mental health services to ascertain resources and style

5. Attend local policymaking meetings, such as town meetings or city council meetings

6. Actively collaborate with community agencies to better serve students

---

Vignette 5.5

School psychologists in the **Nashua Public Schools** participate in "wraparound" meetings for students. During these meetings, representatives from every community agency involved with a student collaborate with the educational system, parents, and student to design improved services. Such collaboration helps schools and agencies inform one another of their services, responsibilities, and limitations. It also promotes problem solving and effective brainstorming. The results greatly enhance services for students (Harvey, 1995).

Families

Understanding individual families-as-systems benefits school psychologists for a number of reasons. Clearly, families have a tremendous influence on students, and enlisting family members as collaborators can have a profoundly positive effect. To facilitate this process, school psychologists should nurture their own ability to perceive parents as partners and become familiar with foundational literature in this field. Although few school psychologists are trained family therapists, they certainly can promote family-school partnerships by adopting a systems/ecological approach to learning problems, deliberately promoting partnerships with parents, and maintaining an "opportunity-oriented, persistent focus when working with families living in challenging circumstances" (Christenson, 2004, p. 83).

Although school psychologists should not attempt family therapy unless they obtain adequate training and supervision, much of the classic family therapy literature provides a helpful perspective that enables school psychologists to avoid the common pitfall of "blaming the parents." For example, Haley's (1985) *Problem Solving Therapy* provides concrete suggestions to foster systemic collaboration to promote student success. *Working With the Families of the Poor* by P. Minuchin, Colapinto, and Minuchin (1998) provides insights into working with families from socioeconomic classes far different from those of typical educators, while Pinderhughes (1989) provides a multicultural perspective that facilitates understanding of families from diverse backgrounds. Additional books of note include *Family Therapy: An Interactional Approach* (Andolfi, 1979); *Steps to an Ecology of Mind* (Bateson, 1972); *Family Therapy: A Systemic Integration* (Becvar & Becvar, 2000); *Family Therapy in Clinical Practice* (Bowen, 1988); *Intensive Structural Therapy: Treating Families in Their Social Context* (Fishman, 1993); *Family Therapy: An Intimate History* (Hoffman, 2002); *Integrating Family Therapy: Handbook of Family Psychology and Systems Theory* (Mikesell, Lusterman, & McDaniel, 1995); *Families and Family Therapy* (S. Minuchin, 1974); *The Family Crucible* (Napier & Whitaker, 1978); *The Process of Change* (Papp, 1983); *Family Therapy Sourcebook* (Piercy, Sprenkle, Wetchler, & Associates, 1996); *Metaphors of Family Systems Theory: Toward New Constructions* (Rosenblatt, 1994); and *Normal Family Processes* (Walsh, 2003).

The Futures Task Force on Family-School Partnerships (2007) has developed modules for training graduate students and practitioners with the intent of ensuring practitioners' inclusion of family members as integral partners in the education of their children. The task force used as its foundation the evidence-based interventions identified in the research literature (C. Carlson & Christenson, 2005) to develop these training modules and materials. Each module provides learning activities, interview forms for training and practice, data collection records, treatment plan summaries, videos, and relationship building goals. Various modules address consulting with families, working with families of preschool children, parent education programs, family intervention programs, and home-school partnerships. These modules are available through www.nasponline.org.

The *Overview Module* of the Futures Task Force on Family-School Partnerships addresses issues relevant to all areas of family-school work, such as multicultural issues and barriers to partnerships. The *Family-School Collaboration Module* was designed to help school psychologists improve family-school collaboration and focuses on developing shared responsibilities among parents and teachers for intervention outcomes. Interventions include positive school-home notes (Blechman, Taylor, & Schrader, 1981), a family literacy program (Morrow & Young, 1997), and involvement in parent-teacher action research (McConaughy, Kay, & Fitzgerald, 1999). The *Parent Involvement Module* targets changing academic achievement and focuses on addressing a single specific activity at a time. Examples of evidence-based approaches include parent tutoring (Duvall, Delquadri, Elliott, & Hall, 1992; Hook & DuPaul, 1999) and parent involvement meetings (Heller & Fantuzzo, 1993). The *Preschool Module* identifies evidence-based strategies for use with parents of preschoolers, such as *The Incredible Years Training Series* (Webster-Stratton, 2001), parent-child interaction therapy (Hembree-Kigin & McNeil, 1995), and dialogic reading (Whitehurst, Epstein, & Angell, 1994).

Parents are particularly appreciative of groups that supply them with information helpful in working with their children. For example, groups for parents of junior high school students appreciate a curriculum that focuses on parenting teenagers, and groups for parents of preschool special education students appreciate information about negotiating the special education system. Programs that help parents understand how to help their children with homework or prepare for high-stakes tests can be quite effective.

Vignette 5.6

Each school psychologist supervised by **Barbara Fischetti** in the Westport, Connecticut, School District holds biannual parent meetings by grade. In other words, all of the parents of third-graders are invited to two meetings per year, and all of the parents in each of the other grades have their own designated meetings. These meetings focus on developmental issues pertinent to children and adolescents. In addition to disseminating information, the meetings familiarize parents with their child's school psychologist and ease future parent–school psychologist communication. The district administrators supports these meetings because they have found them to be invaluable in fostering positive parent-school relationships.

Typically, parent education programs address broad typical developmental topics related to schooling and are geared toward a wider range of parents who come voluntarily to learn about a curriculum or developmental topic. The Futures Task Force on Family-School Partnerships (2007) module that focuses on training school psychologists to work in this domain includes evidence-based parent education programs such as Aware Parenting. This program focuses on increasing parental *support* (praising; encouraging; agreeing; showing affection), *attentiveness* (listening; encouraging sharing), *responsiveness* (acknowledging needs; demonstrating that the child is not alone and that the parent will be there), *guidance* (using effective teaching skills and behaviors; communicating clear expectations and predictable consequences), and *receptivity to emotions* (modeling, accepting, and encouraging expression of emotions and ideas).

The *Parent Consultation Module* of the Futures Task Force on Family-School Partnerships (2007) focuses on conjoint behavioral consultation (Sheridan, Kratochwill, & Bergan, 1996). It provides role-play activities, interview forms for training and practice, data collection records, treatment plan summaries, videos, and relationship building goals that are appropriate for use with parents of children at the prereferral or postreferral level.

The *Families Interventions Module* of the Futures Task Force on Family-School Partnerships (2007) focuses on specific concerns and conditions that interfere with schooling. Typically these programs are used for students who need intensive interventions. The facilitator must have specific training in the technique, and the content must be yoked to relationship process and social learning principles. An example of an evidence-based family intervention program is parent management training, which trains parents in observing and recording behavior, giving positive reinforcements for appropriate behaviors, assigning time-out from reinforcement, deliberately attending to versus using planned ignoring, addressing school issues, problem solving, using family meetings, attending to low-rate behaviors, and effectively reprimanding, compromising, and negotiating.

Supervisors must help their supervisees address the common barriers encountered in working with families (Christenson, 2004). A number of multicultural issues are of significance, and the reader is referred to Chapter 3, but in general, supervisors can address many common structural and psychological barriers by:

1. Obtaining a commitment from administrators to sponsor school psychologists' work with families through resource allocation (e.g., permitting school psychologists to allocate work time to evening hours and funding necessary expenditures for such things as supplies and janitorial coverage).

2. Setting goals regarding the provision of parent education programs, family-school partnerships, and other family work for both the department and individual supervisees and including such work in both job descriptions and performance evaluations.

3. Training school psychologists in evidence-based practices in home-school collaboration.

4. Addressing common difficulties such as time and child care constraints. For example, supervisors can encourage supervisees to routinely offer parent meetings both at midday and in the evening, provide time-limited sessions, and provide necessary child care by service-learning students.

5. Providing close clinical supervision for inexperienced supervises. Conducting parent groups can be intimidating for those inexperienced in this activity! Coleading a group is an effective method of supporting and training inexperienced supervisees, although care must be taken to encourage supervisees to take an active leadership role.

6. Addressing school psychologists as parents. Young school psychologists who are not parents themselves might find their expertise challenged by parents. Supervisors should help supervisees develop a ready response to such challenges. In contrast, supervisees who are themselves parents may find themselves bringing their personal issues into their work with parents, and supervisors will need to help them deal with this tendency. For example, a supervisee who is parenting or has parented an acting-out, drug-involved teenager is likely to have difficulty preventing countertransference issues from affecting his or her work with parents of teenagers.

APPRAISING CHANGE

As discussed in Chapter 4, an essential component of implementing an intervention is determining whether it is effective. This is true for systems-based services as well as those targeting individual students. It is essential to determine a method to provide formative and summative evaluation of systems-based interventions. When measuring the effectiveness of systems-based interventions, one would like to ascertain that the process has had a positive impact on student functioning. During the appraisal phase, the school psychologist and/or supervisor should:

1. Assess the impact of the innovation

2. Recognize and evaluate positive and negative unintended effects of the innovation

3. Reinforce established change to encourage maintenance

The last step, reinforcing established change to encourage maintenance, is extremely important. Without ongoing maintenance, even the most effective changes can quickly disappear with normal staff changes. School psychologists cannot assume that a systems-change program will be sustained simply because it has proven effective. To become institutionalized, change requires supportive planning over a period of 3 to 5 years (Rosenfield, 1992) and must be integrated into the schools' (and districts') budgets, personnel roles, and processes (Knoff, 2000).

Vignette 5.7

Sarah was very proud of having instituted a very successful program in her elementary school during the 5 years before her retirement. She had trained paraprofessionals to conduct Curriculum-Based Measurement thrice yearly and then provide extra reading groups for targeted students. By the third grade, 98% of the children were reading on grade level, there was an extraordinary decrease in referrals for special education, and behavior problems had decreased as well. After having been retired for 6 years, Sarah returned to the elementary school and was shocked to find that the program had completely disappeared. "I thought I had built a program that would last!"

Knoff (2008) recommended that school psychologists act as though "the school year starts in April" and take the last few months of every academic year to plan the transition to the next year. Whenever new staff are hired who are accustomed to "old" methods from previous positions, they need to be trained and supported in the new practices.

Vignette 5.8

Gracia spent several years developing and implementing a successful instructional consultation team at Friendly Elementary School. She then moved to another city. Fifteen years later at a NASP convention, she happened to meet **Roy**, the school psychologist currently working at Friendly School. Gracia was stunned when Roy excitedly told her that he was beginning a new program—an instructional consultation team! It turned out that in the intervening years many of the older teachers had retired. The school psychologist who had immediately succeeded Gracia had a background as a clinical neuropsychologist and was not familiar with instructional consultation. No one had trained either the new faculty or the new psychologist in this approach, and it had disappeared during the intervening years!

Furthermore, many systems-based interventions are *preventative* in nature, and it is very challenging to measure the effects of preventative efforts. Nonetheless, evaluation of preventative efforts is critical; if it does not occur, the programs often become invisible to administrators and consequently very difficult to sustain. They can be quite vulnerable to elimination due to budget cuts or the next educational fad. Supervisors of school psychological services are therefore challenged to build an assessment infrastructure that maintains information regarding student academic and behavioral outcomes relative to systems-based policies and practices. The heart of such assessment infrastructures is program evaluation, described in Chapter 4. Useful tools to evaluate systems interventions and in-service presentations have been developed by Sawyer Hunley from the University of Dayton and are found in Handouts 5.1 and 5.2.

Handout 5.1

EVALUATION OF SYSTEMS INTERVENTION

Teacher _____   School _____   Grade _____   Date _____

	Very Inappropriate	Inappropriate	Adequate	Appropriate	Very Appropriate
Conducts needs assessment	1	2	3	4	5
Selects evidence-based intervention	1	2	3	4	5
Designs intervention plan	1	2	3	4	5
Implements plan	1	2	3	4	5
Monitors intervention progress	1	2	3	4	5
Evaluates plan	1	2	3	4	5
Conducts follow-up	1	2	3	4	5
Collaborates with others in all phases	1	2	3	4	5

Handout 5.2

EVALUATION OF IN-SERVICE PRESENTATION

Psychologist: _____

School: _____

Topic: _____

Date Completed: _____

	Very Inappropriate	*Inappropriate*	*Adequate*	*Appropriate*	*Very Appropriate*
Collaborates in brainstorming possible needs for in-service	1	2	3	4	5
Designs needs assessment	1	2	3	4	5
Conducts needs assessment	1	2	3	4	5
Plans in-service	1	2	3	4	5
Prepares in-service	1	2	3	4	5
Prepares evaluation tool	1	2	3	4	5
Delivers in-service	1	2	3	4	5
Conducts evaluation of in-service	1	2	3	4	5
Summarizes results of evaluation	1	2	3	4	5

SUMMARY

School psychologists often work at the systems level in their work with classrooms, schools, families, and communities. Although challenging, such work can be quite rewarding, since it provides opportunities to effect profound change. These challenges require that school psychologists receive considerable supervisory support and opportunities for professional development.

School psychology has a long history of recommending a systems perspective. Systems-based services are necessary because students' learning problems belong not only to students, but also to the systems—the schools, families, neighborhoods, and communities—in which students live and learn. These systems are pivotal in students' success and failure. School psychologists' work at the systems level can be manifested in many arenas. Because of the many associated challenges, school psychologists must understand principles of organizational change when working within a systems perspective.

School psychologists and their supervisors must gain a comprehensive understanding of the communities in which their students live. School psychologists should also have an understanding of school district, state, and federal educational systems in general as well as of the specific school, district, and state in which the school psychologist is working. This includes knowledge of disagreements in the field over various educational issues. School psychologists must also understand classrooms, both as systems in themselves and as microcosms of the education world. They can assist local school administrators and state departments of education with a number of issues, including the unintended outcomes of high-stakes tests.

School psychologists also need to understand families-as-systems in order to understand individual children and enlist family members as collaborators. The Futures Task Force on Family-School Partnerships has assisted in this pursuit by using evidence-based interventions to develop training modules and materials intended for use in professional development programs and graduate training coursework.

As with systems-based work, systems-based supervision focuses on a search for patterns, hierarchical ordering of facts by complexity, and a holistic approach, with a simultaneous emphasis on theory and empirical investigation. Supervision is active, directive, and collaborative and addresses multiple embedded systems. Supervisors assist with the planning and implementation of change while also supervising family-school partnerships.

REFLECTIVE QUESTIONS

Q5.1. Describe the various systems by which students are influenced.

Q5.2. How do barriers to implementing evidence-based practices relate to systems-based practice?

Q5.3. What are the characteristics of effective organizational development?

Q5.4. How can school psychologists and their supervisors gain and maintain an understanding of the communities in which their students live?

Q5.5. What are some strategies that school psychologists can use to learn about specific schools and educational systems?

Q5.6. How can we understand families-as-systems and enlist family members as collaborators?

Q5.7. How can school psychologists provide assistance with high-stakes testing at the state, community, school and district, classroom, and student levels?

Q5.8. What have been the contributions of the Futures Task Force on Family-School Partnerships in helping school psychologists strengthen school-family collaboration?

Q5.9. How can supervisors address the barriers to successful school-family partnerships?

SUPERVISORY DILEMMAS

SD 5.1

The high-stakes testing program assesses students in the 4th, 8th, and 10th grades and has indicated that many fourth-grade students have significant academic deficiencies in multiple areas. Because of concerns about adverse publicity, the principal has suggested that poorly performing, at-risk students be considered for retention in the third grade. She feels that the extra year will boost scores and help the school avoid being adversely labeled. She has asked for your opinion as the supervising school psychologist. *What are the supervisory considerations? What should be done?*

Authors' thoughts: Unfortunately, the pressures of high-stakes testing may result in reactions that are both ineffective and shortsighted. It is obvious that this situation demands a forceful and proactive response on the part of the school psychologist, who is uniquely positioned to provide both guidance and support. The research literature is clear that retention does not typically benefit students and must be used minimally as an intervention geared toward an individual versus a group. In this scenario, any "positive effects" (e.g., higher test scores) would be, at best, both short term and misleading. The purpose of high-stakes testing is to do exactly what it did—uncover points of curricular weakness that can be addressed and remediated. Initial responses would be to (a) share the literature regarding retention, (b) help develop a plan to examine and rework the curricula for the first three grades (this is not just a third-grade problem!), and (c) help the principal to better understand the benefits and challenges of high-stakes testing. It certainly appears that the principal would profit from some moral support in dealing with the effects of bad publicity.

SD 5.2

After several years, you realize that the expectations for the school psychologist in one building are quite different from the expectations held at the district office. The principal feels that the primary responsibility of the school psychologist is to recommend that students be removed from his school and sent to a different school for special education placement. In contrast, the director of special education perceives that a school psychologist's primary responsibility is to develop programs that will keep students in their neighborhood schools. Your supervisee is tired of being caught in the middle and turns to you for help. *What are the supervisory considerations? What should be done?*

Authors' thoughts: This is a difficult yet probably familiar situation. The reality is that school psychologists do, in fact, serve many masters. As clearly stated in ethical principles, school psychologists always attempt to resolve situations of conflicting interests in a manner that is mutually beneficial while always considering the student(s) to be the primary client(s). When organizational demands conflict with ethical responsibilities, the school psychologist must always make it clear that actions must be dictated by ethical obligations. It is possible that the principal may not understand how it benefits most students with special education needs to remain in their neighborhood schools. Alternatively, it is possible that the principal has observed that students in special education are accorded ineffective or insufficient services within a general education setting. Hence, further information must be sought to determine underlying factors. An appropriate starting point might be for the school psychologist, director of special education, and principal to meet in order to jointly address mutual concerns.

SD 5.3

As a supervising school psychologist, you realize that neither federal nor state laws actually require a full assessment battery for 3-year reevaluations. The district, however, requires that school psychologists conduct 3-year reevaluations identical to initial evaluations, which have the following components: classroom observation, functional behavior assessment, parent interview, teacher interview, individual intelligence test, individual achievement test, and clinical interview. Because 25% of the school-aged population is identified as eligible for special education services, these extensive reevaluations consume an extremely high percentage of school psychologists' time. The members of the school psychology department feel that their time would be better spent providing direct services to students, parents, and teachers. *What are the supervisory considerations? What should be done?*

Authors' thoughts: The best interest of the students must mediate the response to this situation. The current model of service delivery is clearly both regressive and ineffective. A collective action plan that mobilizes the districts' school psychologists should be considered. Neither their time nor efforts are well spent in the above scenario. Introduction of a prevention model should be the first apparent step. A request for funding to investigate implementing a response to intervention model might be a viable proposal. Overall, these school psychologists have an unparalleled opportunity to initiate systems level change for the benefit of students. Such a paradigmatic shift is achieved slowly and with an enormous investment of time and energy. It can be argued that it would be well worth it in this case.

6

Ethical and Legal Issues

Ethical dilemmas are so prevalent in public schools that every practitioner encounters them on a regular basis, regardless of years of experience.

Vignette 6.1

As supervisor **Dottie** reports, "I have been working for more than 20 years, I teach ethics to my interns, and I still need to consult with colleagues about ethical situations that arise constantly! This is the main reason I keep participating in peer supervision every other week."

As Bowser (1995) indicated, many ethical principles appear to be "common sense" that

> sound easy enough in the abstract, from the comfort of one's favorite reading chair. But the real world is full of organizational pressures, conflicting regulations, and personal challenges that can very quickly make fuzzy and grey the sharp, black-and-white distinctions found in a book. (p. 33)

All ethical and legal issues pertinent to the practice of school psychology are also pertinent to the supervision of school psychologists. Supervisors must address complicated and intricate ethical issues across the entire administration-supervisor-client chain (Falender & Shafranske, 2004). They are responsible for ensuring that supervisees are well versed in the ethical and legal issues relevant to the practice of school psychology and that they recognize and successfully resolve ethical dilemmas as encountered. They are also responsible for serving as role models of ethical practice.

Professional licensure and certification are often tied to adherence to professional codes of ethical conduct, even if the psychologist is not a member of relevant professional organizations (Clarke, 2006). Additionally, Nationally Certified School Psychologists are required to adhere to the principles of the National Association of School Psychologists (NASP) even if they are not active members of NASP. In many states, psychologists who hold licenses from licensing boards are required to annually accrue 3 hours of professional development regarding ethical issues to maintain their licenses as are NCSPs. In contrast, school psychologists licensed or certified by state departments of education may not be mandated to accrue professional development focusing on ethics.

Consequently, supervisors of school psychologists may be challenged to meet their obligation to ensure that their supervisees practice ethically; neither the licensing/ certification bodies nor the workplace cultivates ethical knowledge, yet ethical practice is mandated. This chapter provides an overview of ethical guidelines and legal mandates relevant to the supervision of psychological services in schools. It also provides guidelines for ethical decision making, provides suggestions regarding teaching ethical principles to supervisees, offers contextually based ethical dilemma problem solving strategies, and addresses how to appraise the ethical practice of supervision.

BASIC CONSIDERATIONS

Ethical Codes

Both NASP (2000a) and the American Psychological Association (APA; 2002) promote codes of ethics. Unlike the field of counseling psychology (Center for Credentialing and Education, 2001; Supervision Interest Network, 1993), school psychology has not developed a code of ethics specific to supervision. Nonetheless, a number of ethical principles and legal mandates specifically affect the practice of supervision.

Supervisors are ethically responsible on multiple levels: to their clients, to their supervisees, to the public, and to the profession (Storm & Haug, 1997). Because supervisors' decisions have an ethical impact on students, supervisees, the public, and the profession, supervisors must consider all of these elements as they resolve or help resolve ethical dilemmas.

Ethical Violations

Adhering to ethical principles is difficult in that laws conflict with one another, ethics conflict with laws, and laws and ethics conflict with personal values. Psychologists indicate that they break the law and violate ethical code when their personal belief system is at variance.

> **Vignette 6.2**
>
> **Roberto's** supervisee **Uma** raised an ethical dilemma that was causing her severe insomnia. Uma had been providing individual counseling for several months to **Mark**, a fourth-grader who lived with his father and stepmother. Mark's birth mother had recently come to the school and tearfully asked Uma for news of how Mark was doing. Since Uma knew that Mark's mother had lost legal custody of Mark to his father 2 months before, she knew that she was ethically and legally obligated to refuse to disclose any information to Mark's mother. On the other hand, refusing to talk with his mother was in direct conflict with Uma's fundamental beliefs regarding the mother-child bond. As Uma said to Roberto, "How can it be right to refuse to discuss a child with his *mother?*"

Research has revealed that breaches of ethical behavior are distressingly common on the part of psychologists, psychology interns, and supervisors. Pope and Vasquez (1998) and Pope and Vetter (1992) found that the ethical violations reported most often by psychologists tend to be violations of confidentiality, dual relationships, and problems with payment sources. In contrast, the breaches of ethical behavior most often cited by licensing boards tend to be dual (simultaneous personal and professional) relationships and negligent, unethical, or unprofessional practice.

According to Worthington, Tan, and Poulin (2002), psychologists in training jeopardize their own and their supervisors' professional reputations and standing by committing the following violations:

1. Deliberately withholding information from the supervisor that affects their practice and therefore should be addressed in supervision, such as errors or problems (76% reported having withheld this information at least once and 6% reported having withheld this information relatively often), impairing personal problems (47% at least once, 6% relatively often), sexual attraction to clients (45% at least once, 6% relatively often), and strong personal reactions to clients (63% at least once, 3% relatively often)

2. Failing to consult on high-risk cases, such as self-injurious behaviors (20% reported having done this at least once and 1% reported having done this relatively often)

3. Failing to maintain complete, accurate, and up-to-date documentation that indicates that appropriate professional decisions have been made and appropriate care has been provided (85% reported having done this at least once and 22% reported having done this relatively often)

4. Failing to disclose insufficient knowledge or skills to the supervisor and consequently not obtaining appropriate guidance and support (20% to 32% reported having done this at least once and 1% reported having done this relatively often)

5. Failing to disclose their status as a psychologist in training to students or parents (15% reported having done this at least once and 1% reported having done this relatively often)

6. Failing to disclose personal bias regarding clients' religion, race, gender, or sexual orientation (23% to 33% reported having done this at least once and 1% to 1.5% reported having done this relatively often)

7. Using inappropriate methods to deal with supervisor-supervisee conflicts, such as passively or actively refusing to follow directives (48% reported having done this at least once and 3% reported having done this relatively often), obtaining "pseudo" supervision from other supervisors or supervisees (38% at least once, 4% relatively often), gossiping to others about the conflict (83% at least once, 27% relatively often), or making negative statements about the supervisor (28% at least once, 3% relatively often)

8. Violating policies or rules, such as inflating hours of work with clients or supervision hours on reporting forms (32% reported having done this at least once and 1% reported having done this relatively often)

9. Neglecting to engage in supervisor-prescribed professional development activities, such as reading assigned materials (84% reported having neglected to do this at least once and 19% reported having neglected to do this relatively often) or attending meetings, workshops, or training seminars (88% at least once, 31% relatively often)

The most frequent reasons supervisees gave for making these violations were the desire to avoid confrontation, feeling ashamed of errors, a tendency to procrastinate, trying to do what is right, and a heavy workload (Worthington et al., 2002).

According to their supervisees, supervisors are also fairly likely to commit ethical violations. In two studies, one conducted by Ladany, Lehrman-Waterman, Molinaro, and Wolgast (1999) and the other conducted by Worthington et al. (2002), approximately 50% of supervisees reported that their supervisors did not always adhere to ethical principles in that they failed to adequately monitor supervisee activities, provide performance evaluations, adhere to confidentiality regarding supervision, or refrain from providing supervision in areas in which they were not well versed. The majority of supervisees did not discuss these violations with their supervisors, which is not surprising, given the evaluative role that supervisors play. Worthington et al. found that 12% of supervisees often observed but failed to address supervisors' unethical behavior and that 41% did the same at least once.

Even though both APA and NASP require monitoring of ethical behavior by other psychologists, even for nonsupervisees the mandate for peer monitoring is a particularly difficult ethical guideline to follow. Although concerns are supposed to be first addressed informally through direct conversation with the person violating the ethical mandate, if this conversation does not resolve the concern, psychologists are required to refer to the professional ethics committee of a professional organization, the state licensing board, and/or appropriate administrators. Psychologists are cognizant of these guidelines yet tend to be very uncomfortable with the obligation. Pope, Tabachnick, and Keith-Spiegel (1987) found that many psychologists are unwilling to report ethical violations to authorities. Tryon (2001) found that fewer than 50% of advanced graduate students felt prepared to deal with peers' ethical violations.

APPLICATIONS TO SUPERVISION

It is the supervisor's responsibility to help supervisees successfully resolve the inevitable ethical conflicts that arise almost constantly from organizational pressures, conflicting regulations, personal challenges, and time constraints. General ethical responsibilities of supervisors include fostering the ability of supervisees to make appropriate ethical decisions, ensuring that supervisees practice legally and ethically, accepting ultimate responsibility for services provided by clinical supervisees, and continually learning about ethical and legal issues. Supervisors are obligated to take reasonable steps to ensure that supervisees perform services responsibly, competently, and ethically. A lack of knowledge of the ethical principles and laws does not exempt a supervisor from responsibility.

Supervisors should be thoroughly familiar with NASP's (2000a) *Professional Conduct Manual*, APA's (2002) *Ethical Principles*, and S. Jacob and Hartshorne's (2007) *Ethics and Law for School Psychologists*. Haynes, Corey, and Moulton (2003) included excellent chapters regarding ethical considerations in supervision within their book *Professional Supervision in the Helping Professions: A Practical Guide*. Because ethical practice also reflects state and federal law, supervisors should additionally be well versed in pertinent special education laws, such as the Individuals With Disabilities Education Improvement Act of 2004 (IDEA 2004); state special education standards; and laws pertinent to providing multiculturally informed school psychological services (Oakland & Gallegos, 2005). They should also be well versed in state laws pertinent to the provision of mental health services; this information is available in the Law and Mental Health Professionals book series published by APA (e.g., Brandt, 1998).

In addition to reading the above books, it is helpful for supervisors to attend at least one workshop focusing on ethical or legal issues annually and to develop a "buddy" relationship with another school psychology supervisor, within or outside the school district, with whom they can consult regarding ethical dilemmas. Further, supervisors should develop a relationship with a school district or city/town attorney interested in education and special education so that she or he is readily available to consult regarding legal issues.

Ethical responsibilities of supervisors vary according to the level of the supervisee and the power the supervisor has over the supervisee. Practicum students and interns naturally require the most intense supervision. Furthermore, since they are not yet licensed or certified, the clinical supervisor is ethically and legally responsible and therefore vicariously liable for their practice.

Supervisors are less liable for the practice of licensed beginning school psychologists, yet they often must facilitate novice school psychologists' ability to perceive and respond appropriately to ethical dilemmas. Seasoned school psychologists, who need a supervisor's support as they develop professionally and move from competent to expert, often need support as they struggle to balance professional ethical mandates, school system expectations, and their own personal beliefs. Regardless of the school psychologist's experience level, *ultimate legal responsibility and liability lie with the individual who is in a position to hire and fire the individual.*

GENERAL ETHICAL PRINCIPLES

Many professions maintain codes of ethics that are used to inform recommended practice. These vary somewhat according to the expectations of the profession. For example, the ethical code of APA (2002) identifies five core principals of ethical behavior: beneficence and nonmaleficence; fidelity and responsibility; integrity, justice, and respect for people's rights; and dignity. The code of conduct for teachers, passed by the National Education Association (1975), focuses on protecting students' freedom to learn and maintaining ethical and professional standards in teaching. Ethical codes for educational leaders and administrators have been identified by relevant professional organizations, such as the American Association of School Administrators and the Association for Supervision and Curriculum Development. These codes tend to focus on the ethical paradigms of justice, critique, care, and the profession, with students' best interest being the overriding consideration (S. J. Gross & Shapiro, 2004; J. P. Shapiro & Stefkovich, 2001; Stefkovich, 2006).

S. Jacob and Hartshorne (2007) identified four core areas of significance to the ethical practice of school psychologists. These include (a) maintaining integrity in professional relationships, (b) respecting the dignity of persons and protecting the welfare of all, (c) responsible caring and providing competent services, and (d) demonstrating responsibility to the community and society. These core areas are appropriate to consider when addressing ethical and legal issues relevant to the supervision of school psychological services.

Maintain Integrity in Professional Relationships

Integrity in professional relationships is manifested in every professional interaction. As much as possible, supervisors are ethically bound to treat supervisees and children and adolescents fairly, equally, and with respect. An excellent vehicle for maintaining integrity within the supervisory relationship is the written supervision contract.

Effective supervisors are careful to avoid personal (dual) relationships with supervisees that may either impair their ability to judge and evaluate the supervisee accurately or place the supervisee at risk of exploitation. Examples of dual relationships are friendships, social relationships, romantic relationships, and relationships by blood or marriage. Avoiding dual relationships is not always easy and can be particularly problematic in rural or otherwise "small" communities (e.g., a neighborhood in an urban environment) where supervisees and supervisors are likely to share social circles (Helbok, Marinelli, & Walls, 2006). An important strategy in dealing with this issue is to discuss it openly at the beginning of the supervisory relationship.

A blatant example of an inappropriate dual relationship is a sexual relationship between a supervisor and supervisee. Research literature from the fields of clinical and counseling psychology indicates that between 6% and 16% of psychologists have had sexual relationships with supervisees. Although the majority thought these relationships were consensual at the time, in hindsight most supervisees felt some level of coercion. Preexisting couples should not enter into supervisory relationships, and if any relationship emerges during supervision, a new supervisor should be assigned. If this is not possible, the supervisor and supervisee should document their work together and hire a second supervisor to evaluate the supervisee's work (J. M. Bernard & Goodyear, 2004).

Another example of an inappropriate dual relationship occurs when an individual attempts to simultaneously provide supervision and therapy. While it is a responsibility of supervisors to help supervisees identify personal issues that interfere with their work, it is up to the supervisee to obtain appropriate help to resolve them. Supervisors should be careful not to act as a supervisee's therapist (Whiston & Emerson, 1989). To minimize the likelihood of inappropriate dual relationships, Gottlieb, Robinson, and Younggren (2007) recommended the strategies included in Handout 6.1.

Handout 6.1

MINIMIZING DUAL RELATIONSHIPS

(Gottlieb, Robinson, & Younggren, 2007)[1]

1. Openly discuss power differentials in the supervisory relationship.

2. Do not attempt to develop an egalitarian relationship with a supervisee.

3. Focus on fiduciary responsibilities.

4. Emphasize evaluative functions.

5. Directly address the risks of dual relationships.

6. Provide examples of acceptable (e.g., a supervisor and supervisee jointly presenting at a workshop) and unacceptable (e.g., a supervisor and supervisee engaging in an intimate relationship) dual relationships.

7. Minimize the number of roles a supervisor plays.

8. Develop procedures in advance for dealing with situations that arise unexpectedly (e.g., a supervisee suddenly in need of therapy).

9. Encourage group supervision.

10. Increase supervisee power by appointing an ombudsperson who is not an employee and who has direct access to administration.

11. Both formally (through in-service workshops) and informally (through modeling) reinforce a culture with relational boundaries.

12. Keep supervision records.

13. Before entering into even an acceptable dual relationship, consider whether it could be avoided, potentially cause harm, possibly be of benefit, or adversely affect the evaluative role. Additionally, consult with a colleague to maximize the possibility that perceptions regarding these points are accurate.

---

[1]Gottlieb, M. C., Robinson, K., & Younggren, J. N. (2007). Multiple relations in supervision: Guidance for administrators, supervisors, and students. *Professional Psychology: Research and Practice, 38,* 241–247.

Respect the Dignity of Persons and Protect the Welfare of All

Adhering to this principle involves respecting the human rights of all individuals, including supervisees, children, teachers, and parents. The welfare of the child supersedes all else, but the rights of others must also be considered. In a general sense, this means that supervisors should make every effort to do no harm, affirm supervisees' and students' rights to make autonomous decisions (as long as they do not infringe upon the rights of others), ensure that supervisory actions benefit both supervisees and students, treat supervisees and their students fairly and equally, and act in a manner that is truthful, loyal, and reliable (Storm & Haug, 1997). This fundamental principle ensures that school psychologists and their supervisors protect individuals' rights to autonomy, confidentiality, due process, nondiscrimination, privacy, and self-determination. Consultees and students (or parents, in the case of children) have the right to request or refuse services, to protect the release of information about themselves, and to be informed of potential or alternative services. They should also be informed regarding grievance procedures and whether they will be included in program evaluations or research. These issues should be routinely discussed with supervisees, and supervisors should similarly ensure that supervisees routinely discuss them with students, parents, administrators, and consultees.

Respect Autonomy and Self-Determination

This ethical principle is founded on the concept that individuals have the right to autonomously decide what happens to them. Obtaining informed consent is an essential component of adhering to the fundamental principle of respecting individuals. The presumption is that legal guardians, most often parents, have the right to decide what happens to their minor children. In order for consent to be informed, as Reamer (2004) indicated:

- Coercion cannot play a role in obtaining the consent
- Individuals giving consent must be able to understand the language used
- Consent must be given for specific, not general, procedures
- Students (or parents) must be able to refuse or withdraw consent at any time
- Consent must be based on adequate information

Informed Consent for Assessment

When school psychologists obtain informed consent to conduct a psychoeducational assessment, they must provide complete information as specified in IDEA 2004. As Bersoff (1973/2003) indicated, it is helpful when informed consent includes "coadvisement," during which the school psychologist informs the student and parents

> how he functions; informs them of the identity of the referral agent and the purpose for referral; and describes the nature of the assessment devices he will use, the merits and limitations of those devices, what kinds of information will be put in a report, and who might eventually read the report. (p. 296)

In employing coadvisement, the psychologist also asks the student and parents for their perceptions of the purpose and potential consequences of the assessment. At the end of the assessment session or sessions the psychologist shares his or her initial impressions with the student and parents and provides the opportunity to disagree or agree with these impressions as well as to provide further insights. After the assessment is completed and the report written, the psychologist meets with the parents and student to share a copy of the written report and orally interpret the results and recommendations. This provides the opportunity for them to provide additional information. If the parents, student, and psychologist have differing opinions, they can use this opportunity to either reach consensus or develop a dissenting opinion. To effectively meet these coadvisement suggestions, it will be necessary to revise the information presented in the typical consent forms designed to meet legal requirements.

Informed Consent for Treatment

Supervisors ensure that supervisees obtain informed consent before implementing interventions such as individual counseling, group counseling, or behavior intervention plans outside the scope of the general education program. Consent must be attained from legal guardians and should be accompanied by assent on the part of the student. Consent and assent forms should be acquired at the beginning of the treatment and include the type, logistics, and limits of treatment; the potential risks of the treatment; alternative treatments available; the duty of the school psychologist to warn and intervene in dangerous situations; the limits of confidentiality; groups and individuals with whom diagnostic and clinical information will be shared (e.g., Medicaid); the possibility of consultation with colleagues and the supervisor; the possibility of observations by the supervisor; and the possibility of audiotaping or videotaping, how tapes will be used, and how and when tapes will be destroyed.

Privileged Communication

Supervisors should determine and inform students and parents of whether students' communications with school psychologists are privileged and protected from legal proceedings. This varies from state to state; in some states psychologists are required to report crimes already committed and the intention to commit crimes. In other states, school psychologists do not have a legal obligation to report a committed crime unless it involves an act for which reporting is mandated (e.g., child abuse; S. Jacob & Hartshorne, 2007). Supervisors should also ensure that their supervisees inform clients of the limitations to their privilege at the onset of their work with them. This is particularly important with adolescents, who may inform school psychologists of their intent to commit crimes such as selling or distributing illicit drugs.

Vignette 6.3

During school psychology intern **Paula**'s group therapy session for boys with anger management issues, one group member, **Eddie**, was identified as a "mule" for a local drug dealer. Eddie confirmed (somewhat proudly!) that he distributed drugs to other students and, in exchange, was given cocaine for his personal use. He boasted that these transactions didn't take place at or near the school and that the "police will *never* catch him." He also stated that he did not feel he was doing anything wrong or harmful to others. However, two other group members privately expressed concern to Paula regarding the extent of Eddie's drug use and the fact that he often drove his younger brother around town while under the influence of drugs. Furthermore, the principal had announced that there would be increased police surveillance, employment of drug-sniffing dogs, and security cameras placed on the school grounds due to a marked increase in local drug arrests. She had asked for the cooperation of all faculty members in stemming the epidemic of drug use in the schools.

Informed Consent for Psychologists in Training

Whenever informed consent is sought for work to be conducted by a practicum student or intern, it is important to explicitly state that the psychologist is in training. The supervisor's contact information should be provided, and the consent form should indicate that the psychologist in training is likely to consult the supervisor and which supervision techniques will be used, particularly if they might be considered intrusive (i.e., include taping). The consent form should also indicate whether the supervisor is directly available to the parents or students and under what emergency situations the supervisor will be involved. Handout 6.2 contains a sample form.

It can be helpful for supervisors to attend the meetings at which informed consent is obtained regarding services from a psychologist in training to alleviate parental anxiety, to clarify supervisory processes, and to ensure communication clarity (J. M. Bernard & Goodyear, 2004).

Informed Consent From Trainees and Interns

The principle of informed consent also applies to trainees, who must be fully informed of the parameters of their training. For example, applicants to school psychology programs should know the evaluation methods used throughout the program and internship prior to matriculation. They should also know whether they might be required to participate in individual or group counseling as a training component. Similarly, interns and school psychologists should clearly understand both their own and their supervisors' responsibilities. These responsibilities should be included in written program materials and supervision contracts.

Program Evaluations and Research

Maintaining records regarding the progress that students make in response to academic or social-emotional-behavioral interventions is an integral aspect of quality treatment and does not need additional consent beyond the informed treatment consent. However, if the records are to be aggregated and used for research purposes other than archival data collection and program analysis, additional consent must be obtained. This is essential when the aggregated data will be used to generalize results to other populations for publication (Ogles, Lambert, & Masters, 1996).

Before such research is conducted, it must be approved by appropriate administrators (i.e., the district superintendent and/or the university's institutional review board). The approval should be in response to a written proposal that states (a) the researcher or researchers' names and contact information; (b) beginning and ending dates; (c) the rationale for the study; (d) the proposed methodology, including sample assessment tools; (e) HIPAA (Health Insurance Portability and Accountability Act of 1996) and confidentiality compliance information; (f) anticipated participants and sampling information; (g) procedures to protect vulnerable populations, such as students under 18 and students with disabilities; (h) potential risks and benefits to participants; (i) methods to obtain informed consent, including sample consent and assent forms; and (j) procedures to maintain confidentiality of records. The assent (for students under 18) and consent (for parents of minors and students over 18) forms must include the information included in Handout 6.3.

A sample consent form to be used for program evaluations and research can be found in Handout 6.4.

Handout 6.2

PERMISSION STATEMENT

I, the undersigned (parent/legal guardian of a child under 18, or a person over 18), give _____ (name and telephone) permission to provide psychological treatment to my child _____, date of birth _____. This treatment will occur (frequency) _____ until (duration) _____ and include the following:

The goals are to:

Potential benefits of these services are:

Potential harmful effects of these services are:

Alternative treatments available include:

The results of these services will be conveyed to:

I understand that _____ is training as a school psychologist and is being supervised by _____ (telephone_____ ; e-mail_____) using observation, tapes of sessions, and discussion. I understand that all tapes will be destroyed immediately after the supervisor reviews them. Other than those persons listed above, all information will be kept strictly confidential. However, I also understand that confidentiality will be broken if legally mandated, such as if my child appears to be a danger to self or others.

_____   _____
Signature   Date

Handout 6.3

CHECKLIST OF INFORMATION REQUIRED
IN CONSENT TO PARTICIPATE IN A RESEARCH STUDY

___ Indication of willingness to participate as a research subject

___ The topic studied

___ Statement of how the individual was selected to participate

___ Statement of how this treatment differs from traditional treatment

___ Investigator names and contact information

___ Names and contact information of administrators who can answer questions

___ Potential risks and benefits

___ Possible alternatives to participation

___ Assurances regarding confidentiality and privacy

___ An indication that participation is voluntary

___ A statement that participation can be discontinued at any time without penalty

Handout 6.4

SAMPLE RESEARCH CONSENT STATEMENT

You are being asked to allow your child under the age of 18 to participate in a research study concerning Peer Support and Study Skills. Your child was selected to participate as a result of having been identified as having difficulty learning independently. The treatment that your child will receive as a member of this research study differs from traditional treatment of study skills in that it will include participation in a small group in which students will encourage and foster one another's study skills outside of the classroom for 15 minutes per day.

Potential risks to participation include the loss of time in class and the possibility of embarrassment due to participation in the group. Possible benefits to your child include improved study skills, increased peer support for studying, increased knowledge regarding how to improve study skills, and improved academic functioning. The alternative to participation in this research is participation in the general education classroom study skills class.

Your child's progress will be monitored by questionnaires and by grades on homework, quizzes, and tests. All materials will be kept in locked file cabinets. All information and results will be kept strictly confidential unless legally mandated otherwise, such as if there is a danger to self or others.

The results of this research will be compiled in a way that conceals your child's identity. They will be conveyed to school administrators and be used to make future program decisions. They also may be published in journals to inform other educators of the results.

Participation is completely voluntary. Participation can be discontinued at any time without penalty should you (or your child) desire to discontinue it.

If you have any questions, please feel free to ask _____ (names and contact information of investigators) or _____ (names and contact information of administrators who can answer questions).

I, the undersigned (parent/legal guardian of a child under 18, or a person over 18), consent to participation in the research study described above.

_____ (student's name), _____ (date of birth)

_____   _____
Parent/Guardian Consent   Date

_____   _____
Student Assent   Date

Protect Privacy and Confidentiality

Maintaining students' confidentiality is essential, and supervisors must emphasize and reemphasize this point in both individual and group supervision. As Reamer (2004) indicated, to maintain confidentiality supervisors and their supervisees need to be knowledgeable regarding ethical principles, laws, and statutes relative to the disclosure of information regarding a student's being a danger to self or others, alcohol and substance abuse treatment, and high-risk behaviors. They also need to know the parameters of discussing information with teachers and other educators, consultants, the media, child protection services and other social service agencies, and law enforcement officials and during legal proceedings, including divorce litigation, child custody hearings, and criminal proceedings. Supervisors should be aware and should make their supervisees aware of state laws regarding the privilege extended to the psychologist-client relationship.

Record Retention

Supervisors must ensure that accurate and complete records are maintained to ensure appropriate treatment. It is also important that the psychological records be kept in locked files to maintain confidentiality. To minimize the likelihood that inappropriate student records will survive and be abused in the future, supervisors should ensure that school psychologists develop a regular habit of reviewing files, consolidating working notes, and culling obsolete material. State and local laws vary regarding how long psychologists must retain records, and again, supervisors must keep abreast of this information so that they can inform supervisees of the relevant laws and regulations. A. Canter (2001b) suggested that reports and summaries of psychological services be maintained for at least 5 years past high school graduation, while S. Jacob and Hartshorne (2007) indicated that they should be kept until a stable pattern of findings emerges. While ethical and legal regulations differ and supervisors should be well versed in applicable regulations, it is important to keep the welfare of the student uppermost. The purpose of keeping records is to be able to retroactively verify that appropriate decisions were made and effective educational programs were provided until this information is no longer of legal interest. It would seem, therefore, that psychological reports and records of services should be kept until they exceed the statute of limitations, which would in most instances be 7 years after the student reaches the age of majority.

Termination and Transitioning

Supervisors of school psychological services must consider specific legal and ethical issues that arise whenever a practitioner vacates her or his position as a school psychologist. Events such as retirement, termination of employment, transfer to another school, and the conclusion of a specified training period (e.g., practicum or internship) necessitate specific termination activities. Although there may be a vast *quantitative* difference, the school psychologist who retires after 30 years of practice has the same *qualitative* obligations that confront an exiting practicum student. Upon termination of any supervisory relationship, specific plans for the disposal of all notes and students' records should be jointly made by the supervisor and supervisee. Supervisors should ensure that supervisees terminate services with a student or consultee in an ethical and legal manner (Reamer, 2004). For example, school psychologists who provide counseling must ensure that upon termination they provide students with as much advance notice as possible, refer them to appropriate services, and give clear instruction regarding how to handle emergency situations. It may be especially helpful to develop a specific list of activities, which might include the items listed in Handout 12.5 in Chapter 12.

Electronic Records

Supervisors are responsible for ensuring that confidentiality is maintained when student information is stored on computers. This responsibility is becoming more and more difficult with the pervasive increase in hacking, phishing, and identity theft; considerable steps must be taken to reduce risk, and it appears impossible to completely eliminate risk for any computer that is ever attached to the Internet (Pope, 2001).

The APA (1996) ethical guidelines indicate that encoding, encryption, and avoidance of personal identifiers should occur when psychologists enter confidential information into databases or systems of records. However, many school systems are currently storing individualized education plans on local area networks to facilitate information sharing. This occurs even though the networks are minimally secure, and students have been known to break into even "secure" school computer systems to obtain test items and change grades. Furthermore, when using a networked computer, school psychologists may even inadvertently post confidential information on a Web site, as happened to one unfortunate and very unhappy school psychologist (Macklem, 2006).

To minimize the likelihood of these violations, supervisors should consider encouraging their supervisees to (a) electronically store confidential information on external hard drives, USB drives, and flash drives; (b) write confidential reports on stand-alone computers that are never connected to a network or the Internet; (c) minimize identifying information in reports; (d) work on disks or CDs rather than the computer's hard drive (Harvey & Carlson, 2003; Macklem, 2006).

Finally, it is advisable to password-protect documents whenever possible. Computer documents in Microsoft Word and Excel are easily password-protected by selecting "Protect Document" under "Tools." At the beginning of a supervisory relationship, passwords can be mutually selected and applied to all relevant computer documents.

Third-Party Confidentiality

Although school psychologists generally do not bill third-party insurance companies, quite frequently they do share diagnostic and clinical information with independent practitioners housed inside or outside the school walls, who in turn share it with third parties. Furthermore, in some states school psychological services are reimbursable as Medicaid services, and to obtain these reimbursements the school system must submit relevant records. In each of these scenarios, the treatment plans and progress reports can be reviewed by administrative personnel, computer technicians, and investigative government or legal entities who have never met the student in a professional capacity. School psychologists should advise students that information about them may not be completely safeguarded. Supervisors are responsible for ensuring that the formats used by the school district in reporting information minimally infringe upon the confidentiality rights of students and their parents and that supervisees inform others of the limits to their privacy.

E-Mail Confidentiality

E-mails are another potential source of confidentiality violation. School systems do not always use encryption software. Furthermore, e-mails can be forwarded and modified without the original sender's knowledge, resulting in confidentiality breaches. Therefore, it is important that school psychologists' e-mails do not contain identifying information (Harvey & Carlson, 2003). When possible, e-mails should be encrypted and/or password-protected.

Supervisory Techniques

Supervisors must carefully monitor the ethics of any supervisory techniques they employ. While direct observation of supervisees by supervisors greatly facilitates supervision (C. Rogers, 1965), respect for the privacy of the student is still of paramount concern. As described earlier, parents of minors and students themselves should give informed consent before any audio or video recording of sessions with school psychologists occurs. This informed consent must include information regarding the use and disposal of the tapes and the likelihood of supervisors viewing them.

Supervisee Privacy and Confidentiality

Supervisors must also safeguard the confidentiality of supervisees. This means not only that they should protect personal information disclosed by supervisees in a supervisory relationship, but also that they should make clear what information they will share with school district administrators, university supervisors, accrediting agencies, and others. Supervisees' privacy and confidentiality is increasingly being challenged by technological advances such as voice mail, e-mail, and the Internet. As Anthony, Kacmer, and Perrewé (2006) indicated, current electronic systems provide the means for employers to view employees' e-mail messages, listen to voice mail, view networked computer screens, and explore an individual's Internet history. Many places of employment, including schools, have installed surveillance cameras to increase security, but these can also be used to monitor employee behavior. There are questions regarding whether surveillance practices are fair or violate reasonable expectations of privacy. Stringent monitoring is thought to harm "employee morale, strain labor-management relations, and often produce increased stress in employees under surveillance" (p. 570). These technologies have exacerbated the struggle to respect an employee's right to privacy, because employers have been increasingly using them to save expenses and monitor performance.

Policy Development

In addition to addressing the above issues in one-to-one supervisory sessions, supervisors of school psychological services should encourage the development of districtwide policies that promote confidentiality. For example, school personnel should be discouraged from discussing students in public areas, such as hallways and teacher rooms. When supervisors notice school or district policies that violate these ethical principles, they should address changing these policies with appropriate administrators. It is most effective to do so in written form, sending copies to all interested parties.

Vignette 6.4

The first autumn that **Charlene** was employed as a school psychologist in a new school district, she noticed that all of the class lists had two- or three-digit numbers after each student's name. Upon inquiring, she was told that these were the students' IQ scores from the group standardized intelligence tests administered in third grade. School district administrators were surprised when she pointed out that posting IQ scores violated students' rights to confidentiality, but they came to understand her concern and removed the scores from the lists.

Supervisors should determine whether their school district information technology policies are designed to maintain confidentiality. As Macklem (2006) noted, there are a number of relevant questions to ask institutional technology specialists and administrators. The reader might explore these variables by uncovering the answers to questions in Activity 6.1.

Activity 6.1

Assessing School Districts' Technology Security

Ask your administrators and technology experts the following questions:

- Where are confidential data stored? How are they controlled?
- How can you help me ensure my data are protected?
- How do I recover critical data in the event of loss of power, disruption of network services, theft, or inability to access my computer?
- What are the district's backup policies? Are the backups secure?
- Are psychological reports stored electronically? Where and how?
- Is all confidential information stored where it is protected from unauthorized access?
- How are outdated electronic and paper psychological reports destroyed?
- What firewalls and antivirus programs are provided for school psychologists' computers at home? At work?

Similar questions should be raised regarding the storage and disposal of paper documents. Any materials with confidential information, such as students' diagnoses, should be shredded upon disposal.

Maintain Due Process

Due process stems from the legal right of an individual to expect rights and liberties within a given situation, particularly notice and a hearing before the removal of important rights, such as freedom or employment. Supervisors adhere to due process when they are careful to make fair and unbiased judgments by:

- Using unbiased hiring criteria that do not illegally or unethically discriminate on the basis of such factors as race, ethnicity, or disability
- Developing and following a supervision contract that defines supervisory parameters and expectations
- Advising employees of performance requirements and giving sufficient notice when they are not being met so that deficiencies can be addressed
- Designing and providing supervision responsive to the supervisee's skills
- Providing ongoing and constructive feedback
- Adhering to an informal process for listening and responding to supervisee concerns and, when these concerns are not informally resolved, adhering in good faith to district policies regarding complaints and grievances
- Employing reliable and valid evaluation methods that reflect relevant performance standards

Thus supervisors of school psychological services are ethically compelled to develop comprehensive job descriptions for supervisees, and they are ethically compelled to develop and use evaluation tools that reflect these job descriptions.

Promote Fairness and Nondiscrimination

School psychologists and supervisors must respect individual differences and be sensitive to students' physical, mental, emotional, political, economic, social, cultural, ethnic, racial, gender, sexual orientation, and religious characteristics (NASP, 2000a). In adhering to this principle, supervisors consider individual differences as they formulate and inform supervisory recommendations.

As described in greater detail in Chapter 3, supervisors must be aware of appropriate tools and techniques for supervisees' work with ethnically diverse individuals. They should be thoroughly familiar with the "Guidelines for Providers of Psychological Services to Ethnic, Linguistic, and Culturally Diverse Populations" (APA, 1993); the *Standards for Educational and Psychological Testing* (American Educational Research Association, American Psychological Association, & National Council on Measurement in Education, 1999), and the "Guidelines for Psychotherapy with Lesbian, Gay, and Bisexual Clients" (APA, Committee on Lesbian, Gay, and Bisexual Concerns, 2000). They should ensure that their supervisees as well as they themselves assess and improve multicultural competencies. Necessary competencies include:

- Awareness of how one's own age, culture, class, ethnic identity, gender, race, and sexual orientation shape values and attitudes
- Awareness of the backgrounds, beliefs, values, and worldviews of families, students, and educators with whom one works
- The ability to use this awareness to demonstrate sensitivity and respect for cultural differences in all areas of practice, including the selection of assessment methods, the design and monitoring of interventions, and the facilitation of students' and parents' understanding of the American culture, particularly that of schools (Hansen, Pepitone-Arreola-Rockwell, & Greene, 2000; S. Jacob & Hartshorne, 2007; M. R. Rogers et al., 1999)

Provide Responsible Care

It is essential that supervisors manifest the foundations of responsible care provision: being truthful, loyal, and reliable. It is also important that they safeguard the welfare of the students and supervisees with whom they work. To fulfill this responsibility, supervisors must help supervisees determine which of their skills are sufficiently developed, decide which need further development, and then take necessary steps to acquire these competencies.

For example, supervisors are responsible for ensuring that school psychologists under their supervision use software test scoring and report writing programs appropriately and ethically. In particular, supervisors must monitor whether supervisees use software programs to inappropriately practice beyond or outside their levels of expertise (Harvey & Carlson, 2003; S. Jacob & Hartshorne, 2007). Supervisors are responsible for ensuring that psychologists use computer applications to augment rather than replace clinical practice, and only within their areas of competence. The psychologist using software maintains legal responsibility for all treatment effects, good and bad. The psychologist cannot attribute professional responsibility to the software manufacturer, the author of the treatment approach, or the computer programmer (Harvey & Carlson).

Prevent Harm

It is important that supervisors intervene when they see harm being done. While it is obviously legally mandated to report child abuse and neglect, it is further ethically important that supervisors intervene when they observe behaviors or practices that are harmful to others. For example, supervisors should intervene when they perceive that a principal is making such unreasonable demands on a school psychologist that he or she is overwhelmed to the point of being dysfunctional. A supervisor should also intervene when an administrator attempts to force a school psychologist to draw unwarranted conclusions from assessment data. Similarly, some school district policies are unintentionally harmful to students, and it is important for both supervisees and supervisors to work to reverse these policies.

Vignette 6.5

Vanessa, a lead school psychologist, noticed that not only were children in self-contained special education classes bused across town, but their schools were changed almost annually for administrative reasons. She felt that this practice was harmful to the students because they and their parents had no opportunity to belong to a school community. She worked to reverse this policy so that the children attended their home school and their parents could be involved in one school's PTA. Eventually, all of the children returned to their local schools, where they were assigned to a general education homeroom and their files were incorporated into that class's files. This gave each student a homeroom to attend each morning, a class for mainstreaming opportunities and special events such as assemblies and field trips, opportunities to know general education students, and a general sense of belonging.

Promote Beneficence

Supervisors should further strive to ensure that their actions *benefit* children, adolescents, and supervisees. As discussed in Chapters 1 and 4, this mandates that supervisors provide evidence-based practice themselves and require evidence-based practice from their supervisees. It also mandates that supervisors obtain supervision and support when learning new techniques and provide the same for their supervisees.

Promote Accurate and Complete Student Records

While it is important to maintain the confidentiality of records, as previously discussed, it is also important for supervisees to keep comprehensive, high-quality, and thorough documentation of their work. This should include notes regarding referrals to other professionals, with consent, as well as consultations and supervision notes (Reamer, 2004). Such documentation enables the appropriate planning, implementation, and appraisal of services. It also facilitates supervision, fosters accountability, makes meaningful evaluations possible, permits continuity of services from one psychologist to another, and demonstrates appropriate practice.

Maintain Accurate and Complete Supervision Records

Accurate supervision records verify appropriate supervision and document the provision of appropriate services. Each supervision session should be summarized in notes that contain the date and content of all sessions.

Ensure Record Accuracy

As Reamer (2004) indicated, supervisors are responsible to ensure that supervisees' records are accurate. It is important that supervisees do not fraudulently misrepresent services reported to administrators, such as student contact hours.

Maintain Clinical and Professional Skills

Clinical supervisors are responsible for monitoring and developing their own professional or clinical competence sufficiently so that they are more advanced than the supervisee in the areas in which the supervisee is practicing (J. M. Bernard & Goodyear, 2004). If a clinical supervisor is insufficiently experienced in the issues presented by a supervisee's student or consultee, she or he should consult another supervisor or another appropriately qualified professional. If consultation is insufficient, another supervisor should be assigned.

The ethical mandate to provide competent services is made difficult by the high likelihood that school psychologists are generalists and by the rapidly expanding knowledge base. As discussed in Chapter 1, supervisors of school psychological services must not just maintain but also constantly update their clinical and professional skills. This includes keeping abreast of developments in assessment and interventions as well as technological advances to improve services with increased effectiveness and efficiency (Harvey & Carlson, 2003).

Supervisors should keep sufficient records to enable them to assess their own skills. In reviewing their records, they should be able to establish that the recommendations they make to their supervisees are evidence based and known to be effective. There should also be evidence that they have recommended that supervisees modify or terminate interventions that do not result in sufficient progress.

Supervisors should also monitor the services provided by supervisees, such as consultation and professional development workshops, to ensure that they comply with best practices. For example, ethical violations may occur when school psychologists recommend that teachers or paraprofessionals implement behavior management programs but do not provide ongoing consultation over a period of time, because the application of such programs is so likely to be inappropriately executed by poorly trained personnel and result in harm to students (S. Jacob & Hartshorne, 2007).

Develop and Maintain Supervisory Skills

Supervisors are responsible for developing their competence in supervision. This should include participation in fundamental coursework and workshops as well as ongoing collaboration with other supervisors. Obtaining and reviewing raw data, such as taping and reviewing supervisory sessions, can also be extremely helpful in determining their areas of strength and weakness as supervisors. Supervisors should document the time expended in supervision, the supervisee's progress, and supervisory recommendations with enough detail so that accurate summative and formative evaluations can be accomplished.

Balance Competing Demands

Supervisors must respond to the basic principle of providing competent services by appropriately resisting administrative pressure to sacrifice quality of services for expediency (Bowser, 1995). In addition to resisting pressure, supervisors must use conceptual, conflict resolution/problem solving, and planning skills to satisfactorily analyze, address, and resolve these problematic situations. Furthermore, they should help their supervisees develop the same skills, since these are critical skills for balancing accountability, increased demands, and limited resources.

Assume Responsibility for Supervisees' Professional Practice

Supervisors are responsible for the services provided by their supervisees and thus are responsible for ensuring the competence of the supervisees. They must meet the great challenge of simultaneously attending to the needs of both their supervisees and the students with whom they work (J. M. Bernard & Goodyear, 2004). To ensure that supervisees are competent, two approaches are critical. First, supervisors must use direct observation and other sources of raw data, such as tapes, to obtain information regarding supervisee effectiveness. Second, supervisors should help supervisees increase their ability to practice reflectively, self-evaluate, and monitor their own professional skills (Knoff, 1986).

Be Responsible to the Community and Society

This broad principle has several implications for the supervisor of school psychologists. First, as an individual who is preparing and monitoring the growth of school psychologists, the supervisor has an ethical responsibility to safeguard the public from incompetent professionals. Second, the supervisor has a responsibility to ensure that school psychological service programs are effective. This means that the supervisor is ethically mandated to conduct program evaluations. Third, the supervisor has the responsibility to work toward, and to encourage supervisees to work toward, the development of policies that protect students from poor educational programs, toxic family environments, and negative community situations. Finally, the supervisor has the responsibility to ensure that school psychologists uphold federal, state, and local laws relevant to the practice of school psychology.

Safeguard the Public

Responsible Hiring

As previously discussed, it is important for supervisors to adhere to due process by using unbiased criteria when hiring school psychologists. On the other hand, supervisors are legally and ethically responsible to safeguard the public by avoiding *negligent hiring*. Negligent hiring is a legal finding that can result from failure to conduct thorough background checks (e.g., failure to uncover a history of convictions for sexual predation or violent crimes), and a supervisor can be found "responsible for using poor selection procedures after an employee inflicts harm on a third party" (Anthony et al., 2006, p. 251).

When agreeing to supervise an intern, a school psychologist is essentially hiring that intern, whether or not the intern is paid a stipend or salary. Therefore, it is essential that intern supervisors ensure that the school district conducts sufficient background checks to avoid any possibility of negligent hiring.

Professional Development

It is also the responsibility of the supervisor to promote professional competence throughout employment. As discussed previously, this means that supervisors ensure that school psychologists are utilizing up-to-date and evidence-based practices.

Dismissal

While fostering professional competence is obviously the preferred course of action, there are times when supervisors are obliged to take action to dismiss an incompetent school psychologist. As stated by S. Jacob and Hartshorne (2007),

> when a supervisee is suffering from an impairment or engages in serious norma- tive errors, it is ethically appropriate and necessary for the supervisor to recom- mend a failing internship grade, suspend or terminate the internship, deny endorsement for state credentialing, and/or recommend non-renewal of an employment contract or immediate termination of employment. (p. 307)

Supervisors must understand the nature of incompetence, misconduct, and impair- ment. An impaired practitioner is one who is unable to provide competent care due to alcoholism, chemical dependency, mental illness, personal conflict, or physical or emo- tional limitations. A "problem" becomes an "impairment" when the professional does not acknowledge, understand, or address the identified problem. The problem is not simply a skill deficit that can be addressed by training. An impairment negatively affects services provided, impacts more than one area of professional functioning, requires a disproportionate amount of the supervisor's time, and does not change in response to feedback, remediation efforts, and/or the passage of time (Forrest, Elman, Gizara, & Vacha-Haase, 1999, p. 630).

Supervisors should be familiar with warning signs of impairment, make constructive responses (such as requiring counseling), appropriately adjust workloads, and notify appropriate administrators and licensing agencies when necessary (Reamer, 2004). To ensure that actions are not arbitrary, it is important for supervisors to establish formal guidelines for dealing with impaired practitioners that are respectful, institute a thorough review of the situation, and consider the opinions of experts in addition to the opinions of the person initiating the complaint. The guidelines must balance the supervisee's right to due process—notice and a hearing prior to action—and the ethical imperative to pro- tect children and adolescents.

Such actions are obviously difficult for supervisors to take. They are made more dif- ficult by the logistics of dismissing individuals from school system employment, particu- larly after tenure or professional status is attained. However, the ethical imperative is to put the welfare of students first, and to "do no harm" clearly mandates taking action when necessary.

Program Evaluations

Supervisors must ensure that, whether conducted by them or by their supervisees, research and program evaluations are conducted in an ethical manner. Relevant ethical guidelines include practicing within the realm of professional competence and responsibil- ity, considering the welfare of the student, guaranteeing informed consent and maintenance of confidentiality, providing freedom from coercion and minimal risk, avoiding conceal- ment and deception, and providing post–data collection debriefing and desensitization.

Policy Development

Supervisors also promote the ethical principle of protecting the community when they work toward, and encourage supervisees to work toward, the development of policies that protect students and foster social justice (Clark & Croney, 2006). This work can occur at multiple levels. For example, supervisors of psychological services can:

- Address school district policies that are known to adversely affect student functioning (e.g., retention policies or curricula that are not evidence based)
- Work to improve prevention and early intervention services to reduce the likelihood that students are inappropriately diagnosed as disabled because "that's the only way they can get services"
- Establish programs that prevent or ameliorate toxic family environments, such as parent education programs
- Address negative community situations, such as insufficient after-school care, by serving on community agency boards

Adhere to Laws

Ethical codes require that school psychologists know and adhere to current laws, statutes, administrative rulings, and local policies and procedures. Supervisor knowledge of laws is essential for four reasons. First, adhering to laws is mandated by ethical guidelines themselves. Second, laws inform the means by which supervisors should address many of the ethical constraints discussed earlier in the chapter. Third, ethical dilemmas result from conflicts among laws, conflicts between laws and ethical mandates, and conflicts between laws or ethical mandates and personal values. Supervisors will not be able to adequately help supervisees deal with ethical dilemmas unless they have a good understanding of relevant laws. Finally, supervisors cannot develop an effective, broad-based school psychology program unless they are fully aware of all of the laws relevant to public education.

Laws Regarding Public Education

All school psychologists, including supervisors, should be thoroughly knowledgeable regarding federal and state laws affecting public education. The reader is referred to S. Jacob and Hartshorne (2007) and Oakland and Gallegos (2005) for more detailed treatment of the laws affecting public education, school psychologists, and the supervision of school psychological services. In brief, relevant laws include:

1. *Federally mandated accountability standards as designated by the No Child Left Behind Act of 2001 (NCLB).* Title I of NCLB includes goals to improve the academic achievement of the disadvantaged; promote reading and literacy development through early reading programs, family literacy programs, and school library programs; ensure appropriate education for migratory children; provide prevention and intervention programs for neglected, delinquent, and at-risk children and youth; provide assessment of Title I programs; provide comprehensive school reforms; increase access of low-income students to advanced placement courses and exams; and provide school dropout prevention programs. Title III of NCLB focuses on developing the English skills of students with limited English proficiency and requires that they pass the same state tests as all other students. NCLB requires that students attain proficiency on state achievement tests, that

schools demonstrate annual yearly progress, and that districts report test results disaggregated by student socioeconomic status, race/ethnicity, English language proficiency, and disability. Some educators feel that the higher expectations and standards will result in higher levels of academic achievement, while others find "the goal to have all children achieving on grade level to be unrealistic and the requirement that each race and demographic group in a school district show annual improvement on standardized tests to be unattainable" (Oakland & Gallegos, 2005, p. 1057). Importantly, supervisors should be aware of the possible systemic and individual stress that may result from the initiation of high-stakes testing in their districts (Kruger, Wandle, & Struzziero, 2007).

2. *Compulsory school attendance laws* that require, between state-specified birthdays, attendance at either a public school or a setting that provides equivalent instruction. Because compulsory school attendance laws require the attendance of all students regardless of disability, educational background, native language, or immigrant status, schools have increasingly diverse populations.

3. *State laws governing academic curriculum.* Since the implementation of educational programs is delegated to state government, each state has developed and mandated curriculum guidelines and frameworks to govern the teaching of each subject. These address the subjects, instruction, and curriculum required at each grade and for high school graduation; some are so highly specific that hundreds of objectives are listed for a given subject. A profound lack of agreement across states results in highly divergent expectations, which creates difficulties for the many students who change schools when their families move across district and state boundaries.

4. *Laws relevant to multicultural populations*, including regulations enforced by the Office for Civil Rights mandating that schools (a) identify students in need of assistance in learning English, (b) develop a language program that has a reasonable chance for success, (c) hire sufficient staff and purchase and use appropriate curricula, (d) develop and adopt appropriate evaluation standards, and (e) appraise program success and use the results of the appraisal to modify future programs. These laws indicate that evaluations should be conducted by school psychologists bilingual in English and the language in which the student is proficient, that language proficiency in both the native language and English should be determined before assessment instruments are selected, and that if the child is not proficient in English, great care should be taken in instrument selection. Otherwise, assessment results are likely to be invalid (S. Jacob & Hartshorne, 2007; Oakland & Gallegos, 2005). Furthermore, the acculturation of families and students should be determined, since it affects selection of assessment tools and interventions.

5. *Federal laws mandating a free appropriate education to all students*, including those from minority populations and those with disabilities, as mandated by the Civil Rights Act of 1991, IDEA 2004, Section 504 of the Rehabilitation Act of 1973, and the Americans With Disabilities Act of 1990. Section 504 requires reasonable accommodations for students with disabilities that do not result in the need for special education programming. Recent changes to the law defining eligibility for special education programs mandate increased early intervention services prior to the determination of special education eligibility, ongoing monitoring of responses to these and special education interventions, changed procedures for designating students as having learning disabilities, and steps to reduce the disproportionate number of minority students in special education programs. Supervisors will need to plan, develop, and provide considerable training to help veteran school psychologists develop the skills necessary to provide effective services in response to these changes.

6. *Laws regulating acceptable methods to control student behavior.* State laws regulate the use of corporal punishment, physical restraints, and suspensions. Federal law, however, mandates due process prior to denying a student the right to an education via expulsion. For example, IDEA 2004, the Americans With Disabilities Act of 1990, and Section 504 of the Rehabilitation Act of 1973 indicate that students with disabilities cannot be excluded for more than 10 days if it has been determined that the misbehavior is a manifestation of the diagnosed disability. Students also cannot be excluded because of pregnancy.

7. *Laws and school district policies regarding students' freedoms.* A number of court cases have addressed students' freedom of personal expression, speech, and the press as well as student appearance and the right to assemble in groups. While mixed, the cases have tended to support school administrators' rights to develop policies that "protect student health, safety, and school discipline" (Lunenburg & Ornstein, 2004, p. 462).

8. *Laws forbidding sexual harassment,* including the Civil Rights Act of 1964 and Title IX of the Education Amendments of 1972. Sexual harassment can take the form of sexual bribery, sexual imposition, gender harassment, sexual coercion, or sexual behavior. Sexual harassment can appear in relationships between supervisees and supervisors, between supervisees and other school employees, between supervisees and students, and between students and students. Supervisors and school psychologists often need to help others understand what comprises sexual harassment and how to deal with it.

9. *Federal and state laws regarding the protection of religious liberty.* During the past several years there has been an increasing conflict between the protection of religious liberty and respect of the property right to an education. While still controversial, this issue is manifested in a number of practices, including the provision of special education services to students attending parochial schools and the use of school vouchers to attend parochial schools. It is also manifested in controversies such as the teaching of evolution, sex education, and birth control.

10. *Laws regarding educational records and the right to privacy.* Laws that support previously described ethical mandates to maintain privacy and confidentiality include the Family Educational Rights and Privacy Act of 1976 and IDEA 2004. In addition, the Health Insurance Portability and Accountability Act of 1996 (HIPAA; see www.hhs.gov/ocr/hipaa) regulates the sharing of information with third parties, such as Medicaid, and specifically addresses the electronic storage and transmission of confidential information.

11. *Laws regarding mandated reporting.* State laws typically mandate reporting of knowledge regarding specified topics. In Massachusetts, for example, educators are mandated to report knowledge regarding child abuse or neglect, possession or use of a weapon in a school, and fire setting to an appropriate authority. Professionals are also mandated to report knowledge of a child's disease or defect to that child's parents (Clarke, 2006).

12. *Copyright laws* that regulate the copying and distribution of materials. These laws regulate the copying of articles, test materials, and computer software. In general, they permit individuals to make one "fair use" copy but prohibit the making of additional copies unless the holder of the copyright is paid a royalty (Copyright Law of the United States of America, 1996).

13. *Laws regulating the duty to warn.* The Tarasoff ruling (*Tarasoff v. Regents of California*, 1974) and resulting interpretations mandate that psychologists provide adequate warning to threatened individuals. In this case the supervisor was held vicariously responsible for

the lack of appropriate practice by the supervisee. Supervisors of school psychological services must help supervisees determine when it is appropriate to break confidentiality and inform victims of intended harm (Munson, 1991).

Laws Regarding Professional Employment

In addition to public education and student rights, supervisors of school psychological services should be thoroughly knowledgeable regarding laws regulating the employment of professional personnel. These include laws relating to nondiscriminatory employment, safe workplaces, licensing and certification, the right to collectively bargain, employment contracts, and employment termination. Supervisors should also be aware that these laws contain "whistle-blower" provisions that prohibit punishment of individuals who report their employers for violations.

1. *Laws regarding nondiscriminatory employment*, including the Civil Rights Acts of 1964 and 1991, Title IX of the Education Amendments of 1972, the Rehabilitation Act of 1973, the Equal Pay Act of 1963, the Age Discrimination in Employment Act of 1967, the Pregnancy Discrimination Act of 1978, the Americans With Disabilities Act of 1990, and the Family and Medical Leave Act of 1993. These laws indicate that employment practices cannot be influenced by artificial barriers, such as ethnic minority membership, age, gender, religious beliefs, or disability, as long as the individual is "otherwise qualified."

2. *Federal laws mandating a safe and healthful workplace*, including the Occupational Safety and Health Act of 1970, the Civil Rights Act of 1991, and Title IX of the Education Amendments of 1972. "A safe and healthful environment" means a physical environment that is not threatening to the health of employees (e.g., free from toxic mold levels, asbestos, and lead). It also means freedom from sexual harassment, because sexual harassment results in a hostile environment that interferes with work performance. These laws forbid retribution after a violation is reported and are supported by the possibility of punitive measures and compensatory damages (Anthony et al., 2006).

3. *State licensure and certification laws pertaining to employment eligibility, employment continuance, and conditions leading to the revoking of licensure or certification.* Supervisors must be familiar with laws pertaining to employment eligibility. For example, in some states an individual with a master's degree in clinical psychology is eligible for state board of education licensure or certification and therefore employment as a school psychologist, while in other states the individual must have at least a master's degree in school psychology for the same licensure or certification. These laws are also pertinent to employment continuance; for example, states may require that individuals meet requirements for professional licensure or certification within a specified time period. Supervisors may need to find methods to support supervisees in meeting these requirements. Furthermore, each state has regulations and procedures under which licensure or certification as a school psychologist can be revoked for such things as immorality, misconduct, incompetence, or neglect of duty (Lunenburg & Ornstein, 2004).

4. *Federal laws providing employees with the right to collectively bargain for wages, hours, and other employment conditions.* In many school districts, this right has led to union membership and union-negotiated contracts. Supervisors of school psychological services should be thoroughly familiar with union contracts pertinent to school psychologists, teachers, paraprofessionals, clerical staff, and administrators. These contracts specify conditions that affect the provision of school psychological services, such as after-school attendance at meetings and parent workshops. They also specify administrative and

evaluative processes. For example, usually a person cannot be the administrative supervisor of another individual in the same bargaining unit, which means that administrative supervisors of school psychological services must either be included in an administrative unit or negotiate their own working conditions, salary, and benefits.

5. *Statutory laws and regulations governing employment contracts.* Supervisors should clearly understand who has the legal and designated right to hire. In general, the ultimate right to hire is the province of the school board and employment offers must undergo a school board review before they are official (Lunenburg & Ornstein, 2004). On the other hand, contracts are negotiated by a designated administrator, often an associate superintendent, before the recommendation to hire an individual is presented to the school board. It is important for supervisors of school psychological services to know whether they have the authority to discuss salary, contract length, days worked per year, and other employment conditions with job candidates.

6. *Statutory laws and regulations governing employment termination.* Often employment termination in schools is regulated by tenure and union contracts. Contracts can be nonrenewed for any reason before tenure is awarded, usually after a 3- to 5-year probationary period. After tenure has been awarded, employment can be terminated "for cause" and is subject to due process (Lunenburg & Ornstein, 2004). This is particularly relevant if the "cause" involves a stigma that would prevent future employment, such as immoral conduct, serious mental illness, substance abuse, or neglect of duty. Definitions of cause for dismissal vary by state but in all cases must comply with the Americans With Disabilities Act of 1990.

Laws Regarding Negligence, Malpractice, and Liability

Federal law mandates that individuals have a duty to protect others against reasonable risk and to exercise appropriate standards of care such that physical or mental injuries resulting in loss or damage to a person do not occur. This means that school employees must provide guidance regarding student behavior and physical supervision sufficient to prevent student injuries. For example, supervisees should be reminded to never leave students unsupervised.

Supervisees' services can be negligent due to actual malpractice or due to their providing services below acceptable standards. In either situation, students can be "harmed." As Sweitzer and King (2004) indicated, supervisors can be deemed liable when their supervisees are found to be negligent if they:

- Have been remiss in carrying out supervisory responsibilities
- Have given inappropriate advice
- Have failed to attend to a supervisee's comments and therefore failed to understand student needs
- Have assigned tasks beyond the skill level of the supervisee

The extent to which a supervisee's behavior falls within the responsibility of the supervisory relationship is determined by the supervisor's power over the supervisee; the supervisee's assigned duties; the time, place, purpose, and motivation of the behavior; and the likelihood that the supervisor would have been able to anticipate the supervisee's behavior (Disney & Stephens, 1994). As previously mentioned, supervisors are most liable when they have the ability to hire, fire, and control the work of supervisees—as when they are administrative or intern supervisors.

As J. M. Bernard and Goodyear (2004) suggested, to minimize the likelihood of being named a codefendant in a malpractice suit, a supervisor should:

- Maintain open and trusting relationships with supervisees
- Keep up-to-date on ethical and legal issues
- Maintain liability insurance
- Consult with the school district's legal counsel
- Document all supervisory contacts
- Invest adequate time and energy in supervision

TRAINING SUPERVISEES IN ETHICAL PRACTICE

Knowledge of ethics and of ethical decision making is clearly associated with having completed coursework in ethics (Baldick, 1980; Gawthrop & Uhleman, 1992; S. Jacob & Hartshorne, 2007; Tryon, 2001), and all school psychology training programs include exposure to ethical principles. Unfortunately, such training is not sufficient for developing proficiency in ethical decision making. As described at the beginning of this chapter, knowledge of ethics and ethical behavior do not always coincide.

Ethical practice actually develops during practice itself. Fieldwork experience as a practicum student and intern are essential components of the development of ethical practice, and intern supervisors therefore have a particular responsibility to model ethical practice (Sullivan & Conoley, 2008; S. Jacob & Hartshorne, 2007). As Handelsman, Gottlieb, and Knapp (2005) indicated, becoming an ethical psychologist is more complex than following a set of rules or imitating supervisors. In addition to acquiring a sound knowledge of ethical codes and legal mandates, appropriate ethics training involves becoming acculturated into the profession and developing ethical thinking that permeates professional practice. Therefore, supervisors should promote ethical practice by:

- Helping supervisees to consider their own personal ethics

Activity 6.2

Write three to four pages about significant professional or personal events that have created a moral dilemma in your life. State the dilemma explicitly, describe what caused it to be a dilemma, and indicate resolutions you considered.

- Helping supervisees to understand their personal reactions to ethical codes

Activity 6.3

After reading this chapter and rereading the professional ethical standards, reflect on the following question: How does this information influence how I think and feel about my relationship with the students with whom I work and the schools in which I work?

- Regularly addressing ethical dilemmas during individual and group supervision sessions to both model and implement effective problem solving strategies
- Promoting an open and honest supervisory relationship that fosters open discussion of difficult issues
- Discussing and developing preventative measures and policies that meet both ethical and legal mandates
- Modeling keeping abreast of current laws through ongoing consultation with district lawyers and human resource departments
- Modeling seeking assistance from other professionals or professional associations when encountering areas of difficulty
- Discussing situations that are prone to ethical violations

Vignette 6.6

After many years of debate regarding how to handle parental requests for copies of test protocols, **Tom** met with his supervisees to brainstorm strategies that would respect both parents' right to access their children's records and test publishers' right to copyright their materials. They decided to (a) mandate that psychologists routinely invite parents to individual meetings at which test results would be interpreted in parent-friendly language to foster open communication and psychologist-parent relationship building, (b) develop sample items for report templates that were not actual test items, (c) forbid the use of actual test items in oral and written reports, and (d) share copies of completed test protocols only with qualified examiners.

To reduce supervisees' likelihood of violating boundaries, it is imperative that supervisors initiate conversations that bring potential boundary violations into the open. Hamilton and Spruill (1999) recommended that prior to any individual work with students, novice supervisees should be told

- How the emotional disclosure and physical proximity involved in working individually with students are likely to increase feelings of attraction for both the student and the psychologist
- Information from well-respected clinicians regarding their experiences in handling sexual attraction during the therapeutic process
- The importance of maintaining visibility to others while maintaining confidentiality (often through windowed doors)
- Actions to take, particularly consultation with the supervisor, whenever the supervisee has feelings of attraction toward students
- Risk factors for and signs of intimacy (e.g., feelings of similarity to a student, inappropriate self-disclosure, fantasies about or preoccupation with the student)
- Negative consequences of boundary violations on the student
- Techniques to increase skills regarding ethical decision making
- Clear program policies regarding unacceptable actions

Boundary issues are also relevant to the supervisor-supervisee relationship. Although some boundary maintenance is always warranted, it is likely that there will be some variability according to the inherent power differential in the relationship. For example, when supervising practicum and internship students, maintaining "tight" boundaries is advisable at the initiation of the relationship. Boundaries are likely to become more permeable as the supervisee transitions from a supervisory to a collegial relationship. However, "once a supervisor, always a supervisor" may be a good general rule, in that former supervisees often seek letters of recommendation, and the presence of a dual (personal) relationship may make it difficult to write an honest letter.

ETHICAL DECISION MAKING

In any case involving ethical or legal questions, consulting with others to find resolutions that consider the needs of all parties involved is essential. It is very helpful to have a knowledgeable colleague with whom to consult when difficulties arise. It is also helpful to develop a consultative relationship with the school district or city attorney to keep informed of new laws and statutes.

When unethical practice is suspected, the first course of action is to attempt to resolve the issue informally with the person about whom one is concerned. It is most helpful to consider this collaboration rather than confrontation. If this is not effective, both individuals can approach a colleague, state association, or national association for assistance and information. Only after these steps have been taken should the school psychologist file a complaint with the licensing board or professional organization.

When struggling with an ethical decision, school psychologists and supervisors of school psychological services should follow a deliberate decision making process. Handout 6.5 describes appropriate ethical decision making steps.

Activity 6.4

Ethical Decision Making

In individual and group supervision sessions, consider the supervisory dilemmas presented in this book, apply the ethical problem solving strategies described in Handout 6.5, and determine appropriate courses of action.

SUMMARY

Professional licensure or certification is often tied to adherence to professional codes of ethical conduct, and supervisors are responsible for ensuring that supervisees understand, recognize, and resolve ethical and legal dilemmas. Adherence to ethical principles is complicated by conflicting laws, conflicts between laws and ethics, and conflicts with personal values. Breaches of ethical behavior are unfortunately common among school psychologists, interns, and supervisors. Common breaches include those pertaining to confidentiality, dual (including sexual) relationships, and payment sources as well as other areas. Supervisors are expected to foster the ability of supervisees to make appropriate ethical decisions. They must ensure that supervisees practice legally and ethically while also accepting ultimate responsibility for services provided by supervisees. Ethical mandates include maintaining integrity in professional relationships, respecting the dignity of persons and protecting the welfare of all, respecting autonomy and self-determination,

Handout 6.5

ETHICAL DECISION MAKING

(Adapted from S. Jacob & Hartshorne, 2007;[1]
Koocher & Keith-Spiegel, 1998;[2] Reamer, 2004[3])

1. Describe the parameters of the problem, including all individuals, groups, and organizations likely to be affected

2. Define and consider pertinent complementary and conflicting:
   - Ethical guidelines, both broad and specific
   - Federal and state laws
   - District policies
   - Professional duties
   - Personal values

3. Evaluate:
   - The rights, responsibilities, and welfare of all affected individuals
   - Any cultural, racial, and/or linguistic factors that may have an impact
   - Functions that the problematic behavior serves at the individual or organizational level

4. Generate and evaluate alternative decisions possible for each issue
   - Enumerate potential short- and long-term consequences of each possible decision
   - Determine possible risks and benefits
   - Consider who will benefit from and who will be hurt by each decision

5. Thoroughly investigate reasons for and against each possibility; conduct risk-benefit analysis that considers ethical codes, professional best practices, personal values, and the potential to more appropriately carry out functions currently performed

6. Consult with colleagues and appropriate experts, such as supervisors, attorneys, administrators, and ethics consultants

7. Select a course of action, thoroughly document the decision making process in writing, and take the course of action

8. After taking action, appraise the decision making process and the final outcome; determine what worked, what didn't work, and how future practice should be modified

---

[1]Jacob, S., & Hartshorne, T. S. (2007). *Ethics and law for school psychologists* (5th ed.). New York: Wiley.

[2]Koocher, G. P., & Keith-Spiegel, P. (1998). *Ethics in psychology: Professional standards and cases* (2nd ed.). New York: Oxford University Press.

[3]Reamer, F. G. (2004). Ethical decisions and risk management. In M. J. Austin & K. M. Hopkins (Eds.), *Supervision as collaboration in the human services: Building a learning culture* (pp. 97–109). Thousand Oaks, CA: SAGE.

seeking informed consent for treatment, protecting privacy and confidentiality, maintaining due process, promoting fairness and nondiscrimination, providing responsible care, promoting beneficence, maintaining clinical and professional skills as well as supervisory skills, and being responsible to the community and society through such actions as adherence to laws. When faced with ethical decisions, school psychologists and supervisors alike should follow a deliberate decision making process that includes collaboration.

REFLECTIVE QUESTIONS

Q6.1. What ethical violations are most often committed by psychologists in training? What reasons do they give for making these violations?

Q6.2. What are four core areas of significance to the ethical practice of school psychologists as identified by S. Jacob and Hartshorne (2007)? How can school psychologists best adhere to these core practices?

Q6.3. What are the ethical responsibilities of supervisors? What are some ways in which supervisors can promote ethical practice?

Q6.4. Describe why supervisors must be cautious of dual relationships, particularly with supervisees.

Q6.5. What is important in obtaining informed consent for assessment and treatment? How does it differ from informed consent for interns?

Q6.6. What are the ethical guidelines for program evaluations and research?

Q6.7. Describe the issues and challenges involved in protecting privacy and confidentiality. How do they apply to supervisees?

Q6.8. How do supervisors adhere to due process?

Q6.9. What are some of the laws to which school psychologists must adhere?

Q6.10. How can vicarious liability be minimized?

SUPERVISORY DILEMMAS

SD 6.1

In a large district, one of the psychologists disapprovingly observes that a number of colleagues do not follow procedures recommended in NASP's *Best Practices in School Psychology V* (A. Thomas & Grimes, 2008). The school psychologist comes to you, the supervising school psychologist, insisting that his colleagues be immediately reported to NASP for numerous ethical violations. *What are the supervisory considerations? What should be done?*

Authors' thoughts: Take a deep breath! This is a situation in which one would hope to tame or redirect the fervor of this judgmental school psychologist. In school psychology, as in all professions, the unfortunate reality is that not all practitioners vigilantly adhere to optimal practice standards. However, this does not necessarily constitute an ethical violation. Exemplary practice is an aspirational goal, not an adjudicated standard. The supervising school psychologist may conclude that the energy of this school psychologist would be far better spent in developing an in-service training module to offer to his colleagues in a special area of expertise. This would afford a more positive opportunity for all.

SD 6.2

The director of special education turns to you, the supervising school psychologist, to set a policy regarding the sharing of test protocols. A local parent advocate has been recommending that her clients request copies of the inside pages of the WISC-IV protocol to take to their children's private therapists. The state law mandates that parents have full access to all test results. *What are the supervisory considerations? What should be done?*

Authors' thoughts: Probably no other question has been addressed by *so* many *so* often. This is historically one of the most frequent questions to emerge (and reemerge!). Initially, it would be advisable to read the articles written by Andrea Canter (2001a, 2001b; available at www.nasponline.org), which offer invaluable information regarding the release of test protocols. In this particular case, the therapists who want the protocols should obtain releases from the parents. Copies can then be made available to them. Before releasing them, however, it will be important to verify that they are authorized to obtain the instruments themselves (e.g., in this case, are able to meet the publisher's requirements for "authorized users"). Importantly, protocols are typically not released to parents because of copyright law as well as concerns about test security. It is advisable to ask parents to come in for a face-to-face meeting to go over any questions or concerns.

SD 6.3

You are providing supervision for a newly graduated school psychologist. A parent in your district has recently requested help from this psychologist in obtaining a psychoeducational evaluation for her daughter as part of the admissions process for a local private high school. The parent has offered to pay for the evaluation and the school psychologist would be happy to do it in order to earn extra money. *What are the supervisory considerations? What should be done?*

Authors' thoughts: School psychologists who are employed by the school district and/or practice independently in their district may not accept remuneration from clients who are entitled to the same services within that school district. Also, a newly graduated school psychologist may not yet be licensed by her or his respective state for independent assessments. Our recommendation would be to refer this student to a private practitioner.

SD 6.4

You cowrote a federal grant with an intern you are supervising. Although the needs assessment conducted prior to writing the grant indicated a high interest in school-based family therapy, in actuality, after the grant has been awarded and the services have been initiated, very few families actually attend the therapy sessions. Therefore, a large sum of money from the grant remains to be spent. The internship is soon to be concluded and the intern is looking for a job. You would like to hire her but do not have money in the general fund to do so. Someone suggests that you spend the unused "family therapy" grant money to hire the intern as a general school psychologist. *What are the supervisory considerations? What should be done?*

Authors' thoughts: Although creative funding often assists in the procurement of school psychological services, the overarching stipulations of the grant will clearly dictate a course of action. School psychologists must adhere to all federal, state, and local laws and not engage in fraud. The supervisor must adhere to any and all restrictions. To do otherwise would not only break the law and jeopardize her professional license, but also jeopardize future grants for this school district. It might be fruitful for the school psychologist to contact the funding source to discuss the regulations. It is possible, for example, that this intern could be hired if part of her job responsibilities would be to provide family therapy, assuming that she is adequately qualified to do so.

SD 6.5

You have recently been promoted to supervising school psychologist after working 10 years as a practicing school psychologist in the same district. You consider several of the other six psychologists in the district to be among your closest and long-standing friends. You now will be in a position to complete evaluations on these friends. While you recognize this as a dual relationship and a potential conflict of interest, you also are loath to give up your friendships. *What are the supervisory considerations? What should be done?*

Authors' thoughts: While promotions afford status, monetary compensation, and personal satisfaction, they can also be fraught with difficulties that transcend the increased professional responsibility. This situation necessitates that the newly appointed supervisor adeptly juggle her new and old roles. Clearly, while school psychologists consciously avoid *entering* into such dual relationships, they sometimes find themselves *evolving* into them via unforeseen circumstances. The first course of action is to consider each relationship on an individual basis. It is likely that a frank discussion that addresses possible conflicts of interest will ease the situation. One would also hope that, as school psychologists themselves, the supervisees will understand the nature of the problem and try to facilitate a viable plan of action! One possible arrangement would include having a third party complete some evaluative tasks. For example, if one person has been an especially close friend, his evaluation might be done by a third party. If it is clearly not feasible to merge both roles, a decision will have to be made to refuse the promotion, alter some attendant duties, or cool friendships. Importantly, the newly promoted school psychologist exhibits a sound understanding of the intent of the ethical code. This will permit the exploration of multiple possibilities. It is likely that, with open and honest discussion, objectivity and effectiveness in the new role can be developed and maintained while a cordial relationship is upheld with the supervisor's former peers. With openness and inventiveness, this should be a workable promotion.

SD 6.6

Your intern, age 23, discloses that she finds one of the boys in her counseling caseload very attractive and "really sexy." He is 19 years old and is repeating his senior year. She states that she would love to date him but is aware that she can't do so while interning in the school. He has made it more than obvious that he thinks she is attractive. In fact, he has even asked you for her cell phone number! She confides that she would consider dating him after she has finished her internship. You readily notice that she treats him preferentially and dresses more provocatively on days that she is scheduled to counsel him. *What are the supervisory considerations? What should be done?*

Authors' thoughts: This situation is certainly ripe with potential pitfalls and problems. Assuredly, the intern does not appear to demonstrate a genuine understanding of *why* such relationships are inappropriate. As a beginning practitioner, she knows and can recite the "rule" that prohibits dual relationships but seemingly lacks the ability to clearly understand its intent. Most important, she is unable to apply it. She does not appear to have a well-developed appreciation of how potentially detrimental such a relationship might be to the student. APA standards clearly state that sexual intimacy is forbidden for at least 2 years after the cessation of services and further suggests that this would occur only in rare circumstances after consultation with a colleague. Inarguably, for school psychologists, whose clients are typically not adults, the prohibition is even greater. It is far preferable that intimate relationships *never* occur, regardless of how much time has elapsed. Another critical concern is the noticeable preferential treatment, provocative dress, and flirtatious behavior. This suggests that an immediate course of action must be initiated. Future remediation must be determined by the intern's responsiveness and perceived ability to understand the serious nature of her supervisor's concerns. If satisfactory resolution is not immediate, a second meeting should include the university field supervisor. Additionally, the intern will need assistance in terminating or transferring this case. The welfare of the student does, of course, take precedence at all times. It will be critically important for the new clinician to ascertain what might need to be addressed with the student. Without a doubt, stressing and ensuring the maintenance of strict boundaries will be a topic of inestimable importance in upcoming supervision. Other possible scenarios, depending on the intern's reaction and resulting behavior, might range from referral to therapy to termination from the program.

PART II

Clinical Supervision

7

Planning Clinical Supervision

The structure of clinical supervision profoundly influences its potential to be effective.

Vignette 7.1

In Chapter 1 we met **Anne**, a school psychologist who was to be the clinical supervisor of an intern for the first time. She still had vivid memories of the supervision she received as an intern, since it had occurred only 3 years before. She had no difficulty remembering specific techniques her supervisor had used, such as reviewing tapes of consultation sessions. But she had no idea how her supervisor had planned the entire supervision experience. In a panic, Anne called her former supervisor to ask for advice. Her supervisor recommended that she enroll in an online course in supervision to help her plan, execute, and monitor her supervision.

BASIC CONSIDERATIONS

This and the following chapters address clinical supervision—those aspects of supervision that focus on fostering professional skills and competencies. This chapter addresses planning clinical supervision and considers the supervisor's worldview, theoretical orientation, and supervisory models. It then addresses supervision variables such as organization, format, and frequency. It concludes with special considerations in the supervision of practicum students and interns.

SUPERVISOR CONSIDERATIONS

Appropriate clinical supervision techniques depend on multiple factors, each influencing the other (M. L. Friedlander & Ward, 1984). The structure of clinical supervision, often determined at the district or organization level, profoundly influences its practice. In addition, clinical supervision is influenced by characteristics of individual supervisors, such as worldview, theoretical orientation, supervision model, role preference, and supervision techniques.

Worldview and Professional View

A supervisor's worldview has a profound affect on his or her fundamental approach to clinical supervision. Supervisors who perceive supervision as a method of fostering supervisees' cognitive and professional development toward eventual self-actualization have quite a different approach to supervision than those who perceive supervisees as fundamentally untrustworthy and in need of authoritarian structure and close monitoring.

Vignette 7.2

Intern **Fran** had two remarkably different supervisors. At the high school, her supervisor **Sam** was highly suspicious, monitored every minute of her time, and in general made her feel incompetent even at the end of her internship year. Her supervisor at the middle and elementary schools, **Joan**, was the complete opposite—she fostered Fran's professional growth through guided practice and encouraged Fran to take on substantial responsibility. Joan would have liked Fran to take over her position upon her retirement that August, but Fran declined the job offer. Her experience with Sam had so undermined her self-confidence that she left the field of school psychology.

Even before individuals become supervisors, they have foundational beliefs regarding supervision. These include "convictions . . . about how supervisees become competent practitioners" (J. M. Bernard & Goodyear, 2004, p. 210), which in turn affect the selection of supervision interventions and techniques. Clinical supervision can be *directive*, in which "the supervisor models the intervention and students are expected to adopt the supervisor's approach," or more advantageously, *enabling*, in which supervisees are encouraged to develop critical thinking and problem solving skills, metacognitive skills, increased autonomy, and "an inner sense of competence" (Haboush, 2003, p. 232). Clinical supervision is more likely to be enabling when supervisors are responsive to supervisees' varying needs for autonomy and when they develop a secure attachment with their supervisees by being dependable, consistent, and emotionally responsive (D. J. Tharinger, 1998).

In addition to the supervisor's worldview of humanity, her or his fundamental beliefs regarding the practice of school psychology are critical. U.S. licensing and certification laws require that supervision be provided by an individual holding the same license the supervisee seeks, the presumption being that the clinical supervisor should be more expert than the supervisee (Cutliffe & Lowe, 2005). Clinical supervisors incorporate their professional skills with administrative skills (Falender & Shafranske, 2004), which will be discussed later. This model is illustrated in Figure 7.1.

Figure 7.1. Clinical supervision skills.

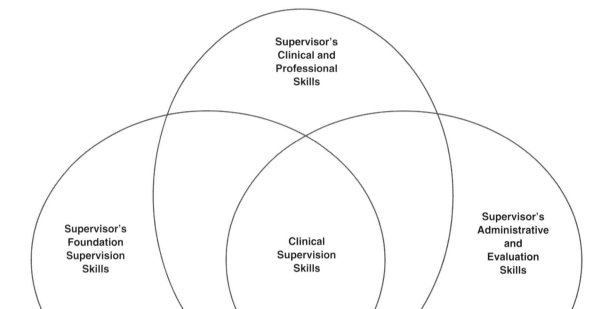

However, this conceptualization suggests a particular worldview. In contrast to the U.S. model, a model sometimes practiced in Europe emphasizes cross-disciplinary supervision (Cutliffe & Lowe, 2005). Obtaining supervision from an individual "different from you" is thought to provide new perspectives and increase the likelihood of being "stretched" (Davies, Tennant, & Ferguson, 2004; Stricker, as cited in DeAngelis, 2006).

Clinical Skills

Because school psychology encompasses a unique set of professional and clinical skills, effective clinical supervision of school psychologists is not the same as clinical supervision provided to therapists and mental health professionals. Such supervision is described in *Clinical Supervision: A Competency-Based Approach* (Falender & Shafranske, 2004); *Managing Clinical Supervision: Ethical Practice and Legal Risk Management* (Falvey, 2001); *Professional Supervision in the Helping Professions: A Practical Guide* (Haynes, Corey, & Moulton, 2003); *Counselling Supervision: Theory, Skills, Practice* (M. Carroll, 2006); and *Fundamentals of Clinical Supervision* (J. M. Bernard & Goodyear, 2004).

School psychology is highly contextual, and expert school psychologists' clinical skills traverse several areas of applied psychology. Table 7.1 contrasts the school psychology domains of training and practice as defined by the National Association of School Psychologists (NASP; 2000b) with the common practices of psychologists who provide only therapy, psychoeducational assessments, or organizational consultation.

Table 7.1   Comparison of Clinical Skills

School psychology domains of training and practice (required competencies; NASP, 2000b)	Providers of individual and group therapy	Providers of psychoeducational assessments	Providers of organizational consulting
2.1. Data-based decision making and accountability (collect data and other information, translate assessment results into empirically based decisions about service delivery, and evaluate the outcomes of services)	Can provide.	Usually do not evaluate the outcomes of interventions.	Can provide.
2.2. Consultation and collaboration at the individual, group, and systems levels	Usually do not consult at the universal or systems level.	Usually do not consult at the universal or systems level.	Usually do not consult at the individual level.
2.3. Effective instruction and development of cognitive/academic skills (develop appropriate cognitive and academic goals for students with different abilities, disabilities, strengths, and needs; implement interventions to achieve those goals; and evaluate the effectiveness of interventions)	Usually do not address cognitive/ academic skills.	Usually do not evaluate the outcomes of interventions.	Usually do not address cognitive/ academic skills.
2.4. Socialization and development of life skills (develop appropriate behavioral, affective, adaptive, and social goals for students of varying abilities, disabilities, strengths, and needs; implement interventions to achieve those goals; and evaluate the effectiveness of interventions)	Can provide.	Usually do not evaluate the outcomes of interventions.	Usually do not address socialization and development of life skills.

(Continued)

Table 7.1 (Continued)

School psychology domains of training and practice (required competencies; NASP, 2000b)	Providers of individual and group therapy	Providers of psychoeducational assessments	Providers of organizational consulting
2.5. Diversity in development and learning (multicultural skills)	Usually do not address cognitive/academic skills.	Can provide.	Can provide.
2.6. School and systems organization, policy development, and climate	Not customary.	Usually do not address.	Can provide if knowledgeable regarding schools.
2.7. Prevention, crisis intervention, and mental health	Prevention programs provided by school counselors. Not usually addressed by private practitioners.	Usually do not address.	Usually do not address crisis intervention and mental health.
2.8. Home/school/community collaboration	Provided by school counselors. Not focus of private practitioners.	Can provide.	Can provide.
2.9. Research, statistics, and program evaluation	Knowledgeable regarding research and statistics. Do not usually provide program evaluations.	Knowledgeable regarding research and statistics. Do not usually provide program evaluations.	Can provide.
2.10. School psychology practice and development (ethical, professional, and legal standards and public policy development applicable to services for students and families)	Knowledgeable regarding ethics. Do not usually provide public policy consultation.	Knowledgeable regarding ethics. Do not usually provide public policy consultation.	Can provide if knowledgeable regarding schools.
2.11. Information technology	Can be knowledgeable regarding professional technology. Do not usually consult regarding assistive technology.	Can provide.	Can provide.

Source: From the National Association of School Psychologists. (2000). *Professional conduct manual, 3rd edition.* Bethesda, MD: Author. Copyright 2000 by the National Association of School Psychologists, Bethesda, MD. Use of this material is by permission of the publisher, www.nasponline.org

Theoretical Orientation and Supervision Models

A clearly articulated theoretical orientation provides practicing psychologists with structures and strategies for making sense of the variables affecting the students and adults with whom they work. An active awareness of the concepts and theories that underlie one's professional practice is essential for integrity in practicing psychology. Similarly, according to C. H. Patterson (1997), thorough grounding in one's theory of choice (in his case, client centered) is necessary in order to provide appropriate, integrated supervision.

In addition to working from theories relevant to school psychology, supervisors of school psychologists work from conscious and unconscious thoughts regarding supervision (J. M. Bernard & Goodyear, 2004; Conoley & Bahns, 1995). Counseling, organizational, and clinical psychology as well as educational administration and business management literature propose several models of supervision. Each of these theories and models has generated information and viewpoints that can be useful to clinical supervisors.

Psychodynamic

Supervision based on psychodynamic and psychotherapeutic (Freudian) principles focuses on relationships and resolution of conflict between and among client, supervisee, and supervisor. The supervision technique employed is self-report. In this model, the supervisor focuses on developing a positive working relationship with the therapist as well as fostering a therapeutic relationship between the client and therapist. It is presumed that the dynamics of the relationship between the supervisor and supervisee mirror those of the relationship between the supervisee and the client. Just as clients are thought to relate to their therapists in the same style in which they relate to others in their lives, especially parents, the supervisee is thought to relate to the supervisor in the same style in which he or she relates to others, including clients. Issues of transference and countertransference are emphasized, and supervisees' and supervisors' unresolved personal issues often emerge. However, it is important to note that supervision is distinct from therapy. When a supervisee has significant personal problems, the supervisor does not conduct therapy but refers the supervisee to another therapist (J. M. Bernard & Goodyear, 2004; Neufeldt, Iversen, & Juntunen, 1995).

Group supervision based on this model focuses on supervisee self-reports of therapy sessions using case notes, free association, and possibly tape recordings. The supervisor and group members identify areas of resistance and model mental activities such as curiosity and thinking out loud. Supervisees are encouraged to use therapy manuals and to learn good questioning techniques. Supervisors must learn to be particularly aware of countertransferance, to establish good working alliances, and to coach appropriately (Binder & Strupp, 1997; Milne & Oliver, 2000).

Most school psychology programs are not grounded in psychodynamic theory. Nonetheless, supervisors should be aware of the likelihood that supervisees' personal issues may interfere with their practice.

Vignette 7.3

Alissa has found that school psychologists she supervises who are children of alcoholics themselves tend to be inappropriately overinvolved, oblivious, or overly distant when they work with children of alcoholics in their practice. She takes care not to attempt to provide them therapy herself, but she is sensitive to their experiencing recurring patterns of difficulty and helps them develop problem solving strategies to address them.

Person Centered

The person- or client-centered approach to therapy, developed by Carl Rogers (1958), indicates that congruence, empathy, unconditional positive regard, and warmth not only are essential in therapy but in and of themselves lead to positive psychological growth. Supervision from a client-centered approach relies on developing similar characteristics in the supervisor-supervisee relationship. It focuses on developing the supervisee's skills in fostering each of the above traits in client relationships through the use of audiotapes, live demonstrations, modeling, and role-plays (J. M. Bernard & Goodyear, 2004; Conoley & Bahns, 1995). Electronic recordings and transcript analyses augment direct observations and self-observations. Direct analysis of the content and process of sessions enables supervisees to recognize a tendency to inadvertently affect the progress of sessions. In this model, supervision is on a continuum with therapy. The focus is on being genuine, warm, and empathic and trusting in the potential of the supervisee to grow toward self-actualization. Potential barriers to success include not believing in the potential of the supervisee, students, teachers, or parents. Supervisors who desire control will have difficulty with this approach.

Behavioral and Cognitive-Behavioral

The behavioral approach assumes that both adaptive and maladaptive behaviors are learned and maintained through consequences and reinforcements (Krumboltz & Thorensen, 1969). Individual therapy sessions and therapy as a whole are characterized by setting long- and short-term goals, carrying out empirically validated treatments, using treatment manuals, and changing observable behavior.

The same principals apply to the behavioral approach to supervision (Neufeldt et al., 1995). Supervision's purpose is to teach supervisees appropriate behaviors and technical skills and to extinguish their inappropriate behaviors. Supervisors and supervisees jointly assess skills and develop goals to remedy areas of weakness. They generate and implement strategies to accomplish these goals, and the supervisor provides frequent feedback to shape supervisee behavior. The supervisor and supervisee appraise success after a supervisory intervention and modify goals accordingly. Preferred supervision techniques include agenda setting, homework assignment and review, behavioral feedback, behavior modification programs, didactic instruction, direct observation of the supervisee, program generalization, programmed instruction, modeling, guided discovery, rehearsing, review of tape recordings, and role-plays. Benefits of this approach include clear communication, frequent feedback, and careful monitoring of supervisees (Conoley & Bahns, 1995).

Cognitive-behaviorists add cognitions and affect to the behavioral dimensions. Therapy addresses connections among thoughts, feelings, and behavior (Kendall & Braswell, 1985; Meichenbaum, 1977). Similarly, a cognitive-behavioral approach to supervision focuses on changing observable behaviors by modifying cognitions, affect, and actions (Kratochwill, Bergan, & Mace, 1981). This approach assumes that adaptive and maladaptive behaviors *and cognitions* are learned and maintained through consequences. Supervision is directed by goals, both for overarching development and for individual supervision sessions, that focus on changing the cognitions, feelings, and behaviors of both supervisees and clients.

Constructivism

Constructivist models suggest that a client's reality is subjective and results from the client's active agency, personal constructions, and personal interpretations. It is presumed that there are multiple truths. Supervision using this model similarly assumes that supervisees are active agents constructing their experiences (Trenhaile, 2005). An example of the constructivist approach is the *narrative* approach, wherein the therapist helps clients (and the supervisor helps supervisees) construct and edit personal "stories" that mentally organize their past experiences and thereby influence their future behavior.

Solution-focused models focus on helping clients "get what they want" rather than focusing on what is wrong with them. The emphasis is on drawing on strengths and making incremental changes to achieve goals. A favored strategy is the "miracle question," during which the client (or supervisee) is told, "Imagine that a miracle has occurred and that the problem for which you are seeking help has magically disappeared. What, specifically, do you notice that tells you that this has occurred? What else do you notice?" Solution-focused supervision "emphasizes collaboration in the supervisory relationship, encourages supervisees to become curious about their own potentials, illuminates the possibilities for continued professional development, and highlights the importance of discovery in the supervision experience" (Presbury, Echterling, & McKee, 1999, p. 148). Rather than discuss them, supervisors model successful strategies and encourage supervisees to self-reflect and rate their work, indicate what might increase the effectiveness of their work, determine what worked well, and suggest what should be changed in the future (Trenhaile, 2005).

Discrimination Model

The discrimination model emphasizes matching supervisor role (consultant, teacher, etc.) with supervisee skill in interventions, conceptualization, and personalization (J. M. Bernard & Goodyear, 2004). According to developmental theorists, supervision that does not match the developmental level of the supervisee will be counterproductive (see Chapter 2). The resultant discord may be interpreted as a "personality clash" when in fact it is a failure of the supervisor to adapt to the supervisee's need for support and direction (Ralph, 2002). Typically, novices prefer supervision processes that provide high levels of both support and direction, but as their skills improve their need for direction diminishes. Thus supervisors need to:

1. Assess the developmental level of the supervisee regarding any given task by asking the supervisee, or by directly or indirectly observing the supervisee perform the task

2. Synchronize the supervision role, style, format, and techniques according to the degree of support and direction needed

3. Continually monitor and appraise the skill acquisition of the supervisee and modify the supervision approach accordingly

Integrative Approaches

When employing an integrative approach, a psychologist *combines* different theories, therapies, and techniques to form a repertoire of conceptual, executive, perceptual, and relational skills to address clients' needs (Messer, 2004; Rigazio-DiGilio, 1997). Integrative models assume that psychologists must adopt a holistic perspective to understand the development and functioning of both humans and systems. They also assume that nonadaptation by clients is not a result of a deficiency or pathology but is instead a logical, natural, and even positive result of the combination of developmental history and context. Furthermore, integrative approaches assume that the wide variety of issues presented by clients render adherence to one theoretical approach insufficient and that flexibility is substantially increased by the opportunity to use multiple theories. Given the complexity of schools and school psychology, it is almost inevitable that skilled school psychologists will adopt integrative approaches in their professional practice. So doing can indicate increased proficiency (Skovholt & Rønnestad, 1992).

Like integrative therapy, integrative supervision combines components of various theories. Supervisors who take an integrative approach introduce their supervisees to various theories and approaches and provide organizational structures to enable them to coordinate aspects of professional practice. They adapt supervision techniques to each particular situation (Pearson, 2001). The integrative supervision model assumes that supervisors must adopt a holistic and recursive perspective in order to understand the development and functioning of supervisees. Supervisory impasses are thought to be natural and to reflect a possible mismatch between the needs of the supervisee and the context of supervision. Multiple approaches are expected to yield many supervision strategies and provide multiple perspectives, schemata, and opportunities for growth.

Integrative supervision of school psychological services applies executive functions to client-centered, systemic, cognitive-behavioral, developmental, and process-based supervision to consider student outcomes, school outcomes, supervisee outcomes, supervisor outcomes, and district outcomes. At each level are three recursive phases: preparation, performance, and appraisal. During the preparation phase, the supervisor collects data, sets goals, and develops a plan. At the student, class, and program levels, data collection focuses on assessing needs, academic skills, and social-emotional-behavioral functioning. At the supervisee and supervisor levels, data collection focuses on assessing and addressing professional skills and dispositions. During the performance phase, regardless of the targeted audience, the supervisor or supervisee implements data-based interventions, makes observations, and modifies the intervention. During the appraisal phase, the supervisor or supervisee assesses progress, reflects, and revises future plans.

Supervisor Role and Style

At any given moment, according to process-based supervision (J. M. Bernard & Goodyear, 2004), a supervisor selects her or his appropriate role according to the situational needs and the developmental level of the supervisee. Supervisors can be teachers, counselors, evaluators, mentors, or consultants. At times a supervisor will take a consultant role and focus on improving the functioning of the supervisee so that future independent functioning is more likely. At other times, a supervisor will take an evaluative role and recommend that a supervisee be awarded (or not be awarded) licensure. Although it can cause clinical supervisors discomfort, all supervisors must assume administrative functions inasmuch as they organize the supervisory experience and evaluate supervisees' clinical skills and fitness to practice (J. M. Bernard & Goodyear, 2004; Falender & Shafranske, 2004).

Multiple clinical supervision purposes and supervisor roles are described in teacher education literature (Clifford, Macy, & Albi, 2005; Pajak, 2000). These can be adapted to the practice of school psychology. In traditional supervision, the supervisor's role is to assist the psychologist in discovering his or her strengths and professional style. In the coaching model, the supervisor helps the supervisee identify strengths and refine skills. In the developmental model, the supervisor evaluates the supervisee's developmental level and decreases support as the supervisee's skill increases in order to foster independence and problem solving skills. When taking the didactic role, supervisors provide information and expert modeling. In the reflective model, supervisors help supervisees appraise their own effectiveness.

Hart and Nance (2003) explored four counselor-supervisor roles: *directive teacher* (high direction, low support), *supportive teacher* (high direction, high support), *counselor* (low direction, high support), and *consultant* (low direction, low support). Hart and Nance found that supervisors preferred to take roles providing high support but not necessarily high direction (counselor or supportive teacher). Supervisees, on the other hand, preferred that supervisors take the role that provides both high support and high direction (supportive teacher). Research regarding the effects of the role and style of supervisors are equivocal, with some studies finding an impact on self-efficacy and effectiveness (Borders, 1990; Fernando & Hulse-Killacky, 2005).

A significant body of literature in educational psychology delineates fundamental learning principals to which supervisors should attend when they design supervisory teaching strategies. These fundamental learning principles (Harvey & Chickie-Wolfe, 2007), with the addition of Boud and Walker's (1998) principles of adult leaning, are summarized in Table 7.2.

Table 7.2   Learning Principles

- Provide experiential learning
- Provide collaborative and interactive learning
- Focus on important information
- Tie new information to known information
- Space and repeat learning trials
- Use multiple senses
- Incorporate corrective feedback
- Encourage the monitoring of learning
- Ensure comprehension
- Foster self-regulation and self-appraisal of learning

Skilled supervisors consider the characteristics of individual learners when they take the teaching role. One method of doing this is to ask supervisees to write "learning narratives" to discover their preferred learning methods. Statements in Activity 7.1 are modifications of questions that Aggett (2004) suggested supervisees might address in writing learning narratives.

Activity 7.1

Writing a Learning Narrative

Compose a learning narrative by answering the following questions:

Your perceptions: What are your early memories of learning in your school, family, and neighborhood? What was learning like for you as a child? As an adolescent? As an adult? What sort of learner were you as a child? As an adolescent? As an adult? What was your preferred learning style as a child? As an adolescent? As an adult? Would you have wanted to make different learning choices? How did your choice of careers affect you learning opportunities? How did your learning opportunities affect your career choice?

(Continued)

(Continued)

> **Your perceptions of others' perceptions:** What messages did you receive from others (teachers, parents, and peers) regarding yourself as a learner? How would they have described your learning style when you were young?
>
> **You and ideas:** What did you think of your own ideas when you were young? What do you think of your own ideas now? What did you think of the ideas of others when you were young? What do you think of others' ideas now? What is an example of your holding on to your own ideas even when others do not agree with you? What ideas did you have as a young child about your future?
>
> **You in groups:** How do you participate in group conversations? What is your style? How do you think the style you have as a group participant affects your ability to learn new ideas in a group? How does it affect whether and how others listen to you? Whether and how they adopt your ideas?
>
> **Your context:** How have you been affected by large political, philosophical, religious, and cultural ideas about learning? How do current situations affect your confidence in your own ideas? Who most influenced your ideas about learning in your family? How was your learning affected by conflicts or upheavals in your family or social group? How did friendships or parenthood affect your learning?
>
> **Your style:** When someone presents a new idea, are you more likely to incorporate it into your preexisting concepts or to try to determine which is correct? Are you more likely to think in metaphors, in mental pictures, or by internal dialogue? If you were to design a teaching situation that would be ideal for you as a learner, what would it look like?
>
> **Your legacy:** Given your ideas regarding learning, how will you be challenged in this learning situation? What philosophy of learning will you pass on to your children and supervisees? How will that differ from the philosophies your teachers, mentors, and supervisors have held?

ORGANIZATIONAL AND DISTRICT CONSIDERATIONS

The structure of clinical supervision tends to be determined, both covertly and overtly, at the organizational level. In schools, this often occurs at the district level. Some administrators recognize supervision of psychologists as so critical that they instruct principals to release supervisors and supervisees during regular school hours for supervision sessions.

Vignette 7.4

Janice found that the most effective schedule for group supervision was every Friday from 1:30 to 3:30. The group thus met for half their session "on school time," but at a time that principals found least objectionable. The second half of the session was "on their own time," but for the most part the supervisees felt comfortable with this arrangement. Since there was no pressure to return to the schools, the conversations were relaxed and highly supportive. As an end-of-the-week debriefing opportunity, the sessions were characterized by a great deal of laughter and tension release. Supervisees left the sessions relaxed and ready to enjoy their weekends. This schedule fulfilled Janice's belief that the fundamental purpose of group supervision is to foster group cohesion and provide peer support for clinical issues. Administrative supervisory directives and information were typically shared through memos, e-mails, and meetings at other times during the week.

Savvy administrators also establish policies that require maintenance of case notes and supervision records and the development of supervision plans with each supervisee. A number of best practices regarding the planning and provision of clinical supervision have emerged in the literature. These include developing supervision goals, writing and signing supervision contracts, determining the supervision format, and determining supervision frequency.

Supervision Goals

Overarching Goals

As Mead (1990) indicated, clinical supervisors and supervisees often differ in their supervision goals, and it is important to reconcile these differences from the beginning. Supervisees and supervisors may have different goals for supervision based on their respective positions. A supervisee's supervision goals may be to

> learn a specific skill or technique, . . . evaluate therapy as a career, search for support and reinforcement, look for an answer to personal problems, seek personal growth and development, or to attempt to evaluate or validate a specific therapeutic model. (p. 59)

Supervisors, on the other hand, have the overarching supervision goal of improving supervisees' skills until they perform like expert practitioners. Subsidiary goals may include ensuring that supervisees learn how to conduct initial interviews, use basic assessment techniques, hypothesize about cases, develop effective treatment plans, and evaluate student progress (Mead, 1990).

Furthermore, supervisors and supervisees may have different goals as a result of the supervisee's developmental level. A beginning practitioner is likely to seek help for a specific case, while supervisors prefer that supervisees develop skills "to deal with a class of problems, rather than finding a technique to fix a specific problem" (Mead, 1990, p. 57). It is probable that supervisors will need to push intermediate supervisees to add new theories and techniques to their repertoire and to encourage advanced supervisees to articulate the theories and principles behind their work.

Therefore, a critical aspect of supervision planning is to develop mutually agreed-upon written supervision goals. Just as it is good practice to have written treatment goals for the provision of students' special education services, it is good practice to have written supervision goals. Written goals improve communication, suggest supervisory interventions, and facilitate evaluations of both supervisees and supervisors. In developing overarching supervision goals, general goals are written in abstract language, and then measurable and observable objectives are listed and reviewed to ensure that an observer could assess the completion of each. The objectives preferably focus on increasing positive behaviors rather than on decreasing negative behaviors. Like a student's education plan, supervision goals are useful only if they contain observable outcomes, specify action steps needed to reach the outcome, and specify evaluation procedures to be followed.

Session Goals

Just as supervisors and supervisees may differ in their overarching goals, they may differ in their goals for individual supervision sessions. Therefore, it is helpful to begin each session by establishing a clear working agenda by reviewing the respective goals held by the supervisee and supervisor for that session. This is followed by dealing with immediate needs and providing support and direction according to the developmental needs of the supervisee. It is also important to allow sufficient time for spontaneous discussions and to check back and make sure that each person's session goals have been met by the end of the session.

Supervision Contracts

Supervision goals are best included in a comprehensive written supervision contract that delineates the methods, techniques, and frequency of supervision. As indicated by Falvey and Cohen (2003), "from a legal perspective, if no written contract exists the courts can assume an implied contract and impose a duty of care solely on the basis of assuming a supervisory role" (p. 68). Thus it is very important for clinical supervisors to develop and adhere to a contract that ensures the welfare of the students with whom the school psychologist works and also addresses the supervisee's professional development.

A number of authors (Blackwell, Strohmer, Belcas, & Burton, 2002; Cobia & Boes, 2000; Falvey & Cohen, 2003; Mead, 1990; Munson, 2002; Osborn & Davis, 1996; Sutter, McPherson, & Geeseman, 2002; J. T. Thomas, 2007) have suggested components of supervision contracts. A compilation, adapted to school psychology, follows in Table 7.3.

The supervision contract should be signed by all stakeholders: the supervisee, supervisor(s), university supervisor (if applicable), and relevant school district administrator(s). Each should keep a copy for their files.

Supervision Format

Various supervision formats (e.g., individual, group, peer, coworking, team) can be used across theoretical orientations, although some formats are better suited to particular models and activities than others. Although individual supervision tends to be most preferred, Milne and Oliver (2000) found other formats to be very highly rated (above 4 on a 5-point scale) as well. In fact, flexible formats wherein the structure of supervision is deliberately varied according to the learning needs of the supervisee and site circumstances are highly recommended.

Individual Supervision

Individual supervision is the most traditional, familiar, frequently practiced, and preferred form of clinical supervision. It provides supervisors with unique opportunities to develop strong supportive relationships with supervisees and is conducive to revealing vulnerabilities, reducing anxiety, increasing the ability to relate to clients, and developing self-awareness (Bogo, Globerman, & Sussman, 2004). Supervision sessions tend to focus on supervisees' presentation of case studies while the supervisor encourages reflection, conceptualization, and case planning. Although individual supervision is inefficient and time consuming, it can provide the ability to focus on specific objectives and closely monitor the quality of services provided by the supervisee. This results in the greatest level of client protection and quality control (Milne & Oliver, 2000). Most supervision techniques and interventions have emerged in the context of individual supervision, but they can be adapted for use in other formats.

Table 7.3   Supervision Contract Components

Supervisor Variables

- Name
- Education (degrees, dates of degrees, and concentrations)
- Licenses and certifications
- Years of experience as a school psychologist
- Areas of professional expertise
- Orientation toward school psychology
- Training in supervision
- Years of experience as a supervisor
- Supervision model
- Supervisor duties and responsibilities
- Commitment to avoid a dual (nonprofessional) relationship with the supervisee
- Commitment to maintain malpractice insurance acknowledging supervision
- Agreement to assign tasks that the supervisee is competent to perform and can reasonably deliver
- Agreement to meet the training needs of the supervisee (e.g., provide experiences in the breadth of school psychology services and throughout the age ranges specified in the license/certification)
- Agreement to provide at least 2 weeks' notice prior to supervision contract termination
- Methods to be used to document supervision and where supervision records will be kept
- Availability for nonscheduled appointments

Supervisee Variables

- Name
- Qualifications for practice
- Clear and specific delineations of areas of strength and weakness
- General and specific skills to be developed
- Commitment to share important information with the supervisor
- Commitment to carry malpractice insurance
- Agreement to provide at least 2 weeks' notice prior to supervision contract termination
- Agreement to maintain required documentation (such as logs) of supervised activities
- Commitment to adhere to ethical codes, legal requirements, and office policies
- Commitment to obtain informed consent and acknowledge supervised status (as appropriate) before providing psychological services

Supervision Variables

- Purpose of supervision
- Goals and objectives of supervision
- Duration of the supervisory relationship

(Continued)

Table 7.3 (Continued)

- Anticipated supervision formats
- Frequency of supervision sessions by format
- Fees
- Anticipated supervision techniques and interventions

Organization Variables

- Official supervisee hours and days (e.g., 7 a.m. to 4 p.m., September 1 through June 5, holidays excepted)
- Type and number of clients to be seen by the supervisee
- Activities in which the supervisee will engage
- Confidentiality (or lack thereof) of supervisory sessions
- Limits to confidentiality (duty to warn or protect, harm to self or others, violations of law or ethical conduct per NASP/APA)
- Frequency and duration of organizationally sanctioned supervision sessions
- Organizational goals and objectives of supervision
- Organizationally sanctioned supervision formats (individual, group, peer, live, e-mail)
- Emergency procedures the supervisee should take in a crisis situation
- Methods the supervisor will use to intervene when the supervisees' actions need modification or merit termination
- Necessary site-specific knowledge and skills, such as expertise with state curriculum frameworks and knowledge of state special education laws
- Expected familiarity with specific assessment tools
- Informal site norms such as dress code, work hours beyond the official hours, and parking provisions
- Means of record keeping
- Protocol regarding sharing e-mails and other forms of communication
- Information regarding lines of authority
- Information regarding supervisor rotation
- Provision of space, equipment, and support services

Evaluation Variables

- Formative evaluation methods
- Written summaries to be provided after each supervision session
- Summative evaluation methods
- Written summaries and evaluations provided to the supervisee
- Frequency of summative and formative evaluation methods
- Methods to assess progress made toward the accomplishment of specific goals of the supervisee, supervisor, and clients
- Manner and frequency of direct observations
- Methods to be used to assess the supervisee's ongoing progress
- Individuals with whom the evaluation will be shared
- Steps to counteract a negative evaluation

Individual Supervision in a Small Group

In this format the supervisor holds supervision sessions with a small group of supervisees but works with each supervisee individually on a rotating basis. This format has the potential to combine the advantages of individual supervision with those of group supervision (Milne & Oliver, 2000). It is more efficient and cost effective than individual supervision and also permits vicarious learning because supervisees observe one another's supervision sessions.

Vignette 7.5

Maxine provides individual supervision to three individuals. During one 90-minute supervision session she conducts a 30-minute session with each of her supervisees and has them observe one another's sessions. She finds that this provides excellent learning opportunities for all of them. However, she does need to take care to manage any competition among the group members.

Group Supervision

In group supervision, supervision is provided collectively regarding common issues as well as to individuals within the group setting. Group supervision has several advantages; not only does it cost less and provide opportunities to observe others both less and more advanced than oneself, but it also enables supervisees to learn from one another and develop a network of professional support so that they do not become overly dependent on the supervisor. It "provides the opportunity to learn from others through sharing knowledge, hearing different perspectives, and discussing issues, both common and unique to each group member" (Bogo et al., 2004, p. 13). Group supervision can normalize experiences, foster group cohesion, and increase supervisees' likelihood of being open to consultation (Riva & Cornish, 1995). It can be an effective method of conveying "informal curriculum" during training (Haboush, 2003). To gain these advantages, supervisors must address critical issues. For example, timing is a consideration: Weekly meetings tend to result in the most professional growth. Biweekly and monthly meetings tend to result in more formal interactions (J. M. Bernard & Goodyear, 2004). In addition, supervisors should consider group composition, stages of group development, and the structure of group supervision sessions.

Group Composition

It is helpful to limit the group size (four to eight supervisees appears optimal) and to consider member characteristics. It is often advantageous to cluster individuals with similar developmental levels or interests.

Vignette 7.6

The 30 school psychologists employed in **Abbott School District** meet together monthly to receive administration supervision and to be informed of current districtwide issues. In addition, each school psychologist takes part in a small peer group for clinical supervision. Every week the psychologists meet in small groups of six to eight according to interest: The school psychologists assigned primarily to students with emotional and behavioral disorders meet as a group, as do those respectively assigned to the elementary schools, the junior high schools, and the high schools.

Stages of Group Development

A number of stages or phases of group development have been proposed by various authors, but the research regarding whether groups actually follow predictable stages is equivocal (Rivera et al., 2004). Nonetheless, supervisors should consciously address those stages of group development that have been established recursively. During the *initial stage* (variously called *formation*, *exploration*, *orientation*, *engagement*, and *forming*), the group leader encourages group members to get comfortable with one another and establish ground rules. During the *intermediate stage*, the supervisor promotes a norm of structured and supportive feedback during group supervision sessions. At some point, the supervisor may need to directly address relationships among members to help them resolve power and competition issues stemming from needs to seem competent, to be favored by the supervisor, to reconcile family-of-origin matters, or to address friendships or previous classroom relationships (Bogo et al., 2004). The *final stage* (variously called *adjourning*, *termination*, and *ending*) occurs when the group disbands. In this stage, the supervisor is challenged to help members simultaneously manage the termination of client relationships and the ending of the group without prematurely disengaging. Adjourning is a natural stage for a time-limited group, such as a group of interns, but occasional addition and subtraction of members needs to be "scheduled" periodically in ongoing groups (J. M. Bernard & Goodyear, 2004; B. W. Tuckman & Jensen, 1977).

Certain predictable variables can interfere with effective group supervision, including problems between members, problems with supervisors, supervisee anxiety, logistical constraints, and poor time management (Enyedy et al., 2003). Therefore, supervisors should take care to proactively address common group phenomena such as competition, scapegoated members, overbearing individuals, and reenactment of family-of-origin issues. Supervisors should ensure that all supervisees benefit from the issues addressed in the group regardless of their expertise or characteristics of their clients. It can be quite difficult to ensure that both beginning and advanced practitioners are simultaneously supported and sufficiently challenged. It can also be difficult to ensure equitable participation; supervisors should monitor each member's contributions and change the group focus accordingly. Furthermore, supervisors should ensure that group sessions have clearly stated objectives, that members feel able to openly communicate, and that feedback regarding the effectiveness of the supervision sessions is regularly attained (Bogo et al., 2004). It is critically important that group supervision not be confused with group therapy, because group supervision that attempts to imitate group therapy can actually be detrimental (Prieto, 1997).

During the initial sessions, the supervisor should establish ground rules, including regular attendance and maintenance of confidentiality regarding both clients and supervisees. It is also important to establish that case presentations will be organized and focused, include written and taped material, include both client and supervisee issues, and lead to constructive feedback from group members as well as the supervisor. The supervisor can make this clear by modeling an effective case presentation at the onset of group sessions (J. M. Bernard & Goodyear, 2004; Bogo et al., 2004; Wilbur, Roberts-Wilbur, Hart, Morris, & Betz, 1994).

Session Structure

At the beginning of each group supervision session, supervisors are advised to have members *check in* by asking them for specific information (Edwards & Heshmati, 2003).

> **Vignette 7.7**
>
> **Karen** begins her group supervision sessions by asking each member to mention a professional success he or she has experienced since the last supervision session. Karen finds that her supervisees look forward to sharing these positive experiences and that they set a positive tone for the entire session. Furthermore, since supervisees tend to bring problems to supervision, this practice enables Karen to hear about successes that her supervisees would otherwise forget to mention.

Structured Group Supervision, in which cases are presented in a systematic format, have been found to result in empirically grounded skill development (Crutchfield et al., 1997; Rivera et al., 2004; Russo et al., 2001; Wilbur et al., 1994). In the first step a group member introduces a problem, challenging event, critical incident, or difficult case and ends with a clear *request for assistance.* Then each group member in turn asks one or more *questions* to gain a better understanding of the situation and its context. After every group member has asked questions, each provides *feedback* (suggestions and insights). Then there is a *pause* during which the presenter reflects on these suggestions and insights, after which she or he *responds* to the suggestions, indicates which will be attempted, and states why those suggestions will be attempted and others will not. Following the presenter's response, the group *discusses* the process. Sufficient time must be allocated for Structured Group Supervision. It can take 60 to 90 minutes to adequately address one case (Russo et al., 2001).

Postsupervision supervisor reflections are a written summary and extension of the discussion that took place during group supervision. The comments are given to the supervisees who have presented a case during the group supervision session as soon as possible after the session. The supervisor uses notes taken during the session as the foundation for these reflections, but also adds news insights and ideas. The comments include (a) reflections regarding the client, (b) reflections regarding the supervisee's interactions with the client, and (c) reflections regarding supervisor and group member responses to questions the supervisee posed. Emphasis is placed on identifying supervisee strengths, providing constructive comments, and using the session as a learning experience (Edwards & Heshmati, 2003).

Peer Supervision

Peer support groups are voluntary relationships among professionals with common interests and are characterized by the mutual sharing of advice, guidance, and social support (Kirschenbaum & Glaser, 1978). Peer support groups have emerged as an important professional development tool in school psychology and provide a means to engage in career-long learning. They also offer a viable means by which professionals can respond to changing educational conditions and increasing demands for accountability. Such groups have evolved in response to a distinct need for professional development and social support that was not adequately met in other ways. Peer consultation and support groups provide a logical, efficient way to meet the obligation to stay abreast of the field in order to implement new ideas (Zins & Murphy, 1996).

In peer supervision, two or more individuals informally supervise one another's work. In both individual and group supervision, the supervisor takes an advisory and evaluative role. Peer supervision is unique in that the relationship is voluntary and generally collaborative, occurs between professionals of equal status, and has no evalua-tive component. Supervisees receiving peer supervision are freer to reject recommended strategies and maintain legal and ethical responsibility for their work. Because peer supervisors are not in a position to evaluate or reprimand the supervisee, they are much less subject to vicarious liability (Kruger & Struzziero, 1997).

Peer support and supervision groups can serve many of the same functions as indi-vidual and group supervision. They can generate suggestions for difficult cases, provide a forum for discussion of ethical dilemmas, ameliorate feelings of stress and isolation, supply an opportunity to learn new methods and techniques, and provide a venue for discussing feelings and attitudes toward students, parents, and teachers (Culbreth, Scarborough, & Banks-Johnson, 2005; Lewis, Greenburg, & Hatch, 1988). They can be effective when composed of members of one discipline, such as school psychologists, or when composed of members of many disciplines (Thomasgard & Collins, 2003). They can be a particularly effective tool for increasing multicultural competencies (Gainor & Constantine, 2002). Peer supervision is particularly well suited for advanced practitioners.

When well carried out, with structured case presentations and attention to the group dynamics previously discussed under group supervision, peer supervision can have many of the advantages of group supervision. Zins and Murphy (1996) conducted a survey regarding peer supervision and consultation among school psychologists and found that several characteristics yield the most effective groups. Borders (1991) similarly elucidated important variables. The recommendations of these authors are summarized in Table 7.4.

Table 7.4   Characteristics of Effective Peer Consultation/Supervision Groups

- Members share similar interests and responsibilities
- Group membership is small
- Group goals and plans have been developed
- Communication is open, with honest and constructive feedback
- A supportive atmosphere is maintained
- Local circumstances are addressed
- Group cohesion is fostered
- A formal structure similar to that employed in formal consultation or group supervision is used
- Participants are asked to analyze case presentations from specific viewpoints (e.g., they might be asked to note nonverbal cues; assume the role of a parent, student, or teacher; or take a particular theoretical orientation)
- Designated moderators coordinate and observe group processes, foster a supportive atmosphere, and keep records of actions and recommendations

Peer support and supervision groups can be ongoing over a period of years. They can also be effective when time limited. Benshoff and Paisley (1996) employed a nine-session structured peer supervision model for school counselors. In the first session, members shared background information regarding their education and work experience, described their typical professional approach, and set goals for themselves and their pro-fessional practice. The second session was devoted to broader program practices in the counselors' schools and concluded with the sharing of session audiotapes for other members' review. The third through eighth sessions were devoted to tape reviews and case study presentations, and the ninth session was devoted to termination. Even when so time limited, peer supervision resulted in increased professional expertise.

Collaborative Work

In this supervision format, the supervisor and supervisee collaboratively work on the same cases by collaboratively conducting assessments, consultations, or counseling. This format can provide a very effective and efficient way for novices or experienced practitioners to learn skills. It also provides ample opportunity to hone observation skills.

Vignette 7.8

Every year **Stuart** supervised interns, and he always began by having each intern collaboratively conduct assessments with him. He completed some assessment tasks, the supervisee completed others, they discussed their observations and results, and then they collaboratively wrote the report. This process provided the intern with ample opportunities to observe an expert at work and also gave Stuart opportunities to verify the intern's skills in assessment practices and case conceptualization.

Team Supervision

In team supervision, multiple supervisors work with the same supervisee and each supervisor has a defined role (Milne & Oliver, 2000). An example of team supervision is triadic supervision, wherein a university supervisor and school supervisor share supervisory responsibilities for a practicum student working in a school. Another example is when a school district assigns various supervisors according to specialty areas. For example, one supervisor might address all district school psychologists' work with students with autism to augment their normal supervision. Regardless of the individuals involved in team supervision, it is important to encourage collaboration and communication regarding the supervision role, model, evaluation processes, and performance criteria.

Vignette 7.9

As a university supervisor, **Ralph** (2002) finds it very helpful to explain the developmental model of supervision to field supervisors at the beginning of the practicum/internship experience, during each university visit, and at the end of the practicum/internship experience. Using the developmental model as a keystone of supervision fosters clear communication among the supervisee, field supervisor, and university supervisor.

Mixed Format Supervision

Many clinical supervisors maximize the advantages of various supervision formats by regularly using more than one. For example, supervisors might schedule a weekly 1-hour individual session with each supervisee and a weekly 2-hour group supervision session. Other supervisors encourage various mixed formats that include peer supervision (Milne & Oliver, 2000).

Supervision Frequency

It is our experience that supervision frequency should vary according to the supervisee's needs and the setting in which the supervisee practices. While NASP (2000b) standards mandate that interns be provided at least 2 hours of face-to-face supervision every week, beginning interns need much more supervision and are commonly "joined at the hip" to their supervisors at the beginning of the internship. Furthermore, it is very rarely (if ever) appropriate for a beginning intern to be the only school psychologist assigned to a school building without the ongoing support of a supervisor who is very familiar with the school's teachers, administrators, and parents. On the other hand, by the end of the internship, the need for supervision should be considerably reduced. However, weekly clinical supervision sessions should be scheduled throughout the first several years of practice. Regularly scheduled (e.g., Wednesday at 2 p.m.) supervision sessions are critical, because otherwise both supervisees and supervisors get caught up in other obligations and supervision does not occur. If a particular session is not needed by a more advanced supervisee, it can always be canceled. However, in addition to regularly scheduled supervision sessions, supervisees of all levels of development must have provisions to obtain additional supervision whenever they encounter an emergency situation or are dealing with a difficult or complex case.

SPECIAL CONSIDERATIONS IN SUPERVISING PRACTICUM STUDENTS AND INTERNS

Successful fieldwork offers an opportunity for growth for all participants. The site supervisor facilitates the intern's learning. In turn, the site supervisor's knowledge and skills are enriched by the current ideas and materials shared by the intern. Both the site supervisor and the intern or practicum student inform the university supervisor and program of current issues in the field and of needed university program adjustments. To maximize benefit to all participants, close cooperation and collaboration among the university supervisor, site supervisor, and intern or practicum student are critically important.

Frequent communication is vital. Written correspondence, phone conversations, and e-mail can be used to supplement face-to-face meetings. Daily communication between interns or practicum students and site supervisors can be facilitated by using notebooks in which either party can pose a question or make an observation to which the other can respond. Another method is to use e-mail correspondence, as long as confidentiality is maintained by avoiding the use of names. Such communication facilitates reflective practice, gives the intern a mechanism for acquiring information almost immediately, and creates a permanent record of ideas, information, and responsibility clarification. Handout 7.1, Internship Supervisor Conference, and Handout 7.2, Internship Learner Conference (included at the end of this chapter), were developed by Christine Merman Woolf of Capella University to facilitate communication among the university supervisor, the field supervisor, and the intern. Based on NASP standards, they provide semistructured interview questions to use during telephone and face-to-face conferences throughout the internship year.

One of the most important responsibilities of both university and field supervisors is to collaborate in the development of a training plan. Within the parameters of professional and university dictates, this comprehensive training plan should be designed according to the needs of the individual student. Students enter fieldwork with vastly different interests, experiences, and competencies. Although mandatory competencies must be achieved by all, it is important to recognize that great variability will exist. The initiation and evolution of an individual training plan is a dynamic, interactive process that involves all participants. Completion of self-assessment by the intern or practicum student regarding skills and competencies offers a logical starting point.

Site Supervisors' Qualifications and Obligations

NASP (2004) recommended that, before becoming supervisors, individuals meet the Nationally Certified School Psychologist credentialing requirements, complete a minimum of 3 years' supervised experience as a school psychologist, and be employed as a school psychologist for at least 1 year. It is very helpful when the site supervisor is employed full time in the district. Although more than one supervisor may supervise an intern, it is advantageous to assign primary supervisory responsibility to one person (Alessi, Lascurettes-Alessi, & Leyes, 1981). Site supervisor competencies are found in Handout 1.1.

School psychologists who decide to supervise interns should do so with the knowledge that it takes considerable time. Ward (1999) found that the average intern supervisor spent 4.7 hours in direct supervision and 4.4 hours in indirect supervision every week, the equivalent of more than a day per week. Therefore, it is important that supervisors have sufficient time allocated. Site supervisors should expect to spend 50% of their time with the intern during the first semester, more at the beginning of the semester than at the end. A common error is allowing (or even requiring) too much independence too soon, forcing the intern to learn from trial and error. On the other hand, it is important to "let go" as the skills of the intern increase, since excessive supervision can smother growth.

In addition to formal qualifications and time allocation, fieldwork supervision requires significant interpersonal skills. It is essential that the supervisor understands, accepts, and positively responds to supervisees' uncertainty. This is accomplished when the supervisor develops a positive emotional climate; accords supervisees professional equality by encouraging, accepting, and implementing their ideas; and treats supervisees as persons of authority in the presence of students, school personnel, and parents.

At the same time, the site supervisor should become familiar with the basic ethical and legal responsibilities and requirements for the fieldwork. This includes being aware of the legal status of interns in the state in which the internship is occurring. The site supervisor should also read the university internship handbook before internship occurs.

University Supervisors' Obligations and Perspectives

The overarching job of the university supervisor is to ensure that university and state requirements are being met. This necessitates interpreting policy, explaining program requirements, orienting the student to academic requirements, making specific suggestions to enhance training, completing appropriate forms, suggesting desirable activities, helping to determine the intern's schedule, and troubleshooting when necessary.

The university supervisor serves as a liaison between the training site and the university program. At the beginning of the internship, the university supervisor should develop a relationship with the site supervisor to consider:

- The basic rationale for the internship program
- The philosophy of the training program and its congruence with the philosophy of the field site

- Objectives and requirements of the internship
- The number of hours of the internship, including consideration of vacations and holidays
- The schedule of observations and conferences between the site supervisor and intern
- Competencies to be achieved by the intern
- Evaluation schedules and forms for assessing the intern, the field site, and the university program
- The types of activities and training plan
- Grading responsibilities

The university supervisor monitors the appropriateness of the site, ensures that requirements are met, serves as a feedback loop between the university training program and the field site, and, by the end of the internship, ensures that the student is sufficiently competent to warrant certification.

Throughout the year, the university supervisor often conducts seminars that provide interns from different sites with opportunities to compare notes, ask questions, and formulate conclusions through peer interaction. The seminars give the university supervisor the opportunity to observe the intern in a different environment, answer questions, and guide discussions regarding problem analysis where alternatives for practice are considered. It is most helpful if the university supervisor has had significant experience working in schools and has achieved at least a proficient level of practice.

Additionally, throughout the internship year, the university supervisor often makes site visits that include direct observations of the intern engaging in various professional activities such as counseling, consultation, and assessment. After such observations, the university supervisor provides feedback and assists the intern in self-evaluation. The university supervisor also meets individually with the field supervisor, solicits his or her impressions, reviews progress toward the fulfillment of university and state requirements, suggests additional experiences for the intern, and summarizes the intern's progress for both the intern and site supervisor from a different perspective. If an intern is having difficulty, whether in practice or in the relationship with the site supervisor, the university supervisor serves as both mediator and problem solver. University supervisors can also extend communication beyond the site supervisor and establish relationships with others in the building who work with the intern, including the principal, teachers, and paraprofessionals. An exchange of views and ideas with these individuals can be beneficial and informative for all involved.

Alessi et al. (1981) offered a model for intern supervision that includes a sequence of goal-directed teaching activities divided into five stages, the length of which varies with the skills of the intern and the demands of the setting. An adaptation follows:

Stage 1: Shadowing and modeling. During the initial phase of supervision, the intern physically shadows the supervisor to directly observe the performance of professional activities from a comfortable, nonthreatening vantage point. The function of the supervisor is to demonstrate tasks while the supervisee observes. During this period, the intern is introduced to various school personnel, views different programs, becomes familiar with the physical facility, learns about the organizational structure of the school, obtains information about the characteristics of the community and school system, and is exposed to formal and informal procedures used in the performance of school psychology tasks. It is helpful for the intern to observe other practitioners in addition to the field supervisor to gain exposure to different skills and techniques in a relatively short time.

To acquire knowledge regarding the scope and sequence of instruction, interns should be scheduled to visit classrooms varying by type, age of pupils, subject matter, and school. Observations should be conducted during general education classes; special education classes; art, music, and gym classes; recess; lunch; afterschool activities; and counseling group meetings. Both expert and novice teachers should be observed.

As a professional courtesy to those being observed, observations should be scheduled in advance. All observations should be maximally active in that the intern critiques and analyzes the observations and discusses them with the site supervisor. Observations are most fruitful when students enter them with specific questions in mind, have time to speak to those observed ahead of time, thank those observed and give constructive comments regarding what has been seen, and analyze the observation with the supervisor. Observations should yield:

- Increased knowledge regarding the facilitation of student learning
- Increased ability to analyze and evaluate practice
- Recognition of theoretical orientations and their implications for practice
- Formulation of a valid concept of effective teaching
- Formulation of a valid concept of effective school psychology
- Formulation of a comprehensive concept of the school's scope and sequence of curriculum and the relationship of various content areas
- Formulation of a concept of education as an integrated whole

Stage 2: Observation and assessment of professional skills. The supervisor closely observes the intern performing both direct (e.g., assessment, interviewing, counseling) and indirect (e.g., consultation) services. The developmental levels of the intern are determined and a specific plan to provide appropriate training experiences is mutually formulated and agreed upon. This training plan considers the individual requirements of the intern and the overarching requirements of the university training program. Before every activity, the intern indicates the goals and objectives, methods and techniques, and timing and sequencing as well as methods of evaluating its effectiveness. The site supervisor should refrain from correcting the intern or interrupting during an observation, because such an interruption can reduce confidence and deteriorate the respect of others; however, interruptions should certainly be made when damage might occur. A planning conference should be able to prevent most difficulties, and most other concerns can be discussed in a conference after the observation.

Stage 3: Guided independent practice. During this stage, interns independently perform specific tasks in which they have demonstrated competence in prior observations. For example, familiar cognitive tests might be administered for reevaluations. Under direct supervision and/or observation, the intern continues to observe and/or perform activities in which more direction and experience are necessary. The training plan is reviewed and revised and decisions are mutually agreed upon.

Cooperative practice, or collaboration of the supervisor and intern on cases, can be an effective method of internship supervision at this stage. When done well, cooperative practice is characterized by mutual goals, shared responsibility, and teamwork. Many activities lend themselves naturally to this practice. For example, interns and their supervisors can conduct different aspects of a student evaluation or colead a counseling group.

Interns should be encouraged to have both long-range and daily plans regarding each case or group with whom they are working. Long-range plans consider a comprehensive design as well as daily or weekly activities. Plans for specific activities should be written and submitted to the supervisor several days in advance to allow for necessary revisions. It is helpful for interns to have access to several model plans so that they may follow them as they write their own plans. These model plans should include resources used by the supervisor, library resources, audiovisual materials, available supplies and equipment, community resources, available funds, and publications.

Stage 4: Increasing independent practice. As interns gain more experience, their scope of professional activities increases. Independent practice is encouraged within the framework of regular supervision. At this stage, interns take more initiative and responsibility for professional activities and become increasingly less dependent on the supervisor. They make independent decisions and discuss them in supervision.

Stage 5: Professional independence. Supervisors should not expect that interns will function completely independently by the end of the internship. Long-term plans for professional development and ongoing supervision should be established during the final stage.

In summary, as Sullivan and Conoley (2008) indicated, internship supervision is most effective when:

- Supervisors make themselves available
- The amount of direction provided meets the intern's developmental level
- Supervisors are knowledgeable, implement research-based practice, and skillfully help interns conceptualize cases
- Expectations are clear
- Supervisors provide interns with a "safe place" that fosters trust and open communication through respect, support, and positive encouragement
- Supervisors stereotype neither supervisees nor their cases according to cultural variables and are particularly sensitive to minority interns
- Supervisors help interns with time management and setting appropriate limits
- Interns are not exploited, and the sacrifice they are taking to complete the internship is acknowledged
- Supervisors are enthusiastic and positive about the profession of school psychology

SUMMARY

Clinical supervision is defined as those aspects of supervision that focus on fostering professional skills and competencies. Appropriate clinical supervision involves multiple factors. These include supervisor characteristics such as worldview, theoretical orientation, supervision model, role preference, and supervision techniques. Even before becoming supervisors, individuals have beliefs regarding supervision that influence their choice of supervision interventions and techniques. Additionally, supervision is influenced by the supervisor's beliefs regarding the practice of school psychology. Because of the differences in roles, clinical supervision of school psychologists is different from the clinical supervision provided to therapists and mental health professionals.

The theoretical orientation that guides the clinical work of school psychologists also provides structures and strategies in supervision. These theoretical frameworks may include psychodynamic principles, person-centered therapy, the cognitive-behavioral approach, constructivism, the solution-focused model, systemic approaches, the discrimination model, and integrative approaches. Supervisors can take the roles of teachers, counselors, evaluators, mentors, and consultants as needed. As described in teacher education literature, multiple clinical supervision purposes and supervisor roles can be adapted to the practice of school psychology. These include the coaching model, the developmental model, and the reflective model. Skilled supervisors consider characteristics of individual learners. The structure of clinical supervision is usually determined at the district level. It is hoped that administrators recognize the importance of supervision and facilitate the use of best practices in the development of supervision goals, the writing and signing of supervision contracts, and the determination of supervision format and frequency.

Supervisors and supervisees often differ in their supervision goals, and it is important that these differences be reconciled and written supervision goals developed. Goals are best included in a comprehensive written supervision contract that delineates the methods, techniques, and frequency of supervision. While individual supervision is most common, various supervision formats (such as group, peer, and team) can also be used. Supervision frequency should vary according to the supervisee's needs and the setting in which the supervisee practices. Particularly for novices, regularly scheduled supervision sessions are critical, since supervision can be overlooked as other obligations arise. Supervisees at all levels must also be able to access supervision in emergencies or when dealing with a difficult or complex case.

REFLECTIVE QUESTIONS

Q7.1. Describe how a supervisor's worldview and views regarding the practice of school psychology can influence how she or he provides clinical supervision.

Q7.2. How does the clinical supervision provided to school psychologists differ from that provided to therapists and mental health practitioners?

Q7.3. Discuss how the various theoretical approaches to the practice of school psychology could impact supervision.

Q7.4. Describe the fundamental learning principals to which supervisors should attend when they design supervisory teaching strategies.

Q7.5. Describe how asking supervisees to write learning narratives could be helpful in supervision.

Q7.6. Discuss the development of supervision goals as part of a comprehensive supervision contract. Why are they important and how should they be formulated?

Q7.7. Describe the various formats of supervision, including the benefits and challenges of each.

Q7.8. Discuss unique aspects of supervising interns and practicum students and delineate methods to address the challenges.

SUPERVISORY DILEMMAS

SD 7.1

As the supervisor of one intern and two practicum students at the high school level, you are asked to "temporarily loan" your intern to one of the district's elementary schools.

The school psychologist who covers that school is out on an unexpectedly long medical leave. To date, your intern has had no experience at the elementary level, and she has stated that she feels quite insecure about handling such responsibility. However, due to her tight financial situation, the intern is very attracted to the idea of being paid for her services. (The district policy provides a per diem stipend of $75 when someone covers medical leave as a substitute.) You have just been confidentially informed that the elementary school psychologist will not be able to return. You anticipate that your intern will be approached to cover the job for the remainder of the year. *What are the supervisory considerations? What should be done?*

Authors' thoughts: Regardless of whether the assignment is short term or long term, the intern's lack of experience and confidence is clearly problematic. This situation certainly does not provide appropriate training opportunities. Hence, allowing the intern to proceed would deprive her of a critically important learning experience. In this scenario, some degree of compromise might be sought. For example, the intern might agree to work 1 day per week under close supervision with the idea that expansion of time could occur in the future. Training should never be bypassed to meet the needs of the district.

SD 7.2

In the late spring, the director of special education noticed that district school psychologists were overloaded with reevaluations. She called a local university and volunteered her school district to serve as a training site for school psychology interns in the fall. Practicing school psychologists were told that things would be easier the following fall because help would be available when the interns arrived. They were also told that they would share the services of the interns and share supervision responsibilities. In the fall, two interns floated from school to school on an as-needed basis to conduct reevaluations. When the interns mentioned that they were not receiving experience in developing prevention programs, monitoring student progress, providing individual and group counseling, or providing consultation to parents, they were told that they had to do what needed to be done and that if time was available at the end of the year, they could consult and counsel. During the budget presentation, district school psychologists requested that an additional position be funded because special education referrals continued to escalate. However, they were told that the following year the district would accept four interns instead of hiring additional positions. *What are the supervisory considerations? What should be done?*

Authors' thoughts: This is, without doubt, a horrific situation that harms *all* participants. Requiring interns to conduct only special education gatekeeping assessments with little to no supervision is intern abuse at its worst! While having interns can be helpful, their purpose is not to alleviate staff shortages. This district's "solution" to the problem of understaffing is shortsighted and ineffective. Short- and long-term plans must be immediately implemented to address this intolerable situation. The interns should contact their university supervisor to intervene on their behalf. This is nothing short of a training emergency. Obviously, agreeing to host interns demands that the contractual training agreement be honored. Moreover, it is likely that the students in the school have not been well served. Given the severity of this situation, local university training directors might want to delete this site from the list of approved placements . . . and fast!

SD 7.3

The university training program requires students to submit audiotapes of selected counseling sessions. Parents have thus far refused to give permission for your intern to do so. Without tapes, the intern's portfolio will be incomplete and she could fail the class. *What are the supervisory considerations? What should be done?*

Authors' thoughts: Obtaining informed consent will always be a nonnegotiable requirement. One approach would be to again reassure the parents that such audiotapes are used for training purposes only and are destroyed after review. If this is fruitless, alternative students might be sought to illustrate the intern's counseling abilities. Importantly, the university supervisor should be consulted in the decision making process. Often some flexibility exists and alternatives can be generated to cover the requirements of the training program. The university may need to work with the intern and supervisor on an alternative method of evaluation.

SD 7.4

You are a supervisor of school psychologists in a district with 20 school psychologists. One of the interns has complained to you that her supervisor has asked her to perform menial tasks such as filing, typing, answering the telephone, making appointments, and even cleaning the office. She would like to change supervisors and work with another district psychologist. *What are the supervisory considerations? What should be done?*

Authors' thoughts: While clerical tasks are often part of a school psychologist's job, it is clearly a violation of the training contract to limit work *exclusively* to such tasks. Obviously, it is never acceptable to exploit interns. The overarching obligation is to train them so that they can be competent school psychologists. The first undertaking should be to gather more information to ascertain that, in fact, the requests are unreasonable. For example, at the beginning of the year, it is hardly unusual for interns to perform the above-mentioned tasks. After encouraging the student to first discuss her concerns directly with the supervisor, a prudent approach would be to discuss the parameters of the training contract with the supervising school psychologist. The district has an obligation to ensure that university requirements are appropriately met. It will be fruitful to determine and delineate the difference between reality and expectations so that mutual understanding about "housekeeping tasks" can occur. After the initial meeting, it would be wise for the district level supervisor to follow up to ensure compliance and satisfaction. Further decisions can be made after examination of the effects of intervention. It is not unusual to have to change course during a yearlong training period; in fact, it is advisable. Changing supervisors should be a last resort. The university supervisor should be included in all decisions.

SD 7.5

You are supervising an intern whose university has very specific expectations for the internship year. The intern is expected to perform the full range of school psychological services, including direct and indirect interventions and assessment. While you were trained in direct interventions such as counseling, your job has been restricted, omitting many of these activities, so that you feel extremely rusty and incompetent. *What are the supervisory considerations? What should be done?*

Authors' thoughts: This would-be supervisor is to be commended for her sound insight. It is so critically important to "know what we don't know!" It would be helpful for this school psychologist to discuss her concerns with the university supervisor. It is possible that they could work together to obtain appropriate supervision. This is also a great opportunity for the supervisor to learn from the intern. Supervision often "teaches the teacher" as much as the student! Hopefully, at the conclusion of the year, this astute supervisor might obtain a voucher for a free course at the training institution.

SD 7.6

One of your veteran school psychologists, Susan, has co-supervised an intern with a colleague every year for the past 5 years. Normally she has been very happy with her interns, but this year it is obvious that the intern will not become an effective school psychologist because of personality traits—he is disorganized, presents himself in an unprofessional manner, has little initiative or self-regulation, has poor time management, and in general has difficulty handling the stress of being a school psychologist. The co-supervisor is in favor of "passing him on" because she feels that the intern is "just immature and will grow out of it." Susan feels these traits are so detrimental that they will preclude the intern's functioning as a school psychologist as well as his ability to help students and adolescents. She believes that, as intern supervisors, she and her colleague are mandated to "gatekeep" for their profession. *What are the supervisory considerations? What should be done?*

Authors' thoughts: School psychologists who supervise interns are obligated to ensure that interns are prepared to work as school psychologists. It can be argued that such poor organizational skills will interfere with the intern's ability to work as a school psychologist. On the other hand, Susan should not dismiss the co-supervisor's opinion that the issue is lack of maturity rather than enduring personality traits. In a helpful fashion, Susan might present evidence of how the intern's organizational skills are problematic. She should also share the problem with faculty from the intern's program so that a plan can be developed under which the intern can improve these skills before graduating and working as a school psychologist.

Handout 7.1

INTERNSHIP SUPERVISOR CONFERENCE

Christine Merman Woolf

Capella University

Date:

Time:

Field Supervisor:

Course:

Learner:

Phone Number:

University Instructor:

1. Is the learner completing 40 hours of fieldwork each week?

2. Is the learner participating in at least 2 hours of individual supervision each week? When does the individual supervision take place? (Goal is to have a consistent day and time for individual supervision.)

3. Is the learner participating in group supervision? If so, what are the qualifications of the individual who is conducting the supervision? Also, describe the educational status of the other learners participating in the group supervision sessions. When does group supervision take place?

4. What are the ages of the students the learner is observing or with whom he/she is working? What are your plans for allowing the learner to gain needed exposure to all age levels? (Goal is to work with students of various ages, e.g., pre-K, elementary school, middle school, high school).

5. To what extent is the learner observing or working with students who have various disabilities? Please identify some of the types of disability categories with which the learner has gained experience. What are your plans for allowing the learner to gain needed exposure to additional disability categories?

6. To what extent is the learner observing or working with students of different ethnicities and cultures or who speak languages other than English? Please identify the groups with whom the learner is gaining experience.

7. To what extent is the learner observing or working with students of various economic levels? Please identify the economic groups with whom the learner is interacting.

8. To what extent is the learner exposed to a variety of school psychological services (e.g., assessment, consultation, collaboration, intervention, participation in team meetings)? Please describe the learner's performance within these activities. In the area of assessment, be sure to identify the instruments with which the learner is gaining experience. If the learner has not been exposed to certain roles, what are your plans for allowing the learner to gain the needed exposure?

9. To what extent does the learner observe the field supervisor using data-based decision making to determine the most appropriate assessment, intervention, and monitoring strategies in the application of school psychological services?

(Continued)

(Continued)

10. To what extent does the learner show the supervisor that he/she can use data-based decision making to determine the most appropriate assessment, intervention, and monitoring strategies in the application of school psychological services? Please provide an example of the learner displaying this skill.

11. To what extent does the learner observe the supervisor using a variety of decision making models (e.g., for academic and behavioral cases, choosing when to use collaboration, consultation, counseling, behavior management, and individual, group, or schoolwide interventions) when working within the field training setting?

12. To what extent does the learner show the supervisor that he/she can use a variety of decision making models when working within the field training setting? Please provide an example of the learner displaying this skill.

13. To what extent does the learner observe the supervisor applying his/her knowledge of learning theory and processes in developing services to improve the academic and cognitive skills of the students with whom he/she works?

14. To what extent does the learner show the supervisor that he/she can apply his/her knowledge of learning theory and processes in developing services to improve the academic and cognitive skills of the students with whom he/she works? Please provide an example of the learner displaying this skill.

15. To what extent does the learner observe the supervisor applying his/her knowledge of human development in creating and evaluating interventions to improve the behavioral, adaptive, and social skills of the students with whom he/she works?

16. To what extent does the learner show the supervisor that he/she can apply his/her knowledge of human development in creating and evaluating interventions to improve the behavioral, adaptive, and social skills of the students with whom he/she works? Please provide an example of the learner displaying this skill.

17. To what extent is the learner gaining an understanding of the system of the schools within which he/she works? To what extent is he/she developing knowledge of the process by which the school system creates and maintains a safe and effective learning environment by conducting interviews, reading school system materials, and participating in school psychological activities?

18. To what extent is the learner observing and/or participating in the use of crisis management? Field training supervisors determine the extent to which learners are ready to put into practice their theoretical understanding of effective services within these situations. If possible, please provide an example of the learner's exposure to these services.

19. To what extent is the learner observing and/or participating in the use of mental health counseling interventions (e.g., conducting individual counseling, group counseling, or social skills training; implementing prevention programs)? If possible, please provide an example of the learner displaying this skill. If the learner is not engaging in these activities, what are your plans for allowing the learner to develop his/her skills in this area?

20. To what extent does the learner observe the supervisor applying his/her knowledge of family systems in his/her work within the school? To what extent does the learner observe the supervisor when he/she is engaged in collaboration with families and school personnel to ensure comprehensive service delivery?

21. To what extent does the learner apply his/her knowledge of family systems in his/her work within the school? To what extent does the learner engage in collaboration with families and school personnel to ensure comprehensive service delivery? Please provide an example of the learner displaying this skill.

22. To what extent does the learner observe the field supervisor applying his/her understanding of program evaluation (e.g., reviewing the use of curriculum, reviewing state-mandated test scores, reviewing progress monitoring data, reviewing special education placement data, reviewing prevention program results) within the setting?

23. To what extent does the learner apply his/her understanding of program evaluation within the setting? Please provide an example of the learner participating in this type of activity. If the learner is not engaging in this activity, what are your plans for allowing the learner to develop his/her skills in this area?

24. In what professional development activities has the learner participated (e.g., faculty meetings, school psychology staff meetings, workshops)? Please describe the topics of the meetings. In what other activities will the learner be participating within the next few months?

25. To what extent does the learner observe the supervisor applying his/her knowledge of the ethics and standards that guide the field of school psychology (e.g., reviewing consent forms and procedural safeguards with parents, reporting abuse or neglect, maintaining confidentiality of information)?

26. To what extent does the learner apply his/her knowledge of the ethics and standards that guide the field of school psychology? Please provide an example of the learner displaying this skill.

27. To what extent does the learner observe the supervisor using technology (e.g., using the student database, the school e-mail system, computer scoring systems, or assistive technology; finding school forms online) in the implementation of his/her services?

28. To what extent does the learner use technology in the implementation of his/her services? Please provide an example of the learner displaying this skill.

29. Considering the amount of time the learner has been participating in internship, does this learner possess adequate writing skills? Please identify some areas of strength in his/her writing and some areas in which he/she needs additional assistance. What activities have been suggested to the learner to improve his/her writing? To what extent has the learner engaged in these suggested activities?

30. Does this learner possess adequate organization and time management skills (e.g., arriving on time for meetings, organizing materials, maintaining a schedule, completing cases within the allotted time)? Please provide some examples of the learner displaying these skills.

31. Overall comments:

Handout 7.2

INTERNSHIP LEARNER CONFERENCE

Christine Merman Woolf
Capella University

Date:

Time:

Field Supervisor:

Course:

Learner:

Phone Number:

University Instructor:

1. What are your overall impressions of the field experience so far?

2. Are there any concerns that you would like me to address with your field supervisor?

3. Are you completing 40 hours of fieldwork each week?

4. Are you participating in at least 2 hours of individual supervision each week? When does the individual supervision take place? (Goal is to have a consistent day and time for individual supervision.)

5. Are you participating in group supervision? If so, what are the qualifications of the individual who is conducting the supervision? Also, describe the educational status of the other learners participating in the group supervision sessions. When does group supervision take place?

6. What are the ages of the students you are observing or with whom you are working? (Goal is to work with students of various ages, e.g., pre-K, elementary school, middle school, high school). What plans are there for allowing you to gain needed exposure to all age levels?

7. To what extent are you observing or working with students of various disabilities? Please identify some of the types of disability categories with which you have gained experience. What plans are there for allowing you to gain needed exposure to additional disability categories?

8. To what extent are you observing or working with students of different ethnicities and cultures or who speak languages other than English? Please identify the groups with which you are gaining experience.

9. To what extent are you observing or working with students of various economic levels? Please identify the economic groups with which you are interacting.

10. To what extent are you exposed to a variety of school psychological services (e.g., assessment, consultation, collaboration, intervention, participation in team meetings)? In the area of assessment, be sure to identify the instruments with which you are gaining experience. Describe your strengths and areas in need of development within these activities. If you have not been exposed to certain roles, what are your plans to gain the needed exposure?

11. To what extent are you using data-based decision making to determine the most appropriate assessment, intervention, and monitoring strategies in the application of school psychological services? Please provide an example of your displaying this skill.

12. To what extent are you using a variety of decision making models (e.g., for academic and behavioral cases, choosing when to use collaboration, consultation, counseling, behavior management, and individual, group, or schoolwide interventions) when working within the field training setting? Please provide an example of your displaying this skill.

13. To what extent are you applying your knowledge of learning theory and processes in developing services to improve the academic and cognitive skills of the students with whom you work? Please provide an example of your displaying this skill.

14. To what extent are you applying your knowledge of human development in creating and evaluating interventions to improve the behavioral, adaptive, and social skills of the students with whom you work? Please provide an example of your displaying this skill.

15. To what extent are you gaining an understanding of the system of the schools within which you work? To what extent are you developing knowledge of the process by which the school system creates and maintains a safe and effective learning environment by conducting interviews, reading school system materials, and participating in school psychological activities?

16. To what extent are you observing and/or participating in the use of crisis management? Field training supervisors determine the extent to which you are ready to put into practice your theoretical understanding of effective services within these situations. If possible, please provide an example of your exposure to these services.

17. To what extent are you observing and/or participating in the use of mental health counseling interventions (e.g., conducting individual counseling, group counseling, social skills training, implementing prevention programs)? If possible, please provide an example of your displaying this skill. If you are not engaging in these activities, what are your plans for developing your skills in this area?

18. To what extent are you applying your knowledge of family systems in your work within the school? To what extent are you engaging in collaboration with families and school personnel to ensure comprehensive service delivery? Please provide an example of your displaying this skill.

(Continued)

(Continued)

19. To what extent are you applying your understanding of program evaluation (e.g., reviewing the use of curriculum, reviewing state-mandated test scores, reviewing progress monitoring data, reviewing special education placement data, reviewing prevention program results) within the setting? Please provide an example of your participating in this type of activity. If you are not engaging in this activity, what are your plans for developing your skills in this area?

20. In what professional development activities have you participated (e.g., faculty meetings, school psychology staff meetings, workshops)? Please describe the topics of the meetings. In what other activities will you be participating within the next few months?

21. To what extent are you applying your knowledge of the ethics and standards that guide the field of school psychology (e.g., reviewing consent forms and procedural safeguards with parents, reporting abuse or neglect, maintaining confidentiality of information)? Please provide an example of your displaying this skill.

22. To what extent do you use technology (e.g., use the student database, the school e-mail system, computer scoring systems, or assistive technology; find school forms online) in the implementation of your services? Please provide an example of your displaying this skill.

23. Considering the amount of time you have been participating in internship, to what extent do you possess adequate writing skills? Please identify some areas of strength in your writing and some areas in which you need additional assistance. What activities have been suggested to you to improve your writing? To what extent have you engaged in these suggested activities?

24. To what extent do you possess adequate organization and time management skills (e.g., arriving on time for meetings, organizing materials, maintaining a schedule, completing cases within the allotted time)? Please provide some examples of your displaying these skills.

25. Overall comments:

8

Computer-Assisted Supervision

The question is not so much whether computers will be used in supervision, but to what extent and how well.

Vignette 8.1

Taj is a university supervisor for a group of six interns. In the spring, she meets with the next year's interns to establish a relationship. She also visits each intern on-site once at the beginning of the academic year so that she has a sense of their location. Other than those meetings, however, her supervision is conducted entirely online. Using e-mail, her students send her brief weekly summaries of their work and relate incidents they've dealt with during the week, how they feel about how they are doing, and any questions or concerns they might have. The entire class meets weekly online for a synchronous audio chat using Wimba. During these chats, the interns present case studies using PowerPoint and other shared files. At times the class conducts "Web safaris" to collaborate on Internet literature searches or to simultaneously research their district's characteristics. In addition to e-mail and synchronous chats, the class communicates with asynchronous threaded discussions. Taj also communicates by "POT" (plain old telephone) with the interns and their site supervisors—more frequently whenever there is a problem. Students log their internship hours according to the domains of practice onto a server. The interns submit case studies and other work to Taj via the class Web site (using Blackboard technology), and she uses the Track Changes feature in Microsoft Word to add comments and other edits. The intern's culminating electronic portfolios include video clips of their work with children, adolescents, parents, and teachers. Taj was quite apprehensive when she began providing online supervision, but with time she has found this multimedia approach dynamic and enriching.

BASIC CONSIDERATIONS

In a relatively short period of time, computers and Internet communication have clearly revolutionized every aspect of the modern world, including the provision of mental health services (McClosky-Armstrong, 2001). Similarly, computer technology has profoundly affected school psychological services. For example:

- Interpersonal communication among school psychologists and between school psychologists and the students, parents, and teachers with whom they work has been greatly facilitated through the use of cell phones, e-mail, and faxes.
- As an enormous library, the Internet makes information regarding best practices and professional research readily available, both through search engines, such as Google Research (http://research.google.com), and through professional Web sites, such as www.apa.org and www.nasponline.org.
- Videoconferenced professional conferences such as the 2002 Conference on the Futures of School Psychology (Cummings et al., 2004) and easily accessible video-conferencing software such as Skype have rendered "virtual attendance" a reality.
- Technology is changing curriculum presentation to children and adolescents. Some high schools provide every student with a laptop, and some colleges are requiring applicants to have taken online classes in high school. Almost universally, elementary and high school students are expected to be able to conduct research on the Internet and to use computers to generate written products. These technological advancements are changing the way in which teachers reach students. Consequently, school psychologists are being called upon to change the way in which they view struggling learners and to make recommendations on how to assist students who have difficulty with these media.
- School psychologists have quickly adopted many technologies, such as test scoring software, writing software, Curriculum-Based Measurement scoring software such as AIMSweb, voice recognition software such as Dragon NaturallySpeaking, iPods to record and listen to presentations and in-services they provide, and personal data assistants (PDAs) to conduct behavior observations and manage work.
- Technology is revolutionizing graduate training through Web sites and synchronous and asynchronous communication tools.
- Computer-assisted peer consultation is providing ongoing collaboration.
- Technology is being used to supplement and sometimes replace face-to-face supervision and professional development opportunities.
- Original research is being conducted via the Internet, allowing instantaneous collaboration among researchers.

Computer-assisted supervision can clearly aid in the provision of psychological services. For example, the Online Clinical Case Study Group (Fenichel et al., 2002) is a peer support and supervision group for individuals providing online counseling through the International Society for Mental Health Online. It is a powerful example of peer collaboration and supervision in an online environment. Members of the group share online resources, suggestions, and support with one another both during case presentations and in response to spontaneous calls for help.

Several effective, rapid, and knowledgeable interventions would not have been possible were it not for the opportunity to utilize both synchronous and asynchronous communication channels to consult with respected peers—around the clock and, in some cases, around the planet. (p. 493)

Computers are tools of communication; they are not themselves methods or techniques of supervision. However, since many of these tools are recently developed, supervisors of school psychologists may have limited experience with them and may be unaware of considerations regarding their use in supervision. This chapter is intended to increase familiarity with and use of these helpful tools.

APPLICATIONS TO SUPERVISION

Typed Communications

E-mail is, of course, an almost universally available asynchronous written computer-based communication tool and is likely the most commonly used technology in supervision (Stamm, 2003). E-mail has been used to supplement or even replace face-to-face counseling services and has been found to have significant positive effects in terms of its potential to facilitate counseling relationships. The therapeutic alliance can be both established and maintained through e-mail (Cook & Doyle, 2002), and in fact, it can be augmented, because e-mail leads to disinhibition (Joinson, 1998) and fosters "self-disclosure, ventilation, and externalization of problems and conflicts" and thereby promotes self-awareness (Barak, 1999, p. 237).

Similarly, computer-based communication can enhance clinical supervision efforts (Clingerman & Bernard, 2004). It can take the form of individual communications between an individual supervisor and supervisee, or it can be used for group consultation, as found in the Global School Psychology Network (Kruger & Struzziero, 1997; Struzziero, 1998). E-mail can augment traditional, face-to-face communication and provide a technologically innovative way to support consultation and supervision efforts among educators. Furthermore, the positive effects of computer-based supervision appear to endure over time (Thurber, 2005).

Written synchronous communications via chat rooms and instant messages share many of the characteristics of e-mail discussed above, with the advantage of occurring in real time. Counseling based on synchronous communication has been found to be quite effective, particularly with clients who might not otherwise seek counseling due to stigmatization, hearing impairments, being homebound, geographic isolation, or social phobia. Online clinical work offers unique elasticity in communication in that online clinicians use a combination of e-mail, instant messaging, chats, and phone calls and clients can express themselves more fully across modalities. The Internet can also provide online support groups for various personal problems ranging from addiction to depression. Computer-based suicide prevention hotlines have been found to be as successful as telephone-based suicide prevention hotlines (Fenichel et al., 2002).

However, a number of concerns regarding the use of written computer-based communication methods prevail. A primary ethical consideration is maintaining confidentiality. E-mails, instant messages, and chat room communications are simply not confidential for a number of reasons. They can be read by technicians during communication, are very difficult to completely erase, can be held by servers for some time, and can be forwarded to others (with modifications!) without the sender's knowledge or consent. As it has been said, using these methods is akin to writing a postcard in pencil; confidentiality is impossible to promise. Supervisors and supervisees must therefore be proactive regarding confidentiality. E-mail encryption can be a useful tool, as can virtual private networks. Most reliable, of course, is not to write anything in an e-mail, instant message, or chat room communication that would be problematic were confidentiality disrupted. At an absolute minimum, names and identifying information should be omitted.

Another critical variable is that nonverbal cues are not always transmitted well via typed communication. Interestingly, readers tend to perceive e-mail communications as more emotionally charged than information conveyed via audio or video modalities (Coomey & Wilczenski, 2005). Like e-mail, synchronous written computer-based supervision has significant limitations because of the loss of nonverbal cues and interpersonal contact. For example, Gainor and Constantine (2002) found that peer supervision using synchronous typed chats was less effective than face-to-face supervision in increasing multicultural skills. Without nonverbal cues, e-mails can be seriously misunderstood. Consequently, e-mails must be crafted very carefully.

Vignette 8.2

Mary Jane wrote an e-mail to her supervisor about frustrations regarding a case. She concluded with the statement, *"So, as I have explained, I am having a really difficult time completing the tasks you recommended. SOB!"* Since she had meant "sob" as in "I am crying," Mary Jane was shocked when her supervisor responded in bold letters, *"JUST DO IT!"* At their next supervision session, Mary Jane was almost in tears and disclosed that she felt "yelled at" by the bold letters. The supervisor responded that he was trying to give cheerful encouragement (like the Nike ads!) and patiently went on to say that he felt pretty generous to have done so after being called an S.O.B. (as in the acronym). Needless to say, a good laugh followed that explanation!

Finally, written synchronous communications via chat rooms and instant messages additionally require facile typing by both parties. They are not appropriate for use with individuals who are not comfortable with writing (e.g., individuals with written language learning disabilities or fine motor deficits). Further, they can pose logistical difficulties because of the challenge of fostering smooth discussions while simultaneously coordinating responses to multiple questions (Wilczenski & Coomey, 2006). On the other hand, synchronous communications have the advantages of feeling more similar to face-to-face communication and of allowing records to be kept, which are helpful for both teaching and supervision.

Audio and Video Communications

Synchronous audio contacts, such as individual telephone calls, conference telephone calls, and synchronous conversations using software such as Centra or Wimba, can provide more facile communication than written communication and have the added advantage of voice tone and other verbal expression. On the other hand, learners can be inhibited during synchronous discussions if sessions are recorded or audited by technicians (Wilczenski & Coomey, 2006). Because many of these technologies are emerging, supervisors can encounter problems as they use them.

Vignette 8.3

Every semester **Melinda** enjoys providing an online seminar for practicum students because it gives them an opportunity to share experiences without the hassle of driving back to campus for a face-to-face meeting. When the university changed the software used for the verbal chats, however, Melinda was quite distressed because the new software did not have emoticons (smiley faces, clapping hands, and other methods to express nonverbal reactions). The lack of these tools was surprisingly detrimental to the class process.

If students do not have access to high-speed Internet, the processes are slowed considerably and there are unnatural delays in the conversation. Some platforms are not compatible with wireless connections. Occasionally, someone will lose a connection and be unable to reconnect from his or her own computer. It is important to have a backup system in place, such as a telephone number whereby individuals can connect to the group via phone.

Videoconferencing can be accomplished with surprising ease. It can be used to provide remote supervision across long distances, as when interns are placed in internship sites at a considerable distance from their university. It can also be used to provide supervision in settings in which travel to a common site can be time consuming or expensive, such as rural areas. Videoconferencing has been used to effectively supervise psychotherapy (Stamm, 1998), social work services (Panos, 2005; Panos, Panos, Cox, Roby, & Matheson, 2002), speech and language services (Dudding & Justice, 2004), psychiatric nursing (Heckner & Giard, 2005), neuropsychological evaluations (Tröster, Paolo, Glatt, Hubble, & Koller, 1995), and psychological services (Chamberlain, 2000).

Dudding and Justice (2004) applied videoconferencing to the supervision of speech and language pathologists and found that, when well designed, videoconferencing differs minimally from traditional models. It enables supervisors to observe sessions, offer feedback to supervisees, and hold supervisory conferences. Supervisees indicated that they found videoconferencing less intrusive and less distracting for clients than direct observation. Social work supervisees report that supervision via videoconferencing can substantially reduce feelings of isolation, particularly when they are working in a location with a predominant culture with which they are unfamiliar (Panos, 2005).

Videoconferencing can be used with an individual, with a number of individuals in multiple settings, with a group in a single setting, or as a broadcast. Each type of conference requires certain software and hardware, as shown in Table 8.1.

Dudding and Justice (2004) recommended that, when selecting videoconferencing equipment, supervisors and administrators consider multiple factors. Equipment factors to consider include portability, ease of setup, the degree to which the interface is intuitive and easily navigable, compatibility with other systems currently in use, minimum bandwidth requirements, the likelihood that the unit can interface with a bridge and permit usage expansion, and connectivity potential (ability to connect with the transmission used by the site as well as the ability to connect with multiple sites and to be used with different protocols and platforms). Additional factors to consider include technology support from the manufacturer and school, versatility, training availability, firewalls installed at the school or university that might prevent videoconferencing (e.g., required popup prevention), and costs for future upgrades and technical support as well as initial expenditures.

Table 8.1   Videoconferencing Capabilities

Type of Conference	Necessary Hardware	Software Available	Recommended Network Connection	Uses
Individual	Computer, headset with microphone, and computer camera	Microsoft NetMeeting, Skype	High speed (cable modem or DSL)	Almost any individual supervision experience: case presentation, PowerPoint presentations, shared text editing
Group Members in Multiple Settings	Computer, headset with microphone, and computer camera	Microsoft NetMeeting, Skype	High speed (cable modem or DSL)	Almost any small group supervision technique: case presentation, PowerPoint presentations, shared text editing
Group Members in One Setting	Computer application to transmit signals, self-focusing camera, and directional microphone	ViewStation (Polycom) or Escort (VCON)	High speed (cable modem or DSL)	Distance learning opportunities
Broadcast	Professional quality sound, cameras, and lighting equipment		Satellite, microwave, ATM, T1, T3	Professional broadcasts with large numbers of viewers

While it has many advantages, videoconferencing can have several disadvantages, including:

- Challenges to maintaining confidentiality
- Limited potential for role-plays and modeling of practice
- Limited opportunities to observe varied contexts (e.g., the entire school or work in rooms other than the designated room)
- Decreased interaction between the supervisee and supervisor
- The possibility of insufficient technical support
- Potential loss of computer connection

Virtual Libraries

Supervisees and supervisors alike now have immediate and easy access to a tremendous amount of information on the Internet. Many libraries permit access to search engines such as PsycINFO, Academic Search Premier, and ERIC. The Internet itself has ready access to search engines (e.g., Google Research, AltaVista, Yahoo!). Many articles are now available online in a full-text format, and for those that are not, many libraries make them available through interlibrary loan.

Vignette 8.4

Rosa found that when she encouraged her supervisees to research a topic of interest, they frequently turned to the Internet first. She found their exploratory endeavors were endangered if they (a) did not know effective methods of restricting their search to avoid obtaining so much information that they were completely overwhelmed, (b) did not know how to tell whether the information they obtained was obsolete or untrustworthy, or (c) did not understand how to change search parameters to increase the search yield. She devoted a group supervision session to helping her supervisees learn (and having them help each other learn) how to do more effective searches.

Supervisors can help their supervisees use search tools effectively by using the search engine's keywords, adding Boolean search cues (e.g., *and*, *or*, *not*, and quotation marks for terms with two or more words) as appropriate, and turning off graphics. It is also helpful for supervisees to conduct extensive searches on topics with which they are already familiar in order to learn how to master search engines.

Since there are virtually no restrictions regarding the Internet, anyone can publish almost any information or opinion. Learning to evaluate information found on the Internet is crucial for both beginning and veteran school psychologists. Supervisors will need to help supervisees determine whether the information they have obtained via the Internet is credible (written by a credentialed author and sponsored by a reputable institution), accurate (with appropriate sources), current, objective (free of advertising and bias), and comprehensive (Kruger, Macklem, Weksel, & Kalinsky, 2001).

Distance Learning

One supervisory role is to teach and oversee professional development, and it is entirely possible that this activity might be conducted online. Therefore, it is appropriate to consider research regarding distance education. A substantial volume of research on the effectiveness of online instruction exists. Much of this literature focuses on determining factors that affect the experiences of students and faculty in online classes. Perreault, Waldman, Alexander, and Zhao (2002) studied methods of overcoming barriers to successful instruction; Petrides (2002) explored the subjective experiences of students; Hoyt and Shirvani (2002) examined factors influencing satisfaction with distance learning; and Hampton (2002) and G. G. Smith, Ferguson, and Caris (2002) investigated the experiences of instructors teaching over the Web.

The strongest theme to evolve from the above research is that, when teaching online, instructors must take deliberate steps to minimize the learner's disengagement and frustration. Gibbons, Mize, and Rogers (2002) indicated that online learning requires a stronger work ethic than face-to-face learning, although individuals enrolling in online learning experiences may mistakenly believe the opposite. C. N. Richards and Ridley (1997) found that satisfaction and persistence in learning via online instruction increased with the individual's computer proficiency, the user-friendliness of the online software, and the applicability of the work to degree and professional development credits. Rovai (2003) indicated that characteristics affecting learners' persistence in finishing online work included their academic preparation, computer literacy, information literacy, time management, reading and writing skills, learning styles, and computer-based interaction skills. Additional personal variables included finances, hours of employment, family responsibilities, outside encouragement, opportunities to transfer, and life crises. Program factors include the learning community, clarity of the program, availability and quality of advising, institutional commitment, interpersonal relationships, accessibility of services, course availability, and teaching styles. Offir, Barth, Lev, and Shteinbok (2003) increased the effectiveness of distance education by collecting data throughout the course and using that data to dynamically modify the course. Their methods are depicted in Table 8.2.

Studies have also explored the effectiveness of Web-based teaching on achievement (Martindale & Ahern, 2001), critical thinking (Astleitner, 2002), and communication in online environments (Miltiadou, 2001). In general, performance assessments tend to find that online learners perform as well as or better than face-to-face learners (M. C. Campbell, Floyd, & Sheridan, 2002; Merisotis & Phipps, 1999). In fact, synchronous tools tend to detract from learning while asynchronous tools seem to result in increased learning (R. M. Bernard et al., 2004). This may be a result of students' having greater opportunities

Table 8.2   Distance Education Formative Evaluation Methods and Results

Evaluation	Method	Result
Student knowledge	Content analysis of students' questions to the help desk	Evaluated students' proficiency in technology and allowed for increased technological support
	Student self-evaluation of content comprehension after each lesson	Allowed for repetition of material if more than a third of students indicated that they had struggled with the material
	Multiple-choice quizzes at the conclusion of each lesson	Allowed analysis of student comprehension and performance
Teacher-student interactions	Analysis of teacher-student interactions	Allowed the determination of interaction patterns and the identification of interactions correlating with positive learning outcomes

to reflect on their learning and control the pace and timing of their learning. Anecdotal evidence indicates that this is particularly the case for learners who are not facile in English, who have learning disabilities or attention deficit disorder, or who are prevented by shyness from open participation in class discussions. Students can submit equivalent work and can attain equivalent levels of content knowledge in online classes when the following variables are present (Harvey, 2005b):

- High-quality, university-supported computers are provided for the faculty
- Course support software, servers, and technical support are provided for the faculty and students
- Synchronous discussion group software (e.g., Centra or Wimba), servers, and technical support are readily available for the faculty and students
- Professors are trained in the use of the provided software
- Additional technical support is provided in streaming video clips and narrated PowerPoint lectures
- Backup is provided during class time for anyone experiencing technological difficulties
- Faculty who already taught courses on campus were paid to develop the online courses
- Full-time faculty are permitted to provide online courses as part of their normal course load
- Extensive online library resources have been developed, including electronic databases, electronic reserves, electronic journals, and electronically available interlibrary loans
- Students are carefully advised regarding time management and planning
- Methods of helping students develop a professional identity and foster a professional network are deliberately implemented

Combining Computer Applications

Computer-assisted supervision offers economies of time, money, and expertise and also transcends geographic barriers (Miller, Miller, & Evans, 2002). It also can foster open discussion of many issues, since electronically mediated communication tends to lower social inhibitions and decrease communication barriers (Weisband, Schneider, & Connolly, 1995). Computer-assisted supervision can provide a variety of instructional formats (e.g., e-mail, Web resources, PowerPoint slides) to enhance the learning experience.

Methods of combining computers and clinical supervision have been developed for a number of activities. Newman and Abbey (2004) combined digital video editing and supervision. Lehr (2005) developed Computer-Assisted Supervision (CAS), a software program that facilitates supervisees' and supervisors' monitoring and analyzing of counseling skills and intentions. Supervisees analyze their tapes according to their intentions to set limits; get information; give information; support the client; focus the discussion; clarify the client's expressions; provide hope; encourage catharsis; identify maladaptive cognitions; identify and provide feedback regarding maladaptive behaviors; encourage self-control; identify and promote acceptance of feelings; foster change; reinforce change; overcome resistance; challenge clients' thoughts, feelings, beliefs, or behaviors; maintain a working alliance; or meet their own needs. Supervisees then graph their intentions on a time line, and the graph and tape are used to focus discussions during the supervision sessions. Because it encourages self-evaluation, CAS promotes reflective practice.

Combining the wide variety of new technologies available to assist in providing supervision as well as combining face-to-face contact with telecommunications technology in an integrated model may address many challenges faced by providers of supervision to school psychologists. Wood, Miller, and Hargrove (2005) recommended providing supervision through four training modules:

- Module 1 provides didactic and hands-on training in specified telecommunication applications. The mechanics and use of the equipment; legal and ethical issues, including professional practice guidelines; and liability related to technology use are addressed.
- Module 2 involves participants in discussions of hypothetical case studies that demonstrate ethical and practice-oriented dilemmas. The supervisor uses a limited-access Web page (e.g., Blackboard) that includes the case studies and useful Web resources (e.g., Web sites, online articles, PowerPoint presentations). Discussions between the supervisor and supervisee(s) can occur through e-mail, closed chat rooms, or a synchronous discussion tool such as Centra or Wimba.
- Module 3 involves participants in group supervision using live videoconferencing.
- Module 4 involves participants in traditional face-to-face supervision. This supplements the videoconferenced supervision.

CHALLENGES IN COMPUTER-ASSISTED SUPERVISION

Although it has many promising aspects, computer-assisted supervision is subject to many of the same shortcomings associated with face-to-face supervision. In both modalities, supervisees may not get what they need from supervision because of variables such as insufficient supervisor time or skills, heavy caseloads, or an overpowering person in the supervision group.

Although the National Association of School Psychologists (NASP) and American Psychological Association (APA) professional and ethical standards do not directly address computer-assisted supervision, several concerns should be addressed when using these tools. These include supervision quantity, supervision quality, security and confidentiality, cost, access and familiarity, licensure, missing information, integrity, and provisions for crisis intervention (Kanz, 2001; Panos et al., 2002; Wilczenski & Coomey, 2006). It is also important to maintain telephone contact with supervisees in order to facilitate communication about topics not appropriate for e-mail or teleconferencing.

Quantity

Computer-assisted supervision tends to be more readily accessible than face-to-face supervision and therefore to have the potential for increased quantity. It can facilitate communication not only between supervisors and supervisees but also among supervisees, such that peer supervision is more readily available. For example, Stamm (1998) conducted a study in which four supervisors provided supervision regarding the treatment of posttraumatic stress to a total of 80 supervisees at 10 sites. The study took place over the course of a year using combined computer applications: daily e-mails, weekly telephone calls, monthly group videoconferences, and faxes and group telephone calls as needed. At the conclusion of the study there had been 20,000 e-mails, 10,000 hours of audiotaped sessions, 1,800 hours of individual consultation, 500 hours of group telephone conversations, 500 hours of videotaped sessions, and 450 (secured) faxed forms!

Quality

The quality of computer-assisted supervision is dependent on the quality of the computer system. Low-end video systems, composed of personal computers with webcams, headsets with microphones, and free conferencing software, are very inexpensive and in recent years have become of high enough quality to support adequate *emotional bandwidth*, "the emotional understanding, support that can be transmitted" (Panos et al., 2002). However, without a high-speed Internet connection, videoconferencing is unusable.

Security and Confidentiality

Computer-assisted supervision poses multiple risks to security and confidentiality. These risks can be reduced by adhering to Health Insurance Portability and Accountability Act of 1996 (HIPAA) standards. These standards dictate that any discussion of health-related information through the supervisory process must be disclosed to patients with the assurance that their privacy will be protected. Clients must be advised of the uses and disclosures of health information, including those that involve quality assessment, evaluations of practitioner and provider performance, training programs, clinical supervision, accreditation, certification, and credentialing activities (United States Department of Health and Human Services, Office of the Secretary, 2000). As mentioned previously, in written communications, encryption programs can be helpful, but the easiest method of maintaining confidentiality is to omit identifying information.

When audioconferencing or videoconferencing is used, it is critical to ensure that adequate security measures are taken at the locations of both the supervisee and supervisor. This includes ensuring each participant's privacy regarding visual (monitor) and auditory (both transmitted and received) material before beginning a supervision session. It also means that actual names and identifying information should be omitted from transmittals. To avoid the danger posed by computer viruses, worms, and other intentionally destructive software, both psychologists and computer system managers must continually update their virus scan programs and firewalls. Finally, clients must give informed consent regarding online supervision as well as to supervision in general before tapes of sessions are shared, perhaps preferably via mail until Internet security is better established (Kanz, 2001).

Cost of Technology

Another challenge in computer-assisted supervision is the cost of acquiring and maintaining hardware and software. E-mail and chat rooms are relatively inexpensive in that only a computer and Internet access are needed. As described previously, videoconferencing requires some additional equipment and a high-speed Internet connection.

Access To and Familiarity With Technology

Several factors render computer-assisted supervision unavailable to some individuals. While it is true that computers and Internet access are becoming increasingly available, not every person has access to high-speed Internet service and high-memory computers that render these tools useful. Although text readers and voice recognition software are becoming more available, individuals with disabilities are not universally able to access every type of computer software or even many Web pages. Regardless of handicapping condition, both supervisors and supervisees require training and ongoing support in the use of these technology tools in order to feel comfortable with them and be able to use them productively.

Licensure

Clinical supervision must be provided by an individual licensed to provide the services being supervised, which can be problematic if the supervisor is not licensed in the state in which the supervisee works. Since psychologists are licensed on a state-by-state basis, it is important for supervisors to check with state licensing boards to ensure that they are appropriately licensed (Kanz, 2001). Acquiring and maintaining multiple licenses could impose an obvious professional and financial hardship for such supervisors. On the other hand, some states are working toward special legislature that permits computer-assisted supervision, and the Association of State and Provincial Psychology Boards (ASPPB) has begun to address issues of license reciprocity among states (Wood et al., 2005). Fortunately, the credential of Nationally Certified School Psychologist (NCSP) is recognized by an increasing number of states, which greatly facilitates resolution of this conundrum for school psychologists.

Missing Information

Online supervisors often do not have access to critical environmental and cultural information. Online supervision of practicum students and interns clearly must be supplemented by on-site supervision. It is particularly helpful when the online supervisor and on-site supervisor communicate frequently with one another and with the supervisee.

Academic Honesty

Another challenge in computer-based supervision is determining whether the individual completing the work is indeed that person. The same issue, of course, arises in face-to-face learning when students knowingly and unknowingly plagiarize papers and other academic work.

Crisis Intervention

As in face-to-face supervision, provisions for crisis intervention must be available in computer-assisted supervision. Because technological failures are common, it is important that supervisors establish more than one method of communication.

SUMMARY

Computers and Internet communication have revolutionized the provision of mental health services, including school psychology. Computer-assisted supervision offers economies of time, money, and expertise and also transcends geographic barriers. Examples include online peer support and supervision groups, the use of e-mail, written synchronous communications via chat rooms and instant messages, synchronous audio contacts, and videoconferencing. Numerous concerns exist regarding the use of written computer-based communication, including the need for confidentiality, and precautions such as e-mail encryption should be taken. Videoconferencing can be very useful in providing services when distance and travel are problematic, although its limitations must be noted.

Supervisors can teach their supervisees to use virtual libraries and search engines, which allow immediate and easy access to information. Distance learning can also be used, although it is critical that potential problems be recognized and minimized. Combining these technologies may address many of the challenges. Methods for doing so include Computer-Assisted Supervision (CAS), a software program that facilitates supervisees' and supervisors' monitoring and analysis of counseling skills and intentions.

Although it is very promising, computer-assisted supervision is subject to many of the same shortcomings associated with face-to-face supervision. These include issues regarding supervision quantity, supervision quality, security and confidentiality, cost, access and familiarity, licensure, missing information, integrity, and crisis intervention. Supervisors must be aware of these limitations and concerns and understand how they can be addressed.

REFLECTIVE QUESTIONS

Q8.1. What are some ways in which computers and Internet communication have revolutionized the field of school psychology?

Q8.2. What are some examples of how computer-assisted supervision can be used?

Q8.3. Discuss the concerns that arise when written computer-based communication is used and the precautions that can be taken.

Q8.4. What are the advantages and disadvantages of videoconferencing?

Q8.5. How can supervisors assist supervisees in their use of virtual libraries, search engines, and Internet material?

Q8.6. What are the advantages and potential problems of distance learning? How can these potential problems be minimized?

Q8.7. What are some methods of combining computer technology and clinical supervision?

Q8.8. What issues regarding computer-based supervision exist in terms of supervision quantity, supervision quality, security and confidentiality, cost, access and familiarity, licensure, missing information, integrity, and crisis intervention?

SUPERVISORY DILEMMAS

SD 8.1

A school psychologist within your district is skillful on the computer and uses e-mail with teachers to facilitate consultation. This gives the psychologist a highly effective method of consultation follow-up. On the other hand, knowing that e-mail is not confidential for a number of reasons, you are concerned that confidentiality may not be maintained. *What are the supervisory considerations? What should be done?*

Authors' thoughts: Given the widespread use of e-mail, it is likely that all readers will have either directly or indirectly experienced the horror that accompanies the act of sending the wrong e-mail to the wrong person! Using e-mail successfully in the practice of school psychology requires intense vigilance and consistent caution. The only "solution" is to encrypt and/or disguise the identity of all parties. The inherent dangers in casual e-mail use are impressive. Avoidance of breaches of confidentiality demands constant care and attentiveness. One must always proceed with utmost caution! Electronic communication is, assuredly, here to stay. Practitioners must vigilantly work to uphold and protect the identity of their constituents. We are fully responsible for our actions and our errors.

SD 8.2

You are a supervising psychologist in a large city. Some school psychologists in private practice have begun using computer-generated reports when conducting third-party assessments. They present the unedited reports as their own work and charge a full fee for the service. The reports seem to make universal recommendations for private school placement and do not consider resources available within the district. *What are the supervisory considerations? What should be done?*

Authors' thoughts: There is little doubt that computers have become very useful in terms of test scoring by helping to eliminate human error in computation and data input. Many software programs offer an efficient way to avoid spending time hand scoring. As programs become increasingly sophisticated, more and more "report writing" is embedded. While an unedited computer report is perhaps helpful as a template, it is clear that it cannot appropriately serve the needs of students. Assessments and the ensuing recommendations must be individualized to address the individual differences of each and every student. Boilerplate recommendations must be edited and crafted to meet the needs of the individual. A secondary danger is that computer-generated reports may allow practitioners access to instruments they do not fully understand. Finally, anyone conducting evaluations should keep abreast of available programs and services. To do less is to do the student a tremendous injustice.

9

Providing Clinical Supervision

Skilled clinical supervision fosters competence, critical thinking, problem solving, metacognitive skills, and autonomy.

Vignette 9.1

Missy was employed as the chief psychologist in a small city. When she attended a meeting where local university school psychology training program faculty explained the rubrics used to evaluate interns' portfolios and case studies, she realized that she needed to revise the techniques used to provide clinical supervision for all of the district school psychologists. Specifically, she realized that she needed to ask all psychologists to submit data that tracked student behavior and academic progress before and after interventions, just as interns were asked to do. She also realized that, as chief school psychologist, she needed to work with the administration to ensure that the psychologists received recognition for this work.

BASIC CONSIDERATIONS

Supervision techniques and interventions serve a number of purposes. They *intervene*, when necessary, in services provided by supervisees and thereby protect students, parents, and teachers from incompetence. They also *provide teaching methods* for the supervisor and *learning opportunities* for the supervisee. Finally, effective supervision techniques *foster supervisee self-appraisal* and thereby encourage reflective practice and increased self-sufficiency.

Falender and Shafranske (2007) advocated that clinical supervisors fully integrate a competency-based approach into the supervisory process. To do so, the clinical supervisor implements the steps listed in Handout 9.1.

Handout 9.1

COMPONENTS OF COMPETENCY-BASED SUPERVISION

(Adapted from Falender & Shafranske, 2007)[1]

1. Self-assess supervisory and professional practice knowledge and skills.

2. Develop a positive supervisory relationship with the supervisee.

3. Commit to evidence-based and ethical practice.

4. Delineate supervisory expectations, standards, rules, and practice.

5. Identify competencies the supervisee must attain.

6. Collaboratively develop a supervisory contract to attain consent and establish goals, activities, and procedures.

7. Link desired competencies with ongoing formative and summative evaluative procedures.

8. Foster the supervisee's self-awareness and reflective practice in the evaluative process.

9. Use tape reviews and case notes to review the supervisee's work.

10. Model self-assessment and metacognitive practice throughout supervision and engage the supervisee in the same.

11. On an ongoing basis, provide verbal and written feedback to the supervisee.

12. Encourage and accept verbal and written feedback from the supervisee.

13. Accept responsibility for maintaining communication.

14. Accept responsibility for observing and addressing problems in the supervisory relationship.

[1]Falender, C. A., & Shafranske, E. P. (2007). Competence in competency-based supervision practice: Construct and application. *Professional Psychology: Research and Practice, 38,* 232–240.

As discussed previously, the same supervision interventions and techniques can be used with different models of supervision, although some of them are better suited to some models than to others. Furthermore, the same interventions and techniques can be used in a variety of supervision formats (individual, group, peer, team) and in computer-assisted supervision as well as face-to-face supervision.

SUPERVISORY INTERVENTIONS AND TECHNIQUES

Supervisory interventions can occur prior to the session in question when the supervisor helps the supervisee appropriately *plan* a course of action by providing didactic instruction, assigning readings, modeling, or role-playing. Interventions can also occur *during* sessions through direct observations and collaborative work on the same cases. Or interventions can occur *after* sessions through review of session tapes, reports, and case process notes. Each technique and intervention has unique advantages and disadvantages.

Interventions and Techniques Used in Planning

It is very important that supervisees plan their work, and supervisors play a pivotal role in facilitating this process. Planning takes place on two levels: the broad and the specific.

Vignette 9.2

Martha spent considerable time helping her supervisee, **Kit**, plan a series of parent-student workshops to facilitate homework completion. At the broad level, Martha helped Kit plan the content of the workshops, obtain materials, design methods to find participants, and determine evaluation methods. On the specific level, Martha helped Kit plan each session before the sessions began. As the series progressed, Martha helped Kit modify session plans according to events that transpired during the sessions. The care that Martha took during this process was pivotal in teaching Kit to provide effective workshops that responded to participants' needs.

Clinical supervisors can help their supervisees plan at both levels. To orient supervisees to upcoming cases and situations, supervisors can provide didactic instruction (i.e., direct teaching and lectures) and find and assign hard copy or Internet-based readings. These two methods provide the supervisee with *content* information necessary for approaching new tasks.

Processes for new tasks are often taught using modeling or role-playing. These methods can help supervisees deal with difficult interpersonal situations often encountered in schools. For example, in Vignette 9.2, the supervisor, Martha, might teach her supervisee Kit how to deal with a parent who brags about belittling his children. The first step might be to model an appropriate response and then conduct a role-play in which the supervisor plays the parent. Modeling and role-playing are also very useful in preparing supervisees for activities such as presenting and interpreting information to parents, chairing team meetings, administering a new assessment tool, or working with an uncooperative teacher.

Case presentations are effective in helping supervisees plan upcoming sessions while in the midst of an intervention. Case presentations can be used during individual, group, and peer supervision sessions. Essential components are listed in Table 9.1.

Table 9.1   Case Presentation Guidelines (Adapted from Wilbur, Roberts-Wilbur, Hart, Morris, & Betz, 1994)

1. The supervisee presents a case along with supporting data, paper documentation, and audiotaped or videotaped segments of an assessment, counseling, or consultation session and then:
   a. Indicates the most salient content, events, and processes of the session
   b. Offers possible explanations for the content, events, and processes
   c. Shares feelings experienced toward the student/teacher/parent
   d. Shares thoughts experienced
   e. Indicates feelings and thoughts believed to be experienced by the student/teacher/parent during the session
   f. Indicates specific feedback desired

2. The supervisor/group supervision members respond to the psychologist by:
   a. Commenting on what they like about the psychologist's approach
   b. Noting student/parent/teacher reactions to the psychologist
   c. Suggesting what might have been added to or subtracted from the session
   d. Indicating what might have been done differently

3. The supervisor/group supervision members respond to the client by:
   a. Noting the student's/parent's/teacher's concerns
   b. Indicating the feelings elicited by the student/parent/teacher
   c. Noting themes and inconsistencies

4. The supervisor/group supervision members respond to the session by:
   a. Noting which goals were accomplished during the session
   b. Indicating the session's major accomplishments and flaws
   c. Suggesting possible future goals and methods to accomplish them

5. A 10- to 15-minute break is taken for the supervisee to reflect on provided feedback.

6. The supervisee responds to the supervisor's/group members' feedback and indicates which statements were helpful, which were not, why they were or were not helpful, and which the supervisee plans to adopt.

7. The supervisor leads a discussion of the entire process.

During-Session Interventions and Techniques

Direct observations enable supervisors to assess supervisees' skills, determine the effects of supervisees on clients, observe supervisees' ability to reason about their impact on clients, and help supervisees improve (Mead, 1990). Traditionally, during direct observations the supervisor does not intervene during the session unless an emergency occurs. This is in contrast to *live supervision* used in family therapy, where supervisors commonly intervene during sessions. Direct observations have several advantages: The supervisor is able to intervene in the event of an emergency, the observations provide a great deal of information to the supervisor, and feedback can be given immediately.

Regardless of the level of the supervisee, it is challenging to provide supervisees with an atmosphere that permits them to feel comfortable while being observed. To minimize the discomfort experienced by most supervisees during observations, it helps to (a) conduct observations frequently enough so that they are routine; (b) avoid interruptions, negative facial expressions, and excessive note taking; and (c) follow every observation with an immediate conference during which notes are shared and collaboratively and constructively analyzed (Henry & Beasley, 1982).

Collaborative work includes coleading group or individual counseling sessions, conducting collaborative assessment, or collaboratively working on consultation cases. It is a highly effective teaching technique and is particularly appropriate for use with beginner practitioners. However, it is also very helpful whenever a supervisee is attempting to learn a new skill. For example, a supervisee and supervisor (or two peer supervisors) might collaboratively assess a student when one of them is learning a new instrument.

Post-Session Interventions and Techniques

Verbal self-reports of the events that transpire during counseling, assessment, and consultation sessions are the oldest and most traditional form of supervision. In self-report, the supervisor meets with the supervisee to hear the supervisee's observations and perceptions of the session, examine the supervisees' hypotheses, and facilitate plans for the case (Mead, 1990). However, as J. M. Bernard and Goodyear (2004) pointed out, "although it is a simple form of supervision in one sense, self-report [is] a difficult method to perform well" (p. 211).

A serious complication with self-report is that the supervisor is dependent on the accuracy of the supervisee's perceptions and reporting, either of which can be affected by unconscious and conscious distortions and omissions. This is particularly problematic with novice supervisees, since supervisees often do not report important events in therapy sessions to their supervisors (Worthington, Tan, & Poulin, 2002). Therefore, supervision literature often recommends that supervisees' observations and perceptions be verified through direct observation or tapes, particularly with novice supervisees or in situations that are highly emotionally charged for the supervisee (e.g., crisis situations or those that elicit transference and countertransference).

Case notes are the records the psychologist keeps of every counseling, consultation, and assessment session and are the professional, institutional, and legal record of the interaction. Suggested components of case notes are listed in Table 9.2.

Table 9.2   Case Note Components

- Signed consent and release forms, including those consenting to taping and supervision review
- Records of all contacts with the students, parents, and teachers
- Notes regarding history and symptomatology
- Session notes
- Interventions used during the sessions
- Recommended courses of action, including those not followed
- Termination and follow-up plans

Case notes can be reviewed during supervision sessions and used as a catalyst for discussions during which the supervisee is challenged to reflect on choices made, to consider cultural dynamics, or to link theoretical processes to practice (J. M. Bernard & Goodyear, 2004). However, case notes are subject to supervisee distortions and omissions, since they are simply a written variation of self-reports.

Process notes are more extensive versions of case notes; the psychologist makes note of the content of the session and analyzes the interactions that occur, her or his feelings about the session, the rationale for choices made, and details about interventions (Goldberg, 1985). Process notes can be quite detailed and are most commonly used in training, although they are beneficial when a supervisor feels the need for an intensive review of the supervisee's interactions.

Process notes can be extremely helpful in supervision, since they are a record not only of what occurred during a session with a student but also of the supervisee's subjective reactions and plans for a future direction. Process notes are reminders of what has occurred previously, provide a developmental overview of the case, and provide a protective function if legal or ethical issues arise (Goldberg, 1985; Pruitt, McColgan, Pugh, & Kiser, 1986). Careful examination of the hypotheses and explanations that emerge in supervisees' process notes provides a method of investigating underlying theories around factors that induce and support student change. A form for supervisees to use for taking process notes while working with students can be found in Handout 9.2.

Audiotape review enables supervisors to obtain more accurate information regarding a psychologist's interactions with students, teachers, and parents than does verbal self-report, case notes, or process notes. It has the advantage of providing direct data and has been noted to result in "exemplary" supervision as rated by supervisees (Magnuson, Wilcoxon, & Norem, 2000). Supervisees are sometimes resistant to the concept of taping sessions and may indicate that their clients are uncomfortable with being taped. As J. M. Bernard and Goodyear (2004) pointed out, however, clients are generally comfortable with taping as long as the prospect of taping for supervision is broached in a professional manner and the clients are reassured that confidentiality will be maintained. In turn, supervisees' discomfort with the prospect of taping tends to dissolve when their tapes are reviewed sensitively and result in helpful and constructive feedback from their supervisors (Benshoff & Paisley, 1996; Ellis, Krengel, & Beck, 2002). While counseling sessions are those most commonly taped and analyzed, the same process can be fruitfully applied to consultation sessions.

Supervision using audiotapes is least effective when used in an unstructured, nonselective manner. At the beginning of a supervisory relationship, it is helpful to listen to at least one entire session to obtain an overview of the psychologist's skills and to preselect segments to review during supervision. With time, the supervisee can select tape portions to review during supervision. Preselected segments can (a) highlight productive or important portions of the session, (b) point out portions in which the supervisee has difficulty or appears frustrated or overwhelmed, (c) highlight indications that cultural variables should be considered, and (d) emphasize recurring themes and important content (J. M. Bernard & Goodyear, 2004).

Rather than listening to portions of audiotapes during supervision sessions, some supervisors prefer to listen to the tapes between sessions and provide written feedback. This method has the advantage of providing a written record of supervision and of allowing the supervisor time to reflect on and formulate feedback.

Another strategy is to have the supervisee transcribe audiotaped sessions and to submit the transcriptions along with a self-analysis. This strategy is commonly used in introductory courses to help the supervisee perceive inappropriate interpersonal actions, such as being overly directive or interrupting. While very time consuming, analysis of audiotape

Handout 9.2

CASE PROCESS NOTES

Date:

Student:

Parent:

Teacher:

School Psychologist:

Supervisor:

Information	Theory/Hypothesis
Student's/client's subjective description of status	
Objective information regarding the student's/client's status (behavioral observations, data collected, external feedback from others, etc.)	
Observations regarding the psychologist's words and behaviors	
Plans, goals, and strategies (intervention homework, future session topics)	

transcriptions can be quite illuminating. With the increased accuracy of speech recognition software such as Dragon NaturallySpeaking, it may be that producing transcripts of audiotapes will become much less onerous and therefore more common.

Videotape review is another option. In counseling psychology, reviewing videotapes of sessions with clients has become the technology of choice (J. M. Bernard & Goodyear, 2004). Even though the processes used are very similar to those used in reviewing audiotapes, videotaping has many advantages over audiotaping. Videotapes provide much more information than audiotapes because the supervisor can observe both the client's and the supervisee's body language. They also provide substantial information to supervisees as they watch themselves provide services. A helpful strategy is Interpersonal Process Recall (Kagan & Kagan, 1997), during which the supervisee and supervisor view a videotaped session, stop it when something important happens, and then explore the thoughts, cognitions, images, and expectations the supervisee recalls having had at that moment. This greatly increases the supervisee's ability to self-monitor.

Despite its advantages, videotaping does have several disadvantages. It is relatively expensive, requires more space than audiotaping, is more intrusive to students and clients, and is not a recognized or accepted component in most public school cultures.

Journal writing can be used by supervisees to evaluate their practice, consider external events, relate relevant emotional experiences, and identify recurring patterns. When reviewed by the supervisor, supervisees' journals can be a powerful supervision tool (J. M. Bernard & Goodyear, 2004; Griffith & Frieden, 2000).

Treatment Summaries

Treatment summaries are the consolidation of material into a format to be shared with others, most often at the conclusion of a counseling or consultation relationship, at the culmination of an assessment, or at the end of a marking period. Treatment summaries facilitate continuity of care and service when cases are transferred from one practitioner to another and as students progress through the grades and schools. It is helpful to develop a series of preprepared forms to guide the collection of desired information (students' developmental and academic history forms, parent consent forms, etc.). Establishing a protocol that determines what is to be kept in various student folders helps to promote consistency of records over time and from one school psychologist to another.

Vignette 9.3

Annette supervises school psychology interns every year, and they traditionally lead social skills groups as part of their internship. Many of the same children participate from one year to the next. Annette ensures that the interns keep good records regarding activities, individual progress, and individual and group goals. These records make it more likely that appropriate continuity will occur so that new interns can avoid repetitious activities and sustain progress.

Selecting Supervision Techniques

Supervision techniques should be selected according to the goals of supervision, the task being completed by the supervisee, the characteristics of the supervisee, and the characteristics of the supervisor. The supervision techniques most commonly used are not necessarily the techniques that are most effective. The most frequently used technique is self-report, even though collaborative work is more effective (Romans, Boswell, Carlozzi, & Ferguson, 1995). Furthermore, techniques requiring the highest levels of supervisee skill—for example, case study presentations—have been found to be used most often (Mead, 1990). Ward (1999) found that supervision of school psychologists consisted of 20% case presentation, 17% review of reports, 15% supervisor modeling, 15% direct observation of the intern, 11% sharing of resources, 9% goal planning and setting, and 9% performance evaluation. Only 0.5% of supervision was spent reviewing tapes, which is the technique with the highest accuracy.

Supervisee Task

Different supervisory techniques are better suited to different supervisee tasks. Many activities traverse myriad domains of practice. Whether or not the school psychologist is consulting regarding student progress, conducting an evaluation, providing counseling, offering parent training sessions, or completing a program evaluation, he or she must establish collaborative partnerships, identify goals, select interventions, and monitor progress. Table 9.3 lists common supervisee tasks and possible supervisory methods.

Supervisee Development

Effective supervisors must be sensitive and responsive to which techniques are most ethical, considering the supervisee's developmental level. Highly structured (supervisor-directed) supervision techniques are closer to the "training" end of the supervisory continuum and are most appropriate for novice supervisees, while less structured techniques (not supervisor directed) are closer to the "consultation" end of the continuum and are more appropriate for proficient practitioners (J. M. Bernard & Goodyear, 2004).

As Mead (1990) indicated, techniques vary in terms of information accuracy, the ability of the supervisor to intervene and quickly modify the supervisee's behavior, reliance on technology, required supervisor time, required level of supervisee skill or development, and degree of intrusiveness. Novice supervisors need techniques that provide high intervention possibilities and low requisite supervisee skill. Given these parameters, supervisors should strive as much as possible to use techniques that maximize information accuracy but minimize intrusion on the client. Supervision techniques and interventions are summarized according to these variables in Table 9.4.

Supervision Session Feedback

All supervisory interventions should be accompanied by feedback to the supervisee. It is best when feedback is specific, timely, offered in a calm manner, balanced in terms of strengths and weaknesses, given with time for reflection and questions, provided with an attitude that invites comments, and presented in a manner that implies methods for improvement. Particularly with beginners and at the initiation of a supervisory relationship, it is important to maintain a positive focus to avoid unnecessary exacerbation of anxiety.

Supervisors and supervisees find it much easier to give and receive feedback regarding some activities than others. For example, many supervisees and supervisors find feedback regarding behavioral observations, test administration, and test interpretation fairly routine. Beginners are likely to be more insecure regarding presenting results at staff meetings, making presentations at teachers' meetings, providing counseling, and writing skills. More difficult feedback would address personal factors, understanding boundaries, interpersonal skills, and professional ethics (Cruise et al., 2000). Nonetheless,

Table 9.3 Supervisee Tasks and Supervision Techniques

Supervisee Task	Applicable Supervision Techniques
Establish rapport and collaborative partnerships; set confidentiality limitations	Role-playing Modeling Collaborative work Direct observation Tape review
Collaboratively identify and analyze the problem	Modeling Collaborative work Direct observation Tape review Review of collected data
Gather data accurately (e.g., administer and score Curriculum-Based Measurement probes or standardized batteries accurately)	Direct observation Tape review Review of collected data
Generate hypotheses and corresponding interventions	Modeling Collaborative work Direct observation Tape review Case process notes and case study presentation
Select and implement interventions	Modeling Collaborative work Direct observation Tape review Case process notes and case study presentation
Appraise success and modify strategies accordingly	Modeling Collaborative work Direct observation Tape review Review of collected data Case process notes and case study presentation
Implement strategies to promote generalization and continual improvement (self-regulation)	Modeling Collaborative work Direct observation Tape review Review of collected data Case process notes and case study presentation
Maintain accurate records and generate effective reports	Modeling Collaborative work Tape review Case process notes and case study presentation Review of psychological reports

Table 9.4 Advantages and Disadvantages of Supervisory Techniques

Supervisory Technique	Information Accuracy	Supervisor's Ability to Intervene	Reliance on Technology	Required Supervisor Time	Required Supervisee Skill Level	Intrusion on Client
Supervision Plan	Not applicable	Low	Low	Low	Low	Low
Supervision Goals	Varies	Low	Low	Low	Low	Low
Monitoring of Treatment Integrity	Varies	Varies	Varies	High	Low	Low
Supervision Records	Varies	Low	Varies	Moderate	Low	Low
Review of Collected Data	Varies	Low	Varies	Moderate	High	Low
Didactic Instruction	Not applicable	Low	Low	Low	Low	Low
Assigned Readings	Not applicable	Not applicable	Low	Low	Low	Not applicable
Modeling	Not applicable	Not applicable	Low	Moderate	Low	Not applicable
Role-Playing	Low; rarely completely reflects practice	High	Low	High	Low	Not applicable
Direct Observation in Room	High	High	Low	Very high; supervisor must be present during sessions and meet with the supervisee before and after to plan and analyze	Low	High
Direct Observation Through One-Way Mirror	High	High, although it requires interruption of the session (unless a "bug in the ear" receiver is used)	Requires one-way mirror	Very high; supervisor must be present during sessions and meet with the supervisee before and after to plan and analyze	Low	Moderate to high

(Continued)

Table 9.4 (Continued)

Supervisory Technique	Information Accuracy	Supervisor's Ability to Intervene	Reliance on Technology	Required Supervisor Time	Required Supervisee Skill Level	Intrusion on Client
Collaborative Work: Co-Counseling, Collaborative Assessment, Collaborative Consultation	High accuracy, but sessions affected by supervisor's presence	Too high; experienced psychologists find it almost impossible not to take over the session	Low	Very high; supervisor must be present during sessions and meet with the supervisee before and after to plan and analyze	Low to moderate	Usually low
Audiotaping of Sessions With Typed Transcript and Analysis	High (although lack of nonverbal behaviors is a serious detriment); typed transcript and analysis of the content and process of the session greatly facilitates supervisee observations	Low; delayed until at least the next session, if not longer	Requires audiotape equipment and the ability to type and analyze the transcript	High; supervisor must listen to tapes (and supervisee must transcribe and analyze them)	Low to moderate	Moderate
Audiotaping of Sessions	High (although lack of nonverbal behaviors is a serious detriment)	Low; delayed until the next session	Requires audiotape equipment and the ability to type and analyze the transcript	High; supervisor must listen to tapes	Moderate	Moderate
Review of Psychological Reports	Moderate; supervisor does not have access to raw data other than test protocols, but the text reveals the thought processes of the supervisee	Very low	Low	Low	All levels	Not applicable

Supervisory Technique	Information Accuracy	Supervisor's Ability to Intervene	Reliance on Technology	Required Supervisor Time	Required Supervisee Skill Level	Intrusion on Client
Case Process Notes, Reviewed in Individual Supervision	Very low; prone to the supervisee's distortion, and the supervisor has neither verbal nor nonverbal client cues	Low; delayed until the next session	Low	Low	High	Not applicable
Case Process Notes, Reviewed in Peer Supervision	Very low; prone to the supervisee's distortion, and peer supervisors have neither verbal nor nonverbal client cues	Low; case presentation is often postponed and interventions are delayed	Low	Low	High	Not applicable
Case Study Presentation	Very low; prone to the supervisee's distortion, and peer supervisors have neither verbal nor nonverbal client cues	Low; case presentation is often postponed and interventions are delayed	Low	Low	High	Not applicable

supervisors must be careful to attend to these difficult issues, since they are often the very variables that cause supervisees the greatest hardship.

Vignette 9.4

Over a number of years as a supervisor, **Haven** found that he was most discomfited when called upon to provide his supervisees with feedback regarding their personal grooming. Once a principal refused to have a particular school psychologist in his building because he wore facial jewelry, another had complained about an intern wearing flip-flops, and a third had objected to a supervisee's excessive perfume. Haven found it difficult to approach his supervisees with these secondhand complaints of a personal nature. He also was struck by the fact that the principals were so uncomfortable addressing these issues themselves.

MAINTAINING SUPERVISION RECORDS

Maintaining accurate and complete records of supervision is important for several reasons: It facilitates effective practice, serves as a method of guiding supervision, and provides a means of accountability. Record keeping in public schools is governed by federal law, state law, and local practice and is critical because supervisors are accountable for supervisees' implemented interventions and decisions. Thus, supervision documentation is a "standard of competent supervisory practice" (Falvey & Cohen, 2003, p. 63).

Vignette 9.5

The Brookfield School District's attorney has advised all administrators and coordinators to keep complete records of supervision sessions to protect themselves and the district in the event of lawsuits and due process cases. **Mia**'s supervision has previously consisted of regular "chats" and report review. She recognizes that, to comply with the attorney's recommendation, she needs to block out time to complete supervision paperwork in her appointment book, much as she blocks out report writing time in her appointment book whenever she has a psychoeducational report to write.

The supervisee's developmental level affects the level of record keeping required, since supervising unlicensed interns requires more comprehensive records than supervising a seasoned practitioner. A supervisor should keep a file for each supervisee. In this file, according to Falvey and Cohen (2003) as well as Munson (2002), the supervisor should keep the materials listed in Table 9.5.

As J. M. Bernard and Goodyear (2004) indicated, a number of tools have been developed to monitor ongoing supervision. They vary in the degree to which they are comprehensive, address risk management, and encourage responses from both the supervisor and the supervisee. Focused Risk Management Supervision (Falvey & Cohen, 2003) provides a format to track the supervisee's caseload, goals and experience, professional development needs, initial assessments, and treatment plans. It also tracks the supervisee's clients' progress, referrals, outcomes, termination, and risk factors. The Clinical Supervision Notes Record Form (Brantly, 2001) has two parts, one completed by the supervisee and one completed by the supervisor. The supervisee form tracks client referrals, the interventions used, the response and progress of the client, concerns, and client issues discussed in supervision. The supervisor form tracks supervisory comments and observations, notations regarding supervisory issues, strategies, and recommendations for professional development.

Just as process notes that supervisees take while working with students provide a great deal of information about their work, supervision process notes can be taken to record the supervision process. Careful examination of the hypotheses and explanations that emerge in supervisors' process notes provides a method of investigating underlying theories around factors that induce and support supervisee change. A form for supervisors to use for taking supervision notes while working with supervisees can be found in Handout 9.3. These notes can be kept privately by the supervisor, but they are also very helpful to share with the supervisee, since they provide opportunities to give feedback in writing.

Handout 9.3

SUPERVISION PROCESS NOTES

Date:

Supervisee:

Supervisor:

Information	Theory/Hypothesis
Supervisee's subjective description of the situation	
Objective information regarding the supervisee's status (behavioral observations, data collected, external feedback from others, etc.)	
Observations regarding the supervisor's words and behaviors	
Plans, goals, and strategies (intervention homework, future session topics)	

Table 9.5 Supervision File Contents (Adapted from Falvey & Cohen, 2003; Munson, 2002)

Supervision files should include:

- The supervision contract
- Records of each supervision session
- Records of canceled or missed sessions
- Notations regarding discussed cases and ensuing recommendations
- Notations of training recommendations made to the supervisee
- Evidence that past supervision records were obtained and reviewed
- Formative evaluations of the supervisee
- Summative evaluations of the supervisee
- Notes of problems encountered during supervision
- Successful and unsuccessful attempts to resolve supervision problems

Supervision files should *not* include:

- Disparaging comments regarding either supervisees or clients
- Opinions that are not supported by objective data

FOSTERING SELF-SUPERVISION BY SUPERVISEES

Todd (1997b) indicated that supervisors should make self-sufficiency a clear goal of supervision and develop a clear description of the behaviors shown by a competent and self-sufficient school psychologist. Supervisors can encourage supervisees to employ a number of strategies to work toward eventual self-sufficiency. These include meta-analysis of supervision and professional work, stress management, and time management.

Meta-Analysis of Supervision

An emphasis on the practice of meta-analysis has become increasingly evident in the counseling psychology supervision literature (Neufeldt, 1999) and is reinforced by the finding that meta-analysis is associated with professional growth and long-term satisfaction (Rønnestad & Skovholt, 2003). It has as its fundamental source the constructivist (Piagetian) approach to education, which recognizes that learning occurs when students are involved in "constructing" their own knowledge. It is augmented by the literature on self-regulated learning, which reveals that encouraging students to use executive skills and metacognition to appraise their learning methods and results yields greatly improved learning (Harvey & Chickie-Wolfe, 2007). Thus supervisors should encourage supervisees to repeatedly consider the three fundamental questions inherent in self-regulation: What did I do? How well did it work? How should I modify my practice in the future?

To foster self-sufficiency, supervisors need to help supervisees assess their own strengths and areas of relative weakness systematically and explicitly and then develop small and specific learning goals related to areas of relative weakness. It is also beneficial to explore supervisees' learning styles by providing a wide range of supervisory activities, observe those which are most effective with each supervisee, and share that information with supervisees. Furthermore, supervisors can help supervisees develop a theoretical framework in which to function so that they can "critique . . . sessions and look for behaviors that would be considered errors within that framework" (Todd, 1997b, p. 21).

Self-sufficiency is also fostered when supervisors encourage supervisees to structure supervision sessions themselves. This can be accomplished by encouraging supervisees to arrive at supervision sessions with clearly defined goals and questions for the session and to carefully select materials to bring to supervisory sessions.

Furthermore, supervisors can use specific strategies to decrease supervisees' dependence on them. They might use supervision sessions to generate alternative hypotheses and collaboratively brainstorm rather than to give the supervisee "correct" answers, and they might ask supervisees what they anticipate the supervisor will ask or recommend before either asking questions or making recommendations. It is also beneficial to obtain structured feedback on the supervisory process by taking a few minutes at the end of each supervisory session to discuss what aspects of the session were particularly helpful. Another strategy is to encourage supervisees to utilize additional forms of supervision, such as peer support groups.

Finally, supervisors should encourage supervisees to obtain feedback from children, parents, and teachers regarding the effectiveness of their practice by routinely conducting follow-up appraisals of student functioning. Supervisors can encourage supervisees to develop skill in both generalizing from one case to another and differentiating one case from another so that they can independently determine when it is appropriate for them to continue a particular intervention and when they should not.

Stress Management

Whether school psychologists are helping failing students succeed, working with teachers struggling to meet the demands of diverse learners in the context of high-stakes testing, providing therapy to distressed adolescents, or attempting to satisfy enraged parents, they can experience considerable stress. As Guy (2000) indicated, "spending hour after hour with troubled individuals in significant distress can take a toll on us after many years of practice" (p. 351). Stress results when environmental demands are greater than an individual's perceived ability to meet those demands (R. S. Lazarus, 1966).

The nature of school psychology, wherein problems that are "solved" disappear and those that are not solved remain for up to 12 years, is inherently stressful. Furthermore, school psychologists may have the highly stressful experience of working with contentious and litigious cases, as when a case is taken to arbitration or due process hearings that result from parental dissatisfaction with educational programs. It is not unreasonable to expect that the stress caused by such hearings may approximate that felt by psychologists experiencing licensing board complaints (J. T. Thomas, 2005). Finally, working in schools appears to be a stress-producing job for general education teachers, special education teachers, and school psychologists alike (Forman & Cecil, 1985). In addition to the pervasively stressful school environment, school psychologists are challenged by attempting to simultaneously meet the needs of students, parents, teachers, and administrators. They may be challenged to simultaneously meet multiple roles, such as school psychologist and team leader. Almost inevitably, they encounter highly stressful situations with students who have high needs, such as those for whom abuse reports must be filed and those who express suicidal ideation. Furthermore, supervisors of school psychologists are typically in a highly stressful situation themselves, since they are responsible for helping their supervisees fulfill responsibilities in the face of pressing demands and emotional stress (Harvey, 2008).

Adverse reactions to stress can be behavioral, cognitive, emotional, or physical and can be manifested by anxiety, apathy, avoidance, burnout, compulsivity, critical attitudes, dependence, deterioration of work performance, frustration, impatience, negative attitudes, procrastination, rejection, retaliation, somatic illnesses, or temper outbursts (Noe, Hollenbeck, Gerhart, & Wright, 1996). Harvey (2005a) compared supervision experiences, workplace characteristics, roles and functions, and methods of stress management with job satisfaction and burnout. Results revealed that the highest job stress was associated with incongruence of the supervisor's values with the school psychologist's values, job responsibilities incongruent with the school psychologist's expectations, inability to meet time demands, policies incongruent with the school psychologist's value system, and dissatisfaction with feedback and guidance. Considerable stress was found to result from supervisors with poor interpersonal skills, administrators with insufficient understanding of special education law and school psychology, and supervisors with little interest in work quality. Additional concerns included poor job structure, excessive workloads, insufficient clerical support, inadequate pay or office space, and outdated technology. School psychologists also expressed frustration with state, federal, and local policies and politics and with the characteristics of teachers, other educators, and parents with whom they worked.

A. A. Lazarus (2000) recommended that psychologists conduct weekly or biweekly self-assessments to counteract stressors of working as a professional psychologist. Relevant questions are listed in Activity 9.1.

Activity 9.1

Psychologist Self-Assessment

Conduct self-assessment by answering the following questions:

1. What behaviors do I want to increase? What behaviors do I want to decrease?

2. What do I want to stop doing? What do I want to start doing?

3. Which emotions do I want to increase? Which emotions do I want to increase?

4. Which sensations do I want to increase? Which sensations do I want to decrease?

5. Which of my mental images could I phase out? What mental image could I deliberately foster to replace those that I phase out?

6. Which ongoing cognitions could I phase out? What cognitions could I deliberately foster to replace those that I phase out?

7. Which negative interpersonal contacts could I phase out? Which could I foster?

8. What biological (e.g., fitness, diet) changes are warranted in my life?

9. What unchangeable situations must I simply learn to accept?

A number of studies have examined the use of self-care strategies by psychologists. J. A. Turner et al. (2005) found that interns most frequently used social supports, active problem solving, and humor, but that seeking pleasurable experiences was also very effective. Dlugos and Friedlander (2001) found that psychologists who are energized and invigorated by their work rather than exhausted and drained are skillful in stress management. Harvey (2005a) surveyed school psychologists and found that they use multiple methods to cope with the stress of being a school psychologist. These methods can be grouped into eight categories: (a) finding satisfaction in the job, (b) maintaining perspective, (c) promoting positive relationships with others, (d) being appropriately assertive, (e) mentoring others, (f) finding ways to laugh, (g) setting boundaries, and (h) "having a life." Examples from each category follow.

To help supervisees find satisfaction in their jobs, supervisors can encourage their supervisees to be aware of and appreciate the differences they make in children's lives, to foster students' and parents' trust and confidence by serving as their advocate, to periodically refocus on students by visiting a preschool or kindergarten class, and to do things they enjoy with students. Supervisees can also participate in early intervention programs (birth to Grade 2) and monitor the progress of the students, keep a running list of students whose lives have benefited from their work, and meet often with parents to promote parental involvement. It is also helpful for them to build variety into their jobs and to take on one different activity each year at work. Finally, it is important for them to consciously celebrate the good to counterbalance that over which they have no control and to avoid focusing on frustrations.

To help supervisees maintain perspective, supervisors can encourage their supervisees to focus on what is most important in their jobs (i.e., helping students) and in their personal lives (e.g., family). It is also helpful for supervisees to keep a "smile file" containing thank you notes from staff, students, and parents so that it is easy for them to remember their successes. Further, supervisees can be encouraged to remain optimistic, yet balance their perspective with realistic expectations.

To help supervisees promote positive interpersonal interactions on the job, supervisors can encourage their supervisees to develop positive relationships with work colleagues. To do so, school psychologists associate with positively minded colleagues; collaborate with colleagues regarding methods to improve difficult work situations; take time to talk with students, teachers, and parents; share compliments with others; have lunch with colleagues; schedule monthly meetings with school counselors and resource teachers; avoid gossiping; stay calm and avoid taking things personally; participate in book group and coffee get-togethers with school personnel after school; maintain good rapport with colleagues to make the environment fun and supportive; develop a wonderful instructional support team; develop good rapport with school staff to make it easier to collaborate; and consult with knowledgeable teachers, speech therapists, and counselors.

To help supervisees develop positive relationships with other psychologists, supervisors can encourage their supervisees to develop a collaborative team with other psychologists; participate in local and state school psychology associations and conferences; meet regularly with other psychologists for lunch and after work to vent, joke, and laugh; have group sessions to talk about problems; develop a network of supportive friends and colleagues; and consult with knowledgeable colleagues on challenging cases.

To help supervisees become appropriately assertive, supervisors can encourage their supervisees to role-play using assertive confrontation with aggressive parents and coworkers and saying no to unreasonable requests.

To help supervisees experience the benefits of mentoring others, supervisors can encourage three-tiered supervision, wherein interns help supervise practicum students and school psychologists supervise the interns and practicum students. In addition, supervisors can help supervisees participate in peer supervision groups.

To help supervisees find ways to laugh, supervisors can foster a positive attitude within the department, find humor in work situations, and share humor and stories from outside of work.

To help supervisees set boundaries, supervisors can encourage their supervisees to separate work from personal life. It is advisable to leave work at work and to enjoy one's family and hobbies at home. Many school psychologists stay late at work a couple of days per week so that they do not have to bring work home. It is also helpful to take a full lunch break, "in a park if possible." Supervisors can encourage their supervisees to be clear about their time constraints and other limitations, to limit others' expectations by giving them an accurate time frame, and to refer students and parents to other practitioners when necessary.

To help supervisees "have a life," supervisors can encourage their supervisees to find time to nurture themselves. Various activities recommended by school psychologists include exercise, yoga, church attendance, vacationing, reading for pleasure, community activities not involving the school, spending time with family and friends, singing, watching films, attending concerts, socializing with others outside the school district who do not identify one as a psychologist, eating a healthy diet, living in a beautiful place, volunteer work, listening to music at work or in the car, lunching with the secretary or a friend, getting to bed earlier, journal writing, relaxing on a daily basis either formally (meditation) or informally (being a couch potato), building breaks into the day (e.g., playing solitaire, taking walks), and participating in hobbies that give concrete results (e.g., woodworking, painting).

Vignette 9.6

Gayle recommends having a passion outside the job that is as intense, as consuming, and as fascinating as the job. This provides another realm in which to feel successful when the job is overwhelming and stressful, and it helps enormously. Her passion is painting, and she spends weeks every summer painting with other artists.

Time Management

One of the greatest challenges faced by beginning school psychologists is the establishment of effective time management and organizational skills. Some of the most attractive aspects of the job—high flexibility, varied activities, unstructured time, challenging expectations—are also the attributes that require a high degree of time management and organization. Time management has been shown to increase both the quantity and quality of time for school psychologists. A lack of effective time management can result in anxiety, stress, and ineffectual practice (Maher & Cook, 1985). A supervisor of school psychology will probably need to help novice school psychologists develop these skills. For good time management, school psychologists need to appreciate time as a scarce resource, understand tasks across the entire school year, and consider time management as an ongoing problem solving process. A survey of several hundred school psychologists resulted in the following suggestions (Harvey, 2005a):

1. Use executive skills:
   - Determine how time is spent by keeping a precise log to ascertain how much time it actually takes to complete various tasks, such as providing ongoing consultation, implementing a behavior management plan, conducting a psychological

assessment, running a parent support group, conducting a program evaluation, implementing an in-service training program, or writing a grant. Consider these time requirements before taking on or assigning new tasks.

- Determine when different tasks are completed most efficiently and take this into consideration when scheduling.
- At the end of the year, aggregate data regarding gender, referral problem, grade, school, and the percentage of referred students found to be in need of services and use this information to plan and develop prevention programs.
- Conduct a parent, student, and administrator satisfaction survey to ascertain appreciation and gain information for future needs.
- Write shorter reports and do less detailed evaluations when appropriate.
- Organize papers every day so that materials are easily found.
- Develop a report template on the computer that prompts entries.
- Continually ask: What did I do? How well did it work? What should I change in the future?

2. Minimize procrastination:
   - Deal with paperwork as soon as it arrives.
   - Do paperwork as soon as an upcoming meeting is scheduled.
   - Keep sticky notes hidden in the mail room for making immediate replies to some mail.
   - Score tests and rating scales immediately.
   - Begin writing a report as soon as a referral is made (background, history, presenting concerns, notes from team meetings, family data, etc.) and plug in additional information as it is received.
   - Answer e-mails immediately.

3. Schedule carefully:
   - Combine meetings.
   - Block time at each building for consultations, meetings, evaluations, and observations.
   - Be organized and efficient.
   - Give realistic time estimates.
   - Hold informal group lunches to talk with team members.
   - Keep desks organized.
   - Schedule and keep an office day every week.
   - Call parents at lunchtime.
   - Arrange to be at a "high need" school for a week straight.
   - Maintain an appointment book and a to-do list.
   - Prioritize tasks.
   - Maintain control of schedules.
   - Maintain copies of a school's recess, lunch, and specials schedules.
   - Break down large tasks into smaller units with deadlines.
   - Designate a day for writing reports.
   - Schedule follow-up meetings during initial meetings.
   - Write non-appointments into calendars.
   - Allocate time every day for phone calls, dealing with mail and e-mail, and scheduling.
   - Develop short- and long-term objectives and mark them on calendars.

4. Delegate:
   - Have secretaries copy, file, and schedule meetings.
   - Teach paraprofessionals to administer Curriculum-Based Measurement probes and conduct behavioral observations accurately.

5. Employ technology:
   - Use voice recognition software to dictate reports.
   - Use tablet PCs to take notes.
   - Use e-mail for communication.
   - Use a personal digital assistant (PDA).
   - Leave oneself voice mail as a memo system.
   - Use computerized test scoring software.
   - Use calculators.
   - Use computer report writing software.

6. Reduce distractions:
   - Work late 1 or 2 days a week to catch up.
   - Arrive at work before students and teachers for uninterrupted time.

7. Use organizers:
   - Employ a flow sheet to manage schedules.
   - Develop and use a good organizational system.
   - Use a pilot bag to wheel materials into schools rather than taking multiple trips.
   - Use folders to organize materials.
   - Keep student lists updated.
   - Keep a running list of referrals and case consultations.
   - Clearly explain to teachers what records they need to keep regarding interventions and provide easy ways for them to maintain them.
   - Keep a checklist stapled to each student's folder and date each item when it is addressed or completed. Handout 9.4 provides an example of such a checklist.

SUMMARY

Supervision serves a number of purposes. It provides interventions and therefore protects students, parents, and teachers. It also provides teaching methods and learning opportunities while fostering self-appraisal and reflective practice. The same supervisory interventions and techniques can be used in a variety of formats.

Supervisors assist supervisees in planning their work. Such planning can be facilitated through the use of didactic instruction, modeling, role-playing, and case presentations. Through direct observation, supervisors can assess supervisees' skills, determine effects on clients, gain insight into supervisees' ability to reason, and provide feedback. Post-session supervisory interventions include case notes, process notes, audiotape and videotape review, and journal writing. The most common post-session supervisory intervention is verbal self-report, which can be made more accurate when supplemented with direct observation or tapes.

In determining which techniques to use, supervisors should consider the task at hand; the supervisee's level of experience, developmental level, learning style, and learning goals; and the goals of supervision. It is critical that supervisory feedback be given in a manner that is specific, timely, calm, and balanced, and in a way that offers time for reflection and questions, invites comments, and implies methods for improvement. Supervisors

Handout 9.4

SUPERVISEE CASE LOG SHEET

Psychologist:

Student:

Date Assigned:

Activity	*Notes*	*Date(s)*
Record review		
Parent interview		
Prereferral team meeting		
Informed consent obtained		
Limits of confidentiality discussed		
Releases needed/obtained		
Student interview		
Areas of concern (abuse/neglect; substance abuse; harm risk/duty to warn; medical exam)		
Problem definition		
Baseline data		
Interventions		
Outcomes		
Supervisee concerns		
Supervisor concerns		
Supervisor recommendations		
Recommendations for supervisee training		
Termination		

must maintain accurate and complete records of supervision. Supervisors should also be aware of their supervisees' stress levels so that they can offer support and management techniques and assist them with time management while also fostering self-supervision.

REFLECTIVE QUESTIONS

Q9.1.   Describe how supervisors assist supervisees in planning their work. What are the essential components of a case presentation? In what supervisory formats can they be used?

Q9.2.   How can supervisors make direct observations more comfortable for their supervisees?

Q9.3.   What are the essential components of case notes?

Q9.4.   Discuss the benefits and challenges of the various post-session supervisory intervention techniques and give suggestions for improving their use.

Q9.5.   What variables account for the selection of supervisory techniques?

Q9.6.   Why is it important that supervisors maintain accurate and complete records of supervision? What do such records consist of?

Q9.7.   Discuss the stressors that school psychologists face and how they can cope.

Q9.8.   Discuss how supervisors can assist supervisees with time management.

Q9.9.   Discuss how supervisors can foster self-supervision.

SUPERVISORY DILEMMAS

SD 9.1

A supervisor adamantly refuses to directly observe his supervisee, require or listen to audiotapes of sessions conducted by his supervisee, or actively collaborate with his supervisee in providing an assessment or intervention. In sum, he has never observed his supervisee's actual performance and bases his supervision sessions and his evaluations of his supervisee's competence solely on the supervisee's self-reports. *What are the supervisory considerations? What should be done?*

Authors' thoughts: While self-report is helpful, there is just no substitute for direct observation. To provide less is a dereliction of one's duty to the supervisee and, more important, to the students as well.

SD 9.2

A school psychologist in your district has 20 years' experience and is well liked by both parents and teachers. It has recently been discovered that he had made consistent scoring errors on the Wechsler Scales for many years. Specifically, the Digit Span and Symbol Search subtest scores have been used erroneously in the computation of scores. Hence, students' IQ scores have been consistently inflated. *What are the supervisory considerations? What should be done?*

Authors' thoughts: This is an extremely unfortunate situation. The first and foremost task is to mitigate possible damage done to students tested by this individual. It is possible that as a result of erroneous test scores, students have been denied services or given insufficient services. Corrective action will necessitate the arduous process of going back over *all* past assessments to individually correct scores and redetermine eligibility for services. Parents will need to be notified as well. Legal counsel should be sought to assure that mitigation is done correctly. One wonders if this would have occurred with better supervision and oversight!

SD 9.3

When initially hired, a staff school psychologist indicated that his strong point was working with secondary students, and he was placed full time at a high school. During the first 2 years of his employment, you observed that he had excellent counseling skills with adolescents but that his assessment and consultation skills were relatively weak. During the past 2 years he has not progressed satisfactorily in these areas, possibly because the high school climate is conducive to the development of neither. Most recently, you have become concerned that even his counseling skills have deteriorated in the laissez-faire atmosphere of the high school. The school psychologist wants to stay at the high school, but you feel that he needs a different assignment for professional growth. *What are the supervisory considerations? What should be done?*

Authors' thoughts: While job satisfaction is an important factor in a field facing shortages, providing optimal services to students remains the most important goal. It appears that students are not well served in this scenario. Reassignment, in isolation, is unlikely to remediate deficient skills. It seems advisable to institute a more structured course of professional development. Although it will likely require a difficult conversation, it is imperative to swiftly intervene with this individual.

10

Supervising Consultation

"No one can whistle a symphony."

—H. E. Luccock

Just as a symphony is produced by collaboration among musicians, successful education results from collaboration among educators, parents, and students. As Murphy, DeEsch, and Strein (1998) eloquently expressed, "current realities make it abundantly clear that it is no longer possible for school personnel to function effectively in isolation" (p. 85). When they provide expert consultation, school psychologists can serve as valuable members of these educational teams.

Vignette 10.1

Supervising school psychologist **Courtney** decided that she would like to help her supervisees move from focusing on assessing for special education eligibility to focusing on consultation prior to referral. She met with the director of special education and said, "It takes a psychologist between 12 and 20 hours to complete a thorough psychological evaluation, write the report, and meet to interpret the findings. If you like, we can continue to do that. Or, we could schedule our time at the school to coincide with the day that the student development team meets to discuss any student of concern. We could then provide consultation regarding those students—reviewing the file, meeting with the teacher, meeting with the parents, possibly observing and meeting with the students, and developing an initial consultation report with possible interventions. That would take about 5 hours. Then we could use the

---

remaining 7 to 15 hours to work directly with the teachers, parents, or (with permission) the student. If after interventions are implemented we still need to do a formal assessment, nothing has been lost, since these activities provide the foundation." The director agreed to the change, and the results were extraordinarily successful. School personnel were so pleased with what they described as "real help" that many principals asked for additional psychologist time in their annual budget.

The *Blueprint for Training and Practice III* (Ysseldyke et al., 2006) reflects the increasing importance of consultation as a foundational skill for efficient, effective practice. During the 2002 Conference on the Future of School Psychology (Meyers, 2002), it was suggested that consultation may become the single most important activity that school psychologists engage in during the 21st century! A study indicated that during the 1999–2000 school year, 40% of school psychologists had participated in over 50 consultation cases (Curtis, Hunley, & Grier, 2002).

With the anticipated expansion of prevention-oriented practices that depend on indirect service delivery, it is likely that school psychologists will increasingly offer consultation regarding both academic and mental health issues as well as help address systems level concerns. Hence, acquiring sound supervision skills to assist school psychologists in their efforts to be effective consultants is of critical importance. This chapter provides a general definition of school-based consultation, links current practice to its historical roots, offers suggestions for best practices in supervision, and discusses challenges in the effective provision of supervision of indirect services. This chapter emphasizes the supervision of consultation that focuses on the functioning of individual or targeted groups of students, or child-centered and consultee-centered consultation. Chapter 5 focuses on providing organizational consultation to prevent learning and adjustment problems through systems change at the school, district, family, and community levels.

BASIC CONSIDERATIONS

Historically rooted in the mental health consultation model (Caplan, 1970; Caplan & Caplan, 1993), the behavioral consultation model (Bergan, 1977; Bergan & Kratochwill, 1990), and organizational consultation (Schein, 1999), contemporary school-based consultation has evolved into an eclectic, ecological, problem solving approach that is guided by data-driven decision making (Kratochwill, Elliott, & Callan-Stoiber, 2002). Although numerous definitions have been advanced, the following reflects the overarching features of school-based consultation regardless of underlying theoretical model:

> Consultation is a collaborative problem solving process in which two or more persons (consultant and consultee) engage in efforts to benefit one or more other persons (client) for whom they bear some level of responsibility, within a context of reciprocal interactions. (Curtis & Meyers, 1989, p. 36)

Consultation involves the development and execution of collaborative problem solving strategies and can occur with administrators, parents, or teachers. Importantly, consultation requires the enlistment and cooperation of others in the actual intervention design and implementation. It is a collaborative process during which school psychologists design and apply interventions regarding individuals, targeted groups of students, or systems. Services provided to the client (e.g., student) are typically indirect, while services provided to the consultee (e.g., the teacher) are direct. The intent of consultation is to provide an experience that is ultimately beneficial to both.

Vignette 10.2

As a supervisor, **Estelle** emphasized the dual nature of consultation with her supervisees. She helped them understand that when they participated in a consultation process for designing, delivering, and assessing the success of an intervention to address a student's unruly, "out-of-seat" behavior, they were striving not only to improve the student's self-regulatory skills, but also to enhance the teacher's behavior management skills.

Although distinct models of consultation have been developed, the seminal work of Gutkin and Curtis (1982) suggested defining characteristics found across all models. Briefly, the commonalties are that:

- Consultation is an indirect approach to service delivery
- The consultee and consultant share a coordinate status and the relationship is nonhierarchical
- The consultee is actively involved in the consultation process at all times
- Consultees have the right to reject the advice and suggestions of the consultant
- The relationship is voluntary
- Confidentiality is maintained
- The focus is on professional problems in the work setting
- The goals of consultation are to enhance the skills of the consultee and to assist the student

Traditional, triadic consultation relationships involve one consultant, one teacher, and one student. In this model, the teacher and school psychologist share responsibility for the success of the targeted client (the student). However, consultation in school-based practice is becoming increasingly collaborative (D. Brown, Pryzwansky, & Schulte, 2006; Dougherty, 2005; Erchul & Martens, 2002). The triadic relationship has expanded to include other educators in instructional consultation and parents in conjoint behavioral consultation. Furthermore, in traditional consultation, the consultant never meets or sees the client. However, to foster data gathering, school psychologists are increasingly engaging in direct contact with students, particularly by observing them in class.

A number of variables have led to these changes in practice. The intent of the Individuals With Disabilities Education Improvement Act of 2004 (IDEA 2004) is to help students with disabilities succeed in the regular education classroom. Consultation services are an invaluable means of providing the support necessary for doing so. IDEA 2004 mandates that evidence-based interventions be attempted *prior* to referral for special education assessment. Accomplishing this charge requires sound consultation skills on the part of school psychologists. Additionally, IDEA 2004 encourages a response to intervention approach to the diagnosis of learning disability in lieu of the traditional discrepancy model. This represents a paradigmatic change that is dependent on effective provision of indirect services. As stated by Albers and Kratochwill (2006), multitiered intervention models are being advocated as a method of providing early intervention services along a continuum in which a student's needs determine the level of services provided. These factors indicate the necessity of having a service delivery model that allows for the provision of services in an efficient, yet cost-effective manner. The provision of services through consultation has the potential to meet these requirements. (p. 971)

The demand for expert consultation has been further expanded by the challenges faced by teachers, who are overwhelmed by attempting to meet the needs of students who are extremely diverse in terms of skills, disabilities, language, and culture. Many general education teachers have minimal training in individualizing instruction to meet the needs of special education students, gifted students, and English language learners, yet they have these students in their classes. Thus problems encountered in a typical classroom are increasingly likely to be diverse and complex.

In summary, evolving practices in education necessitate that new trainees enter the field with well-developed consultation skills and that seasoned professionals constantly refine and develop their own consultation skills. Supervision and ongoing professional development are pivotal in providing effective delivery of indirect services.

CONSULTATION MODELS

The model of consultation that is used mediates the supervision process, because different supervisory techniques and practices appear to be better suited to different models of consultation. Therefore, we will briefly address the major models of consultation and then relate specific strategies useful in the supervision of these indirect services. Consultation models are founded upon distinct theoretical bases and vary according to their structures and the role of the consultant (Dougherty, 2005). As Scholten (2003) indicated, the models

can generally be divided into those that differ in terms of the type of problem *focus* (mental health, behavioral or organizational development), *the level of intervention* (individual child, classroom, or system) and the *approach* taken by the consultant (expert or collaborative). (p. 88)

The adoption of a particular consultation model is dependent on one's theoretical orientation, past experiences, and training. Theories, whether explicit or implicit, provide the structure from which one builds hypotheses, infers causes of behavior, and chooses interventions. It is helpful to consider the various consultation models and examine how tenets of each are reflected in everyday practice. Several of the most widely taught and used consultation models are briefly described below.

Behavioral Consultation

Behavioral consultation is scientifically based, data driven, and well suited for an educational climate that highly values accountability and research-based principles. Additionally, readily available technology has increased educators' ability to accurately monitor and compile data and thereby optimally assess intervention effectiveness. Dougherty (2005) stated that "the major contribution of behavioral consultation has been its emphasis on approaching consultation in a systematic way" and that, with its "emphasis on specifics, [behavioral consultation] has contributed to more effective methods in setting the goals of consultation, gathering data on the perceived problem, and most importantly, in evaluating the effects of consultation" (p. 243).

Behavioral consultation encourages the consultee to be the change agent and is indirect, nonhierarchical, and triadic. It exclusively addresses the concrete, discrete, and observable behaviors of the client. Strongly rooted in applied behavioral analysis, behavioral consultation considers overt behavior to be more important than unconscious themes (Bergan, 1977; Bergan & Kratochwill, 1990). The behavioral consultation model considers the unconscious processes of the consultee to be of little consequence. Because behavioral consultation emphasizes observable behaviors and data collection, the development and examination of interpersonal variables in dyads are not prominent. The emphasis of the consultation interview is analytic, with little focus on the consultee's recollections (Noell & Witt, 1998).

Bergan's (1977) foundational four-stage sequential problem solving model included (a) problem identification, (b) problem analysis, (c) plan implementation, and (d) problem evaluation. Although variations have emerged, these steps are the core of the behavioral consultation model. The consultant defines the targeted problem, isolates those variables that affect the problem, and devises a plan to manipulate the environment in such a way that continuation of the undesired behavior is not supported (Conoley & Conoley, 1988). It is essential that the consultant sequentially implement all four consultation stages.

Repeatedly, studies examining the effectiveness of behavioral consultation have demonstrated that it results in the use of critical problem solving strategies and that student functioning improves in the majority of cases (MacLeod, Jones, Somers, & Havey, 2001; Sheridan, Welch, & Orme, 1996). However, this success depends on consistent, accurate delivery of agreed-upon interventions. No treatment can be successful without the full cooperation and active participation of the consultee. Treatment integrity, which refers to the "degree to which a consultation plan is implemented as intended" (Gresham, 1989, p. 37), is largely dependent on the consultee's acceptance of and investment in the chosen interventions. Therefore, positive outcomes are dependent on the skills of the consultant, the quality of the consultation, and the treatment integrity with which the interventions are implemented. Although behavioral consultation emphasizes technical adequacy, the impact of interpersonal relationships must also be considered as a critical factor because they so profoundly affect the consultation process.

Supervisees' knowledge of operant conditioning, learning theory, and applied behavioral analysis provides the foundation for effective behavioral consultation. Supervision of behavioral consultation involves helping the supervisee operationally define desired behaviors, design intervention plans with appropriate schedules and reinforcers, apply functional behavioral analysis techniques, and examine data and modify practices with technical adequacy and treatment fidelity.

Mental Health Consultation

Gerald Caplan (1970) implemented mental health consultation 50 years ago when he was confronted with the unmanageable task of providing mental health services to thousands of displaced, immigrant children in postwar Israel. Quickly recognizing that traditional models of service delivery were insufficient, he developed and refined an alternative model reflecting the newly emerging prevention movement. Mental health consultation is founded in psychodynamic theory and hypothesizes that many student issues that the teacher perceives as problematic may largely reflect displacement and/or projection on the part of the teacher. The consultant's task is to avoid direct discussion of the teacher's unresolved conflicts yet simultaneously correct misperceptions about the client's problems. Because school psychologists are not typically trained from a psychoanalytic perspective, the original model has evolved to reflect more contemporary training. Four types of mental health consultation have been developed, differing in both foci and goals:

- Client-centered case consultation seeks to help a specific client. A school psychologist employs this type of consultation when consulting with a teacher regarding one student's functioning.
- Consultee-centered case consultation focuses on the development of generalized skills in the consultee. A school psychologist employs this type of consultation when working with a teacher to help her or him improve classroom management skills, or when providing an in-service program to a group of educators regarding nonviolent crisis intervention.
- Program-centered administrative consultation seeks to improve programs. An example of this type of consultation is when a school psychologist helps administrators evaluate and improve a program for students with attention deficit disorder.
- Consultee-centered administrative consultation seeks to develop consultees' skills in dealing with organization-based problems.

Vignette 10.3

Constance worked as a school psychologist in a district that mandated grades of 1 on a 4-point scale for any student achieving below-grade-level benchmarks. This meant that, no matter how hard they worked and what progress they made, all students identified as eligible for special education services received grades of 1. Recognizing that such a mandate would have severely detrimental effects on students' internal locus of control, sense of self-efficacy, and motivation, Constance determined that the policy needed modification. She therefore worked with teachers and administrators to develop effective yet fair grading policies for special education students.

Supervision of mental health consultation focuses on an awareness of relational issues, strict maintenance of objectivity, and the utilization of an indirect, therapeutic approach. Techniques that enhance supervision of mental health consultation include the use of process notes, examination of parallel process issues (which assumes that supervisees unconsciously replicate client issues during supervision), examination of transference and countertransference, and the use of reflection. The use of taping with Interpersonal Process Recall (IRP; see Chapter 9) may also be helpful.

Meyers and Nastasi (1999) adapted Caplan's (1964) mental health consultation model to create a preventative consultation framework to use in schools. They identified *primary prevention* as taking steps to prevent the entire population from developing a learning or social problem, *risk reduction* as taking steps to reduce the likelihood of learning or adjustment problems in an at-risk population, *early intervention* as taking steps to prevent an identified problem from worsening, and *treatment* as applying prevention strategies to reduce the duration and impact of identified disorders, including their effects on others. As Meyers, Meyers, and Grogg (2004) indicated, these strategies readily provide a framework for consultation by school psychologists in response to individual needs as well as in group settings.

Instructional Consultation

Instructional consultation (IC; Rosenfield, 1987) is a collaborative process that focuses on academic and behavioral concerns from an ecological perspective and is a modification of consultee-centered consultation (Rosenfield, 2002). It emphasizes a problem solving approach driven by data-based decision making. Designed to be used schoolwide, IC employs a team that serves as a centralized problem solving unit, models interactive professionalism, and operates as a consultant panel for each of its own members and for teachers in the building (Rosenfield & Gravois, 1996). It has been found to effectively promote the professional growth of consultees away from a pathology-driven medical model (Knotek, Rosenfield, Gravois, & Babinski, 2003) and to reduce referrals for special education services, thereby reducing the disproportionate number of minority students referred to and placed in special education programs (Gravois & Rosenfield, 2006).

As described on the IC Web site (University of Maryland at College Park, Laboratory for Instructional Consultation Teams, n.d.),

> the mission of Instructional Consultation as a model of team functioning is to link people and resources at all levels whereby general, special education, and pupil service personnel share the responsibility for the education of ALL students through the improved quality of service. (¶ 1)

The overarching goal of this approach is to enhance, improve, and increase student and school staff performance. The objective is to develop a systematic support network in each school that includes a trained IC team composed of administrators, general and special educators, and pupil services personnel (Rosenfield, 1995b). This team serves to enhance teachers' skills in best practices of instructional assessment and delivery, develop a schoolwide collaborative problem solving model, use data for classroom and school decisions, focus problem solving on matching instructional methods to students' needs, foster a learning community, and change instructional practices rather than attempting to change the student (Rosenfield, 1995a).

Individual team members serve as case managers who work with classroom teachers in a systematic, data-based, collaborative problem solving process. The case manager and the teacher follow the problem solving stages of:

- Problem identification and analysis
- Collection of specific student data
- Intervention design
- Intervention implementation
- Intervention evaluation
- Follow-up and closure

Supervision is a major component of the IC model (Cramer & Rosenfield, 2003). Techniques of supervision applicable to this model include process notes, the use of reflection, taping, process recall and analysis, problem analysis, monitoring of behavioral intervention plans, mutual examination of data obtained by the teacher and/or supervisee, and exploration of treatment effectiveness.

Conjoint Behavioral Consultation

The steps and processes used in conjoint behavioral consultation (CBC) are similar to those used in behavioral consultation and IC, but CBC emphasizes the importance of including parents and parent figures as full members of the consultation team (Sheridan, Kratochwill, & Bergen, 1996). CBC has been found to be highly effective at increasing academic success and to have long-standing effects (Rhoades & Kratochwill, 1998; Weiner, Sheridan, & Jenson, 1998).

CBC emphasizes that, as consultants develop collaborative relationships with parents, they must explicitly address common barriers to home-school partnerships. These barriers include time constraints due to child care and work schedules, transportation challenges, cultural differences, language barriers, expectations that educators will be unresponsive to needs and desires, previous negative experiences with schools, perceptions that education is solely the province of schools, feelings of inadequacy, limited knowledge regarding or access to resources, and limited resources in terms of time and finances (Christenson, 2004; S. O. Ortiz & Flanagan, 2002).

Again, appropriate supervision techniques are varied. They include reflection, audiotapes, videotapes, process recall and analysis, problem analysis, monitoring of intervention success, exploration of treatment effectiveness, and mutual examination of data obtained by the teacher, parent, and supervisee.

APPLICATIONS TO SUPERVISION

Although school psychologists report that they are interested in providing consultation, they also report that they do not feel adequately trained to do so (Costenbader, Swartz, & Petrix, 1992; Guest, 2000). This perception is not surprising, given that school psychology training programs require minimal coursework in consultation relative to coursework in assessment. Nor do most training programs require a practicum in consultation or provide supervision of consultation applications, other than simulated practice and role-plays (Anton-LaHart & Rosenfield, 2004). Yet the very nature of consultation—collaborating with parents, teachers, and students about "real" problems—requires fieldwork that cannot be duplicated through role-plays (Meyers, 2002). Therefore, practicum and intern supervisors are highly likely to supervise individuals who are completely inexperienced as consultants.

Furthermore, supervisors' consultation skills are likely to be underdeveloped as well. Many school psychologists do not feel expert as consultants, and individuals are disinclined to practice in areas in which they have not received direct supervision themselves (E. S. Shapiro & Lentz, 1985). Although consultation has been recommended for more than 40 years (Bardon, 1969) and has demonstrated effectiveness, it lags behind assessment in terms of time allocation. Thus it is likely that supervisors with inadequate consultation skills are attempting to supervise novice consultants and are thereby perpetuating insufficient and inadequate consultation practice.

All of these factors add to the general challenges to supervision of psychological services described in previous chapters. Consequently, clinical supervisors must ensure that their own skills in consultation are adequate, and that they directly and specifically focus supervision goals on increasing supervisees' consultation skills. To this end, literature in effective consultation skill development will be briefly summarized.

Consultation Skill Development

Several authors have addressed consultation skill development. Although recommended strategies emerge from various consultation models, they have a great deal in common. Strategies suggested by Cramer and Rosenfield (2003), Lepage, Kratochwill, and Elliott (2004), Meyers (2002), and Sheridan, Salmon, Kratochwill, and Rotto (1992) include the following:

1. *Address foundation knowledge.* Supervisors should ensure that supervisees have adequate content knowledge by assigning readings as needed in developmental psychology, learning, authentic assessment, evidence-based interventions, educational psychology, and self-regulated learning (Harvey & Chickie-Wolfe, 2007). Supervisees should also have a deep understanding of the specific population with which they are working. With the increasing cultural, linguistic, and racial diversity found in schools, cross-cultural considerations are of ever-increasing importance (D. Brown et al., 2006; Dougherty, 2005). Consultants must respect and respond to differences of all kinds (S. O. Ortiz & Flanagan, 2002) as well as conform to all legal and ethical expectations. Suggestions for increasing multicultural competencies are addressed comprehensively in Chapter 3.

2. *Address consultation stage and processes knowledge.* Supervisees must master consultation processes and stages, including assessing the problem, identifying intervening variables, generating and examining hypotheses, identifying factors that might influence intervention success, and developing interventions appropriate to the context and student. Assigning readings regarding consultation can be helpful, including *Psychological Consultation and Collaboration* (D. Brown et al., 2006); *Effective Consultation in School Psychology* (E. Cole & Siegel, 2003); *Psychological Consultation and Collaboration in School and Community Settings* (Dougherty, 2005); *School Consultation: Conceptual and Empirical Bases of Practice* (Erchul & Martens, 2002); *Instructional Consultation Teams: Collaborating for Change* (Rosenfield & Gravois, 1996); and *Conjoint Behavioral Consultation: A Procedural Manual* (Sheridan, Kratochwill, et al., 1996). Supervisors might also:

- Have supervisees analyze videotapes or audiotapes of expert consultants
- Model consultation sessions that address "real" problems
- Have supervisees role-play consultation sessions while addressing "real" problems
- Have supervisees videotape or audiotape and analyze their own consultation sessions
- Have supervisees complete process notes regarding consultation sessions
- Encourage supervisees to link theory, research, and consultation practice
- Have supervisees obtain support and feedback via individual or group supervision

3. *Address role and relationship variables.* Excellent communication and interpersonal skills are essential in building and maintaining collaborative relationships. Regardless of the consultation model employed, interpersonal and consultation process skills are essential for effective consultation (Henning-Stout, 1999). Consultation can be rendered ineffective due to unsatisfactory interpersonal relationships, insufficient communication, poor interpersonal skills, or interpersonal insensitivity regarding cultural differences due to race, ethnicity, socioeconomic class, professional identity, sexual identity, or generation. Therefore, it is important for supervisors to address these variables with their supervisees and ensure that they master various interpersonal and problem solving skills (Ingraham, 2000; Kampworth, 2003; S. O. Ortiz & Flanagan, 2002; Rosenfield, 1995b). Essential skills are listed in Handout 10.2 at the end of this chapter.

Furthermore, well-developed communication and interpersonal skills are essential components in the supervision of consultation. Thus, in addition to helping supervisees develop verbal and nonverbal skills, supervisors must monitor themselves to ensure that they are active listeners who elicit both qualitative and quantitative information.

Case discussions with supervisees during supervision sessions are the most common method used in supervising consultation. However, more accurate ways to gather information include regular analysis of tape recordings of consultation sessions as well as review of data generated throughout the consultation process (Anton-LaHart & Rosenfield, 2004). Especially important during the early stages of skill development, these practices allow the detailed and continual feedback necessary for professional growth (Cramer & Rosenfield, 2003). Supervisors can foster interpersonal skills through modeling, role-plays, videotape and audiotape analysis, and post-session supervision. In addition, rating checklists and consultation logs can be helpful.

Supervisors can use similar techniques as they monitor their own supervision of indirect services. Maintaining supervision session process notes, reviewing audiotapes of sessions in which the supervision of consultation has occurred, and consulting with peers will enable supervisors to monitor and increase their own effectiveness.

4. *Develop an understanding of broader contexts and systems.* To provide effective consultation, supervisees need a deep understanding of the classrooms, schools, communities, and families in which consultation is occurring. They also need to understand relevant entry issues, possible resistance, and available interventions. The reader is referred to Chapter 5 for specific strategies in this area.

5. *Promote skill appraisal.* Sheridan et al. (1992) recommended a multi-level evaluation model to assess supervisees' consultation skills across the consultation components. Knowledge of procedures, content, and systems issues can be assessed by quizzes and self-monitoring. Application of procedures, content skills, interpersonal relationships, and field-based experiences can be assessed through analysis of audiotapes and videotapes, relational ratings, and consumer satisfaction measures. Relevant traits are incorporated in Handout 10.2 at the end of this chapter.

6. *Provide ongoing support.* Even when well trained, school psychologists need ongoing support to sustain effective consultation teams (Rosenfield, 2000). Therefore, after a supervisee has demonstrated adequate consultation skills in individual and group supervision sessions, it is helpful to encourage generalization and increased self-sufficiency through peer supervision and ongoing self-evaluation. The same supervision techniques (analysis of videotapes and audiotapes, checklists, consultation logs, etc.) are appropriate.

Record Keeping

Because consultation involves multiple individuals and diverse issues, and occurs over an extended time period, good record keeping is invaluable. An effective supervisor will encourage the supervisee to record both content and process variables that arise during consultation. Because consultation cases often do not include the same time lines and deadlines as referrals for special education services, they can easily be neglected or forgotten. Therefore, it is critically important to schedule and adhere to supervision sessions that address consultation follow-up in order to avoid neglecting consultation cases. Both supervisees and supervisors should keep written records of supervision sessions. Tools included in Chapters 7 through 9 can be helpful to this end.

Consultation With Paraprofessionals and Other School Personnel

School psychologists can fruitfully consult with paraprofessionals and other non-teaching school personnel even when it does not constitute an "official" part of their professional responsibilities. When the collective influence of bus drivers, playground monitors, teacher aides, library assistants, custodians, lunchroom attendants, and clerical personnel is considered, it is obvious that these individuals have a considerable impact on the children they serve and constitute a very important part of each school's ecology. Effective consultation with this group of adults, most of whom have had little formal training in education or psychology, can have a profoundly beneficial effect.

Supervision of consultation with paraprofessionals and other school personnel must enable the supervisee to consider the differences between consulting with these individuals and with those who consider themselves professionals. It is important to consider their roles, abilities, and openness to intervention as well as the nature of the presenting problem. Perhaps most important, the level of intervention must be carefully chosen. The rights of the children must always take precedence.

Challenges in Supervising Consultation

The multiplicity of roles and relationships that exist during supervision of consultation make achieving supervision goals extremely complex. Both consultation and supervision usually occur within dyadic relationships. However, both are actually triadic in that they involve three distinct participants. Some participants customarily have direct, face-to-face contact with each other while others do not. In school-based consultation, participants usually include (a) the consultant, (b) the consultee, and (c) the client (student). In the supervision of counseling and assessment, participants are (a) the supervisor, (b) the supervisee, and (c) the individual with whom the supervisee is working.

In contrast, the supervision of consultation minimally involves four people with multiple roles: (a) the supervisor, (b) the consultant (supervisee), (c) the consultee (teacher), and (d) the student (client). Some interpersonal interactions are direct and always include face-to-face contact, while others remain indirect and rarely include face-to-face contact. Because of the interaction of both process and content variables across these multiple relationships, the supervision of consultation profits from a structured framework to guide both practice and supervision. It may be helpful to consider Figure 10.1.

Effective supervision of consultation demands an awareness of the similarities and differences between the two processes (supervision and consultation). Both are professional relationships that are triadic, confidential, and extend over time. In contrast to the typical egalitarian approach to consultation, however, the supervisory relationship tends to be hierarchical, evaluative, and involuntary. Furthermore, during supervision, administrative supervisors retain ultimate responsibility for the case. In contrast, during consultation, responsibility for the case can either be shared or remain with the consultee.

Supervisee Developmental Level

As is the case for other domains of practice, it can be anticipated that novice consultants undergo predictable development stages as they acquire consultation skills. As previously discussed, effective supervisors vary the intensity of their supervision and

Figure 10.1. Relationships in the supervision of consultation.

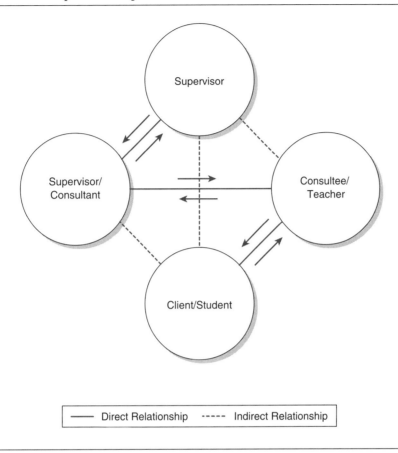

- —— Direct Relationship   ----- Indirect Relationship

their supervisory techniques according to the developmental level of the supervisee. Prescriptive supervisory techniques are more appropriate with beginning consultants, and as the supervisee moves into a higher level of competence the supervisor can rely on supervisory methods that are less prescriptive and more dependent on the supervisee's self-regulation.

In addition, the effective consultation supervisor considers the developmental stage of the supervisee and the nature of the presenting problem when deciding which model of consultation to recommend. Consultation skills are complex and tend to be developed after other skills in assessment and counseling have been mastered (Stoltenberg, 1993). Furthermore, some models of consultation (e.g., behavioral consultation) may be more appropriate for novice practitioners or for particular presenting issues. Others (e.g., consultee-based consultation) require advanced interpersonal and consultation skills.

Further, because the welfare of the student is always of primary concern, the supervisor must first consider the student's needs in the context of the supervisee's developmental level and the nature of the presenting problem. A critical supervision task is determining when and whether direct interaction with the consultee or client is warranted. With novice practitioners, face-to-face observation of the student who is the object of consultation is often advisable.

Vignette 10.4

A group of school psychology supervisors participated in a focus group concerning the supervision of consultation. These practitioners were unanimous in stating that they favored direct contact with the client and consultee while supervising new interns because the novices missed too many important pieces of information. On the other hand, they felt that with more experienced practitioners, such contact was not generally necessary.

Other variables that influence the supervisor's level of direct involvement include the communication and interpersonal skills of the supervisee, the nature and severity of the presenting problem, and the experience and expertise of the supervisee regarding the presenting problems. This finding supports the recommendations of Stoltenberg (1993), who indicated that novice consultants require close supervision in order to develop self- and other-awareness, modulate motivation, and foster autonomy.

As the professional knowledge gap between supervisor and supervisee diminishes, the need for intensive, direct monitoring and observation tends to decrease and supervision becomes increasingly consultative in nature. Peer supervision, for example, usually resembles consultation more than supervision. In such cases, direct contact with the student is much less likely to occur.

Ethical Issues

Ethical principles for supervisors of school psychologists practicing consultation incorporate and reflect the same fundamental ethical principles that guide all mental health professionals. Supervisors have a responsibility to simultaneously monitor and maximize the therapeutic benefits for the student, provide professional training for the supervisee, and ensure that ethical principals are upheld. Heron, Martz, and Margolis (1996) suggested that the inherent complexity of consultation and the intense emotions that often arise from dealing with complicated issues necessitate that consultants have a strong and clear ethical framework dictating their behavior. Further, a concurrent awareness of cross-cultural issues is vital. Hence, one constant supervisory goal is to ensure that supervisees offer consultation services within enduring frameworks of ethical and cultural sensitivity.

Strict maintenance of confidentiality is essential. In consulting, psychologists should not share confidential information leading to the identification of a client or other person or organization with whom they have a confidential relationship unless they have either obtained the prior consent of the person or disclosure cannot be avoided because the student poses a danger to himself or another (American Psychological Association, 2002). Psychologists should share information only to the extent necessary for achieving the purposes of consultation.

Change Is Difficult

As supervisees attempt to provide indirect services through consultation, they often become discouraged when consultees do not implement recommended procedures or when recommended changes are not made. To overcome this challenge, supervisors can encourage their supervisees to (a) gather data that serve as persuasive evidence, (b) gently persevere with the understanding that change takes time, and (c) better understand the dynamics that support the "old way."

Vignette 10.5

After determining that the function of **Johnny**'s misbehavior was to obtain adult attention after being sent "to the office," intern **Suzette** wanted to recommend an evidence-based intervention that required that the teacher provide positive feedback (when appropriate) to Johnny at least once every hour in order to "catch" and reinforce appropriate behavior. Suzette's supervisor helped her understand that sending Johnny to the office was a "solution" for multiple "problems" for the teacher as well as a reinforcement for Johnny, and helped her devise a self-regulating behavior management program for Johnny that used teacher attention at the end of the day as one of the rewards. The program successfully met Johnny's need for attention, diminished the disruptive behavior, and did not require ongoing teacher monitoring that may have overtaxed the teacher's resources.

Funding and Role Differentiation

Effective consultation requires that school psychologists be standing members of each school's student development team. This is necessary so that the psychologist is aware of problems before they have blossomed to the "treatment" stage. Otherwise, it is impossible to provide meaningful prevention activities. Thus supervisors work to ensure that school psychologists' services are rightfully available to the entire student population. Even school psychologists funded under special education funds should be able to participate in such teams; with IDEA 2004, 15% of special education funds can be applied to prevention efforts. Hence, supervisors should encourage school psychologists to provide consultation and prevention services under these auspices.

In some settings, consultation might be thought to belong to behavior specialists or special education consultants. However, it has been our experience that there are more than enough problems to go around. The high needs of students and schools render completely inappropriate attempts at turf protection that can arise from unawareness of others' expertise or fears of reduced status or employment (Murphy et al., 1998). Ethical and responsible professionals foster a culture of collaborative service delivery wherein respective roles are clear, yet all personnel consult and collaborate to create and maintain school environments that foster maximal student growth and achievement. Supervisors can do much to foster these attitudes among educators as well as with their supervisees.

ASSESSING CONSULTATION SKILLS

It is essential to determine a means to provide formative and summative evaluation of supervisees' consultation skills. Because supervisors have an ethical responsibility to inform their supervisees about the methods of evaluation that will be used to monitor progress (Pope & Vasquez, 1998), it is important to share and describe evaluation methods in the early stages of the supervisory relationship.

Evaluating the Consultation Process

Examination of data related to the consultation process can assist the supervisor in guiding both consultation and its supervision. Critical components of behavioral consultation, developed by Flugum and Reschly (1994) and found to be correlated with positive student outcomes (MacLeod et al., 2001), suggest the questions included in Table 10.1.

Table 10.1 Consultation Process Questions

- Was a working alliance established and maintained with all team members?
- Was a consultation contract developed?
- Was an operational and behavioral definition of the target behavior established?
- Were baseline data obtained?
- Was a step-by-step plan for the intervention developed?
- Was the intervention implemented as planned?
- Was a direct comparison of baseline and postintervention performance made?
- Was closure reached?

Additional tools have been developed to assess the consultation process. The Consultation Effectiveness Scale (Knoff, Hines, & Kromrey, 1995) uses a Likert-type scale to assess a consultant's interpersonal skills, problem solving skills, consultation process and application skills, and ethical and professional practice skills. This scale could be completed by consultees, or by supervisors as they review tapes of consultation sessions. In addition, a number of measurements have been developed by Kratochwill and are listed in Lepage et al. (2004). These include the Behavioral Consultation Process Checklist, the Behavioral Consultation Knowledge Test, the Behavior Modification Test, Knowledge of Behavior Principles as Applied to Children, the Behavior Modification Attitude Scale, the Training Satisfaction Scale, the Consultation Training Satisfaction Scale, the Consultation Survey, the Consultation Project Evaluation, and the Consultant Evaluation Form. Handout 10.2, the Consultant Skills Checklist, was compiled from information in Ingraham (2000), Kampworth (2003), Knoff et al. (1995), Meyers (2002), S. O. Ortiz and Flanagan (2002), and Rosenfield (1995b). It can be found at the end of this chapter.

Handout 10.1, the Team Report Evaluation, was developed by Sawyer Hunley of the University of Dayton. This can be used to assess the work of the consultation teams.

Appraising Student Outcomes

When measuring the effectiveness of consultation strategies, one also needs to determine that the process has had a positive impact on student functioning. As discussed in Chapter 5, single-subject design is an obvious way to evaluate the success of consultation efforts to assess client change. Such measurement of progress is a part of the consultation process. However, it is far more difficult to determine change in the consultee or the system. Despite such inherent difficulty, it is possible to gather some objective and subjective data. Stoiber and Kratochwill (2002) developed *Outcomes: Planning, Monitoring, Evaluating (PME)* as a tool to use in planning, monitoring, and evaluating the outcomes of social and academic service delivery programs. It helps identify concerns, consider context, measure baseline performance, monitor student progress, evaluate intervention effectiveness, and plan the next steps.

SUMMARY

With the expansion of prevention-oriented practices, school psychologists increasingly offer consultation regarding both academic and mental health issues. It is important that both new trainees and seasoned professionals constantly develop and refine their consultation skills through ongoing professional development and supervision.

Handout 10.1

TEAM REPORT EVALUATION

	Very Inappropriate	*Inappropriate*	*Adequate*	*Appropriate*	*Very Appropriate*
Plans assessments for referred eligibility determination	1	2	3	4	5
Selects assessment procedures for given eligibility determination and student characteristics	1	2	3	4	5
Describes each assessment procedure (area)	1	2	3	4	5
Provides summary interpretation for each assessment procedure	1	2	3	4	5
Includes instructional implications in the assessment summaries for each procedure	1	2	3	4	5
Provides an integrated summary of multifactored assessment	1	2	3	4	5
Provides instructional implications drawn from integrated multifactored assessment results	1	2	3	4	5
Uses clear and concise language throughout the report	1	2	3	4	5

From the *2006 Handbook of the University of Dayton School Psychology Program*. Dayton, OH: Locally published monograph. Use of this material is by permission of the author, Sawyer Hunley.

Although they share many commonalities, consultation models vary in terms of their structure and the consultant's role. Behavioral consultation is systematic, research based, and data driven and seeks to address the concrete, discrete, and observable behavior of clients. Mental health consultation focuses on changing the skills and attitudes of the consultee as well as the functioning of the client. Instructional consultation emphasizes a problem solving approach driven by data-based decision making regarding both academic and behavioral problems and employs a team that serves as a centralized problem solving unit. Conjoint behavioral consultation emphasizes the importance of including parents and parent figures as members of the consultation team. It is important to consider supervisees' developmental skill level and the presenting problem when selecting a consultation model, since some models of consultation (e.g., behavioral consultation) are more appropriate for novices or for particular presenting issues.

Many school psychologists recognize the importance of providing consultation but do not feel adequately skilled to do so. It is likely that supervisors' consultation skills are underdeveloped as well. In assessing consultation skills, supervisors must examine both the consultation process and student outcomes. Ethical principles for supervisors of school psychologists practicing consultation incorporate and reflect the same fundamental ethical principles that guide all mental health professionals, including those regarding confidentiality.

REFLECTIVE QUESTIONS

Q10.1. Describe how the practice of consultation has changed for school psychologists and how such changes have come about.

Q10.2. Describe the various consultation models. What are the similarities and differences? What variables should be considered when determining which model to use?

Q10.3. Describe consultation training strategies and how they might aid in the development of consultation skills. What other strategies might be employed?

Q10.4. Discuss the importance of considering the supervisee's developmental level when supervising school psychologists in their consultation work.

Q10.5. How might school psychologists handle situations in which consultees do not implement recommended procedures or changes?

Q10.6. What tools might you use in evaluating consultation skills?

SUPERVISORY DILEMMAS

SD 10.1

A new intern, anxious to demonstrate both her knowledge and good intentions, has offered to consult with a third-grade teacher regarding a student with autism. The student, who is in an inclusive, regular education setting, is often disruptive and unruly in the classroom. Although previous teachers have expressed frustration and concern in the past, the present teacher is truly enraged. She claims that in her 30 years of teaching, she has never encountered such a difficult student and that her whole class has been negatively impacted by this student's presence in the classroom. She vigorously demands that he be removed and placed in a substantially separate program. Day after day, her complaints have dominated the lunchroom conversation. Among other threats, she is stating that she is planning to file a grievance with the teachers' union. The staff is becoming extremely polarized regarding this issue. The new intern, who is young, inexperienced, and eager, desperately wants to see if she can help alleviate the growing animosity. She has a brother diagnosed with autism and feels that she "has a handle" on some of the pertinent issues. *What are the supervisory considerations? What should be done?*

Authors' thoughts: Where to even begin! This case requires immediate damage control on multiple levels. The needs of the students, teacher, parents, and unfortunate lunchroom attendees must all be considered. An immediate classroom observation, a functional behavioral assessment, and ongoing consultation are warranted. While these may help alleviate some of the tension, they are probably a temporary measure. The needs of the student with autism—as well as those of his classmates—must be made the priority. It is likely that more and/or different services are warranted. While the intern is to be commended for her willingness to provide assistance, it is also important to determine whether her skills are appropriate and the degree to which her own family experiences drive her. In addition, the teacher must be cautioned to maintain confidentiality. This situation demands immediate supervisory and administrative intervention.

SD 10.2

Mr. Smith has been a bus driver for the school system for almost 20 years. He has recently approached the principal and asked for an immediate transfer. He claims that he is angry and frustrated by the behavior of a sixth-grade girl who rides his bus. She intermittently swears and incessantly picks at the padding of the bus seat. She has produced a large hole in her seat and will not respond to his repeated requests to stop. Her swearing, although usually whispered, offends nearby riders. Because this often leads to further confrontations, the current situation on the bus is unpleasant for all. Parents are beginning to complain as well. Your supervisee, the school psychologist, is called into a meeting for consultation. She is aware that this student was recently diagnosed with Tourette disorder. The parents are extremely sensitive about maintaining strict confidentiality and do not want their daughter's condition disclosed—even to her teacher. *What are the supervisory considerations? What should be done?*

Authors' thoughts: While it may be very helpful for teachers, bus drivers, and other school personnel to know about the student's diagnosis, the parents have voiced their opposition to disclosure. Clearly, ethical guidelines forbid the release of such information without parental consent. This situation calls for an immediate conference with the parents to clarify the disadvantages to their daughter if confidentiality is maintained and to help them understand what the boundaries of disclosure would be. While disclosure might assist the driver in better understanding that the actions of the girl do not constitute disciplinary infractions, it will do little to actually alleviate the situation on the bus. Regardless of the diagnosis, the inappropriate behavior must be addressed using appropriate behavioral interventions.

SD 10.3

A supervisor trained exclusively in the traditional Caplanian model of mental health consultation has been asked to provide supervision in regard to a very problematic elementary school student diagnosed with oppositional defiant disorder, bipolar disorder, and attention deficit hyperactivity disorder. The supervisee, who is very well trained and experienced in behavioral consultation, appears at the initial supervisory session armed with data sheets and behavior charts. The supervisor, who is unfamiliar with behavioral consultation, begins the session by asking about the consultee's possible resistance to intervention and suggests that parables be used. *What are the supervisory considerations? What should be done?*

Authors' thoughts: It is always a megachallenge when the theoretical perspectives of the supervisee and supervisor do not match. As the practice of school psychology evolves, this is inevitable. This scenario provides a wonderful opportunity for both the supervisor and the supervisee to learn from one another. In fact, this is probably one of the most beneficial aspects of the whole supervisory relationship. There is no reason why both approaches cannot be acknowledged as the two work toward developing a consultation plan that is data driven *and* addresses resistance. Importantly, the supervisor will have to make it clear that she does not possess the necessary competence to comprehensively supervise a behavioral consultation case.

SD 10.4

You provide clinical supervision to a new school psychologist who receives administrative supervision from the elementary school principal. State-mandated testing begins next month and will be overseen by your supervisee, who has been clearly told that the district *must* perform better this year than it did last year, or serious funding issues could ensue. In fact, one very real possibility is that the school psychologist's position may be eliminated or reduced. The supervisee approaches you about what possible techniques could be used to aggressively "up the scores." *What are the supervisory considerations? What should be done?*

Authors' thoughts: There is no simple way to "up the scores." However, many sound interventions are feasible. For example, advising parents to be sure that students are well rested and well nourished on the day of the test will have a positive impact. It might also be helpful to teach stress reduction techniques to anxious test takers and to ensure that the curriculum taught in class is in accord with state standards. A far more serious situation is apparent, however, because there appears to be coercion regarding test scores. The school psychologist must, in no uncertain terms, delineate what can be done (as discussed in Chapters 4 and 5) and frankly dismiss any thoughts of unethical or illegal tampering with the scores. Potentially, the school psychologist may wind up in the uncomfortable position of having to disclose the principal's behavior to administrators.

Handout 10.2

CONSULTANT SKILLS CHECKLIST

Rate the consultant on each of the following behaviors according to the following scale:

1 = not at all
2 = to a slight degree
3 = to a considerable degree
4 = to a very large degree

The consultant:

Establishes and maintains rapport, respect, trust, and a collaborative working relationship with and among consultation team members	1	2	3	4
Is empathic	1	2	3	4
Is encouraging	1	2	3	4
Expresses supportive affection	1	2	3	4
Shows respect for the consultee(s)	1	2	3	4
Is warm	1	2	3	4
Maintains an "I'm OK, you're OK" position	1	2	3	4
Is interested and concerned	1	2	3	4
Is approachable	1	2	3	4
Is accepting and nonjudgmental	1	2	3	4
Is tolerant	1	2	3	4
Is tactful	1	2	3	4
Is collaborative and shares responsibility	1	2	3	4
Is pleasant	1	2	3	4
Maintains a positive attitude	1	2	3	4
Self-discloses	1	2	3	4
Encourages ventilation	1	2	3	4
Is open-minded	1	2	3	4
Gives and receives feedback	1	2	3	4
Is flexible	1	2	3	4
Is a team player	1	2	3	4

(Continued)

(Continued)

Is effective at establishing rapport	1	2	3	4
Is willing to get involved	1	2	3	4
Is attentive	1	2	3	4
Explicitly addresses parents' and teachers' time constraints	1	2	3	4
Carefully listens to, attends to, and responds to all participants' input	1	2	3	4
Respects others' cultures and individual differences within cultures	1	2	3	4
Attains consensus that a problem exists and needs to be addressed	1	2	3	4
Is skilled in questioning	1	2	3	4
Is aware of relationship issues within the consultation team	1	2	3	4
Is good at problem solving	1	2	3	4
Is an astute and perceptive observer	1	2	3	4
Develops a common vocabulary/fluency in everyone's "language"	1	2	3	4
Values multiple perspectives by eliciting all participants' descriptions of the problem, attempts they have already made to solve the problem, and other ideas they have to solve the problem	1	2	3	4
Clearly defines and analyzes attributes of the problem, including antecedents, an operational definition of the appropriate and inappropriate behaviors, and maintenance factors	1	2	3	4
Isolates and systematically identifies problem components	1	2	3	4
Anticipates possible consequences	1	2	3	4
Is a good facilitator	1	2	3	4
Is skilled in conflict resolution	1	2	3	4
Is an efficient user of time	1	2	3	4
Is an active listener	1	2	3	4
Takes risks and is willing to experiment	1	2	3	4
Uses the consultation group as a problem solving unit	1	2	3	4
Demonstrates ability to understand appropriate interventions, given the cultures and values of students, parents, and teachers	1	2	3	4
Demonstrates ability to consider the instructional context, including the situation, tasks, and teaching methods	1	2	3	4
Is actively engaged and willing to get involved	1	2	3	4
Documents and gathers data for clear communication	1	2	3	4

Identifies clear goals	1 2 3 4
Reviews client records	1 2 3 4
Specifies the consultation contract for all parties (time, effort, cost)	1 2 3 4
Gives clear, understandable, and explicit directions	1 2 3 4
Pursues issues and follows through	1 2 3 4
Evaluates and focuses ideas	1 2 3 4
Clarifies roles	1 2 3 4
Is able to overcome resistance by addressing participants' strongly habituated responses, cognitive dissonances, and perceptions that the intervention will be threatening	1 2 3 4
Coordinates sufficient support for appropriate implementation	1 2 3 4
Devises interventions that have greater benefits than costs in terms of time, complexity, intrusion, duration, and effectiveness	1 2 3 4
Determines and addresses participants' need for increased knowledge and skills to address the problem	1 2 3 4
Designs and executes appropriate follow-up strategies	1 2 3 4
Summarizes	1 2 3 4
Is emotionally well adjusted and stable	1 2 3 4
Maintains confidentiality	1 2 3 4
Practices in an ethical manner	1 2 3 4
Has a clear sense of identity	1 2 3 4
Employs appropriate personal distance	1 2 3 4
Is trustworthy	1 2 3 4
Is confident	1 2 3 4
Systematically uses all problem solving stages: contract negotiation and problem identification, data collection and problem analysis, intervention development, intervention implementation, evaluation	1 2 3 4
Has teachers (and parents) actively collect and analyze data using practical and acceptable methods (e.g., end-of-the-day anecdotal notes, tallies of infrequent behaviors, time sampling)	1 2 3 4
Develops monitoring forms that can be easily used by the teacher or student	1 2 3 4
Employs a problem solving sheet during consultation sessions	1 2 3 4

11

Supervising Services That Enhance Cognitive and Academic Skills

When school psychologists facilitate multitiered interventions to enhance academic skills, they adopt more meaningful, effective, and ethically appropriate roles than that of "special education gatekeeper."

Vignette 11.1

As an intern, **Alberto** noticed that teachers in his schools generated an enormous amount of data when they administered classroom, state, and national tests to their students, but they were overwhelmed by the volume of information and therefore ignored the data. Furthermore, he was eager to establish routine Curriculum-Based Measurement (CBM) in the primary grades to facilitate early intervention programs for students falling behind in reading and math. He asked whether he could officially become the data manager for his school's achievement data. After this request was granted, Alberto monitored the effectiveness of academic programs for the general population and targeted at-risk students as well as for students in need of intense special education services. This close monitoring resulted in quick referrals into small group instruction, culminating with impressive gains in schoolwide scores. Alberto's supervisor and the district administrators were impressed by how this well-implemented role expansion resulted in more effective programs for all students.

D espite historic controversy and skepticism, cognitive and academic assessments continue to be prominent in education. Major changes in law and policy have given rise to the application of large-scale, high-stakes assessment. Assessment results determine whether students receive remedial services, are deemed eligible for special education services, are promoted or retained, and receive high school diplomas. There appears to be emerging consensus in the fields of both education and school psychology that linking high-quality assessments to evidence-based interventions is key to fostering students' success. Both the No Child Left Behind Act of 2001 (NCLB) and the Individuals With Disabilities Education Improvement Act of 2004 (IDEA 2004) designate prevention-oriented, data-driven models of assessment as favored tools to deliver services to all children. However, these educational assessments differ from traditional psychoeducational assessments that focus exclusively on cognitive functioning.

Further, the ongoing, profound paradigm shift in the field of school psychology (Reschly & Ysseldyke, 2002; Sheridan & Gutkin, 2000; Ysseldyke et al., 2006) is arguably most evident in practices regarding cognitive and academic functioning. The value of cognitive assessment has been seriously questioned and can be considered "one of the most controversial topics in school psychology" (Merrell, Ervin, & Gimpel, 2006, p. 161). It is believed that emerging transformations in educational practice and policy afford school psychologists the opportunity to have more meaningful, effective, and ethically appropriate roles than that of "special education gatekeeper." Since school psychologists provide such broad-based services, this chapter addresses the supervision of school psychologists to promote effective practice in enhancing students' cognitive and academic functioning.

BASIC CONSIDERATIONS

Providing services intended to enhance students' cognitive and academic skills has historically been and continues to be a primary function of school psychologists. These services include administering cognitive and academic assessments of either a traditional (e.g., standardized cognitive testing) or less traditional (e.g., portfolio assessment, authentic assessment, CBM) nature and linking these assessments to appropriate interventions.

Although always focused on problem solving and guided by empirical data, assessments can be conducted for purposes either "outside the classroom" or "inside the classroom" (Howell & Nolet, 2000). Traditionally, school psychologists have spent much of their time conducting outside-the-classroom evaluations to determine eligibility for services through special education or state agencies (e.g., departments of mental retardation). When properly designed, conducted, and interpreted, such assessments diagnose disabilities and also provide the basis from which well-formulated recommendations emerge.

However, controversy regarding the utility of cognitive assessment raises several concerns worth attention. These include cultural bias, theoretical constructs, the appropriateness of subtest interpretation, and the utility of cognitive measures in planning interventions (Merrell et al., 2006). Furthermore, serious concerns have been raised regarding the differential effects of both cognitive assessment and high-stakes testing on minority students and students with learning disabilities (Ysseldyke et al., 2006). Nonetheless, traditional psychoeducational assessment using standardized instruments remains an integral part of many school psychologists' practice. In response to a survey conducted by Hosp and Reschly (2002), school psychologists reported that on average they administered approximately 15 cognitive assessment batteries every month. Even when the numbers of students eligible for special education services decrease as a result of successful early intervention services, cognitive assessments continue to be administered to determine eligibility for services.

School psychologists are expending increasing effort on evaluations conducted for purposes *inside* the classroom. As Merrell et al. (2006, p. 162) indicated, "evaluations conducted for inside purposes are those intended to obtain data to identify students who need specific skills, to inform intervention decisions, and to monitor implemented interventions." Although CBM has been promoted for some time (Tindal, 1989), it has become much more widespread due to increasingly sophisticated technology as well as its compatibility with the response to intervention model suggested in IDEA 2004. CBM's dynamic assessment can provide invaluable feedback regarding the efficacy of interventions and thereby bridge the assessment-to-intervention gap.

Providing such broad-based services and thereby promoting students' cognitive and academic functioning requires that school psychologists carefully plan, implement, and appraise their services. Activities related to each of these phases will be addressed.

PLANNING SERVICES TO ENHANCE STUDENTS' COGNITIVE AND ACADEMIC SKILLS

In planning services to enhance students' cognitive and academic functioning, skillful school psychologists apply theories and research to develop effective prevention programs, design appropriate assessment processes, select evidence-based interventions, maintain ethical practice, and address multicultural issues.

Prevention Programs

A number of prevention programs focusing on enhancing academic functioning have been found to be effective. Some examples are:

1. Attending to and improving the climate and organization of the classroom to ensure that it is socially supportive, promotes academic engagement, and utilizes appropriate teaching strategies (Doll, Zucker, & Brehm, 2004).

2. Ensuring that the general education curriculum is suitable and appropriately delivered, as described by D. Fuchs, Mock, Morgan, and Young (2003) and Reschly (2006). For example, reading instruction addresses phonemic awareness, alphabetic principles, fluency, vocabulary, and comprehension. It is explicit and brisk, provides frequent feedback, and employs modeling, guided practice, learning to automaticity, and integration with other subject matter.

3. Screening all students for basic academic skills three times per year using reading, math, written expression, and spelling probes from the general education curricula or derived from commercially available programs such as DIBELS and AIMSweb; providing targeted interventions along with weekly reassessments for any students in the lowest quartile and modified teaching approaches and strategies for any students making less than satisfactory progress (E. S. Shapiro, 1989).

Selecting Evidence-Based and Appropriate Assessment Tools

When students who have been provided suitable instruction and formative evaluations reveal that they still remain unresponsive to interventions, it is likely that they will be referred for further evaluation. Competent school psychologists select evidence-based and appropriate assessment tools. To safeguard privacy, practitioners and their supervisors also consider how much testing and what kind of testing should be conducted. Sandoval and Irvin (1990) suggested that "a good rule of thumb may be that only the information actually needed for good decision making should be obtained in response to the referral concern or the presenting problem" (p. 99).

Vignette 11.2

Frank wanted to help his supervisees avoid being obligated to administer excessive standardized tests. Because student evaluation teams obtained parental permission for specific test instruments without a psychologist's input, Frank advised his supervisees to serve on the student development teams. This enabled the psychologists to generate appropriate referral questions with the team and, when necessary, develop suitable assessment plans that targeted specific referral questions.

Cognitive Assessment

In response to vigorous challenges directed at traditional psychometric models, revised theories of intelligence have emerged and received increased attention and favor. The Wechsler instruments (Wechsler, 1997, 2002, 2003) remain the most popular measures of cognition used by school psychologists (Merrell et al., 2006). However, the relatively atheoretical basis of the Wechsler instruments remains a major concern of critics who ponder the question, what do intelligence tests measure?

In response to this question, recent developments in cognitive theory and scientifically based research have been accompanied by concerted efforts to construct cognitive assessment instruments based on theoretically sound, integrated models of human cognition. This proliferation of new and revised instruments requires appropriate administration and new and different interpretation skills (Alfonso & Pratt, 1997).

Relatively recent models of intelligence include the triarchic theory (Sternberg, 1988); the Planning, Attention, Simultaneous, Successive (PASS) theory (Das, Naglieri, & Kirby, 1994); cross-battery assessment (Flanagan & Ortiz, 2000); and dynamic/learning potential assessment (Feuerstein, Rand, & Hoffman, 1979; Lidz & Elliott, 2000). These vary according to several characteristics. Some focus on intelligence as involving a general factor (generally referred to as g), while others focus on intelligence as being composed of multiple factors. They also vary in the degree to which they perceive intelligence as a relatively fixed trait (g) as opposed to a highly fluid trait responsive to intervention (dynamic/learning potential; Flanagan & Harrison, 2005).

Another model, multiple intelligences (Gardner, 1999), has gained considerable popularity among teachers. Teachers indicate that maintaining a multiple intelligences perspective promotes success for all children by taking advantage of various strengths, provides an entry point into learning new material for all students, encourages teachers to focus on positive attributes of students, helps *every* student learn due to the use of multiple modalities in teaching, provides opportunities to honor all children for being intelligent in some manner, and does not penalize students who learn in only a certain way. On the other hand, the model has been criticized because it lacks empirical evidence, the intelligences are overlapping rather than separate entities, neurocognitive research does not support the existence of separate brain areas for different types of intelligences, no measurement methods have been devised, and it includes traits more commonly considered talents, such as musical ability, as forms of intelligence (Alexander, 2006).

The Cattell-Horn-Carroll (CHC) theory, which is a compilation of Gf-Gc theory (Horn, 1991; Horn & Noll, 1997) and the Carroll three-stratum theory (J. B. Carroll, 1997), has emerged as one of the most utilized and well-researched theories in the field (Flanagan & Ortiz, 2000; McGrew & Flanagan, 1998). CHC theory "is a hierarchical framework of human cognitive abilities that consists of three strata: general intelligence or g (stratum III), broad cognitive abilities (stratum II), and narrow cognitive abilities (stratum I)" (Evans, Floyd, McGrew, & Leforgee, 2001, p. 247). This theory is operationalized in standardized batteries, for example, the Woodcock-Johnson Battery (McGrew & Woodcock, 2001).

Academic Assessment

The degree to which school psychologists are involved in completing academic assessments varies greatly. Although Merrell et al. (2006) found that many school psychologists do not actually administer achievement tests, in some districts school psychologists are very heavily involved in academic assessment and coordinate the universal CBM assessments of reading, math, and writing skills for all primary level general education students as well as the weekly monitoring of academic progress of students receiving intensive special education instruction (Harvey, 2008; Reschly, 2006). Further, many school psychologists appropriately appraise academic skills using curriculum-based assessment during psychoeducational evaluations to better link assessment to academic and learning interventions (Harvey & Chickie-Wolfe, 2007).

Nationally standardized achievement tests that rank a student's performance relative to the performance of peers are often not in sync with the curriculum. When academic test results do not reflect the school's curricula or when the tests are gross, nonspecific measures, they are of little use in educational planning.

Vignette 11.3

Penelope turned to curriculum-based assessment when she became frustrated with the lack of helpful information obtained during psychoeducational evaluations. Standardized achievement test results invariably indicated that students were performing at grade level, even when they clearly could not meet teachers' expectations. Parents, teachers, and Penelope could never understand that discrepancy.

Since students' performance on standardized instruments relative to normative samples often does not reflect classroom performance, it can be argued that time is better spent using formative evaluations. Formative assessment tools are used throughout the academic year to effectively and efficiently guide instructional practice. The function of formative evaluations is to provide the student and teacher feedback on student progress so that remedial instructional activities can be prescribed and learning improved. Such formative academic evaluations are based on the concept that students should be assessed relative to the skills they are expected to master in their specific curriculum.

One formative assessment tool, CBM (E. S. Shapiro, 1989, 1990), has evolved to include grade level benchmarks and normal rates of knowledge acquisition. CBM measures mastery of specific curriculum learning tasks and can link assessment to intervention by quickly identifying insufficient progress.

Curriculum-based assessment (CBA; Gickling & Rosenfield, 1995) uses curriculum materials as an assessment tool. The assessment is conducted by selecting a task (such as reading a passage from a social studies textbook), assessing students' ability to complete the task, matching assignments to the instructional level and learning strategies, and implementing the instructional strategies in the classroom. A great advantage of CBA is that it can be used for any subject, such as reading, social studies, science, or math, and result in highly meaningful and authentic assessments (Henning-Stout, 1994). Core questions to be addressed when using CBA are:

1. What does the student need to do to be successful within the curriculum?

2. What discrepancies exist between the outcomes anticipated by the teacher and the student's performance?

3. What knowledge and skills are needed for success with this curriculum? Which of these does the student already possess, and which are yet to be acquired?

4. What steps are being taken currently, and what steps can be taken in the future, to match learning activities to the student's skills and learning needs?

5. Is classroom instruction currently being presented in a manner that maximizes this student's learning? To benefit the student, what modifications should be made in the amount of curriculum covered; the presentation of material; instructional approaches; examination requirements; student strategies, practices, or approaches; group size; group structure; and/or teaching strategies?

6. How can student progress be regularly assessed, graphed, monitored, and used to modify instructional practice? (Gickling & Rosenfield, 1995; Sabatino, Vance, & Miller, 1993)

Maintaining Ethical Practice

Psychologists providing services to enhance cognitive and academic skills encounter many legal, ethical, and technical issues. These include selecting and implementing appropriate prevention programs and assessment tools, becoming competent in the use of new or revised tools, determining the effects of retesting, ascertaining the positive and negative outcomes associated with adding more evaluation tools, minimizing bias, and ensuring personal competence.

To meet the ethical mandate for equal protection, all assessment tools must meet stringent requirements for reliability and validity. The American Psychological Association (APA; 2002) and National Association of School Psychologists (NASP; 2000a) ethical guidelines offer specific criteria for practitioners. Briefly, any test must be reliable and valid for the purpose of its use and must be used in conjunction with other tools. Assessments should be conducted such that the extent to which the child needs educational services is determined rather than English language deficiencies, sensory impairments, or motor disabilities. Assessments should be sufficiently comprehensive to identify all educational services needed, including those regarding health, vision, hearing, social and emotional status, general intelligence, academic performance, communicative status, and motor abilities. They should lead to viable evidence-based interventions that are appropriate, pragmatic, valid, and acceptable and ultimately assist classroom performance (IDEA 2004).

Psychologists can violate ethical principles in a variety of ways when they administer assessment tools. They might make errors in standardized administration procedures, use tools for which they have not received adequate training, ignore current scientific knowledge and professional developments, attempt to provide services when impaired (by personal illness, substance abuse, or psychological issues), or recommend practices or interventions that are not based on scientific evidence (APA, 2002).

Furthermore, while the goal of traditional outside-the-classroom evaluations is to determine whether a student is eligible to receive special education services, meta-analysis of research examining the effects of placement in special education does not confirm that such placements are positive (Sheridan & Gutkin, 2000). Instead, it suggests that such placements are actually detrimental (Kavale, Forness, & Siperstein, 1999). Given the ethical imperative to "do no harm" to students, such results raise grave concerns. Recommending programs that are not beneficial, much less those that are harmful, is a clear violation of ethical imperatives.

One of the most often voiced criticisms of individual intelligence tests is that they are culturally biased. Certainly test publishers have made concerted efforts to reduce cultural bias in individual test items. Nonetheless, assessment tools continue to be predominantly in English and grounded in the middle-class American culture despite the increasing linguistic, cultural, and racial diversity of students. This challenges school psychologists and supervisors alike as they attempt to determine the needs of many students. In addition to psychometric validity, it is important to consider the effects of test results. One major concern has been the overrepresentation of minority group members in special education (Reschly, 2006). Assessment processes that result in disproportionate placement of minorities in special education violate the ethical principle of equal protection.

IMPLEMENTING SERVICES TO ENHANCE STUDENTS' COGNITIVE AND ACADEMIC SKILLS

When school psychologists implement services well, they skillfully conduct assessments, synthesize the results with ecological information to determine appropriate interventions and placements, and sensitively and accurately report information to students, parents, and educators both orally and in writing. They then facilitate intervention implementation, monitor student responses to interventions, and modify interventions in light of student progress.

Administering, Scoring, and Interpreting Assessment Results

Both novice and experienced school psychologists must constantly be vigilant to ensure that they accurately and appropriately administer, score, and interpret cognitive and academic assessments (Dumont & Willis, 2003). This requires caution with both procedures and interpretation. A checklist of relevant variables is contained in Handout 11.4 at the end of this chapter.

One of the most challenging facets of assessment interpretation is the diagnosis of disabilities linked to cognitive and academic performance, including mental retardation and learning disabilities. Such diagnoses have profound implications for students, their educational programs, and their futures.

Diagnosis of Mental Retardation

Results of cognitive, academic, and adaptive behavior assessments are combined to determine whether a student is eligible for special education and other services as a result of mental retardation. The American Association on Intellectual and Developmental Disabilities (AAIDD; 2002) defines mental retardation as "a disability [originating before age 18] characterized by significant limitations both in intellectual functioning and in adaptive behavior as expressed in conceptual, social, and practical adaptive skills" (¶ 1). Strengths are thought to coexist with limitations, and the purpose of describing limitations is to identify needed supports. Limitations in functioning are considered within the context of community environments, and assessments must consider cultural and linguistic diversity as well as differences in communicative, sensory, motor, and behavioral factors. The AAIDD is interested in changing the diagnostic label from "mental retardation" to "intellectual and developmental disability" to reduce stigma and enhance the understanding that when appropriate supports are applied over a sustained period, life functioning of individuals with "mental retardation" generally improves. Thus, contrary to historical understandings, this disability is considered a contextual and developmental disorder *that can be modified* with appropriate environmental supports.

Diagnosis of Learning Disabilities

While diagnosis of almost any disorder is challenging, the difficulties of diagnosing learning disabilities are legendary. Recent research-based developments have affected both theory and practice in this diagnosis. The validity of using an aptitude-achievement discrepancy to determine whether a student has a learning disability has been vehemently challenged. Whereas the discrepancy model was previously widespread, broader paradigms have emerged that define learning disabilities as multifaceted and heterogeneous. Reflected in both law and practice, new models view learning difficulties within the context of instructional variables rather than as discrete processing deficits present in the student. Accurate diagnosis and treatment of learning difficulties is considered to be dependent on the interaction of the student with the academic curricula, the classroom, and the teacher, all within the context of the family and social environment.

Vignette 11.4

Julianne attended a student development meeting with her supervisee, **Becca**, to provide support. The first-grade teacher was very frustrated because the referred student, **Andy**, was below grade level in phonics and other basic reading skills. Since Andy had attended a kindergarten that did not emphasize the acquisition of reading skills, Becca agreed that Andy needed extra reading instruction but maintained that incorrect teaching approaches had led to a reading deficit that was not diagnosable as a learning disability.

Determining whether students are eligible for special education services as a result of a learning disability is frustrating due to the lack of consensus regarding appropriate methods to reach this diagnosis. Because every state (and in some states, every community) has latitude in the interpretation of disability eligibility, there is little consistency from one state, community, or school to another in designating students as learning disabled. This issue has been exacerbated by the varied responses to IDEA 2004 and the suggestion that the diagnosis of learning disability be tied to response to intervention. As of this writing, some states and school districts are embracing these practices proactively, while others are adopting a "wait-and-see" attitude. Consequently, a student can easily be identified as eligible for special education services as a result of learning disability in some communities but not in others.

IDEA 2004 indicates that states cannot mandate the use of a cognitive-academic discrepancy formula in the diagnosis of learning disabilities because of several problems with this method. The discrepancy model does not distinguish learning-disabled from non-learning-disabled individuals, does not lead to appropriate differentiated instruction, does not take into consideration the high correlation between tests of cognitive ability and achievement, does not identify needy students in early grades, and tends to "overlook children who are struggling academically but do not manifest a discrepancy between ability and achievement" (Dombrowski, Kamphaus, & Reynolds, 2004, p. 367). Several alternate systems have been suggested. These include the roundtable approach, response to intervention, and the three-tiered approach.

The *roundtable approach* utilizes a method recommended by a collaboration of 10 professional organizations (U.S. Office of Special Education, National Joint Committee on Learning Disabilities, 2006). In this model, learning disabilities are diagnosed through a comprehensive evaluation using multiple measures and methods (student products, student records, standardized tests, observations, teacher logs, and continuous progress monitoring of performance) and multiple sources of information (teacher and parent interviews). All of this information is compiled and compared with the federal definition of learning disabilities to identify a processing deficit using the clinical judgment of team members.

The *response to intervention* (RTI) model uses a dual-discrepancy approach. Assuming that classroom instruction is appropriate (as determined by average student performance on CBM probes), potentially learning-disabled students are first targeted when they score significantly below same-grade peers on a CBM measure of academic performance. They are identified as learning disabled only after they do not make satisfactory progress in response to precisely delivered instruction, measured by ongoing and regular CBM (L. S. Fuchs & Fuchs, 1986; Shinn, 2002). Student performance is compared to baselines after instructional interventions are employed. Assuming that the interventions have been employed with integrity and modified when appropriate, students are expected to demonstrate progress at age-appropriate rates (Reschly, 2006). A lack of such responsivity is presumed to indicate a learning disability (Kovaleski & Prasse, 2004). Districts that are moving to the RTI model can use *Response to Intervention Policy Considerations and Implementation*, published by the National Association of State Directors of Education (2005), to facilitate implementation. However, in so doing they must address some of the complications in the RTI model, including but not limited to the difficulty of applying it at the secondary level and the difficulty of intersecting it with other diagnostic models, such as the *Diagnostic and Statistical Manual of Mental Disorders* (American Psychiatric Association, 2000).

To reconcile these difficulties, the *three-tiered model* has been proposed to encompass both the roundtable approach and the RTI model. As noted by Hale (2006), "the schism between those who advocate for RTI and those who advocate comprehensive evaluation of cognitive processes must be bridged, because politicized professional ideologies do not serve children well" (p. 17).

The three-tiered model entails (a) observing limitations in basic skills, fluency, or application ability in reading, written language, or math that are not due to mental retardation or lack of educational opportunity; (b) documenting those limitations using multiple sources of data, including educational history, standardized measures, multiple-session CBM measures, lack of response to intervention, and teacher, parent, and student reports; and (c) identifying "specific cognitive and/or linguistic correlates that appear to be related to the identified area of underachievement or relative difficultly, after having ruled out alternative explanations for the difficulties" (Mather & Gregg, 2006). As Fiorello and Primerano (2005) stated, "most school psychologists would agree that the way a student processes, stores, retrieves, and analyzes information influences how that student will perform in school" (p. 525). They suggested that this perspective will support continued assessment practices that address individual differences in reference to a standardization group. With this model, cognitive assessment remains a "next step" process for those who do not respond to intervention. This model was adopted by NASP in July 2007 (NASP, 2007).

In contrast to the above models, Dombrowski et al. (2004) recommended that the term *learning disability* be modified to "developmental learning delay." They recommended determining developmental learning delays via (a) a standard score of 85 or less on a nationally norm-referenced individual measure of academic achievement in basic reading skills, reading comprehension, mathematics reasoning, math calculation, spelling, written expression, or oral language *and* (b) evidence of educational impairment on classroom grades, CBA, and teacher ratings (p. 367). This model considers the source of developmental learning delays, like that of other disabilities (e.g., mental retardation, schizophrenia), to be irrelevant. It also ignores cognitive level, other than ruling out mental retardation. Dombrowski et al. recommended considering coexisting factors, such as attention deficit hyperactivity disorder, visual impairment, lack of educational opportunity, and emotional disturbance, when planning interventions, but not using them to deny services. While they recommended the use of global achievement measures such as the Wechsler Individual Achievement Test (Wechsler, 1992) or the Woodcock-Johnson (McGrew & Woodcock, 2001), others recommend more targeted measures such as the Test of Written Language, the Test of Reading Comprehension, the Durrell Analysis of Reading Difficulty, the Comprehensive Test of Phonological Processing, and the Gray Oral Reading Test (Corsi, 2004).

One of the most vexatious challenges faced by current supervisors is addressing this controversy. While policymakers and theoreticians argue, the practical reality is that teachers and school psychologists must determine which students are eligible for services on a daily basis. As systemic leaders, it behooves supervisors to take a leadership role in developing processes and procedures that reconcile differences, incorporate evidence-based research, and maximally benefit students.

Vignette 11.5

In response to their state's revision of the special education standards, **Natalie** and her supervisees met as a group several times to forge an operational definition of learning disability to use when diagnosing students. They used the NASP position statement as a starting point and refrained from mandating specific instruments, cutoffs, or discrepancies out of respect for each individual clinician's professional judgment. They did, however, make procedures and criteria clear enough that there was some universally used approached. Then they discussed cases during every supervision session in an attempt to reach accord.

Determining Appropriate Interventions and Placements

Research has identified evidence-based methods that enhance achievement, develop concentration, foster problem solving, promote study skills, and increase students' self-regulation and self-assessment. These methods can be used to help educators apply learning theory and cognitive strategies to modify and improve the instructional process. Interventions can be implemented at the individual, targeted small group, or universal level of practice.

Sensitively and Accurately Reporting Data

Whether assessment and intervention information is based on CBM and early intervention services or norm-referenced assessments and special education placement, it is important for resultant data to be reported in such a manner that teachers, parents, and students clearly understand the results. Usually this requires both oral and written reporting.

Oral Reports

Psychologists presenting assessment results to students and parents have the challenge of orally interpreting difficult constructs, reporting sometimes unpleasant conclusions, and ensuring that the student and parent truly understand the findings. This requires skill, tact, and resourcefulness. It is very helpful to accompany oral reports with visual aids, such as graphs depicting student progress determined by CBM probes. Otherwise, the complex jargon can be incomprehensible to parents and students.

Vignette 11.6

Sharon was amused while observing her young and attractive supervisee, **Lola**, interpret a psychological assessment to parents. Although the father, **Mr. Johnson,** listened intently, he was obviously having great difficulty understanding Lola's attempt to explain the complex terms. After she finished her presentation, Mr. Johnson said, "Honey, you're very attractive, but I can't understand a word you say."

Written Reports

Traditional psychological reports describe students from a fresh perspective to parents and teachers; communicate information regarding academic, intellectual, and social skills; and provide recommendations to enhance learning. Such reports are more than tools used to determine eligibility for services. Clear, concise, and relevant psychoeducational assessment reports transform diverse pieces of data, observations, test scores, and hypotheses into useful descriptions, diagnoses, and relevant remediation. Unfortunately, written reports are all too frequently written at a level too difficult for the average parent to understand (Harvey, 1997).

In addition, writing comprehensive psychological reports takes a considerable amount of time. Whitaker (1994) found that novice psychologists took 6 to 8 hours to write a report, while veteran psychologists averaged 3 hours per report. Report writing follows many hours of assessment, including review of the records, observation of the student, administration of assessment instruments, and interviews of parents, teachers, and the student. Furthermore, to write at a level that is easily understood by parents and other nonpsychologists takes additional time (Harvey, 2006). Therefore, it is not uncommon for a full psychoeducational evaluation to take from 4 to 24 hours to complete, the median being 11.7 hours (Lichtenstein & Fischetti, 1998). This cost sometimes results in suggestions to streamline psychoeducational reports. Dunham, Liljequist, and Martin (2006) found that streamlined reports with tables of data and bullets could be successful because they affected neither the understanding nor the satisfaction of teachers reading the report. Material presented in a bulleted format had no effect on satisfaction but significantly increased teachers' understanding. Thus, streamlined reports can take less time to write, be more readable, and even be more effective.

Report writing has changed with the advent of computer technology. A number of software programs integrate test results and generate recommendations, including curriculum modifications and special education prescriptions. However, programs that generate reports must be used with extreme caution (Harvey & Carlson, 2003). Questions have been raised regarding insufficient validation (Moreland, 1985, 1992), the illusion of absolute accuracy (Matarazzo, 1985), the neglect of ecological variables (Harvey, Bowser, Carlson, Grossman, & Kruger, 1998; Ownby, 1997), the tendency to fail to examine and evaluate the model used to develop the computer program (Maddux & Johnson, 1993), and the possibility of practicing beyond one's level of competence. Both APA (2002) and NASP (2000a) have standards and ethical principles pertaining to computer-based test scoring and interpretation. They caution against using computer-generated scoring or computer-based reports unless the user is qualified to use the relevant instrument, retains ultimate responsibility for the product, provides understandable explanations, and uses this technology only to improve the quality of services.

Monitoring Student Responses to Interventions

Interventions recommended by school psychologists, regardless of the source of information leading to their recommendation, must be research based, reasonable to implement, carried out as planned, and monitored to ensure fidelity, integrity, and positive outcomes. Such focused monitoring ensures that intervention application positively impacts the student. To that end, a fluid, enduring determination of efficacy must be an integral component of implementation of interventions. Difficulties are often encountered in implementing interventions with fidelity and in consistently and carefully monitoring student progress.

It is important to note that the identification of need is not synonymous with the provision of appropriate services. All too often, school psychologists have conducted assessments and made recommendations but neglected to follow up on the implementation of these recommendations. Salvia and Ysseldyke (1998) noted that "there has been a dramatic shift from a focus on the process of serving students with disabilities to a focus on the outcomes or results of the services provided" (p. 740). It can be anticipated that this emphasis on outcomes and their measurement will have a marked effect on the practice of school psychology. Effective monitoring of intervention outcomes naturally leads to modification of interventions when needed, because there is a constant awareness of student progress.

APPRAISING SERVICES TO ENHANCE STUDENTS' COGNITIVE AND ACADEMIC SKILLS

After providing services to enhance students' academic and cognitive functioning, it is important for school psychologists to appraise the entire process. During the appraisal phase, effective school psychologists review the process to determine what worked well, what did not work well, and which processes and procedures should be modified in the future to provide services that maximally benefit students. Appraisal involves applying meta-analysis to improve professional performance.

APPLICATIONS TO SUPERVISION

Successful supervision of practices to enhance students' cognitive and academic functioning requires that supervisors address a wide variety of activities. Supervisors must ensure that prevention programs are executed appropriately, that assessment tools are administered properly, that psychologists offer appropriate recommendations for interventions, and that student responses to interventions are monitored. For supervisees to become competent in these skills, they must not only complete graduate training but also receive supervised experience and participate in ongoing professional development through workshops, reading, advanced training, research, and scholarship. Competence cannot be assumed. Even at the most basic level, "some psychologists might be competent with intellectual assessment, but might perform cursory, almost useless educational assessments with equal confidence" (Dumont & Willis, 2003, p. 2).

Very little research regarding the supervision of services to enhance cognitive and academic functioning exists, and the extent to which recommendations regarding supervision from the counseling research can be appropriately generalized to assessment is unclear (A. Tuckman & Finkelstein, 1997). Research on supervision of assessment often focuses on the interaction of the supervisee with the client, accurate administration and scoring of assessment tools, and deriving appropriate and valid conclusions. Emotional issues stemming from the supervisee, or from interactions between the supervisee and the client, are much less likely to be the focus of supervision than they are of counseling (DeCato, 2002).

Furthermore, at present the practice of school psychology is straddling two paradigms and practitioners are expected to be able to practice in both. Thus supervisors are likely to be supervising practitioners as they apply new models focusing on prevention and intervention of young children at the same time that they supervise more traditional psychoeducational evaluations. All of these factors result in a need for supervisors to carefully attend to the development, both in themselves and in their supervisees, of skills and practices intended to enhance the cognitive and academic skills of students.

Vignette 11.7

Ellie, a clinical and administrative supervisor of 14 school psychologists in a moderate-sized city, faces a tremendous challenge as she helps her school psychologists retool to be responsive to current laws and best practices. Her school psychologists are of varied ages, levels of training, and experience. While the newer school psychologists are eager proponents of broad-based practice, many of the veteran school psychologists remain most comfortable with the "refer-test-place" model and are apprehensive about any role change. They are especially concerned about the concept of monitoring academic interventions. Furthermore, since they are acutely aware of excellent special education services that have resulted in academic and community success for students with significant disabilities such as Down syndrome and autism spectrum disorders, they are leery of "throwing the baby out with the bathwater." Ellie is unsure of how to provide optimal assistance during this period of professional transition.

Supervising Planning Services to Enhance Cognitive and Academic Skills

To encourage successful planning of services in this area, supervisors must help supervisees maintain ethical practice, appropriately plan prevention programs, determine the assessment process, ensure that they accurately administer and score tests and collect other important data, interpret findings thoughtfully and responsibly, and provide helpful recommendations. Supervision techniques often include observation, collaborative work, review of assessment data, and review of reports. To adequately supervise across this domain, supervisors will need to address their own and their supervisees' knowledge bases, address processes used to enhance students' cognitive and academic skills, address relationship variables, foster an understanding of broader contexts, conduct skill appraisals, promote adequate record keeping, supervise staff development efforts, and promote ongoing support.

Ensuring Adequate Foundational Knowledge

Supervisors should ensure that both they and their supervisees have adequate content knowledge by assigning readings in any areas of deficiency regarding human development, student learning, assessment, and evidence-based interventions. To bolster their understanding of current learning theory and research, supervisees and supervisors can read general educational psychology texts such as *Psychology in Learning and Instruction* (Alexander, 2006), *Cognitive Development and Learning in Instructional Contexts* (Byrnes, 2000), and *Taking Sides: Clashing Views on Educational Issues* (Noll, 2008) as well as specialized books regarding educational interventions such as *Learning Disabilities and Related Disorders: Characteristics and Teaching Strategies* (Lerner & Kline, 2005) and *Interventions for Academic and Behavior Problems II: Preventive and Remedial Approaches* (Shinn, Walker, & Stoner, 2002). A number of Web sites elucidate evidence-based educational practices, such as www.interventioncentral.com and the What Works Clearinghouse (http://ies.ed.gov/ncee/wwc). Evidence-based math programs are described at www.nctm.org, and details regarding evidence-based reading programs are described at http://reading.uoregon.edu/curricula/index.php and www.national readingpanel.org. Finally, to obtain a better understanding of the curriculum expectations encountered by students, it is very helpful to read the curriculum frameworks posted on state department of education Web sites.

To obtain an overview of current practices regarding cognitive assessment, both supervisors and supervisees can refer to *Best Practices in School Psychology IV* (A. Thomas & Grimes, 2002); *Best Practices in School Psychology V* (A. Thomas & Grimes, 2008); and *Children's Needs III: Development, Prevention, and Intervention* (Bear & Minke, 2006). More detailed information can be obtained via current assessment and intervention texts such as *Assessment of Children* (Sattler, in press) and *Clinical Assessment of Child and Adolescent Intelligence* (Kamphaus, 2001); current journal articles; and national and state professional Web sites (e.g., www.nasponline.org).

Fostering Multicultural Competence

As discussed in Chapter 3, supervisees should have a deep understanding of the specific population with which they are working. Supervisors should address multicultural issues as they develop departmental policies regarding assessment and interventions to enhance academic skills. Supervisors can turn to resources such as the *Handbook of Multicultural School Psychology: An Interdisciplinary Perspective* (Esquivel, Lopez, & Nahari, 2007); the *Comprehensive Handbook of Multicultural School Psychology* (Frisby & Reynolds, 2005); and *Multicultural Special Education: Culturally Responsive Teaching* (Obiakor, 2007).

In consultation with staff school psychologists and specialists in English as a second language, the supervisor of school psychological services should develop a policy regarding the assessment and development of interventions that respect multicultural issues. In making the decision regarding eligibility for special education services, the student development team must look at all information, including information provided by the parents, to determine whether a student has an identified handicapping condition, significant underachievement, and a need for special education services that a general education teacher cannot provide in the general education classroom. When considering eligibility for special education services for a student identified as speaking English as a second language (ESL), being an English language learner (ELL), or having limited English proficiency (LEP), a language disorder should be evident in the dominant language as well as in English to be considered a disability. Handout 11.1 incorporates suggestions from A. Ortiz (1997).

Fostering Ethical Practice

As discussed earlier, several variables challenge the provision of ethical practice in enhancing students' cognitive and academic skills. To this end, supervisors have an obligation to teach and model approaches that help supervisees become exemplary consumers and administrators of prevention strategies, assessment tools and processes, and intervention monitoring. This includes emphasizing ethical imperatives to "do no harm" and to refrain from conducting assessments or recommending programs that do not benefit students.

As discussed in Chapter 6, supervisors must help their supervisees ensure that students and their parents give informed consent for assessments. Minimally, informed consent includes knowledge of the potential ramifications of the assessment, reasons for assessment, who will have access to information, and what it will be used to determine. Supervisors are expected to ensure that assessment tools are appropriately selected, administered, interpreted, and used within the time lines mandated by state and federal laws.

It is likely that supervisors will need to revisit standards mandating validity and reliability when facilitating supervisees' selection of assessment tools. As discussed previously, many school psychologists received training in techniques of questionable validity during their graduate programs and continue to use these techniques throughout their careers without reconsidering their appropriateness. Corporations publishing test materials certainly continue to develop and publish tests of questionable validity. It is up to the supervisor and practicing school psychologist to take the time to review and validate instrument suitability in general, determine relevance to specific referrals, and clearly state reliability and validity issues in psychological reports.

Supporting Prevention Programs

Further, most school psychologists have not been trained in providing prevention programs during their graduate programs and therefore will need considerable support in this area. The above resources are useful in furthering supervisees' knowledge of prevention programs. It is also helpful when supervisors incorporate knowledge of prevention programs in supervisees' annual goals, sponsor attendance at prevention program workshops, and encourage supervisees to observe successful prevention programs in action. Finally, prevention programs are an ideal topic to be addressed at group and peer supervision sessions.

Handout 11.1

CONSIDERATIONS IN WORKING
WITH ENGLISH LANGUAGE LEARNERS

- Determine the dominant language.

- Determine whether English skills are at the Basic Interpersonal Communication Skills or the Cognitive Academic Language Proficiency level through parent interviews, questionnaires, direct observations in structured (e.g., classroom) and unstructured (e.g., recess, lunchroom) settings, rating scales, checklists, behavioral sampling, and assessment of work samples.

- Using structured assessments, obtain oral and written language narrative samples in all languages.

- Use standardized and norm-referenced tests only if normative data include the population in question; avoid even nonverbal performance cognitive assessment scales, as they are not culture free.

- Recognize that a student's ability to understand instructions can be hindered in a second language, regardless of ability to complete the tasks, since instructions include abstract terms (*left*, *above*, etc.).

- Rather than focusing on a score, focus cognitive assessment on the process of learning and the ability to adapt and apply skills in various contexts. Consider dynamic assessment using three versions of a task (the first as a pretest, the second to teach the task and observe learning approaches and teaching methods, the third as a posttest).

- Understand that students' knowledge in their native language is likely to differ from their knowledge in a second language. For example, reading skills may be strongest in the native language but science knowledge may be limited to English. Assessing students in only one language gives an incomplete picture of their knowledge, skills, abilities, and instructional needs.

Ensuring Assessment Knowledge

To develop a unique supervision method for each assessment instrument and technique would be insurmountably difficult. Instead, effective supervisors develop a model of assessment supervision that applies to multiple instruments and activities. The goal of supervision should not be to teach a particular test or theory but rather to encourage development of a methodical approach to new instruments

School psychology training programs have a long history of training school psychologists how to conduct individual assessments using standardized instruments and writing psychoeducational reports based on those assessments. As Alfonso, LaRocca, Oakland, and Spanakos (2000) indicated, all school psychology training programs include at least one assessment course during which students learn how to administer tests of cognitive ability. Topics covered include how to interview, establish rapport, record behavioral observations, follow standardized procedures, score results, interpret data, and report results in writing and orally. In 1996, at the time they conducted their survey, Alfonso et al. found that students typically submitted five to six scored protocols, wrote three to four reports, and took a competency exam in these courses. The instruments emphasized were the Wechsler Intelligence Scale for Children (WISC; 92%), the Wechsler Adult Intelligence Scale (80%), the Wechsler Preschool and Primary Scale of Intelligence (WPPSI; 64%), the Stanford-Binet Intelligence Scales (74%), and the Kaufman Assessment Battery for Children (40%). The Bayley Scales of Infant Development, the Woodcock-Johnson, the Differential Ability Scales, and the Kaufman Adolescent and Adult Intelligence Test were required by fewer than 26% of the programs. This study reveals that graduate courses tend to teach the instruments most commonly used in the field and are slow to adopt new instruments due to time limitations and financial constraints (test kits being very expensive). Far too little emphasis is placed on the assessment of multicultural and non–native English speaking students, disabled students (including those with physical disabilities that require accommodations), and infants and preschoolers. Although graduate programs continue to emphasize instruction in the full-length Wechsler scales, emerging trends in cognitive assessment include the greatly increased use of abbreviated tests such as the Kaufman Brief Intelligence Test, short forms of the Wechsler intelligence scales, and team and arena assessments using multiple professionals and family members to assess preschoolers.

In contrast, many training programs have considerably less history, if any, in training prospective school psychologists to use less traditional tools such as CBM. They also have less history than would be desirable in training school psychologists to link assessment to intervention or to monitor the progress of students. Consequently, school psychology supervisors themselves are likely to have received inadequate training in these activities.

Furthermore, a number of tools in which school psychologists were trained in the past have been discredited by research. These include the Bender Visual Motor Gestalt Test for assessment of neuropsychological impairment as well as IQ scores and discrepancy formulas for identifying specific learning disabilities (Norcross, Koocher, & Garofalo, 2006). This presents supervisors with the challenge of convincing supervisees to *stop* using invalid instruments and inappropriate methods in which they themselves were trained and with which they feel competent.

Periodically review the test administration and interpretation skills of supervisees. Both inexperienced and experienced psychologists may not realize the importance of standardized administration or the likelihood of making administrative or scoring blunders that could result in meaningful errors (Dumont & Willis, 2003). It is essential that assessment instruments be administered, scored, and interpreted as designed. However, research has repeatedly shown that students, interns, and practicing school psychologists alike make multiple errors in the administration and scoring of standardized assessment tools. A summary of 14 studies by Alfonso and Pratt (1997) suggests that on the WISC, examiner scoring errors resulted in approximately a 3.5 point difference (5.5 on "difficult" protocols). Hence, "it is logical to suspect that inappropriate diagnostic, placement, and educational planning decisions may occur as a result of tests that have been incorrectly administered or scored" (Alfonso & Pratt, 1997, p. 331).

Supervisors should carefully review test protocols, since even experienced professionals can make errors in basals, ceilings, assignment of bonus points, and scoring (Dumont & Willis, 2003). The same problem is likely true of CBM tools, which require consistent directions and precise timing of probes. Supervisors can ensure that accurate administration is accomplished by direct observation, review of videotapes or audiotapes, or role-playing. Similarly, observations or tapes of interviews are helpful to ensure that supervisees conduct them effectively, tactfully, and in accord with recommended practice (Sattler, in press).

Help supervisees develop skill in self-guided learning of new assessment tools. Considering the wealth of constantly emerging assessment instruments and techniques, learning how to administer and interpret new instruments is an ongoing task. Therefore, a major goal in the supervision of assessment is the development of self-guided learning and self-monitoring. For example, supervisors can help supervisees develop standard procedures to learn a new assessment tool. Handout 11.2 suggests one approach.

Vignette 11.8

In **Talia**'s district, several school psychologists enthusiastically adopted a new instrument as soon as it was published because it was colorful and highly attractive to the preschoolers with whom they worked. After a year, the publisher announced that recent research had revealed that the new instrument misdiagnosed attention deficits as mental retardation. Thus a sizable number of students in the district were mistakenly diagnosed as retarded on the cognitive scale, although not necessarily on the adaptive behavior scale. As a group, the psychologists wrestled with how to address this very serious situation. They decided to inform the parents of what had happened and reassess all of the students using well-established assessment tools. They also decided that, henceforth, they would always administer new instruments in conjunction with more familiar instruments until they felt comfortable interpreting the results.

Fostering Planning Skills

It is very helpful for supervisors to meet with supervisees to help plan the assessment process to prevent flawed evaluations that are difficult to repair. Novice psychologists will, of course, require more frequent meetings and assistance than veteran psychologists, but regardless of the supervisee's level of expertise, a supervisor's help in planning the assessment process prevents the establishment of inappropriate routines. Particularly with novice practitioners, it is very helpful to provide feedback on one case before the supervisee begins the next to avoid the repetition and habituation of errors. During planning, the supervisor and supervisee determine which activities should be included in the assessment process, such as file reviews, portfolio assessments, CBA, CBM, observations, interviews, self-report inventories, questionnaires and rating scales, informal assessment

Handout 11.2

PROCEDURES FOR
LEARNING A NEW ASSESSMENT TOOL

1. When possible, directly observe or view a videotape of an expert administering the tool.

2. When possible, attend a workshop that addresses the tool.

3. Read reviews of the test before selection.

4. Read the manual.

5. Administer the test to oneself.

6. Readminister the test to oneself, tape record the administration, and then review the tape against standardized administration guidelines.

7. Administer the test to another school psychologist who observes for administration errors while role-playing a student who makes test errors.

8. Readminister the test until no administration errors are made.

9. Administer the test to a volunteer.

10. Score the volunteer's answers and review the scoring with another school psychologist.

11. Administer the test to several students as a practice instrument while using other instruments for the actual assessment.

12. Interpret the practice tests and review the results with a colleague in peer supervision.

---

methods, and standardized tests. Planning meetings also provide opportunities to introduce supervisees to new tests and procedures, assign readings, and teach or review critical information and procedures.

Supervising the Implementation of Services That Enhance Students' Cognitive and Academic Skills

Supervising Synthesizing Assessment Results With Ecological Information

Supervisors of school psychologists can steadfastly assert the importance of ecological assessment along with any administration of standardized tests. Even if other team members are officially designated as the individuals who perform classroom observations, achievement testing, and parent interviews, school psychologists can and should make it a practice to observe the student in a natural setting, interview the student, have the student complete some academic work in their presence, and consult with the student's parents. If an administrator questions this practice, the supervising school psychologist can explain that this type of comprehensive evaluation is ethically mandated by professional standards and demonstrate that the inclusion of data gathered from natural observations, student interviews, student completion of academic work, and parent interviews greatly enriches the school psychologist's evaluation, report, and recommendations.

Vignette 11.9

Francine and her supervisees decided that, to better link psychological assessments to student needs, they would adopt a departmental policy mandating that every student assessment completed by a school psychologist include consideration of academic skills. Even when standardized achievement testing was completed by special education personnel, the psychologists observed students completing work and conducted CBA or CBM. This policy immeasurably improved supervisees' ability to make appropriate recommendations.

After gathering data but before reporting the results, supervisees often discuss the results with supervisors. Often it is critical for the supervisor to review raw data and write comments on data sources, such as CBM protocols, behavior management data sheets, and test protocols, and then refer the supervisee to readings or Internet-based resources to facilitate both interpretation and recommendations.

Supervising Determining Appropriate Interventions and Placements

The supervision of evidence-based methods to foster academic skills is not dependent on the specific skill in question but is instead applicable to all academic skills. It is first necessary to ensure that the supervisee has adequately defined the difference between what the student is doing and what is desired. Moreover, supervision must determine that the supervisee is able to exercise an ecological approach that assesses the composition of the classroom, pedagogical issues, ecological and cultural factors, the classroom climate, and characteristics of the individual learner. Helping supervisees determine how to efficiently gather enough information to know whether they should proceed or cease is critical. This requires that supervisors have a sound knowledge of curriculum, good teaching, student-teacher relationships, and community and district expectations. It also requires cultural sensitivity.

To retain the important information that can be gained with appropriate assessment, it is critical that supervisors ensure that practitioners utilize tests and test scores optimally. Because current special education practices emphasize service delivery within the confines of the regular education classroom (with or without modifications), diagnostic testing is less meaningful than it was in the past. Instead, psychologists fruitfully examine classroom products, graph CBM responses, observe in classrooms, review records, or interview teachers regarding expectations.

Vignette 11.10

As **Gayle Macklem** (personal communication, July 2007) suggests, it can be helpful to determine which teachers at the various grade levels are good judges of student work and to collect samples over time to use for comparison. Such comparisons help one avoid making errors by perceiving that a student in a high-functioning class looks worse than she or he would look in a more typical class. This promotes having a broader standard to which work can be compared rather than simply comparing students to the class in which they are currently placed.

Supervising Sensitively and Accurately Reporting Data

To facilitate supervisees' skill in orally reporting information to parents and teachers, supervisors must first determine their skill level through direct observation, role-plays, and tapes of conferences with students and parents. Requesting student and parent feedback can be extremely helpful as well. For example, parents can be requested to fill out a brief survey at the conclusion of the meeting that reveals their understanding of the content of the conference.

For psychologists to improve their report writing skills, it is necessary for supervisors to monitor supervisees' report writing and ask them to rewrite reports at more readable levels when appropriate. In addition, supervisors can request that supervisees obtain information about the readability of their writing through peer review, solicitation of consumer feedback (Ownby, 1997), calculation of reading level, or a computer grammar checking program. When supervisors review draft reports, it is helpful for them to make corrections using word processing tracked changes and to type in comments explaining their reasons for the corrections (e.g., a professional practice principal or grammar rule) rather than simply making them. When the supervisee continually makes similar errors, assigning readings and having discussions relevant to the error are beneficial (Dumont & Willis, 2003).

Standardized assessments are increasingly being accompanied by computer scoring programs, and several instruments are essentially unusable without computer-assisted scoring. When supervisors use computer-assisted scoring, supervisors must ascertain that they are vigilant about data entry, using proper forms, and correctly selecting comparison groups.

Even after a supervisee has demonstrated adequate cognitive and academic assessment and intervention skills in individual and group supervision sessions, it is helpful to encourage generalization and increased self-sufficiency through peer supervision and ongoing self-evaluation. Supervisors might use Handout 11.3, or a modification of it, as a checklist regarding supervisees' reports.

Handout 11.3

REPORT CHECKLIST

_____ All referral questions are explicitly addressed throughout the report.

_____ Assessment tools are clearly and accurately described.

_____ Concrete examples are given.

_____ Findings are related to academic skills, assignments, and classroom performance.

_____ The report is clearly written for the parent, teacher, and student.

_____ Computer-generated reports, if used, are edited by modifying statements, deleting inappropriate hypotheses and recommendations, and integrating results with other information.

_____ The psychologist retains ethical and professional responsibility for the accuracy of the results.

_____ Regardless of whether the student is found to be eligible for special education services, interventions that address the referral concern are suggested.

_____ Tentative recommendations are brought to meetings but not formalized until collaboration with parents and teachers has occurred.

_____ Recommendations are accompanied by handouts, training, and checking back.

Supervising Monitoring Student Progress

It is important for supervisors to ensure that supervisees do not conceptualize the writing of a report as closure to a case. One method of facilitating this perspective is to have supervisees collect ongoing data regarding the student's progress and to share that information with the supervisor. Another method, when supervisees are not involved in the intervention program, is to have them routinely consult with referring parties 1, 3, and 6 months after the completion of a report. Such ongoing processes lead naturally to modification of interventions in light of student progress.

As with all clinical supervision, good record keeping is invaluable in the practice and supervision of services that enhance cognitive and academic skills. A pivotal supervisory issue is providing support in the selection, implementation, and monitoring of interventions. Both supervisees and supervisors should keep written records of supervision sessions, the recommendations that occur, and the eventual results of those recommendations.

SUMMARY

Cognitive and academic assessments determine whether students receive remedial services, are deemed eligible for special education services, are promoted or retained, and receive high school diplomas. Providing support services that enhance students' cognitive and academic skills is a primary function of school psychologists. There is emerging consensus that conducting high-quality assessments linked to evidence-based interventions is pivotal in fostering students' success. Traditionally, school psychologists have spent much of their time conducting evaluations to determine eligibility for services "outside the classroom." Currently there is an increasing tendency to provide assessment and interventions to improve educational programs "inside the classroom."

Psychologists providing services to enhance cognitive and academic skills encounter many legal, ethical, and technical issues. These include selecting and implementing prevention programs, choosing appropriate assessment tools, becoming competent in the use of new or revised tools, determining the effects of retesting, ascertaining the appropriateness of adding more evaluation tools, and minimizing bias. Cultural bias, including the overrepresentation of minority group members in special education, is of special concern.

School psychologists must constantly be vigilant to ensure that they accurately and appropriately administer, score, and interpret cognitive and academic assessments, including the diagnosis of disabilities. There has been a shift away from the traditional diagnosis of learning disabilities by identifying a discrepancy between aptitude and achievement, and IDEA 2004 indicates that states cannot mandate the use of a cognitive-academic discrepancy formula in the diagnosis of learning disabilities because of several problems with this method. Alternatives include the roundtable approach, RTI, and the three-tiered approach, which considers both the student's response to targeted interventions and his or her cognitive processes. In implementing evidence-based interventions, school psychologists must take care when reporting data, monitoring students' responses to interventions, and appraising services.

Supervisors must carefully attend to the development, both in themselves and in others, of skills and practices that support enhancement of cognitive and academic skills. They must help supervisees maintain ethical practice, appropriately plan prevention programs, determine the assessment process, ensure that they accurately administer and score tests and collect other important data, interpret findings thoughtfully and responsibly, and provide helpful recommendations. Appropriate supervision techniques often include observation, tapes, collaborative work, review of assessment data, and review of reports.

REFLECTIVE QUESTIONS

Q11.1. What concerns have been raised regarding cognitive assessment?

Q11.2. Describe the paradigm shift toward conducting evaluations inside the classroom.

Q11.3. Describe the legal, ethical, and technical issues faced by school psychologists who provide services to enhance cognitive and academic skills.

Q11.4. What are the features of an effective academic prevention program?

Q11.5. How do competent school psychologists select evidence-based and appropriate assessment tools? How have changes in cognitive theory influenced this?

Q11.6. What core questions are addressed with the use of CBA?

Q11.7. What are the primary concerns regarding administering, scoring, and interpreting assessment results, particularly when it comes to mental retardation and learning disabilities?

Q11.8. What problems are associated with the discrepancy model of diagnosing learning disabilities? Describe the roundtable approach, RTI, and the three-tiered approach.

Q11.9. How can school psychologists most accurately report data, monitor responses to interventions, and appraise services?

Q11.10. What must supervisors be aware of, and what supervision techniques can be used, to support enhancement of students' cognitive and academic skills?

Q11.11. How can supervisors supervise the implementation of services?

SUPERVISORY DILEMMAS

SD 11.1

A parent known as "difficult" has finally signed permission for an evaluation after many hours of meetings. On the day the psychologist has set aside to conduct the evaluation, she arrives at the school to find a telephone message from the parent withdrawing permission. School personnel want the psychologist to pretend she did not get the message and go ahead with the testing. The school psychologist calls you in a panic for advice. *What are the supervisory considerations? What should be done?*

Authors' thoughts: Although unfortunate, there is little ambiguity in this scenario. Without parental consent, an evaluation simply cannot proceed. Efforts should be spent on determining what elicited the sudden change and caused the withdrawal of permission. Often, providing information about assessment and its potential repercussions quiets parental fears, but it is also helpful to explore the thinking behind the fears. Parents need to feel that an assessment will benefit, rather than stigmatize, their child. Further, school psychologists have a moral and ethical obligation to ensure that this is actually the case.

SD 11.2

As a supervisor of three school psychologists, you are in a position to compare their conclusions as you read their reports. You have noticed that, over time, they have become increasingly divergent in their diagnoses of learning disabilities. Often, a student diagnosed as learning disabled by one of your supervisees would not be diagnosed as learning disabled by another. *What are the supervisory considerations? What should be done?*

Authors' thoughts: This situation is frustratingly common because the diagnosis of learning disabilities remains inconsistent and elusive. It is obviously unfair to have such divergent practices within a district. The supervisor might initiate a review of the assessment methods being used by the three school psychologists, how they are being interpreted, the criteria for eligibility determination and diagnosis, and so forth. Professional development may be necessary to ensure that the district's students are being adequately served, and it would be helpful for the school psychologists to meet as a group to reconcile their differences regarding individual cases.

SD 11.3

The director of special education in your district has recently consulted with you about whether to purchase a neuropsychological assessment battery for the school psychologists in the elementary schools. He expects that this will allow the district to avoid having to refer students to the local hospital's learning disabilities clinic for expensive neuropsychological evaluations. *What are the supervisory considerations? What should be done?*

Authors' thoughts: One need only glance at a recent assessment company catalog to see how many neuropsychological tests have been developed and marketed to school psychologists in the last decade. While it is feasible that the *administration* of the test is within the domain of competency for most school psychologists, it should be argued that the *interpretation* cannot be done judiciously without specialized training. Perhaps the most effective way to address this question is to examine why parents or teachers are seeking a neuropsychological evaluation rather than a psychoeducational evaluation. For example, does the student suffer from a known physical disorder that affects brain functioning? Is the student not responding to well-implemented, evidence-based interventions? Avoiding unnecessary hospital-based evaluations may be in the best interest of the student. However, avoiding them simply to save money clearly is not!

SD 11.4

You are a supervisor of a school psychologist assigned to two elementary schools. One of the schools has a highly intense literacy program at the kindergarten and first-grade levels, including monthly CBM conducted by the school psychologist. The school psychologist has conducted a program evaluation and found that 90% of students in this program read above grade level by the end of second grade. She has tried to convince the teachers in the second elementary school to implement the same program, to no avail, and turns to you for suggestions. *What are the supervisory considerations? What should be done?*

Authors' thoughts: Since it is obvious that the intense literacy program is exceedingly beneficial for the students, it is a worthwhile endeavor to initiate discussion with the school principal and other stakeholders to inform them of the benefits of such a program. This is a case where persistence as a systemic leader is both worthy and necessary. Initially, the teachers could be given a chance to discuss opportunities and barriers to implementation and could mutually problem solve to eliminate identified barriers to implementation. Because resistance often emanates from the unknown and/or misinformation, enlisting the support of teachers from the first school would be helpful. Of inestimable importance, however, is obtaining administrative support. To that end, the principal of the second school should be afforded the opportunity to view the positive results. Ideally, the principal of the first school would also be a helpful resource. In an era of heightened accountability, it is unlikely that the second school will remain resistant for long. One can only imagine the public outcry after the first round of mandated state testing reveals disparate performance between two schools in the same district!

SD 11.5

Your immediate supervisor insists that you, as supervising school psychologist, develop a "standard battery" for the school psychologists to use for all cases that are referred for formal assessments. *What are the supervisory considerations? What should be done?*

Authors' thoughts: Since the formulation of a standard battery would fail to take into account the individual differences and needs of the students, it would clearly be an unethical undertaking. This situation will require the school psychologist to help educate the administrative supervisor about assessment issues as well as special education practices and law.

SD 11.6

A practicum student is enrolled in an individual intelligence testing course. He has sought volunteers for IQ test administration among friends and family. During testing, serious concerns about his cousin's young son have emerged, and there is a strong suspicion of child abuse. The student has come to you for guidance. *What are the supervisory considerations? What should be done?*

Authors' thoughts: As a practicum student soon to be a school psychologist, the student is mandated to report child abuse. As a supervisor, you are responsible for the professional actions of your supervisee. Prudent action would demand that the supervisor and student jointly review the concerns and determine an appropriate course of action. It is important to remember that school psychologists are not responsible for determining the presence of abuse, but rather are responsible for reporting its possible occurrence. Although this is typically an unpleasant task, it is even more distasteful in this situation because the student is a family member. It is likely that the supervisee will profit from support and guidance with the ensuing fallout. As an aside, we would strongly encourage the student to first call the family member to explain why the report was made. To help further protect the supervisee, it may be perfectly acceptable to "share the blame." This presents yet another example of the dangers of recruiting family members to serve as test subjects!

Handout 11.4

CHECKLIST TO ENSURE
APPROPRIATE ASSESSMENT PRACTICE

(Adapted from Dumont & Willis, 2003)[1]

The context of the evaluation has been considered.

____ All assessment results have been integrated and placed in the context of the student's self-reports, school performance, education, family, and medical history. In addition, the referral questions, others' concerns, and findings of previous evaluations are integrated.

____ Commonalties have been noted and disparities discussed.

____ Multiple sources of convergent data have been used in final decisions.

____ Sufficient, bias-free, and appropriate tests have been used that distinguish among unique skills.

Test standardization and norms are respected.

____ Normed standardized tests have not been altered: Basal and ceiling rules were correctly obeyed, instructions and items were read verbatim, timing was adhered to, and demonstrations were given as instructed (no additional help, ad libbing, or unauthorized feedback).

____ Tests were learned and practiced to mastery before use.

____ "Testing the limits" was clearly reported.

____ For students with severe and low incidence disabilities, the examiner *adopted* appropriate tests rather than *adapting* inappropriate ones.

____ Students were tested in their specific native languages (e.g., Puerto Rican vs. Castilian Spanish) with tests normed in that language.

____ The consequences of taking subtests out of context was considered.

____ Scoring keys and test materials were kept secure.

____ Protocols and record forms were originals and not photocopies.

____ All tests were normed on a genuinely representative and sufficiently large sample and appropriately stratified and randomized for sexes, geographic regions, racial and ethnic groups, disabilities, and income and educational levels.

____ The evaluator is aware of possible errors in printed or computerized norm tables and is appropriately skeptical of publishers' claims.

____ The evaluator takes into account the risk of significant changes in scores resulting from movement between norms tables (e.g., the overnight change from Fall norms to Spring norms).

____ Rapport was established with examinees.

Reliability is assured because the evaluator:

____ Takes into account the standard error of measurement (SEM), consistently uses 90% or 95% confidence bands, and clearly explains their meaning in lay terms

____ Recognizes that a test score was obtained once, at a specific time and place, and explains that the confidence band does *not* include errors and problems with test administration and conditions

_____ Distinguishes clearly between reliability and validity

_____ Distinguishes between the standard error of measurement (SEM) and the standard error of the estimate (SEest)

_____ Uses the correct confidence band for the appropriate score: raw, ability, W, standard score, percentile rank, etc.

_____ Understands and makes appropriate decisions about tests that use rigid cutoff scores for decision making

Validity is assured because the evaluator:

_____ Demonstrates an appreciation of the implications of test validity in terms of purpose, groups, sample size, similarity to the referred student, criterion measures, time intervals, and construct validity

_____ Understands the relationship between validity and reliability

_____ Interprets tests only in ways for which validity has been established and demonstrates an appreciation of the limitations of each test

Scoring is accurate because the evaluator:

_____ Employs a straightedge when using scoring tables

_____ Photocopies the norms table and draws lines and circles numbers

_____ Checks the accuracy of tables by inspecting adjacent scores

_____ Reads table titles and headings aloud while scoring

_____ Checks and rechecks all scores

_____ Records the student's name and the date on all sheets of paper

_____ Checks the student's birth date and age with the student and calculates the age correctly by the rules for the particular test

_____ Performs thought experiments with tables (e.g., what if the student had made two lucky or unlucky guesses? What if the student were 6 months older or younger?)

_____ Records all responses verbatim

_____ Keeps raw data for future use

_____ Uses consistent notations for correct and incorrect answers, no responses, "I don't know" responses, and examiner's questions

_____ Ensures that the examinee cannot determine from the number or direction of pencil strokes which notations are being made

_____ Uses templates consistently, carefully, and correctly

_____ Carefully follows computer scoring instructions

_____ Checks the accuracy of computer results by occasionally hand scoring

_____ Is certain to have the latest version of the scoring program, to know of any new errors, and to have the protocols that go with that version

_____ Understands and clearly explains the differences among standard scores, scaled scores, normal curve equivalents, percentile ranks, and other scores

(Continued)

(Continued)

____ Uses age-equivalent ("mental age") and grade-equivalent scores sparingly, if at all; explains them and their myriad limitations clearly; makes sure they have some relationship to reality; and brackets them with 90% or 95% confidence bands, just as with standard scores

____ Follows scoring instructions exactly as described in the test manual, and, when in doubt, obtains a second opinion or asks the test publisher for clarification

In the interpretation of evaluation results, the evaluator:

____ Clearly distinguishes among different tests, clusters, factors, subtests, and scores even when they have similar titles (e.g., "reading comprehension" is not the same skill on different reading tests)

____ Explains with words and figures all statistics used in the reports

____ Explains the differences among statistics for the different tests

____ Explains the names (e.g., "below average") for statistics reported

____ Explains the differences among different names for the same scores on various tests included in the reports

____ Distinguishes clearly between findings and implications

____ Explains the disabilities and programs, not merely the tests

____ Demonstrates a reasoned, clinical judgment, rather than simply an exercise in arithmetic, when diagnosing a disability

____ Offers specific recommendations and gives a rationale for each

____ Eschews boilerplate reports

____ Detects and rejects unvalidated computer software

____ Uses computer reports to help interpret data and plan reports rather than simply including or retyping the actual printouts in reports

____ Recognizes that students' skills in related areas may differ dramatically and unexpectedly

____ Explains the mechanism of the disability

____ Reports genuinely germane observations from sessions while at the same time recognizing that the behaviors may be unique to a particular session

____ Pays attention to the reported observations

____ Considers practice effects when tests are readministered

____ Appraises the entire pattern of the student's abilities, not merely his/her weaknesses

____ Revisits the verbatim record of the student's actual responses before accepting "canned" interpretations from the manual, handbook, or computer printout

____ Bases conclusions and recommendations on multiple sources of convergent data

____ Understands and explains the limitations of norms, especially grade equivalents, for populations differing markedly from the norm sample

____ Has a thorough understanding of standard scores and percentile ranks

____ Keeps up with the field and checks interpretations with other professionals

____ Applies principles of test theory and test interpretation

____ Avoids interpretation beyond the limits of the test

[1]Dumont, R., & Willis, J. O. (2003). Issues regarding the supervision of assessment. *Clinical Supervisor, 22,* 159–176. Reproduced with permission from R. Dumont and J. Willis.

12

Supervising Services That Enhance Wellness, Social Skills, Mental Health, and Life Competencies

Students' emotional regulation, social skills, and mental health directly impact their academic performance.

Vignette 12.1

Herberto, a school psychologist, was startled when **Phil** stormed into his office, threw his books and jacket across the room, and angrily shouted, "I am definitely quitting school!" A 16-year-old freshman with increasing emotional volatility and behavior problems, Phil had just learned that he had not earned sufficient credits to advance to sophomore standing. He was overage because he had already been retained in the third and seventh grades. Presuming this lack of progress was due to multiple moves (seven schools!) and lack of consistent education, student development teams had never found

(Continued)

(Continued)

> Phil eligible for special education services. Phil's school records suggested concerns about behavior and mental health issues stemming from elementary years, but his parents insisted that no counselor had ever been able to help anyone in their family and refused to take Phil to a "pill-throwing shrink." Parental attempts to deal with Phil's problems had been limited to taking him for "rose oil" therapy. Herberto was anxious to help, as he was afraid the teenager was about to make an irrevocable, life-changing mistake.

In addition to providing academic instruction, schools and school psychologists must attend to students' social skills, mental health, and wellness in order to ensure both academic progress and eventual successful adult functioning. Going beyond traditional individual counseling and consistent with the public health model, these services encompass prevention, assessment, intervention, and progress monitoring. They can be provided at any level of service delivery: *universally* to the general population, to *targeted* students in small groups, or to identified individuals or groups receiving *intensive* interventions. This chapter addresses the supervision of these services.

BASIC CONSIDERATIONS

Providing services that enhance students' social skills, behavior, and mental health is a primary function of school psychological services (Ysseldyke et al., 2006). *Primary* (Tier I) prevention programs "seek to change the incidence of new cases by intervening proactively *before* disorders occur" (Hightower, Johnson, & Haffey, 1995, p. 311). *Secondary* (Tier II) prevention addresses "early identification and intervention before problems become severe" (Franklin & Duley, 2002, p. 152). Finally, *tertiary* (Tier III) programs assist the group or individual already identified. Examples relevant to mental health, social skills, and positive behavior development include:

- Tier I: schoolwide and classroomwide prevention programs; positive discipline approaches as well as organized and well-managed classrooms (see www.pbis.org); early identification and treatment of aggression, social isolation, and bullying; social skills instruction for all students
- Tier II: 10- to 20-week intervention programs using behavioral consultation and problem solving for targeted groups and individuals; progress monitoring for participants; crisis intervention
- Tier III: ecological assessment for eligibility determination when appropriate; intensive, sustained special education services employing applied behavior analysis; cognitive-behavioral therapy for anxiety and depression

PREVENTION PROGRAM DEVELOPMENT

Effective school psychologists help design and implement prevention and intervention programs to promote student wellness and resiliency. They help school personnel and parents foster social and life skills and develop challenging but achievable behavioral, affective, and adaptive goals for all students. They also provide leadership in promoting instructional environments that reduce alienation and in which all members of the school community accept diversity and treat one another with respect.

In implementing successful prevention programs, specific steps are followed. These include identifying needs; reviewing extant prevention programs; introducing the program to the system by engaging in professional small talk and making the initial presentation; determining aspects of the program (size, participants, communication system, support structure, integration into the school structure); implementing the program with adequate personnel, supports, and processes; and conducting an evaluation of the program (Hightower et al., 1995).

Needs Assessments and Obtaining Administrative Support

In implementing a prevention program, a high-quality needs assessment is critical. This ensures that the prevention program is responding to a real need and is positioned to obtain administrative support. As Nagle (1995) said, a needs assessment involves determining a gap between a current condition and a desired state.

> In comprehensive needs assessment, once these gaps or needs are identified, the evaluator must also identify and assess existing school and community services and other resources to meet those needs, develop priorities among identified needs, and determine which services should be maintained, altered, or newly developed. (p. 265)

The level of analysis can be as broad as the entire district or as narrow as a classroom. As discussed in Chapter 5, steps in conducting a needs assessment include identifying the problem, establishing an evaluation team, obtaining administrative support, collecting qualitative and quantitative data (using survey questions, interviews, and group assessment tools), analyzing the data, sharing results, and collaboratively developing recommended program modifications.

Selecting Evidence-Based Programs

It is critical that prevention programs be supported by empirical research, monitored on an ongoing (formative) basis, and summatively evaluated regarding outcomes. Fortunately, a number of prevention programs that promote social development and wellness have been identified as effective. These include positive behavior intervention systems, violence and bullying prevention programs, and parenting education programs (see Chapter 5). Ultimately, all prevention programs must be evaluated in terms of four questions (Sugai & Horner, 2006):

1. Is the practice *effective*? What is the likelihood that the desired effects or outcomes will be achieved with the practice?

2. Is the practice *efficient*? What are the costs and benefits of adopting and sustaining the practice?

3. Is the practice *relevant*? Does a contextual fit exist among the practice, the individuals who will use the practice, and the setting or culture in which the practice will be used?

4. Is the practice *durable*? What supports are needed to ensure accurate and sustained use of a practice over time? (p. 248)

Positive Behavior Intervention Systems

It is painfully evident that punitive, "get-tough" discipline policies tend to be ineffective with many students who display inappropriate behavior, and we should be concerned about exclusive reliance on punitive approaches such as suspensions, expulsions, and "zero-tolerance" policies (H. M. Walker & Shinn, 2002). In contrast to traditional, punitive measures, positive behavior intervention systems (PBISs) are *proactive* approaches to discipline that incorporate data-driven assessment and interventions and are based on the reinforcement of positive, prosocial behavior (Crone & Horner, 2003). They can be applied at four main levels: schoolwide, specific, classroom, and individual. Regardless of the level targeted, the goal is to prevent "challenging behavior through proactive interventions for the development of positive social and learning outcomes" (Hendley, 2007, p. 225). PBIS is an amalgamation of behavior-based practices and systems theory and is evidence based, flexible, and consistently monitored. Schoolwide positive behavior support (SWPBS) has been proposed "as a means of increasing the accurate adoption and sustained implementation of effective behavioral practices at the individual student, classroom, and school-wide levels" (Sugai & Horner, 2006, p. 245). However, it is important that the program be implemented as intended.

Vignette 12.2

Josephine's supervisee, **Lakisha**, was assigned to a school that had adopted a PBIS model to manage behavior. During a supervision session, Lakisha reported that the teachers were in an uproar about the program. During the past year it seemed to have completely backfired. A token economy system had been adopted, but the teachers were very frustrated because they were under the impression that they were supposed to be rewarding every instance of positive behavior. The record keeping had become unmanageable. Furthermore, students were stealing tokens from one another and older students were extorting them from younger students on the walk home from school. Josephine agreed to accompany her supervisee to the school and help her salvage the situation.

Violence and Bullying Prevention Programs

Dramatic incidents of school violence, although of national concern, remain relatively rare (Leff, Power, Manz, Costigan, & Nabors, 2001). In an effort to create safe and violence-free school environments, "school administrators, lawmakers, and prosecutors have recently 'cracked-down' on juvenile violence" (Bear, Webster-Stratton, Furlong, & Rhee, 2000, p. 1). "Crime and violence have invaded far too many of our nations' schools. Gunfights are replacing fistfights and crisis drills are replacing fire drills" (Stephens, 2002, p. 47). Lockdowns are common occurrences worldwide in high schools following myriad well-publicized incidents of school violence. Milder forms of aggression, such as bullying, are far more prevalent (Snell, MacKenzie, & Frey, 2002) yet ultimately harmful to both victims and perpetrator (Olweus, 1997).

Relational aggression has received recent attention as a type of bullying that may be as damaging as or even more damaging than aggressive physical, externalizing behavior (Macklem, 2003; E. L. Young, Boye, & Nelson, 2006). It is defined as "harm that occurs through injury or manipulation of a relationship" (E. L. Young et al., 2006, p. 297). Unlike a physical fistfight, relational aggression is especially hard to identify. Often subtle, covert, and indirect, relational aggression requires more subjective judgment.

To address these problems, preventative programs have been developed to target social skills development, anger management, self-management, and social perspective taking. Programs often include a parent component as well (Bear et al., 2000). Whether addressing violence, bullying, or relational aggression, interventions must be developed in a manner that ensures that effects reach "every area of the school and the community in which the school is located" (Macklem, 2003, p. 115). Ease of implementation and sustainability must also be considered. According to Furlong, Felix, Sharkey, and Larson (2005), some effective school violence intervention programs include the Anger Coping Program (Lochman, Curry, Dane, & Ellis, 2000), Second Step (Committee for Children, n.d.), and the Bullying Prevention Program (Olweus, 1997).

Another approach to reducing violence in schools is to teach adults effective methods of dealing with agitation, aggression, and violent acts of students. The beginning steps in nonviolent crisis intervention strategies can be taught to teachers, administrators, and paraprofessionals (e.g., cafeteria monitors) to forestall escalating adult-student confrontations.

Vignette 12.3

Marty, a school psychologist, has obtained certification as an instructor in nonviolent crisis intervention and provides ongoing yearly professional development for district personnel. With school personnel who are unlikely to need to employ physical interventions, such as general education teachers, she limits the training to verbal and nonverbal de-escalation techniques. With school personnel who are likely to be in situations where they are responsible for de-escalating physical altercations (e.g., assistant principals and paraprofessionals working in programs for students with behavior disorders), she teaches more comprehensive techniques and interventions. School personnel find these strategies extremely helpful in preventing small problems from escalating into much bigger problems.

ASSESSING SOCIAL, EMOTIONAL, AND BEHAVIORAL FUNCTIONING

When prevention programs are insufficient, Tier II and III programs are tapped. These initially require assessment of students' social, emotional, or behavioral functioning and then development of achievable social, emotional, and behavioral goals. As stated above, assessments can be provided at any of the levels of service delivery: *universally* to the general population, to *targeted* students in small groups, or to individuals or groups receiving *intensive* interventions.

Appropriate assessment of behavior and personality is multifaceted and encompasses the use of adaptive behavior scales, behavior observations, parent rating scales, projective techniques, self-report inventories, structured and semistructured interviews, teacher rating scales, *Diagnostic and Statistical Manual of Mental Disorders* (*DSM-IV-TR*; American Psychiatric Association, 2000) diagnostic criteria, behavioral diagnosis, and assessment of the school and family context.

Behavioral assessment has been strengthened through psychometric advances in self-report and parent and teacher rating scales. Structured and semistructured interview techniques are increasingly employed. Furthermore, substantial emphasis has been placed on considering the function of the student's behavior in the context where it occurs (Merrell, Ervin, & Gimpel, 2006). Projective techniques are currently viewed with disfavor due to their weak reliability and validity (Norcross, Karpiak, & Santoro, 2005). Personality assessment tools that have been discredited by research include the Bender Visual Motor Gestalt Test for personality assessment, anatomically detailed dolls for determination of sexual abuse, the Blacky test, the Hand Test, the Wechsler scales for personality assessment, the House-Tree-Person test, the Human Figure Drawing test, the Thematic Apperception Test, and office-based cognitive tests for assessment of attention deficit hyperactivity disorder (ADHD; Norcross, Koocher, & Garofalo, 2006).

The assessment of behavior and personality illustrates a difficulty in the intersection of education and psychology. School psychologists are under the guidance of the Individuals With Disabilities Education Act (IDEA; 1990) as educators and are trained in the *DSM-IV-TR* (American Psychiatric Association, 2000) as psychologists. These two sets of criteria do not always comfortably coexist, since there are important distinctions between medical and educational diagnoses. Unless the diagnosis adversely affects academic progress, a student cannot be considered "educationally disabled." This means that students without academic deficiencies who meet *DSM-IV-TR* criteria for depression, schizophrenia, or anxiety may not meet eligibility for special education programming. Furthermore, in the IDEA, the definition of "severe emotional disturbance" excludes students who are "socially maladjusted" unless they also meet criteria for "severe emotional disturbance." Psychologists working outside schools find these distinctions arbitrary and confusing, while psychologists working in schools are often frustrated in their quest to obtain appropriate support for students.

Furthermore, a number of diagnoses are particularly controversial because of easy confusion or frequent comorbidity with other disorders. Students might be diagnosed with attention deficit disorder (ADD) or ADHD when they are in fact suffering from post-traumatic stress disorder (PTSD), anxiety, or another condition. Similarly, students might be diagnosed with bipolar disorder when they are suffering from oppositional defiant disorder or PTSD. Furthermore, diagnostic criteria and common usage change with time. As G. A. Carlson (2002) pointed out, students who previously would have been diagnosed with early-onset schizophrenia, minimal brain dysfunction, or pervasive developmental disorder are now diagnosed with bipolar disorder. Supervisors are frequently asked for guidance in the interpretation and application of these diagnostic criteria.

Vignette 12.4

As a supervisor of school psychologists, **Kelly** was asked to create a separate special education program to address the growing number of students diagnosed with bipolar disorder. The district principals cited the students' overall affective volatility, potentially dangerous behavior, and "high maintenance" as evidence that it was not feasible to maintain the 10 students diagnosed with bipolar disorder in a regular education setting. They also stated that the school nurse was burdened with the frequent administration and monitoring of multiple, ever-changing medications. To help him determine essential program elements, Kelly visited successful day programs for similar populations, and ascertained that interpersonal therapy and cognitive-behavioral therapy were most likely to be effective.

Developmental considerations and a redefinition of the age at which bipolar disorder can be identified (G. A. Carlson, 2002) have contributed to the marked increase in diagnosed cases of early-onset bipolar disorder. Recently it has been generally agreed that "the patterns of illness and symptom definition described in children often vary from the classic description of the disorder in adult" and that "youths in community settings who present with outburst of mood lability, irritability, reckless behavior, and aggression are now receiving a diagnosis of bipolar disorder" (p. 108). To use evidence-based practices in treating this disorder in the school setting, school psychologists must turn to one of the two major treatments supported by empirical research.

Functional Behavior Analysis and Intervention

A functional behavioral analysis (FBA) is mandated by the Individuals With Disabilities Education Improvement Act of 2004 (IDEA 2004) to protect the educational rights of students as well as to afford them the opportunity to optimize their education. This mandate also seeks to provide secondary benefits to all students when classroom disruptions are eliminated or reduced.

FBA is a contextual analysis of behavior and is used to monitor students' progress in addition to serving as an assessment tool. It is a federally sanctioned means of providing efficient, cost-effective, purposeful, and evidence-based interventions. Effective FBA and interventions assist the student in substituting more acceptable behaviors for inappropriate behaviors. Interventions can include coaching, cognitive-behavioral therapy, behavior management plans, modification of the antecedents, or modification of the environment. A variety of methods have emerged to approach FBA (Watson & Steege, 2003), ranging from statistical analysis of direct assessment data to indirect collection of data (although Drasgow & Yell, 2001, indicated that legally challenged FBA cases typically involve reliance on indirect data). In conducting FBA and developing corresponding interventions, the following steps are taken:

1. Define the problem behavior in specific, measurable, and easily understood terms through interviews with the student and teachers. Also describe the circumstances that are thought to maintain the problem behavior. Prioritize problem behaviors according to an agreed-upon criterion (e.g., harm to self or others). Initially target the most critical behavior and focus on one undesirable behavior at a time. Consider how and when the student uses the behavior rather than words to avoid tasks, gain attention, make requests, or communicate feelings in unacceptable ways.

2. Develop testable hypotheses regarding the context, antecedents, and consequences that maintain the behavior. For example, hypotheses regarding incomplete schoolwork could be that the student (a) does not want to do the work, (b) spends very little time doing the work, (c) does not have enough help to do the work, (d) is resisting a change in work requirements, or (e) is being given work that is too hard (Daly, Witt, Martens, & Dool, 1997).

3. Test the hypotheses through additional interviews, observing the student in natural settings, and documenting occurrences, setting events, triggering antecedents, and consequences. Use interventions in hypothesis testing (e.g., the hypothesis that the work is too hard can be tested by giving easier work).

4. Develop a behavioral support plan that has strategies for replacing the defined problem behavior with the desired behavior. Write out the plan and obtain parental and student consent.

5. Teach socially acceptable words or behaviors that serve the same function as the undesirable behavior.

6. Implement the behavioral support plan for at least 3 weeks. If the plan is not effective, revisit the problem definition, regenerate hypotheses, and modify the behavioral support plan as appropriate.

7. When the plan is successful, transition to student-monitored practice. Ensure that the appropriate behavior has been generalized to all relevant settings.

8. With the student, appraise the success of the program.

There is no standardized tool for the assessment of functional behavior or for the formulation of behavior implementation plans, although Watson and Steege's (2003) book provides considerable guidance. In addition to its assessment function, which addresses the underlying purposes (i.e., functions) of specific behaviors exhibited by students, FBA is used to monitor students' progress (as evidenced by the above steps). It is a technique that "looks beyond the overt topography of the behavior, and focuses, instead, upon identifying biological, social, affective, and environmental factors that initiate, sustain, or end the behavior in question" (Quinn, Gable, Rutherford, Nelson, & Howell, 1998, p. 3).

The "competing pathways" visualization (O'Neill et al., 1997) is helpful because it clearly depicts antecedent behaviors and easily suggests (a) antecedent interventions that could be employed to diminish the problem behavior; (b) alternative, more appropriate behaviors that could be taught to the student to replace the problematic response; (c) methods of addressing the problem whenever it occurs to prevent the student from acquiring the secondary gains now being attained; (d) logical baseline and postintervention data to collect; and (e) the elements of a comprehensive behavior support plan. This is graphically portrayed in Figure 12.1.

Manifest Determination Reviews

More than 30 years ago, the U.S. Supreme Court addressed the question of due process rights and suspensions and expulsions from school in the case of *Goss v. Lopez* (1975). It was determined at that time that public education is, in fact, a property right granted by the Constitution. Hence, whenever a student is deprived of his or her right to attend school due to suspension or expulsion, detailed procedures must be followed to ensure due process. Such procedures include provision of oral or written notice of the alleged charges as well as an opportunity for the student to refute them and/or present an alternate viewpoint. As noted by S. Jacob and Hartshorne (2007), grounds for expulsion or suspension may vary by state but typically involve serious behavioral noncompliance; weapon- or drug-related offenses; acts of violence, theft, or vandalism; or

Figure 12.1. Competing pathways.

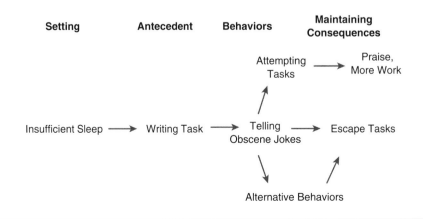

repeated use of obscene language. When students pose an imminent danger to themselves or others, they can be immediately removed from the school setting. In such cases, policies must be implemented as soon as possible, and this usually involves convening a group of interested parties to conduct a suspension/expulsion hearing. The school psychologists' specialized skills and knowledge can be critically important in such hearings.

Reflecting mounting concerns regarding in-school violence, the No Child Left Behind Act of 2001 (NCLB) requires states to craft expulsion laws regarding students who bring weapons to school. Often these laws mandate expulsion. However, considerable discretion is allowed school administrators to address such offenses on a case-by-case basis. Students with disabilities are treated very differently. They are accorded significantly more protection than their nondisabled peers in discipline situations. To prevent students with disabilities from unwarranted exclusion for behavioral infractions due to their disabilities, IDEA 2004 mandates specific procedures and policies.

The following material is intended to provide a cursory overview. It is not intended to represent legal advice or anything beyond a broad assessment of practices that may vary significantly from state to state. For more comprehensive treatment of this subject, the reader is referred to S. Jacob and Hartshorne's (2007) well-written and extremely pragmatic book, *Ethics and Law for School Psychologists.*

Students with disabilities can be excluded for periods of up to 10 days in a manner similar to nondisabled students. However, when the 10-day limit is reached, a manifestation determination hearing must be held to determine if the discipline infraction is related to the student's disability. Selected members of the individualized education plan (IEP) team must determine if the student can be reasonably held responsible for her or his actions. Obviously, this question can be extraordinarily difficult to answer for emotionally impaired students. If the team concludes that the student should be held accountable for the infraction, the exclusion (beyond 10 days) or change in placement can occur. Changes in placement can occur immediately (e.g., interim alternative settings) when safety issues arise, or they may occur only after a manifestation determination review. Provisions for appeal are provided in IDEA 2004, and, during the time that students are removed from school, their educational services must be provided in accordance with their IEPs. Similar rights regarding due process are accorded to students who have Section 504 (Rehabilitation Act of 1973) plans as a result of an identified disability, but they do not necessarily receive educational services during the period of exclusion.

Changing an educational placement or preventing access to the curriculum requires significant deliberation on the part of all involved. Students with disabilities are accorded specific protections, and even those who might possibly have a disability must receive procedural safeguards. For example, if there is an outstanding request for an evaluation, or if parents or teachers have expressed concerns about the possible presence of a disability, the student may have the same rights as those accorded to students who possess IEPs.

INTERVENTION DEVELOPMENT AND IMPLEMENTATION

School psychologists can provide specific skills training in a broad range of areas to foster social development, positive behavior, and emotional growth. At the universal, targeted, and intensive levels, effective school psychologists help school personnel and parents develop and apply methods to enhance appropriate student behavior, conflict resolution, and prosocial problem solving and decision making behaviors. They also help develop and apply sound principles of behavior change for targeted students as well as those in need of intensive interventions. To promote wellness, school psychologists help school personnel address diverse health issues, such as substance abuse, diet, eating disorders, autoimmune deficiency syndrome (AIDS) prevention, and stress management. Furthermore, they recognize and address the behaviors that may be precursors and manifestations of conduct disorders and internalizing disorders. Social-emotional-behavioral interventions include counseling (individual, group, crisis intervention), the implementation of behavioral management plans and functional behavior interventions, specific skills training (e.g., progressive relaxation), and parent training and support groups. Interventions may be prevention oriented (e.g., "friendship groups" for students new to the school) or may address specific identified issues (e.g., students dealing with divorce or chronic illness).

Social-emotional-behavioral interventions can be divided into those that are teacher mediated, parent mediated, peer mediated, self-managed, and pharmacological (Power, 2002). They should be developed, delivered, and assessed in a planned, sequential, and data-driven fashion that addresses the quality indicators identified by Upah and Tilly (2002) in the following steps:

1. *Problem identification,* composed of behavioral definition, baseline data obtainment, and problem validation

2. *Problem analysis*

3. *Plan implementation,* composed of goal setting, intervention plan development, measurement strategy implementation, and decision making plan development

4. *Program evaluation,* composed of progress monitoring, formative evaluation, treatment integrity verification, and summative evaluation

Selecting Interventions

Evidence-based practice in psychology is the integration of the best available research with clinical expertise in the context of patient characteristics, culture, and preferences (American Psychological Association, Presidential Task Force on Evidence-Based Practice, 2006). Interventions for mental and behavioral disorders that have been discredited through research include "angel therapy," aromatherapy, dolphin-assisted therapy, "scared straight" programs to prevent delinquency, and the original Drug Abuse Resistance Education (DARE) programs to prevent drug and alcohol abuse (Norcross et al., 2006). Such "interventions" are commonly the focus of the popular press, and school psychologists frequently encounter desperate parents who subscribe to such questionable practices. Supervisors will need to support their supervisees as they "promote what *does* work and avoid discredited practices to eradicate what does *not* work" (Norcross et al., 2006, p. 522).

A number of references summarize research on *effective* treatments. These include *Best Practices in School Psychology V* (A. Thomas & Grimes, 2008); *Interventions for Academic and Behavior Problems II: Preventive and Remedial Approaches* (Shinn, Walker, & Stoner, 2002); *What Works for Whom?* (Roth, Fonagy, & Parry, 2005); *Behavioral, Social, and Emotional Assessment of Children and Adolescents* (Merrell, 1999); and *Children's Needs III: Development, Prevention, and Intervention* (Bear & Minke, 2006). Weisz, Sandler, and Durlak (2005) reviewed research studies investigating the efficacy of treatments for social and emotional disorders and indicated that for some disorders, certain treatment methods were "well established" or "probably efficacious." These are included in Table 12.1.

Table 12.1 Evidence-Based Treatments for Social-Emotional Disorders (Weisz, Sandler, & Durlak, 2005)

Disorder	Well-Established Treatments	Probably Efficacious Treatments
Attention deficit hyperactivity disorder	Stimulant medication Behavioral parent training Behavioral classroom interventions	Social skills training with generalization components Summer treatment programs
Depression and related disorders	Interpersonal therapy	Cognitive-behavioral therapy Psychotropic medications
Generalized anxiety disorder	None identified at this time	Cognitive-behavioral therapy Modeling In vivo exposure Relaxation training Reinforced practice Family anxiety management
Oppositional defiant disorder and conduct disorders	Parent training based on living with children Videotape modeling Parent training	For preschool-aged children: • Parent-child interaction therapy • Time-out plus signal seat treatment • Parent training program • Delinquency prevention program For school-aged children: • Anger coping therapy • Problem solving skills training For adolescents: • Anger control training with stress inoculation • Assertiveness training • Multisystemic therapy • Rational emotive therapy
Separation anxiety disorder	None identified at this time	Cognitive-behavioral therapy Family anxiety management Modeling In vivo exposure Relaxation training Reinforced practice
Specific phobias	Participant modeling Reinforced practice	Systematic desensitization Cognitive-behavioral therapy

When helping supervisees decide on direct intervention strategies, a supervisor must consider the factors included in Table 12.2.

Table 12.2 Factors to Consider in Selecting Interventions

- The nature of the referral question, problems addressed, and student characteristics, including age, gender, ethnicity, and developmental level
- Knowledge, experience, and theoretical orientation of both the supervisor and supervisee as well as the level of supervision required relative to the severity of the problem and the development of the supervisee
- The prevailing resources and expectations of teachers, parents, administrators, and other professionals
- Ethical considerations
- Intervention plan development
- Methods and frequency of evaluating progress
- Methods of fostering generalization and transfer
- Need for follow-up and booster sessions
- Timing and process of termination

Counseling

Counseling is provided to facilitate change in students and their environments, including the family and school systems, to alleviate the distress of both the student and the referring adult, and to improve the student's functioning. Counseling children is impacted by the fact that they usually do not seek help voluntarily. Most do not have an understanding of the nature of the therapeutic experience, their cognitive and verbal skills are still developing, and they are more influenced by and dependent on their family and school environments (Corey, Corey, & Callanan, 2007). The last consideration means that, particularly with younger students, it can be more effective to work directly with the parents using well-established parent training methods (see Chapter 5) than to work directly with the child.

Providing counseling in schools can be challenging due to limitations on the school psychologist's time, insufficient privacy, and the demands of the school day on the student. On the other hand, school psychologists benefit from unique aspects of counseling students in schools, including easy access to teachers, peers, and the classroom, which can result in readily available feedback about progress, observable social relationships, normative comparison groups, and convenient long-term follow-up.

In today's schools, mental health needs are diverse and pervasive. With the many demands facing school psychologists, it can become difficult to provide individual services for all but the few students who have counseling written into their IEPs. To serve them well, it is important to have a treatment plan developed when the counseling begins and to monitor implementation throughout the period of service delivery. One such model, proposed by Tharinger and Stafford (1995), is provided in Table 12.3.

Counseling objectives must be clearly defined, exact, and measurable. A sample goal with objectives and evaluation techniques is included in Table 12.4.

Table 12.3 School Counseling Model (Tharinger & Stafford, 1995)

Stage 1: Assess appropriateness of referral for school-based counseling.

Stage 2: Plan for counseling and prepare goals.

Stage 3: Begin counseling and establish a working relationship.

Stage 4: Implement the plan for change.

Stage 5: Continue counseling and adjust the plan for change.

Stage 6: Plan for termination.

Stage 7: Evaluate effectiveness.

Table 12.4 Sample IEP Goal

Goal: Improve impulse inhibition and decrease talking out in class

Objectives:

- In the individual counseling setting, Joey will demonstrate the ability to use positive self-talk to gain control over his talking-out impulses.
- In the group counseling setting, Joey will covertly use positive self-talk and overtly use a cognitive-behavioral strategy (visual cueing) to inhibit talking out.
- Joey will decrease talking-out behaviors in class.

Schedule of direct services:

- Weekly individual sessions with a school psychologist lasting 30 minutes
- Weekly group counseling sessions with a school psychologist lasting 60 minutes

Evaluation procedures:

- Case process notes from individual sessions
- Log of talking-out incidents in group counseling
- Weekly memo to Joey's teachers asking them to note his progress
- Monthly observation to assess frequency of talking out

The appropriate counseling technique varies with the referral problem, the context, the experience and availability of the supervisee, and external variables such as space and materials available, expectations of the referring person, and student availability. Student variables include age, mental health needs, cultural and ethnicity factors, gender, and the presenting problem. The development and cognitive level of the student affects the choice of technique: Play therapy may be appropriate for some youngsters, but interpersonal or cognitive-behavioral therapy is preferred for older students.

Play therapy is often used with children under the age of 11, with the presumption that children in the stage of concrete operational cognitive development express themselves best through play with concrete objects. While widely used, its efficacy has been widely debated. A meta-analysis of 93 research studies regarding play therapy concluded that play therapy has an overall treatment effect of .80 when measured by outcomes such as behavior, social adjustment, self-concept, anxiety, family functioning, and adaptive behavior. Neither the site (school or clinic) nor the format (group or individual) resulted in significant differences. Play therapy was most effective when parents were involved and when 35 to 40 sessions occurred (Bratton, Ray, Rhine, & Jones, 2005).

Cognitive-behavioral therapy (CBT; Kendall & Hedtke, 2006; Merrell, 2001) is a well-studied treatment and can be effective with older children and teenagers. CBT focuses on changing negative cognitions and behaviors in order to improve mood. It also focuses on improving communication, problem solving, anger management, relaxation, and social skills. CBT is effective in either a small group or individual format.

Interpersonal therapy (Weissman, Markowitz, & Klerman, 2000) requires more advanced cognitive skills than either play therapy or CBT and can be effective for adolescents. It focuses on understanding and addressing relationship problems with family members and friends and is most often used in individual counseling.

A number of tools have been developed to help supervisors appraise counseling skills. J. M. Bernard and Goodyear's (2004) book *Fundamentals of Clinical Supervision* contains a kit of helpful tools. In addition, Handout 12.1 can be used to facilitate this process.

In addition, Handout 12.6, Professional Counseling Performance Evaluation, can be found at the end of this chapter. Handout 12.2 can also be used to assess counseling skills.

Group Counseling

Given time constraints, group counseling is often the preferred method of providing mental health services in the schools. In addition to efficiency, school-based counseling groups offer an effective way to address the presenting problems commonly found among school-aged students. Groups can foster social skills, and they also permit students to observe others wrestling with and solving the same issues they face.

Critical components in effective group work with students include selection criteria, developmental considerations, group stage characteristics, and outcome evaluation (Van Velsor, 2004). Before beginning a group, psychologists must, of course, obtain parental consent. Additional group-related issues that must be addressed by practitioners and by supervisors of school psychologists are:

- What is the age/grade range of participants? It is best to select group members who are close in age.
- How are they selected for inclusion in the group? Groups should be composed of students who share issues and developmental tasks. On the other hand, the group should be sufficiently balanced to make success possible. Also, students should be carefully chosen to provide one another a supportive peer environment.
- What size should the group be? More than eight members in a school-based group can be unwieldy unless there is a coleader, but optimal group size varies with the ages of the members and the targeted therapeutic issues.
- Which activities should be emphasized? As is fitting for their developmental and cognitive level, groups composed of preschool children are most effective when they utilize play, groups of elementary level students are most effective when they utilize activities with some discussion, and groups of secondary level students are most effective when they utilize discussion with some activities. Activities should be carefully selected, valuable learning experiences.

Handout 12.1

TREATMENT PLAN DEVELOPMENT
(Adapted from Mead, 1990)[1]

1. Problem definition

   - What are the desired outcomes as defined by the student, parent, and teacher?

   - What behaviors would each person like increased?

   - What behaviors would each person like decreased?

   - Write down the values, attitudes, or automatic responses that link the current status to the desired outcome.

   - Make sure that everyone agrees on definitions.

2. Assessment

   - What are the data?

   - What tools could be used to get additional data?

   - Are there patterns in the data?

   - Can the problem be solved by techniques already in the psychologist's repertoire?

   - If not, how could appropriate techniques be acquired?

   - Has the psychologist seen this or a similar problem before?

   - Is there a proven treatment for this or a similar problem?

   - Can the problem be restated or redefined to be more general or more specific, leading to alternative treatment strategies?

   - Can the desired outcome be modified?

3. Hypothesis development

   - What variables control the student's current behavior?

   - What variable may control the desired behavior?

   - How can the student change these variables?

   - How can teachers, parents, or peers change these variables?

   - Are there other contributing variables?

   - What new hypotheses might they suggest?

   - What conceptual framework is being used to tie the data together?

(Continued)

(Continued)

- Are there other conceptual frameworks that fit?
- What hypotheses do the data suggest?
- What theoretical principles are being used?
- What other theories might be used?
- What hypotheses do they suggest?
- What hypotheses can be eliminated based on current data?
- What additional data are needed to eliminate other hypotheses?
- Does this suggest an intervention or series of interventions?
- Write all possible hypotheses.

4. Intervention development
   - Write a proposed treatment plan with enough detail so that another psychologist could take over treatment.
   - Indicate criteria for success, criteria for failure, plans for gathering data and deciding treatment changes, and an estimate of time necessary to reach the desired outcome.

5. Intervention implementation
   - Make sure that the student finds each step to be related to the desired outcome.
   - Make sure that the steps are appropriate in size.
   - Make sure that formative data do not suggest altering the treatment.
   - Address transfer and generalization of skills.

6. Appraisal
   - Does the student think the desired outcome has been reached?
   - Do parents and teachers think the desired outcome has been reached?
   - Do data indicate that treatment made a difference?
   - Can the same result or method be used for some other problem?
   - Have the supervisee's skills improved?
   - Have the supervisor's skills improved?

---

[1]Mead, D. (1990). *Effective supervision: A task-oriented model for the developing professions.* New York: Brunner/Mazel.

Handout 12.2

EVALUATION OF INDIVIDUAL
PROBLEM SOLVING COUNSELING

Pupil _____ School _____ Age ____ Grade ____ Date Completed _____

	Very Inappropriate	Inappropriate	Adequate	Appropriate	Very Appropriate
Obtains permission for counseling following receipt of referral	1	2	3	4	5
Builds rapport	1	2	3	4	5
Leads pupil in exploring the problem	1	2	3	4	5
Confirms identification of the problem with the pupil	1	2	3	4	5
Establishes baseline	1	2	3	4	5
Leads pupil in exploring possible solutions	1	2	3	4	5
Leads pupil in evaluating pros and cons of each possible solution	1	2	3	4	5
Assists pupil in selecting a solution to try	1	2	3	4	5
Assists pupil in designing a solution plan	1	2	3	4	5
Obtains pupil's commitment to the plan	1	2	3	4	5
Assists pupil in monitoring plan implementation	1	2	3	4	5
Assists pupil in evaluating plan effectiveness	1	2	3	4	5
Conducts follow-up evaluation	1	2	3	4	5

- Who should facilitate the group? After teaming with an experienced practitioner and learning to use a well-established treatment manual, a well-supervised practicum student may be capable of independently leading an elementary adjustment group but insufficiently skilled to deal independently with seriously disturbed students. Even advanced practitioners often prefer coleading groups; a moderate-sized group of 10 students can benefit when one adult attends to processes and the other leads.
- What are the rules of the group regarding the time, place, and duration of sessions; confidentiality; attendance; goals; and so forth? How does the supervisee ensure that these rules are followed?
- What theory will underlie group topics and activities? What are the goals for each individual student? For the group?
- How will group stages be handled? During initial meetings, students tend to be anxious and uncomfortable about sharing. At this point, the leader establishes a group identity, clarifies roles, develops norms, and establishes a safe environment. During the middle stage of a group, students take greater responsibility and both comfort and challenge one another. During the termination stage, students may regress or act out in anticipation of the group's dismissal.
- How are goals determined and how is goal attainment measured?
- How will termination occur?

To help in planning group activities, supervisors must help their supervisees design interventions that meet both group and individual goals. Gayle Macklem (personal communication, September 2007) developed the Handout 12.3 Group Planning Sheet to facilitate this process.

After providing group counseling, it is important to assess the success of the process. Handout 12.4 can be used to appraise this success.

Progress Monitoring

After prevention and intervention programs are implemented, they must be monitored closely to ensure that they are delivered as planned. To that end, school psychologists help monitor treatment integrity as well as develop and implement methods to monitor student progress in order to ensure that the chosen intervention has the desired effect. Furthermore, it is important to continue monitoring long enough to ensure that transfer and generalization of skills has occurred. Otherwise, the student is likely to neglect to apply newly learned skills to new situations. These topics are addressed in greater detail in Chapter 4.

Crisis Intervention

Working with school personnel, students, parents, and the general community in the prevention and aftermath of crises constitutes a major challenge for school psychologists and their supervisors. Crises include diverse incidents such as suicide, death, natural disasters, murder, bombs or bomb threats, extraordinary violence, terrorism, and sexual assault. Although schools actually remain one of the safest places for students (Poland & Gorin, 2002), mounting concerns about overall school safety are apparent, especially in light of extreme violence such as in-school shootings. Creating school crisis response and

Handout 12.3

GROUP PLANNING SHEET

(G. Macklem, personal communication, September 2007)

Group and Date _____

Pragmatic Goals (Pertain to all children in the group but especially those with LD or ASD)	Behavioral Goals (Pertain to all children but especially those with ADHD, BD, or executive weaknesses)	Activities (Brief description of activities planned for the session, location, materials if needed)	Generalization (E-mail message with instructions to teachers, paraprofessionals, other specialists, parents)

Handout 12.4

EVALUATION OF SMALL-GROUP COUNSELING

School _____ Ages _____ Grades _____ Date Completed _____

	Very Inappropriate	Inappropriate	Adequate	Appropriate	Very Appropriate
Participates in needs assessment	1	2	3	4	5
Establishes the purpose and goal of counseling	1	2	3	4	5
Obtains permission for counseling	1	2	3	4	5
Participates in pupil selection	1	2	3	4	5
Plans counseling	1	2	3	4	5
Convenes the group	1	2	3	4	5
Establishes baseline	1	2	3	4	5
Implements counseling sessions	1	2	3	4	5
Monitors progress	1	2	3	4	5
Evaluates counseling effectiveness	1	2	3	4	5
Conducts follow-up evaluation	1	2	3	4	5

From the *2006 Handbook of the University of Dayton School Psychology Program.* Dayton, OH: Locally published monograph. Use of this material is by permission of the author, Sawyer Hunley.

safety teams provides a structured and valuable method of crisis intervention. Due to their knowledge and expertise, school psychologists are well suited for crisis team membership. No longer seen as a novel initiative, "plans for the provision of crisis services are expected to be in place, which means that school staff members must have the skills to undertake a variety of immediate and long-term crisis intervention tasks" (Brock, 2002, p. 5). They are most effective when they incorporate community members and agencies as participants (M. A. Young, 2002), and school psychologists are natural liaisons to these external agencies.

Fortunately, there is an emerging literature base and an abundance of available Web-based material regarding crisis intervention strategies. The PREPaRE curriculum (National Association of School Psychologists [NASP], n.d.) was developed to help apply evidence-based resources and consultation to school crisis prevention and response. PREPaRE provides training for school personnel in crisis preparation, prevention, intervention, response, and recovery procedures, with a special emphasis on the role of school-based mental health professionals. In addition, the NASP Web site (www.nasponline.org) contains valuable information that is updated in accordance with need. Web sites such as this provide more specific information than published manuals (on, e.g., responding to Hurricane Katrina). They also address "*postvention*" issues that are of critical importance to school psychologists, who are uniquely positioned to identify groups and individuals who may warrant special attention after a crisis. Supervisors of school psychologists have a responsibility to appropriate and manage services both *during* and *after* crises.

APPLICATIONS TO SUPERVISION

Many of the principles and techniques relevant to clinical supervision of mental health services are addressed in Chapters 7 through 10, since these practices and research foundations undergird clinical supervision. Supervising prevention programs, assessment processes, intervention implementation, and student progress monitoring to enhance wellness, social skills, mental health, and life competencies require that supervisors address all activities within these processes. Just as they do for services that enhance academic functioning, supervisors must ensure that these programs are executed appropriately, that assessment tools are administered properly, that psychologists offer appropriate recommendations for interventions, that student responses to interventions are monitored correctly, and that transfer and generalization of student skills is addressed. Competence cannot be assumed. As in all clinical supervision, good record keeping is invaluable. Both supervisees and supervisors should keep written records of supervision sessions, ensuing recommendations, and eventual results of the recommendations.

Supervisors should ensure that both they and their supervisees have adequate content knowledge to enhance students' mental health and wellness by assigning readings in any areas of deficiency. Supervisees should also have a deep understanding of the specific population with which they are working. To bolster their understanding of current learning theory and research, supervisees and supervisors can read the previously mentioned books or refer to previously mentioned Web sites describing evidence-based mental health practice.

Considering Supervisee Development

As discussed in Chapter 2, supervisors must modify supervision techniques according to the developmental level of the supervisee. Because the developmental level of the supervisee necessarily determines supervisory methodology and techniques, effective supervisors must be competent in addressing various skill levels. It is appropriate for supervisors to assign activities that recognize the needs of beginning practitioners (e.g., coleading social skills groups and dealing with less complex student adjustment issues). More experienced school psychologists should be able to deal with more complicated cases. Practicum students and interns require particular vigilance, and supervisors must have access to raw data such as audiotapes and direct observation. Supervision of interventions at this stage usually has an instructional, didactic focus (Haynes, Corey, & Moulton, 2003). Cases must be chosen carefully because student welfare is always of paramount importance.

Early career professionals should not be encouraged to engage in "high-stakes" counseling activities (e.g., addressing suicidal threats) without considerable support and monitoring (J. M. Bernard & Goodyear, 2004; Falender & Shafranske, 2004). Especially with noncredentialed supervisees, best practice dictates that supervisors *personally* assess and intervene if suicide is a concern; "supervisors cannot assume that supervisees have been adequately trained in suicide assessment and prevention" (Falvey, 2001, p. 100). Even after a supervisee has demonstrated adequate skills in individual and group supervision sessions, it is helpful to encourage peer supervision and ongoing self-evaluation.

Maintaining Ethical Practice

Informed Consent

Both legally and ethically, parents of school-aged children have a clearly defined right to determine whether their minor children participate in school-based psychological services (J. M. Bernard & Goodyear, 2004; Falender & Shafranske, 2004; S. Jacob & Hartshorne, 2007; Pope & Vasquez, 1998). Although emergency services are typically permitted without express parental consent for minor children, written consent should be obtained prior to initiation of either group or individual counseling services (S. Jacob & Hartshorne, 2007). School psychologists should also maintain a permanent, written record of such consent in the student's confidential records. Parents must be fully informed about the nature and intent of any interventions undertaken in the schools, and the student should also be kept informed about treatment goals and methods in a developmentally appropriate manner. Although students are not legally autonomous in their right to initiate or deny psychological treatment, it is clinically and ethically sound to involve them and to obtain their assent for treatment (S. Jacob & Hartshorne, 2007). For students with cognitive or emotional impairments, deliberate, ongoing attempts should be made to assure optimal understanding of the risks and benefits of any treatment (Hoagwood, 2003).

Issues of parental permission can be complex with adolescents under the age of 18. For example, when high school students self-refer for counseling, they may do so with the specific request that their parents not be notified. Prudence dictates that the school psychologist interview the student initially to determine the severity and nature of the presenting problems and then decide how to proceed. The right of minors to seek treatment without parental consent varies with local statutes and state laws, but is generally limited to specific medical concerns (Hoagwood, 2003; S. Jacob & Hartshorne, 2007). Therefore, it is essential for supervisors to be knowledgeable about applicable laws and to ensure supervisees' adherence.

As described in previous chapters, additional considerations must be taken with the work of interns and practicum students. Falvey (2001) recommended that five levels of informed consent be expressly considered when supervising interns and practicum students. It is best to obtain the client's consent to treatment by the supervisee; the client's consent to supervision of his or her case; the supervisor's consent to assume supervisory responsibility for the supervisee; the supervisee's consent to supervision with a given supervisor; and institutional consent to comply with the clinical, ethical, and legal parameters of supervision for the disciplines involved. Exemplars of recommended forms can be found at http://kspope.com.

Confidentiality

As discussed in previous chapters, supervisors are also responsible for ensuring that supervisees explain the limits of confidentiality during their initial meetings with parents and students in an open, clear manner. Both parents and students should know that three situations may obligate the school psychologist to break confidentiality: (a) parental permission for release of information; (b) "duty to protect" provisions, such as danger to self or others; and (c) mandated legal testimony. In addition, when using supervisory techniques that are intrusive (such as videotapes, audiotapes, and direct observation), parents should be informed and written records of their permission obtained. It is important to clarify the nature and purpose of supervision so that parents fully understand why and how information about their child will be shared (J. M. Bernard & Goodyear, 2004). It is also important to be aware that the presence of a third party, tape recorder, and so forth, may have an impact on performance.

One of the most difficult situations concerning confidentiality arises when evidence of sexual, physical, or emotional abuse emerges. It is essential that supervisors of school psychologists be vigilant in following both legal and ethical dictates. Statutes regarding the reporting of abuse must be honored within the appropriate time frames and with the appropriate written follow-up. Supervisors must ensure that their supervisees are aware that law supersedes the maintenance of confidentiality and that in school-based counseling the right of "privileged communication" cannot be typically invoked (S. Jacob & Hartshorne, 2007). Additionally, school policy often demands that principals (or designees) be concurrently notified when mandatory reports of suspected abuse are made to social service or legal agencies. Because these situations are usually highly charged and emotionally taxing, it is important to clarify expectations in advance. Similarly, it is important to provide follow-up, support, and postintervention when appropriate.

Supervising Prevention Programs

Supervisors should keep in mind that many school psychologists have not been trained in providing prevention programs and therefore will need considerable professional development and support in this area. To foster such development, it is helpful to incorporate knowledge of prevention programs in annual goals, sponsor attendance at workshops, and encourage supervisees to observe successful prevention programs in action. Finally, prevention programs are an ideal topic to be addressed in group and peer supervision sessions.

When developing and implementing prevention programs, it is often important for supervisors to take a systemic leadership role and assist supervisees in obtaining administrative support for the program. It can be particularly challenging to negotiate typical school system administrative bureaucracy. Supervisors will also need to provide support in selecting appropriate prevention programs. Hence, effective supervisors will stay abreast of developments in the literature and be prepared to pilot and initiate evidence-based prevention programs themselves.

As new expectations for programmatic development emerge, it becomes necessary for supervisors to help their supervisees research the data supporting program choices and examine, select, implement, and monitor prevention programs with a critical, educated eye. It is not sufficient to implement a plan based on the concept that it's been "somewhat successful in the past" and "seems" to work. Supervisees implementing a prevention program will require substantial emotional and consultative support throughout the implementation. Hightower et al. (1995) recommended developing a network to help supervisees "support, encourage, inspire, assist, reassure, and strengthen each other in the face of day-to-day operations and during occasional, and even formidable, complications" (p. 319).

Vignette 12.5

In Cherry Creek, Colorado, supervisor **Cathy Lines** (personal communication, November 2006) has helped develop building-based mental health teams staffed by school psychologists and social workers. Through prevention and early intervention strategies, the teams provide ongoing support for classroom teachers and administrators to help create safe, caring, and motivating school environments for all students. The intent is to develop student resiliency, support the development of life skills, and incorporate individual students' strengths into "success planning." Key elements include collaborating with staff, parents, and students; communicating with administrators and other school mental health teams; providing professional development and peer support for team members; and setting team goals and monitoring goal attainment. The psychologists meet regularly with one another to provide necessary support and encouragement.

Supervising Assessment

It is likely that supervisors will need to revisit standards mandating validity and reliability when facilitating supervisees' selection of tools to assess social, emotional, and behavioral issues, just as they need to do for cognitive and academic assessment as described in Chapter 11. Corporations publishing test materials certainly continue to develop and publish tests of questionable validity. Additionally, school psychologists may continue to use techniques of questionable validity that they learned in graduate school. Supervisors and practitioners must review and validate instruments in general, determine their appropriateness regarding specific referrals, and clearly state reliability and validity issues in psychological reports. Supervisors may be challenged to convince veteran supervisees to *stop* using invalid instruments with which they feel competent. Furthermore, interns can experience the very uncomfortable position of having a field supervisor who uses methods that they have been taught are inappropriate.

Helping supervisees to conceptualize cases and develop appropriate treatment plans is an essential supervisory task. After gathering data but before reporting the results, supervisees often discuss the results with supervisors. The Treatment Plan Development form, found in Handout 12.1, can be used both to facilitate supervisory sessions and as a tool in assessing supervisee progress.

Supervising Functional Behavioral Analysis

The same questions that guide the practice of FBA guide its supervision. There are several stages of FBA with which supervisees are likely to have the most difficulty. First, beginning school psychologists tend to have difficulty generating multiple hypotheses, particularly regarding the antecedents and consequences of behaviors. Another area that frequently poses difficulty is the collection of data during both the assessment and intervention stages. Meaningful data is collected in a scientific manner, requiring the ability to define behaviors discretely and to devote time to gathering data. Supervisees also need guidance in appropriately choosing and applying evidence-based interventions. Finally, the supervisor must provide support during the inevitable intervention modification that occurs throughout the implementation process. Supervisees often do not realize that behavioral interventions as first designed are rarely the interventions that are finally effective. Obviously, supervisees who have been previously trained in a behaviorist tradition need far less intense supervision than supervisees without such training.

Supervising Manifest Determination

The incredible complexity of manifest determination reviews mandates that supervisors be familiar with the general laws, special education laws, ethical codes, and state regulations that govern their particular state and district. In the opinion of the authors, these situations constitute a notable point of ethical and legal vulnerability and therefore demand the close supervision and support of supervisees. Moreover, it is probably wise to engage the assistance of the school's legal consultants in many cases.

Supervising Interventions

Supervisors should ensure that supervisees read relevant information before developing any treatment plan or attending supervisory sessions. *Every supervisee should have reference books regarding intervention techniques and methodology.* The body of knowledge is expanding so rapidly that attention and effort are required to keep current. This can be done by keeping up with professional publication offerings by either e-mail or mailing lists.

Supervising Counseling

There is considerable literature regarding the supervision of counseling. Readers might explore the Web site of the Association for Counselor Education and Supervision (www.acesonline.net) and the training and ethical guidelines for supervisors delineated by the National Board for Certified Counselors (www.nbcc.org). There are also a large number of helpful books, including *Clinical Supervisor Training: An Interactive CD-ROM Training Program for the Helping Professions* (Baltimore & Crutchfield, 2003); *Fundamentals of Clinical Supervision* (J. M. Bernard & Goodyear, 2004); *Counselor Supervision: Principles, Process, and Practice* (Bradley & Ladany, 2001); *Becoming an Effective Supervisor: A Workbook for Counselors and Psychotherapists* (J. Campbell, 2000); and *Clinical Supervision: A Competency-Based Approach* (Falender & Shafranske, 2004).

As discussed in Chapter 7, it is important for supervisors and supervisees to openly discuss the theories and models that undergird their practice. Reconciling conflicting theories or models is not insurmountable, but it does require conscious effort. Sharing a similar philosophical model with their supervisor is more important to supervisees than having the same professional identity (Townend, 2005). For example, a school psychologist supervisee with a behavioral orientation is more comfortable being supervised by a certified applied behavior analyst than by a school psychologist with a psychoanalytic orientation.

A number of tools can be used to monitor and support the development of counseling skills. Handouts 12.2 and 12.3 can be used to assess the competency levels of supervisees as they provide individual counseling. Another counseling supervision technique that appears to transcend theoretical orientation is microcounseling supervision. This approach enables supervisors to give specific and concrete feedback and results in demonstrable improvements (Russell-Chapin & Ivey, 2004). An effective tool is Russell-Chapin and Sherman's (2001) CD-ROM *Microcounseling Supervision: An Interactive Approach to Teaching Microcounseling Skills.* One component, the Counseling Interview Rating Form (CIRF), is used to provide structured and concrete feedback regarding discrete counseling skills throughout the entire counseling session. Phases include opening the session and developing rapport, exploring and defining the problem, problem solving and defining skills, action and confronting incongruities, closing and generalizing, and professionalism. Each phase has 3 to 18 specific behaviors rated by the observing supervisor. Each time the supervisee uses a defined skill, the supervisor notes a score on the CIRF (1 = used the skill without effect on the client; 2 = used the skill with mastery and the client responded as intended; 3 = the supervisee is teaching or modeling a new skill to the client).

Constructivist reflection is also an effective counseling supervision technique. Strong (2003) recommended the use of conversation analysis (analyzing details of conversations) and discourse analysis (identifying and analyzing forms of talk and interaction) to help supervisees recognize what they must do to reconcile communication differences between them and their clients. Conversation and discourse analysis can be particularly helpful in multicultural counseling, as misunderstandings can result in ineffective treatment. This approach is utilized in Activity 12.1.

Activity 12.1

Conversation and Discourse Analysis

1. Select a 5-minute portion of a counseling session to transcribe.

2. Analyze it according to the following categories (S. Friedlander, 1984):
   Topic shift initiation
   Topic-relevant act
   Terminating turn
   Other metacommunication
   Topic-relevant response
   Off-topic act
   Off-topic response
   Repair initiation
   Passing turn

3. Write a narrative describing what you learned from the exercise.

4. Check the transcript and analysis for accuracy

Supervising Play Therapy

Effective supervision of play therapy involves teaching, modeling, and encouraging responsive skills (Ray, 2004). Basic responsive skills include nonverbal skills (leaning forward, appearing interested, appearing comfortable, using a tone congruent with the child's affect, and using a tone congruent with the psychologist's response) and verbal skills (maintaining high-quality verbal responses, tracking the behavior of the child, reflecting and paraphrasing verbal responses, reflecting feelings, facilitating decision making, facilitating creativity, building esteem, and facilitating the relationship). Advanced skills include enlarging the meaning and facilitating the understanding of the child's play, identifying patterns in the child's play, connecting with the child even when she or he is rejecting or hurtful, and setting limits while simultaneously allowing the child to be self-directing by acknowledging feelings, communicating limits, and targeting an alternative. As Ray suggested, an effective supervision technique is to rate the supervisee on each responsive skill according to whether the supervisee demonstrates it "too much," "to an appropriate degree," "not enough," or "not at all." It is also helpful to convey specific examples and notate the psychologist's strengths and areas for growth (p. 41).

Supervising Behavioral Psychology

Behavioral psychology underlies cognitive-behavioral therapy, social learning theory, applied behavior analysis, and functional behavior analysis and intervention. All of these are characterized by the use of operationally defined target behaviors, evidence-based interventions that provide opportunities to learn more adaptive and socially appropriate behaviors, and outcomes measures that are empirically based and observable. As described in a classic paper by Kratochwill, Bergan, and Mace (1981), supervision is characterized by empirical evaluations using time series analysis in that "during supervision activities, school psychologists provide data documenting that their assessment and intervention efforts have some measurable and desirable outcome" (p. 435). Supervisee training focuses on incrementally increasing supervisees' adaptive behaviors and specific, objectively defined skills. Training components appropriately follow the steps shown in Table 12.5.

Cognitive-behavioral supervision, like cognitive-behavioral therapy, has been shown to be effective when it is systematic and includes consideration of both the behaviors of the supervisee and student outcomes (Milne, Pilkington, Gracie, & James, 2003). This systematic supervision uses a range of direct instructional techniques, including modeling; conducting role-plays; presenting cases; offering didactic information through texts, books, journals, courses, and seminars; viewing and analyzing videotapes of counseling sessions; giving corrective feedback; and providing specific directions (Milne & James, 2000). It can also be very helpful to participate in a self-change as described in Activity 12.2.

Activity 12.2

"Supervise" another professional as he or she designs a self-change project intended to change his or her behavior, following traditional problem solving steps and contracting. Implement the project and monitor your *own* behavior over a period of time. At least biweekly, consult with another person to appraise progress and modify the program as needed.

Table 12.5 Training and Supervision in Behavioral Psychology (Adapted from Kratochwill, Bergan, & Mace, 1981)

- Ability to apply ethical and legal principles
- Awareness of personal values, beliefs, and expectations
- Knowledge of theoretical and empirical literature regarding problematic behaviors, behavioral functioning, and behavioral interventions
- Knowledge of basic data analysis techniques
- Skills in analyzing and synthesizing information
- Skills in case conceptualization, problem identification, and intervention planning
- Skills in clinical judgment
- Procedural skills in implementing assessment and intervention techniques
- Interpersonal skills necessary for assessment and intervention implementation
- Communication skills sufficient to explain interventions and assessment rationales to students, parents, teachers, and paraprofessionals
- Communication skills sufficient to write appropriate reports, communicate student progress, and negotiate contracts
- Skills in developing adaptive student responses through relationship building, support, praise, and encouragement
- Skills in assessing student performance across multiple settings using multiple modalities (direct observation, self-report, educational report; informal measures and formal measures)
- Skills in obtaining repeated samples of student performance across time

Supervising Group Counseling

It is important to determine in advance which technique will be used to supervise group counseling. According to Van Velsor (2004), training supervisees to run groups should include observation of expert practitioners or videotape review, experiential activities such as role-plays, coleadership of groups, journaling, and supervised practice. To provide supervised practice, supervisors can become brief members of the group, observe the group, or listen to tapes. Often, beginning school psychologists greatly benefit from observing their supervisor model. Handout 12.4, Evaluation of Small-Group Counseling, can be used as an appraisal tool.

Supervising Progress Monitoring

The fundamental question in evaluating student progress is whether the goals and objectives of the treatment plan have been met. Consequently, considerable supervision time should be spent helping supervisees develop an adequate treatment plan, including evaluative methods, before an intervention is implemented. Student progress can be measured by observable behaviors, self-report measures of internal states such as anxiety and depression, or student outcome measures such as school attendance, grades, and achievement test scores. In determining which evaluation methods to use, care should be taken to ensure that these methods are congruent with both the referring problem and the selected intervention strategies.

When supervisors evaluate the progress of supervisees providing direct interventions, they should evaluate progress in specific, discrete skills. For example, supervisors should review raw data provided in observations or tape recordings to assess the supervisee's skill in developing a counseling relationship, generating hypotheses, evaluating the process and content of sessions, developing treatment plans, and implementing interventions. In addition, they should assess supervisee growth over time by comparing a sequence of treatment plan development forms, case process notes, and treatment plans.

Supervising Crisis Intervention

Supervising school psychologists must prepare for crisis situations from two perspectives. First, supervisors are responsible for the quality of the crisis intervention services provided by supervisees. Second, since supervising school psychologists are often leaders in the district, it is likely that others will seek guidance from them in developing effective crisis intervention plans.

Supervisors must be adequately prepared to respond to crises in a manner that is deliberate and predictable, reflects best practices, is grounded in theory, and is based on evidence-based principles. Effective supervisors should become familiar with the literature and ensure that the district is prepared for all eventualities. One critical supervisory task is to ensure that supervisees know where to look for guidance and materials (e.g., "facts sheets" for parents and teachers) during a time of crisis. Another task is to appropriately manage services both *during* and *after* crises.

Counseling very troubled students, such as survivors of child abuse, can be so difficult that it results in the counselor experiencing secondary trauma (Sommer & Cox, 2005). Supervisors must help supervisees in this situation "manage the resulting terror, horror, and trauma" (M. Walker, 2004, p. 173). To do so, supervisors must be sensitive when supervisees demonstrate

- Feelings of helplessness and powerlessness
- Difficulty talking about the case
- Feelings of isolation, alienation, and being "frozen"
- Sleepiness, inattentiveness, restlessness, or boredom
- Lack of emotional connection
- Feelings of sexual arousal
- Diffused boundaries
- Desire to rescue the client
- Unwanted recollections, dreams, or reexperiencing of the client's event
- Irritability and anger outbursts
- Difficulty concentrating, hypervigilance, or startle responses
- Signs of stress
- Fear and personal vulnerability

These experiences can be either worsened or ameliorated by supervision. They are worsened when supervisors do not give clear direction, waste time, talk about themselves, deny or ignore the supervisee's experience of vicarious traumatization, or shame or blame the supervisee in some manner.

Supervisees benefit when they are encouraged to share their own feelings and behaviors, describe their reactions to the client, and describe personal feelings regarding the client or supervision. They also benefit from a calming supervisory environment, being encouraged to take care of themselves, and having the phenomenon of secondary traumatization directly addressed. Thus secondary traumatization of supervisees is minimized by supervisors who (a) are sensitive and responsive to supervisees' conscious and unconscious experiences, (b) have a strong theoretical grounding in trauma therapy, (c) maintain a supportive supervisory relationship, and (d) routinely include educational components that address vicarious traumatization in training and supervision (Sommer & Cox, 2005).

Suicide lethality exists on a continuum, and one of the challenges any mental health professional encounters is determining where on this lethality continuum an individual is when he or she mentions suicide. When working with novice supervisees, supervisors appropriately take the teacher role as described in Chapters 1 and 2. In this role, they conduct close and live supervision. In this situation, supervisors help supervisees recognize clues that a student may be suicidal, conduct a suicide assessment, and implement district procedures themselves. Supervisors teach the supervisee to assess lethality (increased lethality exists with more detailed and concrete plans, increased levels in intent to follow the plan, deadlier and more accessible means, previous suicide attempts, and use of drugs or alcohol that might reduce impulse control). They also need to help supervisees deal with the strong emotional reaction evoked by suicidal students.

With more experienced supervisees, supervisors need to monitor supervisees' reactions to suicidal students and help them manage their emotional reactions to both the student's pain and the stress of dealing with bureaucratic organizations. They assist supervisees in becoming more autonomous but still must ensure client safety. When supervisees have extensive professional experience, they are more likely to be able to assess lethality and contextualize their role, but they still will need emotional support and ongoing supervision (McGlothlin, Rainey, & Kindsvatter, 2005). Furthermore, schools are responsible for keeping students safe. It may be that administrators will need to keep a student at school in order to provide a safe environment.

Vignette 12.6

The case *Armijo v. Wagon Mound Public Schools* (1998) involved the suspension of a 16-year-old male student. After making serious verbal threats toward a teacher, the student, Armijo, was immediately suspended and, at the request of the principal, driven home by a school employee. His parents were not contacted and no one was home when Armijo was dropped off. Distraught, he subsequently shot and killed himself. The parents later brought suit against the school and various staff members involved in the incident. Apart from the legal issues, important ethical considerations emerge for all school personnel. S. Jacob and Hartshorne (2007) explicitly stated that "parents should be notified if it is necessary to remove their child from school, and students who are suspended during the school day should not be sent home to an empty house" (p. 260).

Supervising Termination

Methods of terminating interventions enhancing wellness, social skills, and mental health vary according to the type of intervention. Some direct interventions, such as parent training groups or student groups tied to a report period, have a termination date determined at the onset. Others, such as ongoing counseling, have an indeterminate termination point and termination occurs over a period of sessions in which the student's progress is reviewed. Regardless, supervisors will need to help their supervisees design appropriate termination strategies.

In the classic counseling literature, discussions on termination focus on the extent to which the student's issues have been resolved, and termination is expected to occur naturally when evaluations suggest sufficient progress (Egan, 1990). In this era of managed care, school personnel can be better positioned than psychologists practicing in the private sector to postpone termination until adequate student progress has occurred. On the other hand, school psychologists are faced with the challenge of justifying ongoing interventions in the face of competition for students' time with school programs and curricular demands.

Furthermore, it is common for students to change schools and thus transfer from one school psychologist to another before problems are adequately resolved. Rather than termination, this should be considered bridging from one treatment provider to another. Bridging occurs when the student moves from one school to another, particularly from elementary to junior high or from the junior high to the high school. While sharing case process notes and treatment plans is essential, many students greatly benefit from bridging in which the "old" school psychologist personally introduces the student to the "new" school psychologist. A session in which both psychologists meet with the student and review progress and future goals and objectives is particularly beneficial. Handout 12.5 can help ensure that appropriate steps are taken.

SUMMARY

Good supervision that addresses the social, emotional, and behavioral functioning of students is critical. Services typically include assessment and interventions at three levels: universal interventions for the general population (primary), targeted interventions for small groups (secondary), and intensive interventions for individuals or groups (tertiary). Such services include evidence-based assessment, intervention development, progress monitoring, organizational consultation, and crisis intervention. The developmental level of the supervisee determines the appropriate supervisory methodology and techniques, particularly in high-risk situations.

Prevention programs are one means by which to provide social, emotional, and behavioral services to students. Violence and bullying prevention programs especially are becoming more widespread as concern increases about school safety; such programs target social skill development, anger management, self-management, and social perspective taking. When supervisors assist their supervisees in implementing prevention programs, attention must be paid to a high-quality needs assessment, evidence-based programming, obtaining administrative support, and program evaluation. Supervisors might also support their supervisees in implementing positive behavior interventions as an alternative to traditional punitive discipline methods.

The assessment of behavior and personality is multifaceted and encompasses the use of adaptive behavior scales, behavior observations, parent rating scales, projective techniques, self-report inventories, structured and semistructured interviews, teacher rating scales, *DSM-IV-TR* diagnostic criteria, behavioral diagnosis, and assessment of school and family context.

Supervisors assist supervisees in case conceptualization and developing, implementing, and monitoring appropriate treatment plans. Relevant tools include functional behavioral analysis, manifestation determination, individual and group counseling, crisis intervention, behavior management plans, functional behavior interventions, specific skills training (e.g., progressive relaxation), and parent training and support groups.

Handout 12.5

TERMINATION CHECKLIST

_____ I have terminated or transferred all individual counseling cases appropriately.

_____ Records of individual counseling cases are complete and current.

_____ When possible, I have communicated with the person who will replace me.

_____ I have had a supervision session dedicated to discussion of termination and transition issues.

_____ I have terminated all group counseling cases appropriately.

_____ Records of group counseling cases are complete and current.

_____ All counseling records are filed in a secure location.

_____ My supervisor is aware of where I have stored both hard copy and electronic records.

_____ My supervisor is able to access my records and has keys and/or passwords.

_____ All consultation cases have been terminated or transferred appropriately.

_____ I have followed the institutional computer technician's guidelines regarding how to "clean up" my computer.

_____ I have left behind contact information as appropriate.

_____ Protocols have been filed in a secure location.

_____ Personal notes and extraneous information have been culled from all records.

_____ I have checked all test kits to be sure that they are complete.

_____ New protocols are available and stored in a secure location.

_____ I have given my supervisor the passwords for scoring programs.

_____ I have removed personal items from the office.

_____ I have stocked the office with all necessary materials.

_____ I have changed my phone message to reflect departure.

_____ I have terminated my e-mail account.

_____ If desired, I have left a new e-mail address.

_____ I have e-mailed school staff to provide contact information.

REFLECTIVE QUESTIONS

Q12.1. What guidelines should school psychologists follow regarding informed consent and confidentiality?

Q12.2. What are the steps to providing a prevention program? What are the issues around which supervisees require supervision?

Q12.3. What are the issues and supervisor's role in the prevention of violence and bullying, including relational aggression?

Q12.4. How is the positive behavior support model different from traditional discipline? What are the supervision issues?

Q12.5. What are the challenges that school psychologists face in assessing behavior and personality? How do a school psychologist's training in education and training in psychology interact and conflict in assessment of students?

Q12.6. How is a functional behavioral analysis conducted?

Q12.7. What are some of the legal mandates and guidelines that school psychologists must follow?

Q12.8. What must a supervisor consider in determining direct intervention strategies and appropriate supervision methods?

Q12.9. What are the challenges of providing counseling in schools?

SUPERVISORY DILEMMAS

SD 12.1

After weeks of preparation and care in obtaining appropriate parental permission, your intern begins a fourth-grade boys' social skills group. Although she maintains that the group is going well, you immediately sense that she is nervous about the group and dreads meeting with them. After a few weeks, a significant conflict between the intern and the group seems to be brewing, and one day it develops into a confrontation. You pass by the door and observe your intern in a shouting match with several of the boys about whether they have to stay in the group. *What are the supervisory considerations? What should be done?*

Authors' thoughts: Hindsight, yet again, is 20–20! It is likely that the supervising school psychologist will recognize that the intern's observable anxiety and dread constituted a red flag. Now that the situation has escalated, immediate intervention is warranted. A number of options can be explored, ranging from coleading the group (probably the best option) to removing the intern from the task and finding someone else to lead the group. Perhaps most important, for the sake of the group participants, it is essential for them to experience a well-run, goal-oriented group. Establishing clear, enforceable ground rules is an essential initial step. This is a good opportunity for a "corrective experience" for all participants.

SD 12.2

As a supervisor of school psychologists, you hire a newly graduated, certified school psychologist to provide a full spectrum of psychological services at the high school. This school psychologist has received extensive training in dialectical behavior therapy (DBT; Hayes, Follette, & Linehan, 2004) during her internship and university training. She appears to be an advanced beginner in this approach. While you recognize that DBT can be quite effective with adolescents, your own training and experience is grounded in a more traditional interpersonal counseling approach. This advanced beginner psychologist clearly needs supervision in counseling cases, but you are not trained in this approach. *What are the supervisory considerations? What should be done?*

Authors' thoughts: A wonderful opportunity to learn from each another exists in this situation. When the theoretical approach or level of expertise of the supervisor is insufficient to meet the needs of the supervisee, it is important to mutually generate alternatives. One possibility might be for the supervisor to learn more about DBT while asking another person more familiar with this approach to provide supervision for counseling cases. At the same time, there is a mutual opportunity to share each other's approach to counseling.

SD 12.3

Parents of a 16-year-old boy signed permission for counseling sessions on a form that indicated that confidentiality would be maintained unless there was a danger to self or others. The father, however, feels that this restriction does not apply to him and calls your supervisee frequently to ask questions regarding the boy's progress. The boy is angry at his father regarding a number of issues but does not want the school psychologist to discuss them with the father. Your supervisee is uncertain about what to say to the father, feeling conflicted between wanting to respect the boy's wishes and attempting to help the father and son resolve their conflicts. *What are the supervisory considerations? What should be done?*

Authors' thoughts: Confidentiality issues are always challenging and demand walking a fine line that keeps the well-being of the student paramount. Before beginning, it is important to discuss the limits of confidentiality and clearly spell out any limitations. Although minors legally have no right to confidentiality, the therapeutic relationship is likely to be ineffective when it is breached. On the other hand, the importance of parental support cannot be underestimated, and some contact with the curious father is necessary. Providing reassurance and perhaps framing the son's need for privacy as a step in his development will be useful. An important goal of counseling may be to help the student and parent establish more open lines of communication. For example, in the supervisee's work with the son, she might discuss with him what material he *can* share with his father. The father must be reassured that it is in his son's best interest to sustain a relationship of mutual trust with the therapist.

SD 12.4

A school psychologist has been hired through regular education funds to work on a full-time basis at an elementary school. To overcome the delays and hassles associated with obtaining permission for provide counseling and consultation services, he has sent a letter to all parents indicating that individual and group counseling is now available to all students. He has requested that parents notify him if they wish to discuss such services prior to any individual contact with their children. *What are the supervisory considerations? What should be done?*

Authors' thoughts: Obtaining consent for treatment must be an active ("opt-in") process rather than a passive ("opt-out") one. Clearly, the failure to obtain appropriate consent for treatment is an ethical and legal violation. The funding distinction between regular and special education has no bearing on the rights of students and their parents. Additionally, the consent of the student should be sought in a developmentally appropriate manner. In this scenario, immediate corrective action is warranted.

SD 12.5

You have been informed by one of your supervisees (who is a seasoned and highly competent practitioner) that a serious problem may be developing in the high school. One of the adolescent boys he has worked with for 2 years has just returned from a hospitalization due to a serious suicide attempt. It is questionable if the public school setting will be appropriate, but all parties involved have agreed to give it a try. When determining what measures could be established to provide optimal safety, the team addressed the student's tendency to leave the classroom without permission. In the past, after he left the classroom the teacher would notify the office and they would produce an "all-call" announcement on the intercom. The student would respond to the all-call announcement and return. However, the principal has informed you that he will no longer permit any such announcements, since they may be distracting to the other students. Moreover, the principal feels that singling out the student in such a manner betrays confidentiality. *What are the supervisory considerations? What should be done?*

Authors' thoughts: School psychologists must always protect the rights of students in every manner possible, including maintaining confidentiality. This becomes difficult at times, particularly around safety issues, when the costs and benefits of a particular plan must be weighed carefully. While an announcement can't be made discreetly, care can be taken to make it in such a way that it does not advertise why the student is being asked to return. If this plan has worked in the past, it likely makes the student feel safe. Distraction of the other students may be a small price to pay for keeping this student safe. It may be advisable to educate the principal and other staff regarding some basic suicide facts. Importantly, when a situation of this magnitude arises, one must really question the appropriateness of the placement.

Handout 12.6

PROFESSIONAL COUNSELING PERFORMANCE EVALUATION

Supervisee _____ Semester/Year _____
Supervisor/Faculty _____ Course _____

<u>Rating Scale</u>

N = No opportunity to observe

0 = Does not meet criteria for program level

1 = Meets criteria minimally or inconsistently for program level

2 = Meets criteria consistently at this program level

COUNSELING SKILLS AND ABILITIES				
1. The supervisee demonstrates the ability to establish relationships in such a manner that a therapeutic working alliance can be created.	N	0	1	2
2. The supervisee demonstrates therapeutic communication skills, including the following: a. Creating appropriate structure—setting the boundaries of the helping frame (parameters for meeting time and place, time limits, etc.) and maintaining these boundaries throughout the work	N	0	1	2
b. Understanding content—the primary elements of the client's story	N	0	1	2
c. Understanding context—the uniqueness of story elements and their underlying meanings	N	0	1	2
d. Responding to feelings—identifying client affect and addressing those feelings in a therapeutic manner	N	0	1	2
e. Congruence—genuineness, external behavior consistent with internal affect	N	0	1	2
f. Establishing and communicating empathy—taking the perspective of the client without overidentifying, communicating this experience to the client	N	0	1	2
g. Nonverbal communication—effective use of head, eyes, hands, feet, posture, voice, attire, etc.	N	0	1	2
h. Immediacy—staying in the here and now	N	0	1	2
i. Timing—responding at the optimal moment	N	0	1	2
j. Intentionality—client responds with a clear understanding of the therapist's therapeutic intention	N	0	1	2
k. Skillful self-disclosure, carefully considered for a specific therapeutic purpose	N	0	1	2
3. The supervisee demonstrates awareness of power differences in the therapeutic relationship and manages these differences therapeutically.	N	0	1	2
4. The supervisee collaborates with the client to establish clear therapeutic goals.	N	0	1	2
5. The supervisee facilitates movement toward client goals.	N	0	1	2
6. The supervisee demonstrates the capacity to match appropriate interventions to the presenting client profile in a theoretically consistent manner.	N	0	1	2
7. The supervisee creates a safe clinical environment.	N	0	1	2
8. The supervisee demonstrates analysis and resolution of ethical dilemmas.	N	0	1	2
PROFESSIONAL RESPONSIBILITY				
1. The supervisee conducts himself/herself in an ethical manner.	N	0	1	2
2. The supervisee relates to peers, professors, supervisors, and others in a manner consistent with stated professional standards.	N	0	1	2

3. The supervisee demonstrates sensitivity to real and ascribed differences in power between himself/herself and others and does not exploit or mislead other people during or after professional relationships.	N	0	1	2
4. The supervisee demonstrates application of relevant legal requirements.	N	0	1	2
COMPETENCE				
1. The supervisee recognizes the boundaries of his/her particular competencies and the limitations of his/her expertise.	N	0	1	2
2. The supervisee takes responsibility for compensating for his/her deficits.	N	0	1	2
3. The supervisee takes responsibility for ensuring client welfare when encountering the boundaries of his/her expertise.	N	0	1	2
4. The supervisee provides only those services and applies only those techniques for which he/she is qualified by education, training, and experience.	N	0	1	2
5. The supervisee demonstrates sufficient cognitive, affective, sensory, and motor capacities to respond therapeutically to clients.	N	0	1	2
MATURITY				
1. The supervisee demonstrates appropriate self-control (such as anger and impulse control) in relationships with supervisors, faculty, peers, and clients.	N	0	1	2
2. The supervisee demonstrates honesty, fairness, and respect for others.	N	0	1	2
3. The supervisee demonstrates an awareness of his/her own belief systems, values, needs, and limitations and the effects of these on his/her work.	N	0	1	2
4. The supervisee demonstrates the ability to receive, integrate, and utilize feedback from peers, teachers, and supervisors.	N	0	1	2
5. The supervisee exhibits appropriate levels of self-assurance, confidence, and trust in his/her own ability.	N	0	1	2
6. The supervisee follows professionally recognized conflict resolution processes, seeking to informally address the issue first with the individual(s) with whom the conflict exists.	N	0	1	2
INTEGRITY				
1. The supervisee refrains from making statements that are false, misleading, or deceptive.	N	0	1	2
2. The supervisee avoids improper and potentially harmful dual relationships.	N	0	1	2
3. The supervisee respects the fundamental rights, dignity, and worth of all people.	N	0	1	2
4. The supervisee respects the rights of individuals to privacy, confidentiality, and choices regarding self-determination and autonomy.	N	0	1	2
5. The supervisee respects cultural, individual, and role differences, including those due to age, gender, race, ethnicity, national origin, religion, sexual orientation, disability, language, and socioeconomic status.	N	0	1	2

Comments:

Adapted from the Professional Counseling Performance Evaluation created by the Texas State University–San Marcos Counseling Program faculty. Cited in Kerl, S. B., Garcia, J. L., McCullough, C. S., & Maxwell, M. E. (2002). Systematic evaluation of professional performance: Legally supported procedure and process. *Counselor Education and Supervision, 41,* 321–332. Revised July 7, 2005. Reprinted with permission of John Garcia.

PART III

Administrative Supervision

13

Leading and Managing

Hopefully, supervisors are both leaders and managers. As Warren Bennis says, managers empower others to carefully and accurately climb a ladder, while leaders ensure that the ladder is leaning against the correct wall.

Vignette 13.1

Pauline, a speech and language pathologist, assumed a position as a special services coordinator in which she supervised the district school psychologists along with other specialists. She found that throughout the district, counseling was provided in the secondary schools but not in the elementary schools. Districtwide, there was a lack of prereferral interventions, intervention monitoring, and crisis intervention. The school psychologists, Pauline, and her supervisor collaboratively decided to expand the role of school psychologists to include these tasks. The school psychologists became permanent student development team members in each building and coordinated prevention, early intervention, and crisis intervention programs. They supervised paraprofessionals' collection of academic and behavioral data, analyzed the data, and helped modify interventions. They also instituted bullying prevention programs and small group counseling in the elementary schools. They found time to complete these tasks by reducing reevaluation complexity, streamlining reports, and reducing time spent on filing, copying, and preparing mailings by delegating these tasks to office staff and paraprofessionals.

Effective supervision of psychological services requires both leadership and management. In the above scenario, Pauline provided both. She led by evoking a vision that shaped services and by developing a unified team. She managed by providing the structures needed to make the vision a reality.

This chapter addresses leadership and management skills relevant to supervision of school psychological services as a whole. It focuses on leadership and strategic management, decision making, and facilitating change.

LEADERSHIP

Effective leaders orient a group toward goals, make decisions, initiate change, solve conflicts, and mobilize others to face and meet difficult challenges. As Bennis (2007) indicated, exemplary leaders "create a sense of mission, they motivate others to join them on that mission, they create an adaptive social architecture for their followers, they generate trust and optimism, they develop other leaders, and they get results" (p. 5). While leaders are often high achievers, not every high achiever is a leader. Leaders have strong social skills that "influence other by establishing a direction for collective effort and managing, shaping, and developing the collective activities in accordance with this direction" (Zaccaro, 2007, p. 9).

Leadership is not the same as management. As noted at the beginning of the chapter, Bennis (1994) differentiated the two by indicating that managers empower others to carefully and accurately accomplish tasks while leaders ensure that the appropriate tasks are being completed. Both leadership and management are essential. "Strong management with no leadership tends to entrench an organization in a deadly bureaucracy. Strong leadership with no management risks chaos; the organization might walk off a cliff" (Kotter, 1999). A manager (i.e., administrative supervisor) may or may not be a leader. Furthermore, leaders may or may not be managers. In the most favorable scenario, supervisors are both effective leaders and effective managers, as depicted in Figure 13.1.

Leadership Characteristics

Burns (1978) identified leaders as transactional, transformative, or laissez-faire. Vroom and Jago (2007) added contingency (contextual) leadership as a fourth type.

Transactional leaders focus on basic needs and extrinsic reinforcers. To improve performance, they barter salary and benefits with employees. They also "manage by exception," reprimanding supervisees for errors rather than focusing on positive contributions. Such leaders can be autocratic, unilateral decision makers, control seeking, and likely to ignore feedback (Corrigan, Garman, Lam, & Leary, 1998). Supervisors of this type focus on translating the desires and objectives of upper administration to supervisees and act as a buffer between the two groups. This approach assumes that supervisees by nature are lazy, lack

Figure 13.1. Relationships of leadership to supervision/management.

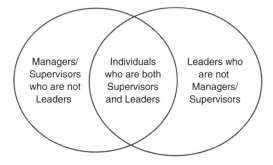

From Harvey, V. S., & Struzziero, J. A. (2000). *Effective supervision in school psychology.* Bethesda, MD: National Association of School Psychologists. Copyright © 2000 by the National Association of School Psychologists, Bethesda, MD. Use of this material is by permission of the publisher, www.nasponline.org.

ambition, prefer to be led, are self-centered, resist change, are indifferent to the needs of the organization, and need strict guidance (McGregor, 1966).

As Sergiovanni and Starratt (2007) explained, often "scientifically" managed schools employ transactional leadership. They focused on controlling supervisees, meeting administrative goals and performance objectives, and increasing efficiency. A typical scenario involves (a) identifying the best way to accomplish a task, (b) developing systems based on the "best way," (c) communicating expectations to supervisees, (d) training supervisees in the system, and (e) monitoring and evaluating supervisees to ensure that they are complying with the "best way."

Vignette 13.2

Seaside City Schools are infused with transactional leadership. The superintendent is highly controlling of principals, and the manner in which he treats the principals is reflected in the manner in which the principals treat the teachers and, in turn, the manner in which the teachers treat the students. The teachers are required to follow scripted curricula and forbidden to deviate from those scripts, even when they know it is in the best interest of the student. This transactional focus became even more pronounced with increased concern about making annual yearly progress (AYP), as teachers have been instructed to "teach to" the high-stakes test.

In contrast, *laissez-faire* leaders do not ensure adequate supervision or program monitoring. They avoid problems and tough decisions. This type of leadership results in insufficient attention to outcomes and neglect of supervisees (Sergiovanni & Starratt, 2007).

Vignette 13.3

The school psychologists in **Lakeside School District** experience laissez-faire leadership. They do not receive clinical supervision and their administrative supervisors—the principals—leave them to their own devices because they do not know how to supervise them. Some school psychologists thrive—those who have high levels of self-regulation, maintain a "constantly learning" approach, and are active in professional organizations. Others, however, experience professional stagnation and subsequent burnout.

Transformative leaders develop and share an idealized vision with supervisees, initiate structures needed to realize that vision, call to others' higher-order needs through inspirational motivational and intellectual stimulation, and unify teams in the pursuit of clearly defined goals. Transformational leaders foster each individual's strengths. This type of leadership is sometimes called *charismatic*, with the understanding that such leaders reframe problematic situations in a manner that makes sense, encourage the application of meaningful solutions, and elicit followers' trust (Avolio, 2007). Transformational leadership is most closely associated with the human resource approach to management. In this model, the goals of the individual and the goals of the organization are integrated and addressed simultaneously. Supervisors develop organizational structures that align supervisees' personal goals with the goals of the larger organization (Sergiovanni & Starratt, 2007). Supervisors take an integrative rather than a buffering role between administrators and supervisees.

Vignette 13.4

Special education director **Barry** served as a transformational leader for his supervisees, the school district, and the state in which he worked. His enthusiastic attitude that "We can make a difference for *all* kids" was so contagious that it spread to the general education administrators and resulted in meaningful collaboration between general education and special education staff and programs. While attentive to the students' needs and the entire school district, Barry also encouraged each individual supervisee to work in the schools and programs that best matched their strengths and interests. Thus Barry focused on and unified others in meeting both the needs of students throughout the district and the needs of individual employees.

Of these three types, transformational leaders are the most successful. Transformational leadership is recommended in school settings (Sergiovanni & Starratt, 2007), is preferred by mental health personnel (Corrigan et al., 1998), is correlated with successful outcomes (Mary, 2005), and results in increased job satisfaction and commitment (Jaskyte, 2003). Transformative leadership appears to be critical in getting supervisees to be willing to adopt evidence-based practice, because it engenders positive attitudes and helps mitigate the stress involved in change (Aarons, 2006).

To some extent, transformational leadership is thought to depend on personal traits of the leader, since some traits make it more likely that an individual will emerge as a leader across situations (O'Mahen & Sloan, 2000). These include cognitive abilities, creativity, personality, values, and motives. Other traits are situation specific and may result in a given individual being a leader in one situation but not in another. Situation-specific traits include domain-related knowledge and expertise, problem solving skills, and social skills (Zaccaro, 2007).

According to Bennis (2007), the most important leadership trait is adaptive capacity, or resilience, that results from "crucible experiences" such as transformative adversity. Adaptive capacity is a function of cognitive complexity, emotional intelligence, metacognitive skills, openness, social intelligence, and tolerance for ambiguity (Zaccaro, 2007). It can be expressed in three ways: adapting to suit the environment, shaping the environment to meet one's own needs, or leaving an unsuitable environment and selecting a new environment in which to work (Sternberg, 2007, p. 38).

On the other hand, leader effectiveness is mediated by the situation in which the leader works. Despite the common tendency to attribute school district success to superintendents, corporate success to chief executive officers, and athletic team success to head coaches, multiple research studies indicate that many variables besides leadership skills affect success. It is very difficult for anyone to be an effective leader with incompetent administrators, incompetent supervisees, or dysfunctional teams (Hackman & Wageman, 2007; Vroom & Jago, 2007).

Furthermore, organizational processes and structures play a role in a leader's ability to be successful. Senge (2006) indicated that when organizational issues occur repeatedly, it is usually the fault of a dysfunctional process or structure in the organization rather than the fault of the people who are struggling to operate within that organization. He encouraged leaders to recognize that recurring problems are not caused by an "amazing coincidence" that all employees are inept, but rather by problems in the organization itself.

In addition, the network of the supervisor affects her or his ability to be effective. Supervisors who have multiple formal and informal connections within complex school districts are more likely to be able to adopt a transformational leadership style because they hold central positions within the district's networks (Bono & Anderson, 2005).

Vignette 13.5

Nicky is an extraordinarily effective supervisor because she has extensive personal connections throughout the entire school district. From many years of both living and working in the city as well as a gregarious nature, she is known and liked not only by every principal and school psychologist in the district but by many teachers and ancillary staff as well. The support she was able to enlist from almost every staff member in the junior high school—from assistant principal to science teachers to janitors—when she instituted a new program for behaviorally disordered students made a tremendous difference in the program's success.

The transformational leadership and human resources management models, with their emphasis on adopting shared decision making practices, appears to be most appropriate for the supervisor of school psychologists, since the ethical imperative for supervisors of school psychologists is to attend to the rights of supervisees, clients, the public, and the profession. However, while this approach is generally preferred in supervising professionals, individual differences will result in differences in appropriate supervisory styles. Transformational leadership is not appropriate for individuals in need of close supervision. Beginning school psychologists, or individuals who are not intrinsically motivated, may require the more traditional, scientific management style.

Changing leadership style in this manner, according to context, has recently been named *contingency leadership* (Vroom & Jago, 2007). This model suggests that effective leaders increase task focus when working with inexperienced supervisees or when the situation is ambiguous. They increase their focus on relationship building with experienced staff and in clearly defined situations. Effective leaders also adjust their leadership style to the organizational context, carefully balancing being responsive both to supervisees and to administrators (Hackman & Wageman, 2007). This theory is most consistent with existing research evidence, and it is also highly relevant to professional practice (Vroom & Jago, 2007).

As previously mentioned, a person can hold a supervisory position yet not be a leader. Unfortunately, a supervisor who is a poor leader can have a seriously detrimental effect. For example, ineffective leaders often attempt to use fear and blame as motivational devices, but these have only short-lived effectiveness; employees soon leave, psychologically if not physically. The most ineffectual leaders undermine supervisees by being overcontrolling, being undercontrolling, or vacillating between being overcontrolling and undercontrolling (Hackman & Wageman, 2007).

Vignette 13.6

As a supervisor, **Alex** vacillated extremely. At times he was undercontrolling and laissez-faire; he did not follow up on requests made by supervisees, ignored supervisees' professional development needs, and allowed litigious parents to harass staff. At other times, he micromanaged details by doing such things as clock watching supervisees' lunch breaks. The morale of his supervisees plummeted; several became very involved in union matters and filed grievances against him. Others submitted applications to neighboring school districts and left. While he held his position as a supervisor for only 2 years, it took a dozen years for the department to recover from his poor supervision.

Supervisors are appointed by administrators, but leaders obtain their position because others choose to follow them (Bennis, 2007; Hackman & Wageman, 2007). If a supervisor is not an effective leader, the group is likely to choose an informal leader whom the members believe will help achieve their objectives. This can be problematic when the informal leader's goals conflict with organization goals (Halloran, 1981).

Modifying Leadership Style

To employ contingency (contextual) leadership and vary leadership style according to the situation, supervisors can take specific actions to increase or decrease the relationship or task focus of supervisory relationships. Strategies suggested by Fiedler and Macauley (1998) are described in Table 13.1.

Table 13.1   Strategies to Change Leadership Style (Fiedler & Macauley, 1998, pp. 346–347)

To increase relationship focus:

- Spend informal time with supervisees at work or outside of work
- Increase availability to supervisees
- Listen to supervisees' problems
- Share information from administration to help supervisees feel included
- Obtain additional rewards for supervisees

To decrease relationship focus:

- Spend less informal time with supervisees
- See supervisees by appointment only
- Keep interactions businesslike
- Avoid becoming involved in supervisees' personal problems
- Introduce new members into the group

To increase task focus:

- Give detailed written instructions
- Assign readings
- Assign training workshops or hire expert consultants
- Break tasks into components
- Solicit more structured assignments
- Keep records of tasks for future reference

STRATEGIC MANAGEMENT

Effective leaders employ strategic management by systematically making informed decisions and taking deliberate actions to shape and guide practice. Such planning helps focus energy on activities that assist in attaining desired outcomes in response to current needs. It is particularly critical in developing innovative strategies to address new challenges encountered in schools while simultaneously addressing day-to-day requirements

(Lane, Bishop, & Wilson-Jones, 2005). The entire strategic management process addresses the questions:

- Where are we now?
- Where do we want to be in the future?
- How will we get there?
- How do we measure our progress? (p. 200)

During the *preparation* phase, the supervisor assesses the readiness of the group to complete a strategic plan and then identifies resources, required steps, and needed organizational structures. The supervisor gains commitment from and explains the entire process to stakeholders. During the *implementation* phase, the supervisor develops a vision; assesses internal and external strengths, weaknesses, opportunities, and threats; develops general goals and specific objectives; develops a strategic plan that integrates policies, goals, objectives, action steps, decision making, and resource allocation into a meaningful and cohesive whole; and implements structures to carry out this plan. During the *appraisal* phase, the supervisor evaluates outcomes and processes and subsequently uses appraisal results to revise the vision, goals, strategic plan, and structures in a recursive cycle.

Developing a Vision

Expressing and articulating a vision that emphasizes underlying purpose is an essential aspect of leadership. To adapt to economic, social, and technological change, leaders must pursue inventive, future-oriented leadership activities associated with vision setting. Leaders who set visions have the strongest effect on innovative practice regardless of environmental variables and organizational characteristics (Shin, 1997).

A quality vision statement comes from the heart; is unique to the setting; is simple, dramatic, and compelling; conveys hope and idealism; and is moral (Block, 1987). Sergiovanni (1990) indicated that effective leaders have a vision that clarifies the present, leads to a commitment to the future, and reflects the dreams, interests, and values of all stakeholders. A vision is a "compass," giving direction and inducing enthusiasm so that stakeholders develop a joint strategic plan. Such leadership is inevitably value laden (Bennis, 2007).

Articulation of a personal vision as a supervisor of school psychologists is informed by uncovering fundamental beliefs about education as well as beliefs about the profession of school psychology. Everyone does not have the same concepts of a "good school psychologist" and a "good school." For example, Barth (1990) described a good school as a community of learners in which principals, teachers, *and* students all *simultaneously* learn, *teach*, and rejoice in individual differences. Not everyone would agree that students should be teachers as well as learners! To analyze their own beliefs regarding education, readers can consider and discuss the questions contained in Activity 13.1.

Activity 13.1

Uncovering Beliefs About Education

Answer the following questions according to your personal beliefs:

1. What is the purpose of education?
2. What should a successful high school graduate know and be able to do?

3. What type of teacher-student relationship fosters learning the best?

4. What should receive the greater emphasis: helping students maximize their individual potentials or preparing them to be good citizens?

5. What is a "good" teacher like? What happens in his or her classroom?

6. What does a "good" school look like?

Supervisors, supervisees, and administrators all hold personal beliefs about school psychology that affect their vision and practice. When tempered by strengths and weaknesses of the school, district, and other school psychologists, a supervisor's personal vision becomes the departmental vision. Although a personal vision may be seemingly (and actually) unattainable, it shapes the supervisor's global direction and thereby pervades all decisions. To analyze personal attitudes, beliefs, and values regarding school psychology, it may be helpful to answer the questions found in Activity 13.2.

Activity 13.2

Uncovering Beliefs About School Psychology

Answer the following questions according to your personal beliefs:

1. What should school psychologists provide for children, adolescents, school personnel, parents, and the community?

2. What functions does a school psychologist serve?

3. How are these functions similar to those of counselors, social workers, behavior specialists, special education teachers, and reading teachers?

4. How are they different from each of the above?

5. How should school psychologists respond to the needs of the general education population? To the special education population? To parents? Teachers? Administrators?

6. How does a "good" school psychologist spend her or his time?

7. If a school psychologist were to receive an award for exemplary practice, what would be the basis of that award?

8. If an ideal school psychology department published a brochure that convinced parents, teachers, and administrators to use the services, what would that brochure say?

9. How do the services described in that ideal brochure compare with services currently provided?

10. What would need to change for those ideal services to be better provided?

11. How do services currently provided compare with professional standards and training?

To address the last question, it is necessary to understand the manner in which the profession of school psychology defines itself. Current competencies held by school psychologists, in which all training programs approved by the National Association of School Psychologists (NASP) must prove graduates competent, are listed in Handout 13.1.

Handout 13.1

NASP DOMAINS OF TRAINING

2.1. Data-Based Decision Making and Accountability: School psychologists have knowledge of varied models and methods of assessment that yield information useful in identifying strengths and needs, in understanding problems, and in measuring progress and accomplishments. School psychologists use such models and methods as part of a systematic process to collect data and other information, translate assessment results into empirically based decisions about service delivery, and evaluate the outcomes of services. Data-based decision making permeates every aspect of professional practice.

2.2. Consultation and Collaboration: School psychologists have knowledge of behavioral, mental health, collaborative, and/or other consultation models and methods and of their application to particular situations. School psychologists collaborate effectively with others in planning and decision making processes at the individual, group, and system levels.

2.3. Effective Instruction and Development of Cognitive/Academic Skills: School psychologists have knowledge of human learning processes, techniques to assess these processes, and direct and indirect services applicable to the development of cognitive and academic skills. School psychologists, in collaboration with others, develop appropriate cognitive and academic goals for students with different abilities, disabilities, strengths, and needs; implement interventions to achieve those goals; and evaluate the effectiveness of interventions. Such interventions include, but are not limited to, instructional interventions and consultation.

2.4. Socialization and Development of Life Skills: School psychologists have knowledge of human developmental processes, techniques to assess these processes, and direct and indirect services applicable to the development of behavioral, affective, adaptive, and social skills. School psychologists, in collaboration with others, develop appropriate behavioral, affective, adaptive, and social goals for students of varying abilities, disabilities, strengths, and needs; implement interventions to achieve those goals; and evaluate the effectiveness of interventions. Such interventions include, but are not limited to, consultation, behavioral assessment and intervention, and counseling.

2.5. Student Diversity in Development and Learning: School psychologists have knowledge of individual differences, abilities, and disabilities and of the potential influence of biological, social, cultural, ethnic, experiential, socioeconomic, gender-related, and linguistic factors in development and learning. School psychologists demonstrate the sensitivity and skills needed to work with individuals of diverse characteristics and to implement strategies selected and/or adapted based on individual characteristics, strengths, and needs.

2.6. School and Systems Organization, Policy Development, and Climate: School psychologists have knowledge of general education, special education, and other educational and related services. They understand schools and other settings as systems. School psychologists work with individuals and groups to facilitate policies and practices that create and maintain safe, supportive, and effective learning environments for children and others.

2.7. Prevention, Crisis Intervention, and Mental Health: School psychologists have knowledge of human development and psychopathology and of associated biological, cultural, and social influences on human behavior. School psychologists provide or contribute to prevention and intervention programs that promote the mental health and physical well-being of students.

2.8. Home-School-Community Collaboration: School psychologists have knowledge of family systems, including family strengths and influences on student development, learning, and behavior, and of methods to involve families in education and service delivery. School psychologists work effectively with families, educators, and others in the community to promote and provide comprehensive services to children and families.

2.9. Research and Program Evaluation: School psychologists have knowledge of research, statistics, and evaluation methods. School psychologists evaluate research, translate research into practice, and understand research design and statistics in sufficient depth to plan and conduct investigations and program evaluations for improvement of services.

2.10. School Psychology Practice and Development: School psychologists have knowledge of the history and foundations of their profession, of various service models and methods, of public policy development applicable to services for children and families, and of ethical, professional, and legal standards. School psychologists practice in ways consistent with applicable standards, are involved in their profession, and have the knowledge and skills needed to acquire career-long professional development.

2.11. Information Technology: School psychologists have knowledge of information sources and technology relevant to their work. School psychologists access, evaluate, and utilize information sources and technology in ways that safeguard or enhance the quality of services.

As indicated by Houle (1984), professions have a constantly changing sense of mission, and school psychology is no different. The above domains are in the process of modification. Leaders in the field of school psychology discussed future directions at the 2002 Conference on the Future of School Psychology, jointly sponsored by NASP, the American Psychological Association, the Society for the Study of School Psychology, the Council of Directors of School Psychology Programs, the Trainers of School Psychologists, the American Academy of School Psychology, the American Board of School Psychology, and the International School Psychology Association (see www.indiana.edu/%7Efutures/sponsors.html). This conference concluded that as experts in child and adolescent learning, behavioral programs, and assessment, school psychologists are ideally trained to develop, implement, monitor, and evaluate evidence-based prevention, early intervention, and targeted intervention programs (Cummings et al., 2004). This vision was expanded in *School Psychology: A Blueprint for Training and Practice III* (Ysseldyke et al., 2006), which stated,

> The goal of education is to help children become competent and caring adults, involved citizens, and productive members of their communities. School psychologists should work to improve competencies for all students, and build and maintain the capacities of systems to meet the needs of all students as they traverse the path to successful adulthood. (p. 3)

A *coordinated vision* results from a covenant among administrators, parents, teachers, and students around shared values, commitments, and dreams. To foster a coordinated vision, it is essential for the supervisor to develop the departmental vision in conjunction with district administration. Administrators must be aware of school psychologists' concepts regarding best practices, leadership vision, reform efforts, and standards of practice (Talley, 1990). While the vision should be responsive to both "external" and "internal" needs, it should also convey a sense of morality and justice in which students, educators, and school psychologists are fairly, equitably, and ethically treated.

It is very helpful for supervisees, supervisors, and administrators to discuss their views of education and school psychological services and then compare these views with the expressed and unexpressed visions of the school or school system. If the views and visions are widely divergent, the supervising school psychologist will need to find methods to reconcile them in order to forge achievable goals and structures (Sergiovanni & Starratt, 2007). Reconciling divergent views is facilitated by remembering that school psychology is, at its most basic level, about helping students to function best, either by empowering the students to change themselves or by changing their instructional environments. Similarly, supervision of psychological services is fundamentally about helping supervisees function best, either by empowering the supervisees to change themselves or by changing something in their environment.

Conducting an Assessment

After the vision has been developed, the supervisor, in collaboration with supervisees, conducts a comprehensive assessment of the environment. It is critical to examine every component that affects how well the department functions. "External scanning" examines factors outside the department, such as laws, funding, and school district factors. "Internal scanning" examines current factors within the department, such as personnel, processes, and costs (Lane et al., 2005). As scanning is completed, a written document is developed that enumerates individual, group, and environmental strengths, weaknesses, opportunities, and threats/barriers (SWOT; Bryson, 1995).

At the *national level*, supervisors must consider the laws relevant to school psychological service delivery and which services are mandated and in what situations. For example, the Individuals With Disabilities Education Improvement Act of 2004 (IDEA 2004) mandates functional behavioral assessments for all students with behavioral issues, even if those behaviors are as commonplace as lack of homework completion. On the other hand, the same law indicates that completing a comprehensive 3-year reevaluation is at the discretion of the team. Supervisors should also consider whether the provided school psychological services meet professional standards and whether opportunities at the national level (e.g., publications, Web sites, grants) are fully utilized.

At the *state level*, supervisors should consider state laws relevant to school psychological service delivery and which services are truly mandated. They should also explore the support available at the state department of education for school psychological services. It is helpful to know whether district school psychologists use the state school psychology organization and other local supports as resources. Supervisors should also consider whether some of the school district's school psychology resources might be appropriately spent at the state level (e.g., work with certification revision committees or work with the department of education to develop methods of student evaluation, curriculum frameworks, and state policies).

Vignette 13.7

In **Illinois** and some other states, collaboration among state department of education personnel, practicing school psychologists, and university training programs has successfully addressed disability diagnoses, unified professional development programs, developed state-supported internships, and provided supervision training for supervisors (M. E. Swerdlik, personal communication, January 2007).

At the *community level*, supervisors should determine whether district school psychologists are knowledgeable about the cultures of the community members and about available community resources for translation, homework supervision, emergency shelter, substance abuse treatment, individual and family therapy, crisis intervention, and suicide prevention. The supervisor might also consider the appropriate role of school psychologists in advocating, providing, or coordinating community services. For example, school psychologists could serve on community boards or local government committees to play a part in decision making and policy building.

Vignette 13.8

School psychologist **Chuck Ott** developed and supervised an after-school program located in a low-income housing project. Local residents, including teenagers, worked at the program for elementary school students. The program improved the behavior of both the children and the adolescents as well as improved homework completion and provided safe after-school care (C. Ott, personal communication, April 1991).

At the *district level*, supervisors should assess policies regarding the provision of school psychological services and whether they match state regulations, federal law, professional standards, and the training of school psychologists. Supervisors might determine how the administrative structures facilitate or hinder the provision of effective school psychology services, how school psychologists' job descriptions compare to national standards for the provision of services, how school psychologists fit into the district organizational structure, whether there are district level committees on which school psychologists might effectively serve, and how conflicts are resolved at the district level. Supervisors should also assess the extent to which the department regularly communicates regarding school psychological services to parents and the community at large through local newspapers, the school Web site, school newsletters, and state and national education newsletters.

Another part of the assessment process is determining how well school psychologists and their supervisors have communicated with school board members, superintendents, principals, teachers, and parents to give them a clear understanding of what school psychologists do, how well they do it, and additional services they are prepared to provide. It is important for supervisors of school psychologists to report departmental accomplishments to teachers, administrators, school board members, and other district constituents at least annually (Franklin & Duley, 2002). Examples of information to communicate include:

- Psychologists' activities and accomplishments
- Data regarding prevention program outcomes, such as the reduction of playground aggression after implementation of violence prevention programs
- Data regarding intervention program outcomes, such as Curriculum-Based Measurement results before and after targeted interventions
- Data regarding consultation outcomes, such as the number of parents who participated in parent training programs, their satisfaction, and data regarding perceived changes
- The amount of time it takes, start to finish, to conduct comprehensive psychoeducational assessments
- Information regarding the conditions under which school psychologists work, including their duties, space, materials, and equipment
- Educational opportunities provided by school psychologists locally and by state associations from which administrators and other educators benefit
- Brief articles and Web-based resources related to school psychology
- Information regarding school psychologists' work at the systems level, such as their serving on districtwide committees

At the *school level*, supervisors should determine each school's strengths and weaknesses and the student population's unique needs. The supervisor might also assess which school personnel have strengths on which school psychologists can draw, which schools have personnel with weaknesses that could be balanced by the strengths of a particular school psychologist, each school's climate, and psychologists' strengths needed for improving that climate. Furthermore, the supervisor should consider each principal's strengths, weaknesses, personal style, and relationship with the school psychologist.

> **Vignette 13.9**
>
> When **Christopher** assigned school psychologists to schools, he was particularly sensitive to the needs of the school principal for the purpose of fostering school psychologist–principal teams. He understood that principals are often in need of someone with whom they can regularly consult regarding school issues, but that effective consultation would occur only if the school psychologist and principal "matched." Therefore, for a school with a principal who loved to aggressively argue, Christopher assigned a school psychologist who was not easily intimidated and who could calmly voice opinions in an intensely emotional climate. For a school with a principal who was meek and overwhelmed, Christopher assigned a school psychologist whose strength was supportive problem solving.

Supervisors should also ensure that there is an easily used mechanism to help resolve conflicts between school psychologists and principals, particularly if school psychologists are evaluated by principals.

At the *school psychology department level*, assessing internal strengths and weaknesses can be completed by considering combined individual performance evaluation results and reviewing results of a departmental program evaluation (see Chapter 15). Additionally, supervisors and department members can compare their department with the characteristics of healthy organizations described by Likert (1967) and Miles (1965) and the characteristics of effective school psychology departments described by Franklin and Duley (2002). These characteristics are contained in Handout 13.2.

At the *individual school psychologist level*, strengths and weaknesses can be formally determined through individual self-examinations and evaluations (see Chapter 15). Less rigorously, strengths and weaknesses can be assessed through informal discussions and brainstorming sessions with department members. Each person can indicate which tasks and activities he or she prefers or at which he or she feels most proficient, as well as which tasks and activities at which he or she feels weakest. The perceptions of the supervisor and other school psychologists also indicate areas of strength and weakness.

Developing the Strategic Plan: Goals, Objectives, Resources, and Activities

The written strategic plan includes the goals, objectives, resources, and activities needed to approach the vision. Goals, or broadly stated intents, are developed in accord with the vision and in response to the assessment. These are long-term (5-year) intentions. It is important to limit the number of goals, since strategic plans often fail because too many goals are identified (Dawson & Guare, 2004). Objectives evolving from the goals should be SMART: specific, measurable, achievable, realistic, and time bound (Lane et al., 2005).

The activities evolve from the objectives and include details regarding exactly what tasks will be completed, by whom, and when they will be completed. Effective supervisors expect adherence to the common values of the "vision," but they are flexible and allow wide discretion in how individuals implement these values in day-to-day decisions. They pay careful attention to social components and reward *team* performance (Huq, 2006).

Handout 13.2

CHECKLIST TO DETERMINE DEPARTMENT HEALTH

(Adapted from Franklin & Duley, 2002;[1] Likert, 1967;[2] Miles, 1965[3])

___ The department has high performance goals that are understood and accepted by the supervisees.

___ The goals have been prioritized and the prioritization fits district priorities.

___ Goals are achievable with available resources.

___ Goals are appropriately congruent with the demands of the broader environment.

___ Group decision making and an equitable distribution of influence exist among members.

___ There is a focus on collaboration rather than coercion or competition.

___ Structures exist to sense problems within the department, develop possible solutions, choose and implement those solutions, and evaluate solution effectiveness.

___ The departmental atmosphere is perceived as supportive.

___ Tasks are appropriately distributed and staff are neither overworked nor underworked.

___ There is good fit between individuals and the roles expected of them.

___ Group members display cohesiveness by showing a desire to stay active members.

___ High morale of individuals is apparent in their demonstration of well-being, satisfaction, and pleasure.

___ The department has functional relationships with other groups that allow for active responsiveness to the total environment.

___ The department has the ability to restructure itself when environmental demands and organizational resources do not match.

___ Communication is distortion free, both vertically and horizontally within the department as well as to those outside the department.

___ There is a movement toward innovation, change, growth, and development.

___ The department has highly qualified practitioners.

___ The department's practitioners have a wide range of expertise.

___ The department provides expansive and comprehensive services that meet the needs of all students.

___ Department members engage in prereferral intervention and prevention activities.

___ Department members participate in school-based collaborative consultation.

___ Department members link assessment to instructional intervention rather than only classification.

___ The department regularly articulates the successes of both individual members and the entire department.

___ The department gathers efficacy data to establish accountability.

___ The department changes focus in response to situational needs.

___ The department emphasizes ongoing professional development.

___ Department members are autonomous.

___ Department members have access to clinical supervision by school psychologists.

___ Department members are evaluated by a supervising school psychologist.

___ Department members are active consumers and conductors of research.

___ Department members are involved in training future school psychologists.

---

[1]Franklin, M., & Duley, S. M. (2002). Best practices in planning school psychology service delivery programs: An update. In A. Thomas & J. Grimes (Eds.), *Best practices in school psychology IV* (pp. 145–159). Washington, DC: National Association of School Psychologists.

[2]Likert, R. (1967). *The human organization: Its management and value.* New York: McGraw-Hill.

[3]Miles, M. (1965). *Planned change and organizational health: Figure and ground. Change processes in the public schools.* Eugene: University of Oregon Center for the Advanced Study of Educational Administration.

As goals, objectives, and activities are developed, it is critical to review them with administrators to ensure that they are compatible with district goals and objectives. Furthermore, strategic planning involves making decisions regarding resource allocation, departmental structure, and goal orientation and compatibility and selecting decision making strategies. Each of these will be briefly discussed.

Resource Allocation

Supervisors allocate resources by determining which tasks to complete, who should do each task, and how much time and money should be devoted to tasks. This is done by delineating a strategy (goal) for each task, listing measurable objectives and major activities that support that goal, setting deadlines, drafting a budget, and obtaining administrative approval (Loen, 1994). It can be very useful for supervisors to calculate the anticipated "dollar impact" for a task or a decision.

Administrative Structure

The administrative structure within a school system can facilitate or hinder the provision of effective school psychological services. As indicated by Talley (1990), the superior to whom school psychologists report has direct bearing on the provision of services. Each prototype appears to have its own advantages and disadvantages. If the supervisor of school psychologists reports directly to a superintendent, there are few levels of bureaucracy, yet there may also be fewer administrators in the system who feel directly benefited by school psychologists. If the supervisor of school psychology reports to the director of pupil personnel services or the director of special education, there may be presumptions and restrictions regarding the population with whom the school psychologist works. If the school psychologist reports to a regional service center that provides services to separate school districts, the psychologist most likely has increased autonomy but decreased networking ability within each district. Many school psychologists report directly to principals; positive effects include the ability to make the school psychologist's services available to all students, while negative effects might include difficulties for the school psychologist in expressing divergent opinions.

While supervisors of school psychologists may have little influence over their position in the school hierarchy, an awareness of the advantages and disadvantages of each structure provides useful ideas regarding potential steps to counteract the negative aspects of one's position. For example, supervisors reporting to a regional service center can counteract the decreased networking ability by assigning each school psychologist to specific schools on a regular schedule rather than assigning school psychologists to individual cases.

Furthermore, regardless of the type of administrative structure, school psychologists need to educate their supervisors about the full range of school psychological services and advocate their appropriate delivery. It is important for supervisors of school psychologists to be sensitive not only to the bureaucracy in which they work, but also to the level of bureaucracy they themselves contribute to the system by adding departmental policies, rules, and regulations.

Another aspect of administrative structure to which the supervisor of school psychologists must be responsive is the administrative structure of the psychological services unit. Although one person can theoretically supervise 12 to 21 individuals, a natural working group is 5 to 9 individuals. Groups of 10 and larger tend to break into smaller groups, each with its own formal or informal leader. Therefore, supervisors with more than 10 supervisees should consider dividing them into smaller subgroups with designated leaders. These subgroups might be peer supervision, peer support, or professional development groups.

In designing a supervisory structure, supervisors must carefully consider the degree of contact and supervision. Supervision is effective only when frequent contact is available. Novice and beginning school psychologists need daily contact with their supervisors, preferably face to face, although telephone and e-mail communication are successful methods of augmenting communication. Experienced school psychologists generally need weekly appointments with their supervisors. Even senior practitioners continue to need supervision, but they will probably be comfortable with peer supervision and scheduling appointments as needed.

On the other hand, excessively close supervision reduces the effectiveness of supervisees for three reasons: Supervisees spend too much time reporting to the supervisor, they feel threatened by constant evaluation, and they feel incompetent. In general, supervisees want just enough supervision to know they are completing their work correctly. The supervisor must determine the amount of supervision necessary to effect that goal (Loen, 1994).

Goal Orientation and Compatibility

Strategic planning is an integral component in business management. It is illuminating to consider a few well-known approaches commonly discussed in management and educational leadership literature because they vary according to their goal orientation, which affects goal compatibility.

Management by objective (MBO) focuses on determining how well previously established goals and objectives have been met. MBO has been found to significantly increase productivity. It minimizes subjectivity because it relies on objective, quantifiable indicators of performance. MBO is likely to be tied to the organization's strategic management plan and is therefore acceptable to administrators, supervisees, and supervisors. It also has the advantage of clearly defining the manner in which performance is to be measured. Stakeholders collaborate in developing the objectives, so they have substantial validity and can be customized to meet specific needs and interests. When done well, MBO greatly facilitates communication among supervisees, supervisors, and administrators (Leonard & Hilgert, 2004; Noe, Hollenbeck, Gerhart, & Wright, 1996).

On the negative side, the ability to achieve objectives can be beyond any individual's control. For example, a department may be unable to meet an objective specifying that professional development be provided to all supervisees if the budget is slashed. Furthermore, not all important aspects of psychological services are easily quantified, which tends to result in an overemphasis on components that are easily measurable. When abused, MBO can result in excessive pressure by the supervisor on the supervisee to produce results.

Total quality management (TQM; Hackman & Wageman, 1995; Hodgetts, 1996; Wilkinson, Redman, Snape, & Marchington, 1998) emphasizes "quality" results rather than simply meeting objectives. "TQM means a total [school or district] effort toward meeting customer needs and satisfaction by planning for quality, preventing defects, correcting defects, and continuously building increased quality into goods and services as far as economically and competitively feasible" (Leonard & Hilgert, 2004, p. 228). Supervision focuses on outcomes, personal qualities of supervisees, and behaviors over which supervisees have control. These foci are chosen in order to increase morale, minimize falsification of results, and provide feedback about areas in which supervisees can improve.

Six Sigma (Eckes, 2000; Huq, 2006) focuses on pleasing consumers, measuring outcomes, *and* increasing "bottom line" results, such as profits and results on high-stakes tests. Six Sigma is intensely data driven and takes a "staggered [rather than total] improvement approach that uses customer preferences, non-intuitive data driven methodology, statistical evidence of quality, diligent attention to detail, and above all, economic justification for each improvement effort" (Huq, 2006, p. 278). While TQM tends to focus on the entire service delivery system, Six Sigma involves selecting smaller units of improvement and carefully choosing and prioritizing projects. The enforcement of high-stakes testing regulations in schools reflects this orientation, wherein the test results are presumed to mirror the effectiveness of the entire system.

Decision Making

Supervisors vary the extent in which they involve supervisees in decision making. Decisions can be made by supervisors autonomously; by consulting with group members to obtain suggestions and then deciding; by using a meeting to define the problem, set solution parameters, and obtain consensus and refusing to exert power over any other group member; or by delegating the decision to the group while simultaneously providing resources, encouragement, and prescribed limits. The extent to which supervisors involve others in making decisions has a decided impact on both the choices made and their implementation (Vroom & Jago, 2007).

Vroom and his colleagues (Vroom, 2000; Vroom & Jago, 2007; Vroom & Yetton, 1973) indicate that different decision making styles are appropriate in different situations and with different types of problems. The more participatory the decision making process, the greater the cost in terms of both elapsed time before the decision is made and time spent in meetings. On the other hand, more participatory decision making processes have greater developmental benefits for group members as long as the issue is not trivial. Increased participation also builds team cohesion and identification with organizational goals. Thus participatory decision making can be more efficient in the long run even though it is more costly in the short term.

According to Vroom (2000, p. 92), effective supervisors should select more participative decision making strategies under the following conditions:

- When the decision is highly significant
- When they need group members to commit to the decision
- When the likelihood of commitment to a unilateral decision is low
- When they lack expertise themselves but group members have high expertise
- When the group works together effectively

When supervisors consider these variables, decisions are almost twice as likely to be successful. However, while situations dictate about two thirds of the choice regarding decision making style, supervisors do tend to have a preferred style that affects their selection. Some individuals almost always select a nonparticipatory (autocratic) style, while others almost always select a participatory style. Interestingly, almost all administrative supervisors are seen by supervisees as more autocratic than they consider themselves to be (Vroom, 2000).

Selecting Decision Making Strategies

Some decisions that supervisees make are repetitive and routine. In response to these decisions, supervisors can unilaterally design appropriate policies and procedures (Leonard & Hilgert, 2004). On the other hand, new and unusual problems require adaptive problem solving. An appropriate decision making process includes:

1. Carefully defining the problem by determining what the problem is, when it occurs, where it occurs, and who is affected (Leonard & Hilgert, 2004)

2. Determining the appropriate level of supervisee collaboration using the criteria discussed above (Vroom & Jago, 2007)

3. Analyzing the problem by gathering facts and information

4. Establishing and prioritizing the desired outcomes of the decision

5. Nonjudgmentally brainstorming about alternative solutions, either verbally or in writing (Leonard & Hilgert, 2004)

6. Evaluating each alternative relative to established criteria and ethical considerations

7. Selecting the alternative that either is "best" or meets at least a minimum standard of satisfaction on the basis of experience, intuition, advice from others, or a pilot study (Leonard & Hilgert, 2004)

8. Implementing the selected alternative

9. Appraising the results by comparing current facts and information with previous problem definition and information

Many variables impact the supervisor's flexibility in making decisions, including the culture of the district and the backgrounds, expectations, and personalities of administrators and supervisees for and with whom the supervisor works. The ability to make decisions also depends greatly on the supervisor's position in the school system. A supervisor with close working relationships with upper administration has substantially greater decision making power. Participative management tends to be valued by supervisees, especially women supervisees. Regardless of sex, supervisees tend to dislike autocratic women (Vroom, 2000). These findings are particularly relevant for supervisors working in schools, where the majority of both supervisees and supervisors are women.

Implementing Structures

Implementing service structures involves making myriad decisions, attending to details, and monitoring implementation. Attempts to improve the quality of programs often fail because of ineffectual implementation or insufficient skills.

Supervisors of school psychological services must frequently make decisions that impact the provision of school psychological services. For example, supervisors must determine how to retool veteran psychologists in updated methods; whether to encourage supervisees to use standard reporting forms and descriptors; and whether and how to modify existing procedures. As discussed earlier, multiple factors must be taken into consideration in making decisions. One of the most important is the degree to which supervisees should be included in the decision making process. Additional factors include cost, availability of school psychologists, the amount of training required, availability of materials, the potential for efficient record keeping, and compatibility with existing procedures. On occasion, supervisors of school psychologists will be consulted regarding other aspects of operation planning, such as site selection and facilities layout.

Vignette 13.10

Richard, a supervising school psychologist in a moderate-sized city, was deeply involved in developing a program for students with emotional disabilities. When a former shop was being converted into classroom and office space for this program, Richard was consulted regarding the most appropriate layout of space in a suite of rooms. Fortunately, he was able to gain approval for office space between the two classrooms for himself as well as for the program coordinator and was also able to have a "quiet" corner set off architecturally in each classroom.

Facilitating Change

Effective leaders incorporate repeated change into their organizations in response to shifts in external factors. To do so, they repeatedly destroy and creatively remake their organizations, abandon old ideas, adopt new and better ideas and methods, and "help each and every employee generate the high levels of positive energy needed to do the same" (Tichy, 1997, p. 24). Effective leaders generate ideas, instill values, create positive energy, and make difficult decisions. They assess current reality and deal with situations as they are, not as they were or as they would like them to be. After assessing reality, leaders decide on a response, determine what actions are needed, mobilize appropriate resources, and ensure that desired actions are appropriately implemented.

Change can be internal (department), external (within the district, community, or state), or technological (in the field). Change is not only inevitable, but it is institutionalized in effective organizations. Despite the need for change, individuals are naturally resistant to change when they are unsure of its effects, suspect that the change will not be in their best interest, are afraid of the unknown, fear economic loss, fear that their current skills and expertise will be devalued, perceive a threat to power, fear inconvenience, or feel that pleasurable social interactions are threatened. To mitigate resistance, change is implemented in several steps:

- Building trust by discussing upcoming changes and involving supervisees in the decision making process
- Presenting new alternatives that are reasonable
- Establishing the new procedure by positively reinforcing the change and making it more attractive than using the old procedure

Supervisors need multiple skills to facilitate change. Leadership skills and the ability to develop a future vision have already been discussed. Skills in recruiting, retaining, evaluating, and monitoring staff are discussed in Chapters 14 and 15. In addition to these skills, supervisors who are facilitating change must have a knowledge of change processes, an understanding of staff needs relative to the future vision, skills and knowledge in the areas of innovation, an understanding of educational change, and willingness to disrupt current practices in favor of new knowledge and skills and to simultaneously create "an alignment of critical elements within the system" (R. Allison, 2002, p. 116). It can be helpful for supervisors to address problem solving by using a systems perspective, which suggests that:

- Behaviors and events are, at least in part, determined by the structures and systems in which they occur
- Problems in a system are usually solved one level above the level where the problem occurs
- Someone who is responsible to address a problem is often part of the problem
- A problem in a specific organization often lies not just in that part but also in the relationships or processes between that part and other parts of the organization
- The longest-lasting change results from the change of systems and structures

ASSESSING THE IMPACT OF LEADERSHIP DEVELOPMENT

Supervisors benefit from feedback on their leadership and management style because it stimulates reflection and self-examination and enables them to deliberately choose a style that fits the situation. Although a very large number of assessment tools have been developed for this purpose, a surprisingly small number have established psychometric validity.

In the spirit of "360-degree feedback," recommended by London and Smither (1995), almost all tools provide both self- and other-report forms to encourage obtaining feedback from a variety of sources "around" leaders. The Campbell Leadership Index (Campbell, 1991) measures leadership, energy, affability, dependability, and resilience. Studies have found the instrument to have strong reliability. The Supervisory Behavior Description Questionnaire (SBD; Fleishman, 1996) has two scales, Consideration and Structure, that have been found to be independent, reliable, and valid (Bugaj, 2003; Roszkowski, 2003). The Leadership Practices Inventory—Delta (LPI-Delta; Kouser & Posner, 1992) assesses "Challenging the Process," "Inspiring a Shared Vision," "Enabling Others to Act," "Modeling the Way," and "Encouraging the Heart." Psychometric properties of an earlier version were well established but have not been established for this version.

A number of scales are grounded theoretically and have been used in research studies but do not have well-established reliability and validity. They may be used to gather information but should not be used to guide personnel actions. These include the Multifactor Leadership Questionnaire (MLQ) Form 5x (Avolio & Bass, 1995), which assesses qualities associated with transformational leadership such as influence, inspirational motivation, intellectual stimulation, and individual consideration; the Leadership Skills Profile (LSP; Jackson, 2003), which measures cognitive managerial skills, interpersonal managerial skills, personal managerial qualities, and teamwork; and the six Situational Leadership instruments (Hersey, 2002), which assess the ability of leaders to adapt their behavior to meet situational demands. Handout 13.3, adapted from special education literature, can be used to assess the leadership provided by school psychology supervisors.

Handout 13.3

LEADERSHIP BEHAVIOR RATING SCALE

(Adapted from L. R. Johnson, 1998)[1]

The supervisor of school psychologists:

1. Brings concerns to staff school psychologists and facilitates collaborative problem solving by participating in group discussions and sharing necessary information	|____|____|____|____| constantly never
2. Delegates tasks and authority effectively	|____|____|____|____| constantly never
3. Openly discusses his/her vision for school psychological services	|____|____|____|____| constantly never
4. Encourages staff school psychologists to share expertise with others and function in leadership roles	|____|____|____|____| constantly never
5. Encourages staff to reflect on current practices and suggest improvements	|____|____|____|____| constantly never
6. Treats staff school psychologists as self-directed professionals who share professional standards	|____|____|____|____| constantly never
7. Meets frequently with staff, both formally and informally	|____|____|____|____| constantly never
8. Shares budget construction, resource management, and program evaluation with staff school psychologists	|____|____|____|____| constantly never

---

[1]Johnson, L. R. (1998). Performance evaluation of special education administrators: Considerations and recommendations. *NASSP Bulletin, 82,* 24–32.

The degree to which leadership qualities can be affected by assessing and addressing them depends on several variables. After conducting a meta-analysis of longitudinal studies addressing the effects of multisource feedback, Smither, London, and Reilly (2005) concluded that changes in skills are most likely to result when

> feedback [from supervisees and administrators] indicates that change is necessary [and] recipients have a positive feedback orientation, perceive a need to change their behavior, react positively to the feedback, believe change is feasible, set appropriate goals to regulate their behavior, and take actions that lead to skill and performance improvement. (p. 33)

After supervisors assess their leadership and management skills, develop a plan to address them, and implement that plan, the resulting change must be appraised in order to determine the need for future change. Even veteran supervisors should appraise these skills on a regular basis. Both clinical and administrative supervisors should include at least one leadership or management goal in their annual goals to ensure continual improvement in these skills.

CHALLENGES IN PROVIDING LEADERSHIP

Many of the challenges inherent in managing and leading psychological services in schools were discussed in Chapter 1. These include the educational context and funding issues; current pressures on the educational system such as educational mandates and legislation; and an increased focus on the need for schools to address the mental health of children and adolescents.

Another concern is that administrative supervisors of psychological services are often assigned far more supervisees than they can reasonably supervise. Management literature suggests that it is possible to closely monitor the performance of six to eight individuals at a time. Larger groups need to be broken down into subgroups and headed by informal leaders or coordinators.

As middle managers, administrative supervisors are challenged to balance the expectations of upper administration, the needs of the school psychologists whom they supervise, and the expectations of teachers, parents, students, and principals. The aforementioned confusion regarding the appropriate roles of school psychologists further complicates this balancing. Even though school psychologists would like increased teacher consultation, parent workshops, and in-service training, school administrators additionally expect school psychologists' current functions. Thus administrative supervisors are challenged to help their supervisees meet conflicting expectations.

The variability among school psychologists in terms of their training and comfort level regarding various roles also challenges administrative supervisors. It can be very difficult to plan strategies and structures when there is considerable difference from one school psychologist to the next in terms of ability to deal with situations such as the diagnosis of low-incidence disabilities or crisis management.

Finally, the shortage of school psychologists challenges administrative supervisors because they often have unfilled positions. This results in their having to choose which services to eliminate in order to avoid overextending the remaining school psychologists and causing them to burn out.

SUMMARY

Well-developed leadership and management skills are supervisory skills. Effective leaders possess good social skills, orient a group toward goals, make decisions, initiate change, solve conflicts, and mobilize others to face and meet difficult challenges. Effective managers keep the current system functioning by planning, staffing, controlling, and problem solving. While different individuals may be in each role, ideally supervisors possess strong skills in both management and leadership.

Leadership can be transactional, transformative, laissez-faire, or contingency based. These leadership styles differ in how they approach problems, interact with staff, and make decisions. Transformational and contingency-based leaders are the most effective. It is problematic when a person in a supervisory position is not an effective leader, since such an individual can be damaging and provides only informal leadership that is incompatible with overarching goals.

In forming a strategic management plan, the supervisor collaboratively develops a vision and considers the strengths and challenges inherent at the national, state, community, district, school, and individual levels. Then goals, objectives, action steps, and time lines are developed. In forming the plan, effective supervisors carefully consider goal compatibility, the decision making process, and methods to facilitate change.

REFLECTIVE QUESTIONS

Q13.1. How does leadership differ from management?

Q13.2. Describe transactional, transformative, laissez-faire, and contingency leadership styles. When each leadership style is utilized, what are the likely results?

Q13.3. Describe the phases of strategic management and give examples of how they are utilized in the school system.

Q13.4. What are some of the challenges faced by administrative supervisors of school psychologists?

Q13.5. What are the most reliable assessment tools designed to measure leadership?

Q13.6. Describe the process involved in effective decision making.

Q13.7. What are the multiple steps involved in the strategic supervision of school psychological services?

Q13.8. In developing a leadership vision, what should a supervisor consider?

Q13.9. When strategically planning school psychology services, how does one consider strengths and challenges at the school, district, community, state, and national levels?

Q13.10. What are some ways in which supervisors can facilitate change?

SUPERVISORY DILEMMAS

SD 13.1

As a supervising school psychologist, you are being pressured by the administration to assign school psychologists inequitably. Two elementary schools, both with populations of 1,000, have historically received relatively equitable school psychology services. Utilization of effective prereferral intervention strategies in one school has reduced the number of referrals for full psychological evaluations by 50%. In sharp contrast, the second school has neglected to implement a prereferral process and thus continues to have a large number of referrals for traditional assessments. The central administration would like school psychology time to be reduced at the school with the prereferral interventions and assigned to the second school to "catch up" their referrals. *What are the supervisory considerations? What should be done?*

Authors' thoughts: This is one of those appalling situations in which one is punished for being good! Such a reassignment of time would be patently unfair to the innovative school psychologist, and it would be terribly unreasonable to remove the services that support such an exemplary program. Clearly, both short-term and long-term solutions are needed. Because evaluations must be completed within circumscribed time lines, it may be initially important to "bail out" the school psychologist at the second school. This should be done in a manner that ensures that this does not become an institutionalized activity that occurs annually. It is critical to brainstorm both how to most effectively bring the new model to the second school and how to more appropriately measure school psychologists' performance.

SD 13.2

One of your supervisees works in a very crowded elementary school without a room designated for his work. Initially, the principal indicated that the school psychologist could work with students in the hallway. When your supervisee indicated that confidentiality would be compromised, the principal said that the school psychologist could use the principal's office. The school psychologist expressed concern that students would feel that they were "in trouble," but the principal insisted that all of the students in the school saw him as "a friend." There is no vacant space in the entire school. *What are the supervisory considerations? What should be done?*

Authors' thoughts: A lack of suitable physical space is a sad reality faced by many school psychologists. There are no easy answers, and great flexibility and inventiveness are required. Most critical, the effect of the location on the student must be addressed. While it is conceivable that the school psychologist might discuss the space dilemma in front of the student and have the principal enthusiastically invite the student and school psychologist to use his office with the assurance that he will be off doing other things, another possibility would be to take advantage of temporarily available spaces (e.g., classrooms vacated by students at lunch or in physical education class).

SD 13.3

You are a supervising school psychologist in a small district with three school psychologists. One of the psychologists is assigned to one small elementary school and is frequently expected to spend considerable time on activities not included in her job description. These include answering office telephones, sending notifications of faculty meetings, and bus and recess duty. In addition, the school's guidance counselor refuses to retire (at age 78), despite having antagonistic relationships with students and parents. Needless to say, parents and teachers alike seek out the services of the school psychologist. She feels more and more overwhelmed each day. *What are the supervisory considerations? What should be done?*

Authors' thoughts: Where to even begin! This overworked school psychologist needs immediate supervisory support. Clarification of her role with the principal of the small school—her supervisor—is a good first step. Avoiding burnout is crucial. Presumably, the supervisor does not have administrative authority over the guidance counselor, so this situation should be handed off to the principal for disposition.

SD 13.4

You are the supervisor of school psychologists in a large urban district. The department has 30 school psychologists, one of whom has recently become very active in the union at both the state and local levels. She has pointed out that the contracted caseloads in the department have been typically ignored. She has surveyed her fellow workers and determined that each school psychologist, on average, has 2.5 more students in his or her caseload than initially agreed upon. She is demanding immediate rectification of the situation. Interestingly, it appears that only a vocal minority want to have their caseloads reduced. As a group, they appear to attribute the problem to a recent override of the school budget. A notable schism is rapidly developing in the department. *What are the supervisory considerations? What should be done?*

Authors' thoughts: The reality is that union contracts do govern working conditions. Hence, when workers in the bargaining unit choose to adhere to contractual language, they have every legal right to do so. This is a prime example of how law and ethics collide. It can be assumed that no school psychologist wants to harm students. To that end, this supervisor may want to invite supervisees (particularly the most disgruntled school psychologist!) to be part of a work group that will focus on solutions. The best short-term solution is to come to an agreement about how to balance the needs of the students with union workload limitations. This is a difficult situation for all involved that demands facile negotiations on both formal and informal levels.

14

Recruiting
and Orienting

Filling staff vacancies with outstanding personnel is a critically important supervisory responsibility.

Vignette 14.1

During his third year as a school psychologist in Mountain View, a rural school district, **Raymond**'s only colleague suffered a sudden and fatal stroke. To find a replacement, the pupil personnel director placed ads in the newspaper, but these yielded no results. The district then suggested that Raymond attend the NASP convention and interview applicants at Career Services. Although Raymond enjoyed meeting the candidates, he was overwhelmed by their questions. He was able to answer, "What would be the advantages of working in Mountain View?" "What is the caseload?" "What system is used to evaluate professional performance?" and "What are the local cultural opportunities?" He could not answer, "How does financial compensation compare to that in other districts across the country?" "Would the school district help my spouse find a position?" or "Would the district fund the interview visits?" He was particularly challenged by the question "How would working in Mountain View be better than my other six choices?"

This chapter provides information regarding recruiting, hiring, and orienting providers of school psychological services. Supervisors are often responsible for supervising social workers, teachers, counselors, clerical staff, and paraprofessionals as well as school psychologists. Although the examples given in this chapter address the selection of school psychologists, the same principles apply to the selection of staff regardless of the position.

BASIC CONSIDERATIONS

Filling staff vacancies with outstanding personnel is a critically important supervisory responsibility. Good leaders are effective team builders, and hiring an outstanding team is pivotal to developing a strong department. Furthermore, because of the increasing shortage of school psychologists (Curtis, Grier, & Hunley, 2004),

> only those districts that identify that they are in a highly competitive hiring environment, and who take aggressive action to compete for the best talent, will have the resources necessary to provide excellent educational programs for students in the future. (Lee, 2005, p. 263)

Recruiting and orienting school psychological service providers is made considerably more complicated by the scarcity of school psychologists. It can be tempting to hire any licensed school psychologist to fill a vacancy, or even to hire unqualified individuals under an "exemption waiver." Supervisors must guard against hiring undesirable or unqualified persons just to fill a vacancy. Undesirable individuals, such as those with poor interpersonal skills, can create havoc by undermining relationships among students, parents, administrators, teachers, other school personnel, and the school psychology department. Unqualified and inadequately trained persons can harm students by inappropriate or unethical practice, such as incompetent counseling or misdiagnosis of disabilities. "Hiring errors" can have costly effects on children and district resources. Incompetent psychologists can harm children, undermine the work of others, and take an extraordinary amount of supervisors' time.

Thus it is important for administrators to make recruitment, interviews, selection, and support of highly skilled candidates a top priority. While hiring, orienting, and training new employees is expensive in terms of the time invested by supervisors and support staff (Anthony, Kacmer, & Perrewé, 2006), hiring errors are even more expensive. Hiring processes that are well carried out—in which applicants are thoroughly screened, interviewed, oriented, and trained—can result in a successful department with longevity because the right person was selected in the first place (p. 245).

RECRUITING

Due to the importance of recruiting and selecting staff, business management literature has extensive information on this topic. It addresses the selection process, pre-interview strategies, interview strategies, post-interview strategies, and considerations regarding promotion, orientation, and increasing job satisfaction (Chapman, Uggerslev, Carroll, Piasenin, & Jones, 2005).

Determining the Hiring Process

The first step is for administrators and the supervisor to determine the hiring process. In designing this process, these questions should be answered:

- Who formally hires the school psychologist and offers the job?
- How negotiable are the salary and benefits? If determined by a union contract, what factors determine the placement of the new hire in the salary schedule?

- How does the position offered compare to those in other districts in terms of job characteristics, opportunities for innovative practice, available supervision, coworkers, pay, benefits, district culture, community supports, and professional development opportunities?
- Given the opportunities provided by other districts, why would the best school psychologists want to work for this district? How can these variables be improved?
- What recruitment methods will be used?
- What information and work samples will applicants be asked to supply?
- Who will initially screen the applicants, and what criteria will be used?
- Who will telephone candidates to invite them in for interviews?
- What semistructured interview questions or assignments will be asked of each candidate?
- What biases are the individuals conducting screenings and interviews likely to have, and how can these biases be minimized?
- What type of references will be contacted? Who will telephone them? What questions will be asked? How will the responses be evaluated?
- What will be the format of the interviews? Who will participate as interviewers? Will interviewees be asked to provide an impromptu work sample?
- How will background information be verified?

To avoid the frustration of completing the hiring process only to have job offers refused, supervisors and administrators must consider and address factors that influence whether a candidate will accept a job as they design this process. Relevant factors include promptness of the job offer, pay level, challenge and responsibility, job security, advancement opportunities, geographic location, opportunities for part-time work, opportunities for flexible hours, salary, benefits, and sign-on bonuses. The following steps can ensure that candidates feel valued during the hiring process:

- As much as possible, reduce bureaucracy and required paperwork.
- Designate one contact person to answer questions regarding openings, requirements, the selection process, and time lines.
- Ensure that all individuals involved in the recruitment process can accurately answer applicants' questions and know the importance of focusing on future job satisfaction, being courteous and friendly, taking interest in the candidate, and conveying high organizational morale (Wiles & Spiro, 2004).
- Select recruiters for personable characteristics and train them to provide consistent and correct information. Organizational position, gender, race, and age are less relevant (Chapman et al., 2005).
- Keep applicants continually informed of where they stand.
- Personalize all communication.
- Ensure that everyone—receptionists, human resource personnel, administrators— treat applicants professionally and with courtesy.
- Carefully plan recruitment activities to reflect positively on the district.
- Avoid distractions and interruptions during interviews.
- Use interviews to gather information regarding traits and attributes.
- Include highly qualified individuals in the interview process and be sure to acknowledge their participation (Lee, 2005).
- Before any offers are extended, have applicants complete a questionnaire regarding what they liked and disliked about the recruitment process, whether they obtained

enough and consistent information, and what suggestions they might have to improve the process.

- After offers are extended and refused, use questionnaires or telephone interviews to obtain information regarding why the offer was refused, where the individual accepted an offer, and why.
- Use information attained in questionnaires and interviews to modify the application process in the future (Lee, 2005).

Making the Work Setting Attractive

Perceived attractiveness of the work setting affects the likelihood that a candidate will even apply for a position. Professionals want to work in a setting that is "a great place to work" and has a friendly environment, smart colleagues, high standards, teams that work well together, staff who are focused on continual improvement, honest and humane supervisors, and jobs that are likely to result in personal satisfaction (Mulcahy & Betts, 2005). Applicants begin to assess the attractiveness of a position when they first encounter information, whether that information is deliberately stated (such as a statement that the district seeks diverse applicants) or covertly conveyed (such as a complicated application procedure that reveals excessive bureaucracy). Candidates tend to generalize information to the entire organization.

> **Vignette 14.2**
>
> When **Suzy** was applying to several districts as a school psychologist, she assumed that Apple School District was emotionally supportive because the receptionist and recruiter were friendly and interested. Conversely, she assumed that Bureaucratic School District's impersonal and complicated application processes indicated that working in that environment would be similarly unpleasant.

Applicants perceive individual interviews, submitting evidence of work-related skills, reference checks, and résumés to be appropriate recruitment tools (Hausknecht, Day, & Thomas, 2004; Reeve & Schultz, 2004). They also perceive being interviewed by high-level administrators as a sign that positions (and, potentially, they) are highly valued. Consequently, Lee (2005) recommended that all professional applicants be interviewed by a district superintendent. He felt that such an interview reinforces the importance of the hiring process, provides a quality check, and sets a standard for the district.

A primary concern of applicants is determining that resources and expectations associated with the position are congruent with their needs and skills (Dubinsky, Howell, & Ingraham, 1986). Applicants are most concerned that they are selecting an environment in which they are likely to attain job satisfaction (Chapman et al., 2005; Wiles & Spiro, 2004). Unfortunately, human resource recruiters tend to overemphasize salary and training opportunities, grossly underestimating the importance of potential job satisfaction (Wiles & Spiro, 2004). As Lee (2005) indicated, applicants are attracted to positions that will enable them to:

- Work in a collegial environment that is professionally stimulating, fun, and exciting
- Enjoy supportive supervision and leadership
- Gain competitive salary, benefits, and hiring incentives such as loan forgiveness

- Provide innovative practice
- Be a member of a respected team of professionals who have a record of excellent outcomes
- Work with state-of-the art materials and resources
- Participate in positive parent-educator partnerships

Positive attributes of the position should be consistently and clearly evident in all printed and online materials regarding both the position and the district. They should also be evident in the recruitment and selection process.

Developing a Comprehensive Job Description and Specifications

It is critical to develop accurate job descriptions and specifications, because their accuracy is directly related to the potential for success. The first step is to conduct a *job analysis*, which is "the building block of everything that personnel does" (Noe, Hollenbeck, Gerhart, & Wright, 1996, p. 172). It affects selection of personnel, performance appraisal, training and development, individual performance evaluation, career planning, and work redesign. When supervisors conduct a job design, they ask, "How is the job to be performed? Who is to perform the job, and where?" In school psychology, job design is immensely complex because different individuals react differently to the same job due to varied levels of interest, training, experience, development, and skill. In addition, a job in one school will be markedly different from the same job in another school. To effectively conduct a job analysis, one must understand the larger context, identify the desired outcomes, specify standards of quality for these outcomes, examine the processes used to generate outcomes (e.g., team meetings), and identify the inputs used in the development of those outcomes (human skills, equipment, and supplies). Supervisors should ensure that their priorities are aligned with the priorities of the administrators who formally offer the job and negotiate salary.

Vignette 14.3

When **Peggy** was attempting to recruit a highly experienced school psychologist who would be able to successfully handle a program for seriously emotionally disturbed adolescents, she was frustrated when the assistant superintendent attempted to insist on hiring a new graduate who would start at the bottom of the salary scale. She successfully argued for hiring the more experienced candidate by discussing the financial costs that would be incurred by a poor hire—either in terms of the individual quitting or in terms of students failing and being referred to expensive out-of-district placements.

After a job analysis is conducted, a *job description* is written that indicates the characteristics of the job being advertised and its requirements, duties, observable actions, and tasks. Information about job dimensions and tasks can be developed by holding a meeting in which individuals identify four to eight groups of major, interrelated tasks. In school psychology, these can be derived from the *Professional Conduct Manual* of the National Association of School Psychologists (NASP; 2000) and modified to fit the needs of the setting. The group then brainstorms regarding (a) the tasks that encompass each dimension, identifying the abilities, knowledge, and skills necessary to perform the tasks effectively; (b) environmental and technological factors that are likely to change in the next 5 years that will affect the tasks or necessary abilities, knowledge, and skills; and (c) the impact these changes will likely have on the future job.

Most often, school psychology job descriptions describe generalists. Currently, there is some movement in the direction of specialists, such as a school psychologist with a specialization in working with children diagnosed with autism spectrum disorders. In large departments, specialization has some benefits in terms of promoting specialized areas of competence, and dividing labor increases efficiency in each unit. On the other hand, specialization can lead to a fragmentation of services. Further, if there are subgroups of specialists and generalists within a department, it may have the unintended side effect of subgroups developing goals that conflict with departmental goals.

Finally, the *job specification* that indicates the education, experience, knowledge, and skills desired in the applicant is developed (Certo, 2006). For best results, both the job description and job specification should be included in promotional material. They should both be coordinated with:

- The mission, goals, and vision of the school district
- The departmental vision of school psychological service provision
- Performance evaluation tools and procedures
- Specialized skills needed for a particular position

Formal training and certification as a school psychologist are obviously prerequisites for a position as a school psychologist. However, formal training does not guarantee that a candidate has the skills necessary for a particular opening. Many training programs do not provide training in specialty areas, such as crisis intervention, preschool assessment, and parent training.

Besides formal training, certain personal characteristics are essential to job success. Supervisors should hire on the basis of integrity, motivation, capacity, understanding, knowledge, and experience. "Without integrity, motivation is dangerous; without motivation, capacity is impotent; without capacity, understanding is limited; without understanding, knowledge is meaningless; without knowledge, experience is blind. Experience is easy to provide and quickly put to use with the other qualities" (Dee Hock, as quoted by Mornell, 1998, p. 168).

For several reasons, graduation from a reputable school psychology program unfortunately does not guarantee that individuals possess these traits. University programs can and do make admissions errors, despite using references and interviews as well as standardized tests and grade point averages to screen candidates. Following admissions, programs monitor the professional skills of students and "counsel" students ill suited for the profession into a more appropriate profession. However, university programs have little legal ground to eliminate students on the basis of mediocrity. Furthermore, some students who are ill suited to the profession are excellent academically, and their academic skills overshadow weak application skills in many courses. Formal courses provide enough structure so those students who work well only in structured settings do not surface as problematic until their internships. Although practica and internships serve as additional screening opportunities, performance under close supervision is not necessarily predictive of performance as an independent practitioner.

Many would agree that excellent school psychologists possess the skills described by Fagan and Wise (2000): listening skills; skills in oral expression; writing skills; an ability to respond to constructive criticism professionally; overall emotional maturity; an ability to work with children; an ability to work with peers, parents, and school or agency personnel; a willingness to go beyond basic requirements; flexibility in adapting to change; observance of protocol and rules; responsivity to professional ethics; and a respect for individual and group differences. A great challenge in hiring is to discriminate among qualified candidates on the basis of these characteristics while using selection methods that are reliable, valid, and legal.

Vignette 14.4

After years of hiring school psychologists, **Terri** indicated that she had finally settled on the critical variables. After determining that the applicant had appropriate certification as a school psychologist, she didn't look for particular skills because she found that she could train a person in those qualifications. She did look for intelligence, integrity, and a sense of humor. "Without a sense of humor— without being able to laugh at all the crazy things that happen in this job—they can't last as good school psychologists," she maintained.

Handouts 14.1 and 14.2 are illustrations of job descriptions. Another example of job expectations is contained in Handout 14.7 at the end of the chapter.

Generating Applicants

There are a number of recruitment methods in the management literature, each with its own benefits, drawbacks, and success rates. Possible methods include internal hiring, hiring direct or referred applicants, contacting training programs, convention recruitment, hiring temporary employees, placing local and professional newspaper advertisements, and advertising on general or professional databases.

Internal hiring is hiring a person from within the district. Advantages are that the abilities of the applicant are already well known, the applicant is already familiar with the job parameters, the adjustment period of the new hire is decreased, vacancies are filled more quickly, and less expense is incurred. Furthermore, internal hiring provides the potential for internal job changes and promotions, which increases general job satisfaction and improves morale. Union contracts often mandate internal job postings prior to recruitment of outside applicants. In school psychology, internal hiring most commonly occurs by hiring a person who has obtained certification as a school psychologist but is currently a teacher or counselor in the district. These candidates have either obtained this certification on their own or were encouraged to obtain certification by district personnel.

One disadvantage to internal hiring is that there are often insufficient qualified internal applicants. Even more important, external hires often bring new ideas and fresh perspectives and thereby generate professional growth in the department and district. Relying entirely on internal hires can lead to stagnation because there are no sources of new ideas (Certo, 2006). Further, internal hiring can lead to "political infighting" for positions and decreased morale in those who apply for positions and are not hired (Rue & Byars, 1997).

Direct applicants are individuals who contact the school system to inquire about a position without being aware of an opening, while *referrals* are individuals who have been urged to apply by someone already working for the school system. The primary advantage of recruiting from these groups is that, at least to some extent, they have already investigated

Handout 14.1

SAMPLE JOB DESCRIPTION: SUPERVISING SCHOOL PSYCHOLOGIST

POSITION TITLE: Supervising School Psychologist
REPORTS TO AND IS EVALUATED BY: Director of Special Education
SUPERVISES: School psychologists, counselors, social workers, and educational examiners
COORDINATES WITH: School administrators and personnel

The Supervising School Psychologist provides student psychological services and recommends appropriate programs and placements at designated programs. The Supervising School Psychologist also coordinates and supervises the provision of psychological services throughout the district.

Principal Duties

1. Provides effective psychological consultation services to school personnel and parents (e.g., observation, review of records, teacher conferences, parent conferences, student interviews, brief reports, staffing).

2. Conducts comprehensive psychological evaluations (e.g., all of the above as well as administration and interpretation of psychological instruments).

3. Prepares psychological reports on individual students.

4. Recommends and implements effective intervention strategies as required and appropriate.

5. Provides and assists in providing effective psychological therapy for individual students.

6. Provides facilitative psychological consultation to counselors and therapists for students with emotional and behavioral disorders.

7. Participates effectively in building and district level team meetings.

8. Provides effective clinical supervision for staff school psychologists via weekly individual and biweekly group meetings.

9. Holds bimonthly meetings with educational examiners that result in improved practice.

10. Provides clinical supervision and consultation to district social workers that result in improved practice.

11. Provides administrative supervision to staff school psychologists, educational examiners, and district social workers (e.g., hiring, evaluating, and planning) in an effective manner.

12. Performs other duties within the general scope of the position that may be assigned by the Director of Special Education.

Subsidiary Activities

1. Provides training for staff and parents.

2. Makes on-site visits to out-of-district placement locations and determines their appropriateness.

Combination Tasks

1. Makes programmatic recommendations for individualized education plans in coordination with the placement team.

2. Exchanges information with external agencies for purposes of student assessment and programs.

Minimum Requirements

Has attained certification as a school psychologist. Possesses knowledge of and a willingness to implement statutes and ethical guidelines related to psychology and special education. Displays good communication and interpersonal skills. Some training or experience in supervision preferred.

Handout 14.2

SAMPLE JOB DESCRIPTION: SCHOOL PSYCHOLOGIST

POSITION TITLE: School Psychologist

REPORTS TO AND IS EVALUATED BY: Director of Special Education and Supervising School Psychologist (who also provides direct supervision and consultation)

SUPERVISES: None

COORDINATES WITH: Other staff psychologists and school personnel

The School Psychologist provides student psychological services and recommends and implements appropriate programs and placements.

Principal Duties

1. Provides effective psychological consultation services to school personnel and parents (e.g., observation, review of records, teacher conferences, parent conferences, student interviews, brief reports, staffing).

2. Conducts comprehensive psychological evaluations (e.g., all of the above as well as administration and interpretation of psychological instruments).

3. Prepares psychological reports on individual students.

4. Recommends and implements effective intervention strategies as required and appropriate.

5. Provides and assists in providing effective psychological therapy for individual students.

6. Provides facilitative psychological consultation to counselors and therapists for students with emotional and behavior disorders.

7. Participates effectively in building and district level team meetings.

8. Performs other duties within the general scope of the position that may be assigned by the Director of Special Education.

Subsidiary Activities

1. Provides training for staff and parents.

2. Makes on-site visits to out-of-district placement locations and determines their appropriateness.

Combination Tasks

1. Makes programmatic recommendations for individualized education plans in coordination with the placement team.

2. Exchanges information with external agencies for purposes of student assessment and programs.

Minimum Requirements

Meets requirements for state certification as a school psychologist and is qualified to assess emotional and behavioral disorders. Possesses knowledge of and willingness to implement statutes and ethical guidelines related to psychology and special education. Displays good communication and interpersonal skills.

the position and drawn the conclusion that there is a "good fit." Individuals who have been referred often know a fair amount about the district because they have spoken with the person(s) who urged them to apply. Hiring direct applicants and referrals also has the advantage of reducing recruitment cost.

In *networking*, the supervisor, other school psychologists in the district, and other school personnel contact potential candidates and invite them to apply. Sources might be school psychologists who know other interested school psychologists, university professors, special educators, general educators, administrators, or community agency personnel. Colleges and universities are also excellent sources of prospective applicants. Campus placement services (and often school psychology programs themselves) offer links to current students and graduates of school psychology programs. Some supervisors report that a chief benefit of teaching a course for a school psychology program is the opportunity to observe and recruit future applicants. Like contacting training programs, attending and interviewing at *professional conferences* has the advantage of providing contact with individuals who are known to be qualified.

Some organizations hire *temporary workers* for a specific project or time period. For example, a school district might hire a temporary worker to replace an individual on maternity leave. Temporary workers typically take a "fill-in" role and are unlikely to be able to perform broad-based interventions. The advantage of hiring temporary workers is that it provides an extended period during which an individual's working style, strengths, and relative weaknesses can be observed (Anthony et al., 2006). In school psychology, temporary employees can be long-term substitutes and interns. Supervisors must be vigilant in ensuring that sufficient supervision is provided to such individuals. Even when paid a full salary, interns require considerable supervisory time. To hire an intern and not provide adequate supervision is unethical and results in considerable vicarious liability.

Vignette 14.5

Marc accepted a position as an intern in a state 900 miles from his home, signed a 1-year apartment lease, and moved over the summer. The first day of his internship he was informed that the field supervisor who had agreed to supervise his internship had resigned and that he was expected to handle two schools without on-site supervision. The second day of his internship, a high school student stood in a third-story window and threatened to jump, and Marc was expected to provide crisis intervention without supervision. Marc called a meeting with his (off-site) field supervisor and university supervisor and explained that he was not prepared to work without supervision and that he believed it was an ethical violation for the district to expect him to do so.

It is preferable to leave a position unfilled rather than to hire an undesirable or unqualified individual, or to place an unqualified individual such as an intern in an unsupervised situation. In leaving a position unfilled, however, it is important to prioritize activities of the remaining staff who are obligated to provide services for a higher number of students. It is not appropriate to leave one school entirely unstaffed and provide full services for an adjacent school.

Local newspapers are a traditional method of recruitment. They have the advantage of reaching a large number of individuals in a given geographic area, of having a short lead time, and of being relatively inexpensive. However, they can become expensive when lengthy enough to contain sufficient information for readers to accurately assess their qualifications for the position. They often reach and are responded to by a large number of unqualified people and are not read by individuals who are not actively job searching.

Advertisements in *professional newspapers* such as state association newsletters and the *Communiqué* are more efficient, because they reach only qualified individuals yet also attract the interest of individuals who are not actively job searching. On the other hand, they do not reach individuals who are not dues-paying members of the organization. They also create additional expense and require substantial lead time relative to the short time line under which school systems commonly operate.

Online job databases such as Monster (www.monster.com) and Yahoo! HotJobs (http://hotjobs.yahoo.com) reach an even larger audience than newspapers and are increasingly relied on by job seekers and employers alike (Certo, 2006; Reeve & Schultz, 2004). Like newspapers, such databases generate a large number of applicants, many of whom are unqualified. Because of the very large number of applicants, employers often utilize automated responses or screening devices that advance applications with only specified keywords. This can result in employers' experiencing considerable frustration. While 60% of computer companies indicate that they find computer applications helpful, only 4% of consumer goods, telecommunication, and health care industries find them so (Certo, 2006). Furthermore, computer applications can cause applicants frustration as well. They often do not receive meaningful responses, resulting in the feeling that they sent their application to a "black hole." In addition, responding to databases often removes applicants' opportunity to control the appearance of their applications because formatting is lost in transition. Since individuals who are hiring can determine some personality characteristics through résumé review (M. S. Cole, Field, & Stafford, 2005), both applicants and recruiters are negatively impacted by this loss.

Professional databases, such as those of state and national professional associations (e.g., www.nasponline.org), reach a more limited and qualified audience and can be an excellent source of personnel. Like professional newspapers, however, they are typically available only to dues-paying members.

Screening Applicants

The purpose of the initial screening is to narrow the pool of applicants to the number that the interviewer would like to meet. Often the initial screening is conducted by the human resources (HR) department. Supervisors should be careful to ensure that the screening processes employed by the HR department do not prevent potentially attractive applications from reaching them.

Vignette 14.6

Rachel, a supervisor in a large urban district, received a telephone call from **Yvette**, an applicant whose résumé she had never seen. She was distressed to find out that the human resources department had kept back Yvette's application because her degree read "Educational Psychology" rather than "School Psychology," even though she had completed a school psychology program, internship, and licensure process in another state. After this experience, Rachel met with the HR department to broaden their understanding of the relevant qualifications and encourage them to forward applications directly to her.

Eliminating Bias

Avoiding bias during the hiring process is necessary to conform to both ethical standards and federal laws. Standards of reliability, validity, generalizability, and legality must be met. Methods must be relatively free of random error, associated with success on the job, and conform to current law. Unfortunately, many methods commonly used to discriminate applicants do not meet standards of reliability or validity. Interviews are notoriously unreliable. Grade point averages above a certain minimal level have little ability to predict job success and thus do not have predictive validity. References have become so universally positive that they are minimally helpful. Therefore, to avoid hiring errors, supervisors must combine multiple measures and methods of comparison, including multiple opportunities to see applicants "in action" (Mornell, 1998).

Reviewing employment laws is relevant, as described in Chapter 6. These laws include the Equal Pay Act of 1963, the Civil Rights Act of 1964, the Age Discrimination in Employment Act of 1967, the Rehabilitation Act of 1973, the Americans With Disabilities Act of 1990, and the Civil Rights Act of 1991. In sum, these laws prohibit discrimination on the basis of race, color, sex, religion, national origin, and age (40 to 70) concerning hiring, compensation, and working conditions (Leonard & Hilgert, 2004). For example, the Americans With Disabilities Act of 1990 protects individuals with a history of current physical or mental disabilities. This law requires employers to make "reasonable accommodations" for those who are "otherwise qualified" for the job. Reasonable accommodations include modifying equipment or work schedules, providing readers, and restructuring jobs (Noe et al., 1996).

As a result of these laws, employers must be able to prove that the methods used in employee selection measure traits and behaviors essential to job success. While these laws specifically address hiring and firing practices, it is important to understand that discrimination also occurs and is similarly unacceptable in other areas essential to job success, such as communication, mentoring, networking, evaluation, and promotion (Leonard & Hilgert, 2004).

If selection methods do not measure traits essential to job success and discriminate on the basis of variables such as race, color, sex, religion, national origin, disability, and age, the laws permit jury trials and awarding of punitive damages. During the past 30 years, such trials have led to large monetary awards for those with successful lawsuits. Hence, supervisors must be vigilantly aware of potential litigation and liability. Laws restrict what supervisors can ask applicants and forbid questions about an applicant's race, ethnicity, gender, religion, national origin, age, or disabilities. They also restrict discriminatory screening methods and measures. To make sure that a hiring process is legally sound, it is highly recommended that a standardized hiring process be developed and reviewed by the school district's personnel director and legal counsel. Before beginning the screening or interviewing process, supervisors should determine and minimize biases regarding age, sex, ethnicity, and race. It is helpful to compose a hiring team that reflects the composition of the school population.

In taking deliberate steps to avoid bias in hiring school psychologists, it should be noted that "minority" is a relative term. In school psychology, minorities include men as well as ethnic and racial minorities. To ensure compliance with legal antidiscrimination laws, supervisors are advised to maintain a file of not-hired minority applicants (including males) and contact them when an opening occurs (Rue & Byars, 1997); enlist males and members of ethnic minorities as recruiters, screeners, and interviewers; advertise in media directed toward minorities; include the phrase "equal opportunity employer" in all materials; and encourage men and members of ethnic minorities to enter and complete school psychology programs.

This is a particularly important variable because of the insufficient diversity among school psychologists. Although many school psychology training programs have deliberately and methodically increased the number of students from diverse backgrounds, a far smaller percentage of school psychologists are from ethnic minority backgrounds than there are students and parents from the same. This is particularly problematic regarding students and parents who are not native English speakers. While an increasing number of school psychologists are bilingual in English and Spanish, there are still few enough that they tend to be asked to cover a large number of schools. The problem is even more acute for the many languages spoken by even fewer (or no) bilingual school psychologists. Many state associations maintain lists of bilingual school psychologists that school districts can hire on a contractual basis, but contracted services are unlikely to be broad based or preventative in nature.

Application Materials

Applicants for school psychologist positions should be asked to submit:

1. A letter of application

2. A résumé

3. Undergraduate and graduate college and university transcripts

4. At least three letters of reference, particularly from supervisors

5. Relevant job evaluations, such as internship evaluations

6. Evidence of school psychology certification

7. A completed formal job application

8. A signed release to allow contact of references via telephone

9. Work samples. School psychologists often submit several psychoeducational reports as work samples, but, to demonstrate a breadth of skills, they should be strongly encouraged to submit other materials such as in-service workshop materials they developed and presented, consultation progress notes, authentic or functional assessments, intervention plans and evaluations of the results, grant applications they wrote, or other materials that prove their ability to perform the professional practice of school psychology at a high level.

After the applications have been reviewed for completeness, a team of three to five diverse individuals screens them. The screening eliminates applicants who are not qualified and determines which applicants to invite for interviews. At this stage, it is preferable to be generous rather than highly critical. It is important not to exclude all but the "top" candidates solely on the basis of a paper evaluation, as highly qualified candidates may be excluded. For example, a candidate with a range of grades from B to A may ultimately be as competent as a candidate with all A's. However, an applicant with close to failing grades or many C's at the graduate level is obviously not a strong candidate.

The screening team should verify the résumés against the transcripts and other information for consistency, since a large proportion of job applicants misrepresent or falsify information (Mornell, 1998). The applications should also be screened for indications of problematic behavior. It is not uncommon for the manner in which individuals present themselves in their cover letter and résumé to reveal essential characteristics such as literacy, integrity, and stability (M. S. Cole et al., 2005). For example, a candidate might state one grade point average on a résumé while the transcript lists quite another. Submitting a reference letter written by a relative reveals a lack of understanding of the fundamental ethical principle of avoiding dual relationships. Since past behavior tends to indicate future behavior, attending to past patterns can be illuminating. If a candidate has skipped among fields or positions in the past, she or he may be likely to do so in the future.

After the screening committee generates a list of applicants to be interviewed, they are telephoned to set up the initial interview. It is best if the supervisor makes these telephone calls, rather than a secretary, as this demonstrates a level of respect for the candidate, and his or her responses can provide additional information.

During this telephone call, the applicant can be asked to complete a brief pre-interview assignment that reveals how she or he carries out tasks. This task can be as simple as visiting the district's Web page or city library to obtain information about district schools and then sharing impressions and observations during the interview (Mornell, 1998). The completion of the assignment before the interview indicates the tendency to follow through in general; the supervisor can also assess the accuracy and helpfulness of the observations.

Interviewing

The fundamental purpose of interviewing is to obtain information not available on the résumé and related paperwork. The most important variables are interpersonal and verbal communication skills. Interviews also give the supervisor the opportunity to ask more detailed questions regarding information contained in the résumé as well as give applicants the opportunity to ask questions that help them decide whether they would like to accept the position. Although interviews are the most common hiring selection process, research indicates that they can be unreliable and subjective. To increase the likelihood that interviews will be reliable and legal, interviews should be

> structured, standardized and focused on . . . quantitative ratings on a small number of dimensions that are observable (e.g., interpersonal style or ability to express oneself), and avoid ratings of abilities that may be better measured by tests (e.g., intelligence). (Noe et al., 1996, pp. 320–321)

Deliberately *minimizing bias in interviews* is important, because all of us have prejudices and personal experiences that color our perceptions and can adversely affect the hiring process. To minimize the effect of these issues, interviewers should first identify and then sensitize themselves to their own biases regarding age, sex, ethnicity, and race before interviewing candidates (Halloran, 1981). It is also helpful to involve more than one person. To increase the number of persons involved in the screening process, some supervisors turn to teleconferencing or videoconferencing interviews. However, there is evidence that face-to-face interviews yield more accurate results (Garman & Lesowitz, 2005).

Initial interviews generally include the supervisor and at least one other person, although a large (e.g., eight-person) panel of interviewers can actually be detrimental to the process (Garman & Lesowitz, 2005). Developing a roster of semistructured interview questions is important. Consistent use of the same questions across applicants minimizes bias and results in consistent information. On the other hand, the open-ended nature of semistructured questions provides critical information regarding the applicant's personality (Garman & Lesowitz, 2005).

Initial interviews are often short but critical. They serve to eliminate "paper tigers who have great résumés but are less impressive in person" (Mornell, 1998, p. 49). Interviews test "how well someone interviews" because "a good con artist can con you every time" (p. 55). Although personal chemistry, or likability, can be significant, it certainly is not appropriate as a sole criterion. Candidates' responses to the questions posed are important, but their behavior is also important. Inexplicable or inappropriate behavior may indicate significant issues, such as alcoholism. On the other hand, during the interview it is important to avoid judgment errors, such as making decisions on a personal bias. To counteract the tendency to make a decision based on first impressions, such as the quality of the interviewee's handshake, it is helpful to listen carefully, keep questions simple and clear, ask questions that balance the information the candidate presents, and always check past records (Certo, 2006; Mornell, 1998).

As previously mentioned, to comply with the Americans With Disabilities Act of 1990, the interviewer cannot ask any questions that would disclose a disability, including whether the candidate has or has had a physical illness, mental disability, or issues with substance abuse. On the other hand, it is not only permissible but required to ask questions that reveal the candidate's ability to successfully perform the job. For example, if it is a job requirement for school psychologists to be on-site during school hours, it is permissible to ask whether candidates would be able to arrive by the time school opens at 7 a.m. These questions can be asked both of candidates and of their references.

As Certo (2006) suggested, to conduct a successful interview during which one can accurately appraise the candidate, interviewers should:

- Review the candidate's materials before the interview to find patterns of accomplishments, strengths, and attributes to explore
- Discuss the candidate's work history and patterns in that work history
- Eliminate visual distractions, interruptions, and phone calls to present a professional atmosphere
- Establish rapport
- Avoid inducing additional stress
- Conduct a "conversation" rather than an "interrogation," using open-ended questions to enable the applicant to reveal feelings and ideas (the candidate should do 80% of the talking)
- Describe the school and district
- Provide a "realistic job preview" by describing attractive aspects as well as the challenges the candidate will encounter in the position
- Provide accurate information regarding benefits
- Provide opportunities for questions
- Discuss the next step in the hiring process and provide as much feedback as possible

It is very important to avoid questions that elicit information that might lead to illegal discrimination. These would be questions pertaining to:

- Age
- Race
- Ethnicity
- Religion

- Citizenship of parents or spouse
- Type of military discharge
- National origin or ancestry
- Languages spoken, unless they are job related
- Arrests or convictions, unless they are job related
- Height
- Weight
- Marital status
- Number of dependents
- Plans to have children in the future
- With whom the candidate lives
- Personal finances, such as bankruptcy or home or car ownership, unless it is job related
- Membership in any organization that is not job related
- Health history
- Disabilities

Additionally, a set of standardized questions that raise issues the candidate is likely to encounter as a school psychologist are helpful. These can be based on the interviewees' own experiences or may draw on future problem solving capabilities. In a typical interview, a candidate can be asked to respond to four or five such questions. Examples are included in Handout 14.3.

These questions do not necessarily have correct or incorrect answers. The candidates' responses can be evaluated, nonetheless, on several dimensions mentioned previously as characteristics necessary for school psychologists, including oral expression; ability to respond to constructive criticism professionally; overall emotional maturity; ability to work with children; ability to work with peers, parents, and school or agency personnel; willingness to go beyond basic requirements; flexibility in adapting to change; observance of protocol and rules; ability to act in accord with professional ethics; and ability to respect individual and group differences. Some individuals prefer to hand each candidate a typed list of the questions at the beginning of the interview. This gives candidates the opportunity to exhibit their organizational skill and makes it less likely that interviewers will dominate the conversation (Mornell, 1998). Others prefer to ask questions as the interview progresses, thereby fostering a more conversational interview.

In academia and business, it is common to expect applicants to *perform a task* during the interview. The task might be to teach a class, give a lecture, solve a "problem," or analyze a work sample. Such experience-based approaches can be quite valid predictors of job performance (Garman & Lesowitz, 2005). Another approach is to assign a task, such as reading and discussing a case study or solving hypothetical problems. Examples are included in Handout 14.8, found at the end of the chapter.

Besides delineating the interview questions and methods to evaluate the responses, the supervisor lists the additional traits that are to be observed during the interview (e.g., curiosity, general attitude, interpersonal skills, punctuality, energy, enthusiasm, and humor). Again, to comply with legal requirements, whatever traits the supervisor notes in the interview should be observed and noted for all candidates and must be relevant to the job. After the interview, the applicant is rated according to the previously determined criteria. Sample rating forms are included in Handouts 14.4, 14.5, and 14.6.

Many organizations follow successful initial interviews with *second interviews* with a few finalists. Second interviews provide the opportunity for both the candidate and the

Handout 14.3

POTENTIAL SEMISTRUCTURED INTERVIEW QUESTIONS

Describe a case about which you feel particular success.

Describe a difficult case where you wished you had done something differently. How would you approach a similar situation differently in the future?

What would your former supervisor(s) say about your work, including both positive and negative aspects?

What would you describe as your greatest professional strength? In what circumstances does that strength become a weakness? What do you do in those circumstances?

What factor regarding your work would you most like to improve? How will you go about improving it?

School psychology is a constantly changing field. Describe how you go about learning new techniques. How do you decide which techniques to learn? How do you acquire the necessary skills?

What methods have you developed to cope with the inevitable stress that results from being a school psychologist? How do you release tension?

What would you like to be doing professionally in 10 years?

With what type of person do you find it most difficult to work? How do you deal with that difficulty?

What metaphor would you use to describe the profession of school psychology?

What metaphor would you use to describe schools?

What three things would you change about your current or most recent job?

Pretending that you were your former supervisor, how would you structure your job differently?

Which professional books have most profoundly affected your thinking and professional work?

What led you to leave your last positions?

What responsibilities as a school psychologist do you like least, and how do you deal with them?

What responsibilities as a school psychologist do you like most, and why?

What work environment is most likely to induce your best performance?

How do you approach working with individuals whose language or class is different from yours?

What do you think are the most important characteristics for a school psychologist to have? Which of these characteristics do you display?

Handout 14.4

APPLICANT RATING

Name: _____   Rating: _____

Undergraduate School: _____   Undergraduate Major: _____

Undergraduate GPA

0	1	2	3
(Below 3.0)	(3.0–3.39)	(3.40–3.79)	(3.80–4.0)

Graduate Institution _____   Graduate Major _____

Graduate GPA

0	1	2	3
(Below 3.0)	(3.0–3.39)	(3.4–3.79)	(3.8–4.0)

Cover Letter

0	1	2	3
(Weak)	(Fair)	(Good)	(Excellent)

Academic Honors

0	1	2
(None noted)	(Yes)	Type: _____

Depth of Thought

0	1	2	3

Quality of Writing Style

0	1	2	3

Relevant Work Experience

0	1	2	3
(None noted)		(Very relevant)	

Interview   (Weak)   (Excellent)

1. Verbal Articulation   1   2   3   4   5

Community Service

0	1	2	3
(None noted)		(High degree)	

2. Professional
   Development   1   2   3   4   5

Letter of Recommendation #1

0	1	2
(Weaknesses noted)	(No weakness noted)	(Strong)

3. Cognitive Flexibility   1   2   3   4   5

Letter of Recommendation #2

0	1	2
(Weaknesses noted)	(No weakness noted)	(Strong)

4. Realistic Self-Appraisal   1   2   3   4   5

5. Commitment   1   2   3   4   5

Letter of Recommendation #3

0	1	2
(Weaknesses noted)	(No weakness noted)	(Strong)

6. Overall Estimate of   1   2   3   4   5
   Cognitive, Clinical, and
   Interpersonal Skills

Overall Likelihood of Success

Total Points _____   Ranking _____

From the *2006 Baltimore County, Maryland, Public Schools School Psychologist Handbook.* Baltimore, MD: Locally published monograph. Use of this material is by permission of the author, William Flook.

Handout 14.5

INTERVIEW RATING FORM

Name of Applicant: _____ Interviewer: _____

Interview Content (Inspiration, Initiative, Metaphor, Additional Information)

1. Verbal articulation: Expresses thoughts and feelings clearly, logically, and convincingly. Listens and responds appropriately. Makes eye contact.

   1   2   3   4   5

   (inadequate)   (average)   (outstanding)

2. Professional development: Active involvement in pursuing described goals (e.g., conference attendance, workshops, courses, reading journals, belong to professional organizations).

   1   2   3   4   5

   (inadequate)   (average)   (outstanding)

3. Cognitive flexibility: Openness to different ideas, experiences, roles, people, etc.

   1   2   3   4   5

   (inadequate)   (average)   (outstanding)

4. Realistic self-appraisal: Awareness of professional and personal strengths and weaknesses relative to goals. Genuine interest in children, sense of humor, etc.

   1   2   3   4   5

   (inadequate)   (average)   (outstanding)

5. Commitment: realistic expectations of time required, flexibility in personal schedule, etc.

   1   2   3   4   5

   (inadequate)   (average)   (outstanding)

6. Overall estimate of cognitive, clinical, and interpersonal skills.

   1   2   3   4   5

   (inadequate)   (average)   (outstanding)

_____ Strong Candidate _____ Acceptable Candidate _____ Not Acceptable Candidate

Handout 14.6

CANDIDATE INTERVIEW RATING FORM

Name of Candidate: _____ Date of Interview: _____

Position Interviewed for: _____ Location of Interview: _____

Interview Team Captain: _____

(Team Captain completes one rating form for the applicant based on team input)

Interview Team Members: _____

_____

_____

Rating Scale: 1 = Unacceptable (U), 2 = Acceptable (A), 3 = Strong (S), 4 = Outstanding (O)

	Criteria	*Rating*	*Comments*
A.	Academic Profile/Potential for Learning	1 2 3 4	
B.	Quality of Training/Experience	1 2 3 4	
C.	Knowledge of School Psychology	1 2 3 4	
D.	Clinical Skills and Judgment	1 2 3 4	
E.	Communication Skills	1 2 3 4	
F.	Personal Qualities		
	(Energy/Enthusiasm; Imagination/ Curiosity; Sense of Humor)	1 2 3 4	

Rating Score ☐ /24

Overall Rating ☐ U ☐ A ☐ S ☐ O

22–24	O
18–21	S
15–17	A
14 and below	U

interviewer to gather second impressions and additional information. Interaction skills exhibited in second interviews, when a candidate is often less nervous, can offer more accurate indications of the candidate's general persona than the first interview. These interviews are structured to include more interviewers and interview sessions. A one-to-one session with the supervisor, a session with potential colleagues (other school psychologists), and a session with administrators (including the director of special education and either a principal or assistant superintendent) are all appropriate. It is thoughtful and efficient to coordinate questions so that candidates are not asked by different interviewers to reply to the same questions repeatedly.

At the end of each interview, each candidate meets again with the supervisor and is provided a final opportunity to raise questions. Just before the end of the final session, the supervisor should indicate that the interview is almost over. Frequently, the questions raised at this time are the most important (Mornell, 1998). Finally, the candidate is asked for the names and telephone numbers of additional references, including previous supervisors, school administrators, school psychologists, and teachers.

Post-Interview Strategies

Checking background variables that are job related is a critical aspect of the hiring process. According to management research, 30% of applicants falsely represent themselves on their applications (Mornell, 1998). The vast majority of supervisors (90%) who conduct background and reference checks have found that at least one applicant falsified information (Certo, 2006). Lies range from an exaggeration of educational background to the hiding of criminal records. Employers can be held responsible and legally liable for crimes committed by employees who have been hired without adequate background checks that would have revealed problems such as a history of pedophilia. This liability has led many school districts to require criminal background checks for all individuals (even volunteers) working in schools. Verification of background information can include checks on driving records and criminal records, education verification, and employment verification. Often these variables are routinely checked by HR departments, but supervisors should not presume that to be the case.

Checking references is also essential. Unfortunately, information conveyed by references is not necessarily a reliable indicator of future job performance. This stems from two sources. First, candidates request references only from those who they expect will give good reports. Second, references are hesitant to give negative responses due to justifiable fear of lawsuits (Anthony et al., 2006). Some businesses will refuse to convey any information other than the dates of employment. Consequently, written references are often notoriously vague, resulting in interviewers' attempting to "read between the lines." Telephone references often yield more information, particularly when conducted by persons in comparable positions (e.g., special education administrators calling special education administrators, principals calling principals, school psychologists calling school psychologists). The references of the strongest candidates should be telephoned and asked about the candidate's:

1. Technical competency as a school psychologist

2. Intelligence

3. Energy, motivation, and initiative

4. Ability to display good interpersonal skills with children, teachers, parents, other school psychologists, administrators, and supervisors

5. Professional and ethical attitude and behavior

Finally, each reference should be asked, "Is there anything that I haven't asked?" (Mornell, 1998, p. 141). It is critical to listen carefully to the responses and to allow the reference to disclose freely. In checking references, supervisors are still obligated to refrain from asking questions that might violate employment laws but have a right and obligation to ask questions about ability to perform the job.

Follow-up tasks can provide additional information. For example, asking candidates to telephone on a certain day to discuss any additional thoughts they have or to raise additional questions provides yet another opportunity to observe whether candidates act responsibly by following through with tasks (Mornell, 1998). Candidates might be assigned a post-interview project, such as analyzing a case, editing a report, or writing up the responses to a critical issue currently faced by the school district. The finished result can be analyzed for accuracy, timeliness, attention to detail, and problem analysis.

Sample Postinterview Projects

Describe what you believe should be included in a workshop for teachers on functional behavior assessment.

Describe how you would help a school develop and implement a crisis intervention plan.

Delineate a recommended set of procedures for the district in approaching children who are learning English as a second language and who are also experience considerable academic difficulties.

Making the Hiring Decision

Some organizations designate one individual to make the hiring decision, while others involve a group decision making process. The advantages and disadvantages of group decision making have been discussed in the previous chapter. Certainly there is considerable advantage to having both the administrative and clinical supervisor involved in the decision to hire a school psychologist. It is not wise to hire someone who will be supervised by an individual not committed to the new hire's success.

In many situations, upper level administration accepts the recommendation of the supervising school psychologist in the selection of an intern or school psychologist but retains the right to actually offer the job and negotiate salary. Although employers appropriately strive to minimize expenditures, often negotiation must occur if qualified applicants are to be successfully hired. For example, some administrators believe a school psychologist without experience as a contracted school district employee should start at the lowest pay level. However, a certified school psychologist with 10 years' experience working in a mental health clinic is unlikely to be willing to enter a school system at that level. If the applicant has worked for a number of years in a clinic setting, the supervising school psychologist should negotiate to have those years credited on the salary scale.

In making the final selection, some organizations add up the "points" obtained by applicants, while others use a "global perspective." Using a combination of both approaches seems to have the best predictive validity (Garman & Lesowitz, 2005). After the decision has been made, the job offer must be negotiated by the appropriate administrator.

Documentation regarding the hiring process is often required. This involves providing a written record of reasons for the choices made in screening, interviewing, and hiring. Such justifications may be needed in the future if any of the decisions are challenged due to perceived discrimination, nepotism, or other factors.

ORIENTING AND TRAINING NEW SUPERVISEES

Supervisors should strive to make the transition into employment as smooth and positive as possible. This requires providing support such that the new supervisee quickly becomes "an accepted member of the departmental work team and a contributing, productive employee" (Leonard & Hilgert, 2004, p. 351). Supervisors should let others know about positive attributes of the new hire, personally introduce the new supervisee to individuals and groups with whom he or she will work, and take care to orient the new psychologist. Orientation also involves providing initial training. This training may be provided on the job or through off-site resources such as colleges. Initial training should naturally evolve into a plan for ongoing professional development.

Orientation is both formal and informal. Informal and unofficial orientations, particularly from colleagues and school personnel, can unfortunately be misleading and inaccurate. In contrast, well-planned formal orientations facilitate adjustment to the work environment and reduce stress, startup costs, turnover rates, and integration time (Leonard & Hilgert, 2004). *Mentoring*, or "having a more experienced person provide guidance, coaching, or counseling to a less experienced person" (Leonard & Hilgert, 2004, p. 351), is very helpful. Supervisors can assign every new hire at least one mentor who can help him or her transition, and often more than one mentor is appropriate.

Part of orientation is helping supervisees understand where they fit into the school system's organization and how the work of the school psychology department fits into the functioning and success of the school system. Describing formal structures is generally straightforward and can be accomplished using organizational charts. The most common complication is that more than one person claims ownership of the psychologist's time and loyalty. For example, the school psychologist may directly report to the supervising school psychologist, who reports to the assistant superintendent, the director of pupil personnel services, or the director of special education. However, principals in a school psychologist's assigned schools also frequently have supervisory responsibilities. As long as competing demands and role conflicts are clarified, reporting to multiple "bosses" can be managed.

Informal structures develop primarily from social relationships and are the main route for informal communication in a school district. Orienting new hires to informal structures is more difficult than orienting them to the formal structure, because informal structures tend to be unstable, complex, and unexposed. Many school personnel are originally from the area and have blood relatives, in-laws, former in-laws, long-standing friends and enemies, or casual acquaintances working within the school district. These relationships result in informal communication channels that affect the work of school psychologists to an extraordinary degree, particularly if they are insensitive to or unaware of the relationships. Failing to orient the new school psychologist thoroughly can lead to unintentional breaches of protocol that can ultimately lead to bad feeling.

Vignette 14.7

Yvonne, a school psychology intern, was not informed about informal parking rules. While she carefully avoided parking in the spots marked "Principal" and "Nurse," she consistently parked in the (frequently empty) spot next to the side door. Only after several months did she realize that she had consistently taken the spot "belonging" to the director of pupil personnel—who happened to be her administrative supervisor.

Information Provision

Often the school district personnel department conducts a formal orientation and presents topics of relevance and interest to all employees. Usually this orientation provides new employees with a packet of information, including the school calendar, benefits and insurance information, school district regulations and work policies, and union information.

The supervisor typically conducts the departmental and job orientation. New school psychologists should be given copies of school district and departmental regulations, tools used for individual performance evaluations, administrative organizational charts, and policy and procedure handbooks. Helpful information additionally includes:

- Demographics of the populations served in the schools
- The philosophy, objectives, and mission statement of the district
- District characteristics, facilities, and services
- The schedule of faculty meetings and staff development days
- Discipline procedures and policies
- Student and faculty dress code, if applicable
- Available student activities
- Emergency procedures
- General education forms, grades, and reports
- Prereferral and special education procedures, forms, and time lines
- Availability of and procedures regarding pupil records
- Class schedules, schedules for specials (art, music, physical education, library), and schedule deviations (early release days or delayed openings)
- School and staff directories
- School and district handbooks
- Maps of the district and each school
- School calendars

School psychologists new to the district should also be given clear guidelines regarding work policies. For example, they should have a clear understanding of expected work hours, responsibilities, attendance during inclement weather days, methods of reporting absence, report formats, and whether they are expected to complete paperwork and make parent contacts after school hours (on their "own" time).

New employees also appreciate information regarding available facilities, materials, computer and audiovisual equipment, and support services. They also need to know various procedures (reproducing materials, obtaining supplies and assessment tools, submitting travel reimbursement forms, etc.). Not infrequently, space is an issue. From the beginning, every school psychologist needs a desk and access to other office equipment, such as a telephone and computer. Individual offices may be difficult to obtain, but all school psychologists and second-semester interns should have individual space to facilitate autonomy. Issues regarding compensation, contracts, and insurance issues should also be clarified. These policies should be reviewed orally and supplied in written form. A well-organized and comprehensive handbook, as described in Chapter 2, is the most efficient manner in which to convey essential information.

Training

Even when appropriately credentialed psychologists have the necessary professional skills, they will not know the processes and procedures used in a particular setting. While indubitably every school psychologist is familiar with the administration of standardized assessment tools, a training program cannot possibly cover every instrument. Therefore, it is necessary for the clinical supervisor to provide training for new hires, or to designate another person more knowledgeable or skillful in a given area. For example, if a new supervisee is deficient in applied behavior analysis (ABA), he or she may be assigned to shadow and learn from an individual with very strong ABA skills.

Promoting Job Satisfaction

Promoting job satisfaction has been an area of interest in industrial psychology for several decades. Job satisfaction is personally associated with self-esteem, general life adjustment, physical health, and mental health. Professionally, it is associated with attendance, attitude, turnover, effort, job performance, and productivity (E. M. Levinson, 1990; E. M. Levinson, Fetchkan, & Hohenshil, 1988). As mentioned previously, job satisfaction is critically important to employees.

Hundreds of studies have linked job dissatisfaction to consequent physical or psychological job withdrawal (Noe et al., 1996). When employees are dissatisfied, they first express that dissatisfaction by trying to change the conditions under which they work. This can take the form of confrontations with supervisors, negatively focused union involvement, whistle-blowing, or the filing of grievances against the employer. If these efforts to promote change are unsuccessful, employees are likely to physically or psychologically withdraw from the job. Transferring to another job, being absent, or being late manifests physical withdrawal. Psychological withdrawal is manifested through minimal job involvement, low organizational commitment, or physical or mental health problems (Noe et al., 1996). Studies examining job dissatisfaction have found that between 35% (Solly & Hohenshil, 1986) and 14% (Anderson, Hohenshil, & Brown, 1984) of school psychologists are dissatisfied. Sources of school psychologists' dissatisfaction have been identified as:

- Restriction of activities and roles to psychoeducational assessment (Guidubaldi, 1981; Jerrell, 1984; E. M. Levinson, 1990; D. K. Smith, 1984)
- Excessive caseloads, insufficient time, and lack of appreciation (Reiner & Hartshorne, 1982)
- Disagreement with school system policies and practices, lack of advancement opportunities, insufficient compensation, poor working conditions, and insufficient supervision (Solly & Hohenshil, 1986) and,
- High student-psychologist ratios, disagreement with school district policies and practices, or the lack of the opportunity for advancement (Anderson et al., 1984)

In contrast, school psychologists' job satisfaction has been found to correlate with age, experience, ratio of psychologist to students, diversity of roles, participation in research, and membership in professional organizations (E. M. Levinson et al., 1988). Role diversity and "boundary spanning functions" such as interdisciplinary work (Jerrell, 1984) as well as role function and perceived control (E. M. Levinson, 1990, 1991) have been correlated with increased job satisfaction and decreased burnout (Huberty & Huebner, 1988). School psychologists working in large districts tend to be more dissatisfied with school district policies and opportunities for advancement than school psychologists in smaller districts (E. M. Levinson, 1991).

As indicated by Littrell, Billingsley, and Cross (1994), supervisors can increase job satisfaction by providing (a) emotional support; (b) constructive and frequent feedback and clear guidance regarding responsibilities and improvement; (c) help with work-related tasks through the procuring of materials, space, resources, administrative support, and appropriate scheduling; and (d) information and instruction needed for supervisees to improve.

Providing Emotional Support

The amount of emotional support provided by supervisors is the most significant variable in promoting job satisfaction and preventing burnout for educators (Littrell et al., 1994; Russell, Altmaier, & Van Velzen, 1987), factory workers (House, 1981), mental health workers (R. R. Ross, Altmaier, & Russell, 1989), and nurses (Constable & Russell, 1986). A significant source of emotional support stems from the social environment, determined by positive relationships among supervisees and peers as well as between supervisee and supervisor.

A supervisor can facilitate a positive social environment by several methods. First, supervisors improve the social environment when they encourage supervisees to develop a network of support among themselves rather than relying solely on the supervisor for problem solving. Because of the isolation of school psychologists, this requires deliberate planning and team assignments. Basically, the supervisor seeks to form a department with lines of communication between all members rather than a department in which all communications are directed to the supervisor as though the supervisor were a hub in a spoked wheel.

In addition, the supervisor encourages school psychologists to develop positive and professional networks within their schools. School psychologists feel less isolated when they psychologically become members of schools. This requires that the supervisor assign department members to schools and programs on a predictable and continuous basis. The degree to which school psychologists have predictable schedules determines their ability to take part in community building activities such as parent-teacher association meetings, potlucks, and faculty meetings.

Finally, supervisors increase social support by encouraging participation in professional organizations. Such participation positively correlates with job satisfaction (E. M. Levinson et al., 1988), and school psychologists are more likely to become active members of local, state, and national school psychology associations with their supervisor's support and example. Encouraging supervisees' participation in international associations and Internet consultation groups can also increase their sense of professional community.

Supervisors additionally foster emotional support when they both privately and publicly show esteem, maintain an open communication system, demonstrate appreciation, and consider the ideas of each supervisee. McInerney (1985) recommended the following methods to foster positive working relationships:

1. Address supervisees' concerns. If it is not possible to address the concerns, communicate them to higher authorities.

2. Keep staff informed and provide rationales for decisions.

3. Ask staff how they feel about what they are doing and give them opportunities to talk about their work.

4. Be physically and psychologically present for both formal meetings and informal discussions.

5. Observe staff in action.

6. Give direction clearly.

7. Ensure that sufficient time and resources are allocated.

8. Provide reinforcers for good work, such as monetary rewards, personal thanks and praise, a positive memorandum to a higher authority, and opportunities for further training or recognition.

Promoting a Positive Physical Environment

Another major consideration in fostering job satisfaction is that of the physical environment. While schools are generally not thought to be harsh physical environments, supervisors of school psychologists are frequently in a position where they must attend to the physical work environment of their supervisees. Because of the overcrowded nature of schools and the itinerant nature of school psychology, it is common to hear "horror stories" of school psychologists who are asked to work in highly unsuitable or undesirable settings such as hallways and storage closets. Exposure to adverse physical work conditions should be of limited duration. These recommendations are reflected in the NASP *Standards* (2000b) and *Professional Conduct Manual* (2000a).

Often school psychologists themselves feel unable to negotiate for adequate workspace and so supervisors must negotiate for them. Of course, in negotiating for appropriate space it is necessary to be reasonable about resource availability. To demand "deluxe accommodations"—a private office with a telephone and window in every school—would certainly adversely affect relationships between the school psychologist and other school personnel. Often reasonable space can be achieved by taking into account the schedules of other itinerant specialists when developing school psychologists' schedules.

Vignette 14.8

Madelyn had to ask her supervisor for help in dealing with a most adverse work setting. The only room available on her scheduled days in the school was a former locker room adjacent to the gym. The small room had only a metal grill between it and the gymnasium, in which physical education classes were held all day. The noise—particularly when the PE classes played basketball—was so extreme that she could not hear children speaking to her. She met with her supervisor, and, in collaboration with the principal, it was decided to change her schedule so that she would be at the school on the days the speech and language pathologist was at other schools so that they could share work space.

Facilitating Job Enrichment

To counteract job dissatisfaction stemming from monotony, a supervisor can accomplish job enrichment through careful analysis of the roles and responsibilities of the job and by advocating increased complexity, greater involvement in cases prior to referral for special services, and greater involvement in research. Job rotation can be accomplished by changing school or program assignments every 3 to 5 years.

Promoting

It cannot be presumed that, because an individual functions successfully at one level, she or he will succeed at the next level. In management lore, the "Peter Principle" suggests the opposite: that individuals are promoted to their level of incompetence (Rue & Byars, 1997). Promoting an intern to the position of a school psychologist, or a school psychologist to the position of supervising school psychologist, requires the same level of attention in developing a job description, recruiting, screening, selecting, and orienting as described previously.

ASSESSING THE RECRUITING AND ORIENTING PROCESS

After completing a hiring process, it is important to assess the success of that process. Each of the steps described above (determining the hiring process, conducting a job analysis, developing a job description and specifications, generating applicants, screening, interviewing, and implementing post-interview strategies) should be carefully reviewed. Gathering information from applicants and individuals who did not accept job offers can be very helpful, as can meeting with individuals who leave the district in favor of another position. After the assessment is completed, the results should be used to modify hiring procedures in the future.

SUMMARY

Recruitment of high-quality school psychologists is an important supervisory responsibility, particularly in light of the shortage of school psychologists and the high cost to children, colleagues, schools, and the district when errors in hiring are made. The application process and the hiring process, as well as job descriptions, should be comprehensive and thorough. Management literature includes numerous methods of generating applicants, each with its own benefits, drawbacks, and success rates. When screening applicants, care must be taken to avoid bias, since this is mandated by both ethical standards and federal laws. Interviews allow for the evaluation of qualities not evident on a résumé, particularly interpersonal and verbal communication skills. Interviews can, however, be unreliable, subjective, and biased. They should be conducted in a standardized manner to minimize these risks. Checking backgrounds is an important tool in screening applicants, since research indicates that many applicants falsely represent themselves. To further assess candidates, it is common to ask applicants to provide work samples, to perform a task during the interview process, or to complete follow-up tasks.

There is considerable advantage to having both the administrative and clinical supervisor involved in the decision to hire a school psychologist. It is important to document choices made in screening, interviewing, and hiring processes should decisions later be challenged. Once an individual is hired, supervisors should strive to make the transition as smooth and positive as possible through thorough and well-planned orientations and deliberate efforts to increase job satisfaction. Finally, it is important to assess the success of the hiring process. After the assessment is completed, the results should be used to modify hiring procedures in the future.

REFLECTIVE QUESTIONS

Q14.1. What factors are important in determining whether a candidate will accept a job offer? What steps can be taken to ensure that a candidate feels valued?

Q14.2. How should job descriptions and specifications be developed?

Q14.3. What are the benefits and challenges of hiring internally and externally?

Q14.4. What are the important factors in screening applicants? How can one avoid bias?

Q14.5. Discuss the important components of an interview. How would you design a first and second interview?

Q14.6. If reference checks can be unreliable, how can we best utilize them and minimize the risks of inappropriate hires?

Q14.7. How would you design orientation and training to be comprehensive and helpful in transitioning new staff?

Q14.8. What work samples might you ask a candidate to submit that would demonstrate a breadth of skills? Which skills would you be most concerned that they demonstrate?

Q14.9. How does job satisfaction affect an employee's performance, and what are the possible implications of dissatisfaction? How can supervisors promote job satisfaction, provide support, and foster stress management?

SUPERVISORY DILEMMAS

SD 14.1

A school psychology intern was assigned to two different schools, one elementary and one secondary. After several months, she discovered that the social worker in one building was sister to the speech therapist in the other building, that the secretary in the elementary school was living with the assistant superintendent, and that the guidance counselor in the secondary school was the roommate of her administrative supervisor, the director of special education. Her site supervisor, a school psychologist, had not advised her of any of the informal structures in the school system, and the intern felt that she might have said or done something inappropriate. *What are the supervisory considerations? What should be done?*

Authors' thoughts: At one time or another, similar situations will inevitably be encountered. The world does seem to get smaller and smaller! This is largely an issue of etiquette and good old common sense. A good rule to follow is to use the good listening skills learned in training to try to deduce some of the covert relationships and alliances present in all organizations. (One of the authors remembers with abject horror having criticized the cleanliness of a classroom only to discover that the superintendent's son was the school's custodian!) It will be helpful for supervisors to advise supervisees to be conscious of the many relationships that typically exist within the school and community at large. Often supervisors are not privy to all the overt and covert alliances that permeate the various systems. Hence, consistent application of the Golden Rule is advised. When intricate relationship issues complicate communication and actions (and they surely do), proceed professionally with kindness, diplomacy, and sound observational skills. Finally, it does help to remind the supervisee that it takes time to discover the myriad social alliances that exist and that many of us have made statements we would pay to retract!

SD 14.2

You are working in the district school that houses the program for (signing) deaf students. The director of special education has inadvertently hired a teacher of the hearing impaired without realizing that her graduate program was oral/aural and that she does not sign. You feel that the students are not being adequately served, but the director indicates that the posting stipulated only that the person be qualified to teach the deaf, not that signing be used to do so. In addition, the administration indicates that the teacher was offered and signed a contract and therefore must finish the school year. *What are the supervisory considerations? What should be done?*

Authors' thoughts: This situation is fraught with adverse consequences for all students in the program. Essentially, this is no different than appointing a non–English speaking teacher to teach the class. As an "educational emergency," it demands immediate resolution. This occurrence certainly illustrates a major flaw in the hiring process. An error in hiring does not justify violating the students' rights and welfare. (We have a hunch that some angry parents will soon provide support for the initiation of change!) While it might be possible to help the teacher acquire signing skills at the district's expense, developing the requisite competency will be a time-consuming process. To serve the needs of the students in the program, it will be necessary to immediately procure a teacher who is appropriately trained.

SD 14.3

Your district has just changed its service delivery model. Each time a guidance counselor's position is vacated, a school psychologist is hired instead. Some unforeseen difficulties have emerged that are causing a great deal of dissention within the school system. For example, in the past, guidance counselors always assisted the principal with recess duty, lunch duty, and bus duty. They would then handle any discipline problems that emerged during these periods. These responsibilities have never been part of the school psychologists' jobs, and they are not interested in acquiring them! You approach the director of pupil personnel with your concerns. He adamantly responds that this *will* be part of the new job and will make no accommodations. *What are the supervisory considerations? What should be done?*

Authors' thoughts: It is difficult to simultaneously serve in a "helping role" and a disciplinary role. A first chore will be to brainstorm with the principal about how job duties can be adjusted to fit the new situation. This systems level change is likely to affect all participants in the same manner. A concerted effort to explain the role conflict should help in eliminating the punitive role. A beneficial outcome for all concerned would be for the school psychologists to take this opportunity to institute a schoolwide positive behavior support system.

SD 14.4

You are responsible for supervising a school psychologist who, although well seasoned and very experienced, is new to your district. Within the first month, multiple complaints have emerged regarding a variety of concerns, including accusations of (a) intimidation (e.g., the preschool teachers feel that they have been strongly discouraged from offering services and programs); (b) failure to complete paperwork for a grant, resulting in ineligibility for further funding; and (c) general inconsistency in paperwork completion. When you discuss the issues with the supervisee, she loudly (rudely, actually!) denies all accusations. *What are the supervisory considerations? What should be done?*

Authors' thoughts: Since issues of poor job performance appeared immediately, it is probable that this is a classic bad hire. Within the contractual obligations, a series of structured observations, concrete data collection regarding job performance, and provision of additional support should be initiated immediately. Personality issues are more subjective and harder to deal with. However, forfeiting a grant by failing to complete paperwork in a timely manner constitutes a straightforward dereliction of duties. Under these circumstances, it may be necessary to explore the contractual language and resulting options and steps for dismissal. Often, an opportunity for early termination exists (e.g., within the first 60 days). This is, of course, a somewhat extreme step that would be taken only if the supervisor made a good faith determination that remediation was not feasible. If it is determined that a plan of remediation is viable, it will have to be well crafted, monitored closely, and mutually agreed upon. In this scenario, it appears unlikely that the school psychologist would be a good candidate for remediation because there is no ownership of the problem. On another note, it would be important to consider hiring practice and policy to determine how and why the bad hire occurred and determine what might help to avoid this in the future. For example, were references checked? Was the interview thorough? It could be a very long year!

SD 14.5

You are a supervising school psychologist in a large district. Because you are assigned to three schools, you are able to meet with your supervisees only once a week for individual supervision and every other week for group supervision. Within a few weeks of the beginning of the school year, numerous complaints surface from principals and parents about the new school psychologist in the district. These complaints, along with your own observations, make it obvious that you made a serious hiring error. The new school psychologist is in need of substantial, daily supervision. He has a yearlong contract. *What are the supervisory considerations? What should be done?*

Authors' thoughts: Daily supervision is not likely to be a viable option. Hence, alternatives must be explored. If permitted by the contract, termination might be an option. Minimally, a warning should be placed in the psychologist's personnel file. It appears that serious skill deficits exist. A conversation must ensue that generates quantifiable, achievable expectations. It may be possible to assign another school psychologist in the district to act as a mentor. Finally, hiring practices should be reviewed to determine if something might be put in place to avoid similar situations in the future.

SD 14.6

Your department's most recently hired school psychologist has changed her style of dress considerably. At the time of her interview, she dressed traditionally. After being hired, she began to sport various body, ear, nose, lip, and tongue piercings; dyed her hair maroon; and stopped shaving her legs and underarms. Because of her scanty clothing, an impressively large tattoo is frequently observable. Some school administrators are indicating to you, the supervising school psychologist, that they would prefer that she not be assigned to their schools because of her appearance. Your supervisee maintains that she has the freedom to express herself in her dress. *What are the supervisory considerations? What should be done?*

Authors' thoughts: While all school psychologists are free to pursue their unique personal interests and tastes, it is necessary to modify their behavior when their ability to fulfill their professional responsibilities is adversely affected. Receiving complaints from multiple administrators certainly suggests that this is the case. Hence, it will be necessary to sensitively talk with her about her appearance. Such discussion could focus on how parents and others might perceive her and how her colleagues' disapproval could affect her career and job satisfaction. In addition to discussing formal policies, it is important to orient new school psychologists to the informal mores of the school district, including professional dress. While school psychologists do not dress as formally as principals do, they do typically dress similarly to assistant principals and department heads—certainly less casually than graduate students. In our experience, we have found new practitioners to be quite responsive to well-delivered suggestions.

Handout 14.7

PERFORMANCE EXPECTATIONS FOR SCHOOL PSYCHOLOGISTS

It is expected that school psychologists will exhibit demonstrable competence in all of these competencies:

1. Plans and effectively implements programs and interventions to achieve objectives
   a. Provides students with the opportunity for appropriate academic and/or personal counseling individually and/or in small or classroom groups
   b. Selects and applies appropriate procedures for counseling with parents about their child's individual growth and development
   c. Selects and provides students with guidance and information to help them in their personal, educational, and vocational decision making as appropriate
   d. Plans and develops articulation programs and procedures to help students with transitions to new grade levels
   e. Designs and develops procedures for preventing disorders, promoting mental health, and improving effective educational programs
   f. Assists in the planning and development of educational programs appropriate to the individual needs of all students

2. Effectively communicates with students, staff, family members, and members of the community
   a. Provides outreach and support to parents, staff, and students
   b. Consults and collaborates with other community professionals in providing a continuum of services and advocacy for children in need
   c. Consults with administrators to assist in resolving school issues and crises that have implications for the psychological well-being of students and staff
   d. Assists the school community in developing a respect for individual differences
   e. Assists in identifying, planning, and implementing nonschool referrals to outside agencies and resources for individual students
   f. Works cooperatively with staff to plan, develop, and implement mutual educational and professional goals to ensure that the school appropriately meets the educational, social, and developmental needs of students

3. Effectively assesses student needs and progress
   a. Clearly, concisely, and accurately reports psychological evaluation findings, both written and oral
   b. In order to facilitate learning, acts as a liaison between the school and the community and identifies unmet academic, social-emotional, and vocational needs of students
   c. Selects, administers, and interprets appropriate individual and group tests and evaluative techniques to assess student achievement ability and social-emotional development

4. Effectively meets the needs of special education students
   a. Demonstrates understanding of the behaviors resulting from mental, physical, emotional, sensory, speech, or any other handicapping conditions
   b. Assists staff and parents in understanding the handicapping condition and how it interferes with the child's school functioning

5. Demonstrates knowledge of the theory and practice of school psychology
   a. Demonstrates knowledge of human growth and development as it relates to the teaching-learning process and the educational environment
   b. Participates in and contributes to curriculum research, planning, and development in terms of learning and human development theory

6. Demonstrates ethical and professional behavior
   a. Conducts services in a manner that protects the due process rights of students and their parents as defined by state and federal laws and regulations
   b. Participates in supervision and evaluation of all services provided in order to maintain and improve the effectiveness of these services
   c. Is aware of, contributes to, and participates in the aims and activities of relevant professional organizations
   d. Participates in programs for individual and departmental professional growth

From the *2006 Westport School District School Psychologist Handbook.* Westport, CT: Locally published monograph. Use of this material is by permission of the author, Barbara Fischetti.

Handout 14.8

SCHOOL PSYCHOLOGY POSITION INTERVIEW QUESTIONS

Name: _____   Date: _____

Interviewer: _____   License: _____

Please tell us about your experience as a school psychologist (e.g., grade level, disabilities, languages, settings, etc.).

Why are you interested in working in our school district?

Foundational Competencies	Mismatch		Superior	
Interpersonal and Collaborative Skills				
1. The IEP of a student with Asperger syndrome calls for you to consult with his teachers on classroom strategies. In your first meeting with one teacher, she tells you that she has been teaching longer than you have been alive and doesn't need help—especially since the kid is clearly smart and doesn't need any special management at all. In fact, your observation is that the student is having a harder time focusing and working in this class than in other classes. How would you deal with this situation?	1	2	3	4
2. You are working with a student who is truly mentally ill. When on her medications and properly supported, she does reasonably well in general education. When she is off her medications and home/community supports are not in place, she does very poorly and is sometimes hospitalized. The school team is aware of this cycle and has noticed her starting to deteriorate. What steps would you take?	1	2	3	4
Diversity Awareness and Sensitive Service Delivery				
3. The school district is working with the federal Office for Civil Rights to reduce the disproportionate placement of African American students in special education. What might be some reasons behind this disproportion? What are some strategies that might help reduce bias in referral, evaluation, and placement of children of color?	1	2	3	4
4. This district serves children who speak more than 80 languages. How would you approach a referral for special education eligibility for a student who is an English language learner? What questions would you ask in planning the evaluation? What evaluation approaches would you use? How would you ensure an accurate and fair evaluation and eligibility decision?	1	2	3	4

<u>Professional, Legal, Ethical, and Social Responsibility</u> 5. Over the course of the year, you have assessed three students from one teacher's classroom. Each one has complained that his/her teacher frequently says mean and hurtful things to his students. What step or steps would you take in response to these complaints?	1	2	3	4
Functional Competencies <u>Data-Based Decision Making and Accountability</u> 6. IDEA 2004 says that states can no longer mandate the use of an ability-achievement discrepancy to identify students with a learning disability. Why was this change made? What other approaches could schools take to identify students with learning difficulties? What role or roles would school psychologists play in these approaches?	1	2	3	4
<u>Systems-Based Service</u> 7. Budget shortfalls, decreased enrollment, and the increased needs of students and families have a negative impact on the climate in a school. What would you recommend to an administrator trying to improve the climate of a school?	1	2	3	4
<u>Enhancing the Development of Cognitive and Academic Skills</u> 8. A second-grade teacher is concerned about one of her student's reading skills. What questions would you ask to determine the nature of the problem?	1	2	3	4
9. You learn that the student has only a few sight words and has difficulty blending sounds. What intervention strategies would you recommend to the teacher?	1	2	3	4
<u>Enhancing the Development of Wellness, Social Skills, Mental Health, and Life Competencies</u> 10. An out-of-state student enrolls in a fifth-grade classroom. He has never, to anyone's knowledge, received special education services. He is verbally aggressive to staff and students on a daily basis and physically aggressive to peers at least twice a week. The teacher asks you for help. What would you do?	1	2	3	4
11. A student in your school is killed in a drive-by shooting on Saturday night. The principal calls you on Sunday and asks for your advice on how to handle things on Monday morning at school. What would you suggest?	1	2	3	4
12. Based on your experience, whether as a school psychology intern or professional, what one improvement in your practice would you most like to make? Why is this important to you?	1	2	3	4
13. Is there anything else you would like to tell us about yourself?	1	2	3	4
14. Do you have any questions for us?	1	2	3	4

Use of this material is by permission of the author, Andrea Canter.

15

Performance Evaluations and Professional Development

To overcome discomfort about evaluating supervisees, supervisors should consider it an opportunity *to provide information and professional development—with the ultimate goals of both protecting students and helping supervisees improve.*

Vignette 15.1

Patrick was promoted from director of special education to associate superintendent of pupil personnel. With this promotion he was required to supervise school psychologists whose professional performance had not been appraised in many years. When he met with them to discuss the appraisal process, Patrick found that the psychologists were in essence practicing different professions. One had been a special education teacher and concentrated his work on academic interventions. Another was a clinical psychologist who focused on adolescents' intrapsychic dynamics. A third had been trained in a systems approach and spent time in policy meetings at the school and district levels. A fourth thoroughly enjoyed assessments and devoted all of her time to completing detailed psychoeducational reports. Patrick started by having the group collaboratively develop a tool that could evaluate performance across such diverse "job descriptions." He then had them construct a departmental professional development program that would enable them to function successfully within the evidence-based practice paradigm.

As Armistead (2008) stated, "it is widely accepted that completion of a graduate training program . . . is just the beginning of a school psychologist's professional development" (p. 1975). School psychologists need ongoing professional development throughout their careers, and this should be linked to individual and departmental performance evaluations. Just as assessments conducted with students should be linked to interventions, performance evaluations should be linked to professional development plans. This chapter addresses conducting formal performance evaluations and developing associated professional development plans for supervisees, supervisors, and school psychology departments.

These activities are summarized in Handout 15.6, Checklist of Performance Appraisal and Professional Development Strategies, at the end of the chapter. They are normally conducted by administrative supervisors who have the ability to hire, fire, mandate remediation plans, and endorse psychologists for professional licensure. Less formal methods to appraise, monitor, and develop discrete clinical skills have been addressed in earlier chapters.

BASIC CONSIDERATIONS

A supervisor has a fundamental obligation to promote the best possible school psychological services for students and educators. Performance evaluations are essential to achieving this goal. Individual and departmental performance evaluations serve several purposes for multiple constituents. They benefit the greater organization because they monitor service quality and ensure accountability. They benefit students, educators, and parents with whom school psychologists work by protecting clients' rights and controlling the school psychologists' behavior. For the supervisee, they assess and recognize quality of service, guide future professional development activities, and provide direction for future practice. For the supervisor, they offer an opportunity to ascertain what the supervisee actually does and provide information that helps plan professional development programs (Tsui, 2005).

However, performance evaluations are effective only within the context of a performance management process that includes job analysis, formative performance feedback, and subsequent improvement (Leonard & Hilgert, 2004). Therefore, to conduct meaningful performance appraisals of school psychologists, even administrative supervisors without a school psychology background must have a working knowledge of school psychology (Chafouleas, Clonan, & Vanauken, 2002).

Just as no one assessment method is appropriate for all students in all settings, no one appraisal method is appropriate for all settings. Responsible performance evaluations and associated professional development plans are both context responsive and context specific. They involve:

- Establishing performance expectations and communicating them through departmental objectives, job descriptions, and job specifications
- Developing performance appraisal methods that are linked to these expectations and communicated in writing to supervisees and administrators
- Observing and appraising individual performance relative to these expectations
- Reinforcing appropriate performance and providing professional development opportunities to remedy deficiencies
- Addressing impairments
- Assessing the performance appraisal process and modifying it appropriately

DESIGNING APPRAISAL PROCESSES AND PROCEDURES

Whether the performance evaluation addresses the work of a practicum student, intern, veteran school psychologist, supervisor, or entire department, the same principles apply. Effective appraisals determine whether psychologists use critical thinking, exercise professional judgment, respond to context, and use self-reflection to evaluate and modify practice as appropriate (Kaslow, 2004). Evaluations should determine whether psychological practice, knowledge, skills, and behavior meet professional standards and local, state, and federal guidelines. The underlying question is, are quality services provided that have a positive impact on the functioning of students and staff?

Appraising the performance of school psychologists is made challenging by a number of variables. First of all, many supervisors must overcome a reluctance to conduct the evaluation process at all. To do so, they must understand that conducting evaluations is less about passing judgment than about providing information. They also must understand that protecting the welfare of students is their primary responsibility. Keeping these two facts in mind empowers supervisors to accept responsibility for completing evaluations, hold school psychologists accountable for their work, and provide honest appraisals even at the risk of receiving complaints or experiencing discomfort.

Furthermore, as in any evaluation method, techniques used should avoid inappropriate bias and adhere to valid measurement criteria as much as possible. First, the process should be carefully planned. Then data is collected, reports are written, feedback is provided, and objectives are developed. After the evaluation is complete, a professional development plan is developed and implemented. Finally, the effectiveness of the evaluation process is assessed.

Planning

The supervisor plans the appraisal process by determining sources of information, methods of data collection, and indicators of effective performance for each area of performance. Effective processes have a well-defined purpose, are well timed, and are reliable, valid, meaningful, acceptable, practical, and respectful.

Effective Appraisal Processes Have a Well-Defined Purpose

Performance appraisals can be *summative* or *formative*. Evaluations that occur at the end of a specified time period and emphasize conclusions and gatekeeping are summative, while those that occur on an ongoing basis and emphasize corrective feedback are formative. The appraisal process is most effective when it integrates formative and summative processes, and a combination of both types to evaluate school psychologists has been recommended for some time (Bennett, 1988; Maher, 1984; Mowder & Prasse, 1981; M. Q. Patton, 1982; B. W. Tuckman, 1985). Unfortunately, many school psychologists are evaluated with summative evaluations only every year or two or even less frequently. Furthermore, these summative evaluations are often conducted by administrators using inappropriate teacher evaluation forms, which cannot possibly address critical skills, knowledge, and behaviors. Appropriate appraisal methods are multi-informant, multi-method, and multitrait and address psychological practice (Kaslow, 2004).

Vignette 15.2

In **Busy City School District**, the union contract mandated that school psychologists be evaluated using only teacher evaluation forms. This was a source of considerable frustration for all concerned. Supervising principals were obligated to force-fit the items, while school psychologists were frustrated by receiving irrelevant feedback. Finally, the school psychologists sent a member of the department to the union to request a revised evaluation form addressing the attributes, behaviors, and outcomes necessary for successful school psychology practice. Negotiations with the administration and union to effect this change were time consuming but satisfying in the long run.

Effective Appraisal Processes Are Well Timed

The desired frequency of performance appraisals depends on the supervisee's developmental level. Beginning practitioners, particularly interns, should be evaluated continuously. Continuous evaluation is a process, rather than a product, during which plans, procedures, alternatives, and implications are continuously evaluated. Following each evaluation, the supervisee formulates a profile that indicates areas of strength and weakness and generates a plan for the activities within the next time frame. Effective continuous evaluations are objective, focus on skills and techniques essential for good practice of school psychology, provide the next steps for professional development, and furnish an objective description of ability and potential (Henry & Beasley, 1982; Leonard & Hilgert, 2004; Mead, 1990). While continuous evaluation emphasizes formative evaluation, it yields summative evaluations at specific points, such as midterm and year end for interns and annually for advanced practitioners. Even for experienced practitioners and supervisors, formal summative evaluations should be completed at least once a year, and monitoring of progress toward goals should occur more frequently.

Effective Appraisal Processes Are Reliable

As much as possible, evaluation methods must be reliable and consistent across raters and time. One source of poor reliability is contrasting individuals with one another rather than using an objective standard; this results in average performers' looking weak in the company of outstanding performers or strong in the company of low achievers. Reliability is also reduced when supervisors fail to use the full range of rating scales and restrict responses to either the high or low ends of a scale. Yet another reliability threat occurs when evaluators do not consider each category independently, resulting in "halo effects" wherein those who are superior (or inferior) in one area are presumed to be superior (or inferior) in others.

To ensure reasonable reliability, supervisors should base individual performance appraisals on behaviors or outcomes rather than solely on attributes. They can also foster vigilant self-awareness and consult with a knowledgeable colleague when evaluating persons from backgrounds dissimilar from their own to avoid inflating the ratings of supervisees with whom they share characteristics. Reliability is further enhanced by developing operational definitions of excellent, satisfactory, and unsatisfactory performance to use as an objective standard rather than contrasting individuals with one another. Furthermore, supervisors should take care to use the full ranges of the rating scale and consider each category independently.

Vignette 15.3

Brianna developed an evaluation scale that helped her overcome her inclination toward unreliable evaluations. Previously, to maintain positive relationships with supervisees, she had tended to score them at the top of every evaluation scale item. To overcome this habit, she used two rating scales for each item: one indicating "acceptability for developmental level" the other indicating "competence." That way she felt comfortable rating supervisees as "not yet competent" because she could simultaneously rate them as "acceptable for developmental level."

Effective Appraisal Processes Are Valid

Evaluation methods also must be valid and measure relevant aspects of performance. The effective practice of psychology can be difficult to clearly define, and the field has been challenged to identify uniform standards and expectations. It is important not to "define competencies in a manner that reduces the profession to a collection of specific skills that might or might not require extensive educational/experiential training and as a result train technicians rather than professionals" (Kaslow, 2004, p. 779). Furthermore, appraisals should not discriminate on the basis of personal characteristics that are not job related. Evaluation methods must impart clear information to supervisees regarding expectations and the manner in which to achieve them. Further, appraisals should have minimal contamination by elements outside the individual's control.

Vignette 15.4

Supervisee **Elise** was in a panic as the appointment with her supervisor to review her annual objectives approached. She had not met her objective specifying that "all evaluations are completed within 2 weeks of the referral," and she was afraid that she would lose her job as a result. However, **Rick**, her supervisor, understood that Elise worked at the vocational high school in an urban district with an extremely high truancy rate. Instead of taking her to task for not meeting this objective, Rick had her gather information that separated out the data regarding chronically truant students. He also had her rewrite her objectives to be more realistic for the context in which she worked.

To ensure that evaluations are valid and in sync with quality performance, supervisors should develop performance appraisal procedures from a job analysis that appropriately identifies important aspects of job performance (see Chapter 14). It is also helpful to consider quality as well as quantity of work, avoid focusing on isolated instances of accomplishment or failure, tie behavior to goal development, and base evaluation on records of performance maintained throughout the evaluation period rather than those written just prior to the evaluation.

Strengths should be addressed as well as deficiencies, and deficiencies should not become the main focus of the evaluation. To prevent deficiencies from being emphasized, supervisors can employ a "fair pair" approach and focus on strengths as much or more than weaknesses. They also can minimize criticism, help the supervisee develop specific goals for improvement, and focus discussions on behavior and results more than on personal attributes.

Effective Appraisal Processes Are Meaningful and Acceptable

Meaningfulness and acceptability are dependent on the development of common understandings regarding appropriate performance on the part of principals, teachers, parents, students, administrators, supervisees, and supervisors in light of the education context. They also should be strategically congruent and consistent with the current goals, strategy, and culture of the school system and school psychology department. The entire appraisal process must be in sync with quality performance, professional standards, and ethical conduct.

Vignette 15.5

Novice supervisor **Charlene** found that her district school psychologists' appraisal forms focused almost entirely on compliance with state special education regulations (e.g., "Completes 3-year reevaluations of special education students on time"). Charlene understood that such a focus would overemphasize compliance issues, so she collaborated with others to modify the appraisal form. They added psychological services that the administrator, school psychologist, and teachers wanted to see increased. This led to inclusion of items regarding designing and monitoring behavior management plans as well as providing collaboration consultation with teachers and parents. As would be expected, those behaviors then increased.

Evaluations have increased meaning when they are incorporated into both personal and organizational professional development plans. It helps to involve supervisees in setting goals and time lines for progress review over the coming year. It also helps to have upper level administrators review all performance ratings.

Sometimes supervisees feel disconnected from the evaluation process. To ameliorate this disconnection, it is helpful to have supervisees *self-evaluate* by rating and reflecting on their performance, determining their strengths and deficiencies, and developing their own professional development strategies before the evaluation session. The supervisor can then make the evaluation session a problem solving meeting during which the supervisor and supervisee collaboratively brainstorm about problem solutions in an atmosphere of mutual respect.

Effective Appraisal Processes Are Practical

Evaluation methods must also be practical to implement. Methods that are overly cumbersome will not be used.

Vignette 15.6

Supervisor **Nelson** developed a terrific assessment plan that was extraordinarily detailed. At more than 30 pages, it described a multifaceted process that incorporated feedback from students, teachers, administrators, parents, and psychologists. It delineated action items across departments and schools and indicated time frames and persons responsible for all actions. Unfortunately, it was so complex that it was never implemented. Even worse, because this complex plan existed, the simple tools that had been in place before Nelson developed the assessment plan were abandoned. Consequently, no assessments occurred for some time and valuable information was lost.

Effective Appraisal Processes Are Respectful

The evaluation process must protect the due process rights of supervisees. Supervisees should never be surprised by an evaluation outcome. To avoid surprises, supervisors should give frequent and honest feedback so that supervisees already know forthcoming results prior to the formal evaluation. Supervisors should always voice concerns immediately upon becoming aware of them. Concerns should be discussed along a continuum and through a variety of modalities to respect varied learning styles. Supervisors should follow verbal statements with written feedback that includes time lines and specific criteria for the measurement of improvement. By the time a negative evaluation occurs, the supervisee should have received multiple verbal and written communications about any concern. Supervisees should not be given a negative final evaluation, dismissed from a training program, or dismissed from a job without having been given adequate notice of inadequate performance, specific criteria for improvement, and time to improve that performance (J. M. Bernard & Goodyear, 2004).

Vignette 15.7

As a person who considered herself supportive and kind, **Harriet** found it so difficult to give supervisees corrective feedback that she found herself avoiding it altogether. She finally realized that it was indeed *not* kind to refrain from giving them feedback when that resulted in their "digging themselves in deeper and deeper" and exacerbating others' frustration with their work to the point of no return. She began to write down notes regarding any concern as soon as she became aware of it and to share a copy of her notes with supervisees at their regularly scheduled supervision sessions. Because she was more apt to write down issues than to speak them, her notes prompted the supervisees to ask questions regarding topics that Harriet would normally have glossed over. This process gave Harriet detailed records of expressed concerns and the dates on which she expressed them. It also provided both written and oral feedback for her supervisees.

Sources of Information

Administrative supervisors, such as principals, are appropriate sources of evaluative information because they have opportunities to directly observe supervisees in action. On the other hand, their observations are limited because they are not omnipresent. In addition, they often lack knowledge regarding best practices in school psychology and may not know the critical behaviors to observe. Clinical supervisors suffer from other difficulties: While they may be well aware of critical behaviors, they have even fewer opportunities to observe the school psychologist in action. Furthermore, an evaluation conducted by only one person is easily colored by biases such as the halo effect.

For these reasons, obtaining appraisal information from multiple sources is highly beneficial. When supervisory roles are filled by two different individuals (such as administrative and clinical supervisors, or supervisors in two different schools), they can collaborate in conducting formal appraisals of school psychologists. In addition, soliciting others' opinions can be very helpful. An increasingly common practice is to employ a "360-degree evaluation" for which evaluative feedback is obtained from peers, clients, and subordinates (Atkins & Wood, 2002). Although school psychologists generally do not have subordinates, they do have a substantial number of "clients" who can provide feedback regarding performance. These include general education teachers, nurses, occupational therapists, parents, physical therapists, physicians, principals, psychologists in private practice, remedial teachers, school counselors, social workers, special education administrators, special education teachers, speech and language therapists, upper level administrators, and students. Information can be gathered by asking these individuals to respond verbally or in writing regarding the attributes, behaviors, or objectives in question. To use these approaches, it is necessary to have both administrative and union approval. It is also necessary to design methods that ethically maintain confidentiality and respect the privacy of all involved.

Peers may notice problematic situations that supervisors are not aware of, yet not know how to deal with that knowledge. For example, Rosenberg, Getzelman, Arcinue, and Oren (2005) found that trainees were more aware of peers' difficulties than faculty, but because they did not have appropriate avenues to deal with this information they withdrew or gossiped with one another. In school districts, peers and colleagues may similarly be aware of serious concerns before supervisors are. To foster "early interventions" that could lead to appropriate remediation, supervisors could develop mechanisms to encourage peers to ethically and professionally share critical information, especially if an environment that fosters supportive help is nurtured (Rosenberg et al., 2005).

Finally, supervisees themselves are a rich source of information. Although individuals might deflate or inflate their own performance, they often provide helpful information when responding to a well-developed scale (Leonard & Hilgert, 2004). Self-evaluations, along with supporting documentation, can be submitted prior to the evaluation session and used by the supervisor to augment the formal evaluation. To facilitate the process, the supervisee might provide others with evaluation forms, gather the written responses, and cite them in his or her own written self-appraisal.

Selecting and Designing Tools

Performance evaluation methods can focus on attributes of the supervisee, behaviors of the supervisee, results the supervisee obtains, or a combination thereof. According to the U.S. Equal Employment Opportunity Commission (n.d.), *performance appraisals must objectively measure behaviors related to specific tasks that are under the employee's control and are essential to job success.* Appraisals should not reflect race, sex, disability, or other variables that do not impact performance. Furthermore, supervisees should be informed well ahead of their evaluation regarding explicit criteria for appraisal. They also should be informed of the procedures available in the event that they have questions or wish to challenge the evaluation. A number of appraisal techniques, each with its own strengths and weaknesses, can be used.

Graphic rating scales require the evaluator to rate desirable attributes numerically on a Likert-type scale following formal or informal observations. They are extremely popular in both business and education (Certo, 2006). Graphic rating scales have the substantial advantage of being relatively "easy." However, their validity is often low because they are not aligned with current goals and objectives. They are prone to poor reliability because they are highly subjective—one supervisor's "excellent" may be another's "satisfactory." Furthermore, supervisors tend to adopt a response set; one supervisor may rate all supervisees highly while another rates all supervisors more stringently. Table 15.1 is a sample of a graphic rating scale.

Table 15.1 Sample Graphic Rating Scale

Please rate the supervisee's attributes as follows:
4 = Excellent, 3 = Good, 2 = Fair, 1 = Poor, NA = No basis for appraisal

___ 1. Listening skills

___ 2. Oral expression

___ 3. Written expression

___ 4. Acceptance of constructive criticism

___ 5. Emotional maturity

___ 6. Ability to work with students

___ 7. Ability to work with parents and educators

___ 8. Flexibility

___ 9. Meets job requirements

___10. Observes protocol and rules

___11. Acts in accord with professional ethics

___12. Shows respect for cultural differences

Behaviorally anchored rating scales require raters to rate supervisees on operationally defined attributes. The process of constructing these operational definitions can be quite enlightening because it forces the evaluator to clearly define behavioral requirements of the job and corresponding data points. Other benefits of this approach are that it can link performance to strategic goals; it can be reliable, valid, and acceptable; and it can provide clear and specific guidelines for performance improvement. The main disadvantage of this method is the lengthy time it takes to complete the job analysis, develop the scale, and gather the data. Furthermore, it can be difficult to develop such scales for complex positions in which essential behaviors (e.g., "rapport") are not easily quantified. Table 15.2 is an example of a behaviorally anchored rating item from the SUNY Plattsburgh School Psychology Program's Professional Dispositions questionnaire; the entire scale is found in Handout 15.7 at the end of this chapter, courtesy of Dale Phillips.

When using the *critical incident approach*, supervisors keep records of both effective and ineffective supervisee performance. Records include actions taken, individuals involved, dates, and other details. It is most helpful to maintain ongoing records of "critical incidents" and ask supervisees for examples of specific incidents in which their performance was adequate or inadequate (Leonard & Hilgert, 2004). During the appraisal process, the supervisee is given the opportunity to respond to each incident. This approach has the benefit of focusing on behaviors. On the negative side, using the critical incident approach requires very close supervision, is time consuming, can result in a focus on negative behaviors more than positive ones, and is not well suited to complex jobs (Certo, 2006). Below is a sample critical incident approach.

Table 15.2   Sample Behaviorally Anchored Rating Scale Item

Please use the following scale:

1 = Poor. Fails to meet expectations. Consistently performs poorly and needs improvement. A specific plan and period of time should be established to improve performance. If improvement is not made, then the supervisee's suitability for this field of work should be evaluated.

2 = Below Standard. Performance is below average. A supervisee whose performance consistently falls in this range requires improvement to function effectively in a professional environment.

3 = Standard. Most candidates will possess skills and judgment sufficient to meet professional demands in this area, and a large proportion will remain in this range. The performance of supervisees in this range meets normal expectations.

4 = Above Standard. Performance and judgment of supervisees in this category is decidedly better than average. Shows sensitivity, judgment, and skill beyond what is normally expected or displayed by peers.

5 = Outstanding. Performance is recognizably and decidedly better than that of a large proportion of other supervisees.

N = Not Observed. This rating should be used when the activity in question is not part of class or placement expectations or the rater has not had the opportunity to observe or rate the candidate on the item.

1. Respect for Human Diversity

    a. Candidate is sensitive to racial issues.   1 2 3 4 5 N

    b. Candidate is sensitive to cultural issues.   1 2 3 4 5 N

    c. Candidate is sensitive to the needs of all learners.   1 2 3 4 5 N

    d. Candidate is sensitive to people of all sexual orientations. 1 2 3 4 5 N

    e. Candidate professionally encourages inclusion in school settings. 1 2 3 4 5 N

    f. Candidate is aware of challenges diversity issues pose in the schools. 1 2 3 4 5 N

Sample Critical Incident Approach

To ensure that the school psychologist conveys assessment results to parents in a meaningful manner, the supervisor observes the school psychologist conveying information to parents and makes note of parental feedback that indicates understanding. The supervisor maintains a log of observations and parent responses throughout the year.

Another method is to *enumerate discrete behaviors.* The advantage to this approach is that the behaviors are observable and administrators have a high interest in such data. Furthermore, by its very existence, enumeration increases the occurrence of measured behaviors. The disadvantages to enumeration are that it cannot possibly reflect all relevant aspects of the job, takes substantial time to maintain, and ignores performance quality (Sandoval & Lambert, 1977; Zins, 1984). On the other hand, most administrations require some type of enumeration to justify school district expenditures, including school psychologist positions. The most frequently enumerated behavior regarding school psychologists' performance is the number of psychoeducational evaluations completed, yet there are many other possible measures. Given that "what is counted gets done," supervisors should have supervisees enumerate the behaviors that they would most like to see. Table 15.3 lists some possibilities.

Management by objective (MBO), as discussed in Chapter 13, focuses on meeting performance objectives through the following steps:

1. The supervisee and supervisor meet at the beginning of the year and agree upon measurable objectives and time lines for the supervisee. Objectives are compatible with organizational goals, measurable, challenging, and realistic.

2. The supervisee keeps record of activities completed toward the objectives.

3. Periodically through the year, the supervisor and supervisee conduct a joint review of progress toward the objectives.

4. The supervisor completes the individual performance appraisal based on the supervisee's progress in meeting objectives.

Because MBO relies on objective, quantifiable indicators of performance, it minimizes subjectivity. It also has the advantage of clearly defining the manner in which performance is to be measured. Because the supervisee writes the objectives, they have substantial validity for the individual and can be customized to meet specific needs and interests. Furthermore, MBO can greatly facilitate communication between supervisees and supervisors. When done well, MBO empowers supervisees to be responsible for their own professional growth.

On the negative side, MBO can be significantly contaminated by elements beyond the supervisee's control. It is difficult to set reasonable goals in advance because outside variables have marked influences. Furthermore, not all important aspects of a position—particularly positions as complicated as school psychology—can be quantified. Consequently, there may be an overemphasis on aspects of the job that are easily measurable. When abused, MBO can result in excessive pressure by the supervisor on the supervisee to produce results (Noe, Hollenbeck, Gehart, & Wright, 1996). Tables 15.4 and 15.5 are examples of performance objectives for school psychologists and supervisors, respectively.

Outcomes evaluations are a variation of total quality management and Six Sigma as discussed in Chapter 13. Instead of focusing on professionals' meeting objectives, as is done in MBO, the focus is on improvements in *students'* behavior and learning. Much of the research on the relationship between supervision and client outcomes, even in the field of counseling supervision with its substantial body of literature, tends to be poorly designed with ambiguous results (Freitas, 2002). There are some studies, however, that have found correlations. Triantafillou (1997), for example, found that compared to administrative supervision, supervision focusing on solutions and client outcomes resulted in increased supervisee job satisfaction and improved client outcomes. Table 15.6

Table 15.3   A Menu of Activities to Enumerate

Academic assessment data analyzed
Assessments completed
Behavior assessments completed
Behavior plans developed
Behavior plans implemented and monitored
CBM assessments completed among the general population
CBM assessments completed with students receiving targeted or intensive interventions
Classroom observations conducted
Contacts with outside agencies and professionals
Direct interventions
Early intervention activities
Functional behavioral assessments completed
Grants implemented
Grants received
Grants written
Group counseling sessions
Indirect interventions
Individual counseling sessions
In-service workshops conducted
Intervention referrals received
Interventions modeled for parents
Interventions modeled for teachers
Manifest determinations completed
Newsletters distributed
Number of assessed students identified as disabled
Number of assessed students placed in special education
Number of staff trained in in-service workshops
Number of students counseled in groups
Number of students counseled individually
Number of students monitored for progress
Parent conferences held
Parent e-mails sent
Parent information sessions held
Parent interviews and telephone calls made
Parent training workshops held
Postassessment meetings attended
Prereferral intervention strategies and activities
Prevention programs implemented
Program development activities
Program evaluation activities
Programs implemented
Programs modified
Psychoeducational assessments completed
Referrals received
Research distributed
Research reviewed
School records reviewed
Teacher assistance team meetings attended
Teacher interviews conducted and contacts established
Time spent providing direct services
Yearly goals attained

Table 15.4   Sample Supervisee Objectives

- The school psychologist will implement a violence prevention program in which 80% of the second-grade students participate.
- The school psychologist will participate in the prereferral process for at least 90% of individual referrals throughout the school year.
- The school psychologist will initiate all formal psychoeducational evaluations within 5 days of the referral and complete them within 30 days.
- The school psychologist will oversee ongoing progress monitoring for designated students and provide graphic data by the end of each school week 90% of the time.
- The school psychologist will complete a 2-day workshop in conflict resolution and effectively apply the acquired skills in at least six situations.
- The school psychologist will coordinate a monthly "parent-teacher coffee" that addresses study skills, social skills, and behavior of sixth-grade students.
- The school psychologist will collaborate with the fourth-grade team by October 15 to identify students at risk of failing the high-stakes test, help develop targeted interventions, and coordinate progress monitoring on a weekly basis.

Table 15.5   Sample Supervision Goal and Objectives

Goal 1: Facilitate the professional development of supervisees.

Objective 1.1: Collaboratively develop a professional development plan with each supervisee by September 15.

Objective 1.2: Collaboratively develop a group departmental professional development plan by September 15.

Objective 1.3: Sponsor attendance at relevant workshops through budgetary allocation.

Objective 1.4: Sponsor group department development by funding guest speakers at four department meetings per year.

Objective 1.5: Facilitate the dissemination of workshop information by devoting 50% of department meeting time to professional development conversations.

Objective 1.6: Encourage the acquisition of new skills through biannual supervision of individual psychologists' professional development plans.

is an example of possible outcome measures regarding students with whom a school psychologist has worked.

The *portfolio* method involves collecting multiple work samples over time that demonstrate competence. This method is widely used in university training programs, and L. R. Johnson (1998) recommended using portfolios to supplement the evaluation of employed supervisees. Components of portfolios for interns and supervisees should include information regarding future goals and perceived areas of strength and weakness; placement information; and evidence of skills in all domains of practice. Evidence-based practice should be demonstrated in reports, data from intervention progress monitoring, and process notes. Table 15.7 indicates possible components to include in an intern portfolio.

Table 15.6 Sample Student Outcomes

- Percentage of students who attended 90% of assigned classes
- Percentage of students who demonstrated progress on weekly CBM measures
- Percentage of students who passed all subjects with grades of C or better
- Percentage of students who were promoted
- Percentage of students whose discipline reports decreased
- Percentage of students whose suspensions decreased
- Percentage of students whose academic anxiety decreased per psychometric measures

Table 15.7 Sample Intern Portfolio Components

1. A narrative summary of intern experience including the objectives, experiences, and competencies initially designated at the beginning of the internship as well as an analysis of success in attaining them

2. Daily logs of activities by domain

3. Case log

4. Completed intern evaluation of internship site

5. An evaluation team report written by the intern

6. A case study focusing on *academics* that demonstrates skillful consultation (problem solving, intervention implementation, and progress monitoring)

7. A case study focusing on *behavior* that demonstrates skillful consultation (problem solving, intervention implementation, and progress monitoring)

8. A case study focusing on a *classwide intervention* program that demonstrates skillful systems level problem solving, intervention implementation, and progress monitoring

9. An *individual counseling* plan, audiotapes, and case process notes demonstrating the plan's successful implementation

10. A small *group counseling* plan, audiotapes, and case process notes demonstrating the plan's successful implementation

11. An *in-service presentation* developed and implemented by the intern

12. A *parent education plan*, audiotapes, and notes demonstrating the plan's successful implementation

13. A plan for evaluating the services provided by the intern and the results of the implementation of that plan

14. A written evaluation of the internship experience to which both the intern and the field supervisor have contributed

From the *2006 Handbook of the University of Dayton School Psychology Program*. Dayton, OH: Locally published monograph. Use of this material is by permission of the author, Sawyer Hunley.

Components of a supervisor's portfolio should reflect the job description of the supervisor as well as contain evidence related to critical supervisory skills.

Vignette 15.8

At the end of his supervision course, **Thomas** submitted a portfolio that demonstrated his knowledge and skills. He included:

- Tape analyses demonstrating his communication and interpersonal skills
- An analysis of areas of concern regarding ethics and relevant laws
- An analysis of his preferred clinical supervision models, theories, and techniques
- A plan for recruiting and selecting staff
- Two brochures regarding his department's services, one describing current services and one describing ideal services
- Sample formative and summative individual performance appraisals he had completed with supervisees
- Supervision process notes that demonstrated, over a period of time, his skills in advancing his supervisees' performance in providing consultation, services to improve academic functioning, and services to improve social-emotional-behavioral functioning
- A plan for his future development as a supervisor

The *comprehensive method* employs a combination of attribute evaluation, MBO, and outcomes measurement. This approach uses a variety of information sources and therefore reduces reliability and validity errors. The steps indicated in Handout 15.1 are followed.

Sample Supervisee Appraisal Tools

A number of appraisal tools that have been developed to assess school psychologist competencies are included at the end of this chapter. These include Handout 15.8, the School Psychologist Evaluation Form of the University of Massachusetts Boston, provided by Virginia Harvey; Handout 15.9, the School Psychologist Competency Observation Form of Baltimore County, Maryland, Public Schools, provided by Bill Flook; Handout 15.10, the School Psychologist Professional Development and Evaluation Plan of the Westport, Connecticut, School District, provided by Barbara Fischetti; and Handout 15.11, the intern evaluation form of the University of Dayton, provided by Sawyer Hunley.

Special Considerations in Practicum Student and Intern Evaluations

Evaluations constitute major components of practicum student and intern supervision processes. They should include regular, systematic feedback concerning strengths and weaknesses along with ways to improve functioning. All of the previously discussed considerations apply to conducting practicum student and intern performance appraisals. However, appraising practicum students and interns is further complicated because it is cooperatively conducted with the university supervisor. Collaboration is seriously compromised (resulting in unfairness to the intern) if the university supervisor and site supervisor do not have the same expectations for the intern. Thus, in addition to ensuring that the intern's job description or prospectus is aligned with school district goals, intern supervisors must ensure that their expectations (and those of the school and district) for the intern are aligned with university requirements. This alignment requires skilled communication among all parties.

Handout 15.1

STEPS IN THE COMPREHENSIVE EVALUATION OF SUPERVISEES

1. The supervisor updates and aligns the job description and evaluation materials.

2. The supervisee is interviewed to discuss updated job requirements relative to training, prior experience, and personal strengths and weaknesses.

3. After ensuring that expectations are clear, the supervisor observes the supervisee while engaged in multiple activities such as consulting, conducting an assessment, running a support group, working with a team of educators, and meeting with parents.

4. Data is gathered via interviews or written evaluation forms completed by principals, teachers, and parents who work with the supervisee.

5. Additionally, the supervisor reviews samples of the supervisee's work since the last appraisal and reviews the personnel file.

6. The supervisor then drafts an evaluation.

7. The supervisee simultaneously completes a self-evaluation.

8. During a one-to-one meeting with the supervisee, the supervisor discusses the draft evaluation and compares it to the self-evaluation.

9. The supervisor and supervisee then collaboratively develop individual goals and objectives.

10. The supervisor and supervisee meet regularly and review progress regarding the completion of goals, objectives, and activities. These meetings are informed by data presented by the supervisee.

11. After the appraisal cycle is completed, the supervisor and supervisee revise goals, objectives, activities, and desired outcomes in preparation for the coming year.

12. Periodically, the supervisor revisits the entire appraisal process to ensure its appropriateness.

> ### Vignette 15.9
>
> In the vignette that opened Chapter 4, **Anne** was faced with supervising her intern **Zoe** as she completed six case studies using research design. Anne did not know where to begin, so she contacted the university supervisor to clarify expectations. With this prompting, the university supervisor scheduled an online videoconference during which all site supervisors and university supervisors discussed the requirements and achieved a greater understanding of the appropriate process.

Questions to facilitate this communication have been developed by Christine Merman Woolf of Capella University and can be found in Handouts 7.1 and 7.2 in Chapter 7. Based on the training standards of the National Association of School Psychologists (NASP; 2000b), these contain parallel forms for university supervisors to use as they speak with both field supervisors and learners (interns and practicum students).

Furthermore, it is important for university supervisors to include training site information in the evaluation process. Training sites must be prudently recruited, selected, and monitored and regularly evaluated. It is helpful for university supervisors, site supervisors, and exiting interns to all participate in this evaluative process. Such ongoing evaluations can help to eliminate ineffective, problematic training sites or site supervisors.

> ### Vignette 15.10
>
> For many years, the practicum students and interns from the School Psychology Department at **Eastern University** had completed their fieldwork in the **Countryside School District.** Recently the superintendent at Countryside had retired and was replaced by a superintendent who restricted school psychologists' activities to completing psychoeducational evaluations as a special education gatekeeping function. This provided insufficient experiences in prevention, consultation, and direct service delivery for the practicum students and interns. The Eastern University faculty were forced to inform the district that without modification, Countryside was not an appropriate training site and students and interns would no longer be permitted to complete field placement experiences in the district.

Handout 15.12, the Internship Site Information form of the University of Massachusetts Boston, provided by Virginia Harvey, is an example of a tool that can be completed by interns, field supervisors, and university supervisors to provide information to the training program. Similarly, Handout 15.13, the field supervisor application of the School Psychology Department of San Diego Public Schools, provided by Michelle Bronson and Valerie Cook-Morales, and Handouts 15.14 and 15.15, the "general" and "specific" Intern Evaluation of Internship forms of the University of Dayton School Psychology Program, provided by Sawyer Hunley, are examples of forms developed to provide information regarding internship sites. These forms can be found at the end of this chapter.

Special Considerations in Supervisor Evaluations

Effective supervisor evaluations have multiple benefits. They improve performance, focus professional development activities, identify and improve programs and procedures, provide professional recognition, and document effectiveness (Bolton, 1980).

Evaluations of school psychology supervisors are essential to the health of the school psychology department. Like supervisee evaluations, supervisor evaluations should address critical skills. Critical supervisor skills include ethical practice, communication and interpersonal skills, multicultural skills, data-based decision making, clinical planning and provision, and administrative supervision.

An example of a comprehensive approach to supervisor evaluations was described by L. R. Johnson (1988). Using this approach, the supervisor's professional behaviors, leadership, program management, and professional development are assessed using information from a variety of sources as indicated in Handout 15.2.

At the end of this chapter are two forms that have been used to evaluate supervisors. Handout 15.16, a supervisor evaluation form based on NASP standards, was developed by Virginia Harvey of the University of Massachusetts Boston. Handout 15.17 was developed by Barbara Fischetti of Westport, Connecticut, to appraise clinical supervisors.

Improved functioning of supervisees and of students is perhaps the most valid assessment of supervision effectiveness. To this end, Cherniss (1986) advocated direct observation of the supervisor's method, style, and content communication with supervisees. Lambert and Hawkins (2001) suggested considering client outcomes as a measure of supervisor effectiveness. As Mead (1990) indicated, the development of the supervisor subsumes the system of the practitioner, and the system of the practitioner subsumes practice itself.

Communicating Evaluation Feedback

Communication with supervisees both before and after the performance appraisal is critical. Insufficient communication results in supervisees' perceiving the process as capricious and arbitrary. Miscommunication can result in supervisees' feeling disconnected from the evaluation process, misunderstanding or being surprised by the feedback, and ignoring the results to the point that they are not incorporated into professional development plans.

After appraisal information is gathered, the supervisor meets personally with the supervisee to review the appraisal and make plans. As mentioned earlier, it is helpful to encourage self-assessment by asking the supervisee to bring a written self-appraisal to the feedback session. The supervisor can also draft a written appraisal ahead of time.

The feedback session should be conducted privately, without interruptions (e.g., not answering the telephone). The supervisor should begin the feedback session with a detailed discussion of strengths, then address weaknesses simply, clearly, and explicitly. It is important to make positive and specific suggestions for improvement, emphasize performance and activities rather than the person, state suggestions for improvement positively, convey criticisms clearly and specifically, and provide specific examples regarding areas in need of change. The supervisor should encourage supervisees to express their feelings regarding the evaluation and empower them to provide honest reactions. It is also helpful to ask supervisees what can be changed to help them do their jobs better. To determine an appropriate course of action when difficulties have been previously identified yet little progress has been made, the supervisor should explore whether the difficulties stem from a skill deficit or whether an underlying problem exists that requires referral to outside services. If there are serious concerns, the supervisor should give multiple written warnings before finalizing a formal negative review, indicating that, "The review will say [this] if [the following] does not change." Throughout the feedback session, the supervisor should be honest, straightforward, and kind. At the conclusion of the feedback session, the supervisor should link the supervisee's individual learning needs to organizational objectives, develop a plan of action, and summarize the session.

Handout 15.2

STEPS IN THE COMPREHENSIVE EVALUATION OF SUPERVISORS

1. An evaluation process that reflects the supervisor's role description is developed.

2. Rating scales are completed by the supervisor, the administrator, and peers to evaluate the supervisor's professional behaviors, leadership behaviors, and program management.

3. Supervisees complete rating scales regarding general professional behaviors.

4. The supervisor develops a portfolio that provides evidence of technical skills, including personnel management, program leadership, program development, training and consultation, public relations, and program evaluation.

5. The supervisor meets with his/her administrator to review the gathered information and develop goals, objectives, and activities for the coming year.

ADDRESSING IMPAIRMENT

Unfortunately, performance evaluations sometimes reveal that a psychologist is seriously impaired. An increasing body of information suggests that a disconcerting percentage of psychologists in training (Huprich & Rudd, 2004; Vacha-Haase, Davenport, & Kerewsky, 2004) and psychologists (Forrest, Elman, Gizara, & Vacha-Haase, 1999; Gizara & Forrest, 2004) are so impaired that their character and fitness to practice are greatly compromised.

Impairment can be manifested in the inability to acquire and integrate professional standards, the inability to achieve competence in professional skills, and/or the "inability to control personal stress, psychological dysfunction, or emotional reactions that may affect professional functioning" (Lamb, Cochran, & Jackson, 1991, p. 292). It is also associated with a disinclination to respect appropriate boundaries regarding sexual contact, social contact, gifts, self-disclosure, language, use of power, and dual relationships (Lamb, 1999). The most common concerns in trainees are adjustment disorders, anxiety problems, depression, personality disorders, substance abuse, sexual misconduct, and ethical violations (Huprich & Rudd, 2004; Vacha-Haase et al., 2004). Impairment can also result from a temporary personal crisis, such as a difficult divorce, or from a personal predisposition, such as a prejudicial attitude, interpersonal insensitivity, a need to control others, or a tendency to rigidly assume a parental role (Bhat, 2005).

If impaired psychologists continue to provide (inadequate) services, they and their supervisors violate both professional standards and ethical principles (American Psychological Association, 2002). As much as possible, supervisors must protect clients from the ill effects of being subject to impaired professionals while still protecting the due process rights of supervisees. To ensure that due process rights are not ignored, supervisors can provide regular, ongoing, and goal-directed supervision to supervisees so that they have adequate opportunity to improve skills before dismissal. Identifying and dealing with impairments is one reason that it is very important for job descriptions and specifications and appraisal materials to reflect all critical aspects of job performance. It is particularly helpful when the appraisal materials include descriptions of how an expert practitioner performs in behavioral terms, along with a scale on which the rater indicates how frequently the supervisee objectively displays such expert behaviors. Furthermore, it is important to clearly define remedial steps and communicate the appeal system in the employee handbook. Steps in dealing with impaired personnel are indicated in Handout 15.3.

Intern Impairment and Incompetence

To assess potential impairment, training programs use periodic appraisal of students' basic communication skills, basic clinical skills, ethical practice, and personality or behavioral traits that might impact professional functioning, such as impulse control, anger control, empathy, maturity, professional demeanor, conflict resolution, and professional standards. For example, the Professional Counseling Performance Evaluation (PCPE; Kerl, Garcia, McCullough, & Maxwell, 2002), found in Handout 12.6, was developed at Texas State University to assess professional dispositions in classes as well as fieldwork. It can be used in every class and can be the basis for failing a class even when academic work is satisfactory. The PCPE is printed in triplicate so that instructors, students, and the program director all have copies; students who are found to have persistent difficulties are referred to a faculty review committee.

Handout 15.3

STEPS IN DEALING WITH IMPAIRED PERSONNEL

(Adapted from Forrest, Elman, Gizara, & Vacha-Haase, 1999;[1]
Lamb, Cochran, & Jackson, 1991;[2] Muratori, 2001[3])

1. Using objective and observable evidence, target the concern by identifying specific problem behaviors that keep a supervisee from meeting job expectations.

2. Determine the negative impact of the behavior on service delivery.

3. Identify ethical or legal repercussions.

4. Consult with colleagues to delineate possible interventions, as it is very important that decisions be made by more than one person.

5. Meet with the supervisee to provide feedback and to ensure that the supervisee understands due process rights.

6. Provide necessary training.

7. Allow time for the supervisee to change.

8. Document the results of the above measures.

9. Consult with colleagues to determine intervention effectiveness.

10. Determine whether (a) the psychologist cannot acknowledge or address the problem, (b) the behavior does not improve with training or feedback, (c) service provision is adversely affected, (d) the problem is manifested in more than one area of practice, (e) the problem behavior leads to ethical or legal violations, and (f) the behavior may reflect seriously and negatively on the organization.

11. Consult with administrators prior to finalizing the review to ensure that due process procedures have been followed.

12. Determine and implement a course of action (additional interventions, probationary status, dismissal).

13. Address the repercussions of the impaired supervisee's actions with administrators, other supervisees, other educators, clients, and others involved with the psychologist.

14. If dismissal is necessary, address the repercussions of the dismissal with administrators, other supervisees, other educators, clients, and others involved with the psychologist.

---

[1]Forrest, L., Elman, N., Gizara, S., & Vacha-Haase, T. (1999). Trainee impairment: A review of identification, remediation, dismissal, and legal issues. *Counseling Psychologist, 27,* 627–686.

[2]Lamb, D. H., Cochran, D. J., & Jackson, V. R. (1991). Training and organizational issues associated with identifying and responding to intern impairment. *Professional Psychology: Research and Practice, 22,* 291–296.

[3]Muratori, M. C. (2001). Examining supervisor impairment from the counselor trainee's perspective. *Counselor Education and Supervision, 41,* 41–56.

Interns often have problems specific to their role. These can include severe financial difficulties, feelings of inadequacy, and difficulty relating to others as an adult. For example, they may relate to students as peers or dress inappropriately and convey that they do not have the skills, responsibility, and authority of other adults in the school. Furthermore, financial obligations that require "outside" jobs on top of heavy academic workloads can result in overextended schedules and severe stress.

Vignette 15.11

As an intern, **Jeanne** was under tremendous financial stress, and this led to many problems during her internship. Because of financial circumstances, she was forced to live in an apartment some distance from her internship site, which caused her to have great difficulty getting to the site on time in the morning due to rush hour traffic. After working a full day as an intern, she worked as a waitress every evening until 1 a.m., which led to constant exhaustion. She spent a great deal of time complaining about her problems. Even when meeting with high school students, she talked so much about her situation that she neglected theirs!

One serious issue that must be addressed is that some interns are below the advanced beginner level and are subsequently unable to progress in their field placement. Often these students have progressed to an advanced level in graduate school because they are proficient academically but have difficulties in less structured settings.

The vacuum in which supervisors work is problematic across all supervisory skills. It becomes an even more serious problem when supervisors are faced with addressing incompetence or impairment in their supervisees. Regardless of their level of training or their knowledge of the supervision literature, supervisors tend to feel ill prepared to address serious competence problems. Since the evaluative process causes supervisors considerable discomfort, they need ample professional development in this area themselves. To become effective evaluators, supervisors need explicit support to move past their need to be liked by their supervisees (Gizara & Forrest, 2004). Consequently, in addressing impaired supervisees, it is imperative to draw on a network of supervisory colleagues and administrators.

Sometimes these difficulties are a result of problems with self-regulation and time management. Diagnosed disabilities, such as learning disabilities and attention deficit disorder (ADD), do not in themselves render one unable to become a school psychologist. In fact, some individuals with learning disabilities and ADD who have developed adequate compensatory strategies have become highly skilled practitioners. On the other hand, critical skills in the practice of school psychology include sequential processing, working memory, spatial orientation, directionality, time management, organization, quick completion of work, simultaneous management of multiple tasks, and skillful written and oral expression. Individuals with learning disabilities or ADD may have severe challenges in these areas. Supervisors can provide guidance in time management and organization or can direct supervisees to compensatory tools such as voice recognition software.

In other cases, interns may have difficulty communicating, being culturally aware, expressing themselves, or relating interpersonally. These difficulties may be the result of developmental delays, lack of motivation, or unresolved interpersonal or intrapersonal concerns such as early childhood abuse, unhappy adult relationships, or substance abuse

(Stoltenberg, McNeill, & Delworth, 1998). Such individuals should be referred for therapy of their own.

When interns' difficulties are not amenable to remediation, occasionally it is necessary to "counsel them into a different profession." Both the university and site supervisor must document an intern's poor performance through recordings and written records. Difficulties most frequently arise when site supervisors fail to identify the problem early enough for a remediation plan to be developed, fail to keep complete records, or fail to notify the university when incompetence is evident.

Impaired Supervisors

Just as impairment and incompetence can be serious issues with supervisees and interns, they can be serious issues for supervisors. The literature on impairment has glossed over supervisor impairment (Muratori, 2001). This is a severely distressing problem, whether it is a result of sexual misconduct, burnout, substance abuse, or emotional or mental disorders. Supervisor impairment is exacerbated by the little attention given to developing skills unique to supervision in both graduate training programs and the organizations in which supervisors work. Furthermore, supervisors often work in isolation, and organizations tend to adopt a "hands-off" policy regarding supervision. Consequently, "supervisors are essentially left in a vacuum to develop their own knowledge and skills" (Gizara & Forrest, 2004, p. 138). As discussed in Chapter 1, impaired supervisors can do considerable harm to their vulnerable supervisees due to their powerful evaluative role. Muratori described considerations supervisees should address if they find themselves in the unfortunate situation of having a supervisor they suspect is impaired. When supervisees' answers to these questions indicate that they are being supervised by an impaired supervisor, they must consider this a serious ethical situation and follow the ethical problem solving steps described in Chapter 6 (see Handout 6.5). His points are summarized in Handout 15.4.

EVALUATING SCHOOL PSYCHOLOGICAL SERVICES

In addition to the individual performance evaluations of school psychologists, supervisors of school psychologists are responsible for the evaluation of services provided by the entire department. Evaluating a department's services improves performance, guides professional development, and provides opportunities for professional recognition. In addition, it identifies and leads to the improvement of programmatic and procedural weakness, documents services, and can be used to promote the effectiveness of psychological services. An evaluation of school psychological services can profoundly impact practice and employment. When school psychologists assess their functioning by documenting professional activities, funds allocation can be justified and a need for change can be demonstrated (Zins, 1985).

Planning

The first step in planning an evaluation is to develop a steering committee to guide the process and determine which questions to answer. In developing a steering committee, the supervising school psychologist should be careful to include upper level administrators and school board members, since their involvement in the process is most likely to result in desired changes.

Handout 15.4

QUESTIONS TO CONSIDER REGARDING SUPERVISOR IMPAIRMENT

(Muratori, 2001, p. 51)[1]

- Which of my supervisor's observable behaviors suggest impairment?

- How am I affected by these behaviors?

- How might my professional development needs influence my reaction to my supervisor?

- How are students with whom I work affected by my supervisor's behavior?

- How are the school district's policies and processes affected?

- What needs do I have that may be affecting my judgment?

- What repercussions do I anticipate if I take action?

- How might I be affected if I do not take action?

- How might the students with whom I work be affected if I do not take action?

- How might future supervisees be affected if I do not take action?

- Do I fear retribution from either my supervisor or the district?

---

[1]Muratori, M. C. (2001). Examining supervisor impairment from the counselor trainee's perspective. *Counselor Education and Supervision, 41,* 41–56.

The underlying question in assessing school psychological services is whether the services provided are of high quality. However, quality can be defined from different perspectives: whether services comply with local, state, and federal guidelines; whether services meet professional standards; whether services have an impact on students and staff; whether consumers are satisfied with the services; whether policies and resources are adequate; and whether the services are cost effective.

1. *Do school psychology services have an impact on students and staff?* Answering this question requires gathering outcome data. Since the overriding goal of school psychological services is to improve the functioning of children, the ultimate outcome of school psychological services should be that referral problems are alleviated and student functioning is improved. Assessment of student outcomes has been discussed in Chapter 5, and the reader is referred to that chapter for methods and procedures.

2. *Do school psychological service procedures comply with local, state, and federal guidelines?* This question can be answered by conducting file reviews to determine variables such as the average number of days from initial referral to initial contact; the average number of days from initial referral to implementation of counseling and/or behavior management consultation; the average number of days from parent permission for assessment to parental receipt of written results; the appropriateness of assessment techniques, including the use of multifaceted assessments and the use of valid and reliable instruments; the appropriateness of assessments to the handicapping conditions; use of the student's dominant language; whether the data gathered justify recommendations; and whether reports are jargon free, readable, and professional in appearance.

3. *How do school psychological services compare with professional standards?* This question can be addressed by using questionnaires based on NASP standards of practice. Handouts 15.8, 15.12, and 15.16 were developed using the NASP (2000a) *Professional Conduct Manual*. The reader can similarly develop individually tailored questionnaires using the same resource. One questionnaire can be designed to be completed by school psychologists themselves. Others can be designed to be completed by parents, school personnel such as teachers and counselors, and administrators. Finally, questionnaires can be developed to address issues applicable to school systems that contract psychological services. It is particularly helpful to key questions to facilitate comparison across surveys. That is, questions appearing in the administrator survey would be numbered A1, A2, and so forth; parallel questions in the school psychologist survey would be numbered S1, S2, and so forth; and parallel questions in the school personnel and parent surveys would be keyed with appropriate cross-references.

4. *Do administrators, parents, and teachers consider school psychological services adequate?* This question can be addressed by gathering information from administrators, parents, and teachers via questionnaires, as described previously. Interviews with administrators, parents, teachers, and students can also address this question. Interview questions might include the items found in Handout 15.5.

5. *What are the school psychology department's policies and resources?* Policy variables include guidelines regarding referral systems, inclusion in prereferral teams, paperwork procedures; diagnosis, crisis intervention, and confidentiality and other ethical mandates. Personnel resources include psychologists and other staff who provide psychological services in schools (e.g., counselors, behavior specialists, social workers, contracted agencies); their qualifications; ratios of staff to students; staff schedules and frequency of visits

Handout 15.5

QUESTIONS REGARDING THE ADEQUACY
OF PSYCHOLOGICAL SERVICES

1. In an ideal world, what impact would school psychological services have on students, teachers, parents, the school, the district, and the community?

2. Do you find the wide spectrum of school psychology services, including program evaluation and research, desirable?

3. Are school psychologists sufficiently accessible to students, teachers, administrators, and parents? What would make them more accessible?

4. Do school psychologists help analyze, understand, and solve problems?

5. Are school psychologists' recommendations appropriate?

6. What psychological services would you like increased? Decreased?

to assigned schools; available supervision; available peer support and communities of learners; and clerical support. Physical resources include funding; available office space in schools and elsewhere; assessment tools, books, and other materials; and storage of student records.

6. *Are school psychology services cost effective? What would be the cost of these services if externally contracted psychologists provided them?* This question is best answered by document analysis, enumeration of the school psychologists' activities, and comparison of the school psychologists' compensation with fees charged by consultants for the same amount of time. District school psychologists can submit enumerations of activities to the supervisor, who can aggregate the information and submit it to the administration and school board in an easily digestible format. In conducting such an analysis, it is important to look at the full range of the school psychologists' activities. A menu of possible activities to enumerate can be found in Table 15.3.

Implementation

After the evaluation questions are defined and procedures have been determined, the evaluation of school psychological services follows the same stages as those of general program evaluations described in Chapter 5. After strengths and weaknesses have been determined, the results should be shared first with all school psychologists and the steering committee to develop a list of potential recommendations. The strengths, weaknesses, and recommendations are then shared with the larger community and used to devise departmentwide professional development plans. Thus formal performance appraisals of both individual practitioners and entire departments should lead naturally to generation of professional development goals and objectives.

DEVELOPING AND PROVIDING PROFESSIONAL DEVELOPMENT

Supervisors are responsible for training and professional development from several perspectives. They orient and train school psychologists new to the district, facilitate the ongoing professional development of veteran school psychologists, and maintain their own professional development. If the district has school psychology interns, the supervisor oversees the training provided to the interns by the district's school psychologists. In large districts, supervisors assist in the development of additional supervisors of school psychologists.

Facilitating professional development is a pivotal supervisory role. "The most important role that the supervisor of school psychology plays . . . is that of teacher, mentor, and catalyst for change and growth" (E. Smith, 1987, p. 39). If, as is said to be true for teachers, school psychologists "peak out" after 5 to 7 years of practice, supervisors must pay intense attention to supervisees' professional development to maintain enthusiasm and the capacity for change.

Furthermore, since effective school psychology departments provide professional development activities for school district teachers, administrators, and paraprofessionals (S. K. Green, 1995), supervisors often either plan professional development programs themselves or supervise district school psychologists as they plan and provide them. A supervisor of school psychologists is likely to be involved in many of the above activities simultaneously, as exemplified in the following vignette.

Vignette 15.12

After a tragic series of student-teacher assaults in **Urban School District** resulted in significant teacher injuries, upper level administrators and the supervisor of school psychologists concurred that the school psychologists should become more active in crisis prevention and intervention across the district. In the preparation phase, baseline data were gathered by examining the discipline reports at all schools for the past 2 years. In addition, a needs assessment was conducted by surveying school personnel. Both of these confirmed the impression that the entire district needed development in nonviolent crisis intervention. The district school psychologists then implemented individual and group activities to increase their own levels of expertise. They read professional literature, attended professional seminars and workshops regarding mediation, obtained certification as nonviolent crisis intervention instructors, held departmental seminars, and consulted with specialists in crisis prevention. During the implementation phase, the school psychology department coordinated the development of a crisis management handbook for the district. Psychologists who had obtained training and instructor certification conducted workshops for teachers, paraprofessionals, counselors, and administrators in crisis prevention and nonviolent crisis intervention. These workshops continued to be held in subsequent years to facilitate training of new employees and professional development of seasoned employees. Every year these activities were evaluated using workshop evaluation forms and outcome data based on student discipline reports.

Planning Professional Development

Professional development activities range from those directed by supervisors and administration to those chosen by the individual. At one extreme, professional development programs do not involve supervisors at all. Such self-managed professional development has some advantages. Assuming responsibility for ongoing professional development is a professional obligation. Self-managed programs that include the examination, planning, and evaluation of one's professional development needs through a self-assessment package can be helpful. However, they do not address the difficulty of helping supervisees sustain a commitment to professional development (Rosenfield, 1981). Furthermore, the goals that an individual develops may be quite independent of the school or district goals.

At the other extreme, traditional management approaches to staff development have supervisors initiate and coordinate the programs. This approach is most appropriate when the entire staff have deficits in knowledge or skills, such as when new technology, strategies, and professional tools are adopted departmentwide. A number of benefits result when supervisors of school psychologists take some responsibility for the professional development of supervisees rather than leaving their professional growth to chance or intermittent workshop attendance. Knowledge is increased, intradepartmental cooperation and respect are promoted, all group members benefit from improved skills, and supervisors consequently spend less time in corrective activities.

An intermediate planning approach involves both the supervisor and supervisee. This approach complements literature describing adult learners as self-directed and experiential yet needing encouragement to critically evaluate their assumptions, practices, and values (S. K. Green, 1995). Effective staff development programs are characterized by individualized training according to each person's chosen goals and activities, methods that require active involvement, multiple sessions that permit spaced learning, and multiple evaluations of changes in the attitudes and behaviors of participants. As Milne, Woodward, et al. (2003) indicated, professional development programs are most effective when learning is experiential, the training is closely aligned with organizational objectives, barriers (e.g., funding and motivation) to implementing the newly learned skills have been addressed, and skill generalization is planned and monitored.

Basic steps in planning effective training programs are (a) conducting a needs assessment; (b) ensuring the readiness of employees for training; (c) creating a learning environment, including identifying goals and objectives; and (d) selecting appropriate materials and methods. After the training program is implemented, an evaluation of its effectiveness should follow.

Conducting Needs Assessment

Probably the most common but perhaps the least important reason that training is undertaken by school personnel, including school psychologists, is the requirement for professional development hours to maintain certification and licensure. More important reasons for training include changes in technology, job redesign, new legislation, and changes in the demographics or needs of the school district population. Other reasons include emerging strategies and techniques, performance problems, deficiencies in basic skills, and complaints from or requests by school personnel or parents. "Continuing professional development is an ethical and professional responsibility, necessary for initial professional competence, required for continuing competence and to cope with changing roles, helpful during professional transitions, essential for development of a specialty, and required for maintaining credentials" (Armistead, 2008, p. 1976).

Before initiation of a professional development program, a systematic needs assessment should be conducted to determine school district, departmental, and individual needs. Assessing the appropriateness of a professional development program from the school district perspective involves taking into account several factors, including:

- The self-perceived needs of the staff
- The compatibility of training objectives with the objectives and values of the school district or department
- The degree to which administrators support participation in training activities
- Resources (time, budget, and expertise) available to support training and the potential to take time for the collaboration necessary for meaningful change
- The effectiveness of the district's procedures, norms, and communication processes
- The degree to which administrators and peers support application of newly learned skills and behaviors (S. K. Green, 1995; Noe et al., 1996; Schmuck & Runkel, 1994)

Areas in which individuals need additional training can be determined through annual performance appraisals, brainstorming, committee meetings, conferences, consultants, interviews, observations, surveys, and questionnaires. To assess individual psychologists' continuing professional development needs, the supervisor collaborates with every school psychologist to review each skill and knowledge area required in professional practice; rate the individual psychologist in each knowledge or skill area as "satisfactory," "questionable," or "needing improvement" based on information provided by the individual, the supervisor, peers, and consumers such as teachers and administrators; determine the importance of each skill area relative to current expectations; and assign priority weights to each continuing professional development goal (Fowler & Harrison, 1995).

In addition to development in the fields of their profession, many individual school psychologists find it fruitful to seek training in related fields such as remedial reading, special education, speech and language therapy, school administration, program evaluation, mediation, and family therapy. On a voluntary basis, many school psychologists also feel they benefit from development in areas not related to their occupation, such as art, music, and philosophy. These activities are broadening, facilitate creativity, and provide intellectual stimulation to counterbalance

> the boredom and routine often produced by professional practice. In too many cases, work dominates life, and what an individual does becomes a symbol for what he or she is . . . life comes to be viewed in the increasingly rigid framework of a single profession. (Houle, 1984, p. 49)

When a problem with a particular school psychologist is identified, the supervisor must determine whether the apparent need for training stems from a lack of knowledge, motivational issues, or personal issues. Regardless, seeking personal or professional growth should be viewed as an indication of strength and never be interpreted as a symptom of incompetence.

Ensuring Readiness for Training

For training to be worth resource expenditure, participants must be motivated to learn, believe that they can successfully learn, and be inclined and able to practice new skills and behaviors. To achieve this readiness for training, it is important to reach agreement on the nature of the problem, goals to solve the problem, and the need for training. It is also important to prepare participants for the content before training begins, give choices on participation in training programs, and provide materials, time, and evaluative feedback so that participants are likely to practice and apply the newly learned skills and behaviors (Certo, 2006).

Armistead (2008) suggested that specific activities can be undertaken to foster opportunities for lifelong learning. These include:

- Joining and actively participating in local, state, and national associations
- Taking leadership positions in professional associations
- Regularly assessing professional development needs in a problem solving cycle
- Focusing continuing professional development needs on students' needs and improving outcomes
- Working within the school psychology department to coordinate professional development throughout the unit
- Strategically selecting professional development activities that address specific professional needs, are effective training activities, involve active participation, and actually result in increased knowledge, skill development, and generalization of skills to practice
- Participating in peer support activities such as online discussion groups, regional supervision groups, peer supervision groups, and mentoring

Creating a Learning Environment

To create the learning environment necessary for effective training, objectives are developed, employees are given opportunities to observe others practicing the desired skills, and training programs are coordinated and well organized. It is helpful when varied teaching strategies are used and guided practice is employed, wherein trainees perform the new task several times under direction and then are given opportunities to practice it independently. Furthermore, performance standards should be developed and used in formal evaluations. This practice encourages supervisees to actually use the skills and also gives them feedback regarding their proficiency in skill application. An emphasis on student outcomes suggests that the most important goals and objectives will address the delivery of services to students and their increased learning and functioning (Wise & Leibbrand, 1996).

Selecting and Designing Training Methods

Professional development activities should employ fundamental learning principals such as spaced trials and enablement of the learner to assign personal meaning to the material. The traditional method of providing professional development in one-time lectures is among the least effective teaching strategies. The most frequently used strategies, self-study and reading professional materials (Lam & Yuen, 2004), are difficult to transfer to applied practice. Furthermore, in addition to addressing content, effective professional development activities employ supervisees' own executive functioning to the extent that they develop metacognitive awareness of their own learning and learning methods. A number of instructional methods are effectively used in training and professional development, each having its own advantages and disadvantages. These are summarized in Table 15.8.

Generalization

Effective professional development programs provide continued support for staff until the new skill is maintained and generalized (S. K. Green, 1995). Often individuals need mentoring and participation in ongoing support groups to sustain a change, even when a skill has been well learned. If ongoing and organizational supports are not engaged, the new skill is not performed (Milne & Roberts, 2002; Rosenfield, 2000).

Evaluating Professional Development Activities

Professional development activities are evaluated using surveys, observations, focus groups, personnel records, or ratings by participants' supervisors or peers. The evaluation method is determined by the training objectives. Results of training and professional development can occur in a number of areas:

1. Integrity: Was the professional development training conducted as planned?
2. Acceptability: Did the participants find the training acceptable?
3. Affect: Did the attitudes of the participants change in desired areas?
4. Cognition: What concepts, facts, and principles did the participants learn?
5. Skills: Did the participants' skills change as a result of the training?
6. Behavior: Did the participants' behavior change after the training?
7. Long-term results: Did training yield increased program effectiveness, improved student outcomes, reduced costs, reduced turnover, or other benefits?

Table 15.8   Professional Development Methods

Method	Advantages	Disadvantages
A. Experiential learning: exposure to videotaped vignettes followed by interactive discussion, appraisal, and feedback	Highly effective teaching tool	Requires structured learning processes, detailed pedagogical techniques, and instructor feedback
B. Lecture supplemented by question and discussion (e.g., professional and in-service workshops)	Quickly provides information to large groups Inexpensive and least time consuming	Effectiveness depends on audience's ability to listen Effectiveness depends on presenter's ability to present clearly and incorporate active participation, case studies, examples, and exercises Ineffective when presented as a "one-shot" workshop without experiential components
C. Simulated case study presentations in which participants think through problems, propose solutions, choose among alternatives, and analyze consequences of the decision	Brings a note of realism Can be used in small or large groups	Simulated cases are usually simpler than real-life cases Because participants are not actually involved in the case, lacks emotional involvement and common complications
D. Distance learning: two-way communication via audioconferencing, videoconferencing, document sharing, or Internet-based synchronous and asynchronous tools	Permits collaborative learning among geographically dispersed individuals Saves travel costs	Potential lack of interaction Misunderstandings can result from lack of nonverbal feedback An on-site facilitator is needed to answer questions
E. Audiovisual techniques such as overheads, slides, prepared videos, videotaping of participants, and PowerPoint presentations	Trainer can vary speed of presentation in response to needs of the audience Trainees are exposed to material not easily demonstrated or presented verbally Instruction can be made consistent from one training session to another When used in conjunction with role-playing, videotaping permits participants to see their own performance Often engages interest	Time necessary to prepare materials can be considerable (estimated video editing time is 1 hour of editing per 1 minute of finished video)

(Continued)

Table 15.8 (Continued)

Method	Advantages	Disadvantages
F. Formation of a peer group that focuses on collaborative problem solving or practicing new skills	Increased morale, networking, familiarity with resources, and participation in professional organizations Improvement of skills	School psychologists practicing in isolation may have difficulty developing such a group Time pressures and geographic distances may preclude scheduling meetings frequently enough to be effective
G. Role-playing of assigned roles in "realistic" situations	Encourages active learning and participation When used in conjunction with videotaping, effectiveness is increased through review and critique	Success depends on willingness of individuals to role-play realistically
H. Behavior modeling, in which interpersonal skills (such as communication of ideas) are taught by: • Giving the rationale behind the desired behaviors • Showing a videotape of the modeled behaviors • Providing trainees practice opportunities in role-play • Requiring trainees to evaluate a model's performance • Giving feedback regarding how closely the trainee's behaviors match those of the model • Having trainees indicate how they plan to use the desired skills on the job	Effective method to learn interpersonal skills Videotaping facilitates self-observation	Relies on willingness of participants to role-play Relies on availability of modeled behavior samples
I. Group building techniques designed to build group identity through shared ideas and experiences; examples include adventure learning (developing teamwork though outdoor activities) and team training (coordinating the performance of individuals who work together to achieve common goals)	Increases understanding of interpersonal dynamics Increases knowledge of one's own and of colleagues' personal strengths and weaknesses	Success limited by team members' ability to identify and resolve errors, coordinate decisions, and reinforce one another

Method	Advantages	Disadvantages
J. Provision of access to professional journals, monographs, books, manuals, and digests through a professional library, dissemination of articles, and book purchases	Readily available Less expensive than the alternatives	Additional support required for effective implementation (i.e., for moving from knowing "about" to knowing "how"; E. Smith, 1987) Does not provide guided practice or feedback
K. Self-directed learning through readings, CD-ROMs, or personal computer instruction	Trainees can participate in accordance with their own schedules Trainees have responsibility for their own training Computer learning provides immediate feedback, multiple learning opportunities, and self-paced instruction	Motivation must be high for the program completion
L. Simulations (including virtual reality simulations) that represent real-life situations in which the trainee's decisions have outcomes similar to those that would occur on the job	Allows trainees to see the impact of their performance in a risk-free environment Effective in teaching interpersonal skills	Virtual reality technology is neither fully developed nor readily available
M. On-the-job training during which the trainer: • Breaks down tasks into steps • Obtains equipment and supplies • Demonstrates the task • Explains key points of the behaviors involved • Demonstrates the task a second time • Has the trainee perform the task in incremental steps • Praises correct performance and provides corrective feedback • Provides additional supervised practice until independent practice is achieved	Novice has opportunity to observe proficient or expert practitioners, imitate them, and practice under direct supervision Effective in giving experience in all job aspects Training occurs in a realistic situation before responsibility is assumed	Novice is likely to acquire poor as well as good practices demonstrated by the trainer Requires the trainee to shadow the trainer, which may be expensive and time consuming

(Continued)

Table 15.8 (Continued)

Method	Advantages	Disadvantages
N. Mentoring: voluntary relationships for both the mentor and protégé that can be ended at any time; the programs have clearly understood purposes, specified projects and activities, a specified duration, a minimum level of contact, opportunities for protégés to contact one another, a formal evaluation process, and rewarded participation	Novice develops his/her own approach while still under the guidance of a more proficient practitioner Formal mentoring programs are accessible to minorities and women, not just to those with previous "network" connections (unlike informal mentor programs) Mentoring relationships benefit both parties: mentors have opportunities to develop interpersonal skills, increase feelings of self-worth, and gain knowledge about new developments Protégés are benefited by receipt of career, psychosocial, and emotional support	Bad practices can be passed on to the novice Mentor might neglect responsibilities Mentor may have difficulty understanding the protégé's situation when only verbal descriptions are available All novice practitioners do not seek informal mentoring Formal mentoring programs may result in attempts to develop relationships inadequately matched for interests, values, and mutual regard
O. On-campus university coursework	Most effective when participants have little knowledge Provides supervision, active learning, and feedback	Not always available in areas of interest Requires repeated travel Can be costly and time consuming
P. Online university coursework	Most effective when participants have little knowledge Provides supervision, active learning, and feedback	Not always available in areas of interest Technology not universally available Can be costly and time consuming

ASSESSING EVALUATION AND PROFESSIONAL DEVELOPMENT PROCESSES

After the evaluation and professional development processes have been completed, the supervisor should consider supervisees' opinions and suggestions to modify these practices. Whether considering the appraisal process for discrimination on the basis of race, ethnicity, culture, gender, age, or disability or attempting to determine how well the entire process works, supervisors should continually foster a metacognitive perspective and self-evaluation processes. It can be a relief to understand that perfection is not possible. There is always room for improvement and there is always a need for change. Therein lies the great challenge, and reward, in supervision of psychological services in the schools.

Vignette 15.13

After 33 years in the field of school psychology, 29 of them as a supervisor, **Tessa** changed her concept of her work. Previously, she had thought of the practice and supervision of school psychology as similar to building a house: a challenge in design, coordination, resource procurement, and management. More recently, Tessa realized that the house building metaphor implied that one could be "finished," but that practice and supervision in school psychology is never finished. There is always progress to be monitored, practices to refine, new evidence to incorporate. Therefore, Tessa thought a more useful metaphor would be farming in New England. Due to sandy soil, a proliferation of rocks, and harsh climate, farming in New England is very hard work that never ends. If constant effort is not applied, the land quickly reverts back to blackberry briar patches and scrub pine. Farming also requires great skill in discerning the appropriate steps to take, knowledge regarding which plants to encourage and which to eliminate, and as much nurturing as one can muster. Like farming, practicing and supervising school psychology is both incredibly challenging and phenomenally rewarding.

SUMMARY

Performance appraisals are an important function of supervisors in school psychology. They are effective only within the context of a performance management process that includes job analysis, performance feedback, and subsequent improvement. For both formative and summative evaluations, the supervisor and supervisee determine indicators of effective performance, collect data, monitor and report effectiveness, and develop a plan.

A number of issues render conducting individual performance appraisals challenging. Evaluations must be reliable, valid, meaningful, acceptable, useful, specific, and practical while also avoiding discrimination and protecting due rights. Evaluation methods must comply with union contracts and include steps for dealing with impaired supervisees. In conducting an evaluation, information should be gathered from teachers, school administrators, parents, clients, and the school psychologist himself. It is also helpful to include other personnel such as nurses, therapists, and social workers. Evaluations of school psychology supervisors are a key component of healthy school psychology departments as well as supervision of interns and practicum students.

Supervisors can take a number of steps to meet the challenges of the evaluation process. They must begin by overcoming their reluctance to conduct the evaluation and understanding that protecting the welfare of students is their primary responsibility. This empowers them to accept responsibility for completing evaluations and to hold school psychologists accountable for their work. It also helps them complete honest appraisals even when they receive complaints or experience discomfort.

After evaluations are conducted, the supervisor meets personally with the supervisee to discuss strong and weak points and to make plans to address areas of weakness. This includes the development of professional development plans. It is recommended that both the supervisor and supervisee be involved in the development of a plan for continuing professional development and that the newly acquired skills be incorporated into the individual and group performance evaluation process.

Unfortunately, performance evaluations sometimes reveal that a psychologist is seriously impaired. If impaired psychologists continue to provide (inadequate) services, they and their supervisors violate both professional standards and ethical principles. Supervisors must protect clients from the ill effects of being subject to impaired professionals while still protecting the due process rights of supervisees.

In addition to the individual performance evaluations of school psychologists, supervisors of school psychologists are responsible for the evaluation of services provided by the entire department. Evaluating a department's services improves performance, guides professional development, and provides opportunities for professional recognition. In addition, it identifies and leads to the improvement of programmatic and procedural weakness, documents services, and can be used to promote the effectiveness of psychological services. An evaluation of school psychological services can profoundly impact practice and employment. When school psychologists assess their functioning by documenting professional activities, funds allocation can be justified and a need for change can be demonstrated.

Facilitating professional development is a pivotal supervisory role. Supervisors orient and train school psychologists new to the district, facilitate the ongoing professional development of veteran school psychologists, and maintain their own professional development. If the district has school psychology interns, the supervisor oversees the training provided to the interns. In large districts, supervisors assist in the development of additional supervisors of school psychologists. The traditional method of providing professional development in one-time lectures is among the least effective teaching strategies. A number of other instructional methods can be effectively used in training and professional development, each with its own advantages and disadvantages.

REFLECTIVE QUESTIONS

Q15.1. Describe the steps in conducting a performance appraisal.

Q15.2. What variables should appraisals measure? What variables should not be reflected?

Q15.3. Describe the various methods of appraisal.

Q15.4. Describe the components of an effective professional development plan, including methods for training. How can the success of training be evaluated?

Q15.5. Describe the challenges of conducting performance appraisals. What are the issues and how can they be dealt with?

Q15.6. How can supervisors gather information about supervisee performance?

Q15.7. What are the steps of a comprehensive method of performance evaluation?

Q15.8. How can a supervisor best communicate evaluation feedback?

Q15.9. Describe methods for evaluating supervisors.

Q15.10. Discuss the evaluation issues specific to interns and practicum students.

Q15.11. Describe the processes to use in determining whether a supervisee is so impaired that it is not possible to permit continued employment.

Q15.12. Design a process to evaluate the school psychological services provided in your district. Make sure that it focuses on the skills and behaviors that you most value.

Q15.13. Conduct a comprehensive evaluation of school psychological services and present the results to both school psychologists and administrators.

Q15.14. Design a multisession, multimodality professional development program for a group of supervisees regarding a topic you consider critically important.

Q15.15. Provide a multisession, multimodality professional development program and appraise its effectiveness.

SUPERVISORY DILEMMAS

SD 15.1

A school psychologist and his supervisor determine that his training is obsolete and decide that he should enroll in a class at a local university. The following year the building principal writes a negative comment in the school psychologist's evaluation, indicating that his need for training revealed incompetence. The school psychologist feels that the receipt of training should not be reflected in his evaluation unless he has been warned ahead of time that this might be the case. *What are the supervisory considerations? What should be done?*

Authors' thoughts: This case illustrates the necessity of advance, clear communication among pertinent parties when evaluating personnel. Obtaining training to update skills should not be responded to in a punitive manner. This case well illustrates the problems that arise when administrators without adequate knowledge of psychology serve as supervisors. One option would be for the supervisor to advocate for the supervisee and/or participate in the evaluative process.

SD 15.2

One of your supervisees approaches you, asking you to write a personal letter of reference. He is seeking a job as a school psychologist in a neighboring town. The pay is more and the commute will be easier. Unfortunately, you are aware of a number of performance issues that have been problematic in the past. For example, his assessment reports are frequently late and are typically computer generated (with notably few edits). You have also been told by teachers in the building that he is considered ineffective by parents, students, and staff alike. He has stated on many occasions that he prides himself on being the first staff member to leave the building at the end of the day. He staunchly refuses to do any work beyond that which is contractually required. On one hand, you would hardly consider his departure a loss for the district, but you are concerned about writing a dishonest letter of reference. *What are the supervisory considerations? What should be done?*

Authors' thoughts: This presents a difficult situation that most supervisors will confront at some point. It is clearly difficult to navigate these messy waters, fraught with conflicting demands. Although tempting for the good of the district, it is obviously unethical to write an inaccurate letter of recommendation. Many supervisors have learned how to effectively write a letter that says so little that it says everything! (Due to litigation concerns, in business settings, it is not uncommon practice to limits letters of recommendation to stating only the length of time and position in which the job applicant worked.) Another issue is helping the supervisee develop better communication and professional skills (to say nothing of commitment to the profession!) so that students are better served. (Good luck!) Finally, the supervisor must examine why this individual has been allowed to remain in his current position without corrective action. This request can be considered an opportunity for effective change.

SD 15.3

You have become suspicious that your supervisee, a school psychologist in his mid-40s, is developing a habit of drinking on the job. He brings a thermos to work daily, and when you visit him on-site he quickly hides his cup. You have not noticed any change in his work, yet feel uncomfortable ignoring the issue. *What are the supervisory considerations? What should be done?*

Authors' thoughts: If the supervisee is indeed drinking on the job, this situation must be confronted vigorously. It would be advisable to explore what services are available (e.g., through the employee assistance program or health insurance). The reality is that, if left untreated, the situation is most likely to deteriorate and adversely affect students. Close supervision and monitoring are warranted. The supervisor will need to assess whether there is imminent danger to students and, if so, take disciplinary action to remove the supervisee immediately. Consultation with the administration is also advisable.

SD 15.4

You have recently been named the supervising school psychologist in a district and are quite pleased with the work of six of your supervisees. One district school psychologist, however, has extremely deficient skills. When you attempt to address these deficiencies, she informs you that every previous evaluation has been extremely positive. After pulling her personnel file, you discover that this is indeed the case. *What are the ethical dilemmas? What can be done?*

Authors' thoughts: It is likely that the earlier positive evaluations were symptomatic of the previous supervisor's discomfort with the evaluation process rather than of adequate skills. They were a disservice to the psychologist and, even worse, to the students. The current supervisor must remedy the situation by taking the time to carefully and honestly complete evaluation procedures and provide professional development. If these procedures to not yield effective results, steps to determine and deal with impairment must be followed.

SD 15.5

A second-year student in a specialist level school psychology program has disclosed to the director of the program that in the past he has periodically suffered from clinical depression. At this point, he is a stellar student, but he is afraid that the challenge of working as an intern will precipitate feelings of inadequacy and may lead to a depression. The program director cannot decide whether he should warn the internship supervisor of the intern's need for additional support and the possibility that he might suffer from debilitating depression. *What are the supervisory considerations? What should be done?*

Authors' thoughts: This student is aware that a personal problem may interfere with his work and is taking appropriate measures by seeking support. Since he clearly wants support, it is likely that he would be equally candid with the internship supervisor. The program director can encourage this, and should also let the supervisor know that he is a stellar student who has held up well to the rigors of graduate school. The program director should also let the student know that she will remain available to him for support.

Handout 15.6

CHECKLIST OF PERFORMANCE APPRAISAL
AND PROFESSIONAL DEVELOPMENT STRATEGIES

Plan the appraisal process:
Update the supervisee's job description.
Design an appraisal process that incorporates the supervisee's job description, information from multiple informants, and varied methods; assesses multiple traits; and contains valid and specific criteria.
Ensure that the supervisee and supervisor are in agreement regarding the purpose of the appraisal and make the process as nonthreatening as possible.
Interview the supervisee to discuss updated job requirements relative to training, prior experience, and personal strengths and weaknesses.
Gather information:
Observe the supervisee in several settings (e.g., consulting, assessing, running a support group, working with a team of educators, meeting with a parent).
Speak with and/or have appraisal forms completed by principals, teachers, and parents who work with the supervisee.
Review samples of the supervisee's work since the last appraisal.
Review personnel files.
Draft an appraisal based on the previously described steps.
Ask the supervisee to complete a written self-appraisal and bring it to the feedback session.
During the appraisal feedback session:
Meet privately to discuss the draft appraisal and compare it to the self-appraisal.
Focus attention and avoid interruptions.
Begin the feedback session with a detailed discussion of strengths.
Address weaknesses simply, clearly, and explicitly.
Make positive and specific suggestions for improvement, emphasizing performance and activities.
Establish a climate of open communication; encourage expression of feelings and honest reactions.
Ask the supervisee what might be changed about his/her job or the supervision process that could help.
Explore the source of difficulties to determine a course of action and give written warnings.
Be honest, straightforward, and kind.
Develop individual goals and objectives that link individual needs to organizational objectives.
Conclude with a summary and plan for the future.

(Continued)

(Continued)

After the appraisal feedback session:
Modify supervision in accord with supervisees' opinions and suggestions.
As appropriate, modify supervisees' job assignments based on their opinions, suggestions, and strengths.
Make provisions for appropriate training by (a) needs assessment, (b) ensuring readiness, (c) creating a learning environment and identifying goals, and (d) selecting appropriate materials and methods.
After the training program is implemented, evaluate its effectiveness.
Review progress in goal completion regularly through the examination of data provided by the supervisee.
Address problematic situations:
Identify specific problem behaviors via objective and observable evidence.
Determine the negative impact of these behaviors on service delivery and identify ethical or legal repercussions.
Consult with colleagues to delineate possible interventions.
Meet with the supervisee to provide feedback and ensure that he/she understands due process rights.
Allow a specified time for the supervisee to change independently.
Provide needed training.
Document the results of the above measures and consult with colleagues to determine intervention effectiveness.
Determine whether or not an impairment exists.
Consult with administrators to ensure that due process procedures have been followed.
Determine and implement a course of action (additional interventions, probationary status, dismissal).
Address repercussions with administrators, other supervisees, other educators, clients, and others.
Appraise the appraisal process:
Monitor the appraisal process for discrimination on the basis of race, ethnicity, culture, gender, age, or disability.
Periodically review and modify the appraisal process.

Handout 15.7

PROFESSIONAL DISPOSITIONS

Name: _____   Rater: _____

Please rate your candidate on the questionnaire provided. Use the following scale.

1 = Poor. Fails to meet expectations. Consistently performs poorly and needs improvement. A specific plan and period of time should be established to improve performance. If improvement is not made, then the candidate's suitability for this field of work should be evaluated.

2 = Below Standard. Performance is below average. A candidate whose performance consistently falls in this range requires improvement to function effectively in a professional environment.

3 = Standard. Most candidates will possess skills and judgment sufficient to meet professional demands in this area, and a large proportion will remain in this range. The performance of candidates in this range meets normal expectations.

4 = Above Standard. Performance and judgment of candidates in this category is decidedly better than average. Shows sensitivity, judgment, and skill beyond what is normally expected or displayed by peers.

5 = Outstanding. Performance is recognizably and decidedly better than that of a large proportion of other students.

N = Not Observed. This rating should be used when the activity in question is not part of class or placement expectations or the rater has not had the opportunity to observe or rate the candidate on the item.

Acceptable performance on these professional work characteristics is an important component of our students' evaluation. Please review the items carefully.

Professional Dispositions

1. Respect for Human Diversity
   a. Candidate is sensitive to racial issues.   1 2 3 4 5 N
   b. Candidate is sensitive to cultural issues.   1 2 3 4 5 N
   c. Candidate is sensitive to the needs of all learners.   1 2 3 4 5 N
   d. Candidate is sensitive to people of all sexual orientations.   1 2 3 4 5 N
   e. Candidate professionally encourages inclusion in school settings.   1 2 3 4 5 N
   f. Candidate is aware of challenges diversity issues pose in the schools.   1 2 3 4 5 N

2. Effective Communication Skills
   a. Candidate's written work is free of spelling errors.   1 2 3 4 5 N
   b. Candidate's written work is free of grammatical errors.   1 2 3 4 5 N
   c. Candidate's spoken language is free of grammatical errors.   1 2 3 4 5 N
   d. Candidate can clearly express ideas in writing.   1 2 3 4 5 N
   e. Candidate can clearly express ideas verbally.   1 2 3 4 5 N
   f. Candidate can explain complex ideas in simple language.   1 2 3 4 5 N

(Continued)

(Continued)

3. Effective Interpersonal Relations
   a. Candidate demonstrates understanding of others' points of view.   1 2 3 4 5 N
   b. Candidate is empathic of others.   1 2 3 4 5 N
   c. Candidate is supportive of others.   1 2 3 4 5 N
   d. Candidate resolves conflict situations in a professional manner.   1 2 3 4 5 N
   e. Candidate approaches others for assistance when needed.   1 2 3 4 5 N

4. Ethical Responsibility
   a. Candidate has demonstrated knowledge of ethical guidelines of the profession.   1 2 3 4 5 N
   b. Candidate can apply ethical guidelines to situations within practice.   1 2 3 4 5 N
   c. Candidate does not exceed areas of competence in professional practice.   1 2 3 4 5 N

5. Self-Awareness, Self-Evaluation, and Self-Reflection
   a. Candidate has adapted to the academic demands of the program.   1 2 3 4 5 N
   b. Candidate is aware of the potential impact of personal values and beliefs on clients, peers, and faculty.   1 2 3 4 5 N
   c. Candidate independently identifies problem situations.   1 2 3 4 5 N
   d. Candidate engages in problem solving to address problem situations.   1 2 3 4 5 N
   e. Candidate has adapted to the emotional demands of the program.   1 2 3 4 5 N

6. Initiative and Dependability
   a. Candidate is organized.   1 2 3 4 5 N
   b. Candidate meets important deadlines.   1 2 3 4 5 N
   c. Candidate anticipates the needs of students/clients.   1 2 3 4 5 N

7. Openness to Processes of Supervision
   a. Candidate welcomes performance feedback.   1 2 3 4 5 N
   b. Candidate receives feedback in a thoughtful and reflective manner.   1 2 3 4 5 N
   c. Candidate actively seeks to resolve issues raised in supervision.   1 2 3 4 5 N

The questions below should be completed only if applicable.

8. Resolution of Issues or Problems That Interfere With Professional Development
   a. Candidate responded professionally to negative feedback or reprimand.   1 2 3 4 5 N
   b. Candidate successfully completed a remediation plan.   1 2 3 4 5 N
   c. Candidate sought out assistance in dealing with a critical professional issue.   1 2 3 4 5 N
   d. Candidate entered and completed therapy to resolve issues or problems.   1 2 3 4 5 N

Do you have any comments about this candidate that you would like to add?

From the *2006 SUNY Plattsburgh School Psychology Program Handbook.* Plattsburgh, NY: Locally published monograph. Use of this material is by permission of the author, Dale Phillips.

Handout 15.8

SCHOOL PSYCHOLOGIST EVALUATION FORM

Supervisee name: _____ E-mail: _____

Placement: _____

Evaluation period: _____ Date of evaluation: _____

Supervisor: _____ Site: _____

Street: _____ City: _____ Zip: _____

Phone: _____ E-mail: _____

- Please review this form at the beginning of the evaluation period with the supervisee (and university supervisor for students) and collaborate in developing a work plan at that time.
- Please complete the form twice each evaluation period, once at the midpoint and once at the end.
- Share a copy with the supervisee (for students, send the original to the university).
- Please rate each item twice, once for *competency* and once for *acceptability*.

   First, indicate the extent to which the psychologist demonstrates competency for each domain:
      1 = Novice
      2 = Advanced Beginner
      3 = Competent
      4 = Proficient or Expert (not expected but occasionally seen in experienced students)

   Second, indicate the acceptability of the level of competency demonstrated:
      1 = Not Acceptable
      2 = Marginally Acceptable
      3 = Acceptable (as expected for the placement level)
      4 = Exceeds Expectations

If you have no basis for appraisal, **please leave blank.**

DEFINITIONS

Novices are rule bound, have simplistic and partial understandings, have difficulty understanding contextual issues, tend to be anxious, do not integrate well, and are highly motivated and dependent. They require close supervision and a high degree of structure.

Advanced beginners focus on the mastery of technical aspects, begin to perceive recurring situations, start considering context, and are more autonomous than novices. They have difficulty setting priorities and determining the relative importance of information.

Competent practitioners are better able to see relationships and patterns, balance skills and empathy, and plan and think ahead. They tend to feel responsible and analyze their own skills well. They still need access to a supervisor for ongoing consultation.

Proficient and expert practitioners recognize patterns and context, work successfully with very complex cases, have decreased reliance on guidelines, and utilize self-analysis.

(Continued)

(Continued)

	Competency Scale	Acceptability Scale
	1 = Novice	1 = Not Acceptable
	2 = Advanced Beginner	2 = Marginally Acceptable
	3 = Competent	3 = Acceptable/Expected
	4 = Proficient or Expert	4 = Exceeds Expectations

DOMAIN 1: Data-Based Decision Making and Accountability

The psychologist:	Competency	Acceptability
Knows varied models and methods of assessment that yield information useful in identifying strengths and needs, in understanding problems, and in measuring progress and accomplishments		
Uses varied models and methods as part of a systematic process to collect data and other information		
Uses varied models and methods to translate assessment results into empirically based decisions about service delivery		
Uses varied models to evaluate the outcomes of services		
Practices such that data-based decision making permeates every aspect of professional practice		

Please offer specific suggestions for growth in these areas.

DOMAIN 2: Consultation and Collaboration

The psychologist:	Competency	Acceptability
Knows behavioral, mental health, collaborative, and/or other consultation models and methods		
Applies behavioral, mental health, collaborative, and/or other consultation models and methods appropriately to particular situations		
Collaborates effectively with others in planning and decision making processes at the individual, group, and systems levels		

Please offer specific suggestions for growth in these areas.

DOMAIN 3: Effective Instruction and Development of Cognitive and Academic Skills

The psychologist:	Competency	Acceptability
Understands human learning processes, techniques to assess them, and direct and indirect services applicable to the development of cognitive and academic skills		
Develops, in collaboration with others, appropriate cognitive and academic goals for children and adolescents with different abilities, disabilities, strengths, and needs		
Implements interventions, including instructional interventions and consultation, to achieve the above goals		
Evaluates the effectiveness of such interventions		

Please offer specific suggestions for growth in these areas.

<u>Competency Scale</u>

1 = Novice
2 = Advanced Beginner
3 = Competent
4 = Proficient or Expert

<u>Acceptability Scale</u>

1 = Not Acceptable
2 = Marginally Acceptable
3 = Acceptable/Expected
4 = Exceeds Expectations

DOMAIN 4: Socialization and Development of Life Skills

The psychologist:	*Competency*	*Acceptability*
Knows human developmental processes, techniques to assess these processes, and direct and indirect services applicable to the development of behavioral, affective, adaptive, and social skills		
Develops, in collaboration with others, appropriate behavioral, affective, adaptive, and social goals for children and adolescents of varying abilities, disabilities, strengths, and needs		
Implements interventions, including consultation, behavioral assessment and intervention, and counseling, to achieve the above goals		
Evaluates the effectiveness of these interventions		

Please offer specific suggestions for growth in these areas.

DOMAIN 5: Diversity in Development and Learning

The psychologist:	*Competency*	*Acceptability*
Knows individual differences, abilities, and disabilities and the potential influence of biological, social, cultural, ethnic, experiential, socioeconomic, gender-related, and linguistic factors in development and learning		
Demonstrates the sensitivity and skills needed to work with individuals of diverse characteristics		
Implements strategies selected and/or adapted based on individual characteristics, strengths, and needs		

Please offer specific suggestions for growth in these areas.

DOMAIN 6: School and System Organization, Policy Development, and Climate

The psychologist:	*Competency*	*Acceptability*
Demonstrates knowledge of general education, special education, and other educational and related services		
Understands schools and other settings as systems		
Works with individuals and groups to facilitate policies and practices that create and maintain safe, supportive, and effective learning environments for children and adolescents		

Please offer specific suggestions for growth in these areas.

(Continued)

(Continued)

<table>
<tr><td colspan="2">

<u>Competency Scale</u>

1 = Novice
2 = Advanced Beginner
3 = Competent
4 = Proficient or Expert
</td><td colspan="2">

<u>Acceptability Scale</u>

1 = Not Acceptable
2 = Marginally Acceptable
3 = Acceptable/Expected
4 = Exceeds Expectations
</td></tr>
</table>

DOMAIN 7: Prevention, Crisis Intervention, and Mental Health

The psychologist:	Competency	Acceptability
Understands human development, psychopathology, and associated biological, cultural, and social influences on human behavior		
Provides or contributes to *prevention* programs that promote the mental health and physical well-being of children and adolescents		
Provides or contributes to *intervention* programs that promote the mental health and physical well-being of children and adolescents		

Please offer specific suggestions for growth in these areas.

DOMAIN 8: Home-School-Community Collaboration

The psychologist:	Competency	Acceptability
Demonstrates knowledge of family systems, including family strengths and influences on child and adolescent development, learning, and behavior, and of methods to involve families in education and service delivery		
Works effectively with families, educators, and others in the community to promote and provide comprehensive services to children, adolescents, and families		

Please offer specific suggestions for growth in these areas.

DOMAIN 9: Research and Program Evaluation

The psychologist:	Competency	Acceptability
Demonstrates knowledge of research, statistics, and evaluation methods		
Evaluates research studies and translates research into practice		
Understands research design and statistics in sufficient depth to plan and conduct investigations and program evaluations for improvement of services		

Please offer specific suggestions for growth in these areas.

Competency Scale	Acceptability Scale
1 = Novice	1 = Not Acceptable
2 = Advanced Beginner	2 = Marginally Acceptable
3 = Competent	3 = Acceptable/Expected
4 = Proficient or Expert	4 = Exceeds Expectations

DOMAIN 10: School Psychology Practice and Professional Development

The psychologist:	Competency	Acceptability
Demonstrates knowledge of the history and foundations of the profession; of various service models and methods; of public policy development applicable to services for children, adolescents, and families; and of ethical, professional, and legal standards		
Practices in ways that are consistent with applicable standards		
Is involved in the profession		
Has the knowledge and skills needed to acquire career-long professional development		

Please offer specific suggestions for growth in these areas.

DOMAIN 11: Information Technology

The psychologist:	Competency	Acceptability
Knows relevant information sources and technology		
Accesses, evaluates, and utilizes information sources and technology in ways that safeguard and enhance service quality		

Please offer specific ways or suggestions for growth in these areas.

PERSONAL QUALITIES

	Acceptability
Punctuality and attendance	
Attendance at training and supervisory sessions	
Professional appearance and demeanor, including speech	
Consistency, perseverance, industry, and initiative	
Flexibility; adaptability to novel and unexpected situations	
General attitude and interest in program and assignment	
Insight, sensitivity, commitment, and active participation	
Poise, tactfulness, and rapport with staff and others	
Preparation and organization of material	
Ability to handle constructive criticism professionally	
Ethical practice	

(Continued)

(Continued)

FINAL EVALUATION

Please give your impression of the overall performance of the school psychologist.

How has the psychologist's presence benefited the children and adolescents with whom he/she has worked?

Please give your impression of the psychologist's personal and professional growth as a result of this fieldwork experience.

Please give recommendations for future professional development.

_____

Supervisor's Signature

From the *2007 University of Massachusetts Boston School Psychology Field Work Handbook*. Boston, MA: Locally published monograph. Use of this material is by permission of the author, Virginia Harvey.

Handout 15.9

SCHOOL PSYCHOLOGIST COMPETENCY OBSERVATION FORM

School Psychologist:

Date:

Student Name (if applicable):

School/Location:

Activity Observed: _____ IEP Team _____ Student Support Team _____ Other:

Ratings: 4 = Exceeds Expectations, 3 = Satisfactory, 2 = Needs Improvement, 1 = Unsatisfactory

Professional/clinical skills:
____ Displays knowledge of ethical practices
____ Demonstrates knowledge of child development, learning, and evaluation
____ Adheres to procedures
____ Engages in effective data collection
____ Assists in planning additional data collection (if needed)
____ Presents information accurately
____ Assists in integrating and interpreting information and assessment findings
____ Demonstrates effective consultation
____ Offers meaningful suggestions for prevention, intervention, and/or referral

Comments:

Human relations skills:
____ Engages in active listening
____ Demonstrates empathy
____ Shows respect for colleagues and parents
____ Communicates clearly and effectively
____ Demonstrates appropriate responsibility and leadership
____ Shows willingness to offer assistance
____ Assists with problem solving and conflict resolution
____ Facilitates closure and consensus

Comments:

Management:
____ Shows evidence of planning with colleagues
____ Knows background and issues
____ Is ready with a written report if appropriate
____ Assists with priority setting and decision making
____ Facilitates process
____ Assists with planning and follow-up

Comments:

Overall: ____ Exceeds Expectations ____ Satisfactory ____ Needs Improvement ____ Unsatisfactory

_____   _____
Supervisor's Signature   Psychologist's Signature

From the *2006 Baltimore County, Maryland, Public Schools School Psychologist Handbook.* Baltimore, MD: Locally published monograph. Use of this material is by permission of the author, William Flook.

Handout 15.10

SCHOOL PSYCHOLOGIST
PROFESSIONAL DEVELOPMENT AND EVALUATION PLAN

School Psychologist: School:

Assignment: Supervisor:

Visitation Date(s):   Conference Date(s):

Activity: Number of Individuals Present:

Code: 1 = Excellent Progress, 2 = Satisfactory, 3 = Area for Growth, 4 = Unsatisfactory

	1	2	3	4
1. Demonstrates knowledge of the theory and practice of school psychology				
a. Demonstrates knowledge of human growth and development as it relates to the teaching-learning process and the educational environment				
b. Participates in and contributes to curriculum research, planning, and development in terms of learning and human development theory				
2. Effectively assesses student needs and progress				
a. To facilitate learning, acts as a liaison between the school and community in identifying unmet needs of students				
b. Selects, administers, and interprets appropriate individual and group tests and evaluative techniques to assess student achievement, ability, and social-emotional development				
3. Plans and effectively implements programs and interventions to achieve objectives				
a. Provides students with the opportunity for appropriate academic and/or personal counseling individually or in small groups				
b. Selects and applies appropriate procedures for counseling with parents about their child's individual growth and development				
c. Selects and provides students with guidance and information to help them in their personal, educational, and vocational decision making as appropriate				
d. Plans and develops articulation programs and procedures to help students with transitions to new grade levels				
e. Designs and develops procedures for preventing disorders, promoting mental health, and improving effective educational programs				
f. Assists in the planning and development of educational programs appropriate to the individual needs of all students				
4. Effectively communicates with students, staff, family members, and members of the community				
a. Reports psychological evaluation findings, both written and oral, in clear, concise, and accurate terms				
b. Provides outreach and support to parents, staff, and students				

	1	2	3	4
c. Consults and collaborates with other community professionals in providing a continuum of services and advocacy for children in need				
d. Consults with administrators to assist in resolving school issues and crises that have implications for the psychological well-being of students and staff				
e. Assists the school community in developing a respect for individual differences				
f. Assists in identifying, planning, and implementing nonschool referrals to outside agencies and resources for individual students				
g. Works cooperatively with staff to plan, develop, and implement mutual educational and professional goals to ensure that the school appropriately meets the educational, social, and developmental needs of students				
h. Establishes rapport with students and staff and fosters positive interactions				
5. Effectively meets the needs of special education students				
a. Demonstrates understanding of the behaviors resulting from mental, physical, emotional, sensory, speech, or any other handicapping conditions				
b. Assists staff and parents in understanding the handicapping condition and how it interferes with the child's school functioning				
c. Implements school psychology as a related service, when appropriate				
d. Assesses individual needs as they relate to the special education process				
6. Demonstrates ethical and professional behavior				
a. Conducts services in a manner that protects the due process rights of the students and their parents as defined by current state and federal laws and regulations				
b. Participates in supervision and evaluation of all services provided in order to maintain and improve the effectiveness of these services				
c. Is aware of, contributes to, and participates in the aims and activities of relevant professional organizations				
d. Participates in programs for individual and departmental professional growth				

Comments:

_____ is recommended for reemployment for the 20 _____ –20 _____ school year.

_____   _____   _____   _____

Staff Member's Signature   Date   Supervisor's Signature   Date

My signature indicates that I have read this document. It does not indicate agreement or disagreement with its contents.

From the *2006 Westport School District School Psychologist Handbook*. Westport, CT: Locally published monograph. Use of this material is by permission of the author, Barbara Fischetti.

Handout 15.11

OUTLINE OF OBJECTIVES, COMPETENCIES, EXPERIENCES, AND ASSIGNMENTS BY THE NATIONAL ASSOCIATION OF SCHOOL PSYCHOLOGISTS' ELEVEN DOMAINS OF PROFESSIONAL PRACTICE

1. **Data-Based Decision Making and Accountability**

The intern is able to assess strengths and needs to gain an understanding of problems, measure progress and accomplishments, translate assessment results into empirically based decisions about service delivery, and evaluate the outcomes of services.

Initiated by the end of   Fall   Spring

Evaluation			
Competency/Skill/Activity	**Entry**	**Midterm**	**Final**

Overall Rating: _____

Comments:

Sep	Dec	Jun	*Specific Skills*
			a. **Selecting and applying appropriate assessment methods** – Test administration and interpretation (norm referenced, criterion referenced) – Behavioral assessment: interviewing, systematic direct observation, functional assessment/analysis – Curriculum-based assessment – Ecological/environmental assessment (home, classroom, school, community) – Assessment of student characteristics (cognitive, emotional, and motivational factors affecting performance) – Permanent products inspection (e.g., work products, school records) – Integration of assessment results in written reports *Comments:* b. **Understanding and using assessment in a problem solving context** – Use of data to demonstrate student problems/needs – Use of data to demonstrate student outcomes *Comments:* c. **Understanding and using assessment in an accountability context** – Use of assessment to identify systems level needs (e.g., classwide intervention, improved parent-school communication, more effective problem solving team functioning, less reliance on testing) – Use of assessment to identify outcomes of systems level practices, activities, and projects – Use of assessment information to make decisions regarding special education eligibility *Comments:*

2. Consultation and Collaboration

The intern is able to listen well, participate in discussions, convey information, and work together with others at the individual, group, and systems levels. The intern has knowledge of behavioral, mental health, collaborative, and/or other consultation models and methods and of their application to particular situations.

Initiated by the end of   Fall   Spring

Evaluation			
Competency/Skill/Activity	Entry	Midterm	Final

Overall Rating: _____

Comments:

Sep	Dec	Jun	Specific Skills
			a. Displays appropriate interpersonal communication skills – Listens attentively to others – Displays appropriate empathy – Paraphrases, summarizes, and questions appropriately – Participates in group discussions – Displays appropriate communication with educational personnel and parents *Comments:*
			b. Conveys information accurately and effectively – Writes clearly, coherently, and effectively – Speaks clearly, coherently, and effectively *Comments:*
			c. Works collaboratively with others – Solicits and considers the viewpoints of others – Establishes trust in relationships; is reliable – Promotes collaboration through modeling and facilitative skills *Comments:*

			d. Displays knowledge and skill in consultative problem solving
			– Models support for problem solving initiatives at the individual, school, and systems levels
			– Applies a complete and systematic problem solving process that includes:
			  o Identification and clarification of the problem situation
			  o Analysis of factors related to the problem
			  o Implementation and monitoring of interventions
			  o Evaluation of outcomes and follow-up
			Comments:

(Continued)

(Continued)

3. Effective Instruction and Development of Cognitive and Academic Skills

The intern has knowledge of human learning processes, techniques to assess these processes, and direct and indirect services applicable to the development of cognitive and academic skills

Initiated by the end of   Fall   Spring

Evaluation			
Competency/Skill/Activity	**Entry**	**Midterm**	**Final**

Overall Rating: _____

Comments:

Sep	Dec	Jun	*Specific Skills*
			a. **Interprets, recommends, and supports accountability standards and procedures** – Is familiar with federal, state, and local accountability standards and procedures (e.g., proficiency testing, standardized group testing program, "handicapped count") – Recommends and assists with appropriate procedures for demonstrating attainment of standards *Comments:* b. **Knows when and how to use empirically validated academic intervention strategies** – Knows empirically validated components of effective academic intervention (e.g., immediate feedback, opportunities to respond, contingencies for accuracy) – Knows empirically validated instructional interventions (e.g., peer-assisted learning, listening, previewing, practice strategies) *Comments:* **Suggests and is able to apply appropriate intervention monitoring methods** – Understands intervention acceptability as a factor influencing use of interventions – Supports intervention integrity through development of appropriate monitoring techniques – Assists in designing and implementing data collection procedures that are appropriate to the nature of the intervention, its goals, and relevant child and environmental factors *Comments:*

4. Socialization and Development of Life Competencies

The intern has knowledge of human developmental processes, techniques to assess these processes, and direct and indirect services applicable to the development of behavioral, affective, adaptive, and social skills.

Initiated by the end of   Fall   Spring

Evaluation		
Competency/Skill/Activity	**Entry**	**Midterm**	**Final**

Overall Rating: _____

Comments:

Sep	Dec	Jun	*Specific Skills*
			a. Knows when and how to use empirically validated behavioral intervention strategies – Knows empirically validated components of effective behavioral interventions (e.g., cueing, reinforcement, skill training) – Knows empirically validated behavioral interventions (e.g., reinforcement plans, self-regulation, problem solving routines) *Comments:*
			b. Knows when and how to use one or more short-term counseling approaches – Develops and implements appropriate counseling plans for individual students – Develops and implements appropriate counseling plans for groups of students *Comments:*
			c. Suggests and is able to apply appropriate intervention monitoring methods – Understands intervention acceptability as a factor influencing use of interventions – Supports intervention integrity through development of appropriate monitoring techniques – Assists in designing and implementing data collection procedures that are appropriate to the nature of the intervention, its goals, and relevant child and environmental factors *Comments:*

(Continued)

(Continued)

5. Student Diversity in Development and Learning

The intern has knowledge of individual differences, abilities, and disabilities and of the potential influence of biological, social, cultural, ethnic, experiential, socioeconomic, gender-related, and linguistic factors in development and learning. The intern evidences sensitivity and the ability to work effectively with a wide variety of people.

Initiated by the end of   Fall   Spring

Evaluation			
Competency/Skill/Activity	Entry	Midterm	Final

Overall Rating: _____

Comments:

Sep	Dec	Jun	Specific Skills
			– Possesses an adequate knowledge base regarding age, race, ethnicity, gender, disability, sexual orientation, and culture-related issues – Demonstrates respect for diversity and awareness of his/her own biases and their impact on his/her own behavior – Is able to identify needs and appropriate modifications related to student diversity *Comments:*

6. School and Systems Organization, Policy Development, and Climate

The intern has knowledge of general education, special education, and other educational and related services, as well as an understanding of schools. The intern collaborates to facilitate policies and practices that create and maintain safe, supportive, and effective learning environments for children and others.

Initiated by the end of   Fall   Spring

Evaluation			
Competency/Skill/Activity	Entry	Midterm	Final

Overall Rating: _____

Comments:

Sep	Dec	Jun	Specific Skills
			a. Knows the components of effective problem solving team structure and operation – Is familiar with the components and operating procedures of effective school-based teams (membership, agenda, observation of time limits, written records, action plans, frequency and length of meetings)

Sep	Dec	Jun	*Specific Skills*
			– Demonstrates effective "process" skills in team activities (inviting, redirecting, conflict management, summarizing, eliciting agreements, role assignments) *Comments:* b. **Is able to conceptualize change-related phenomena (resistance, crisis, etc.) in "systems" terms, and to recommend/implement corresponding and effective strategic responses** – Avoids "joining" resistance (blaming, giving up, faultfinding); maintains professional objectivity – Describes behavioral phenomena in systems terms (power relationships, healthy/ unhealthy resistance, crisis response, etc.) – Suggests/implements strategies to respond to change-related system phenomena (e.g., enhancing ownership, demonstrating need/results, "Just do it") *Comments:* c. **Conducts training activities for professional staff and parents/caregivers** – Assesses potential training needs – Develops a training plan – Conducts/assists with training, working toward an effective presentational style – Evaluates training impact/outcomes *Comments:* d. **Facilitates the development of attitudes and practices that foster a positive school climate** – Demonstrates knowledge of effective disciplinary policies and practices (classwide, schoolwide) – Demonstrates knowledge of institutional practices that foster a positive school climate (shared decision making, frequent communication, parent involvement, high standards, etc.) – Participates, when feasible, in activities and programs to foster a positive school climate *Comments:*

7. Prevention, Crisis Intervention, and Mental Health

The intern has knowledge of human development and psychopathology and of associated biological, cultural, and social influences on human behavior. The intern contributes to prevention and intervention programs that promote the mental health and physical well-being of students.

Initiated by the end of   **Fall**   **Spring**

Evaluation			
Competency/Skill/Activity	**Entry**	**Midterm**	**Final**

Overall Rating: _____

Comments:

(Continued)

(Continued)

Sep	Dec	Jun	*Specific Skills*
			– Knows and recognizes behaviors and personal risk factors that are precursors to conduct and other disorders or threats to wellness – Is familiar with prevention and risk reduction programs and activities – Knows and is able to apply principles for responding to crises (suicide, death, natural disaster, murder, violence, sexual harassment) *Comments:*

8. Home-School-Community Collaboration

The intern has knowledge of family systems, including family strengths and influences on student development, learning, and behavior, and of methods to involve families in education and service delivery. The intern works effectively with families, educators, and others in the community to promote and provide comprehensive services to children and families.

Initiated by the end of   Fall   Spring

Evaluation			
Competency/Skill/Activity	**Entry**	**Midterm**	**Final**

Overall Rating: _____

Comments:

Sep	Dec	Jun	*Specific Skills*
			– Knows how family characteristics and practices affect patterns of attitudes, feelings, and behavior – Accommodates parent/caregiver needs, preferences, values, and cultural characteristics – Promotes home-school collaboration through effective communication with parents/caregivers – Assesses potential parent/caregiver training needs; develops/implements/evaluates a training program – Creates and strengthens linkages with community-based agencies and resources *Comments:*

9. Research and Program Evaluation

The intern knows current literature on various aspects of education and child development, is able to translate research into practice, and understands research design and statistics in sufficient depth to conduct investigations and program evaluations for improvement of services.

Initiated by the end of				Fall	Spring	

Evaluation					
Competency/Skill/Activity			Entry	Midterm	Final

Overall Rating: _____

Comments:

Sep	Dec	Jun	*Specific Skills*
			– Knows basic principles of research design, including single-subject designs – Accurately distinguishes between good and inadequate research – Understands measurement practices and outcomes and is able to recommend and explain them to others (teachers, parents) – Is able to design an evaluation or investigation relevant to his/her own work *Comments:*

10. School Psychology Practice and Professional Development

The intern takes responsibility for developing as a professional and practicing in ways that meet all appropriate ethical, professional, and legal standards to enhance the quality of services, and to protect the rights of all parties.

Initiated by the end of				Fall	Spring	

Evaluation					
Competency/Skill/Activity			Entry	Midterm	Final

Overall Rating: _____

Comments:

Sep	Dec	Jun	*Specific Skills*
			a. Knows and applies laws and regulations governing special education identification and placement activities – Is familiar with special education eligibility criteria under IDEA and Ohio *Operating Standards for the Education of Children With Disabilities* (OS) – Is familiar with parent and child rights under IDEA and Ohio OS – Is familiar with due process and procedural safeguard provisions of IDEA and Ohio OS – Is familiar with requirements related to evaluation activities and IEP development per IDEA and Ohio OS *Comments:*

(Continued)

(Continued)

Sep	Dec	Jun	*Specific Skills*
			b. Knows and applies pertinent legal and ethical standards in professional activities – Is familiar with/observes the codes of ethics of state and national professional associations – Is familiar with/observes laws pertaining to the delivery of professional services (e.g., child abuse reporting, status offenses, confidentiality, informed consent) *Comments:*
			c. Participates in appropriate professional development activities (e.g., state and local professional association meetings, conferences) – Attends conferences, meetings, etc. – Engages in continuous learning (readings, class participation, seminars, etc.) *Comments:*
			d. Displays appropriate attitudes and behavior related to professional and employment status – Identifies his/her own strengths/weaknesses – Shows respect for the expertise and contributions of other professionals – Accepts responsibility for his/her own behavior (acknowledges errors, works toward improvement) – Accepts and responds constructively to criticism and suggestions – Cooperates with directives of the intern supervisor – Persists in completing assigned tasks with minimal oversight (locates and obtains needed information and materials, follows through on tasks and needs without reminders, etc.) – Employs effective organizational strategies (calendar, caseload tracking and management, prioritizing, time management) – Is flexible in altering routines to meet novel demands – Returns telephone calls and e-mail messages and responds to communication promptly – Recognizes his/her own limitations; seeks advice and information as circumstances dictate – Respects the authority of the intern supervisor, school administrators, etc. – Adheres to district policies and procedures (attendance and punctuality, dress and personal hygiene, case-related policies/procedures, employment-related policies/procedures) *Comments:*

11. Information Technology

The intern has knowledge of information sources and technology relevant to the practice of school psychology and is able to access, evaluate, and utilize information sources and technology in ways that safeguard and enhance the quality of services.

Initiated by the end of   Fall   Spring

Evaluation			
Competency/Skill/Activity	**Entry**	**Midterm**	**Final**

Overall Rating: _____

Comments:

Sep	Dec	Jun	*Specific Skills*
			– Is familiar with electronic information resources available via the Internet and World Wide Web – Knows how to use electronic technology for communication purposes and how to access information relevant to professional practice. – Knows how to locate, evaluate, and make appropriate use of software supporting professional activities (e.g., test scoring, statistical analysis, reporting, computer-assisted instruction) *Comments:*

Documentation of Involvement With Diverse Populations

Evaluation	
(Key: 1 = Exposed or Observed, 2 = Served)	

Sep	Dec	Jun	
			By age/grade level: – Early childhood (Ages 0–4) – Primary (Grades K–3) – Intermediate (Grades 4–6) – Junior High (Grades 7–9) – Secondary (Grades 10–12) *By population:* – Regular (general) education – Developmentally delayed – Emotionally disturbed – Learning disabled

(Continued)

(Continued)

Sep	Dec	Jun	*Specific Skills*
			– Multiple disabilities – Sensory impaired (vision, hearing) – Orthopedically/health impaired – Gifted/talented – Low incidence (autism, traumatic brain injury, etc.) – Other:

Initial Recommendations for the Internship Experience

Results of this evaluation, completed on _____ , suggest that the following competencies/ skills/activities should be emphasized during the early months of the internship:

Midterm Recommendations for the Internship Experience

Results of this evaluation, completed on _____ , suggest that the following competencies/ skills/activities should be emphasized during the next phase of the internship:

Certification of Satisfactory Completion of School Psychology Internship

It is the professional judgment of the University Supervisor and the Field Supervisor that has completed the activities and experiences planned for the School Psychology Internship, and that he/she has achieved a satisfactory level of performance in the skills and competencies specified herein.

University Supervisor_____ Date _____ Field Supervisor _____ Date _____

Intern _____ Date _____ Field Supervisor _____ Date _____

From the *2006 Handbook of the University of Dayton School Psychology Program*. Dayton, OH: Locally published monograph. Use of this material is by permission of the author, Sawyer Hunley.

Handout 15.12

INTERNSHIP SITE INFORMATION

District/Agency: _____   Contact Person: _____

Day Telephone: _____   E-mail: _____

Ages at this site with which an intern can work (please check all that apply):

____ High school ____ Junior high/middle school ____ Elementary school ____ Preschool

Non–special education populations with which an intern can work (please check all that apply):

Normal-developing (non–special education) native English speaking children and adolescents

Interns can ____ assess, ____ diagnose, ____ provide treatment, ____ monitor progress

Children and adolescents at risk, eligible for early intervening services, or eligible under Section 504

Interns can ____ assess, ____ diagnose, ____ provide treatment, ____ monitor progress

Normal-developing (non–special education) bilingual students or English language learners

Interns can ____ assess, ____ diagnose, ____ provide treatment, ____ monitor progress

At this site, interns have the opportunity to work with the following populations eligible for services under IDEA (please check all that apply):

Children and adolescents with pervasive developmental disorders and autistic spectrum disorders

Interns can ____ assess, ____ diagnose, ____ provide treatment, ____ monitor progress

Children and adolescents with developmental delays and mental retardation

Interns can ____ assess, ____ diagnose, ____ provide treatment, ____ monitor progress

Children and adolescents with emotional impairment or behavior disorders

Interns can ____ assess, ____ diagnose, ____ provide treatment, ____ monitor progress

Children and adolescents with physical or sensory impairments

Interns can ____ assess, ____ diagnose, ____ provide treatment, ____ monitor progress

Children and adolescents with specific learning disabilities

Interns can ____ assess, ____ diagnose, ____ provide treatment, ____ monitor progress

Children and adolescents with sensory deficits (blind, deaf, hard-of-hearing, visually impaired)

Interns can ____ assess, ____ diagnose, ____ provide treatment, ____ monitor progress

Preschool children with developmental difficulties

Interns can ____ assess, ____ diagnose, ____ provide treatment, ____ monitor progress

Children and adolescents with other disabilities _____

Interns can ____ assess, ____ diagnose, ____ provide treatment, ____ monitor progress

(Continued)

(Continued)

How would you describe the site's population in terms of ethnicity and socioeconomic status?

Is this site urban, suburban, or rural?

Are the facilities adequate for school psychology practice (supplies, testing and equipment, clerical assistance, office space, privacy, etc.)? If not, please explain:

Is the supervisor accessible beyond scheduled supervision times to assist with crisis situations?

How would you describe the orientation of the supervision available at this site?

Are expectations clear?

Is appropriate support provided and helpful and constructive feedback given?

On a 0 to 5 scale (0 = no opportunity at all, 5 = extremely good opportunities), please rate the opportunities available at this site to practice across the following domains of school psychology:

___ Data-based decision making and accountability

___ Consultation and collaboration with teachers and parents

___ Assessment of cognitive/academic skills and assessment of ongoing development

___ Assessment and development of socialization and life skills and assessment of ongoing progress

___ Diversity in development and learning

___ School and system organization, policy development, and climate

___ Prevention, crisis intervention, and mental health

___ Home-school-community collaboration

___ Research and program evaluation

___ School psychology practice and professional development

___ Information technology

Can interns work at this site at times other than the normal school day (in the evening, during weekends, or in the summer)?

Is this site accessible by public transportation?

Hours per week available for individual supervision:

Hours per week available for group supervision:

Annual stipend for a school psychology intern:

On a 0 to 5 scale (0 = couldn't be worse and 5 = couldn't be better), how strongly would you recommend this site for future interns?

Comments:

From the *2007 University of Massachusetts Boston School Psychology Field Work Handbook*. Boston, MA: Locally published monograph. Use of this material is by permission of the author, Virginia Harvey.

Handout 15.13

APPLICATION FOR APPROVED SUPERVISOR
AND FIELD EXPERIENCE SITE STATUS

Name of Applicant: _____

Work Phone: (_____) _____   E-Mail: _____

Business Address: _____

_____ (Zip) _____

Levels at which you desire to supervise: o Practicum/Fieldwork o Internship

Are you teaching at a university in the area of school psychology? If so, please provide the name of the university.
_____

Are you working as a university supervisor with any interns or practicum level students (inside or outside the district)? Please list names if students are in the district. _____

How many years have you been in San Diego City Schools? _____

What types of leadership activities have you been involved in within the district or with outside organizations?

Current Position: __School Psychologist __ Administrator (specify) _____

Site(s) where services will be provided—Name(s) of school(s): _____

_____

Experience supervising trainees or interns from other universities (briefly describe):

PART I. For each category, please rate the degree to which you will be able to provide:

(a) *Administrative supervision* (i.e., arrange exposure/opportunities to practice)
(b) *Model practice* in the area
(c) *Clinical supervision* (e.g., spend time reviewing cases in detail)

I.A. *Professional School Psychology*—includes legal and ethical mandates; ongoing involvement with professional development, such as workshops, conferences, in-service trainings; leadership; comprehensive service delivery model.

	Not able to provide				Amply able to provide
Administrative Supervision	1	2	3	4	5
Modeling	1	2	3	4	5
Clinical Supervision	1	2	3	4	5

(Continued)

(Continued)

I.B. *Research and Program Evaluation*—includes evaluating and using research, design, and analysis of service delivery, and research with diverse populations.

	Not able to provide				Amply able to provide
Administrative Supervision	I	2	3	4	5
Modeling	I	2	3	4	5
Clinical supervision	I	2	3	4	5

I.C. *Social and Cultural Sensitivity and Advocacy*—includes understanding own and others' cultures; issues with social or cultural bases which influence the delivery of school services; cross-cultural transactions; general attention to this arena in interactions and service.

	Not able to provide				Amply able to provide
Administrative Supervision	I	2	3	4	5
Modeling	I	2	3	4	5
Clinical Supervision	I	2	3	4	5

I.D. *Assessment for Intervention*—includes orientation to the assessment process as driving interventions; experience with a broad range of assessment tools appropriate across cultures.

	Not able to provide				Amply able to provide
Administrative Supervision	I	2	3	4	5
Modeling	I	2	3	4	5
Clinical Supervision	I	2	3	4	5

I.E. *Interventions*—includes a broad range of interventions, from systemic (dealing with change of a larger unit, such as a class, school, or family) to individual, and knowing when to target each; breadth includes, for instance, counseling interventions, behavioral interventions, instructional interventions, school-to-home interventions, program development.

	Not able to provide				Amply able to provide
Administrative Supervision	I	2	3	4	5
Modeling	I	2	3	4	5
Clinical Supervision	I	2	3	4	5

I.F. *Psychological Foundations*—includes knowledge and grounding in individual differences, learning, life span development, and biological factors influencing referral situations.

	Not able to provide				Amply able to provide
Administrative Supervision	I	2	3	4	5
Modeling	I	2	3	4	5
Clinical Supervision	I	2	3	4	5

I.G. *Educational Foundations*—includes knowledge of the school as a culture and a system, historical influences and current educational policy issues and practice influencing ethnolinguistically diverse groups, and categorical programs, especially special education services.

	Not able to provide				Amply able to provide
Administrative Supervision	1	2	3	4	5
Modeling	1	2	3	4	5
Clinical Supervision	1	2	3	4	5

PART II. Please rate yourself on the following aspects of interpersonal supervisory style, which may or may not characterize you as a supervisor.

	Strongly disagree				Strongly agree
1. I encourage and support discussion of my trainees'/interns' concerns	1	2	3	4	5
2. I expect to contribute to my trainees' knowledge and competence in school psychology	1	2	3	4	5
3. I expect to conduct formally scheduled face-to-face supervision	1	2	3	4	5
4. I communicate ideas clearly and effectively	1	2	3	4	5
5. I give frank and constructive feedback	1	2	3	4	5
6. I regularly recognize and affirm my trainees' successes in the field	1	2	3	4	5
7. I strive to understand professional issues raised by my trainees/interns	1	2	3	4	5
8. I encourage my trainees/interns to try their own ideas	1	2	3	4	5
9. I am responsive to and considerate of trainees/interns as people	1	2	3	4	5
10. I willingly help my trainees/interns to build effective links with their schools or other parts of the system when necessary	1	2	3	4	5
11. I believe that school psychologists currently are able to effect important changes in a way that can benefit children and communities	1	2	3	4	5
12. I believe that school psychology has a powerful future	1	2	3	4	5

(Continued)

(Continued)

PART III: Terms and Conditions

The purpose of supervision is to build the capacity of competent School Psychologist candidates within the field and to enhance the professional development of credentialed School Psychologists who have worked within the schools. Internships within San Diego City Schools are based on the guidelines set forth by the National Association for School Psychologists (NASP).

- I will follow the District's structure for scheduling the intern to have the greatest possibility of experiences over the course of the year.
- I will attend and participate in the scheduled in-services for supervisors with the lead/senior psychologist(s) to discuss agenda topics and any concerns related to the intern's experience.
- I will act as a liaison with the UNIVERSITY coordinator for internship.
- I will commit to a minimum of 2 hours a week of face-to-face supervision so that student progress can be monitored.

I hereby apply for consideration as an approved supervisor of a school psychology student at the _____ school psychology practicum (3rd year) and/or _____ internship level. I agree to the above-mentioned terms and conditions.

_____   _____

Signature   Date

PLEASE ATTACH YOUR VITAE OR RESUME AND RETURN TO THE TRANSDISCIPLINARY OFFICE BY SEPTEMBER 15.

From the School Psychology Program, San Diego State University (Carol Robinson-Zañartu, author) as adapted for use in San Diego Unified School District (by Michele Bronson). Use of this material is by permission of both parties.

Handout 15.14

INTERN EVALUATION OF INTERNSHIP (GENERAL)

Please rate the following domains of the internship experience. Any comments that you add to explicate your ratings will be appreciated.

Preparation for Internship Through Course Work	Inadequate			Excellent	
Assessment	1	2	3	4	5
Consultation	1	2	3	4	5
Educational foundations	1	2	3	4	5
Psychological foundations	1	2	3	4	5
Legal and ethical	1	2	3	4	5
Intervention	1	2	3	4	5
Availability and Support From the University Supervisor	Inadequate			Excellent	
Materials and forms found in the field experience manual	1	2	3	4	5
Communication	1	2	3	4	5
On-site visits	1	2	3	4	5
Clarity of expectations	1	2	3	4	5
Emotional support from the university supervisor	1	2	3	4	5
Assessment of Field Supervision	Inadequate			Excellent	
Quality of the training plan	1	2	3	4	5
Level of supervision	1	2	3	4	5
Opportunity for independent work	1	2	3	4	5
Range and diversity of training	1	2	3	4	5
Support From Host School(s)	Inadequate			Excellent	
Initial orientation and welcome	1	2	3	4	5
Explanation of rules, procedures, and policies	1	2	3	4	5
Office space and access to support materials	1	2	3	4	5
Access to secretarial support	1	2	3	4	5
Opportunities for in-service training	1	2	3	4	5
Coordination of activities, if more than one school	1	2	3	4	5

Comments:

Intern   Date:

From the *2006 Handbook of the University of Dayton School Psychology Program.* Dayton, OH: Locally published monograph. Use of this material is by permission of the author, Sawyer Hunley.

Handout 15.15

INTERN EVALUATION OF INTERNSHIP (SPECIFIC)

_____   _____   _____
(School District)   (Internship Year)   (Intern)

INSTRUCTIONS: Using the key below, in front of the dashes in the left margin of these pages, please provide your responses to the following items, in evaluation of the degree of opportunity you had to successfully complete the objectives of your internship. Indicate those portions of an objective that may not have been experienced during the internship by drawing a line through the relevant wording, or indicate those portions that were experienced by underlining the relevant wording.

| **N = No** | **L = Limited** | **S = Sufficient** | **E = Excellent** |
| **Opportunity** | **Opportunity** | **Opportunity** | **Opportunity** |

1. **Data-Based Decision Making and Accountability**

   The intern is able to assess strengths and needs to gain an understanding of problems, measure progress and accomplishments, translate assessment results into empirically based decisions about service delivery, and evaluate the outcomes of services.

   a. **Select and apply appropriate assessment methods**
      - Test administration and interpretation (norm referenced, criterion referenced)
      - Behavioral assessment: interviewing, systematic direct observation, functional assessment/analysis
      - Curriculum-based assessment
      - Ecological/environmental assessment (home, classroom, school, community)
      - Assessment of student characteristics (cognitive, emotional, and motivational factors affecting performance)
      - Permanent products inspection (e.g., work products, school records)
      - Integration of assessment results in written reports

   b. **Understanding and using assessment in a problem solving context**
      - Uses data to demonstrate student problems/needs
      - Uses data to demonstrate student outcomes

   c. **Understanding and using assessment in an accountability context**
      - Uses assessment to identify system level needs (e.g., classwide intervention, improved parent-school communication, more effective problem solving team functioning, less reliance on testing)
      - Uses assessment to identify outcomes of system level practices, activities, and projects

2. **Consultation and Collaboration**

   The intern is able to listen well, participate in discussions, convey information, and work together with others at the individual, group, and systems levels. The intern has knowledge of behavioral, mental health, collaborative, and/or other consultation models and methods and of their application to particular situations.

   a. **Displays appropriate interpersonal communication skills**
      - Listens attentively to others
      - Displays appropriate empathy
      - Paraphrases, summarizes, and questions appropriately
      - Participates in group discussions
      - Displays appropriate communication with educational personnel and parents

   b. **Conveys information accurately and effectively**
      - Writes clearly, coherently, and effectively
      - Speaks clearly, coherently, and effectively

   c. **Works collaboratively with others**
      - Solicits and considers the viewpoints of others
      - Establishes trust in relationships; is reliable
      - Promotes collaboration through modeling and facilitative skills

d. Displays knowledge and skill in consultative problem solving
- Models support for problem solving initiatives at the individual, school, and system levels
- Applies a complete and systematic problem solving process that includes:
  - Identification and clarification of the problem situation
  - Analysis of factors related to the problem
  - Implementation and monitoring of interventions
  - Evaluation of outcomes and follow-up

3. Effective Instruction and Development of Cognitive and Academic Skills

The intern has knowledge of human learning processes, techniques to assess these processes, and direct and indirect services applicable to the development of cognitive and academic skills.

a. Interprets, recommends, and supports accountability standards and procedures
- Is familiar with federal, state, and local accountability standards and procedures (e.g., proficiency testing, standardized group testing program, "handicapped count")
- Recommends and assists with appropriate procedures for demonstrating attainment of standards

b. Knows when and how to use empirically validated academic intervention strategies
- Knows empirically validated components of effective academic intervention (e.g., immediate feedback, opportunities to respond, contingencies for accuracy)
- Knows empirically validated instructional interventions (e.g., peer-assisted learning, listening, previewing, practice strategies)

c. Suggests and is able to apply appropriate intervention monitoring methods
- Understands intervention acceptability as a factor influencing use of interventions
- Supports intervention integrity through development of appropriate monitoring techniques
- Assists in designing and implementing data collection procedures that are appropriate to the nature of the intervention, its goals, and relevant child and environmental factors

4. Socialization and Development of Life Competencies

The intern has knowledge of human developmental processes, techniques to assess these processes, and direct and indirect services applicable to the development of behavioral, affective, adaptive, and social skills.

a. Knows when and how to use empirically validated behavioral intervention strategies
- Knows empirically validated components of effective behavioral interventions (e.g., cueing, reinforcement, skill training)
- Knows empirically validated behavioral interventions (e.g., reinforcement plans, self-regulation, problem solving routines)

b. Knows when and how to use one or more short-term counseling approaches
- Develops and implements appropriate counseling plans for individual students
- Develops and implements appropriate counseling plans for groups of students

c. Suggests and is able to apply appropriate intervention monitoring methods
- Understands intervention acceptability as a factor influencing use of interventions
- Supports intervention integrity through development of appropriate monitoring techniques
- Assists in designing and implementing data collection procedures that are appropriate to the nature of the intervention, its goals, and relevant child and environmental factors

5. Student Diversity in Development and Learning

The intern has knowledge of individual differences, abilities, and disabilities and of the potential influence of biological, social, cultural, ethnic, experiential, socioeconomic, gender-related, and linguistic factors in development and learning. The intern evidences sensitivity and the ability to work effectively with a wide variety of people.

- Possesses an adequate knowledge base regarding age, race, ethnicity, gender, disability, sexual orientation, and culture-related issues

(Continued)

(Continued)

    – Demonstrates respect for diversity and awareness of his/her own biases and their impact on his/her own behavior
    – Is able to identify needs and appropriate modifications related to student diversity

6. **School and Systems Organization, Policy Development, and Climate**

The intern has knowledge of general education, special education, and other educational and related services, as well as an understanding of schools. The intern collaborates to facilitate policies and practices that create and maintain safe, supportive, and effective learning environments for children and others.

  a. **Knows the components of effective problem solving team structure and operation**
    – Is familiar with the components and operating procedures of effective school-based teams (membership, agenda, observation of time limits, written records, action plans, frequency and length of meetings)
    – Demonstrates effective "process" skills in team activities (inviting, redirecting, conflict management, summarizing, eliciting agreements, role assignments)

  b. **Is able to conceptualize change-related phenomena (resistance, crisis, etc.) in "systems" terms, and to recommend/implement corresponding and effective strategic responses**
    – Avoids "joining" resistance (blaming, giving up, faultfinding); maintains professional objectivity
    – Describes behavioral phenomena in systems terms (power relationships, healthy/unhealthy resistance, crisis response, etc.)
    – Suggests/implements strategies to respond to change-related system phenomena (e.g., enhancing ownership, demonstrating need/results, "Just do it")

  c. **Conducts training activities for professional staff and parents/caregivers**
    – Assesses potential training needs
    – Develops a training plan
    – Conducts/assists with training, working toward an effective presentational style
    – Evaluates training impact/outcomes

  d. **Facilitates the development of attitudes and practices that foster a positive school climate**
    – Demonstrates knowledge of effective disciplinary policies and practices (classwide; schoolwide)
    – Demonstrates knowledge of institutional practices that foster a positive school climate (shared decision making, frequent communication, parent involvement, high standards, etc.)
    – Participates, when feasible, in activities and programs to foster a positive school climate

7. **Prevention, Crisis Intervention, and Mental Health**

The intern has knowledge of human development and psychopathology and of associated biological, cultural, and social influences on human behavior. The intern contributes to prevention and intervention programs that promote the mental health and physical well-being of students.

  – Knows and recognizes behaviors and personal risk factors that are precursors to conduct and other disorders or threats to wellness
  – Is familiar with prevention and risk reduction programs and activities
  – Knows and is able to apply principles for responding to crises (suicide, death, natural disaster, murder, violence, sexual harassment)

8. **Home-School-Community Collaboration**

The intern has knowledge of family systems, including family strengths and influences on student development, learning, and behavior, and of methods to involve families in education and service delivery. The intern works effectively with families, educators, and others in the community to promote and provide comprehensive services to children and families.

  – Knows how family characteristics and practices affect patterns of attitudes, feelings, and behavior
  – Accommodates parent/caregiver needs, preferences, values, and cultural characteristics
  – Promotes home-school collaboration through effective communication with parents/caregivers
  – Assesses potential parent/caregiver training needs; develops/implements/evaluates a training program
  – Creates and strengthens linkages with community-based agencies and resources

9. Research and Program Evaluation

The intern knows current literature on various aspects of education and child development, is able to translate research into practice, and understands research design and statistics in sufficient depth to conduct investigations and program evaluations for improvement of services.

- Knows basic principles of research design, including single-subject designs
- Accurately distinguishes between good and inadequate research
- Understands measurement practices and outcomes and is able to recommend and explain them to others (teachers, parents)
- Is able to design an evaluation or investigation relevant to his/her own work

10. School Psychology Practice and Professional Development

The intern takes responsibility for developing as a professional and practicing in ways that meet all appropriate ethical, professional, and legal standards to enhance the quality of services, and to protect the rights of all parties.

a. Knows and applies laws and regulations governing special education identification and placement activities
- Is familiar with special education eligibility criteria under IDEA and Ohio *Operating Standards for the Education of Children With Disabilities* (OS)
- Is familiar with parent and child rights under IDEA and Ohio OS
- Is familiar with due process and procedural safeguard provisions of IDEA and Ohio OS
- Is familiar with requirements related to evaluation activities and IEP development per IDEA and Ohio OS

b. Knows and applies pertinent legal and ethical standards in professional activities
- Is familiar with/observes the codes of ethics of state and national professional associations
- Is familiar with/observes laws pertaining to the delivery of professional services (e.g., child abuse reporting, status offenses, confidentiality, informed consent)

c. Participates in appropriate professional development activities (e.g., state and local professional association meetings, conferences)
- Attends conferences, meetings, etc.
- Engages in continuous learning (readings, class participation, seminars, etc.)

d. Displays appropriate attitudes and behavior related to professional and employment status
- Identifies his/her own strengths/weaknesses
- Shows respect for the expertise/contributions of other professionals
- Accepts responsibility for his/her own behavior (acknowledges errors, works toward improvement)
- Accepts and responds constructively to criticism and suggestions
- Cooperates with directives of the intern supervisor
- Persists in completing assigned tasks with minimal oversight (locates and obtains needed information and materials, follows through on tasks and needs without reminders, etc.)
- Employs effective organizational strategies (calendar, caseload tracking and management, prioritizing, time management)
- Is flexible in altering routines to meet novel demands
- Returns telephone calls and e-mail messages and responds to communication promptly
- Recognizes his/her own limitations; seeks advice and information as circumstances dictate
- Respects the authority of the intern supervisor, school administrators, etc.
- Adheres to district policies and procedures (attendance and punctuality, dress and personal hygiene, case-related policies/procedures, employment-related policies/procedures)

11. Information Technology

The intern has knowledge of information sources and technology relevant to the practice of school psychology and is able to access, evaluate, and utilize information sources and technology in ways that safeguard and enhance the quality of services.

- Is familiar with electronic information resources available via the Internet
- Knows how to use electronic technology for communication purposes and how to access information relevant to professional practice
- Knows how to locate, evaluate, and make appropriate use of software supporting professional activities (test scoring, statistical analysis, reporting, computer-assisted instruction)

Handout 15.16

SUPERVISOR EVALUATION FORM BASED ON NATIONAL ASSOCIATION OF SCHOOL PSYCHOLOGISTS STANDARDS

I. The supervisor . . .	
Ia. Effectively supervises the overall development and implementation of district school psychological services.	|_____|_____|_____|_____| Almost Always Almost Never
Ib. Articulates school psychological service programs to others in the agency and constituent groups.	|_____|_____|_____|_____| Almost Always Almost Never
Ic. Provides leadership by promoting innovative service delivery systems that reflect best practices in the field of school psychology.	|_____|_____|_____|_____| Almost Always Almost Never
Id. Leads the school psychology services unit in developing, implementing, and evaluating a coordinated plan for accountability and evaluation of all services.	|_____|_____|_____|_____| Almost Always Almost Never
Ie. Uses measurable objectives in both program and individual performance evaluations.	|_____|_____|_____|_____| Almost Always Almost Never
If. Conducts program and individual performance evaluations that are both formative and summative.	|_____|_____|_____|_____| Almost Always Almost Never
Ig. Evaluates and revises evaluation plans on a regular basis through the systematic collection, analysis, and interpretation of process and performance data.	|_____|_____|_____|_____| Almost Always Almost Never
2. The supervisor provides supervision. . .	
2a. At a level adequate to ensure the provision of effective and accountable services.	|_____|_____|_____|_____| Almost Always Almost Never
2b. Through an ongoing, positive, systematic, collaborative process.	|_____|_____|_____|_____| Almost Always Almost Never
2c. That focuses on promoting professional growth and exemplary professional practice.	|_____|_____|_____|_____| Almost Always Almost Never
2d. For at least 2 hours per week, in a face-to-face format, for interns and first-year school psychologists.	|_____|_____|_____|_____| Almost Always Almost Never

2e. Within the guidelines of the training institution and NASP Standards for Training and Field Placement Programs in School Psychology.	|____|____|____|____|	Almost Always Almost Never
2f. Or peer review for experienced school psychologists to ensure ongoing professional development.	|____|____|____|____|	Almost Always Almost Never
3. The supervisor provides professional leadership . . .		
3a. Through participation in school psychology professional organizations.	|____|____|____|____|	Almost Always Almost Never
3b. By coordinating the activities of the school psychological services unit with those of other professional service units.	|____|____|____|____|	Almost Always Almost Never
3c. Through active involvement in local, state, and federal public policy development and national, state, and local educational organizations.	|____|____|____|____|	Almost Always Almost Never
4. The supervisor's credentials include . . .		
4a. Certification as a Nationally Certified School Psychologist (NCSP).	|____|____|____|____|	Almost Always Almost Never
4b. Designation as a supervisor responsible for school psychology services.	|____|____|____|____|	Almost Always Almost Never
4c. A minimum of 2 years of experience as a practicing school psychologist.	|____|____|____|____|	Almost Always Almost Never
4d. A state school psychologist credential.	|____|____|____|____|	Almost Always Almost Never
4e. Training and/or experience in the supervision of school personnel.	|____|____|____|____|	Almost Always Almost Never

Handout 15.17

SUPERVISOR EVALUATION

The following is a questionnaire to help me learn the extent to which I am providing adequate and appropriate supervision to staff members. I would appreciate your candor in responding. You do not have to sign this evaluation. (Add a short statement to clarify rating if necessary.)

Rating Scale: 5 = Always,   4 = Usually,   3 = Sometimes,   2= Rarely,   1 = Never

A. Supervisor's Awareness

1. Understands the problems confronting me as I carry out my responsibilities.	5 4 3 2 1
2. Understands children and their developmental levels.	5 4 3 2 1
3. Demonstrates a broad background in curriculum and program issues.	5 4 3 2 1

B. Supervisor's Communication and Support

1. Is readily available to discuss problems or concerns.	5 4 3 2 1
2. Responds promptly to written communication.	5 4 3 2 1
3. Is receptive and supportive when I request help in solving a problem.	5 4 3 2 1
4. Provides useful suggestions for solving problems.	5 4 3 2 1
5. Treats me with courtesy and respect.	5 4 3 2 1
6. Keeps me informed of building or systemwide issues that relate to my school or program.	5 4 3 2 1
7. Communicates effectively with staff.	5 4 3 2 1
8. Communicates effectively with parents.	5 4 3 2 1
9. Communicates effectively with the central administration.	5 4 3 2 1
10. Supports me when I have a conflict with students or parents.	5 4 3 2 1
11. Assists in the resolution of personnel matters quickly and appropriately.	5 4 3 2 1

C. Supervisor's Decision Making

1. Actively encourages collaborative decision making on substantive issues.	5 4 3 2 1
2. Provides adequate time and opportunity for expression of opinions of those concerned.	5 4 3 2 1

D. Supervisor's Observations

  1. Could make the observations process more helpful to me in the following ways:

E. Professional Development

1. In-service workshops are relevant to my needs and development.	5 4 3 2 1

F. Meetings

1. I have adequate opportunity to contribute to the agenda of the department meeting.	5 4 3 2 1
2. The content of the department meeting is relevant to my needs.	5 4 3 2 1

G. Clinical Supervision

1. Individual supervision assists with my development as a professional.	5 4 3 2 1
2. Group supervision assists with my development as a professional.	5 4 3 2
3. Peer supervision is helpful to my professional development.	5 4 3 2 1
4. Adequate time is available to participate in supervision activities.	5 4 3 2 1

H. Supervisor's Overall Performance

1. On a scale of 5 to 1, with 5 representing "outstanding" and 1 representing "unsatisfactory," I would rate *overall* performance as follows:	5 4 3 2 1
2. I would make the following suggestions for improvement:	

From the *2006 Westport School District School Psychologist Handbook.* Westport, CT: Locally published monograph. Use of this material is by permission of the author, Barbara Fischetti.

References

Aarons, G. A. (2006). Transformational and transactional leadership: Association with attitudes toward evidence-based practice. *Psychiatric Services, 57*, 1162–1169.

Abramson, J. S., & Fortune, A. (1990). Improving field instruction: An evaluation of a seminar for new field instructors. *Journal of Social Work Education, 26*, 273–286.

Age Discrimination in Employment Act of 1967, 29 U.S.C. § 621 *et seq.* (2000).

Aggett, P. (2004). Learning narratives in group supervision: Enhancing collaborative learning. *Journal of Systemic Therapies, 23*(3), 36–50.

Agnew, T., Vaught, C. C., Getz, H. G., & Fortune, J. (2000). Peer group clinical supervision program fosters confidence and professionalism. *Professional School Counseling, 4*, 6–12.

Ailes, R. (1988). *You are the message.* Homewood, IL: Dow Jones-Irwin.

Albers, C. A., & Kratochwill, T. R. (2006). Teacher and principal consultations: Best practices. In C. Franklin, M. B. Harris, & P. Allen-Meares (Eds.), *The school services sourcebook: A guide for school-based professionals* (pp. 971–976). New York: Oxford University Press.

Alberto, P. A., & Troutman, A. C. (2006). *Applied behavior analysis for teachers* (7th ed.). Upper Saddle River, NJ: Pearson Education.

Alessi, G. J., Lascurettes-Alessi, K. J., & Leyes, W. L. (1981). Internships in school psychology: Supervision issues. *School Psychology Review, 10*, 461–469.

Alexander, P. A. (2006). *Psychology in learning and instruction.* Upper Saddle River, NJ: Prentice Hall.

Alfonso, V. C., LaRocca, R., Oakland, T. D., & Spanakos, A. (2000). The course on individual cognitive assessment. *School Psychology Review, 29*, 52–64.

Alfonso, V. C., & Pratt, S. I. (1997). Issues and suggestions for training professionals in assessing intelligence. In D. P. Flanagan, J. L. Genshaft, & P. L. Harrison (Eds.), *Contemporary intellectual assessment: Theories, tests, and issues* (pp. 326–344). New York: Guilford Press.

Allen, G. J., Szollos, S. J., & Williams, B. E. (1986). Doctoral students' comparative evaluations of best and worst psychotherapy supervision. *Professional Psychology: Research and Practice, 17*, 91–99.

Allison, K. W., Echemendia, R. J., Crawford, I., & Robinson, W. L. (1996). Predicting cultural competence: Implications for practice and training. *Professional Psychology: Research and Practice, 27*, 386–393.

Allison, R. (2002). Best practices in supervision of school psychology staff. In A. Thomas & J. Grimes (Eds.), *Best practices in school psychology IV* (pp. 115–129). Bethesda, MD: National Association of School Psychologists.

Alonso, A., & Rutan, J. S. (1988). Shame and guilt in supervision. *Psychotherapy, 25*, 576–581.

American Association on Intellectual and Developmental Disabilities. (2002). *The AAIDD definition of mental retardation.* Retrieved January 26, 2008, from www.aaidd.org/Policies/faq_mental_retardation.shtml

American Educational Research Association, American Psychological Association, & National Council on Measurement in Education. (1999). *Standards for educational and psychological testing* (2nd ed.). Washington, DC: American Educational Research Association.

American Psychiatric Association. (2000). *Diagnostic and statistical manual of mental disorders* (4th ed., text revision). Washington, DC: Author.

American Psychological Association. (1981). Specialty guidelines for the delivery of services by school psychologists. *American Psychologist, 36*, 670–681.

American Psychological Association. (1993). Guidelines for providers of psychological services to ethnic, linguistic, and culturally diverse populations. *American Psychologist, 48*, 45–48.

American Psychological Association. (1996). Report of the ethics committee. *American Psychologist, 51*, 1279–1286.

American Psychological Association. (2002). Ethical principles of psychologists and code of conduct. *American Psychologist, 57*, 1060–1073.

American Psychological Association. (2003). Guidelines on multicultural education, training, research, practice, and organizational change for psychologists. *American Psychologist, 58,* 377–402.

American Psychological Association. (2007). *Guidelines and principles for accreditation of programs in professional psychology.* Washington, DC: Office of Program Consultation and Accreditation.

American Psychological Association, Committee on Lesbian, Gay, and Bisexual Concerns. (2000). Guidelines for psychotherapy with lesbian, gay, and bisexual clients. *American Psychologist, 55,* 1440–1451.

American Psychological Association, Presidential Task Force on Evidence-Based Practice. (2006). Evidence-based practice in psychology. *American Psychologist, 61,* 271–285.

Americans With Disabilities Act of 1990, Pub. L. No. 101–336, 104 Stat. 328 (1991).

Amrein, A. L., & Berliner, D. C. (2003). The effects of high-stakes testing on students' motivation and learning. *Educational Leadership, 60*(5), 32–38.

Anderson, W. T., Hohenshil, T. H., & Brown, D. T. (1984). Job satisfaction among practicing school psychologists: A national study. *School Psychology Review, 13,* 225–230.

Andolfi, M. (1979). *Family therapy: An interactional approach.* New York: Plenum Press.

Anthony, W. P., Kacmer, K. M., & Perrewé, P. L. (2006). *Human resource management: A strategic approach.* Mason, OH: Thomson.

Anton-LaHart, J., & Rosenfield, S. (2004). A survey of preservice consultation training in school psychology programs. *Journal of Educational & Psychological Consultation, 15,* 41–62.

Arkowitz, S. W. (2001). Perfectionism in the supervisee. In S. Gill (Ed.), *The supervisory alliance: Facilitating the psychotherapist's learning experience* (pp. 35–66). Lanham, MD: Jason Aronson.

Armijo v. Wagon Mound Public Schools, 159 F.3d 1253 (10th Cir. 1998).

Armistead, L. D. (2008). Best practices in continuing professional development for school psychologists. In A. Thomas & J. Grimes (Eds.), *Best practices in school psychology V* (pp. 1975–1990). Bethesda, MD: National Association of School Psychologists.

Astleitner, H. (2002). Teaching critical thinking on-line. *Journal of Instructional Psychology, 29*(2), 53–77.

Atkins, P. W. B., & Wood, R. E. (2002). Self- versus others' ratings as predictors of assessment center ratings: Validation evidence for 360-degree feedback programs. *Personnel Psychology, 55,* 871–904.

Atkinson, D. R. (2004). *Counseling American minorities* (6th ed.). Boston: McGraw-Hill.

Avolio, B. J. (2007). Promoting more integrative strategies for leadership theory-building. *American Psychologist, 62,* 25–33.

Avolio, B. J., & Bass, B. M. (1995). *Multifactor leadership questionnaire.* Redwood City, CA: Mindgarten.

Bailey, J. S., & Burch, M. R. (2002). *Research methods in applied behavior analysis.* Thousand Oaks, CA: SAGE.

Baker, S., Daniels, T., & Greely, A. (1990). Systematic training of graduate-level counselors: Narrative and meta-analytic reviews of three major programs. *Counseling Psychologist, 18,* 355–421.

Baldick, T. L. (1980). Ethical discrimination ability of intern psychologists: A function of training in ethics. *Professional Psychology: Research and Practice, 11,* 276–282.

Baltimore, M. L., & Crutchfield, L. B. (2003). *Clinical supervision training: An interactive CD-ROM training program for the helping professions.* Boston: Allyn & Bacon.

Bandura, A. (1986). *Social foundations of thought and action: A social cognition theory.* Englewood Cliffs, NJ: Prentice Hall.

Bandura, A. (1997). *Self-efficacy: The exercise of control.* New York: Freeman.

Barak, A. (1999). Psychological applications on the Internet: A discipline on the threshold of a new millennium. *Applied & Preventive Psychology, 8,* 231–245.

Bardon, J. I. (1969). Your present is our past: Implications for a school psychology of the future. *Professional Psychology, 1,* 8–13.

Barnett, D. W., Daly, E. J., Jones, K. M., & Lentz, F. E. (2004). Response to intervention: Empirically based special service decisions from single-case designs of increasing and decreasing intensity. *Journal of Special Education, 38,* 66–79.

Barona, A., & Garcia, E. E. (1990). *Children at risk: Poverty, minority status, and other issues in educational equity.* Washington, DC: National Association of School Psychologists.

Barth, R. S. (1990). A personal vision of a good school. *Phi Delta Kappan, 71,* 512–515.

Bartholeme, L. (1998). *The misteaching of academic discourses.* Boulder, CO: Westview Press.

Bateson, G. (1972). *Steps to an ecology of mind.* Northvale, NJ: Jason Aronson.

Bear, G. G., & Minke, K. M. (2006). *Children's needs III: Development, prevention, and intervention.* Silver Spring, MD: National Association of School Psychologists.

Bear, G. G., Webster-Stratton, C., Furlong, M. J., & Rhee, S. (2000). Prevention of school violence. In K. M. Minke & G. C. Bear (Eds.), *Preventing school problems—promoting school success: Strategies that work* (pp. 1–69). Bethesda, MD: National Association of School Psychologists.

Beck, A. T. (1986). Cognitive therapy: A sign of retrogression or progress. *Behavior Therapist, 9*, 2–3.

Becvar, D. S., & Becvar, R. J. (2000). *Family therapy: A systemic integration* (4th ed.). Boston: Allyn & Bacon.

Bem, S. L. (1974). The measurement of psychological androgyny. *Journal of Consulting and Clinical Psychology, 42*, 155–162.

Benner, P. (1984). *From novice to expert: Excellence and power in clinical nursing practice.* Menlo Park, CA: Addison-Wesley.

Bennett, R. C. (1988). Evaluating the effectiveness of alternative delivery systems. In J. L. Graden, J. E. Zins, & M. J. Curtis (Eds.), *Alternative educational delivery systems: Enhancing instructional options for all students* (pp. 513–534). Washington, DC: National Association of School Psychologists.

Bennis, W. (1994). *On becoming a leader.* Reading, MA: Addison-Wesley.

Bennis, W. (2007). The challenges of leadership in the modern world: Introduction to the special issue. *American Psychologist, 62*, 2–5.

Benshoff, J. M., & Paisley, P. O. (1996). The structured peer consultation model for school counselors. *Journal of Counseling and Development, 74*, 314–318.

Bergan, J. R. (1977). *Behavioral consultation.* Columbus, OH: Merrill.

Bergan, J. R., & Kratochwill, T. R. (1990). *Behavioral consultation and therapy.* New York: Plenum Press.

Bernard, J. M., & Goodyear, R. K. (2004). *Fundamentals of clinical supervision* (3rd ed.). Boston: Allyn & Bacon.

Bernard, R. M., Abrami, P. C., Lou, Y., Borokhovski, E., Wade, A., & Wozney, L. (2004). How does distance education compare with classroom instruction? A meta-analysis of the empirical literature. *Review of Educational Research, 74*, 379–439.

Bersoff, D. N. (2003). The ethical practice of school psychology: A rebuttal and suggested model. In D. N. Bersoff (Ed.), *Ethical conflicts in psychology* (3rd ed., pp. 296–299). Washington, DC: American Psychological Association. (Original work published 1973)

Bertalanffy, L. von. (1956). General systems theory. In L. von Bertalanffy & A. Rapoport (Eds.), *General systems: Yearbook of the Society for the Advancement of General Systems Theory* (Vol. 1, pp. 1–10). Ann Arbor, MI: Society for General Systems Research.

Bhat, C. (2005). Enhancing counseling gatekeeping with performance appraisal protocols. *International Journal for the Advancement of Counselling, 27*, 399–411.

Binder, J. L., & Strupp, H. H. (1997). Supervision of psychodynamic psychotherapies. In C. F. Watkins (Ed.), *Handbook of psychotherapy supervision* (pp. 44–62). New York: Wiley.

Blackwell, T. L., Strohmer, D. C., Belcas, E. M., & Burton, K. A. (2002). Ethics in rehabilitation counselor supervision. *Rehabilitation Counseling Bulletin, 45*, 240–247.

Blechman, E. A., Taylor, C. J., & Schrader, S. M. (1981). Family problem solving versus home notes as early intervention with high-risk children. *Journal of Consulting and Clinical Psychology, 49*, 919–926.

Block, P. (1987). *The empowered manager: Positive practical skills at work.* San Francisco: Jossey-Bass.

Blumstein, P., & Schwartz, P. (1983). *American couples: Money, work, and sex.* New York: William Morrow.

Bogo, M., Globerman, J., & Sussman, T. (2004). The field instructor as group worker: Managing trust and competition in group supervision. *Journal of Social Work Education, 40*, 13–26.

Bolton, D. L. (1980). *Evaluating administrative personnel in school systems.* New York: Teachers College Press.

Bono, J. E., & Anderson, M. H. (2005). The advice and influence networks of transformational leaders. *Journal of Applied Psychology, 90*, 1306–1314.

Borders, L. D. (1990). Developmental changes during supervisees' first practicum. *Clinical Supervisor, 8*, 157–167.

Borders, L. D. (1991). A systematic approach to peer group supervision. *Journal of Counseling and Development, 69*, 248–252.

Borders, L. D., & Brown, L. L. (2005). *The new handbook of counseling supervision.* Mahwah, NJ: Lawrence Erlbaum.

Bordin, E. S. (1983). A working alliance model of supervision. *The Counseling Psychologist, 11*, 35–42.

Boud, D., & Walker, D. (1998). Promoting reflection in professional courses: The challenge of context. *Studies in Higher Education, 23*, 191–206.

Boulding, K. (1956). General systems theory: Skeleton of a science. *General Systems, 1*, 11–17.

Bowen, M. (1988). *Family therapy in clinical practice* (2nd ed.). Northvale, NJ: Jason Aronson.

Bowlby, J. (1982). *Attachment and loss.* New York: Basic Books.

Bowser, P. B. (1995). Best practices in professional conduct: Meeting NASP's ethical standards. In A. Thomas & J. Grimes (Eds.), *Best practices in school psychology III* (pp. 33–39). Silver Spring, MD: National Association of School Psychologists.

Bradley, L. J., & Ladany, N. (Eds.). (2001). *Counselor supervision: Principles, process, and practice* (3rd ed.). New York: Brunner-Routledge.

Brandt, J. (1998). *Law and mental health professionals: Massachusetts* (2nd ed.). Washington, DC: American Psychological Association.

Brantly, A. P. (2001). A clinical supervision documentation form. In L. Vande-Creek & T. L. Jackson (Eds.), *Innovations in clinical practice: A source book* (Vol. 18, pp. 301–307). Sarasota, NY: Professional Resources Press.

Bratton, S. C., Ray, D., Rhine, T., & Jones, L. (2005). The efficacy of play therapy with children: A meta-analytic review of treatment outcomes. *Professional Psychology: Research and Practice, 36,* 376–390.

Breiman, K. S. (2001). An analysis of ways in which supervisors of school psychologists and school social workers make sense of their urban educational work environment. *Dissertation Abstracts International, 62* (02), 526A. (UMI No. AAI3004901)

Bridges, N. A. (1999). The role of supervision in managing intense affect and constructing boundaries in therapeutic relationships. *Journal of Sex Education & Therapy, 24,* 218–225.

Briggs, J., & Miller, G. (2005). Success enhancing supervision. *Journal of Family Psychotherapy, 16,* 199–222.

Brock, S. (2002). Crisis theory: A foundation for the comprehensive crisis prevention and intervention team. In S. E. Brock, P. J. Lazarus, & S. R. Jimerson (Eds.), *Best practices in school crisis prevention and intervention* (pp. 5–18). Bethesda, MD: National Association of School Psychologists.

Bronfenbrenner, U. (1979). *The ecology of human development: Experiments by nature and design.* Cambridge, MA: Harvard University Press.

Brown, D., Pryzwansky, W. B., & Schulte, A. C. (2006). *Psychological consultation and collaboration* (6th ed.). Boston: Allyn & Bacon.

Brown, D., & Trusty, J. (2005). *Designing and leading comprehensive school counseling programs: Promoting student competence and meeting student needs.* Belmont, CA: Brooks/Cole.

Brown, T. L., Acevedo-Polakovich, I. D., & Smith, A. M. (2006). In T. K. Neill (Ed.), *Helping others help children: Clinical supervision of child psychotherapy* (pp. 73–88). Washington, DC: American Psychological Association.

Brown-Chidsey, R., & Steege, M. W. (2005). *Response to intervention: Principles and strategies for effective practice.* New York: Guilford Press.

Brown-Chidsey, R., Steege, M. W., & Mace, F. C. (2008). Best practices in evaluating the effectiveness of interventions using case study data. In A. Thomas & J. Grimes (Eds.), *Best practices in school psychology V* (pp. 2177–2192). Bethesda, MD: National Association of School Psychologists.

Bryant, A. S., & Demian, R. (1994). Relationship characteristics of American gay and lesbian couples: Findings from a national survey. *Journal of Gay & Lesbian Social Services, 1,* 101–117.

Bryson, J. M. (1995). *Strategic planning for public and nonprofit organizations: A guide to strengthening and sustaining organizational achievement.* San Francisco: Jossey-Bass.

Bugaj, A. M. (2003). Review of the Supervisory Behavior Description Questionnaire. In B. S. Plake, J. C. Impara, & R. A. Spies (Eds.), *The fifteenth mental measurements yearbook* [Electronic version]. Available from the Buros Institute's *Test Reviews Online* Web site: http://buros.unl.edu/buros

Burkard, A. W., Johnson, A. J., Madson, M. B., Pruitt, N. T., Contreras-Tadych, D. A., Kozlowski, J. M., et al. (2006). Supervisor cultural responsiveness and unresponsiveness in cross-cultural supervision. *Journal of Counseling Psychology, 52,* 288–301.

Burke, W., Goodyear, R., & Guzzard, C. (1998). Weakenings and repairs in supervisory alliances: A multiple-case study. *American Journal of Psychotherapy, 52,* 450–462.

Burns, J. M. (1978). *Leadership.* New York: Harper & Row.

Byrnes, J. P. (2000). *Cognitive development and learning in instructional contexts* (2nd ed.). Boston: Allyn & Bacon.

Cagnon, J., & Russell, R. K. (1995). Assessment of supervisee developmental level and supervision environment across supervisor experience. *Journal of Counseling and Development, 73,* 553–558.

Cameron, K. S. (1980). Critical questions in assessing organizational effectiveness. *Organizational Dynamics, 9,* 66–80.

Campbell, D. (1991). *The Campbell leadership index.* Minneapolis, MN: NCS Assessment.

Campbell, J. (2000). *Becoming an effective supervisor: A workbook for counselors and psychotherapists.* London: Taylor & Francis.

Campbell, M. C., Floyd, J., & Sheridan, J. B. (2002). Assessment of student performance and attitudes for courses taught on-line versus onsite. *Journal of Applied Business Research, 18,* 45–51.

Canter, A. (2001a, May). Test protocols Pt. 1: Right to review and copy. *Communiqué,* pp. 30–32.

Canter, A. (2001b, September). Test protocols Pt. 2: Storage and disposal. *Communiqué,* pp. 16–19.

Caplan, G. (1964). *Principles of preventative psychology.* New York: Basic Books.

Caplan, G. (1970). *The theory and practice of mental health consultation.* New York: Basic Books.

Caplan, G., & Caplan, R. B. (1993). *Mental health consultation and collaboration.* Long Grove, IL: Waveland Press.

Cardemil, E. V., & Battle, C. L. (2003). Guess who's coming to therapy? Getting comfortable with conversations about race and ethnicity in psychotherapy. *Professional Psychology: Research and Practice, 34,* 278–286.

Carlson, C., & Christenson, S. L. (2005). Evidence-based parent and family interventions in school psychology: Overview and procedures. *School Psychology Quarterly, 20,* 345–351.

Carlson, G. A. (2002). Bipolar disorder in children and adolescents: A critical review. In D. Shaffer & B. Waslik (Eds.), *The many faces of depression in children and adolescents* (Vol. 21, pp. 105–128). Washington, DC: American Psychiatric Association.

Carrington, G. (2004). Supervision as a reciprocal learning process. *Educational Psychology in Practice, 20,* 31–42.

Carroll, J. B. (1997). The three-stratum theory of cognitive abilities. In D. P. Flanagan, J. L. Genshaft, & P. L. Harrison (Eds.), *Contemporary intellectual assessment: Theories, tests, and issues* (pp. 122–130). New York: Guilford Press.

Carroll, M. (2006). *Counselling supervision: Theory, skills, practice.* Thousand Oaks, CA: SAGE.

Center for Credentialing and Education. (2001). *Approved clinical supervisor code of ethics.* Greensboro, NC: Author.

Certo, S. C. (2006). *Supervision: Concepts and skill building* (5th ed.). Boston: McGraw-Hill.

Chafouleas, S. M., Clonan, S. M., & Vanauken, T. L. (2002). A national survey of current supervision and evaluation practices of school psychologists. *Psychology in the Schools, 39,* 317–325.

Chamberlain, J. (2000). Point, click, and learn: Educators exhibited the cutting-edge technology they're using to enhance their classrooms. *Monitor on Psychology, 31,* 56–57.

Chan, C. C. (2004). Taking supervision forward: The beginning of a new curriculum on supportive supervision in counseling. *Asian Journal of Counseling, 11,* 55–77.

Chapman, D. S., Uggerslev, K. L., Carroll, S. A., Piasenin, K. A., & Jones, D. A. (2005). Applicant attraction to organizations and job choice: A meta-analytic review of the correlates of recruiting outcomes. *Journal of Applied Psychology, 90,* 928–944.

Cherniss, C. (1986). Instrument for observing supervisor behavior in educational programs for mentally retarded children. *American Journal of Mental Deficiency, 91,* 18–21.

Christenson, S. L. (2004). The family-school partnership: An opportunity to promote the learning competence of all students. *School Psychology Review, 33,* 83–104.

Civil Rights Act of 1964, 42 U.S.C. § 2000d *et seq.* (2000).

Civil Rights Act of 1991, 42 U.S.C. § 1981a (2000).

Clark, J. J., & Croney, E. L. (2006). Ethics and accountability in supervision of child psychotherapy. In T. K. Neill (Ed.), *Helping others help children: Clinical supervision of child psychotherapy* (pp. 52–72). Washington, DC: American Psychological Association.

Clarke, A. (2006, December). *Massachusetts Teachers Association general counsel.* Paper presented at the fall conference of the Massachusetts Association of School Psychologists on Ethics and Law in School Psychology, Woburn, MA.

Clifford, J., Macy, M., & Albi, L. (2005). A model of clinical supervision for preservice professionals in early intervention and early childhood special education. *Topics in Early Childhood Special Education, 25,* 167–176.

Clingerman, T., & Bernard, J. (2004). An investigation of the use of e-mail as a supplemental modality for clinical supervision. *Counselor Education and Supervision, 44,* 82–95.

Cloud, H. (2006). *Integrity: The courage to meet the demands of reality.* New York: Collins.

Cobia, D. C., & Boes, S. R. (2000). Professional disclosure statements and formal plans for supervision: Two strategies for minimizing the risk of ethical conflicts in post-master's supervision. *Journal of Counseling and Development, 78,* 293–296.

Cole, E., & Siegel, J. A. (Eds.). (2003). *Effective consultation in school psychology* (2nd ed.). Cambridge, MA: Hogrefe & Huber.

Cole, M. S., Field, H. S., & Stafford, J. O. (2005). Validity of resumé reviewers' inferences concerning applicant personality based on resumé evaluation. *International Journal of Selection and Assessment, 13,* 321–324.

Committee for Children. (n.d.). *Second Step overview.* Retrieved January 28, 2008, from http://www.cfchildren.org/programs/ssp/overview/

Conoley, J. C., & Bahns, T. (1995). Best practices in supervision of interns. In A. Thomas & J. Grimes (Eds.), *Best practices in school psychology III* (pp. 111–122). Silver Spring, MD: National Association of School Psychologists.

Conoley, J. C., & Conoley, C. W. (1988). Useful theories in school-based consultation. *Remedial and Special Education, 9,* 14–20.

Constable, J. F., & Russell, D. (1986). The effect of social support and the work environment upon burnout among nurses. *Journal of Human Stress, 12,* 12–26.

Constantine, M. G. (1997). Facilitating multicultural competency in counseling supervision. In D. B. Pope-Davis & H. L. K. Coleman (Eds.), *Multicultural counseling competencies* (pp. 310–324). Thousand Oaks, CA: SAGE.

Constantine, M. G., & Sue, D. W. (Eds.). (2005). *Strategies for building multicultural competencies in mental health and educational settings.* Hoboken, NJ: Wiley.

Constantine, M. G., Warren, A., & Miville, M. (2005). White racial identity dyadic interactions in supervision: Implications for supervisees' multicultural counseling competence. *Journal of Counseling Psychology, 52,* 490–496.

Cook, J. E., & Doyle, C. (2002). Working alliance in online therapy as compared to face-to-face therapy: Preliminary results. *CyberPsychology & Behavior, 5,* 95–105.

Coomey, S. M., & Wilczenski, F. L. (2005). Implications of technology for social and emotional communication. *Journal of Applied School Psychology, 21,* 127–139.

Cooper, J. O., Heron, T. E., & Heward, W. L. (1987). *Applied behavior analysis.* Upper Saddle River, NJ: Prentice Hall.

Copyright Law of the United States of America, 1996, 17 U.S.C. (2000).

Corey, G., Corey, M. S., & Callanan, P. (2007). *Issues and ethics in the helping professions* (7th ed.). Belmont, CA: Brooks/Cole.

Corrigan, P., Garman, A., Lam, C., & Leary, M. (1998). What mental health teams want in their leaders. *Administration and Policy in Mental Health, 26,* 111–123.

Corsi, R. (2004). Identification and intervention of reading disabilities: One school district's approach. *Massachusetts School Psychologists Association Newsletter, 22*(2), 1–8.

Costa, L. (1994). Reducing anxiety in live supervision. *Counselor Education and Supervision, 34,* 30–40.

Costenbader, V., Swartz, J., & Petrix, L. (1992). Consultation in the schools: The relationship between preservice training, perception of consultative skills, and actual time spent in consultation. *School Psychology Review, 21,* 95–108.

Cramer, K., & Rosenfield, S. A. (2003). Clinical supervision of consultation. *Clinical Supervisor, 22,* 111–124.

Cresci, M. B. (2001). How does supervision teach? In S. Gill (Ed.), *The supervisory alliance: Facilitating the psychotherapist's learning experience* (pp. 123–138). Lanham, MD: Jason Aronson.

Crone, D. A., & Horner, R. H. (2003). *Building positive behavior support systems in schools.* New York: Guilford Press.

Cruise, T., Kelly, R., Wise, P., Berjohn, M. K., Sanna, B., Sibley, D., et al. (2000, March). *Intern supervision: Development of entry-level skills on how to provide constructive feedback to interns.* Symposium conducted at the 22nd Annual Convention of the Illinois School Psychologists Association, Arlington Heights, IL.

Crutchfield, L. B., & Borders, L. D. (1997). Impact of two clinical peer supervision models on practicing school counselors. *Journal of Counseling and Development, 75,* 219–230.

Crutchfield, L. B., Price, C. B., McGarity, D., Pennington, D., Richardson, J., & Tsolis, A. (1997). Challenge and support: Group supervision for school counselors. *Professional School Counseling, 1,* 43–46.

Culbreth, J., Scarborough, J., & Banks-Johnson, A. (2005). Role stress among practicing school counselors. *Counselor Education and Supervision, 45,* 58–71.

Cummings, J. A., Harrison, P. L., Dawson, M. M., Short, R. J., Gorin, S., & Palomares, R. S. (2004). The 2002 Conference on the Future of School Psychology: Implications for consultation, intervention, and prevention services. *Journal of Educational & Psychological Consultation, 15,* 239–256.

Curtis, M. J., Castillo, J. M., & Cohen, R. M. (2008). Best practices in systems-level change. In A. Thomas & J. Grimes (Eds.), *Best practices in school psychology V* (pp. 887–902). Bethesda, MD: National Association of School Psychologists.

Curtis, M. J., Grier, J. E. C., & Hunley, S. A. (2004). The changing face of school psychology: Trends in data and projections for the future. *School Psychology Review, 33,* 49–66.

Curtis, M. J., Hunley, S. A., & Grier, J. E. C. (2002). Relationships among the professional practices and demographic characteristics of school psychologists. *School Psychology Review, 31,* 30–42.

Curtis, M. J., & Meyers, J. (1989). Consultation: A foundation for alternative services in the schools. In J. L. Graden, J. E. Zins, & M. J. Curtis (Eds.), *Alternative educational delivery systems: Enhancing instructional options for all students* (pp. 3–15, 36). Washington, DC: National Association of School Psychologists.

Curtis, M. J., & Yager, G. G. (1981). A systems model for the supervision of school psychologists. *School Psychology Review, 10,* 425–433.

Curtis, M. J., & Yager, G. G. (1987). A systems model for the supervision of school psychological services. In R. H. Dana & W. T. May (Eds.), *Internship training in professional psychology* (pp. 340–352). Washington, DC: Hemisphere.

Cutliffe, J. R., & Lowe, L. (2005). A comparison of North American and European conceptualizations of clinical supervision. *Issues in Mental Health Nursing, 26,* 475–488.

Daly, E. J., Witt, J. C., Martens, B. K., & Dool, E. J. (1997). A model for conducting a functional analysis of academic performance problems. *School Psychology Review, 26,* 554–574.

D'Andrea, M., & Daniels, J. (2001). Expanding our thinking about white racism: Facing the challenge of multicultural counseling in the 21st century. In J. G. Ponterotto, J. N. Casas, L. A. Suzuki, & C. M. Alexander (Eds.), *Handbook of multicultural counseling* (pp. 289–310). Thousand Oaks, CA: SAGE.

D'Andrea, M., Daniels, J., & Heck, R. (1991). Evaluating the impact of multicultural counseling training. *Journal of Counseling and Development, 70,* 143–150.

Darling-Hammond, L. (2001). *The right to learn: A blueprint for creating schools that work.* San Francisco: Jossey-Bass.

Das, J. P., Naglieri, J. A., & Kirby, J. R. (1994). *The assessment of cognitive processes: The PASS theory of intelligence.* Boston: Allyn & Bacon.

Davies, E. J., Tennant, A., & Ferguson, E. (2004). Developing models and a framework for multiprofessional clinical supervision. *British Journal of Forensic Practice, 6*(3), 36–42.

Dawson, P., & Guare, R. (2004). *Executive skills in children and adolescents: A practical guide to assessment and intervention.* New York: Guilford Press.

DeAngelis, T. (2006). How to change your practice. *Monitor on Psychology, 37,* 60–61.

DeCato, C. M. (2002). A quantitative method for studying the testing supervision process. *Psychological Reports, 90,* 137–138.

DeLeon, P. H., Ball, V., Loftis, C. W., & Sullivan, M. J. (2006). Navigating politics, policy, and procedures: A firsthand perspective of advocacy on behalf of the profession. *Professional Psychology: Research and Practice, 37,* 146–153.

Delpit, L. (1995). *Other people's children: Cultural conflict in the classroom.* New York: New Press.

Dickens, F., & Dickens, J. B. (1991). *The black manager.* New York: American Management Association.

Disney, M. J., & Stephens, A. M. (1994). *Legal issues in clinical supervision.* Alexandria, VA: American Counseling Association.

Dlugos, R. F., & Friedlander, M. L. (2001). Passionately committed psychotherapists: A qualitative study of their experiences. *Professional Psychology: Research and Practice, 32,* 298–304.

Dodenhoff, J. T. (1981). Interpersonal attraction and direct-indirect supervisor influence as predictors of counselor trainee effectiveness. *Journal of Counseling Psychology, 28,* 47–52.

Doll, B., Zucker, S., & Brehm, K. (2004). *Resilient classrooms: Creating healthy environments for learning.* New York: Guilford Press.

Dombrowski, S. C., Kamphaus, R. W., & Reynolds, C. R. (2004). After the demise of the discrepancy: Proposed learning disabilities diagnostic criteria. *Professional Psychology: Research and Practice, 35,* 364–372.

Dougherty, A. M. (2005). *Psychological consultation and collaboration in school and community settings* (4th ed.). Belmont, CA: Brooks/Cole.

Downs, A. (2005). *The velvet rage: Overcoming the pain of growing up gay in a straight man's world.* Cambridge, MA: Perseus.

Drasgow, E., & Yell, M. L. (2001). Functional behavioral assessments: Legal requirements and challenges. *School Psychology Review, 30,* 129–145.

Dreyfus, H., & Dreyfus, S. (1991). Towards a phenomenology of ethical expertise. *Human Studies, 14,* 229–250.

Duan, C., & Roehlke, H. (2001). A descriptive "snapshot" of cross-racial supervision in university counseling center internships. *Journal of Multicultural Counseling and Development, 29,* 131–146.

Dubinsky, A. J., Howell, R. D., & Ingraham, T. N. (1986). Salesforce socialization. *Journal of Marketing, 50,* 192–207.

Dudding, C. C., & Justice, L. M. (2004). An e-supervision model: Videoconferencing as a clinical training tool. *Communications Disorders Quarterly, 25*(3), 145–151.

Duffy, S., & Rusbult, C. (1986). Satisfaction and commitment in homosexual and heterosexual relationships. *Journal of Homosexuality, 12,* 1–24.

Dufresne, B. A., Noell, G. H., Gilbertson, D. N., & Duhon, G. J. (2005). Monitoring implementation of reciprocal peer tutoring: Identifying and intervening with students who do not maintain accurate implementation. *School Psychology Review, 34,* 74–86.

Dumont, R., & Willis, J. O. (2003). Issues regarding the supervision of assessment. *Clinical Supervisor, 22,* 2, 159–176.

Dunham, M., Liljequist, L., & Martin, J. (2006). Streamlining psychological reports. *Trainer's Forum: Periodical of the Trainers of School Psychologists, 25*(4), 9–14.

Duvall, S. F., Delquadri, J. C., Elliott, M., & Hall, R. V. (1992). Parent tutoring procedures: Experimental analysis and validation of generalization in oral reading across passages, settings, and time. *Journal of Behavioral Education, 2,* 281–303.

Dye, H. A., & Borders, L. D. (1990). Counseling supervisors: Standards for preparation and practice. *Journal of Counseling and Development, 69,* 27–29.

Eckes, G. (2000). *The Six-Sigma revolution.* New York: Wiley.

Education Amendments of 1972, 20 U.S.C. § 1681 *et seq.* (2000).

Edwards, T. M., & Heshmati, A. (2003). A guide for beginning family therapy group supervisors. *American Journal of Family Therapy, 31,* 295–304.

Efstation, J. F., Patton, M. J., & Kardash, C. M. (1990). Measuring the working alliance in counselor supervision. *Journal of Counseling Psychology, 37,* 322–329.

Egan, G. (1990). *The skilled helper: A systematic approach to effective helping* (4th ed.). Pacific Grove, CA: Brooks/Cole.

Ellis, M. V., Krengel, M., & Beck, M. (2002). Testing self-focused attention theory in clinical supervision: Effects on supervisee anxiety performance. *Journal of Counseling Psychology, 49,* 101–116.

Ellis, M. V., & Robins, E. S. (1993). Voices of care and justice in clinical supervision: Issues and interventions. *Counselor Education and Supervision, 32,* 203–212.

Enyedy, K. C., Arcinue, F., Puri, N. N., Carter, J. W., Goodyear, R. K., & Getzelman, M. A. (2003). Hindering phenomena in group supervision: Implications for practice. *Professional Psychology: Research and Practice, 34,* 312–317.

Epstein, J. L. (2001). *School, family and community partnerships: Preparing educators and improving schools.* Boulder, CO: Westview Press.

Equal Pay Act of 1963, 29 U.S.C. § 206(d) (2000).

Erchul, W. B., & Martens, B. K. (2002). *School consultation: Conceptual and empirical bases of practice* (2nd ed.). New York: Kluwer/Plenum.

Ericsson, K. A., & Charness, N. (1994). Expert performance: Its structure and acquisition. *American Psychologist, 49,* 725–747.

Ericsson, K. A., Krampe, R. T., & Tesch-Romer, C. (1993). The role of deliberate practice in the acquisition of expert performance. *Psychological Review, 100,* 363–406.

Erikson, E. (1950). *Childhood and society.* New York: Norton.

Esquivel, G. B., Lopez, E. C., & Nahari, S. G. (Eds.). (2007). *Handbook of multicultural school psychology: An interdisciplinary perspective.* Mahwah, NJ: Lawrence Erlbaum.

Evangelista, N. (2006, April). *Clinical supervision of the practicing school psychologist: Teaching supervision at Alfred University.* Paper presented at the annual convention of the National Association of School Psychologists, Anaheim, CA.

Evans, J. J., Floyd, R. G., McGrew, K. S., & Leforgee, M. H. (2001). The relations between measures of Cattell-Horn-Carroll (CHC) cognitive abilities and reading achievement during childhood and adolescence. *School Psychology Review, 31,* 246–262.

Fadiman, A. (1997). *The spirit catches you and you fall down.* New York: Farrar, Straus and Giroux.

Fagan, T. K., & Wise, P. S. (2000). *School psychology: Past, present, and future* (2nd ed.). New York: Longman.

Falender, C. A., Cornish, J., Goodyear, R., Hatcher, R., Kaslow, N., Leventhal, G., et al. (2004). Defining competencies in psychology supervision: A consensus statement. *Journal of Clinical Psychology, 60,* 771–785.

Falender, C. A., & Shafranske, E. P. (2004). *Clinical supervision: A competency-based approach.* Washington, DC: American Psychological Association.

Falender, C. A., & Shafranske, E. P. (2007). Competence in competency-based supervision practice: Construct and application. *Professional Psychology: Research and Practice, 38,* 232–240.

Falvey, J. E. (2001). *Managing clinical supervision: Ethical practice and legal risk management.* Belmont, CA: Brooks/Cole.

Falvey, J. E., & Cohen, C. R. (2003). The buck stops here: Documenting clinical supervision. *Clinical Supervisor, 22,* 63–80.

Family and Medical Leave Act of 1993, 29 U.S.C. § 2601 *et seq.* (2000).

Family Educational Rights and Privacy Act of 1974, Pub. L. No. 93-380, § 513, 88 Stat. 484 (1974).

Fenichel, M., Suler, J., Barak, A., Zelvin, E., Jones, G., Munro, K., et al. (2002). Myths and realities of online clinical work. *CyberPsychology & Behavior, 5,* 481–497.

Fernando, D. M., & Hulse-Killacky, D. (2005). The relationship of supervisor styles to satisfaction with supervision and the perceived self-efficacy of master's level counseling students. *Counselor Education and Supervision, 44,* 293–304.

Feuerstein, R., Rand, Y., & Hoffman, M. B. (1979). *The dynamic assessment of retarded performers: The Learning Potential Assessment Device (LPAD).* Baltimore: University Park Press.

Fiedler, F. E., & Macauley, J. L. (1998). The leadership situation: A missing factor in selecting and training managers. *Human Resource Management Review, 8,* 335–350.

Finkelhor, D. (1986). *A sourcebook on child abuse.* Beverly Hills, CA: SAGE.

Fiorello, C., & Primerano, D. (2005). Research into practice: Cattell-Horn-Carroll cognitive assessment in practice: Eligibility and program development issues. *Psychology in the Schools, 42,* 525–536.

Fischetti, B. A., & Crespi, T. D. (1999). Clinical supervision for school psychologists: National practices, trends, and future implications. *School Psychology International, 20,* 278–288.

Fischetti, B. A., & Lines, C. L. (2003). Views from the field: Models for school-based clinical supervision. *Clinical Supervisor, 22,* 75–86.

Fishman, C. (1993). *Intensive structural therapy: Treating families in their social context.* New York: Basic Books.

Flaks, D., Ficher, I., Masterpasqua, F., & Joseph, G. (1995). Lesbians choosing motherhood: A comparative study of lesbian and heterosexual parents and their children. *Developmental Psychology, 31,* 105–114.

Flanagan, D. P., & Harrison, P. (2005). *Contemporary intellectual assessment* (2nd ed.). New York: Guilford Press.

Flanagan, D. P., & Ortiz, S. O. (2000). *Essentials of Cross-Battery Assessment.* New York: Wiley.

Fleishman, E. A. (1996).*The supervisory behavior description questionnaire.* Chicago: Reid London House.

Fleming, D. C., Fleming, E. R., Roach, K. S., & Oksman, P. F. (1985). Conflict management. In C. A. Maher (Ed.), *Professional self-management: Techniques for special services providers* (pp. 65–84). Baltimore: Brookes.

Flugum, K. R., & Reschly, D. J. (1994). Prereferral interventions: Quality indices and outcomes. *Journal of School Psychology, 32,* 1–14.

Fontagy, P., Target, M., Cottrell, D., Phillips, J., & Kurtz, Z. (Eds.). (2002). *What works for whom? A critical review of treatments for children and adolescents.* New York: Guilford Press.

Forman, S. G., & Burke, C. R. (2008). Best practices in selecting and implementing evidence-based school interventions. In A. Thomas & J. Grimes (Eds.), *Best practices in school psychology V* (pp. 799–812). Bethesda, MD: National Association of School Psychologists.

Forman, S. G., & Cecil, M. A. (1985). Stress management. In C. A. Maher (Ed.), *Professional self-management: Techniques for special services providers* (pp. 45–63). Baltimore: Brookes.

Forrest, L., Elman, N., Gizara, S., & Vacha-Haase, T. (1999). Trainee impairment: A review of identification, remediation, dismissal, and legal issues. *Counseling Psychologist, 27,* 627–686.

Fowler, E., & Harrison, P. L. (1995). Continuing professional development for school psychologists. In A. Thomas & J. Grimes (Eds.), *Best practices in school psychology III* (pp. 81–90). Silver Spring, MD: National Association of School Psychologists.

Franklin, M., & Duley, S. M. (2002). Best practices in planning school psychology service delivery programs: An update. In A. Thomas & J. Grimes (Eds.), *Best practices in school psychology IV* (pp. 145–159). Bethesda, MD: National Association of School Psychologists.

Franklin, M., Stillman, P., Burpeau, M., & Sabers, D. (1982). Examiner error in intelligence testing: Are you the source? *Psychology in the Schools, 19,* 563–569.

Frawley-O'Dea, M. G., & Sarnat, J. E. (2001). *The supervisory relationship: A contemporary psychodynamic approach.* New York: Guilford Press.

Freitas, G. J. (2002). The impact of psychotherapy supervision on client outcome: A critical examination of 2 decades of research. *Psychotherapy: Theory/Research/Practice/Training, 39,* 354–367.

Friedlander, M. L., Keller, K. E., Peca-Baker, T. A., & Olk, M. E. (1986). Effects of role conflict on counselor trainees' self-statement, anxiety level, and performance. *Journal of Counseling Psychology, 33,* 73–77.

Friedlander, M. L., & Ward, L. G. (1984). Development and validation of the Supervisory Styles Inventory. *Journal of Counseling Psychology, 31,* 541–557.

Friedlander, S. (Ed.). (1984). Psychotherapy talk as social control. *Psychotherapy, 21,* 335–341.

Frisby, C. L. (2005). The politics of multiculturalism in school psychology (Pt. 2). In C. L. Frisby & C. R. Reynolds (Eds.), *Comprehensive handbook of multicultural school psychology* (pp. 81–134). Hoboken, NJ: Wiley.

Frisby, C. L., & Reynolds, C. R. (Eds.). (2005). *Comprehensive handbook of multicultural school psychology.* Hoboken, NJ: Wiley.

Fuchs, D., & Fuchs, L. S. (2005). Responsiveness-to-intervention: A blueprint for practitioners, policymakers, and parents. *Teaching Exceptional Children, 38,* 57–61.

Fuchs, D., Mock, D., Morgan, P. L., & Young, C. L. (2003). Responsiveness-to-intervention: Definitions, evidence, and implications for the learning disabilities construct. *Learning Disabilities: Research & Practice, 18,* 157–171.

Fuchs, L. S., & Fuchs, D. (1986). Effects of systematic formative evaluation on student achievement: A meta-analysis. *Exceptional Children, 53,* 199–208.

Fuentes, C., Olmos, E. J., & Ybarra, L. (1999). *Americanos: Latino life in the United States.* Boston: Little, Brown.

Fuqua, D. R., & Newman, J. L. (2002). The role of systems theory in consulting psychology. In R. L. Lowman (Ed.), *The California School of Organizational Studies handbook of organizational consulting psychology: A comprehensive guide to theory, skills, and techniques* (pp. 76–105). San Francisco: Jossey-Bass.

Furlong, M. J., Felix, E. D., Sharkey, J. D., & Larson, J. (2005, September). Preventing school violence: A plan for safe and engaging schools. *Student Counseling,* pp. 11–15.

The Future of School Psychology. (n.d.). *Resources.* Retrieved December 7, 2007, from http://www.indiana.edu/%7Efutures/resources.html

Futures Task Force on Family-School Partnerships. (2007). *Future of school psychology task force on family-school partnership: Family-school partnership training modules.* Unpublished training package and support materials. Available from http://fsp.unl.edu/index.html

Gainor, K. A., & Constantine, M. G. (2002). Multicultural group supervision: A comparison of in-person versus Web-based formats. *Professional School Counseling, 6,* 104–121.

Gardner, H. (1999). *Intelligence reframed.* New York: Basic Books.

Garman, A. N., & Lesowitz, T. (2005). Research update: Interviewing candidates for leadership roles. *Consulting Psychology Journal, 57,* 266–273.

Garrett, M. T., Borders, L. D., Crutchfield, L. B., Torres-Rivera, E., Brotherton, D., & Curtis, R. (2001). Multicultural superVISION: A paradigm of cultural responsiveness for supervisors. *Journal of Multicultural Counseling and Development, 29,* 147–158.

Gatmon, D., Jackson, D., Koshkerian, L., Martos-Perry, N., Molina, A., Patel, N., et al. (2001). Exploring ethnic, gender, and sexual orientation variables in supervision: Do they really matter? *Journal of Multicultural Counseling and Development, 29,* 102–113.

Gawthrop, J. C., & Uhleman, M. R. (1992). Effects of the problem-solving approach in ethics training. *Professional Psychology: Research and Practice, 23,* 38–42.

Gediman, H. K. (2003). The supervisory alliance: Facilitating the psychotherapists' learning experience. *Journal of the American Psychoanalytic Association, 51,* 1060–1066.

Gibbons, A., Mize, C. D., & Rogers, K. L. (2002, June). *That's my story and I'm sticking to it: Promoting academic integrity in the on-line environment.* Paper presented at the 2002 World Conference on Educational Multimedia, Hypermedia, and Telecommunications, Denver, CO. (ERIC Document Reproductive Service No. ED477016)

Gickling, E. E., & Rosenfield, S. (1995). Best practices in Curriculum Based Assessment. In A. Thomas & J. Grimes (Eds.), *Best practices in school psychology III* (pp. 587–596). Silver Spring, MD: National Association of School Psychologists.

Gill, S. (2001). Narcissistic vulnerability in supervisees. In S. Gill (Ed.), *The supervisory alliance: Facilitating the psychotherapist's learning experience* (pp. 19–34). Lanham, MD: Jason Aronson.

Gilligan, C. (1982). *In a different voice.* Cambridge, MA: Harvard University Press.

Gilman, R., & Gabriel, S. (2004). Perceptions of school psychological services by education professionals: Results from a multi-state survey pilot study. *School Psychology Review, 33,* 271–286.

Gizara, S., & Forrest, L. (2004). Supervisors' experiences of trainee impairment and incompetence at APA-accredited internship sites. *Professional Psychology: Research and Practice, 35,* 131–140.

Glickman, C. D., Gordon, S. P., & Ross-Gordon, J. M. (2006). *SuperVision and instructional leadership: A developmental approach* (7th ed.). Boston: Allyn & Bacon.

Goldberg, D. A. (1985). Process notes and videotape: Modes of presentation in psychotherapy training. *Clinical Supervisor, 3,* 3–13.

Golumbok, S., Spencer, A., & Rutter, M. (1983). Children in lesbian and single parent households: Psychosexual and psychiatric appraisal. *Journal of Child Psychology and Psychiatry, 24,* 551.

Goode, T. D. (2002). *Self-assessment checklist for personnel providing services and supports to children and their families.* Retrieved December 7, 2007, from http://www.nasponline.org/resources/culturalcompetence/checklist.aspx

Goss v. Lopez, 419 U.S. 565 (1975).

Gottlieb, M. C., Robinson, K., & Younggren, J. N. (2007). Multiple relations in supervision: Guidance for administrators, supervisors, and students. *Professional Psychology: Research and Practice, 38,* 241–247.

Gourdine, R., & Baffour, T. (2004). Maximizing learning: Evaluating competency-based training program for field instructors. *Clinical Supervisor, 23,* 33–53.

Grandin, T. (2006). *Thinking in pictures: My life with autism* (Expanded ed.). New York: Random House.

Gravois, T. A., & Rosenfield, S. A. (2006). Impact of instructional consultation teams on the disproportionate referral and placement of minority students in special education. *Remedial and Special Education, 27,* 42–52.

Gray, L. A., Ladany, N., Walker, J. A., & Ancis, J. R. (2001). Psychotherapy trainees' experience of counterproductive events in supervision. *Journal of Counseling Psychology, 48,* 371–383.

Gray, S. W. (1963). *The psychologist in the schools.* New York: Holt, Rinehart & Winston.

Green, R. (1982). The best interests of the child with a lesbian mother. *Bulletin of the American Academy of Psychiatry & the Law, 10,* 7–15.

Green, S. K. (1995). Implementing a staff development program. In A. Thomas & J. Grimes (Eds.), *Best practices in school psychology III* (pp. 123–134). Silver Spring, MD: National Association of School Psychologists.

Gresham, F. M. (1989). Assessment of treatment integrity in school consultation and prereferral intervention. *School Psychology Review, 18,* 37–50.

Gresham, F. M., MacMillan, D. L., Beebe-Frankenberger, M. E., & Bocian, K. M. (2000). Treatment integrity in learning disabilities intervention research: Do we really know how treatments are implemented? *Learning Disabilities: Research & Practice, 15,* 198–205.

Griffith, B. A., & Frieden, G. (2000). Facilitating reflective thinking in counselor education. *Counselor Education and Supervision, 40,* 82–93.

Griffith, J. L., & Griffith, M. E. (2002). *Encountering the sacred in psychotherapy: How to talk with people about their spiritual lives.* New York: Guilford Press.

Gross, S. J., & Shapiro, J. P. (2004). Using multiple ethical paradigms and turbulence theory in response to ethical dilemmas. *International Studies in Educational Administration, 32,* 47–62.

Gross, S. M. (2005). Student perspectives on clinical and counseling psychology practica. *Professional Psychology: Research and Practice, 36,* 299–306.

Guest, K. E. (2000). Career development of school psychologists. *Journal of School Psychology, 38,* 237–257.

Guidubaldi, J. (1981). On the way to Olympia. *Communiqué, 10*(3), 1–2.

Gutkin, T. B., & Curtis, M. J. (1982). School-based consultation: Theory and techniques. In C. R. Reynolds & T. B. Gutkin (Eds.), *The handbook of social psychology* (pp. 796–828). New York: Wiley.

Guy, J. D. (2000). Holding the holding environment together: Self-psychology and psychotherapist care. *Professional Psychology: Research and Practice, 31,* 351–352.

Gysbers, N. C. (2006). Improving school guidance and counseling practices through effective and sustained state leadership: A response to Miller. *Professional School Counseling, 9,* 245–247.

Haboush, K. L. (2003). Group supervision of school psychologists in training. *School Psychology International, 24,* 232–255.

Hackman, J. R., & Wageman, R. (1995). Total quality management: Empirical, conceptual, and practical issues. *Administrative Science Quarterly, 40,* 309–342.

Hackman, J. R., & Wageman, R. (2007). Asking the right questions about leadership. *American Psychologist, 62,* 43–47.

Hage, S. M. (2006). A closer look at the role of spirituality in psychology training programs. *Professional Psychology: Research and Practice, 37,* 303–310.

Hale, J. (2006). Implementing IDEA 2004 with a three-tier model that includes response to intervention and cognitive assessment methods. *School Psychology Forum: Research in Practice, 1,* 16–27.

Haley, J. (1985). *Problem solving therapy.* San Francisco: Jossey-Bass.

Halfhill, T. R., Huff, J. W., Johnson, D. A., Ballentine, R. D., & Beyerlein, M. M. (2002). Interventions that work (and some that don't): An executive summary of the organizational change literature. In R. L. Lowman (Ed.), *The California School of Organizational Studies handbook of organizational consulting psychology: A comprehensive guide to theory, skills, and techniques* (pp. 619–644). San Francisco: Jossey-Bass.

Halloran, J. (1981). *Supervision: The art of management.* Englewood Cliffs, NJ: Prentice Hall.

Hamilton, J. C., & Spruill, J. (1999). Identifying and reducing risk factors related to trainee-client sexual misconduct. *Professional Psychology: Research and Practice, 30,* 318–327.

Hampton, N. Z. (2002). Teaching a vocational assessment course on-line: Design and implementation. *Rehabilitation Education, 16,* 357–371.

Handelsman, M., Gottlieb, M., & Knapp, S. (2005). Training ethical psychologists: An acculturation model. *Professional Psychology: Research and Practice, 36,* 59–65.

Haney, W. (2000). The myth of the Texas miracle in education. *Educational Policy Analysis Archives, 8*(41). Retrieved December 7, 2007, from http://epaa.asu.edu/epaa/v8n41/

Hansen, N. D., Pepitone-Areola-Rockwell, F., & Greene, A. F. (2000). Multicultural competence: Criteria and case examples. *Professional Psychology: Research and Practice, 31,* 652–660.

Hansen, N. D., Randazzo, K. V., Schwartz, A., Marshall, M., Kalis, D., Frazier, R., et al. (2006). Do we practice what we preach? An exploratory study of multicultural psychotherapy competencies. *Professional Psychology: Research and Practice, 37,* 66–74.

Harris, M., & Turner, P. (1985–1986). Gay and lesbian parents. *Journal of Homosexuality, 12,* 101–113.

Harry, B., Allen, N., & McLaughlin, M. (1996). "Old-fashioned, good teachers": African American parents' views of effective early instruction. *Learning Disabilities: Research & Practice, 11,* 193–201.

Hart, G. M., & Nance, D. (2003). Styles of counselor supervision as perceived by supervisors and supervisees. *Counselor Education and Supervision, 43,* 146–159.

Harvey, V. S. (1995). Interagency collaboration: Providing a system of care for students. *Special Services in the Schools, 10,* 165–181.

Harvey, V. S. (1997). Improving readability of psychological reports. *Professional Psychology: Research and Practice, 28,* 271–274.

Harvey, V. S. (2005a, April). *The effect of supervision variables on school psychologists' job burnout.* Paper presented at the annual convention of the National Association of School Psychologists, Atlanta, GA.

Harvey, V. S. (2005b, August). Evaluations of on-line courses and programs. In N. Z. Hampton (Chair), *Pedagogy and technology: Issues related to teaching Web-based psychology courses.* Symposium conducted at the annual convention of the American Psychological Association, Washington, DC.

Harvey, V. S. (2006). Variables affecting the clarity of psychological reports. *Journal of Clinical Psychology, 62,* 5–18.

Harvey, V. S. (2008). *Qualitative investigations into clinical, administrative, and systemic supervision of school psychologists.* Unpublished manuscript.

Harvey, V. S., Bowser, P., Carlson, J. F., Grossman, F., & Kruger, L. (1998, April). *School psychologists and high technology: Ethical dilemmas and considerations.* Symposium conducted at the annual convention of the National Association of School Psychologists, Orlando, FL.

Harvey, V. S., & Carlson, J. F. (2003). Ethical and professional issues with computer-related technology. *School Psychology Review, 32,* 92–107.

Harvey, V. S., & Chickie-Wolfe, L. A. (2007). *Fostering independent learning: Practical strategies to promote student success.* New York: Guilford Press.

Harvey, V. S., & Struzziero, J. A. (2000). *Effective supervision in school psychology.* Bethesda, MD: National Association of School Psychologists.

Hausknecht, J. P., Day, D. V., & Thomas, S. C. (2004). Applicant reaction to selection procedures: An updated model and meta-analysis. *Personnel Psychology, 57,* 639–683.

Hayes, S. C., Follette, V. M., & Linehan, M. M. (2004). *Mindfulness* and *acceptance: Expanding* the *cognitive-behavioral tradition.* New York: Guilford Press.

Haynes, R., Corey, C., & Moulton, P. (2003). *Professional supervision in the helping professions: A practical guide.* Pacific Grove, CA: Brooks/Cole.

Hays, P. A. (2001). *Addressing cultural complexities in practice: A framework for clinicians and counselors.* Washington, DC: American Psychological Association.

Health Insurance Portability and Accountability Act of 1996, Pub. L. No. 104-191, 110 Stat. 1936 (1996).

Heckner, C., & Giard, A. (2005). A comparison of on-site and telepsychiatry supervision. *American Psychiatric Nurses Association Journal, 11*(1), 35–41.

Hehir, T. (2002). Eliminating ableism in education. *Harvard Educational Review, 72*(1), 1–32.

Hehir, T. (2007). Confronting ableism. *Educational Leadership, 64*(5), 9–15.

Helbok, C. M., Marinelli, R. P., & Walls, R. T. (2006). National survey of ethical practices across rural and urban communities. *Professional Psychology: Research and Practice, 37,* 36–44.

Heller, L. R., & Fantuzzo, J. W. (1993). Reciprocal peer tutoring and parent partnership: Does parent involvement make a difference? *School Psychology Review, 22,* 517–535.

Helms, J. E., & Cook, D. A. (1999). *Using race and culture in counseling and psychotherapy.* Boston: Allyn & Bacon.

Hembree-Kigin, T. L., & McNeil, C. B. (1995). *Parent-child interaction therapy.* New York: Plenum Press.

Hendley, S. L. (2007). Use positive behavior support for inclusion in the general education classroom. *Intervention in School and Clinic, 42,* 225–228.

Henning-Stout, M. (1994). *Responsive assessment: A new way of thinking about learning.* San Francisco: Jossey-Bass.

Henning-Stout, M. (1996). ¿Que podemos hacer? Roles for school psychologists with Mexican and Latino migrant children and families. *School Psychology Review, 25,* 152–164.

Henning-Stout, M. (1999). Learning consultation: An ethnographic analysis. *Journal of School Psychology, 37,* 73–98.

Henry, M. A., & Beasley, W. W. (1982). *Supervising student teaching the professional way: A guide for cooperating teachers* (3rd ed.). Terre Haute, IN: Sycamore Press.

Herlihy, B., Gray, N., & McCollum, V. (2002). Legal and ethical issues in school counseling supervision. *Professional School Counseling, 6,* 55–60.

Hernandez, M., & Issacs, M. R. (1998). *Promoting cultural competence in children's mental health services.* Baltimore: Brookes.

Heron, T. E., Martz, S. A., & Margolis, H. (1996). Ethical and legal issues in consultation. *Remedial and Special Education, 17,* 377–385.

Hersey, P. (2002). Paul Hersey defines situational leadership terms. *Journal of Leadership Studies, 8,* 87.

Heru, A., Strong, D., Price, M., & Recupero, P. (2004). Boundaries in psychotherapy supervision. *American Journal of Psychotherapy, 58,* 76–89.

Hightower, A. D., Johnson, D., & Haffey, W. G. (1995). Best practices in adopting a prevention program. In A. Thomas & J. Grimes (Eds.), *Best practices in school psychology III* (pp. 311–323). Silver Spring, MD: National Association of School Psychologists.

Hirsch, E. D. (1999). *The schools we need and why we don't have them.* New York: Anchor Books.

Hoagwood, K. (2003). Ethical issues in child and adolescent psychosocial treatment research. In A. E. Kazdin & J. R. Weisz (Eds.), *Evidence-based psychotherapies for children and adolescents* (pp. 60–75). New York: Guilford Press.

Hodgetts, R. M. (1996). *Implementing TQM in small and medium size organizations: A step-by-step guide.* New York: AMACOM.

Hoffman, L. (2002). *Family therapy: An intimate history.* New York: Norton.

Hofstede, G. (1993). Cultural constraints in management theories. *Academy of Management Executive, 7,* 81–90.

Holloway, E. L. (1995). *Clinical supervision: A systems approach.* Thousand Oaks, CA: SAGE.

Hook, C. L., & DuPaul, G. J. (1999). Parent tutoring for students with attention-deficit-hyperactivity disorder: Effects on reading performance at home and school. *School Psychology Review, 28,* 60–75.

Horn, J. L. (1991). Measurement of intellectual capabilities: A review of theory. In K. S. McGrew, J. K. Werder, & R. W. Woodcock (Eds.), *The Woodcock-Johnson revised technical manual.* Chicago: Riverside.

Horn, J. L., & Noll, J. (1997). Human cognitive capabilities: Gf-Gc theory. In D. P. Flanagan, J. L. Genshaft, & P. L. Harrison (Eds.), *Contemporary intellectual assessment: Theories, tests, and issues* (pp. 53–91). New York: Guilford Press.

Horvath, A. O., & Greenberg, L. S. (1989). Development and validation of the Working Alliance Inventory. *Journal of Counseling Psychology, 36,* 223–233.

Hosp, J. L., & Reschly, D. J. (2002). Regional differences in school psychology practice. *School Psychology Review, 32,* 11–29.

Houle, C. O. (1984). *Continuing learning in the professions.* San Francisco: Jossey-Bass.

House, J. S. (1981). *Work stress and social support.* Reading, MA: Addison-Wesley.

Houser, R. (1998). *Counseling and educational research: Evaluation and application.* Thousand Oaks, CA: SAGE.

Howell, K. W., & Nolet, V. (2000). *Curriculum-based evaluation: Instruction and decision-making.* Belmont, CA: Wadsworth.

Hoyt, B. R., & Shirvani, S. (2002). A study of the factors influencing satisfaction with distance learning. *International Journal on E-Learning, 1,* 14–19.

Huberty, T. J., & Huebner, E. S. (1988). A national survey of burnout among school psychologists. *Psychology in the Schools, 25,* 54–61.

Huck, S. W. (2007). *Reading statistics and research* (5th ed.). Needham Heights, MA: Allyn & Bacon.

Hunley, S. A., Harvey, V. S., Curtis, M. J., Portnoy, L. A., Grier, J. E. C., & Helffrich, D. (2000). School psychology supervisors: A national study of demographics and professional practices. *Communiqué, 28*(8), 32–33.

Hunsley, J. (2007). Training psychologists for evidence-based practice. *Canadian Psychology, 48*(1), 32–42.

Hunt, W. (2001). The use of the countertransference in supervision. In S. Gill (Ed.), *The supervisory alliance: Facilitating the psychotherapist's learning experience* (pp. 165–180). Lanham, MD: Jason Aronson.

Huprich, S. K., & Rudd, M. D. (2004). A national survey of trainee impairment in clinical, counseling, and school psychology doctoral programs and internships. *Journal of Clinical Psychology, 60,* 43–52.

Huq, Z. (2006). Six-Sigma implementation through competency based perspective. *Journal of Change Management, 6,* 277–289.

Hyrkäs, K. (2005). Clinical supervision: Burnout and job satisfaction among mental health and psychiatric nurses in Finland. *Issues in Mental Health Nursing, 26,* 531–556.

Illback, R. J., & Morrissey, W. M. (1985). Personnel management. In C. A. Maher (Ed.), *Professional self-management: Techniques for special services providers* (pp. 149–162). Baltimore: Brookes.

Individuals With Disabilities Education Act, Public L. No. 101-476, 104 Stat. 1142 (1990).

Individuals With Disabilities Education Improvement Act of 2004, Pub. L. No. 108-446, 118 Stat. 2647 (2004).

Ingraham, C. L. (2000). Consultation through a multicultural lens: Multicultural and cross-cultural consultation in schools. *The School Psychology Review, 29,* 320–343.

Inman, A. G. (2006). Supervisor multicultural competence and its relation to supervisory process and outcome. *Journal of Marital & Family Therapy, 32,* 73–85.

Institute for the Development of Educational Achievement. (n.d.). *Effective, research-based reading programs.* Retrieved December 8, 2007, from http://reading.uoregon.edu/curricula/index.php

Institute of Education Sciences, What Works Clearinghouse. (n.d.). [Web site]. Retrieved December 10, 2007, from http://ies.ed.gov/ncee/wwc/

Ivey, A. E., & Ivey, M. B. (2006). *Intentional interviewing and counseling: Facilitating client development in a multicultural society.* New York: Thomson Learning.

Jackson, D. N. (2003). *Leadership skills profile (LSP).* Port Huron, MI: Sigma Assessment Systems.

Jacob, B. A. (2001). Getting tough? The impact of high school graduation exams. *Education Evaluation and Policy Analysis, 23,* 99–121.

Jacob, S., & Hartshorne, T. S. (2007). *Ethics and law for school psychologists* (5th ed.). New York: Wiley.

Jamison, K. R. (1995). *The unquiet mind.* New York: Random House.

Jaskyte, K. (2003). Assessing changes in employees' perceptions of leadership behavior, job design, and organizational arrangements and their job satisfaction and commitment. *Administration in Social Work, 27,* 25–39.

Jerrell, J. M. (1984). Boundary-spanning functions served by rural school psychologists. *Journal of School Psychology, 22,* 259–271.

John, J. (2002). *Black baby white hands: A view from the crib.* Silver Spring, MD: Soul Water Rising.

Johnson, D. W., & Johnson, F. P. (1994). *Joining together: Group theory and group skills.* Boston: Allyn & Bacon.

Johnson, L. R. (1998). Performance evaluation of special education administrators: Considerations and recommendations. *NASSP Bulletin, 82,* 24–32.

Joinson, A. (1998). Causes and implications of disinhibited behavior on the Internet. In J. Gackenbach (Ed.), *Psychology and the Internet: Intrapersonal, interpersonal, and transpersonal implications* (pp. 43–60). San Diego, CA: Academic Press.

Joyce, B., & Showers, B. (1995). *Student achievement through staff development.* White Plains, NY: Longman.

Kagan, H. K., & Kagan, N. I. (1997). Interpersonal Process Recall: Influencing human interactions. In C. E. Watkins (Ed.), *Handbook of psychotherapy supervision* (pp. 296–309). New York: Wiley.

Kaiser, T. L. (1997). *Supervisory relationships: Exploring the human element.* Pacific Grove, CA: Brooks/Cole.

Kamphaus, R. W. (2001). *Clinical assessment of child and adolescent intelligence* (2nd ed.). Boston: Allyn & Bacon.

Kampworth, T. J. (2003). *Collaborative consultation in the schools: Effective practices for students with learning and behavior problems.* Upper Saddle River, NJ: Merrill.

Kanz, J. E. (2001). Clinical-supervision.com: Issues in the provision of online supervision. *Professional Psychology: Research and Practice, 32,* 415–420.

Kaslow, N. J. (2004). Competencies in professional psychology. *American Psychologist, 59,* 774–781.

Kaufman, R. A. (1972). *Educational systems planning.* Englewood Cliffs, NJ: Prentice Hall.

Kavale, K. A., Forness, S. R., & Siperstein, G. N. (1999). *Efficacy of special education and related services.* Washington, DC: American Association on Mental Retardation.

Kavanagh, D. J., Spence, S. H., Strong, J., Wilson, J., Sturk, H., & Crow, N. (2003). Supervision practices in allied mental health: Relationships of supervision characteristics to perceived impact and job satisfaction. *Mental Health Services Research, 5,* 187–195.

Keith, T. Z. (2008). Best practices in using and conducting research in applied settings. In A. Thomas & J. Grimes (Eds.), *Best practices in school psychology V* (pp. 2166–2176). Bethesda, MD: National Association of School Psychologists.

Kendall, P. C., & Beidas, R. S. (2007). Smoothing the train for dissemination of evidence-based practices for youth: Flexibility within fidelity. *Professional Psychology: Research and Practice, 38,* 13–20.

Kendall, P. C., & Braswell, L. (1985). *Cognitive-behavioral therapy for impulsive children.* New York: Guilford Press.

Kendall, P. C., & Hedtke, K. (2006). *Cognitive-behavior therapy for anxious children: Therapist manual* (3rd ed.). Ardmore, PA: Workbook.

Kerl, S. B., Garcia, J. L., McCullough, C. S., & Maxwell, M. E. (2002). Systematic evaluation of professional performance: Legally supported procedure and process. *Counselor Education and Supervision, 41,* 321–332.

Kirkpatrick, M., Smith, C., & Roy, R. (1981). Lesbian mothers and their children. *American Journal of Orthopsychiatry, 51,* 545–551.

Kirschenbaum, H., & Glaser, B. (1978). *Developing support groups.* LaJolla, CA: University Associates.

Kiselica, M. S. (1998). *Confronting prejudice and racism during multicultural training.* Alexandria, VA: American Counseling Association.

Knoff, H. M. (1986). Supervision in school psychology: The forgotten or future path to effective services? *School Psychology Review, 15,* 529–545.

Knoff, H. M. (2000). Organizational development and strategic planning for the millennium: A blueprint toward effective school discipline, safety, and crisis prevention. *Psychology in the Schools, 37,* 17–32.

Knoff, H. M. (2002). Best practices in facilitating school reform, organizational change, and strategic planning. In A. Thomas & J. Grimes (Eds.), *Best practices in school psychology IV* (pp. 235–253). Bethesda, MD: National Association of School Psychologists.

Knoff, H. M. (2008). Best practices in strategic planning, organizational development, and school effectiveness. In A. Thomas & J. Grimes (Eds.), *Best practices in school psychology V* (pp. 903–916). Bethesda, MD: National Association of School Psychologists.

Knoff, H. M., Hines, C. V., & Kromrey, J. D. (1995). Finalizing the Consultant Effectiveness Scale: An analysis and validation of the characteristics of effective consultants. *School Psychology Review, 24,* 480–500.

Knotek, S. E., Rosenfield, S. A., Gravois, T. A., & Babinski, L. M. (2003). The process of fostering consultee development during instructional consultation. *Journal of Educational & Psychological Consultation, 14,* 303–328.

Koocher, G. P., & Keith-Spiegel, P. (1998). *Ethics in psychology: Professional standards and cases* (2nd ed.). New York: Oxford University Press.

Kotter, J. P. (1999). *John P. Kotter on what leaders really do.* Boston: Harvard Business School Press.

Kouser, B. K., & Posner, J. M. (1992). *Leadership process inventory.* San Francisco: Jossey-Bass.

Kovaleski, J. F., & Prasse, D. P. (2004, February). Response to instruction in the identification of learning disabilities: A guide for school teams. *Communiqué, 32*(5), Insert.

Kozol, J. (1991). *Savage inequalities: Children in America's schools.* New York: HarperCollins.

Kozol, J. (2005). *The shame of a nation: The restoration of apartheid schooling in America.* New York: Crown.

Krashen, S. D. (1982). *Principals and practice in second language acquisition.* New York: Pergamon Press.

Kratochwill, T. R., Bergan, J. R., & Mace, F. C. (1981). Practitioner competencies needed for implementation of behavior psychology in the schools: Issues in supervision. *School Psychology Review, 10,* 434–444.

Kratochwill, T. R., Elliott, S. N., & Callan-Stoiber, K. (2002). Best practices in school-based problem-solving consultation. In A. Thomas & J. Grimes (Eds.), *Best practices in school psychology IV* (pp. 583–608). Bethesda, MD: National Association of School Psychologists.

Kratochwill, T. R., & Stoiber, K. C. (2002). Evidence-based interventions in school psychology: Conceptual foundations of the Procedural and Coding Manual of Division 16 and the Society for the Study of School Psychology Task Force. *School Psychology Quarterly, 17,* 341–389.

Kruger, L. J., Macklem, G., Weksel, T., & Kalinsky, R. (2001, April). *Professional development and the Internet: What school psychologists should know.* Paper presented at the annual convention of the National Association of School Psychologists, Washington, DC.

Kruger, L. J., & Struzziero, J. A. (1997). Computer-mediated peer support of consultation: Case description and evaluation. *Journal of Educational & Psychological Consultation, 8,* 75–90.

Kruger, L. J., Wandle, C., & Struzziero, J. (2007). Coping with the stress of high stakes testing. In L. J. Kruger & D. Shriberg (Eds.), *High stakes testing: New challenges and opportunities for school psychologists* (pp. 109–128). Binghamton, NY: Haworth Press.

Krumboltz, J. D., & Thorensen, C. E. (1969). *Behavioral counseling: Cases and techniques.* New York: Holt, Rinehart & Winston.

Kurdek, L., & Schmitt, J. (1987). Relationship quality of partners in heterosexual married, heterosexual co-habiting, and gay and lesbian relationships. *Journal of Personality and Social Psychology, 14,* 57–68.

Ladany, N., Constantine, M. G., Miller, K., Erickson, C. D., & Muse-Burke, J. L. (2000). Supervisor countertransference: A qualitative investigation into its identification and description. *Journal of Counseling Psychology, 41,* 102–115.

Ladany, N., Hill, C. E., Corbett, M. M., & Nutt, E. A. (1996). Nature, extent, and importance of what psychotherapy trainees do not disclose to their supervisors. *Journal of Counseling Psychology, 43,* 10–24.

Ladany, N., Inman, A. G., Constantine, M. G., & Hofheinz, E. W. (1997). Supervisee multicultural case conceptualization ability and self-reported multicultural competence as functions of supervisee racial identity and supervisor focus. *Journal of Counseling Psychology, 44,* 284–293.

Ladany, N., & Lehrman-Waterman, D. E. (1999). The content and frequency of supervisor self-disclosures and their relationship to supervisor style and the supervisory working alliance. *Counselor Education and Supervision, 38,* 143–160.

Ladany, N., Lehrman-Waterman, D., Molinaro, M., & Wolgast, B. (1999). Psychotherapy supervision ethical practices: Adherence to guidelines, the supervisory working alliance, and supervisee satisfaction. *Counseling Psychologist, 27,* 443–475.

Ladany, N., & Walker, J. A. (2003). Supervision self-disclosure: Balancing the uncontrollable narcissist with the indomitable altruist. *Journal of Clinical Psychology, 59,* 611–621.

Ladany, N., Walker, J. A., & Malincoff, D. S. (2001). Supervisory style: Its relation to the supervisory working alliance and supervisor self-disclosure. *Counselor Education and Supervision, 40,* 263–275.

LaFromboise, T. D., Coleman, H. L. K., & Hernandez, A. (1991). Development and factor structure of the Cross-Cultural Counseling Inventory—Revised. *Professional Psychology: Research and Practice, 22,* 380–388.

Lam, S., & Yuen, M. (2004). Continuing professional development in school psychology: Perspective from Hong Kong. *School Psychology International, 25,* 480–494.

Lamb, D. H. (1999). Addressing impairment and its relationship to professional boundary issues: A response to Forrest, Elman, Gizara, and Vacha-Haase. *Counseling Psychologist, 27,* 702–711.

Lamb, D. H., Cochran, D. J., & Jackson, V. R. (1991). Training and organizational issues associated with identifying and responding to intern impairment. *Professional Psychology: Research and Practice, 22,* 291–296.

Lambert, M. J., & Hawkins, E. J. (2001) Using information about patient progress in supervision: Are outcomes enhanced? *Australian Psychologist, 36,* 131–138.

Lane, R. J., Bishop, H. L., & Wilson-Jones, L. (2005). Creating an effective strategic plan for the school district. *Journal of Instructional Psychology, 32,* 197–204.

Lappin, J., & Hardy, K. V. (1997). Keeping context in view: The heart of supervision. In T. C. Todd & C. L. Storm (Eds.), *The complete systemic supervisor: Context, philosophy, and pragmatics* (pp. 41–58). Boston: Allyn & Bacon.

Laszlo, E. (1972). *The systems view of the world: The natural philosophy of new developments in the sciences.* New York: George Braziller.

Lau v. Nichols, 414 U.S. 563 (1974).

Lazarus, A. A. (2000). Multimodal replenishment. *Professional Psychology: Research and Practice, 31,* 93–94.

Lazarus, R. S. (1966). *Psychological stress and the coping process.* New York: McGraw-Hill.

Lee, D. M. (2005). Hiring the best teachers: Gaining a competitive edge in the teacher recruitment process. *Public Personnel Management, 34,* 263–269.

Leff, S. S., Power, T. J., Manz, P. H., Costigan, T. E., & Nabors, L. A. (2001). School-based aggression prevention programs for young children: Current status and implications for violence prevention. *School Psychology Review, 30,* 343–360.

Lehr, R. (2005). Using Computer-Assisted Supervision in counsellor education programs. *Canadian Journal of Counselling, 39,* 29–39.

Lehrman-Waterman, D., & Ladany, N. (2001). Development and validation of the evaluation process within Supervision Inventory. *Journal of Counseling Psychology, 48,* 168–177.

Le Maistre, C., Boudreau, S., & Paré, A. (2007). Mentor or evaluator? Assisting and assessing newcomers to the professions. *Journal of Workplace Learning, 18,* 344–354.

Leonard, E. C., & Hilgert, R. L. (2004). *Supervision: Concepts and practices of management* (9th ed.). Mason, OH: Thomson South-Western.

Lepage, K., Kratochwill, T. R., & Elliott, S. N. (2004). Competency-based behavior consultation training: An evaluation of consultant outcomes, treatment effects, and consumer satisfaction. *School Psychology Quarterly, 19,* 1–28.

Lerner, J., & Kline, F. (2005). *Learning disabilities and related disorders: Characteristics and teaching strategies.* Boston: Houghton Mifflin.

Levinson, E. M. (1990). Actual/desired role functioning, perceived control over role functioning, and job satisfaction among school psychologists. *Psychology in the Schools, 27,* 64–74.

Levinson, E. M. (1991). Predictors of school psychologist satisfaction with school system policies/practices and advancement opportunities. *Psychology in the Schools, 28,* 256–266.

Levinson, E. M., Fetchkan, R., & Hohenshil, T. H. (1988). Job satisfaction among practicing school psychologists revisited. *School Psychology Review, 17,* 101–112.

Levinson, H. (2002). Assessing organizations. In R. L. Lowman (Ed.), *The California School of Organizational Studies handbook of organizational consulting psychology: A comprehensive guide to theory, skills, and techniques* (pp. 314–343). San Francisco: Jossey-Bass.

Lewis, G. J., Greenburg, S. L., & Hatch, D. B. (1988). Peer consultation groups for psychologists in private practice: A national survey. *Professional Psychology: Research and Practice, 9,* 81–86.

Lichtenstein, R., & Fischetti, B. A. (1998). How long does a psychoeducational evaluation take? An urban Connecticut study. *Professional Psychology: Research and Practice, 29,* 144–148.

Lidz, C., & Elliott, J. (2000). *Dynamic assessment: Prevailing models and applications.* New York: JAI Press.

Likert, R. (1967). *The human organization: Its management and value.* New York: McGraw-Hill.

Lilienfeld, S., & O'Donohue, W. (2007). *The great ideas of clinical science: 17 principles that every mental health professional should understand.* New York: Routledge.

Littrell, P. C., Billingsley, B. S., & Cross, L. H. (1994). The effects of principal support on special and general educators' stress, job satisfaction, school commitment, health, and intent to stay in teaching. *Remedial and Special Education, 15,* 297–310.

Lochman, J., Curry, J. F., Dane, H., & Ellis, M. (2000). The Anger Coping Program: An empirically-supported treatment for aggressive children. *Residential Treatment for Children & Youth, 18,* 63–73.

Loen, R. O. (1994). *Superior supervision: The 10% solution.* New York: Lexington Books.

London, M., & Smither, J. W. (1995). Can multi-source feedback change perceptions of goal accomplishments, self-evaluations, and performance-related outcomes? Theory based applications and directions for research. *Personnel Psychology, 48,* 803–839.

Long, J. K. (1997). Sexual orientation: Implications for the supervisory process. In T. C. Todd & C. L. Storm (Eds.), *The complete systemic supervisor: Context, philosophy, and pragmatics* (pp. 59–71). Boston: Allyn & Bacon.

Lunenburg, F. C., & Ornstein, A. C. (2004). *Educational administration: Concepts and practices* (4th ed.). Belmont, CA: Thomson/Wadsworth.

Lynch, E. W., & Hanson, M. J. (1998). *Developing cross-cultural competence: A guide to working with children and their families* (2nd ed.). Baltimore: Brookes.

Macklem, G. L. (2003). *Bullying and teasing: Social power in children's groups.* New York: Kluwer Academic/Plenum.

Macklem, G. L. (2006, December). *Technology 101: Safety, security, professional responsibility and common sense.* Paper presented at the fall conference of the Massachusetts School Psychology Association, Woburn, MA.

MacLeod, I. R., Jones, K. M., Somers, C. L., & Havey, J. M. (2001). An evaluation of the effectiveness of school-based behavioral consultation. *Journal of Educational & Psychological Consultation, 12,* 203–216.

Maddux, C. D., & Johnson, L. (1993). Best practices in computer-assisted assessment. In H. B. Vance (Ed.), *Best practices in assessment for school and clinical settings* (pp. 177–200). Brandon, VT: Clinical Psychology.

Magnuson, S., Wilcoxon, S. A., & Norem, K. (2000). Clinical supervision of pre-licensed counselors: Recommendations for consideration and practice. *Journal of Mental Health Counseling, 22,* 176–188.

Maher, C. A. (1984). *Planning and evaluating special education services.* Englewood Cliffs, NJ: Prentice Hall.

Maher, C. A., & Cook, S. A. (1985). Time management. In C. A. Maher (Ed.), *Professional self-management: Techniques for special services providers* (pp. 23–44). Baltimore: Brookes.

Martindale, T., & Ahern, T. C. (2001). The effects of three Web-based delivery models on undergraduate college student achievement. *International Journal of Educational Telecommunications, 7,* 379–393.

Mary, N. L. (2005). Transformational leadership in human service organizations. *Administration in Social Work, 29,* 105–118.

Maslow, A. H. (1954). *Motivation and personality.* New York: Harper & Row.

Maslow, A. H. (1970). New introduction: Religions, values, and peak-experiences. *Journal of Transpersonal Psychology, 2,* 83–90.

Matarazzo, J. D. (1985). Clinical psychology test interpretations by computer: Hardware outpaces software. *Computers in Human Behavior, 1,* 235–253.

Mather, N., & Gregg, N. (2006). Specific learning disabilities: Clarifying, not eliminating, a construct. *Professional Psychology: Research and Practice, 37,* 99–106.

McClosky-Armstrong, T. (2001). Mental health. In S. Burgiss, R. Sprang, & J. Tracy (Eds.), *Telehealth technology guidelines.* Available from the Health Resources and Services Administration Web site: http://ask.hrsa.gov/detail.cfm?PubID=HRS00283.

McColley, S. H., & Baker, E. L. (1982). Training activities and styles of beginning supervisors: A survey. *Professional Psychology: Research and Practice, 13,* 283–292.

McConaughy, S. H., Kay, P. J., & Fitzgerald, M. (1999). The achieving, behaving, caring project for preventing ED: Two-year outcomes. *Journal of Emotional and Behavioral Disorders, 7,* 224–239.

McGlothlin, J., Rainey, S., & Kindsvatter, A. (2005). Suicidal clients and supervisees: A model for considering supervisor roles. *Counselor Education and Supervision, 45,* 135–146.

McGoldrick, M. (1998). *Re-visioning family therapy: Race, culture and gender in clinical practice.* New York: Guilford Press.

McGregor, D. (1966). The human side of enterprise. In W. G. Bennis & E. H. Schein (Eds.), *Leadership and motivation: Essays of Douglas McGregor* (pp. 10–37). Cambridge, MA: MIT Press.

McGrew, K. S., & Flanagan, D. P. (1998). *The intelligence test desk reference.* Needham Heights, MA: Allyn & Bacon.

McGrew, K. S., & Woodcock, R. W. (2001). *Woodcock-Johnson battery* (3rd ed.). Itasca, IL: Riverside.

McInerney, J. F. (1985). Authority management. In C. A. Maher (Ed.), *Professional self-management: Techniques for special services providers* (pp. 129–148). Baltimore: Brookes.

McIntosh, D. E., & Phelps, L. (2000). Supervision in school psychology: Where will the future take us? *Psychology in the Schools, 37,* 33–38.

McIntosh, P. (1989, July/August). White privilege: Unpacking the invisible knapsack. *Peace and Freedom,* pp. 10–12.

McMahon, M., & Patton, W. (2000). Career counsellors, support and lifelong learning: A case for clinical supervision. *International Journal for the Advancement of Counselling, 22,* 157–169.

McMahon, M., & Simons, R. (2004). Supervision training for professional counselors: An exploratory study. *Counselor Education and Supervision, 43,* 301–309, 349.

McNeill, B. W., Stoltenberg, C. D., & Romans, J. S. C. (1992). The Integrated Developmental Model of supervision: Scale development and validation procedures. *Professional Psychology: Research and Practice, 23,* 504–508.

McWhirter, D., & Mattison, A. (1984). Stages in the development of gay relationships. In J. DeCecco (Ed.), *Gay relationships* (pp. 161–168). New York: Harrington Park.

Mead, D. (1990). *Effective supervision: A task-oriented model for the developing professions.* New York: Brunner/Mazel.

Meichenbaum, D. (1977). *Cognitive-behavior modification: An integrative approach.* New York: Plenum Press.

Merisotis, J. P., & Phipps, R. A. (1999). What's the difference? (College-level distance and classroom-based education). *Change, 31,* 12–18.

Merrell, K. W. (1999). *Behavioral, social, and emotional assessment of children and adolescents.* Mahwah, NJ: Lawrence Erlbaum.

Merrell, K. W. (2001). *Helping students overcome depression and anxiety: A practical guide.* New York: Guilford Press.

Merrell, K. W., Ervin, R. A., & Gimpel, G. A. (Eds.). (2006). *School psychology for the 21st century.* New York: Guilford Press.

Messer, S. B. (2004). Evidence-based practice: Beyond empirically supported treatments. *Professional Psychology: Research and Practice, 35,* 580–588.

Meyers, J. (2002). A 30 year perspective on best practices for consultation training. *Journal of Educational & Psychological Consultation, 13,* 35–54.

Meyers, J., Meyers, A. B., & Grogg, K. (2004). Prevention through consultation: A model to guide future developments in the field of school psychology. *Journal of Educational & Psychological Consultation, 15,* 257–276.

Meyers, J., & Nastasi, B. K. (1999). Primary prevention in school settings. In T. B. Gutkin & C. R. Reynolds (Eds.), *The handbook of school psychology* (3rd ed., pp. 764–799). New York: Wiley.

Mikesell, R. H., Lusterman, D. D., & McDaniel, S. H. (Eds.). (1995). *Integrating family therapy: Handbook of family psychology and systems theory.* Washington, DC: American Psychological Association.

Milan, F., Parish, S., & Reichgott, M. (2006). A model for educational feedback based on clinical communication skills strategies: Beyond the "feedback sandwich." *Teaching and Learning in Medicine, 18,* 42–47.

Miles, M. (1965). *Planned change and organizational health: Figure and ground. Change processes in the public schools.* Eugene: University of Oregon Center for the Advanced Study of Educational Administration.

Miller, K. L., Miller, S. M., & Evans, W. J. (2002). Computer-assisted live supervision in college counseling centers. *Journal of College Counseling, 5,* 187–192.

Milne, D. L., & James, I. A. (2000). A systematic review of effective cognitive-behavioural supervision. *British Journal of Clinical Psychology, 39,* 111–127.

Milne, D. L., & Oliver, V. (2000). Flexible formats of clinical supervision: Description, evaluation, and implementation. *Journal of Mental Health, 9,* 291–304.

Milne, D. L., Pilkington, J., Gracie, J., & James, I. (2003). Transferring skills from supervision to therapy: A qualitative and quantitative N=1 analysis. *Behavioural and Cognitive Psychotherapy, 31,* 193–202.

Milne, D. L., & Roberts, H. (2002). An educational and organizational needs assessment for staff training. *Behavioural and Cognitive Psychotherapy, 30,* 153–164.

Milne, D. L., Woodward, K., Hanner, S., Iceton, J., Fitzsimmons, A., & Rochester, J. (2003). An illustration of delivering evidence-based practice through staff training: Multidimensional process, outcome, and organizational evaluation. *Behavioural and Cognitive Psychotherapy, 31,* 85–89.

Miltiadou, M. (2001). Computer-mediated communication in the on-line classroom. *International Journal of Educational Telecommunications, 7,* 407–420.

Minuchin, P., Colapinto, J., & Minuchin, S. (1998). *Working with the families of the poor.* New York: Guilford Press.

Minuchin, S. (1974). *Families and family therapy.* Boston: Harvard University Press.

Mithaug, D. K., & Mithaug, D. E. (2003). Effects of teacher-directed versus student-directed instruction on self-management of young children with disabilities. *Journal of Applied Behavior Analysis, 36,* 133–136.

Miville, M. L., Rosa, D., & Constantine, M. G. (2005). Building multicultural competence in clinical supervision. In M. G. Constantine & D. W. Sue (Eds.), *Strategies for building multicultural competencies in mental health and educational settings* (pp. 192–211). Hoboken, NJ: Wiley.

Mooney, J., & Cole, D. (2000). *Learning outside the lines.* New York: Simon & Schuster.

Morales, E. (2003). *Living in Spanglish: The search for Latino identity in America.* New York: St. Martin's Press.

Moreland, K. L. (1985). Validation of computer-based test interpretations: Problems and prospects. *Journal of Consulting and Clinical Psychology, 53,* 816–825.

Moreland, K. L. (1992). Computer-assisted psychological assessment. In M. Zeidner & R. Most (Eds.), *Psychological testing: An inside view* (pp. 343–376). Palo Alto, CA: Consulting Psychologists Press.

Mornell, P. (1998). *Hiring smart.* Berkeley, CA: Ten Speed Press.

Morrow, L. M., & Young, J. (1997). A family literacy program connecting school and home: Effects on attitude, motivation, and literacy achievement. *Journal of Educational Psychology, 89,* 736–742.

Moskowitz, S. A., & Rupert, P. A. (1983). Conflict resolution within the supervisory relationship. *Professional Psychology: Research and Practice, 14,* 632–641.

Mosley-Howard, G. S. (1995). Best practices in considering the role of culture. In A. Thomas & J. Grimes (Eds.), *Best practices in school psychology III* (pp. 337–345). Silver Spring, MD: National Association of School Psychologists.

Mowder, B. A., & Prasse, D. P. (1981). An evaluation model for school psychological services. *Evaluation and Program Planning, 4,* 377–383.

Mulcahy, C., & Betts, L. (2005). Transforming a culture: An exploration of unit culture and nursing retention within a neonatal unit. *Journal of Nursing Management, 13,* 519–523.

Munson, C. E. (1991). Duty to warn and the role of the supervisor. *Clinical Supervisor, 9,* 1–6.

Munson, C. E. (2002). *Handbook of clinical social work supervision* (3rd ed.). New York: Haworth Press.

Muratori, M. C. (2001). Examining supervisor impairment from the counselor trainee's perspective. *Counselor Education and Supervision, 41,* 41–56.

Murphy, J. P. (1981). Roles, functions, and competencies of supervisors of school psychologists. *School Psychology Review, 10,* 417–424.

Murphy, J. P., DeEsch, J. B., & Strein, W. O. (1998). School counselors and school psychologists: Partners in student services. *Professional School Counseling, 2,* 85–87.

Nagle, R. J. (1995). Best practices in conducting needs assessment. In A. Thomas & J. Grimes (Eds.), *Best practices in school psychology III* (pp. 265, 421–430). Silver Spring, MD: National Association of School Psychologists.

Nam, V. (Ed.). (2001). *YELL-oh girls! Emerging voices explore culture, identity, and growing up Asian American.* New York: Perennial Currents/HarperCollins.

Napier, A., & Whitaker, C. (1978). *The family crucible.* New York: Harper & Row.

Nathan, P. E., & Gorman, J. M. (Eds.). (2002). *A guide to treatments that work.* New York: Oxford University Press.

National Association of School Psychologists. (n.d.). *PREPaRE: School crisis prevention and intervention training curriculum.* Retrieved January 20, 2008, from http://www.nasponline.org/prepare/index.aspx

National Association of School Psychologists. (2000a). *Professional conduct manual* (3rd ed.). Bethesda, MD: Author.

National Association of School Psychologists. (2000b). *Standards for training programs and field placement programs in school psychology. Standards for the credentialing of school psychologists.* Bethesda, MD: Author.

National Association of School Psychologists. (2004). *NASP position statement on supervision in school psychology.* Retrieved January 22, 2008, from http://www.nasponline.org/about_nasp/positionpapers/supervision.pdf

National Association of School Psychologists. (2005). *NASP position statement on prevention and intervention research in schools.* Retrieved Feburary 3, 2008, from www.nasponline.org/about_nasp/positionpapers/prevention.pdf

National Association of School Psychologists. (2007). *NASP position statement on identification of students with specific learning disabilities.* Retrieved January 28, 2008, from www.nasponline.org/about_nasp/positionpapers/SLDPosition_2007.pdf

National Association of State Directors of Special Education. (2005). *Response to intervention policy considerations and implementation.* Alexandria, VA: Author.

National Council of Teachers of Mathematics. (n.d.). *Curriculum focal points for prekindergarten through Grade 8 mathematics.* Retrieved December 8, 2007, from http://www.nctm.org/focalpoints.aspx?ekmensel=c580fa7b_10_48_btnlink

National Education Association. (1975). *Code of ethics of the education profession.* Retrieved December 8, 2007, from http://www.nea.org/aboutnea/code.html

National Reading Panel. (2001). *Put reading first: The research building blocks for teaching children to read.* Available from http://www.nationalreadingpanel.org/Publications/researchread.htm

Nelson, M. L., & Friedlander, M. L. (2001). A close look at conflictual supervisory relationships: The trainee's perspective. *Journal of Counseling Psychology, 48,* 384–395.

Neufeldt, S. A. (1999). Training in thoughtful processes in supervision. In E. Holloway & M. Carroll (Eds.), *Training counselling supervisors: Strategies, methods and techniques* (pp. 92–105). London: SAGE.

Neufeldt, S. A., Iversen, J. N., & Juntunen, C. L. (1995). *Supervision strategies for the first practicum.* Alexandria, VA: American Counseling Association.

Newman, J., & Abbey, P. (2004). Microskills based counselor training using digital video editing software. In C. Crawford et al. (Eds.), *Proceedings of Society for Information Technology and Teacher Education International Conference 2004* (pp. 1303–1306). Chesapeake, VA: Association for the Advancement of Computing in Education.

Nichols, C. W. (1991). *Assessment of core goals (ACG).* Palo Alto, CA: Mind Garden.

Nieto, S. (2004). *Affirming diversity: The sociopolitical context of multicultural education* (4th ed.). Boston: Allyn & Bacon.

Nilsson, J., & Anderson, M. (2004). Supervising international students: The role of acculturation, role ambiguity, and multicultural discussions. *Professional Psychology: Research and Practice, 35,* 306–312.

Nilsson, J., & Dodds, A. (2006). A pilot phase in the development of the International Student Supervision Scale. *Journal of Multicultural Counseling and Development, 34,* 50–62.

No Child Left Behind Act of 2001, Pub. L. No. 107–110, 115 Stat. 1425 (2002).

Noe, R. A., Hollenbeck, J. R., Gerhart, B., & Wright, P. M. (1996). *Human resource management: Gaining a competitive advantage* (2nd ed.). Boston: McGraw-Hill.

Noell, G. H., Duhon, G. J., Gatti, S. L., & Connell, J. E. (2002). Consultation, follow-up, and implementation of behavior management interventions in general education. *School Psychology Review, 31,* 217–234.

Noell, G. H., & Witt, J. C. (1998). Toward a behavior analytic approach to consultation. In T. S. Watson & F. M. Gresham (Eds.), *Handbook of child behavior therapy* (pp. 41–57). New York: Plenum Press.

Noll, J. W. (2008). *Taking sides: Clashing views on educational issues* (14th ed.). Dubuque, IA: McGraw-Hill.

Norcross, J. C. (Ed.). (2002). *Psychotherapy relationships that work: Therapist contributions and responsiveness to patients.* New York: Oxford University Press.

Norcross, J. C., Karpiak, C. P., & Santoro, S. O. (2005). Clinical psychologists across the years: The division of clinical psychology from 1960 to 2003. *Journal of Clinical Psychology, 61,* 1467–1483.

Norcross, J. C., Koocher, G. P., & Garofalo, A. (2006). Discredited psychological treatments and tests: A Delphi poll. *Professional Psychology: Research and Practice, 37,* 515–522.

Oakland, T., & Gallegos, E. M. (2005). Selected legal issues affecting students from multicultural backgrounds. In C. L. Frisby & C. R. Reynolds (Eds.), *Comprehensive handbook of multicultural school psychology* (pp. 1048–1078). Hoboken, NJ: Wiley.

Obiakor, F. E. (2007). *Multicultural special education: Culturally responsive teaching.* Upper Saddle River, NJ: Pearson Education.

Occupational Safety and Health Act of 1970, 29 U.S.C. § 651 (2000).

Offir, B., Barth, I., Lev, Y., & Shteinbok, A. (2003). Teacher-student interactions and learning outcomes in a distance learning environment. *Internet and Higher Education, 6,* 65–75.

Ogles, B. M., Lambert, M. J., & Masters, K. S. (1996). *Assessing outcome in clinical practice.* Boston: Allyn & Bacon.

Okun, B., Fried, J., & Okun, M. L. (1999). *Understanding diversity.* Pacific Grove, CA: Brooks/Cole.

Olk, M. E., & Friedlander, M. L. (1992). Trainees' experiences of role conflict and role ambiguity in supervisory relationships. *Journal of Counseling Psychology, 39,* 389–397.

Olweus, D. (1997). Tackling peer victimization with a school-based intervention program. In D. P. Fry & K. Bjorkqvist (Eds.), *Cultural variation in conflict resolution: Alternatives to violence* (pp. 215–234). Mahwah, NJ: Lawrence Erlbaum.

O'Mahen, H. A., & Sloan, P. (2000). Looking ahead: Preparing psychologists for administrative roles in medical centers. *Professional Psychology: Research and Practice, 37,* 278–282.

O'Neill, R. E., Horner, R. H., Albin, R. W., Sprague, J. R., Storey, K., & Newton, J. S. (1997). *Functional assessment and program development for problem behavior: A practical handbook* (2nd ed.). Pacific Grove, CA: Brooks/Cole.

Ortiz, A. (1997). Learning disabilities occurring concomitantly with linguistic differences. *Journal of Learning Disabilities, 30,* 321–332.

Ortiz, S. O., & Flanagan, D. P. (2002). Best practices in working with culturally diverse children and families. In A. Thomas & J. Grimes (Eds.), *Best practices in school psychology IV* (pp. 337–351). Bethesda, MD: National Association of School Psychologists.

Osborn, C. J., & Davis, T. E. (1996). The supervision contract: Making it perfectly clear. *Clinical Supervisor, 14,* 121–134.

Ownby, R. L. (1997). *Psychological reports: A guide to report writing in professional psychology* (3rd ed.). New York: Wiley.

Pajak, E. (2000). *Approaches to clinical supervision* (2nd ed.). Norwood, MA: Christopher-Gordon.

Palmer, D. J., Stough, L. M., Burdenski, T. K., & Gonzales, M. (2005). Identifying teacher expertise: An examination of researchers' decision making. *Educational Psychologist, 40,* 13–25.

Panos, P. T. (2005). A model for using videoconferencing technology to support international social work field practicum students. *International Social Work, 48,* 834–841.

Panos, P. T., Panos, A., Cox, S. E., Roby, J. L., & Matheson, K. W. (2002). Ethical issues concerning the use of videoconferencing to supervise international social work field practicum students. *Journal of Social Work Education, 38,* 421–437.

Papp, P. (1983). *The process of change.* New York: Guilford Press.

Pargament, K. I. (1997). *Psychology of religion and coping: Theory, research, and practice.* New York: Guilford Press.

Patterson, C. H. (1997). Client-centered supervision. In C. E. Watkins (Ed.), *Handbook of psychotherapy supervision.* New York: Wiley.

Patterson, C. J. (1994). Children of the lesbian baby boom: Behavioral adjustment, self-concepts, and sex role identity. In B. Greene & G. Herek (Eds.), *Lesbian and gay psychology* (pp. 156–175). Thousand Oaks, CA: SAGE.

Patton, M. J., & Kivlighan, D. M. (1997). Relevance of the supervisory alliance to the counseling alliance and to treatment adherence in counselor training. *Journal of Counseling Psychology, 44,* 106–115.

Patton, M. Q. (1982). *Practical evaluation.* Beverly Hills, CA: SAGE.

Payne, R. K. (2001). *A framework for understanding poverty.* Highlands, TX: Aha! Process.

Peace, S. D., & Sprinthall, N. A. (1998). Training school counselors to supervise beginning counselors: Theory, research, and practice. *Professional School Counseling, 1,* 2–8.

Pearson, Q. (2000). Opportunities and challenges in the supervisory relationship: Implications for counselor supervision. *Journal of Mental Health Counseling, 22,* 283–294.

Pearson, Q. (2001). A case in clinical supervision: A framework for putting theory into practice. *Journal of Mental Health Counseling, 23,* 174–183.

Pennington, L. (1989). Supervision of school psychologists. In *School psychology in Wisconsin: Programs and practices* (Bulletin No. 9265). Madison: Wisconsin State Department of Public Instruction. (ERIC Document Reproduction Service No. ED307518)

Peplau, L., & Cochran, S. (1990). A relational perspective on homosexuality. In D. McWhirter, S. Sanders, & J. Reinisch (Eds.), *Homosexuality/heterosexuality: Concepts of sexual orientation* (pp. 321–349). New York: Oxford University Press.

Perez, R. M., DeBord, K. A., & Bieschke, K. J. (Eds.). (2000). *Handbook of counseling and psychotherapy with lesbian, gay, and bisexual clients.* Washington, DC: American Psychological Association.

Perreault, H., Waldman, L., Alexander, M., & Zhao, J. (2002). Overcoming barriers to successful delivery of distance-learning courses. *Journal of Education for Business, 77,* 313–320.

Perrotto, D. S. (2006). The working alliance as predictor of successful school psychology internships. *Dissertation Abstracts International, 66*(09), 5072B. (UMI No. AAI3187934)

Petrides, L. A. (2002). Web-based technologies for distributed (or distance) learning: Creating learning-centered educational experiences in the higher education classroom. *International Journal of Instructional Media, 29*(1), 69–78.

Peyton, P. R. (2004). Bullying in supervision. *Counseling and Psychotherapy Journal, 15,* 36–37.

Piaget, J., & Inhelder, B. (1969). *The psychology of the child.* New York: Basic Books.

Piercy, F. P., Sprenkle, D. H., Wetchler, J. L., & Associates. (1996). *Family therapy sourcebook* (2nd ed.). New York: Guilford Press.

Pinderhughes, E. (1989). *Understanding race, ethnicity and power: The key to efficacy on clinical practice.* New York: Free Press.

Pintrich, P. R., & Schunk, D. H. (2002). *Motivation in education: Theory, research, and applications* (2nd ed.). Upper Saddle River, NJ: Merrill/Prentice Hall.

Plante, T. G., & Sharma, N. K. (2001). Religious faith and mental health outcomes. In T. G. Plante & N. K. Sharma (Eds.), *Faith and health* (pp. 240–261). New York: Guilford Press.

Plas, J. M. (1986). *Systems psychology in the schools.* New York: Pergamon Press.

Poland, S., & Gorin, S. (2002). Preface. In S. E. Brock, P. J. Lazarus, & S. R. Jimerson (Eds.), *Best practices in school crisis prevention and intervention* (pp. xv–xviii). Bethesda, MD: National Association of School Psychologists.

Ponterotto, J. G., Casa, J. M., Suzuki, L. A., & Alexander, C. M. (2001). *Handbook of multicultural counseling.* Thousand Oaks, CA: SAGE.

Ponterotto, J. G., Gretchen, D., Utsey, S. O., Rieger, B. P., & Austin, R. (2002). A revision of the Multicultural Counseling Awareness Scale (MCAS). *Journal of Multicultural Counseling and Development, 30,* 153–180.

Pope, K. S. (2001). *Security of clinical records on computers: Viruses, firewalls, & the Golden Rule.* Retrieved December 9, 2007, from http://www.kspope.com/ethics/security.php

Pope, K. S., Tabachnick, B. G., & Keith-Spiegel, P. (1987). The beliefs and behaviors of psychologists as therapists. *American Psychologist, 42,* 993–1006.

Pope, K. S., & Vasquez, M. J. T. (1998). *Ethics in psychotherapy and counseling: A practical guide* (2nd ed.). San Francisco: Jossey-Bass.

Pope, K. S., & Vetter, V. A. (1992). Ethical dilemmas encountered by members of the American Psychological Association: A national survey. *American Psychologist, 47,* 397–411.

Pope-Davis, D. B., Coleman, H. L. K., Liu, W. M., & Toporek, R. L. (Eds.). (2003). *Handbook of multicultural competencies in counseling and psychology.* Thousand Oaks, CA: SAGE.

Pope-Davis, D. B., Toporek, R. L., & Ortega, L. (1999). *The multicultural supervision scale.* College Park, MD: Authors.

Pope-Davis, D. B., Toporek, R. L., & Ortega-Villalobos, L. (2003). Assessing supervisors' and supervisees' perceptions of multicultural competence in supervision using the Multicultural Supervision Inventory. In D. B. Pope-Davis, H. L. K. Coleman, W. M. Liu, & R. L. Toporek (Eds.), *Handbook of multicultural competencies in counseling and psychology* (pp. 211–224). Thousand Oaks, CA: SAGE.

Porter, N. (1994). Empowering supervisees to empower others: A culturally responsive supervision model. *Hispanic Journal of Behavioral Sciences, 16,* 43–56.

Power, T. J. (2002). Preparing school psychologists as interventionists and preventionists. In M. R. Shinn, H. M. Walker, & G. Stoner (Eds.), *Interventions for academic and behavior problems II: Preventive and remedial approaches* (pp. 1047–1065). Washington, DC: National Association of School Psychologists.

Power, T. J., Blom-Hoffman, J., Clarke, A. T., Riley-Tillman, T. C., Kelleher, C., & Manz, P. H. (2005). Reconceptualizing intervention integrity: A partnership-based framework for linking research with practice. *Psychology in the Schools, 42,* 495–507.

Pregnancy Discrimination Act of 1978, 42 U.S.C. § 2000e(k) (2000).

Presbury, J., Echterling, L. G., & McKee, J. E. (1999). Supervision for inner-vision: Solution-focused strategies. *Counselor Education and Supervision, 39,* 145–155.

Prieto, L. R. (1997). Separating group supervision from group therapy: Avoiding epistemological confusion. *Professional Psychology: Research and Practice, 28,* 405.

Pruitt, D. B., McColgan, E. B., Pugh, R. L., & Kiser, L. J. (1986). Approaches to psychotherapy supervision. *Journal of Psychiatric Education, 10,* 129–147.

Quinn, M. M., Gable, R. A., Rutherford, R. R., Nelson, C. M., & Howell, K. W. (1998, January 16). *An IEP team's introduction to functional behavioral assessment and behavior intervention plans.* Workshop conducted at the Center for Effective Collaboration and Practice, Washington, DC.

Ralph, E. (2002). Mentoring beginning teachers: Findings from contextual supervision. *Journal of Personnel Evaluation in Education, 16,* 191–210.

Rambo, A. H., & Shilts, L. (1997). Four supervisory practices that foster respect for difference. In T. C. Todd & C. L. Storm (Eds.), *The complete systemic supervisor: Context, philosophy, and pragmatics* (pp. 83–92). Boston: Allyn & Bacon.

Ramos-Sanchez, L., Esnil, E., Goodwin, A., Riggs, S., Touster, L., Wright, L., et al. (2002). Negative supervisory events: Effects on supervision satisfaction and supervisory alliance. *Professional Psychology: Research and Practice, 33,* 197–202.

Ray, D. (2004). Supervision of basic and advanced skills in play therapy. *Journal of Professional Counseling: Practice, Theory, and Research, 32,* 28–41.

Reamer, F. G. (2004). Ethical decisions and risk management. In M. J. Austin & K. M. Hopkins (Eds.), *Supervision as collaboration in the human services: Building a learning culture* (pp. 97–109). Thousand Oaks, CA: SAGE.

Reeve, C. L., & Schultz, L. (2004). Job-seeker reactions to selection process information in job ads. *International Journal of Selection and Assessment, 12,* 343–355.

Rehabilitation Act of 1973, Pub. L. No. 93–112, § 504, 87 Stat. 394 (1973).

Reiner, H. D., & Hartshorne, T. S. (1982). Job burnout and the school psychologist. *Psychology in the Schools, 19,* 508–512.

Reschly, D. J. (2006, October). *Response to intervention in general, remedial, and special education.* Paper presented at the fall convention of the New Hampshire Association of School Psychologists, Concord, NH.

Reschly, D. J., & Ysseldyke, J. E. (2002). *Paradigm shift: The past is not the future.* In A. Thomas & J. Grimes (Eds.), *Best practices in school psychology IV* (pp. 3–20). Bethesda, MD: National Association of School Psychologists.

Rhoades, M. M., & Kratochwill, T. R. (1998). Parent training and consultation: An analysis of a homework intervention program. *School Psychology Quarterly, 13,* 241–265.

Rhodes, R. L., Ochoa, S. H., & Ortiz, S. O. (2005). *Assessing culturally and linguistically diverse students: A practical guide.* New York: Guilford Press.

Richards, C. N., & Ridley, D. R. (1997). Factors affecting college students' persistence in on-line computer managed instruction. *College Student Journal, 31,* 490–496.

Richards, P. S., & Abergin, A. E. (Eds.). (2000). *Handbook of psychotherapy and religious diversity.* Washington, DC: American Psychological Association.

Rigazio-DiGilio, S. A. (1997). Integrative supervision: Approaches to tailoring the supervisory process. In T. C. Todd & C. L. Storm (Eds.), *The complete systemic supervisor: Context, philosophy, and pragmatics* (pp. 195–216). Boston: Allyn & Bacon.

Riggs, S. A., & Bretz, K. M. (2006). Attachment processes in the supervisory relationship: An exploratory investigation. *Professional Psychology: Research and Practice, 37,* 558–566.

Riley, W. T., Schumann, M. F., Forman-Hoffman, V. L., Mihm, P., Applegate, B. W., & Asif, O. (2007). Responses of practicing psychologists to a Web site developed to promote empirically supported treatments. *Professional Psychology: Research and Practice, 38,* 44–53.

Rishel, C. (2007). Evidence-based prevention practice in mental health: What is it and how do we get there? *American Journal of Orthopsychiatry, 77,* 153–164.

Riva, M. T., & Cornish, J. A. E. (1995). Group supervision practices at psychology predoctoral internship programs: A national survey. *Professional Psychology: Research and Practice, 26,* 523–525.

Rivera, E. T., Wilbur, M., Roberts-Wilbur, J., Phan, L. T., Garrett, M. T., & Betz, R. L. (2004). Supervising and training psychoeducational group leaders. *Journal for Specialists in Group Work, 29,* 377–394.

Riveria, R. (1987). Legal issues in gay and lesbian parenting. In F. Bozett (Ed.), *Gay and lesbian parents* (pp. 199–227). New York: Praeger.

Rogers, C. (1951). *Client-centered therapy: Its current practice, implications, and theory.* Boston: Houghton Mifflin.

Rogers, C. (1958). Characteristics of a helping relationship. *Personnel & Guidance Journal, 37,* 6–16.

Rogers, C. (1965). *Client-centered therapy.* Boston: Houghton Mifflin.

Rogers, M. R., Ingraham, C. L., Bursztyn, A., Cajigas-Segredo, N., Esquivel, G., & Hess, R. (1999). Providing psychological services to racially, ethnically, culturally, and linguistically diverse individuals in the schools: Recommendations for practice. *School Psychology International, 20,* 243–264.

Romans, J. S. C., Boswell, D. L., Carlozzi, A. F., & Ferguson, D. B. (1995). Training and supervision practices in clinical, counseling, and school psychology programs. *Professional Psychology: Research and Practice, 26,* 407–412.

Rønnestad, M. H., & Skovholt, T. M. (2003). The journey of the counselor and therapist: Research findings and perspectives on professional development. *Journal of Career Development, 30,* 5–44.

Rosenberg, J. I., Getzelman, M. A., Arcinue, F., & Oren, C. Z., (2005). An exploratory look at students' experiences of problematic peers in academic professional psychology programs. *Professional Psychology: Research and Practice, 36,* 665–673.

Rosenblatt, P. C. (1994). *Metaphors of family systems theory: Toward new constructions.* New York: Guilford Press.

Rosenfield, S. (1981). Self-managed professional development. *School Psychology Review, 10,* 487–493.

Rosenfield, S. (1985). Professional development management. In C. A. Maher (Ed.), *Professional self-management: Techniques for special services providers* (pp. 85–104). Baltimore: Brookes.

Rosenfield, S. (1987). *Instructional consultation.* Hillsdale, NJ: Lawrence Erlbaum.

Rosenfield, S. (1992). Developing school-based consultation teams: A design for organizational change. *School Psychology Quarterly, 7,* 27–46.

Rosenfield, S. A. (1995a). Instructional consultation: A model for delivery in schools. *Journal of Educational & Psychological Consultation, 6,* 297–316.

Rosenfield, S. A. (1995b). The practice of instructional consultation. *Journal of Educational & Psychological Consultation, 6,* 317–327.

Rosenfield, S. A. (2000). Crafting usable knowledge. *American Psychologist, 55,* 1347–1355.

Rosenfield, S. A. (2002). Developing instructional consultants: From novice to competent to expert. *Journal of Educational & Psychological Consultation, 13,* 97–111.

Rosenfield, S. A., & Gravois, T. A. (1996). *Instructional consultation teams: Collaborating for change.* New York: Guilford Press.

Ross, J. (1995). Social class tension within families. *American Journal of Family Therapy, 23,* 329–341.

Ross, R. P., & Goh, D. S. (1993). Participating in supervision in school psychology: A national survey of practices and training. *School Psychology Review, 22,* 63–80.

Ross, R. R., Altmaier, E. M., & Russell, D. W. (1989). Job stress, social support, and burnout among counseling center staff. *Journal of Counseling Psychology, 36,* 464–470.

Roszkowski, M. J. (2003). Test review of the Supervisory Behavior Description Questionnaire. In B. S. Plake, J. C. Impara, & R. A. Spies (Eds.), *The fifteenth mental measurements yearbook* [Electronic version]. Available from the Buros Institute's *Test Reviews Online* Web site: http://buros.unl.edu/buros

Roth, A., Fonagy, P., & Parry, G. (2005). *What works for whom? A critical review of psychotherapy research.* New York: Guilford Press.

Rovai, A. P. (2003). In search of higher persistence rates in distance education on-line programs. *Internet and Higher Education, 6,* 1–16.

Royse, D., Thyer, B. A., Padgett, D. K., & Logan, T. K. (2006). *Program evaluation: An introduction* (4th ed.). Belmont, CA: Brooks/Cole.

Rue, L. W., & Byars, L. L. (1997). *Management: Skills and applications* (8th ed.). Chicago: Irwin.

Russell, D., Altmaier, E. M., & Van Velzen, D. (1987). Job-related stress, social support, and burnout among classroom teachers. *Journal of Applied Psychology, 72,* 269–274.

Russell-Chapin, L. A., & Ivey, A. (2004). Microcounselling supervision: An innovative integrated supervision model. *Canadian Journal of Counselling, 38,* 165–176.

Russell-Chapin, L. A., & Sherman, N. (2001). *Microcounseling supervision: An interactive approach to teaching microcounseling skills* [CD-ROM]. Framingham, MA: Microtraining Associates.

Russo, P., Bahr, M. W., Jagodzinski, M., Ehrhardt, G., Smith, N., & Arra, C. (2001, April). *Recent advances in structured group supervision.* Paper presented at the annual convention of the National Association of School Psychologists, Washington, DC.

Sabatino, D. A., Vance, H. B., & Miller, T. L. (1993). Defining best diagnostic practices. In H. B. Vance (Ed.), *Best practices in assessment for school and clinical settings* (pp. 1–27). Brandon, VT: Clinical Psychology.

Safran, J. D., & Muran, J. C. (2000). Resolving therapeutic alliance ruptures: Diversity and integration. *Journal of Clinical Psychology, 56,* 233–243.

Salvia, J., & Ysseldyke, J. E. (1998). *Assessment* (7th ed.). New York: Houghton Mifflin.

Sandoval, J., & Irvin, M. G. (1990). Legal and ethical issues in the assessment of children. In C. R. Reynolds & R. W. Kamphaus (Eds.), *Handbook of psychological and educational assessment of children: Intelligence and achievement.* New York: Guilford Press.

Sandoval, J., & Lambert, N. M. (1977). Instruments for evaluating school psychologists' function and service. *Psychology in the Schools, 14,* 172–179.

Sarason, S. B. (1996). *Revisiting "The culture of school and the problem of change."* New York: Teachers College Press.

Sattler, J. (in press). *Assessment of children* (5th ed.). San Diego, CA: Jerome Sattler.

Schein, E. H. (1999). *Process consultation revisited: Building the helping relationship.* New York: Addison-Wesley.

Schlechty, P. C. (2005). *Creating great schools: Six critical systems at the heart of educational innovation.* San Francisco: Jossey-Bass.

Schmuck, R., & Runkel, P. (1994). *The handbook of organizational development in schools* (4th ed.). Palo Alto, CA: Mayfield.

Scholten, T. (2003). What does it meant to consult? In E. Cole & J. A. Siegel (Eds.), *Effective consultation in school psychology* (2nd ed., pp. 33–52, 88). Cambridge, MA: Hogrefe & Huber.

Schultz, J. C., Ososkie, J. N., Fried, J. H., Nelson, R. E., & Bardos, A. N. (2002). Clinical supervision in public rehabilitation counseling settings. *Rehabilitation Counseling Bulletin, 45,* 213–222.

Seidman, I. (2006). *Interviewing as qualitative research: A guide for researchers in education and the social sciences* (3rd ed.). New York: Teachers College Press.

Senge, P. M. (2006). *The fifth discipline: The art and the practice of the learning organization.* New York: Doubleday.

Sergiovanni, T. J. (1990). *Value-added leadership: How to get extraordinary performance in schools.* New York: Harcourt Brace.

Sergiovanni, T. J., & Starratt, R. J. (2007). *Supervision: A redefinition* (8th ed.). New York: McGraw-Hill.

Shapiro, E. S. (1989). *Academic skills problems: Direct assessment and intervention.* New York: Guilford Press.

Shapiro, E. S. (1990). An integrated model for curriculum-based assessment. *School Psychology Review, 19,* 331–349.

Shapiro, E. S., & Lentz, F. E., Jr. (1985). A survey of school psychologists' use of behavior modification procedures. *Journal of School Psychology, 23,* 327–336.

Shapiro, J. P., & Stefkovich, J. A. (2001). *Ethical leadership and decision making in education: Applying theoretical perspectives to complex dilemmas.* Mahwah, NJ: Lawrence Erlbaum.

Sheridan, S. M., & Gutkin, T. B. (2000). The ecology of school psychology: Examining and changing our paradigm for the 21st century. *School Psychology Review, 29,* 485–502.

Sheridan, S. M., Kratochwill, T. R., & Bergan, J. R. (1996). *Conjoint behavioral consultation: A procedural manual.* New York: Plenum Press.

Sheridan, S. M., Salmon, D., Kratochwill, T. R., & Rotto, P. J. C. (1992). A conceptual model for the expansion of behavioral consultation training. *Journal of Educational & Psychological Consultation, 3,* 193–218.

Sheridan, S. M., Welch, M., & Orme, S. F. (1996). Is consultation effective? *A review of outcome research. Remedial and Special Education, 17,* 341–354.

Shin, J. (1997). The effects of executive leadership on organizational innovation in nonprofit, human service organizations. *Dissertation Abstracts International, 57*(12), 5298A. (UMI No. AAG9715473)

Shinn, M. R. (2002). Best practices in using Curriculum-Based Measurement in a problem-solving model. In A. Thomas & J. Grimes (Eds.), *Best practices in school psychology IV* (pp. 671–697). Bethesda, MD: National Association of School Psychologists.

Shinn, M. R., Walker, H. M., & Stoner, G. (2002). *Interventions for academic and behavior problems II: Preventive and remedial approaches.* Bethesda, MD: National Association of School Psychologists.

Shriberg, D. (2007). The school psychologist as leader and change agent in a high-stakes era. *Journal of Applied School Psychology, 23,* 151–166.

Sigelman, C. K., & Rider, E. A. (2006). *Life-span human development* (5th ed.). Belmont, CA: Thomson Wadsworth.

Skinner, B. F. (1953). *Science and human behavior.* New York: Macmillan.

Skovholt, T. M., & Rønnestad, M. H. (1992). *The evolving professional self: Stages and themes in therapist and counselor development.* Chichester, UK: Wiley.

Smith, D. K. (1984). Practicing school psychologists: Their characteristics, activities, and populations served. *Professional Psychology: Research and Practice, 15,* 798–810.

Smith, E. (1987). Individualized growth of professionals. In J. Grimes & D. Happe (Eds.), *Best practices in the supervision of school psychological services* (pp. 37–46). Des Moines: Iowa State Department of Education. (ERIC Document Reproduction Service No. ED293037)

Smith, G. G., Ferguson, D., & Caris, M. (2002). Teaching over the Web versus in the classroom: Differences in the instructor experience. *International Journal of Instructional Media, 29,* 61–68.

Smither, J. W., London, M., & Reilly, R. R. (2005). Does performance improve following multisource feedback? A theoretical model, meta-analysis, and review of empirical findings. *Personnel Psychology, 58,* 33–66.

Snell, J., MacKenzie, E., & Frey, K. (2002). Bullying prevention in elementary schools: The importance of adult leadership, peer group support, and student social-emotional skills. In M. R. Shinn, H. M. Walker, & G. Stoner (Eds.), *Interventions for academic and behavior problems II: Preventive and remedial approaches* (pp. 351–372). Bethesda, MD: National Association of School Psychologists.

Sodowsky, G. R., & Plake, B. S. (1991) Psychometric properties of the American-International Relations Scale (AIRS). *Educational and Psychological Measurement, 51,* 207–216.

Sodowsky, G. R., Taffe, R. C., Gutkin, T. B., & Wise, S. L. (1994). Development of the Multicultural Counseling Inventory: A self-report measure of multicultural competencies. *Journal of Counseling Psychology, 41,* 137–148.

Solly, D. C., & Hohenshil, T. H. (1986). Job satisfaction of school psychologists in a primarily rural state. *School Psychology Review, 15,* 119–126.

Sommer, C., & Cox, J. (2005). Elements of supervision in sexual violence counselors' narratives: A qualitative analysis. *Counselor Education and Supervision, 45,* 119–134.

Spooner, S. E., & Stone, S. C. (1977). Maintenance of specific counseling skills over time. *Journal of Counseling Psychology, 24,* 66–71.

Sprinthall, N. A., Reiman, A. J., & Thies-Sprinthall, L. (1993). Role-taking and reflection: Promoting the conceptual and moral development of teachers. *Learning and Individual Differences, 5,* 283–299.

Sprinthall, N. A., Reiman, A. J., & Thies-Sprinthall, L. (1996). Teacher professional development. In J. Sidula (Ed.), *Handbook of research in teacher education* (pp. 666–703). New York: Macmillan.

Squire, C. (2000). *Culture in psychology.* London: Routledge.

Stamm, B. H. (1998). Clinical applications of telehealth in mental health care. *Professional Psychology: Research and Practice, 29,* 536–542.

Stamm, B. H. (Ed.). (2003). *Rural behavioral health care: An interdisciplinary guide.* Washington, DC: American Psychological Association.

Stefkovich, J. A. (2006). *Best interest of the student: Applying ethical constraints to legal cases in education.* Mahwah, NJ: Lawrence Erlbaum.

Stephens, R. (2002). Promoting school safety. In S. E. Brock, P. J. Lazarus, & S. R. Jimerson (Eds.), *Best practices in school crisis prevention and intervention* (pp. 47–66). Bethesda, MD: National Association of School Psychologists.

Sternberg, R. J. (1988). *The triarchic mind: A new theory of intelligence.* New York: Viking Press.

Sternberg, R. J. (2007). A systems model of leadership: WICS. *American Psychologist, 62,* 34–42.

Stiles, W. B. (2006). *Session Evaluation Questionnaire: Structure and use.* Retrieved December 10, 2007, from http://www.users.muohio.edu/stileswb/session_evaluation_questionnaire.htm

Stoiber, K. C., & Kratochwill, T. R. (2002). *Outcomes: Planning, Monitoring, Evaluating (PME).* San Antonio, TX: PsychCorp.

Stoltenberg, C. D. (1993). Supervising consultants in training: An application of a model of supervision. *Journal of Counseling and Development, 72,* 131–138.

Stoltenberg, C. D. (2005). Enhancing professional competence through developmental approaches to supervision. *American Psychologist, 60,* 857–864.

Stoltenberg, C. D., & Delworth, U. (1987). *Supervising counselors and therapists: A developmental approach.* San Francisco: Jossey-Bass.

Stoltenberg, C. D., McNeill, B., & Delworth, U. (1998). *IDM supervision: An integrated developmental model for counselors and therapists.* San Francisco: Jossey-Bass.

Stone, C. B., & Dahir, C. A. (2007). *School counselor accountability: A MEASURE of student success* (2nd ed.). Upper Saddle River, NJ: Pearson Education.

Storm, C. L. (1997). Teaching therapists to become supervisors. In T. C. Todd & C. L. Storm (Eds.), *The complete systemic supervisor: Context, philosophy, and pragmatics* (pp. 363–372). Boston: Allyn & Bacon.

Storm, C. L., & Haug, I. E. (1997). Ethical issues: Where do you draw the line? In T. C. Todd & C. L. Storm (Eds.), *The complete systemic supervisor: Context, philosophy, and pragmatics* (pp. 26–40). Boston: Allyn & Bacon.

Storm, C. L., Todd, T. C., McDowell, T., & Sutherland, T. (1997). Supervising supervisors. In T. C. Todd & C. L. Storm (Eds.), *The complete systemic supervisor: Context, philosophy, and pragmatics* (pp. 373–388). Boston: Allyn & Bacon.

Strong, T. (2003). Engaging reflection: A training exercise using conversation and discourse analysis. *Counselor Education and Supervision, 43,* 65–77.

Struzziero, J. A. (1998). *Computer-mediated consultation.* Unpublished doctoral dissertation, Northeastern University, Boston.

Substance Abuse and Mental Health Services Administration. (n.d.). *SAMHSA model programs* [Web page]. Retrieved December 10, 2007, from http://ncadistore.samhsa.gov/catalog/results.aspx?h=drugs&topic=169

Sue, D. W. (2003). *Overcoming our racism: The journey to liberation.* San Francisco: Jossey-Bass.

Sue, D. W., & Sue, D. (1999). *Counseling the culturally different: Theory and practice* (3rd ed.). New York: Wiley.

Sugai, G., & Horner, R. R. (2006). A promising approach for expanding and sustaining school-wide positive behavior support. *School Psychology Review, 35,* 245–259.

Sullivan, J. R., & Conoley, J. C. (2008). Best practices in the supervision of interns. In A. Thomas & J. Grimes (Eds.), *Best practices in school psychology V* (pp. 1957–1974). Bethesda, MD: National Association of School Psychologists.

Supervision Interest Network. (1993). Standards for counselor supervisors. *Journal of Counseling and Development, 69,* 30–32.

Sutherland, J. W. (1973). *A general systems philosophy for the social and behavioral sciences.* New York: George Braziller.

Sutter, E., McPherson, R. H., & Geeseman, R. (2002). Contracting for supervision. *Professional Psychology: Research and Practice, 33,* 495–498.

Sweitzer, H. F., & King, M. A. (2004). *The successful internship: Transformation and empowerment in experiential learning* (2nd ed.). Belmont, CA: Brooks/Cole.

Talley, R. C. (1990). Best practices in the administration and supervision of school psychological services. In A. Thomas & J. Grimes (Eds.), *Best practices in school psychology II* (pp. 43–62). Washington, DC: National Association of School Psychologists.

Tarasoff v. Regents of California, 118 Cal. Rptr. 129, 529 P.2d 553 (Cal. 1974).

Task Force on Evidence-Based Interventions in School Psychology. (2003). *Procedural and coding manual for review of evidence-based interventions.* Retrieved January 9, 2008, from http://www.sp-ebi.org/documents/_workingfiles/EBImanual1.pdf

Tatum, B. C., & Nebeker, D. M. (2002). A strategic approach to measuring organizational performance. In R. L. Lowman (Ed.), *The California School of Organizational Studies handbook of organizational consulting psychology: A comprehensive guide to theory, skills, and techniques* (pp. 692–729). San Francisco: Jossey-Bass.

Tatum, B. D. (1997). *Why are all the black kids sitting together in the cafeteria?* New York: Basic Books.

Tawney, J. W., & Gast, D. L. (1984). *Single-subject research in special education.* Columbus, OH: Merrill.

Tepper, B. J., Duffy, M. K., Henle, C. A., & Lambert, L. S. (2006). Procedural injustice, victim precipitation, and abusive supervision. *Personnel Psychology, 59,* 101–123.

Tharinger, D., & Stafford, M. (1995). Individual counseling of elementary aged students. In A. Thomas & J. Grimes (Eds.), *Best practices in school psychology III* (pp. 893–908). Silver Spring, MD: National Association of School Psychologists.

Tharinger, D. J. (1998). School psychologists: Promoting secure and autonomous attachment: A focus on supervision. *School Psychologist, 52,* 106–123.

Thomas, A., & Grimes, J. (Eds.). (2002). *Best practices in school psychology IV.* Bethesda, MD: National Association of School Psychologists.

Thomas, A., & Grimes, J. (Eds.). (2008). *Best practices in school psychology V.* Bethesda, MD: National Association of School Psychologists.

Thomas, J. T. (2005). Licensing board complaints: Minimizing the impact on the psychologist's defense and clinical practice. *Professional Psychology: Research and Practice, 36,* 426–433.

Thomas, J. T. (2007). Informed consent through contracting for supervision: Minimizing risks, enhancing benefits. *Professional Psychology: Research and Practice, 38,* 221–231.

Thomas, T. (1992). Psychoeducational adjustment of English-speaking Caribbean and Central American immigrant children in the United States. *School Psychology Review, 21,* 566–576.

Thomasgard, M., & Collins, V. (2003). A comprehensive review of a cross-disciplinary, case-based peer supervision model. *Families, Systems, & Health, 21,* 305–319.

Thurber, S. L. (2005). *The effect of direct supervision on therapist behavior: An initial functional analysis.* Doctoral dissertation, Brigham Young University, Ann Arbor, MI. Retrieved December 10, 2007, from http://contentdm.lib.byu.edu/ETD/image/etd739.pdf

Tichy, N. M. (1997). *The leadership engine: How winning companies build leaders at every level.* New York: HarperCollins.

Tindal, G. (1989). Curriculum-Based Measurement. In J. L. Graden, J. E. Zins, & M. J. Curtis (Eds.), *Alternative educational delivery systems: Enhancing instructional options for all students* (pp. 111–136). Washington, DC: National Association of School Psychologists.

Todd, T. C. (1997a). Problems in supervision: Lessons from supervisees. In T. C. Todd & C. L. Storm (Eds.), *The complete systemic supervisor: Context, philosophy, and pragmatics* (pp. 241–252). Boston: Allyn & Bacon.

Todd, T. C. (1997b). Self-supervision as a universal supervisory goal. In T. C. Todd & C. L. Storm (Eds.), *The complete systemic supervisor: Context, philosophy, and pragmatics* (pp. 17–25). Boston: Allyn & Bacon.

Torrey, E. F. (2006). *Surviving schizophrenia: A manual for families, patients, and providers* (5th ed.). New York: Collins.

Townend, M. (2005). Interprofessional supervision from the perspectives of both mental health nurses and other professionals in the field of cognitive behavioural psychotherapy. *Journal of Psychiatric and Mental Health Nursing, 12*(5), 582–588.

Trant, R. P. (2001). *Elements and outcome of school psychologist internship supervision: A retrospective study.* Unpublished doctoral dissertation, Northeastern University, Boston.

Trenhaile, J. (2005). Solution-focused supervision: Returning the focus to client goals. *Journal of Family Psychotherapy, 16,* 223–228.

Triantafillou, N. (1997). A solution-focused approach to mental health supervision. *Journal of Systemic Therapies, 16,* 305–328.

Tromski-Klingshirn, D. M., & Davis, T. E. (2007). Supervisees' perceptions of their clinical supervision: A study of the dual role of clinical and administrative supervisor. *Counselor Education and Supervision, 46,* 294–304.

Tröster, A. I., Paolo, A. M., Glatt, S. L., Hubble, J. P., & Koller, W. C. (1995). Interactive videoconferencing in the provision of neuropsychological services to rural areas. *Journal of Community Psychology, 23,* 85–88.

Tryon, G. S. (2001). School psychology students' beliefs about their preparation and concern with ethical issues. *Ethics & Behavior, 11,* 375–394.

Tsui, M.-S. (2005). *Social work supervision: Contexts and concepts.* Thousand Oaks, CA: SAGE.

Tuckman, A., & Finkelstein, H. (1997). Distinguishing the supervision needs of assessment and therapy trainees. *Professional Psychology: Research and Practice, 28,* 595.

Tuckman, B. W. (1985). *Evaluating instructional programs* (2nd ed.). Needham Heights, MA: Allyn & Bacon.

Tuckman, B. W., & Jensen, M. A. C. (1977). Stages of small group development revisited. *Group and Organizational Studies, 2,* 419–427.

Turner, J., & Fine, M. (1997). Gender and supervision: Evolving debates. In T. C. Todd & C. L. Storm (Eds.), *The complete systemic supervisor: Context, philosophy, and pragmatics* (pp. 72–82). Boston: Allyn & Bacon.

Turner, J. A., Edwards, L. M., Eicken, I. M., Yokoyama, K., Castro, J. R., Tran, A., et al. (2005). Intern self-care: An exploratory study into strategy use and effectiveness. *Professional Psychology: Research and Practice, 36,* 674–680.

United States Department of Health and Human Services. (2005). *Code of Federal Regulations Part 46: Protection of Human Subjects.* Retrieved December 7, 2007, from www.hhs.gov/ohrp/humansubjects/guidance/45cfr46.htm

United States Department of Health and Human Services, Office of the Secretary. (2000). *Standards for privacy of individually identifiable health information.* Retrieved February 3, 2008, from http://www.hhs.gov/ocr/combinedregtext.pdf

University of Maryland at College Park, Laboratory for Instructional Consultation Teams. (n.d.) *IC team model.* Retrieved December 9, 2007, from http://www.icteams.umd.edu/icteammodel.html

Upah, K., & Tilly, W., III. (2002). Best practices in designing, implementing, and evaluating quality interventions. In A. Thomas & J. Grimes (Eds.), *Best practices in school psychology IV* (pp. 483–501). Bethesda, MD: National Association of School Psychologists.

Urwick, L. F. (1938). *Scientific principles and organizations.* New York: American Management Association.

U.S. Equal Employment Opportunity Commission. (n.d.). *Discriminatory practices.* Retrieved December 10, 2007, from http://www.eeoc.gov/abouteeo/overview_practices.html

U.S. Office of Special Education, National Joint Committee on Learning Disabilities. (2006). *Learning disabilities and young children: Identification and intervention.* Retrieved February 3, 2008, from http://www.ldonline.org/article/11511

Utsey, S., Gernat, C., & Hammar, L. (2005). Examining white counselor trainees' reactions to racial issues in counseling and supervision dyads. *Counseling Psychologist, 33,* 449–478.

Vacha-Haase, T., Davenport, D. S., & Kerewsky, S. D. (2004). Problematic students: Gatekeeping practices in academic professional psychology programs. *Professional Psychology: Research and Practice, 35,* 115–122.

Van Velsor, P. (2004). Training for successful group work with children: How and what to teach. *Journal for Specialists in Group Work, 29,* 137–146.

Vargas, L. A., & Koss-Chioino, J. D. (Eds.). (1992). *Working with culture: Psychotherapeutic interventions with ethnic minority children and adolescents.* San Francisco: Jossey-Bass.

Vroom, V. H. (2000). Leadership and the decision-making process. *Organizational Dynamics, 28,* 82–94.

Vroom, V. H., & Jago, A. G. (2007). The role of the situation in leadership. *American Psychologist, 62,* 17–24.

Vroom, V. H., & Yetton, P. W. (1973). *Leadership and managerial decision making.* Pittsburgh, PA: University of Pittsburgh Press.

Walker, H. M., & Shinn, M. R. (2002). Structuring school-based interventions to achieve integrated primary, secondary, and tertiary prevention goals for safe and effective schools. In M. R. Shinn, G. Stoner, & H. M. Walker (Eds.), *Interventions for academic and behavior problems: Preventive and remedial approaches* (pp. 1–25). Silver Spring, MD: National Association of School Psychologists.

Walker, M. (2004). Supervising practitioners working with survivors of childhood abuse: Counter transference; secondary traumatization and terror. *Psychodynamic Practice: Individuals, Groups and Organisations, 10,* 173–193.

Walsh, F. (Ed.). (2003). *Normal family processes* (3rd ed.). New York: Guilford Press.

Ward, S. (1999). Field-based intern supervision: A study of practices. *Communiqué, 28*(3), 32–33.

Watson, T. S., & Steege, M. W. (2003). *Conducting school-based behavioral assessments: A practitioner's guide.* New York: Guilford Press.

Webster-Stratton, C. (2001). The incredible years: Parents, teachers, and children training series. *Residential Treatment for Children & Youth, 18,* 31–45.

Wechsler, D. (1992). *Wechsler individual achievement test.* San Antonio, TX: PsychCorp.

Wechsler, D. (1997). *Wechsler adult intelligence scale* (3rd ed.). San Antonio, TX: PsychCorp.

Wechsler, D. (2002). *Wechsler preschool and primary scale of intelligence* (3rd ed.). San Antonio, TX: PsychCorp.

Wechsler, D. (2003). *Wechsler intelligence scale for children* (4th ed.). San Antonio, TX: Harcourt Assessment.

Weiner, R. K., Sheridan, S. M., & Jenson, W. R. (1998). The effects of conjoint behavioral consultation and a structured homework program on math completion and accuracy in junior high schools. *School Psychology Quarterly, 13,* 281–308.

Weisband, S. P., Schneider, S. K., & Connolly, T. (1995). Computer-mediated communication and social information: Status salience and status differences. *Academy of Management Journal, 38,* 1124–1151.

Weissman, M. M., Markowitz, J. C., & Klerman, G. L. (2000). *Comprehensive guide to interpersonal psychotherapy.* New York: Basic Books.

Weisz, J. R., Sandler, I. N., & Durlak, J. A. (2005). Promoting and protecting youth mental health through evidence-based prevention and treatment. *American Psychologist, 60,* 628–648.

Wester, S. R., & Vogel, D. L. (2002). Working with the masculine mystique: Male gender role conflict, counseling self-efficacy, and the training of male psychologists. *Professional Psychology: Research and Practice, 33,* 370–376.

Wester, S. R., Vogel, D. L., & Archer, J., Jr. (2004). Male restricted emotionality and counseling supervision. *Journal of Counseling and Development, 82,* 91–98.

Whiston, S. C., & Emerson, S. (1989). Ethical implications for supervisors in counseling of trainees. *Counselor Education and Supervision, 28,* 318–325.

Whitaker, D. (1994). *How school psychology trainees learn to communicate through the school psychological report.* Unpublished doctoral dissertation, University of Washington, Seattle.

White, V. E., & Queener, J. (2003). Supervisor and supervisee attachments and social provisions related to the supervisory working alliance. *Counselor Education and Supervision, 42,* 203–218.

Whitehurst, G. J., Epstein, J. N., & Angell, A. L. (1994). Outcomes of an emergent literacy intervention in Head Start. *Journal of Educational Psychology, 86,* 542–555.

Wickstrom, K. F., Jones, K. M., LaFleur, L. H., & Witt, J. C. (1998). An analysis of treatment integrity in school-based behavioral consultation. *School Psychology Quarterly, 13,* 141–154.

Wilbur, M. P., Roberts-Wilbur, J. M., Hart, G., Morris, J. R., & Betz, R. L. (1994). Structured group supervision (SGS): A pilot study. *Counselor Education and Supervision, 33,* 262–279.

Wilczenski, F., & Coomey, S. (2006). Cyber-communication: Finding its place in school counseling practice, education, and professional development. *Professional School Counseling, 9,* 327–331.

Wiles, M. A., & Spiro, R. L. (2004). Attracting graduates to sales positions and the role of recruiter knowledge: A reexamination. *Journal of Personal Selling & Sales Management, 24,* 39–48.

Wiley, M. O., & Ray, P. B. (1986). Counseling supervision by developmental level. *Journal of Counseling Psychology, 33,* 439–445.

Wilkinson, A., Redman, T., Snape, E., & Marchington, M. (1998). *Managing with total quality management: Theory and practice.* Hong Kong: Macmillan Business.

Winum, P. C., Nielsen, T. M., & Bradford, R. E. (2002). Assessing the impact of organizational consulting. In R. L. Lowman (Ed.), *The California School of Organizational Studies handbook of organizational consulting psychology: A comprehensive guide to theory, skills, and techniques* (pp. 645–667). San Francisco: Jossey-Bass.

Wise, A. E., & Leibbrand, J. (1996). Profession-based accreditation: A foundation for high-quality teaching. *Phi Delta Kappan, 78,* 202–206.

Wolters, C. A. (1998). Self-regulated learning and college students' regulation of motivation. *Journal of Educational Psychology, 90,* 224–235.

Wolters, C. A. (2004). Advancing achievement goal theory: Using goal structures and goal orientations to predict students' motivation, cognition, and achievement. *Journal of Educational Psychology, 96,* 236–250.

Wood, J. A. V., Miller, T. W., & Hargrove, D. S. (2005). Clinical supervision in rural settings: A telehealth model. *Professional Psychology: Research and Practice, 36,* 173–179.

Woody, R. H., LaVoie, J. C., & Epps, S. (1992). *School psychology: A developmental and social systems approach.* Boston: Allyn & Bacon.

Worthen, V., & McNeill, B. W. (1996). A phenomenological investigation of "good" supervision events. *Journal of Counseling Psychology, 43,* 25–34.

Worthington, R. L., Tan, J. A., & Poulin, K. (2002). Ethically questionable behaviors among supervisees: An exploratory investigation. *Ethics & Behavior, 12,* 323–351.

Young, E. L., Boye, A. E., & Nelson, D. A. (2006). Relational aggression: Understanding, identifying, and responding in schools. *Psychology in the Schools, 43,* 297–312.

Young, M. A. (2002). The community crisis response team: The national organization for victim assistance protocol. In S. E. Brock, P. J. Lazarus, & S. R. Jimerson (Eds.), *Best practices in school crisis prevention and intervention* (pp. 333–354). Bethesda, MD: National Association of School Psychologists.

Yourman, D. B. (2003). Trainee disclosure in psychotherapy supervision: The impact of shame. *Journal of Clinical Psychology: In Session, 59,* 601–609.

Ysseldyke, J. E., Burns, M., Dawson, P., Kelley, B., Morrison, D., Ortiz, S., et al. (2006). *School psychology: A blueprint for training and practice III.* Silver Spring, MD: National Association of School Psychologists.

Zaccaro, S. J. (2007). Trait-based perspectives of leadership. *American Psychologist, 62,* 6–16.

Zins, J. E. (1984). Scientific problem-solving approach to developing accountability procedures for school psychologists. *Professional Psychology: Research and Practice, 15,* 56–66.

Zins, J. E. (1985). Best practices in improving psychological services through accountability. In A. Thomas & J. Grimes (Eds.), *Best practices in school psychology* (pp. 493–503). Kent, OH: National Association of School Psychologists.

Zins, J. E., & Murphy, J. J. (1996). Consultation with professional peers: A national survey of the practices of school psychologists. *Journal of Educational & Psychological Consultation, 7,* 61–70.

Zins, J. E., Murphy, J. J., & Wess, B. P. (1989). Supervision in school psychology: Current practices and congruence with professional standards. *School Psychology Review, 18,* 56–63.

Author Index

Subject Index

**CORWIN
PRESS**

The Corwin Press logo—a raven striding across an open book—represents the union of courage and learning. Corwin Press is committed to improving education for all learners by publishing books and other professional development resources for those serving the field of PreK–12 education. By providing practical, hands-on materials, Corwin Press continues to carry out the promise of its motto: **"Helping Educators Do Their Work Better."**

**NATIONAL
ASSOCIATION OF
SCHOOL
PSYCHOLOGISTS**

The National Association of School Psychologists represents and supports school pschology through leadership to enhance the mental health and educational competence of all children.